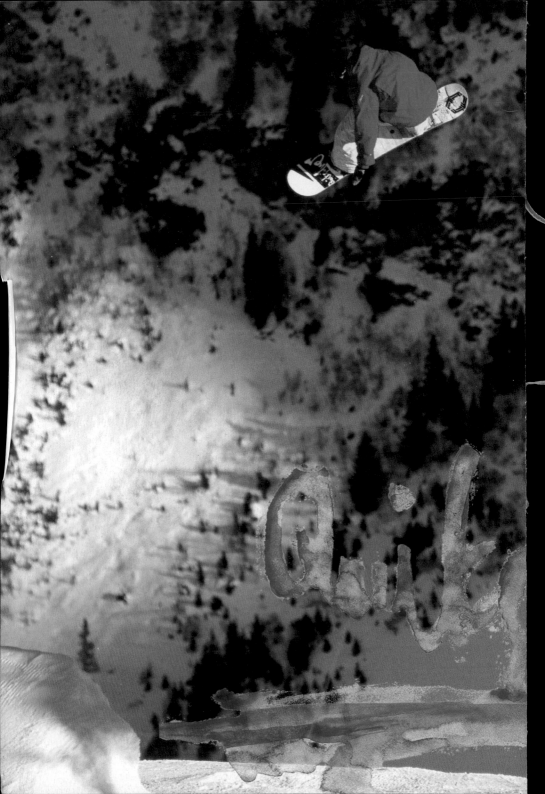

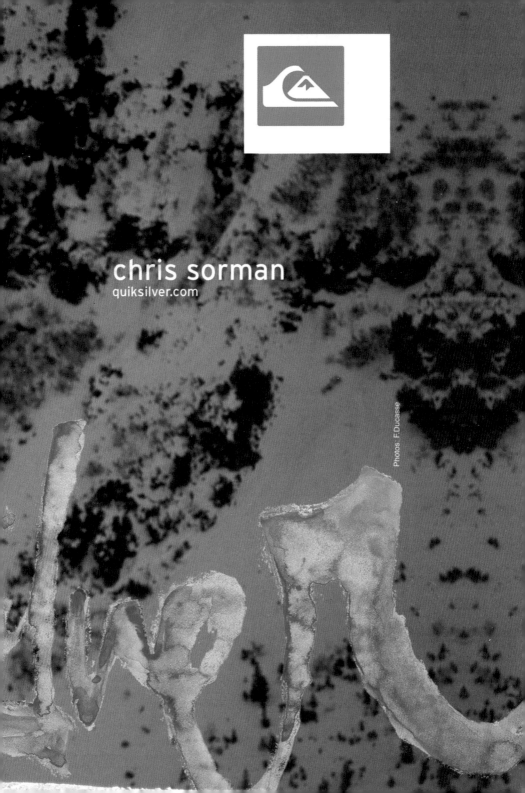

chris sorman
quiksilver.com

Photos: F.Ducasse

Compiled, written & edited by
Steve Dowle & Pete Coombs

Front cover: Location: Lech/Zürs am Arlberg **Rider**: Mäx Holzer **Photo**: Reen West
Back cover: photo: atlinheliski.com, Canada (page 63)
Additional photos: Zoe Webber

Book design & layout by Steve Dowle

Contributions (full reviews in brackets):
Tim Wilkinson - New Zealand (Olympus, Potts), USA (Schweitzer, bridger bowl, Solitude), various Canada. **Emma Taylor** - Whistler review. **Melanie Leando** - Avoriaz/ Morzine update. **Dmitri Paranyushkin** - all Russia reviews & language. **Edward Land** - Austria (Pitzal), Norway, Sweden, USA (northstar, alpine). **Nigel Fisher,** France. **Nicolas Ramirez** - Chile (Al Arpa). **Keith Stubbs** - (Kirkwood,Keystone). **Simon Gorbould, Woody** - German language, **Claire Hickman** - health on the hill, **Sonic** - Zermatt review

Big thanks to: Susie Smith for much support, Woody, Bob & Joan Dowle, Jason Horton, the Mitchells, Per-Hampus Stålhandske, Flynn Seddon, Rob of RTM, Jenny from Soul Sports, Steph for the advertising, Tony F, the Olympic/SIGB team. All the resorts who have helped us out with access & info, and all the photographers used. Tony Brown for starting this. Without the support from our advertisers this book wouldn't be possible, so cheers. El Rafa Benitez & LFC

WORLD SNOWBOARD GUIDE 2006
ISBN 0-9548014-1-5

10th edition – September 2005
First published 1996

Published by:
World Snowboard Guide Ltd
Medius House, 2 Sheraton Street
London W1F 8BH
England

Telephone: +44 (0)207 748 6136
Fax: +44 (0)207 748 6137
Email: info@worldsnowboardguide.com
Web: www.worldsnowboardguide.com

UK distribution by:
Vine House Distribution Ltd
Telephone: +44 (0)1825 723 398

USA distribution by:
SCB Distributors
Tel: +1 (800) 729-6423
Tel: +1 (310) 532-9400
Fax +1 (310) 532-7001

Printed in England by:
Bemrose Booth Ltd
Telephone: +44 (0) 1332 294 242

wsg | 2006
Contents

Before you book that holiday or jump in your car, ask yourself what is it you want from a resort. Do you need instruction? Are you there for the boarding or the night life? Freeride or Freestyle? Do you need a hotel to pamper you or do you want the freedom of your own apartment? And the big one how much cash do you have?

In the **Northern Hemisphere** most resorts open fully mid December but some will open mid November, offering cheap lift tickets, and if you get early snow you could find yourself alone on the slopes. Resorts generally close late April, with some high altitude resorts remaining open into the summer, with boarding on glaciers. Christmas, New Year, February half term and Easter are steer clear times, the resorts are always packed and accommodations at a premium. If you have to go at these times pick a resort with an extensive lift system or you'll find you're queuing more than boarding. The choice of holiday options has never been better and greatly helped by budget airlines. If you want to spend big, you can, with some European resorts offering 5 star hotels on the piste. If cash is short you can often find a bunk house. You can also get great last minute deals with tour operators offering hassle free half board chalet based weeks.

ALTITUDE

Altitude can be vital; some of the lower resorts struggle for snow and often rely on artificial snowmaking. Higher normally means better snow fall and piste coverage, although some high resorts suffer from strong winds, which damages the off piste conditions as well as the piste. Altitude of the resorts town as well as it slopes is important, again the higher the better, or you may find yourself picking your way through rocks and grass, if you want to board back to your accommodation. The higher resorts mostly come with a higher price. If moneys no problem head high it could mean the difference between a great trip and a good one.

SMALL MAY BE BETTER

Often small resorts which maybe cheaper, will join up with a huge interlinked area, such as the Port du Soleil, which links 14 resorts in France and Switzerland. Before rushing to a huge area and paying that hard earned cash for an expensive lift pass, think about your standard. Beginners will only use a few pistes, so why pay loads of cash on a lift pass you won't full utilise. Some riders just hit the fun parks and don't even need a lift pass, some resorts sell cheap terrain park specific passes. In most resorts you can buy a daily upgrade on your pass which allows you to board other adjoining valleys. This could save you money if the weather turns bad and the top lifts are shut all week, and gives you the freedom to decide on the day.

Alpes D'Huez, France (see page 148)
© nuts.fr/JP NOISILLIER/OT ALPE D'HUEZ

FREERIDE OR FREESTYLE?

Our reviews are broken down into four main snowboarding genres Freeride, Freestyle, Pistes, and Beginners.

Freeriding is exactly what it suggests, riding freely around the mountain, be it on the piste, through the trees or best of all descending virgin snow at mach 20, leaving a cloud of snow in your wake. If that's your thing this guide will tell you if a resort has trees, if there's easy access to off piste, what the lift systems like and most importantly what part of the resort to head for. Be warned never take on anything above your ability and if you do go off piste always wear a transceiver, carry a shovel and follow the resorts advice on avalanche risk.

their technique and riding style. Riders are informed of the best slopes for speed, and of a resorts track record on slope maintenance.

BEGINNERS are advised of a resorts suitability. Many resorts will have a designated beginner's area, often with a Magic carpet lift (a small ground level lift, great for first timers). Beginners should always look closely at the level of instruction a resort can offer. Look for a specialized snowboard school. Being taught to board by an Austrian with little English who normally teaches skiing just won't do.

Don't think you won't need lessons, a good posture and stance leads to good balance, which is everything

Freestylers are the big air merchants who love fun parks and half pipes. It's all about the moves, there's no point in going big if there's no style involved, a huge floating grabbed 360 looks far better than a rushed 540. If methods and misty flips are your tip then let WSG inform you of a resorts terrain park and pipes. Many resorts claim to have fun parks and when you turn up its a few bumps on an icy piste. A resort with any snowboarding credibility will have got a pro rider or at least the local riders to help with the design and building of the park. Good parks will have a fulltime team of employees, designated to the upkeep of the hits and pipe. If not you could ask for a shovel at the lift hut and do some pipe-shaping yourself, but only wield a shovel with permission and knowledge. If you don't know what you're doing and destroy a pipe wall, or spoil a hits take off you'll be liable to get a slap.

Piste is mainly for intermediate riders, who want to improve

in snowboarding. You may get away with leaning back and swinging your arms around on the nursery slopes, but once you reach an intermediate level your progress will be hindered by your early bad habits; how can you ever expect to land a jump if you're unbalanced on the approach. A top tip is don't try to teach your spouse, it's bound to end in a fight and there's nothing more annoying than wasting your holiday standing on a green run wishing you were somewhere else.

LIFTS

Lifts will vary around the world, the most basic are **Drag lifts** which normally entail sticking something uncomfortable between your legs and letting it pull you up the hill. Beginners will often find themselves being dragged up the mountain with their face in the snow. Beginners are advised to travel on drag lifts with their rear foot released from its binding, as it allows for a quick getaway should you fall off, and just try and relax your body and look forward.

Chair lifts make for a more comfortable journey and should also be used with your rear foot out of its binding, just remember to keep the board flat and pointing straight when getting on and off.

Bubble/Gondola and **Cable Cars** are enclosed shells, normally with seats which are suspended from a cable and usually the fastest way to the top of the mountain. Some resorts have Funiculars which are underground trains that are incredibly efficient. Some resorts won't let you on the lifts without a leash on your board. This is a completely pointtless strap that connects your boot to your binding, supposidly so your board won't fall off on a lift - as if. Stick one in your pocket in case you meet a fussy lift operator.

LIFT PASSES

Most resorts offer a range of lift passes which can usually be bought on a daily or multiple-day basis. **Weekly tickets** will normally require an attached picture, so take a passport-sized photo with you. Riders staying for a few months can buy season passes, and although expensive, you will make a massive saving in the long run. You may have the choice of one resort or an interlinked area, sometimes you may even get a free day in a nearby affiliated resort. Ask at the office when you buy your pass. Discounted passes are available for kids, old age pensioners, locals and sometimes students. You'll also find prices changes during the season; at low season you can pay around 25% less. Resorts have their own polices on reimbursement if lifts are shut.

Many resorts offer **beginner packages** that offer good value for money. You get a lesson, full equipment hire and a lift pass that gives you access to the beginners slopes. Its also possible to get terrain park only lift passes at some resorts, and a few even have a few free beginner lifts, so make sure you check before shelling out on a full pass if you're not going to use it.

Lift Chairs, Zoë Webber

from £79

GATWICK – GRENOBLE

RETURN INCL. TAXES

Have you clicked yet? **ba.com**

INSURANCE

Shine a torch into the ear of a boarder without insurance and sure enough there'll be light coming out the other side. Only a fool would hit the slopes without good insurance. The main things to check in the small print of your policy is that it states:

- Snowboarding
- Off Piste (you don't want to be crawling back to the piste with a busted leg)
- Personal Injury including repatriation.
- Personal Belongings including your board
- Curtailments, cancellation of flights etc

If hiring kit make sure it's insured on your policy or covered by the hire shop. If its your own kit then make sure your all your kit is covered and that there's not a tiny maximum limit on a single item.

It's possible to get insurance with your lift pass in some countries but this will normally only cover getting you off the slopes and to the hospital.

There's a huge choice out there so pick wisely. If you're going to go on holiday more than a couple of times a year, then get an annual policy, but do watch the maximum number of ski/board days that they always hide in there.

EUROPEAN HEALTH INSURANCE CARD

All EU nationals (inc UK) can get the free European Health Insurance Card (EHIC) which has replaced the old E111, pick up the form from the post office. Its valid for 3-5 years and basically allows you to the same medical treatment that a regular member of that country is eligable to.

You can apply online by going to www.ehic.org.uk or phone (UK) 0845 606 2030, or pick up a form from the post office.

This is no replacement for insurance but it makes sure you're covered for basic medical care and not charged, and is valid across all EU member states and Switzerland.

THEFT

At least once when you go boarding you'll hear the story that a van turned up at the resort and nicked a load of boards from outside a bar. Make sure you look after your board and that your insurance policy covers the full value of it. Its worth spending a tenner and buying a board lock. It may not look cool, but it'll save you when you stumble back to the bar you started drinking in 8 hours ago trying to find it.

If you do get anything stolen then contact the police, you probably won't get it back, but it will help with your claim.

Lake Tahoe sunset, USA
pic WS

we carry your
snowboarding
equipment for free

Book early for this and many more
snowboarding destinations

Don't dress just to look fly! Make sure you're wearing the right kit. Outer layers should be water and wind proof and if possible breathable. The best way to stay warm is to wear layers rather than one huge jumper, so that the air is trapped between the layers and warmed from your body heat. You can buy technical tops to wear next to your skin which are designed to be fast drying and whip the sweat away. if you sweat in cotton it stays wet.

Hiring Kit

If you plan to rent snowboard equipment, it may be better to hire in-resort. That way you only pay for the days you use the equipment, and it gives you the freedom to change the board and boots if they are not right. Another plus side is if you like the set up you maybe able to buy it less the rental price at the end of the hire. Don't settle for substandard kit, things are much better than they used to be and most resorts will have a snowboard specialist. Gone are the days when you had to choose between a few old boards in the back of a ski hire shop. A positive side to hiring before you leave is there maybe a wider choice and if you wanted a specific brand or size you should be able to reserve it, also many shops will offer a standard package or you can pay more to hire top of the range kit.

The main things to check are that the base and edges are in good condition, and that the bindings are set up for you, not just screwed on any old way, and make sure there's no excessive boot overhang. The board should come up to your chin. A short board is good to learn on, but once you start picking up speed a longer board will be more stable. Always check on screws and other parts of your kit; if bits do come loose on the mountain, then look for maintenance tools located at most lift stations. It's a good idea to buy, and carry, a mini-binding tool when on the slopes.

Kids

As more kids take up snowboarding the rental equipment for little people has improved. A good store should have genuine children's kit. It's a good idea to hire a safety helmet and wrist-guards as you don't want to spend your time down the valley with little Billy while he gets put back together.

pic Woody

HEALTH ON THE HILL

To get the most out of any snowboard trip you should have a reasonable level of fitness. You need not be an Olympic athlete but to avoid feeling like you've been hit by a truck do some exercise before reaching the slopes. In resort the best things to do each day to prevent injury is do a warm up before that first run, even if it's just a few stretches warm mussels won't tear as easily as when cold.

Just because a resort has hotels and chair lifts don't let it fool you, it's still a mountain and should be treated with respect. There's less oxygen at altitude and you'll find yourself puffing even on a short up hill walk. Add that to the 15 pints of beer you drank last night and the cold air, and suddenly dehydration is a real issue so drink plenty of water. The sun is really strong in the mountains and reflects off the snow, making your face redder than pie eating football fan's beer belly in Benidorm. Get 100%UV approved goggles and sunglasses, wear high factor sun screen and remember to reapply.

OFF THE SLOPE

There's often loads to do in resorts other than boarding. Some resorts can offer ice-climbing, snowmobiling, paragliding, some even offer tandem freefall parachute jumps. Lots of resorts will have indoor sports facilities like swimming pools, ice rinks, bowling alleys and gyms. Most importantly all will have pubs, bars, night clubs and restaurants. It shouldn't take long to find the best places to hang out, just ask a local to point you in the right direction. Try to stay away from the humourless hat wearing skiers bars that play euro pop and sell cocktails with stupid names. Restaurants on the mountain are always more expensive than those in the town, some criminally so. Most places will have a wide range of eateries from street food to fine dinning.

Snowboarding is there for you to enjoy. Party Hard but Ride Harder.

Steamboat Colorado, USA (see page 350)
Larry Pierce/Steamboat Resort

Hassle-free car hire

Easy Rider

Alamo is WSG's car hire partner, and with locations throughout the world and a great choice of cars, we've got it covered.

Our inclusive rates are designed for ease and peace of mind, with all the protection you need – and quick and efficient service to send you on your way.

So just relax and enjoy the ride.

call **0870 191 6938** quoting **WSG**

click **worldsnowboardguide.com/alamo**

Please give that man a beer. Who was it that came up with the idea of budget airfares? If you're lucky enough to live near an airport serviced by a budget airline, and you want to go to the Alps, get a map out, take your driving licence, and you may find yourself a short drive from the slopes for less money than you'll spend on the first round of beers. The cheapest way is to book as far in advance as possible, but of course that means you won't know what the snow conditions will be. If you can fly early morning and mid week it's far cheaper than on a weekend. A lot of the arrival airports are in the middle of a cow field, so if you can't rent a car do some research into public transport before you arrive or you maybe turning up in the resort on the back of a bull. A down side to budget airlines is if it goes wrong there's little back up. If your flight is cancelled you're

ROLLING YOUR OWN
If you're taking your own kit with you, make sure you check to see if they charge you for the privilege. Most of the tour operators do, and for the budget airlines it's a given, expect to be charged around £20. It looks like Ryan Air won't even allow you to take your kit with you, so check the situation out before you turn up to the airport.

FLY DRIVE
Fly drive is always a winner in North America, it also gives you the freedom to roam resorts at will and follow the snow. If you're boarding in one of the more remote parts of the world then you should defiantly go it alone, and try to hang with the locals, not just steamroller through their country in the back of a motor.

normally met with a long queue and only the offer of a flight in a few days time or your money back.

GOING IT ALONE
The main benefit of going alone is the freedom, as you can visit many resorts in a week. Look on the web find the best snow and head straight to it, but be careful if you're trying to do it on the cheap side as you could find yourself stuck in a full resort and stumping up for an expensive room. When looking for accommodation in a resort try the Tourist Info Office first, they can normally help you with finding and sometimes booking accommodation, and they'll usually speak good English.

TOUR OPERATORS
If time is short tour operators can be great. They will sort out your flights and arrange a transfer to and from resort. If you've booked half-board you'll get breakfast, afternoon tea, and with dinner often free wine. You may have to hold your nose to get it down but it's free. They can also arrange hotels and self-catering apartments. Be careful to find out exactly where your accommodation is located or you could have a long bus ride or walk to the lifts each morning. The two main draw backs to organized holidays is if there's no snow your scuppered, and the holiday reps will try to bleed you dry by wanting to sell you stupid après ski fondue nights.

TRAINS
Many resorts are close to major train links. It sure beats bus services for speed, but make sure that you plan ahead and don't turn up to the airport without knowing the next step. From London you can hop on the snow train on a Thursday night and hop out at Bourg St.Maurice at 7am ready for the lifts to open in Les Arcs.

COACHES
20 hours in a coach doesn't sound like fun, and make no mistake, its not. But then again, if you're small and want a cheap getaway then perfect. There's many companies offering very cheap boarding weekends and holidays by coach, that leave from various parts of the UK to various places in France. You'll travel overnight and possibly get there in time for a few hours on the slope, or at worst first at the bar. Stateside many of the large towns on the east and west coasts run boarding day trips. You'll leave at the crack of dawn, get there by 9am and head off at 4pm. Its a long day, but the price can include your lift pass be a bargain/

wsg | board test

Terrorist attacks, floods, mud slides, a broken rib, a lacerated hand, a pregnancy, a broken aeroplane, snow blindness and miles of motor way driving in torrential rain - not to mention the hangovers and the sun burn. And all I wanted to do was organise a board test.

Picked up the phone and was greeted with *"Pete, I can't come"*.
- *"What "*!
- *"I'm,,,, well, I'm pregnant"*
It's ok, it isn't as bad as it sounds - I'm not the father.
- *"The doctors told me not to go boarding"*
Ok, so we're one girl boarder down - not too much of a problem, still got two others, and Jo agrees to the painful job of sitting at the WSG base camp co-ordinating aka. watching everyone board then helping them to change bindings and set up boards.
Phone goes again. *"Pete mate, got really pissed on a stag do, and have slashed my hand open while dressed as a 118 runner, curly wig, vest, the lot. I've had a doctor picking little bits of glass out of my hand all morning"*.
- *"Ouch, can you still board"*?
- *"Yep I just can't get it wet, or fall on it"*
- *"Ok cool, so don't fall over"*.
Ok, so a pregnancy and a slashed hand, what next?
Phone rings again. *"Pete, you're not going to believe it"*.
- *"What Sam, what"*?
"I was playing cricket and two of us went to catch the same ball, I got a flying knee to the ribs, I think it's broken".
"Did you catch it"?
"No, he did".
"So can you move"? (all compassion lost by this point.)
"Yes, I'll get some pain killers and take it easy for the first few days".

It's now the day before the test. The accommodation is sorted in **Schladming**, the people at the **Dachstein Glacier** know we're coming and have set up a WSG test centre at the bottom of the terrain park. The cars are booked and ready for collection from **Alamo** at **Munich** airport. The test team is in place, albeit a little wounded, and increased by one-still-to-be-born future rider. All but the Rossignol boards are either clogging up my girl-friends flat, or have been delivered to the **Burton Superpark** on the Dachstein Glacier. Time to relax.

Thursday morning. A nice relaxing day. I just need the Rossignol boards to be delivered to the girlfriends flat, and then I can kick back before the flight.

Boooooooooooommmmmmmmmmm London's been blown up, tube trains and bus seemingly exploding everywhere.
(The bombs were a terrible thing to happen, and I'm sorry for the people who lost loved ones, but this is a story about a board test not an article on terrorism).

So London comes to a stand still. I'm now not so worried about the Rossignol boards arriving, as I am about getting myself across London to Heathrow airport, and the whole test going ahead at all. Finally after many calls, I'm sorted - I can get a taxi (for a huge price), but at least I can get to the airport. The Rossignol boards are stuck in a van somewhere and I will have to leave without them. Steve - who lives in central London - has a harder job with his logistics, and ends up walking out of central London, dragging all his kit behind him, one ear to his phone for travel updates Finally he makes it south of the river to meet up with Tony's over priced taxi. Woody is travelling down from Bristol on a bus and is ok, if running a little late. So we've made it to Heathrow even if we've spent a lot - and I mean a lot - of beer money on getting there.

Dodski's infamous 90 ass plant

Friday is spent setting up the test centre and giving the new Burton Vapour and Ride Timeless a blast through the powder – yes, powder - on the **Dachstein Glacier** in July. Friday night, the rest of the team arrive late in **Schladming** only to find no one at home. After a few calls they locate us in the pub, fully cut and with a huge pile of miniature Jagermeister bottles scattered all over our table. Woody insists on another Jagermeister for the road (in fact I think he insisted on all the bloody Jagermeister's!).

Saturday, it's time for the test proper. Down at the apartment it's pissing with rain and the hangovers are in full force, fingers crossed it's dumping on the Dachstein Glacier. Sure enough it is – and it's great to see a line of spanking new boards stuck in the fresh snow, and the WSG team picking whatever board they want. Our team is an assortment of seasonaires, instructors and beginners. Not a pro in sight, but hey, when was the

last time a pro had to buy a board, and more importantly, when did you ever hear a pro-rider slagging off their sponsor's kit?

Dodski, a beginner with 4 weeks of boarding under his ever-so-large belt (who's famed for his 90 degree arse plants and full commitment to never landed jumps) takes the **Burton Vapour** a £650 board and proceeds to get the biggest air of the weekend; man that boy can fly, if only he would learn to land them!

Steve takes a 163 **Ride Profit** while Tony takes the 157 - both are impressed but still prefer the **Timeless** from the day before. .

Sam (the one with the busted rib) grabs the **Salomon DB** 157 and heads straight to the **Burton Superpark** and the rails. We almost have to bust another of his ribs to get the

Rider: Pete

board back off him, so we can test it!

Sonic takes the **Sapient Seduction** 155, which has a woman in a leather cat suit, whip in hand, on the front - a popular graphic with the lads. While Riggs, our 5'4" Norwegian girl rider, takes out a 152 **Burton Feel Good** and gets some good air. I take out the Burton Triumph 163, which is a little to big for me but I find I can stomp my landings with ease. Woody (who still stinks of last nights booze) gives the **Sapient Coast** a blast and agrees with the word on the street that it's a great board, but it has to be ridden real hard.

After testing 3 or 4 boards each we head back to Schladming, where it's still raining and there's a mad alphorn blowing music festival going on. Someone points out that, despite the fact that we've been in snow clouds all day, we're all sporting a fine pair of goggle marks. Shit,

what a school boy error! By 8 o'clock, Woody's eyes start to water. By 9 there not watering anymore, they're just red, like he's in a photo taken with the red-eye reducer turned off. Woody thinks the best course of action is to bathe his stomach in as much Jagermeister as possible - it seems to work as he stops rubbing his eyes, but he

We all join in, and another night of bad Austrian cough mixture - which they pass off as a nice drink - is followed by the final day of the test.

The rain still hasn't stopped and the snow on the glacier is a little wet, but we're not deterred and give the remaining boards a full days riding. Sonic over did the cough mixture the night before and takes to the test centre to sleep it off.

The **Salomon** boards got a good testing today, with all in agreement that they really are making

Rider: sam

some great boards now, although the bindings could still do with some work. With all the boards tested, and a very tired and wet looking test team, we head back down from the snow and into the rain.

With the main test over, half the team head off to the airport and back to the UK summer. The rest of us drive to **Sölden** for a days boarding. Five rain swept hours later, we pull up in Sölden, and each rider picks their favourite board for a full days ride tomorrow. Sam, being worse than a package-deal holiday maker with his towel on a sun lounger, sleeps with the **Salomon DB** and the **Ride SPi** bindings to state his claim. The morning brings the same as the last few: rain. A short drive up to the glacier, and we're sitting on a chair lift clutching our boards in a total white out. The winds really strong, and the hard hail-like snow is smacking us in the face. July in Europe? it's more like January in Canada! After the chair there's a gondola (which is at least warm and dry) that takes us up to the park. Although we can't see much, the snow's great - a good foot of fresh powder, and, apart form another small group of boarders, we've got the mountain and park to ourselves.

Knackered after a hard day on the slopes, we climb into the car. Switching on the radio we hear of mudslides in Kitzbühel, Salzburg being on flood alert with the distinct likelihood of the city being evacuated, and are told of loads of rivers which are about to burst their banks. After a record quick loading of the van, the 3 hours we've given ourselves to get to Munich airport for the flight home, is looking decidedly dodge.
Shit the rain's heavy, the windscreen wipers are giving it their all but the rain just keeps coming. We pass a river, which if it rises at all will flood the autobahn, and still the rain gets heavier. Suddenly there's sunshine - the first we're seen since London - but then, shit, even more rain! In fact,

Rider: Dietmar Pichler Photo: Jan Zach
Dachstein Tourism

more rain than you've ever seen; more than a monsoon in Laos, more than a summers day in Scotland. It's like driving under the Niagara Falls, and then parking up for a bit. Then just before we reach the airport the traffic grinds to a stand-still: that's the flight missed then. Nothings moving other than the rapid backwards and forwards of the windscreen wipers. Then, slowly at first, but then faster and faster, the traffic starts to move. Pulling up at the curb-side drop off zone at the airport, the team runs to check in, whilst Steve and I do mach 10 across the airport to drop off the van. Wow, that was close - but hang on, it's not over yet. The rain has closed the airport and our plane has been diverted, and the interior lights of the replacement plane aren't working. Finally, 5 hours late, we land back in London to find that there's no public transport whatsoever still running…its taxi time again. Arriving back at the girlfriends flat, I unlock the front door as quietly as I can so I don't wake her up. Suddenly I'm being attacked by a dark shape - I drop my bags and brace myself for a blow. Thwack! I get it to the head, seconds later I come round with a huge pile of Rossignol boards on top of me. So they arrived after all.

We had biblical floods, July powder, a pregnancy, wounds and breaks, terrorist attacks, broken aeroplanes, mudslides, sunburn, sun blindness and hangovers. Yes, it was emotional; yes, I returned home a beaten man, but wow - we had a great time. I rode more brand new boards in a weekend than in my twelve previous years of boarding. There's nothing quite like peeling the plastic off a new board, strapping it to your feet for an hour or two, then going back to the test centre and saying "yep, it was good, but I'd now like to try that one". That's a luxury you don't get in a high street shop. Our test was set up to inform the average rider/holiday maker on what the boards are like this year. It wasn't about a group of pros hanging out together, spewing pre-prepared advertising spiel, it was a test by average riders, aimed at helping out the fellow average rider who's looking for a new board.

If you fancy getting involved in next years test, keep an eye on our website **www.worldsnowboardguide.com** towards the end of next season, for information on our next test.

Take care, ride hard, but most of all don't believe all the marketing hype.

Pete and the WSG Test Team.

The board testers

Name	Gender	Level	Style	History	Feet	Height	Weight	Current	Favourite
Dodski	Male	Beg/Int	All Mountain	3 years, 2 weeks per year	UK 9	176cm	83kg	Hire	Timeless & Vapour
Pete	Male	Advanced	Freerider	12 years inc 6 full seasons	UK 9 1/2	171cm	66 kg	Ride Concept, Jeff Brushie bindings	Ride Timeless
Riggs	Female	Beginner		Converted skier, boarding 1 year	UK 3	158cm	49 kg	Hire	Ride Solace
Sam	Male	Advanced	Freestyle	11 years inc 3 full seasons	UK 8 1/2	177cm	66 kg	Forum/GNU boards + Ride bindings	Salomon DB
Sonic	Female	Intermediate	Freerider	4 years, 2 weeks per year	UK 6	174cm	64 kg	Burton custom	Timeless
Steve	Male	Adv/Int	All Mountain	5 years, 5 weeks per year	UK 10 1/2	192cm	68 kg	Burton Custom & Carbon P1's	Burton Vapour
Tony	Male	Intermediate	All Mountain	6 years, 3 weeks per year	UK 9	172cm	73kg	Libtech Jamie Lynn, Burton custom bindings	Ride Prophet
Woody	Male	Adv/Int	All Mountain	7 years inc 2 full seasons	UK 9	178cm	73 kg	Burton Rippey 2000, mission bindings	Timeless

Rider: Riggs

Rider: Tony

sapient COAST

"Is a traditionally designed Freeride board. With a softer nose to initiate turns and a stiffer tail to help stomp those rock drops."

STYLE	
FREERIDE	
PRICE	
329 UK	
SIZES	
148, 153, 156, 159, 163	
FEET	
NORMAL	

TOP   BASE

Tester's comments

Woody - Really good for jumping and easy to land, even when hung-over. I like it a lot! Not sure how it would cope in deep powder though but lots of fun.

Tony - Like all Sapients I tried this also faired very well. A very good stable all-round board, but not as flexible as the seduction or PNB1. Nice work Sapient!

Pete - Fine, but needs to be ridden hard to get the most out of it. Very little vibration when straight lining it

Steve - The 159 felt very flexible without needing to work it. A very nice board that required little effort in making it go where I wanted it to go.

RIDE SOLACE

"A girls all mountain, which will go down well with girls, who want to tour the mountain but feel stable on a jumps run up."

STYLE	
ALL MOUNTAIN	
PRICE	
230 UK	
SIZES	
138, 142, 146, 150, 154	
FEET	
NORMAL	

TOP   BASE

Tester's comments

Riggs - Sweet! Very smooth ride and responsive when turning. Graphics looked good.

Rider: Pete

Rider: Steve

◩ RIDE PROPHET

"A karang board for the park rider. Put on the tunes and hit the park hard, the Prophet won't let you down."

STYLE
FREESTYLE
PRICE
400 UK
SIZES
152, 156, 159, 163
FEET
NORMAL

TOP　　　BASE

Tester's comments

Sonic - much longer than i usually board with, and felt very encouraging

Steve - Didn't do it for me on the pistes, at 163 slightly longer than my normal board but didn't feel too boat like when turning, and fine for my size 10 feet. I needed a shorter board to start getting some spring out of it, even ollie's were hard work.

Tony - Slightly too large for me and therefore had to work it very hard. Very stable on piste but not that flexible when messing around.

Woody - Okay(ish), but nothing special. Same base as the timeless which makes a whistling noise when boarding. Not a big fan of the heavy metal graphics

Dodski - Gave a smooth firm ride, but nothing spectacular on the piste, A great board to learn and improve with; felt like the girl next door, safe secure and comfortable

Pete - Just what you expect from a Ride board; strong, stiff and great edge hold. Handled the park with ease. When ridden shorter than normal it became much easier to work the board into doing more springy

◩ RIDE TIMELESS

"Ride just can't stop doing it. This board is really timeless, just when you thought the timeless would get no better they bring out this all mountain gem"

STYLE
ALL MOUNTAIN
PRICE
370 UK
SIZES
152, 156, 159, 161, 164, 168, 172
FEET
NORMAL

TOP　　　BASE

Tester's comments

Dodski - Fucking loved it. It does exactly what it says on the tin; gives you a timeless ride you'll never forget. Can I keep it?

Tony - Redder than your mums slapped sun burnt ass [the 156]. Felt very stable on the piste, but more difficult through the powder. Found it quite stiff and wouldn't want to take it into the park

Woody - The dogs, but graphics are a little boring. Very zippy and easy to make tiny fast turns. However makes a horrible noise as it cuts through the snow - supposedly a noise reduction system, but it sounds even noisier than a normal board.

Sonic - Great graphics and a top board.

Sam - Good on the piste, rode just as well switch as normal. Good edges, no flapping and comfortable at speed. Good all-round mountain board, and fine on jumps and rails.

Pete - Very confident when changing edge, a real stiff board, very unforgiving, but when ridden hard it responds to you and allows you to take on the mountain. Loved the simple, understated graphics

Steve - Great board, gave me confidence in pretty much anything I threw at it. It did sound a bit like the Nightrider car when hacking it down the pistes. Stability landing jumps maybe the only issue, but that's probably not the board ... Loved the graphics, very understated without being boring and bright without be garish.

ROSSIGNOL
PURE MOUNTAIN COMPANY®

Decoy

"Bringing a twin tip revival to the slopes, the Decoy has much flex and is great in the park. A true twin tip in the old school way"

STYLE	
FREESTYLE	
PRICE	
370 UK	
SIZES	
153, 157, 161	
FEET	
NORMAL	

TOP   BASE

ROSSIGNOL
PURE MOUNTAIN COMPANY®

Alias

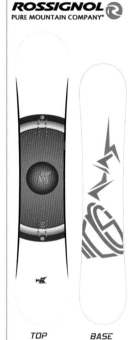

"JF Plechat the Canadian pro designed this board, for the rider who wants to stand in the centre of the board and wants to spend some of his cash in the pub nit just in the board shop."

STYLE	
FREESTYLE	
PRICE	
240 UK	
SIZES	
149, 153, 157, 161, 154+ ,158+	
FEET	
NORMAL/BIG	

TOP   BASE

ROSSIGNOL
PURE MOUNTAIN COMPANY®

Sultan

"Beginners get ready, the Sultan is for you. A great board at a great price. Designed with a longer nose and a short tail for those who want to go forward everywhere."

STYLE	
ALL MOUNTAIN	
PRICE	
180 UK	
SIZES	
150, 155, 159 164, 155+, 159+, 163+	
FEET	
NORMAL/BIG	

TOP   BASE

ROSSIGNOL
PURE MOUNTAIN COMPANY®

Zena

"A woman's all mountain board, with a girls version available @£120. A great board, for the girl who wants to tour the mountain, and still hit the park on occasion. Another good board at a good price from Rossignol"

STYLE	
ALL MOUNTAIN	
PRICE	
220 UK	
SIZES	
139, 143, 148, 153, 157	
FEET	
NORMAL	

TOP   BASE

WWW.SAPIENTSNOWBOARDS.COM

sapient
SNOWBOARDS

Sapient is a division of
A Mordo & Son Ltd

□ sapient SEDUCTION

"Is a full on girls freestyle, it's not for the hot chocolate drinking chalet girl. Designed for a girl that wants to kick the boys arses in the park."

STYLE	
FREESTYLE	
PRICE	
329 UK	
SIZES	
147, 152, 155	
FEET	
NORMAL	

TOP   BASE

Tester's comments

Tony - Slightly too light and sank in the powder. Good nose and tail flex; landed my first forward roll with it!

Woody - Good fun and very manouverable but a bit small for powder. Great for jumping and spins, and would suit beginners to good intermediates alike.

Sonic - Very comfortable in the park, and performed better than average out of it. Very inappropriate graphics - especially for a female board [Ed - the board we tested had last years graphics - a women in leather and a whip ;-)]

□ sapient PNB1

"This team designed board is full on, and set up for the advanced rider. Carbon and Kevlar inserts and a new fusion core make it responsive when ridden hard."

STYLE	
FREESTYLE	
PRICE	
399 UK	
SIZES	
151, 153, 157	
FEET	
NORMAL	

TOP   BASE

Tester's comments

Pete - Great board but very slow in the slush, like the Coast it needs to be pushed hard before you start seeing a return above the norm.

Tony - Felt very solid landing jumps and nice and flexible doing ground tricks.

Sam - Did not enjoy this board, seemed neither good at one thing or another. All full tilt it didn't respond well, and in the park not much better

Woody - The 153 felt too short, the 157 much better. Didn't feel particularly like a freestyle board.

Dodski - Felt a bit sluggish when turning and needed to be bullied into some speed to start getting the most out of it.

OUCH!
WE MAKE
ONLINE SHOPPING
PAINLESS

blue-tomato.com
ONLINE-SNOWBOARDSHOP

info@blue-tomato.at | www.blue-tomato.com
Info Hotline: +43 (0)3687-24 22 344

TOP   BASE

TRIUMPH

BURTON

"the Triumps slightly tappered shape redifines the balance of float, speed and agility"

STYLE
FREERIDE
PRICE
350 UK
SIZES
156,160, 164,169, 173
FEET
MID SIZE

Tester's comments

Pete - Good spring in the nose and tail and very forgiving when landing jumps. At 163 I would have thought it would have been a bit too big, but it rode like a short board with the bonus of that long board stability when ridding at speed and in the pow

Steve - I suffer from the old toe drag, but hated my old wide board so this was going to be interesting. Very pleasantly surprised, no overhang, and yet I was able to turn; both long sweepers and little ones. As expected in the powder it didn't sink, and in the park it felt big, but had some good pop in the nose without having to really try.

TOP   BASE

VAPOUR

BURTON

"Ultra-light and ultra-responsive, the vapur rides like an extension of your mind - you think, it reacts"

STYLE
ALL MOUNTAIN
PRICE
650 UK
SIZES
154, 157, 160
FEET
NORMAL

Tester's comments

Tony - Burtons lightest board, but i didn't notice it when it was strapped to my feet! Very expensive and probably great for experts and the rich, but it only felt like an above average board to me.

Woody - Far too expensive and unjustifyably so. Very light but that was about it, rode a bit like a light Burton Custom. Gimicky see through core on the base.

Sonic - Completely out of my league this one. I'm sure the pros are gonna love it but I struggled holding an edge and getting a response.

Dodski - Exciting board, held edges well at speed and the faster you rode it the better it seemed to get. Great at carving and a joy to ride, the only fault is the price. You can have almost as much fun on a cheaper board; best for those with deep pockets or more money than sense.

Pete - Too soft but the softness gives it a very forgiving nature which is great help when landing jumps, but a bit worrying when at speed on a bumpy piste. A good board, but at the price you want more than good.

Steve - My most eagerly anticipated board, but if I thought I was suddenly going to start pulling huge tricks then I was mistaken. Amazingly springy nose and tail, so easy to ollie with but first impressions on the piste were that it would lose edges and I struggled to straightline it without bouncing everywhere. Swapped to the shortter 157 later on, and it felt so much better. It's the equivalent of a mini; it didn't get me there any quicker but it was a laugh all the way. I'll find it hard to justify shelling out that amount of cash ...

![BURTON] FEELGOOD

"The first truly specific female board, treating women right for over a decade"

TOP   BASE

STYLE	
ALL MOUNTAIN	
PRICE	
380 UK	
SIZES	
140,144, 149, 152, 156	
FEET	
NORMAL	

Tester's comments

Tony - Felt like a good first board, didn't do anything wrong but didn't set the world alight either. God awful graphics!

Riggs - Would be fine for beginners, but didn't feel particularly special. Extremely boring and unimaginative graphics.

SALOMON SNOWBOARDS

PATROL

"Arguably the lightest mid-wide on the market. It reopens the fun-factor "

STYLE	
ALL MOUNTAIN	
PRICE	
319 UK	
SIZES	
159, 163, 167	
FEET	
BIG	

TOP   BASE

Tester's comments

Woody - Far too big for me. Very stable but not responsive to quick turns.

Steve - I've always shied away from big foot boards, after painful memories of owning a second hand Burton Floater a good few years back. No toe drag at all, and the slightly raised centre did seem to help getting extra grip when initiating big turns at speed. It still felt like a boat though, and wasn't particularly manoeuvrable trying short turns on the piste. I'll stick to a little toe-drag still.

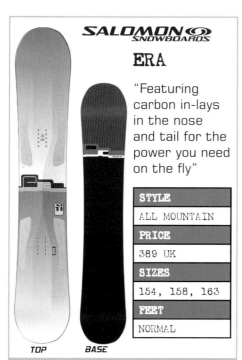

SALOMON SNOWBOARDS
ERA

"Featuring carbon in-lays in the nose and tail for the power you need on the fly"

STYLE	
ALL MOUNTAIN	
PRICE	
389 UK	
SIZES	
154, 158, 163	
FEET	
NORMAL	

TOP   BASE

Tester's comments

Sam - Took time to get used to, too big and not responsive enough on the piste. However excellent when ridden at speed and in the powder it proved to be fun to ride and responsive.

Pete - money graphics, very 70's

Tony - Too big and very unwieldly, but could plough easily through anything, so good for taking out skiers. Ugliest board i've seen - reminds me of 1960's council estate carpets!

Woody - Strange shaped nose, and I found it quite difficult to turn. Looked like a quality street chocolate, not particularly impressed.

Dodski - Seemed to give a heavy, slow somewhat sluggish ride. Too much effort was needed to make the board turn, and it had the turning circle of the QE2. Looks good though, but shame about the ride.

SALOMON SNOWBOARDS
PROSPECT

"Transworld top 10 board, will make you stand out in any any crowd"

STYLE	
FREESTYLE	
PRICE	
299 UK	
SIZES	
150, 153, 157, 160, 163	
FEET	
NORMAL	

TOP   BASE

Tester's comments

Pete - Sold as a freestyle board, but it needs to work very hard to make it happen in the park. However when you push it, it responds. This firmness lends itself very well in the powder and to the rest of the mountain. So a great board for those who ride hard in the park, but also to those want to kick ass when freeriding

Steve - The 160 was perfect for me, no overhang from my size 10's and it felt zippy and responded well. Wasn't sure how a freestyle board would handle the rest of the mountain, but it always felt right and i always felt in control. A true revelation in the powder, the nose never sank into the snow and I never had to lean back. In the park it stuck to the rails, but needed extra effort to pop off jumps, but it landed sooo smoothly.

Photo: Rudi Wyhlidal **Rider**: Bernd Mandlberger

SALOMON SNOWBOARDS

DB

"Pro riders board for the full on freestyler. With a central stance this board rides smooth forwards backward on its tail and on it's tip. A real park board."

STYLE	
FREESTYLE	
PRICE	
399 UK	
SIZES	
155.5	
FEET	
NORMAL	

TOP   BASE

Tester's comments

Sonic - Nice board but nothing special. Felt more at home on jumps than on the piste. Graphics very plain

Sam - Fun, fun, fun. Everything I like about this board, definitely a board for playtime. Good on the piste, excellent for ground tricks, jumps and rails, and will get you through days of all mountain riding. My absolute pleasure to ride, loved it, would sell my granny for one.

Pete - Fantastic board for the park and ground tricks but in the powder its a real leg killer. If you want a board just for the park, then this is it.

Board test conclusions

The big question when putting together this test was once you remove all the talk and marketing, would we actually notice anything significant between the boards? The answer was categorically yes. It was the first time that we'd ever had the opportunity to test this many boards over such a short period, and every rider in the test noticed fundamental differences between the boards.

These days' manufacturers don't produce shit boards. As with anything they are talked up, but all of boards we tested performed well, so it was pretty much down to personal preference.

We hid the brochures and price list before people tested. After each test, the rider was asked to complete the review sheet. Then they were allowed to look at what the manufacturers wrote, and how much it cost.

From the tests it became apparent that picking a board was only half the story. Your weight and height play such a significant part in finding a comfortable board. Testing the same board but of different lengths proved to

be enlightening, and often felt like a completely different board.

You should try and take any opportunity you get to test a number of boards before you buy one. Differences can be picked up within a run or two, so the more boards you can try, the better your choice will be. You can't just tell how a board will perform by reading about it, or bending it in the shop. Borrow your mates' boards, hire a demo board and get out there and try as many boards as you can.

Finally a big thanks to the following:

Juergen and Jan of Action Scouts
Bernd of Dachstein & the resort staff
Neil of Blue Tomato
Ash & Ed of Secret Distributions
Tara and Joerg of Ride
Richard of Salomon
Rob of AGM group
Birgit of Burton

BACKCOUNTRY GUIDE

Back in those dark days before snowboarding, when people were thinking of new ways to descend a slope it wasn't the green run to the café or a 540 they had in mind. It was havin-it down a wide open powder field at full speed sending a plume of light fluffy snow skyward in their wake. That's what Snowboards were made for and anyone who's had the joy of doing it will tell you there's nothing else like it. Those first turns in virgin snow will have you screaming with joy and boring your mates rotten in the bar for days.

Like any extreme sport there's a cost and in Back Country/ Off piste Boarding it can be high. People die every year in avalanches boarding Back Country, 90% of people who are caught in an avalanche either set it off themselves or someone in their party did.

Prior Preparation Prevents Piss Poor Performance. Before you think of heading Back Country there is knowledge and equipment you must have. Read any information on avalanches and back country travel you can get your hands on, watch videos, look at the web and don't skimp on equipment if you have a transceiver and no shovel all you can do is find where you should be digging. Over 90% of people buried in an avalanche survive if dug out within 15 minuets, try digging in avalanche debris with the end of your board, it doesn't work. Pack your back pack for all eventualities. Remember the weather in the mountains can change fast, because you started the day in sunshine doesn't mean that you won't end it stuck Back Country in a white out. Always be prepared to stay over night.

There is advice out there, so seek it out and take note of it. Avalanche Risk Warnings are posted in resorts, often there's an advice line you can call for information on the weather and snow conditions. The resort mountain staff will know the mountain well, local inside knowledge is invaluable. Check if there's any Back country tours available, take a local registered guide, if you can't afford one at least ask their advice. Many resorts will have Heli-boarding or a snowcat service which is a fantastic and easy way to access the back country, most commercially run trips will include a local guide in the price.

BRITISH AIRWAYS

Rider: Frederik Kalbermatten
Photo: Jeff Curtes, Burton Snowboards

BACKCOUNTRY GUIDE

Canadian Rockies

INSURANCE

Never go back county alone or without adequate Insurance, check the small print make sure it states back country or off piste. If you brake a leg and need airlifting out you're going to be paying for it for a long time if your insurance won't cover it.

If you are going on a pre-organised trip with a specialist snowboard or ski organisation, check their insurance cover. Find out if their instructors and guides are properly qualified with a recognised certificate and have public liability insurance.

BACKCOUNTRY LAW

In Europe, you are warned not to ride outside restricted areas. However, you are seldom stopped and in many cases it is not actually illegal, although some areas are National Parks and therefore protected, get caught in these and you could get a fine. In France if you set off an avalanche which ends up killing someone on the piste below you'll be charged with manslaughter.

In the US and Canada, riding in marked-off areas is simply not tolerated. The patrols are extremely strict about riding 'out-of-bounds' and apart from getting yourself kicked off the slopes, you could also face police charges.

SCOTT BACKCOUNRTY PACK
Unfolds to hold board, includes hard-shell pockets for shades

ACCESS

Back Country Terrain can sometimes be accessed straight off a lift or you may have to hike to it. Both should be treated with the same respect just because you hopped off a piste doesn't make it safe. Choosing the size of and who's in your party is very important. When hiking four is a good size for a group it's easy to monitor each other and if someone has an accident one can stay with the casualty and the other two can go for help. All members of the party must be competent riders, be trusted to keep cool and help if it all goes belly up and most importantly have the correct equipment and know how to use it. It's also important to have an experienced party leader, decisions on route finding and if you should turn back or change the objective should fall to one person. Never split the party unless you need to send for help.

SNOWSHOE
Makes lighter work of hiking, by MSR contact www.msrcorp.com for more details

ROUTE FINDING

Route Finding is vital to safe travel in the back country. Always listen and watch the mountain for activity and try to avoid narrow valleys or gullies as they can channel avalanches. Note the profile of the slopes, are they straight, convex or concave? How steep is the area and what features exist? Gullies, bowls or ridges? Do you know what landscape lies under the snow? Grass, bushes, rocks or trees?

Avoid travelling along routes after heavy snowfalls where you can see previous avalanche activity, such as damaged trees, snow cookies or dirty snow slopes. If possible, always travel high and stay above large stashes of snow. If walking along a corniced ridge stay to the windward side as the cornices edge may well be unstable and could fracture with your extra weight.

Descending or crossing a face should be done one at a time so as not to overload the slope. You should always try to enter a slope or snow stash at its top, if you enter its middle and it slides all the snow from above could come down on you. When choosing your line down try to keep it narrow, don't cut across the whole slope if there is a trigger point you're much more likely to find it by traversing across the whole thing. Once you've got to the bottom move to a safe place to watch you friends descend, if they set off a slide and your standing in its path your in trouble. Never ever cut across a slope if someone is on it below you, if you do then you deserve the smack in the mouth your likely to get. Once your friend has descended safely take a line next to theirs. Avoid jumping on a suspect slope as the extra weight from the landing could trigger a slide.

AVALANCHES

Avalanches are the biggest killer of back country boarders. If you don't know about the power of avalanches then you shouldn't even start to think about going off piste. The 12 people who died in their chalets on 9th February 1999 in the Montroc Avalanche Chamonix France probably felt safe, until 300,000 cubic meters of snow travelling at 60miles/hr destroyed 14 buildings. If a building can be flattened think what it could do to you.

As a guide slopes less than 30 degrees aren't steep enough to slide and slopes over 60 degrees normally can't hold enough snow to slide. 38 is the magic number, slopes of 38 degrees are the most likely to slide, can you tell the difference between a safe slope of 30 and a potentially dangerous one at 38? No so get a slope inclinometer a handy little piece of kit for measuring slope angles. Snow pits are the best way to assess a slopes stability learn how to dig one and how to read the snow pack. Look for indicator slopes a slope of similar angle and position to the sun as the one your thinking of descending. If it has avalanche debris

AVALANCHE VIDEO
Distributed by Black Diamond Films

on it then it's highly likely yours will slide to. Rain on fresh snow leads to a high avalanche risk as does high wind and severe temperature change. Get as much information as you can, piece it all together and make a decision.

pic - Les Deux Alps Tourism

RESCUE

If you get caught in an avalanche try to board out of its side. Try to grab at a grounded object such as a tree. If you get knocked over swim with the slide trying to stay near its surface, if you feel the slide slowing try to clear an air pocket around your mouth and reach for the surface.

Transceivers save lives. They are a small device which sends out a signal and can be switched to receive if one of your party gets buried. You and all the people in your party must wear them and know how to use them.

Survival after an avalanche is all down to the response time of your party 92% after 15mins falls to 25% after 45mins so knowledge of your kit is vital, every minute counts. If one of your party gets caught then watch their path if you lose sight of them under the snow follow the snows path where they were until it stops.

All new transceivers use the same frequency world wide, read and follow the manufactures guide lines carefully. If you carry a mobile phone, also check that the phone doesn't interfere with transceiver. Always wear them under your jacket, never put them in a pocket or in your back

BACKCOUNTRY GUIDE

TENT, & BOOT
Compact mountaineering tent by Black Diamond, Ride boots (UK size 10)
www.ridesnowboards.com

GENERAL ITEMS

Over-boots & Gaiters
Clothing layers
Spare torch batteries
Mobile 'phone & batteries
Collapsible poles
Snowprobe poles
Board tune-up kit
Spare binding screws
Spare binding parts
10m of avalanche cord

FOR ICE & GLACIERS

Crampons & Ice axe
Safety helmet
Carabiners, Rope/Harness

NIGHTWISE

Tent & Sleeping bag
Stove & Cooking utensils

MUST HAVE ITEMS

• Avalanche Transceiver
• Maps & Compass
• Shovel
. Slope inclinometer
• First-aid kit
• Whistle & Torch
• Emergency survival food and water
• Probing poles
• Survival sack, blanket or light- weight tent
• Snowshoes (forget split-boards)
• A Complete set of spare thermal clothing
• Hat & face Protection
• Goggles and glasses
• Multi-use pocketknife

The following is a very basic guide for immediate first aid, to help relieve pain and to stop further injury until help is at hand. General rules when helping a casualty: clear the airways and check the patient frequently. Arrest bleeding, apply dressings and immobilise broken limbs. Finally treat for shock, relieve pain and then evacuate the casualty A.S.A.P. If in doubt, do as little as possible to avoid worsening the situation

Never go backcountry riding without a well equipped first-aid kit.

pack. Practice finding them and always check them before you leave home.

Recco produce a small reflector which when worn can be detected by rescue services in most major mountain resorts, the main problem here is response time. However you can purchase a pair for around £25, and they never need batteries. Contact www.Recco.com for more info.

One person should take charge of a rescue search, all transceivers should be turned to receive, someone should be posted to look out for secondary avalanches and you should always make sure you have an escape route you're not going to be of any help if you get buried as well.

Between 1985-2003 2694 people died in avalanches in alpine resorts world wide, around 100 a year die in the alps don't be one of them.

FIRST AID

Mountain first aid is a skill that needs to be learnt and practised. Nothing could be worse than seeing a close friend in pain, when all you can do is stand there looking dumb without a clue of what to do. Buy a book on mountain first aid procedures and learn the basics before you go away. Even better, enrol on a professional first aid course.

FIRST AID ESSENTIALS

Waterproof plasters,
Bandages and safety pins
A sling
Antiseptic cream
Gauze pads
First Aid tape
Asprin or other pain relief
Splint

WEATHER INJURIES

Hypothermia (exposure) is caused by body heat loss to below 37C. To prevent, eat properly and wear technical, waterproof, warm clothing. To treat, get the casualty under shelter and out of wet clothing, while doing all you can to increase body heat.

Frostbite/Frostnip is full or partial freezing of the skin and its tissues, causing numbness and no reaction to pain. To prevent, avoid exposure of bare skin, and wear correct clothing. To treat, warm the affected areas but never apply direct heat.

Snowblindness is temporary, partial, or total blindness, caused by direct and indirect ultra- violet light, even on dull days when the sun can't be seen. To prevent, wear suitable eyewear that has a 100% UVA & UVB rating. To treat, cover eyes and apply wet cloth to the forehead. Keep out of bright areas.

Dehydration occurs because of depleted fluids. Dizziness and nausea are early warning signs of dehydration. To prevent, drink regular amounts of fluid, such as water or healthy sport drinks. To treat, take a rest and drink as much fluid needed to re-hydrate your system.

WATER CARRIER
Fits inside most backcountry packs

built for riding

real snow
real fun
year round

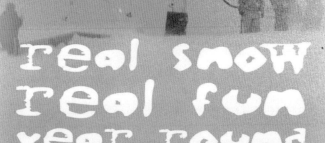

DINE · BOWL · DANCE · SNOW · ICE · CLIMB · SKATE · MOVIES · SHOP

XSCAPE X

WWW.XSCAPE.CO.UK

sessions, events, freestyle nights

WWW.XSCAPE.CO.UK

the uk's premier indoor real snow slopes

  XSCAPE 32 M62

  XSCAPE 14 M1

  XSCAPE 26 M8

castleford, leeds   milton keynes   braehead, glasgow

DINE   BOWL   DANCE   SNOW   ICE   CLIMB   SKATE   MOVIES   SHOP

Orange
AIM SERIES

So you live in the UK, and you want to compete. Maybe you dream of competing in the Olympics or you just want to put your snowboarding skills to the test against your piers. Well the best place for you is the Orange AIM Series.

Since its start in 2001 the Orange AIM Series has attracted snow sports enthusiasts as the official British Championship for snowboarding and freestyle skiing. In fact some of the UK's top snow sport athletes, and Olympic hopefuls, have developed their competitive skills through the series. Competitions are open for all ages and performance levels, so if you fancy a day out don't be put off by thinking it's not for you. Beginners are encouraged to push themselves while the sponsored riders are pushed by the up and coming unknowns.

The Orange AIM Series runs its events on Artificial, Indoor snow slopes and Mountain venues across the UK, and Europe. This enables riders a natural platform for development and a chance to compete without having to have a huge travel budget. The Series also helps to promote the great all year round facilities the UK has, and gets riders from around the country together. So those of

you who do not want to store away your boards or skis over the summer months, get them out of the cupboard and get riding.

This seasons Orange AIM Series is based around five events in the UK, three dryslope and two indoor snow slope competitions, all of which hold a national championship status. The UK events then culminate in the British Championships, which are always held in a European resort in March (this year it's in Laax 11th/18th March '06, packages from £249). Snowboarders and skiers can compete in Board/ Skier cross, Slopestyle, Halfpipe and Big Air. At all the events there's loads of freestyle action, cutting edge DJs, a movie lounge and free lessons for beginners. The national championships are held at some of UK's best facilities, including Bracknell, Rossendale and Milton Keynes. The organisers change the venues yearly to enable new local talent to compete and more beginners to be encouraged to take a free lesson.

Moving the events also helps the Orange AIM Series Schools Tour reach numerous school children around the UK. The Orange AIM Series isn't just about competing; it's about the promotion of snowsports. Thus the Orange

Credit: Nathan Gallagher/ Orange Brits

Join Snowboard Club UK

£100 of FREE snowboard gifts...

Free gifts include...

- Xscape boarding session
- Snowdome boarding session
- Ignite/ SCUK beanie
- Snowboard or Surf DVD
- Snowboard UK mag
- Loads of discounts
- Special benefits
- Cheap insurance

SCUK annual membership
- £25 Junior
- £30 Adult
- £70 Family
visit snowboardclub.co.uk
for more information

SCUK
SNOWBOARD CLUB.CO.UK

Orange
AIM SERIES

AIM Series Schools Tour takes to the road each year in June, with the mission of promoting snow sports to the UK youth, maybe even find the next UK champ. The tour visits two schools in the area of each of the UK events. A crew of professional snowboarders and skiers take over a school PE lessons for a day and with the help of; videos, a trampoline display, and some interactive activities they introduce the youth to boarding and skiing, as well as explaining the various career paths and opportunities within the industry. The team of pros changes, but always includes the UK's top riders and past champions; the 05 team includes the likes of Mike Wakefield, Mollie Percival and Sonia Shaw. The School tour also offers students the chance of a free board/ski introductory lesson at the actual events themselves.

Mrs. Helen Hilton, Head of PE, Tappton School, Sheffield
"The day was marvellous. The pupils really enjoyed the whole experience, from the video, to the demos, to meeting the team. The presentation has enthused some of them to get involved in the activities"

If you want to find out more about the Orange AIM Series, or the Orange Brits and how to book a free lesson log on to
www.orangeaimseries.com

Photos:
Main: Ben Kilner, Brits - 2Alpes Credit; Nathan Gallagher/ Orange Brits
Inset large: School tour, Bracknell Other: rider unknown Small: Mollie Percival

Olympic Dreams

2006 Winter Olympics

It's winter Olympic time again. Those of us in Britain are thinking of Eddie the Eagle and the fact that we've never won a winter Olympic medal. Alain Baxter came close last time out when he won a skiing medal, only to have it taken away over a bloody American Vicks inhaler. Ok, ok, so Torvil and Dean won a gold, and four Scottish house wives beat the world to Gold in Salt Lake City, but sliding stones along the ice while a couple of people thrash about with few brooms, or spinning around a lot while wearing a load of lycra don't do it for me (Although I did secretly get into the curling last time).

I'm talking about snowboarding which is a discipline where we've never won anything. So why watch I hear you ask? We'll let me tell you, you should watch because there's a British Snowboard team that's been breaking their arses and their wallets trying to get enough FIS points (Fédération Internationale de Ski) to be able to compete in Turin. As with all our Olympic athletes it's cash and time which is short but not effort.

So who are the team, what are their hopes and how do you get to compete in Turin?

This Olympics there will be three disciplines; **Half Pipe**, **Board Cross**, and **Parallel Giant Slalom**. The GB Team are all concentrating on the Half Pipe, apart from **Zoe Gillings** who's qualified for the Board Cross, it's the first time Board Cross has been an Olympic sport. **Lesley Mckenna** has qualified for the half pipe, while **Kate Foster**, **Dan Wakeham**, **Dom Harington**, and **James Foster** are all hoping to gain enough FIS points over the coming few months to make the grade. No British male snowboarder has ever gained enough points to compete in the Olympics, so just getting there would be a fantastic achievement.

Here's the deal, the lads need either two top 25 finishes or one top 20 placing within 05/06 season, as well as 120 FIS points or higher. While the lasses need either two top 20 finishes or one top 15 placing within 05/06 season, as well as 120 FIS points or higher.

With FIS events being in places like Chile, Austria and Canada, gaining enough points isn't just down to skill level but Cash. While GB riders are gaining recognition for their contributions to the sport, help from sponsorship is slow in coming forward. The catch, and it's a big one, is that to get sponsored you need to be successful, and to be successful you need to do well in FIS events, and yes you've guessed it, you need the cash to get to the events, vicious circle or what.

History of snowboarding in the Olympics

There's only been two winter Olympics incorporating snowboarding before. The first was Nagano 1998 which saw the International Olympic Committee recognise snowboarding as a skiing discipline. This pissed off a lot of people, including Terje Håkonson, who was undoubtedly the main man at the time, Terje eventually boycotted the games. Then to the great delight of those who didn't want to see snowboarding an Olympic discipline, Canadian Ross Rebagliati tested positive for marijuana, after winning the Giant Slalom Gold. He was stripped of his Gold by the IOC only to see it returned, by the Court of Arbitration for Sport, because marijuana was deemed not to be a performance-enhancing drug. Salt Lake City 2002 saw the Giant Slalom become a parallel event, with two riders racing each other to progress to the next round, as apposed to the clock. Salt Lake also saw an American clean sweep of the male half pipe medals, with Ross Powers adding a Gold to the bronze he won in 1998, and Kelly Clark also of the US winning

the woman's half pipe. So can anyone this time round stop the US's dominance? Antti Auti of Finland is throwing down some sick runs as are the Swiss riders Nicolas Muller and Romain de Marchi. The Slovenia's are also surprising a few people, but most are looking no further than another US dominated games.

Can I still go boarding while the events are on

All of the resorts hosting events will not be open for regular snowboarding during an event. Most of the resorts hosting an event will close the affected areas off a good month or so before the Olympics, but the rest of the resort will be open as normal. If you're looking to head off to one of the resorts featured, then make sure you check the resort review in this book for opening dates, and take a peek at the resorts website before you head off.

Wheres the action?

Ninety KM from Turin is the resort of Bardonecchia, which will be home to the Olympic 2006 Snowboarding competition. The Snowboard events are being held over six days with individual event being completed in one day with Qualifying in the morning and the Finals in the afternoon. It all kicks off with the men's Half Pipe on the 12th February

with the women's Half Pipe the following day.

Tickets can be bought online from **www.torino2006. ticketone.it** and cost €90 or €35 for the cheap seats. Your tickets cover event qualification and the finals.

For more information visit:
www.torino2006.org
www.fis-ski.com
www.snowsportgb.com

www.lesleymckenna.co.uk
www.zoe.org.im

Snowboarding Events Schedule	
Sunday 12th February	10:00-11:30 Mens Halfpipe qualification 14:00-15:30 Mens Halfpipe finals
Monday 13th February	10:00-11:30 Womens Halfpipe qualification 14:00-15:30 Womens Halfpipe finals
Thursday 16th February	10:00-11:00 Mens Boardercross qualification 14:00-15:00 Mens Boardercross finals
Friday 17th February	10:00-11:00 Womens Boardercross qualification 14:00-15:00 Womens Boardercross finals
Wednesday 22nd February	10:00-11:00 Mens Parallel Giant Slalom qualification 13:00-14:30 Mens Parallel Giant Slalom finals
Thursday 23rd Febuary	11:00-12:00 Womens Parallel Giant Slalom qualification 14:00-15:30 Womens Parallel Giant Slalom finals

All photos copyright of LaPresse unless otherwise stated:
Front page: Bardonacia Pipe & Boardercross
Top right: Bardonacia Olympic village
Bottom right: Bardonacia halfpipe in the summer
Top left: Bardonacia halfpipe
Opposite left: Bardonacia town
Opposite right: Turin

Team GB

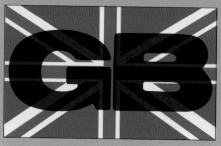

Dom Harington

Kate Foster

We caught up with the members of the GB snowboard team and pitched them a few down to earth questions.

WSG - When, where, and why was the last time you fell off a drag lift?

Dom Harington - "Ha ha. I do that quite a lot. I fell off the t bar at sheffield the other week because I was carrying a burger and chips to the top of the slope and was trying to eat and was not looking where I was going!"

WSG - Ever owned an all in one ski suit, and if yes, what colour was it?

Kate Foster - Yes....when I was about 6.......it was neon green and purple with bright pink flashes to top it off.

WSG - Do you think there's enough help given in this country for people trying to compete in the Olympics?

Dan Wakehan - I'm put in to a situation where I feel like I am really moving forward in my progression but the money doesn't seem to follow. Its hard when I am at events and there all these guys from the states with a team of assistants, a few coaches, physio's, board preps. I saw Ross Powers coach holding goggle lenses to the sky to decide which color lens he should wear. They all seem to have so much support and so many opportunities that it's hard for us to compete.

To think that the U.K. has only had a world cup team for about two years now and we've been doing ok, Zoe Gillings finished the season 4th in the world, Lesley finished high and I am the European champ. We have no support from snow sport GB we have to pay £200 a month for the privilege of being on the team. Thats £2400 a year, that's a lot out of my Nike travel budget. Every thing is expected to come from our personal sponsorship.

WSG - What's your ambition for this Olympics?

Dom Harington - My aim is just to qualify! No other male from Great Britain has done so before so it would be wicked just to go.

WSG - What's your biggest interest outside the sport?

Kate Foster - Football....watching and playing.

WSG - Ever been caught in an Avalanche, if yes what happened?

Dan Wakehan - Nothing to bad, just a little slip, but enough to make you shit your pants and wish you had a transceiver.

WSG - When did you know you wanted to be a professional snowboarder?

Dom Harington - When I was 16 I left school because the only thing I wanted to do was snowboard. I wouldn't count myself as a pro yet though!

TELUS

Zoe Gillings

Lesley McKenna

James Foster

Dan Wakehan

All photos courtesy of snowsportgb unless otherwise stated:

This: brits 05 in Laax
rider: Lesley McKenna
photo: Natalie Mayer
Top right: Whistler
rider: Zoe Gillings
Top middle: Valle Nevado, Chile
rider: Zoe Gillings
Top left: Whistler
rider: James Foster
Opposite top: brits 05, Laax
rider: Don Harrington
Opposite bottom: Whistler
rider: Dan Wakeman

Summer lovin

It's May, Summers a coming and there's shed loads of boarding still to be had. In that upside-down world of the Southern Hemisphere, people are starting to put the surf boards and mountain bikes back in the garage, and blow the dust off their snowboards. That's all well and good for the upside-down ones, but what about us right-way-up lot?

Don't be disheartened, there are still plenty of options, and they're not all a long haul flight away. Summer Camps and high altitude Glaciers are still open all over Europe. Sadly there will be no wide open powder faces to track, but if you want to tune up or even start up your freestyle, look no further than our authoritative guide to summer riding in the Northern Hemisphere, as well as some not so obvious places down South.

Where to Go

If you do have loads of cash, and have got time on your hands, undoubtedly your best option is to head south for the winter to **New Zealand**, **Australia** or **South America** (see the country resort review).

These are a bit far for a weekend or even a week, so instead you could head for the Alps or North to Norway or Iceland, the lands of the midnight sun. You may even get to see the Northern Lights while boarding, and you don't have to get out of bed before the sun melts everything. How cool is that?

Another option, if the God of wealth is smiling down on you, is Heliboarding in the Himalayan massif, Kyrgyzstan and Kazakhstan are both great places to travel through as well as board, and really cheap (excluding the Helicopter!). One thing to keep an eye on is the stability of some countries: Kyrgyzstan had a revolution in March 2005 and they're planning an election soon, so it may kick off again.

Kashmir in late spring is also a great place to Heliboard but until recently was a war zone and could well be again by the time you plan a visit. The Caucasus Mountains in Russia are also great for summer boarding as long as you don't mind getting shot by the Chechen rebels or robbed by the Russian army who haven't been paid in months.

Having said that, successful camps have run on Mount Elbrus for the last few years, without any problems. The best thing to do when travelling far a field is check out www.fco.gov.uk for the latest travel advice.

Park life

Watching locals giving it some in the park in the winter can be a bit intimidating for the not so gifted amongst us, so why not take a week out of your summer and get some instruction form the people who know best? Summer Camps are great for anyone looking for instruction in the park.

Normally they run on a week long basis, in June and July and pull together some of the best riders around to teach you new moves and how to put a tweak into old ones. Some camps do offer beginner freestyle courses so don't be put off whatever your standard. Just contact the organisers before you book. Girlie Camps run through the summer in various locations in Europe, and yes, they're just for girls.

What Do I Need At A Camp?
As always in the mountains the weather can change from hour to hour. The day could start in bright sunshine and by the time you've stomped your first 360 of the day the sun has gone and the temperature has plummeted, so be prepared.

Always take your own:
- Board and Boots (most hire shops will be shut)
- waterproof breathable boarding jacket+trousers
- warm under clothing
- helmet (must have)
- back protector (should have)
- goggles/sunglasses
- gloves hat/baseball cap
- sunscreen total block (just make sure you can rub it in)
- lip protection
- backpack (to put all of the above in)
- skateboard (for the afternoon)

Glacier Riding

Summer Glacial riding is a great way to give first timers an introduction to the sport, and if they still don't like it, you shouldn't have to look too hard for a crevasse to push them down. It's also good for those of you who've only done a few weeks to keep in practise for next season. There's nothing worse than finishing a holiday thinking you've got it sussed, then bigging yourself up to your mates all summer, only to find that 8 months off the board has seen your new found skills disappear like a turd down the u-bend.

Many of the Glacial resorts in Europe have restricted or stopped their summer programs, due to climate change and the erosion caused by boards and skis. That said, many glacial resorts give access to their higher reaches during the mornings and early afternoon, leaving most of the afternoon free for the skate park or a whole other range of summer sports. If you want to chill in the afternoons, then just sit back in the sun, drink some beer and wait for the lifts to open again.

On the slopes there's often a park to play in and normally a few short runs to keep you amused.

The Fake Stuff

Riding indoors on fake snow or outside on the plastic stuff, (dendex or snowflex), is a thing we Brits do well. When you've got no reliable snow fall or even mountains, like the Dutch, then there's not much choice and of course if you're not boarding on snow then you don't need the winter. Most centers have a good scene going on, and many have snowboard only nights when they bring out a few rails and a jump or two.

The Fake stuff is good for freestyle practice, and for complete beginners to get used to the feel of the board and the use of edges. However, runs are short and even the diehard boarder will be bored quickly unless there are some freestyle distractions.

AUSTRIA

Austria has one of the largest options for summer snowboarding as well as some of the best glaciers. Burton Snowboards holds most of its training camps on Austria's glaciers and many national teams train here during summer. Resorts offer good local services and slopes are crowd free, although glaciers like Stubai and others within easy reach of Innsbruck do tend to get a lot of one day two-plankers on special tourist trips. Summer riding in Austria is cheaper than in winter but note some village services close during parts of May and June.

Dachstein

This very small resort, 20 minutes drive from Schladming, is often ignored in the winter, but being the most easterly glacier in the Alps and claming to have the "best snowpark for far and wide"! its worth a good look in the summer at least. In 7 minutes the Dachstein Gondola takes you from 1700m glacier at 2700m, and from there you'll find the park designed by Bernd Mandlbergero. The park has number of big booters and long rails, and its certainly not for the uninitiated, but kept in top condition. Depending on snow cover, there are also a few smaller kickers away from the main park, and the team don't generally mind if you want to wield the shovel and build something small yourself. If you're not into jumping then you'll get bored pretty quickly, the 3 runs are all fairly short, but you still occasionally get powder days even in the summer to spice things up from the summer slush.

The Dachstein glacier and park, opens mid May and, snow permitting, stays open until late autumn. The mountain opens at 8:15 until around 4pm, but depending on the weather it can close earlier. There are 6 lifts, 2 of which

are new and its €27/day for a pass. You'll need transport to get to the bottom of the gondola station; you can stay in Ramsau which is dull as dishwater but close. However the much better option is to stay in Schladming which has plenty of accommodation and some decent nightlife. There is also some very good climbing in the area. Salzburg airport is 90km away and Munich airport is 220km.

www.planai.at

Kaprun

Kaprun is a favourite summer destination where snowboard teams spend a lot of time training. The ride area is located on one of Austria's best glaciers, the **Kitzsteinhorn Glacier,** which reaches an altitude of 3,203 metres, making it a perfect place to ride. Being a glacier resort, you can ride here all year and no matter what month you visit, riders of all levels will find something to shred. There is a terrain park & pipe located off the **Magnetkopfellifte T-bar.** Lift tickets are €27 per day. More info is available at www. kitzsteinhorn.at

Hintertux

The Hintertux glacier is sat at the far end of the Zillertal valley about half an hour from Mayrhofen and its highest peak, Olperer rises to 3476m. You can board here any day of the year, and in the summer (May to October) it is open from 8.15 am to 4.30 pm. For the 29.50 day pass you can board from 3250 to 2660m and access 23km of pistes and a great terrain park.

The park, designed by Wille Kaufmann, is situated next to the Olperer drag lift. There's a pro line consisting of 4 10-15m table-tops, and a mortal's line with 6 kickers. There's also a number of a rails, a spine, and last but certainly not least, a 100m half-pipe. You'll find plenty of accommodation in the small villages close the lifts , collectively called Tux, but if you want any form of nightlife the biggest town is Mayrhofen, and is probably worth the daily commute.

www.hintertuxergletscher.at

Sölden

Summer sees both Sölden's glaciers, Tiefenbach and Rettenbach, open with a nearby car park at their base. Its a good size for a summer slide, and steep enough to ensure you'll never has to skate no matter how slushy things get. There are buses from town to the glacier (45mins), or to drive, follow the main town road as if driving to Obergurgl then take a right as you leave town at the sign for the glacier. At the bottom of Rettenbach glacier, you'll find a restaurant, the excellent Salomon bar and a couple of shops. The Base summer terrain park is located off run 32, and includes a stack of rails; straight, kinked, rainbow, gondola pods, you

know the things, and also various size kickers.

SUMMER PERIODS: Open end of June to beginning of August
Lift Passes: €30/day
LIFTS OPEN: 2 Gondolas, 1 Chair, 5 T-bars
ELEVATION: 2796m to 3309m
TERRAIN PARKS: 2

Summer Camp BASE run 5 camps from the end of June to the end of July. The Burton and Salomon teams are regular visitors. A 6 day camp costs from €210 for camping or €365 for a half board hotel. Packages include lift ticket, product testing and accommodation, but not coaching. You can pay by day if you prefer, which costs €30/day. Base Camp Sölden Phone:+43-676-436-0025, Website: www.base.soelden.com

Stubai

45 minutes drive from the centre of Innsbruck is the Stubai Glacier. Stubai claims to be Austria's largest glacier ski resort although in the summer the ski area shrinks to only 4 T-bars, and a couple of runs. The lifts are open from 8am to 4:15pm daily

CANADA

The Blackcomb Mountain and glacier are the only areas which offer all year round snowboarding in the country. Nearly all of Canada's other resorts close at the end of April with a few closing in mid-May if the snow is still good.

Blackcomb

Blackcomb and its neighbour, Whistler, are located on the west coast just north of Vancouver. You don't have to be on a camp to ride here during the main summer months, but you may not be allowed in the pipe or park if you are not.

112 acres of terrain are open from June until August, from 12pm to 3pm and serviced by 2 T-bars. It takes 45 minutes from the base of Blackcomb to get to the glacier, involving 3 chairs and a bus. Once there you'll find the terrain park has between 4-6 rails/jibs, 2 spine jumps and a halfpipe. Tickets are $45CDN per day.

Summer Camp In addition to the facilities offered by the resort, there are a number of specialist Summer Camps with access to their own private terrain parks & pipes. Prices start from $600CDN a week including tuition, but most cost much more. Loads of summer snowboard camps are held for kids, so if you've got some cash and want your kid getting gold in the Olympics then send them along! www.campofchampions.com

If you're a big person, take a look at **www.glaciersnowboardcamp.com Glacier Camps** have been running week long courses out of Whistler since 1996. Based around a private half pipe, cut by the new 17-foot super dragon, they offer camps with small group sizes no more then 5 campers to 1 instructor, with a maximum of 40 campers a week. They also offer a snowboard park with jumps, hips, and a variety of rails, as well as the natural free riding around Blackcomb glacier and daily video analysis. There are 5 sessions in June and July and a session costs £650 lasting a week, with a rest day in the middle.

WSSC run fully inclusive summer camps on their own private park & pipe on the glacier. $1225CDN (£570) will get you 3 days coaching, 4 nights in a hotel, all meals and some goodies, they also run a 8 day camp for $1995 (£930) where you get 6 days coaching/boarding. Camps run from early June to the end of Jully. Visit **www.whistlersnowboardcamps.com** for more info

FRANCE

It's surprising that a country with so many good winter resorts has so little to offer for summer snowboarding. 99% of French resorts switch off their lift systems at the end of April regardless of how much snow is still on the slopes. The few resorts that do operate in summer provide a lot of high altitude services with snowboarding only a small part of the mountain activities on offer. Climbing and mountain biking are considered the main attractions here.

La Plagne

Ski pass €24.50 a day. There are some easy runs up on the Glacier de la Chiaupe (3250 meters). Some of the board schools should be open, but there are no camps as such, and no park or pipe, just 3 or 4 easy short pistes. Open from 26/6 to 28/8, it is a great spot for beginners.

Les Deux Alps

Often considered the best European summer riding resort, Les Deux Alps is a great place to visit in the summer. The high glacier allows for some fine summer riding in T-shirts, and you can reach the board area from the middle of the town in a cable car. The park is a good size and is well known for its good snow conditions and variety of hits.

Open from mid June to late August from 7:30am to 1:30pm, there are 8 runs and 11 lifts to get you around. Tickets are €30 per day. The town is also full of off-hill sporting activities and has a kicking night life.

BIG A runs camps here for all abilities, from competitors waiting to know what judges are looking for, to first timers. The park is 650m long and is at an altitude of 3500m. It offers 2 pipes, 2 funboxes, a massive hip, a big jump and plenty of kickers for any level of riding. 2 skilifts and a handlift service the park and there is a barbecue area. It's also got boardercross courses and mountain bike courses. The Big A summer session is from June-August. www.big-a.it

Girlie Camps are here most summers. They are an organisation promoting board sports to girls. Their girl only (16-40) snowboard camps have top female riders from Burton and Roxy instructing you and are open to all abilities. Around €600 will get you a weeks accommodation and riding with 4 hours a day instruction in groups of 8 riders, plus video analysis to keep up with your progress, test gear from their sponsors, plus off slope activities like: Climbing, Ice-skating, Yoga, Gymnastics, and Spa. www.girlieproduction.com

Kommunity run freestyle summer camps in the last 2 weeks of July. Prices are £545 per week and include tuition with British Pro riders, lift pass and half-board accommodation. For more information check out www.kommunity.com

Rossignol run excellently organised camps over a two week period in July. All the Rossignol Snowboards and Scratch teams attend the camp, offering 2 hours instruction per day (for an additional cost) while the rest of the day is yours. Prices start at €330 for the basic package and raise to €640 to stay in the Rider's hotel on a full board basis. For those of you with kids there is even a one week option for under sixteens, so you can ride with the kids and the Pros. www.rossignolsummercamp.com.

Photo credits: this page main photo Rossignol Summer Camp, Deux Alps July 05 © WSG Opposite page, main photo rider Andy Cantelon, other photo Brian Smith. Photographer © Yaz Jallad,

Tignes

Tignes is one of the major snowboard resorts in France, and has long been hosting national and international events. Tignes lies at 2,100m, and is without doubt, the best summer snowboard destination in France and a match for any of the top glacier resorts of Austria and Switzerland. Access to the glacier area is from mid June to early September and is accessed by taking the underground funicular (pronounced fanny-licker) train located at Val Claret. In the summer, the glacier is home to 25km of pistes with 750m of vertical. A day lift pass will set you back €30. The Snowpark has a range of table tops and rails to suit all levels, and there is beginners and super pipe.

Summer Camp Snocool is now in its eighth year and offers freestyle coaching along with many other balance based sports. There are filmed sessions everyday with viewing at night. There's a Burton test centre and an occasional visit from a big name French Pro rider. Prices range from €220 for instruction only to €580 for a week long package.

Val Thorens

Due to maintenance work on the Peclet Funitel, there has been no summer boarding on the Glacier for the last few years. There was still no news of opening when we went to print.

GERMANY

Garmisch

Germanys first super pipe. Zugspitze plateau skate park
Summer camp Gap run 5 one week camps in May and June. Options range from 2 day park access up to 7 days riding with accommodation and a chance to do a photo shoot with the Pros. That will set you back €800 euros. Red Bull have built a new skate park in the town, and there is a good mountain bike course and even Paint Balling is available.

BRITISH AIRWAYS

ICELAND

Summer Camp Iceland Park Project, now in its 5th year, run 3 fantastic one week camps, the first two of which the park is fully serviced, and the last called Trash week, where literally you trash the park. The organisers claim it to be "the most tranquil spot on the planet to do freestyle snowboarding where the sun never sets." And they just might be right.

The camps start in late May. Accommodation is in a sea side hostel in the small fishing village of Arnarstapion on the beautiful Snaefell peninsula, 250 kilometres north west of Reykjavik.

The park itself is located on the Snaefellsjökull glacier which gets ample snow over the winter to shape into a great park, albeit without a pipe. There is a chance to surf over a sand based break but it is cold, a skate ramp in a tent and if you're into nature then you can enjoy view whales, artic turns and some mad cliffs.

The draw backs are that there is no instruction, although people are there to offer advice. The camp is for intermediates and advanced riders, so not one for beginners. The price of around £450 does not include flights. Note that you need to get to Keflavik Airport which is a ½ hour flight from Reykjavik or a breathtakingly beautiful drive around the coast. Anyone who's seen the photos on the very informative website will want to go. www.icelandparkproject.com

Photo credits: this page main photo red as f*ck, insets rider Chad Photographer: © Tash
Opposite page, main photo Garmisch © GAP 1328 camp

ITALY

Italy offers some of the cheapest summer snowboarding opportunities in the whole of Europe. However, don't expect a great deal in terms of the size and difficulty of the terrain available. Italy's summer snow cover on its glaciers is okay but, not as good as Austria or Switzerland. You won't find many summer halfpipes or parks to ride, but there are snowboard camps with hits to get air from. One place that does hold camps is Passo Stelvio Glacier. It's the highest glacier resort in Europe and not far from Bormio. Here you get the chance to ride a good park and pipe throughout May and June.

Val Senales

Val Senales is a resort for all snowboarders and skateboarders who want to keep busy in the summer. It is near Bolzano in South Tirol, and the Glacier there offers a good park with a large range of kickers.

Summer camp Big A run camps in July and the hotel they use has a big skate park nearby.

Cervinia

Summer boarding at Cervinia is up at the Plateau Rosà Glacier which, at 3500-3800 metres, always has good snow. It is open from the end of June until early September. The park, known as Indian Park, has a number of kickers, rails and a superpipe. Big A run summer camps here from mid July to mid September with all-in prices from €350 for the week. Check out: www.big-a.it

NORWAY

Stryn

Stryn is located at the base of the **Jostedalsbreen glacier** in amongst the fjords, and is Norway's most famous summer resort (in fact the only one of note really). The glacier gets so much snow during the winter, (five metres or more), that the lifts are usually totally buried so they couldn't run them in the winter even if they wanted to!

The glacier opens at the end of May to late July. There are some beginners runs, but it's best to head for the park. It's got the usual arrangement of various kickers and rails but no pipe, although if there's enough snow they have the ability to build one. Lift passes are 280 NOK/day or 1200 NOK for 6 days.

Summer Camp Snowboard Norge have been running camps in Stryn for almost 20 years so they must be doing something right. The courses start at the end of June and prices are roughly £250 for a week long camp including instruction and lift pass but not accommodation. With the motto "No one too experienced, no one too inexperienced" this is truly a camp for all.

You can also bring the kids but anyone under 14 must be accompanied. Groups are split by ability and given instruction suited to their needs over the 5 days. It's not just freestyle-they also do basic beginners tuition as well. Depending on the snow they normally have 20 or so jumps and a boarder cross track.

There's the option of camping in your own tent 50 NOK/ night or staying in a camp hut 135 NOK/175 NOK night, or if you have some cash you can book a Hotel www.hjelle. com There is also a big skate park to check out in the long warm evenings, and some great hiking. www.snowboard. no/camp

Girlie Camps run a camp here in June, with top female riders instructing Girls only, (see Les Deux Alps in this section). Price is a little over €600 for a week riding and Hotel. All standards are welcome and many people travel to their camps alone.

Folgefonna

Folgefonna is a small glacial resort a mere 1200 metres above sea level but with the snow dumped on it all winter there's plenty left for a bit of boarding in the summer. The highest point on the glacier is 1640meters and although the runs aren't all that long, the park should keep you happy. The resort is located on the west coast of Norway about 90 minutes drive including the ferry from Bergen or 7 hours from Oslo. www.folgefonna.no

Summer Camp

Folgefonn Camp has 4 one week camps here, in June and July the camps are resort run and have a minimum age of 14, but are tailored to an older age group. The park has pipes, boxes, slides, jumps, a boarder cross, music and a demo centre where you can test next years boards and equipment. Outside the park there's a full sized indoor skate ramp, mini ramps, 5 trampolines to practice inverted tricks, and there's also a small stream and a lake where you can go boating, fishing, windsurfing, swimming and wakeboarding. You can ride with tuition from 10 till 4 everyday and with basic accommodation you'll have to part with €450.

Photo credits: this page main photo Stryn summer 05
Opposite: main Big A Camp in Val Senales. Cervinia. Others Giacomo Kratter in the pipe, B/slide Filippo Kratter

RUSSIA

Mt Elbrus

In the heart of the Caucasus mountains is **Mt Elbrus**, just north of the Georgian boarder. At 5642 meters, it's the highest mountain in Europe, it has a glacial system which covers over 145km sq and ice over 400meter deep.

Summer Camp

More importantly it's home to the **SPC summer camps**. Run in June and July they are a great laugh if you fancy some good snow, and a lot of vodka. The park (see picture) is built at around 4000 meters, so be sure to take it easy until you've acclimatised.

Once you're there its cheap-a pint is about 50p and Dinner isn't much more. There's a large indoor space at the camps Hotel which provides (bizarrely) a gun shooting room and more tamely a billiard bar, and two table tennis courts. Camps are available from one to four weeks and cost 350 euros for 8 days when booked through the very good SPC site. However, this price excludes international flights. www.spcrussia.com

SWITZERLAND ✚

Switzerland ranks equal with Austria as being the best country in Europe for offering summer snowboarding facilities. The Swiss boast a number of great destinations which all provide halfpipes or funparks and, like everything else in Switzerland, they are of a very high standard. One of the main places to check out is Saas Fee which boasts of having Europe's only all year round halfpipe and terrain park where loads of Pro-riders hold camps. Swiss local services are good and, in most cases, lodging is available at the base area of the slopes or close by.

Saas-Fee

Saas-Fee has been a resort well known to snowboarders for many years. With its high altitude glacier, Saas-Fee also provides a mountain where you can ride fast and hard in the summer months, indeed for some, this is the only time worth visiting.

The glacier opens in early July until September with access to 20km off pistes and a terrain park with kickers, ¼ pipe, tabletops, rails and a half-pipe. A lift pass will set you back 60CHF a day.

Summer Camp **Team Nitro** run 3 one week camps with their Pro team in July and freestyle camps during July. For more info check out www.nitro-snowboards.ch

Les Diablerets

The glacier is open from mid June 19th to the end of July offering 4 easy pistes. The cable car runs from 8.20am until 4.50pm. One slope is open and the snowpark and the halfpipe. There are a number of summer boarding camps Euroboardtours (www.demonium-mc.com) and Choriqueso Camps (www.choriqueso-camps.ch). Visit www.glacier3000.ch for more information

Engelberg

The **Mount Titlis** glacier is open for summer riding and is accessed from the town by Gondola. This also allows you to take your mountain bike up and there's also some wakeboarding possible nearby. The glacier isn't the biggest around but the park is cool and has a half pipe and a selection of kickers. Always check **www.titlis.ch** to ensure they are open as sometimes they close due to lack of snow.

Summer Camp Iceripper have been running camps here since 1988 and have gained a good reputation. There's instruction for freestyle from half pipe to rails and room for beginners. In the afternoons there's good climbing, wakeboarding, tennis, golf, mountain biking, and ice hockey. **CHF 590** gets you 6 nights B+B accommodation with 5 days riding and instruction and a t-shirt. The camp has halfpipe, big airs, corner, rails, chairlift, drag lift, skatepark and some great snowside tunes with an occasional BBQ. **www.iceripper.com**

Photo credits: this page main photo Saas-Fee halfpipe © SaasFee Resort
Opposite page: top: rider Marc-André Tarte. All photos © SPC Russia

Zermatt

High up on the **Klein Matterhorn**, Zermatt has the largest summer boarding area in Switzerland. The glacier opens in June until September and there are a number of easy/intermediate runs and a terrain park all serviced by T-bars. The **Gravity Park** has a series of kickers and rails and a super-pipe alongside the lift. A lift pass will cost you 60CHF, but the area is only open from 7:30 to 1:30pm so you need to get up early before it starts getting slushy. In the afternoon you can take a look at the World's highest ice pavilion at 3810m, if you're that way inclined.

Stoked runs for 2 weeks next summer from July 23rd until August 5th 2006. A 6 night package including tuition, accommodation and lift pass will set you back €630. For more info take a look at www.stoked.ch

USA

Camps in America are mainly aimed at Kids so before you book read the small print or you may find yourself boarding amongst a bunch of twelve year olds. Parents sick of having "Queens of the Stone Age" blaring out of the stereo, and want the calm of their dodge hippy tunes enveloping the house, just pack their kids bags and send them off to a snowboard camp. There are camps for adults, but as with the kids camps they cost much $, and if you're based in Europe you're best of staying there.

Alaska

Summer Camp You can board pretty much all year in Alaska if you've got the cash for a helicopter. If not then camps are run by Boarderline in June and July. They are for kids, have 24/7 supervision, and are centred around a compound in Anchorage. The kids are transported each day to the park in Alyeska. The park has all the norms and in the evenings there's a good skate park in the compound. A week costs $800 with lodging $350 without. www.boarderlinealaska.com

OREGON

Mount Hood in North West America has a good summer riding area, with a mile long piste (long for a summer run) which is great for beginners. The resort is open from late November until August so plenty of riding is available. There is a park but it's out of bounds as it's restricted to High Cascade camp members. See www.skihood.com for prices and timings.

Summer Camp World renowned is almost a realistic claim for High Cascade summer camps with 2 pipes a huge selection of rails, hips, boxes and jumps all designed and built by Pat Malendoski of Planet Snow Design, builder of the 2002 Salt Lake City Olympic Superpipe. There are no restrictions on riding standard with even complete beginners are welcome.

Campers are split into ability groups and with jumps from 5 to 70 foot there truly is something for everyone. Places are available for 9 year olds to adults. Adult camps are aimed at all levels of progressive freestyle with a maximum of four snowboarders to every coach, and use video analysis. All camps are held in High Cascades private park and pipes. It all sounds great, but here is the drawback: $1800 gets you a one week adult camp, kids camps start at $1400. www.highcascade.com

Windells also run camps at Mt Hood mainly for kids, see www.windells.com

Photo credits: Danny Kass competing in the Burton Aboninable snowjam in June 2005 at Mt.Hood ©2005 Dean Blotto Gray. **Opposite page.** photos © Stoked Summer Camps

HELiboarding

You hit the deck as the "thud thud thud" turns into a continual motorised drone. You look at the floor as a wall of powder, projected by the blades, envelopes you finding its way down your back and onto any uncovered skin. A short stooped run, and the next thing you know the floors dropping away and you're heading for virgin powder and the ride of your life. Heliboarding is untouchable, it's the ultimate. Some think it's just for the rich and famous. It's not, you don't have to be famous.

Imagine it: "Oh Mr Pilot can you drop me on the top of that, I'm just going to ride that virgin snow, and then if you wouldn't mind you could pick me and my friends up at the bottom and take us straight back to the top of that peak over there."

Having the use of a helicopter for a day or better a week, is the dream of any self-respecting boarder. Costs can vary from plain criminal to "you're having a laugh". Although it costs a lot of money, if you can wrangle a deal it may be the best money you ever spent. Instead of falling for all the marketing hype of needing the latest kit each season, blow the cash on a helicopter. Just don't buy a new board or the latest jacket, keep the old one and instead have a day you'll be bragging about years.

In Europe you have a few winter options; Switzerland has a healthy policy to heliboarding. Most of the larger resorts allow you access to the back country without you having to breaking into a sweat, other than when you hand over the cash that is. You can also Heliboard in Spain, Georgia, Turkey or pretty much anywhere there's a mountain with snow on it if you've got the cash you can board it.

If you want to heliboard in Europe's summer then you have to head for the Central Asia or the southern Hemisphere. The US and Canada have some amazing possibilities: Fernie, Red Mountain and Whistler in Canada, Colorado in USA and the big boy Alaska, and that's just to name a few. The main difference between Europe and North America is that in Europe it's normally day hire or even ½ day. In North America it's predominantly sold as a week long package, including being airlifted in to a back country lodge and flying around the area for a week before being flown back to civilisation, with a granted number of vertical feet boarded, but this is not always the case. Some places will offer day trips as well as week long trips that cost thousands of dollars.

The most important things to find out are safety record and garneted vertical decent metres. If they don't want to discuss it, spend your cash elsewhere. Insure they insist that everyone has a transceiver and shovel and knows how to use them. Also find out what their money back policy is for bad weather days and ask if the guide will be boarding or skiing. Being the only boarder on a drop will not necessarily lead to a bad day, but it would be better to be in a group of boarders. Ensuring the guide is a boarder will guarantee you're taken to suitable terrain.

canada

Within Canada there are many options with most major resorts having a Heli-operator. Few offer day trips but shop around and you may be able to strike a deal for a day riding.

Chilkoot Mountains

The Chilkoot mountains are a huge range that run North / South throughout the Yukon. Klondike Heliski offer trips to 23 different areas with over 300 descents to choose from, which encompass an area of 6,000 square km. Based out of Atlin, B.C. almost $7000 can will get you 32,000 true vertical meters of boarding over a week with fully catering. Yep loads of cash, but also loads of boarding.
www.atlinheliski.com

Photo credits
this page: © atlinheliski.com, Canada   opposite page: © Canadian Heli-ski

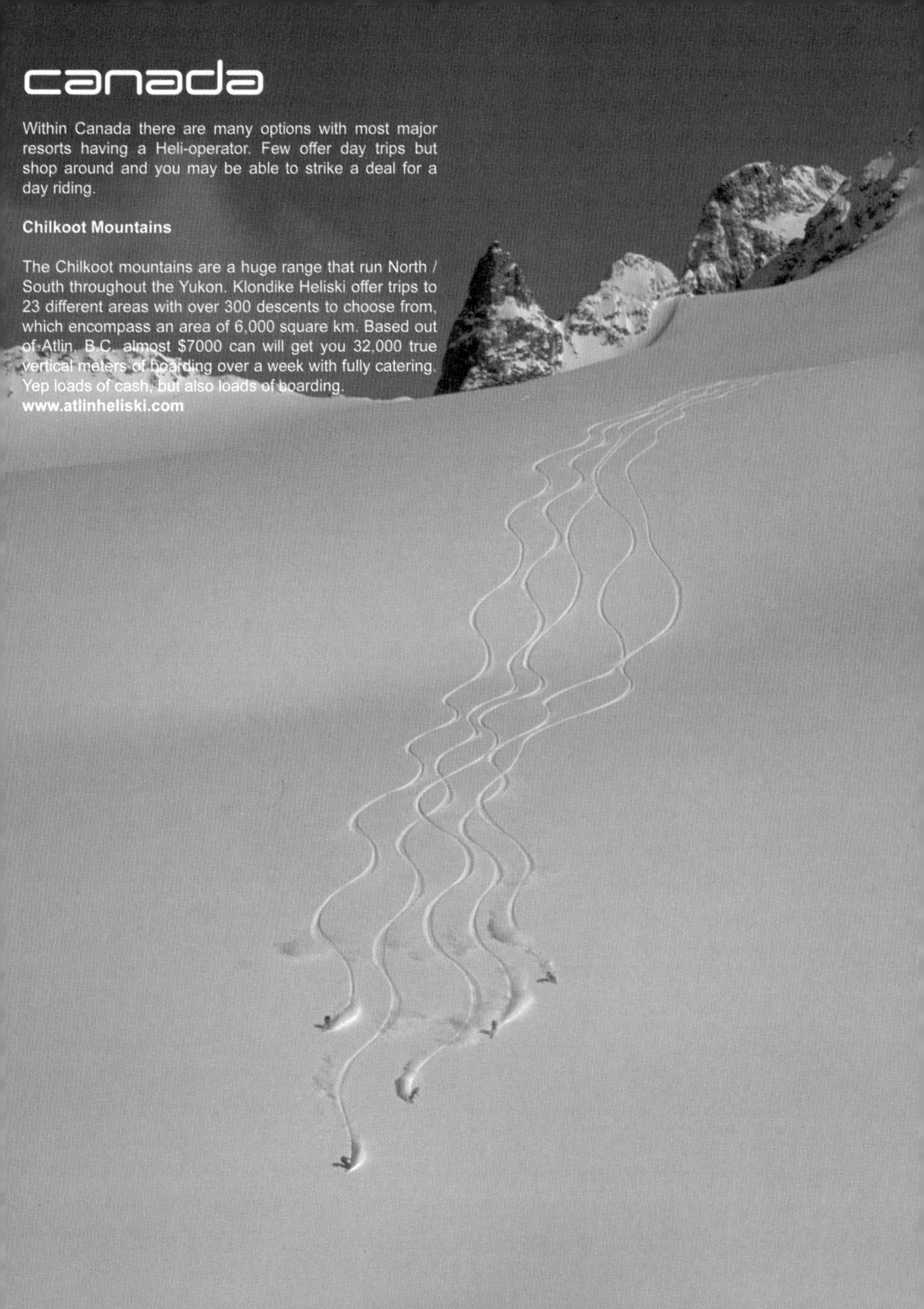

BRITISH AIRWAYS

Kicking Horse/ Golden

Purcell Helicopter Skiing Ltd run day trips with 3 or 5 descents for $610 and $730 with the chance of additional descents at $65pp with a minimum group of 8. They claim to have close to 200 runs offering every conceivable type of mountain terrain and exposure, and will transfer you by bus from Lake Louise and Banff for $40. www.purcellhelicopterskiing.com

Great Canadian Heli Skiing offers 3 day and week long packages out of the village of Golden. Trips are based out of Heather Mountain Lodge on the boundary of the Glacier National Park and near Rogers Pass, where peaks resemble the Matterhorn. Most of the boarding take place in the nearby Purcell Mountains with small groups being lead by a local guide with a guaranteed 15,250 vertical meters in a 3 day package or 30,500 m in the 7 days. www.canadianheli-skiing.com

Chilcotin Mountains

Bring it on. Only 65km north of Whistler, is the Chilcotin mountain range. This is a huge area where you can pick and choose your slopes. There are around 300 different runs, which have around an 800 meter of vertical descent, and there are also some great tree runs. This area gets a massive snowfall of 14 to 18 meters a season, so it should be steep and deep which is just what you're looking for. All this, as always, comes at a cost. Two days with lodge accommodation is $2400. Now that is a lot of cash. Elemental Adventure offers a week trip at £2658, without international flights.

Skeena Mountains

In the far North West of Canada just south of Alaska are the Skeena Mountains. This is a vast area of 9,000sq/km and that's big. An area that size has runs for all and endless fresh tracks. Based out of the town of Terrace, Northern Escape run heli trips in this area for 3, 4 or 7 days. A week costs $6590. If you're in the UK you can book trips with Elemental Adventure.

Photo credits. top 3 photos, © Purcell Helicopter Skiing Ltd
bottom photo © Canadian Heli-ski
Opposite page: © atlinheliski.com, Canada

France

Heliboarding is banned in France, unless you gain special permission, as most undeveloped areas are National Park. You can fly over the border into Italy for a couple of runs, but why bother? Unless you're holidaying in France, you may as well start in Italy. From Chamonix and Tignes you fly over the border and board in the Val Grisenche and Monte Rosa areas.

Greenland

Greenland is accessible via Copenhagen. Maniitoq is right on the Artic Circle trips are run here by www.eaheliskiing.com .The season lasts from March to Mid June. From April the sun never really sets, allowing for some late night boarding, and with loads of the runs ending on the beach, this is truly a mad place to board. Most of the mountains are under 2000meters and the majority of the boardable runs are around 1000meters of vertical decent. While in the area you can also go Whale watching and sea kayaking.

Here as always is the draw back: €7500 gets you a week without international flight or insurance, and things are expensive once you're there so make sure you get some booze at the duty free.

Georgia

In the town of Gudauri you can catch a twin turboengine MI-8-MTB-1 helicopter which can carry a capacity of four tons. The cabin seats 24 passengers so there's plenty of room for your board. There's good snow and lots of varied terrain. www.alpintravel.ch has been running trips here since 1989 so it can't be all bad. The best thing about heliboarding here is that the price of around €3000 will get you a week long trip with a vertical descent guarantee of 15,000 meters, a hotel with sauna and pool, food and most importantly a transceiver and ABS avalanche airbag system. Runs are between 1,500 m and 4,200 m, the average run being 800 to 1,200 m long, which is small in comparison to many places but then so the cost.

India

Surprisingly India has commercial Heliboarding operations running throughout the winter into early April. The best locations are in the Himalayan region of Hanuman Tibba, Deo Tibba, Rohtang Pass and Chandrakhani Pass, all close to the Manali valley which is a wild place where loads of marijuana is grown. Yhe Gulmarg in the Kashkir regions also offer heliboarding, but only experienced travellers and boarders should try these places, as if you have an accident, it's a long way for any help. www.himachal.com run heliboarding trips out of a small village north of Manali but expect to pay $6500 for a week trip. The main attraction of heliboarding in India is the guarantee of great light fluffy snow and the chance to take on some fantastic Oak tree runs.

Italy

Heliboarding in Italy is limited to a few areas. There's still some good riding in the Aoste Valley especially the Monte Rosa area which is high with a summit of 4633m. Val Grisenche normally has good snow when others are suffering. Most agencies within resorts can arrange day trips for you.

kazakhstan

Using old soviet military helicopters which will seat up to 20 people, Kazakhstan is another adventurous place to heliboard. The choice of terrain is endless and being the only helicopters with the ability to land (and more importantly take off again!) at altitudes of nearly 6000 meters you really can just choose any hill you want. The main draw back other than cost, is the cold with temperatures of -10 a winter norm in Alam-Ata, the capital, and the high peaks can easily drop below -30. Having said that, with hundreds of peaks higher than Mont Blanc, you can forget about boarding in January and go in the summer. The cheapest and easiest way is to stay at Karkara base camp (you will need a Kyrgyzstan visa) and take a short 20min flight into the mountains. If you don't fancy camping or being stuck in only the base camp bar listening to stories of the days riding then you could stay in Alma-Ata. However, it's an hour flight and at around £1000/hr to keep the helicopter in the air, the cash could be better spent flying in the mountains than back to the city. A flight to Inylchek Glacier to see Khan-Tengri and peak Pobedy is a must. You can sleep at the climber's base camp but take a good sleeping bag. Check out www.khantengri.kz.

kyrgyzstan

Cheaper than its larger neighbour Kazakhstan, Kyrgystan offers access to the same mountains at less cost. July and August are the best time to Heliboard in the Tien Shan Mountains. This is really high, ranging from 4500m up to 5800m. Using a Russian Helicopter you can fly from Karkara base camp up to the Northen Tien Shan. In a week's program it's possible for 7/8 dissents of 700/800meters a day. After a few days acclimatising to the altitude you will board from 5500 meters down to 4000meters up to 4 times in one day. On the last day if you're lucky you can board from Semeyonov Peak (5816m) down to 4000m. That's well over a vertical mile of untracked powder and there aren't many places in the world with that on offer.

Photo credits. this page, Pete © WSG
Opposite page: Gudauri Caucasus Mountains © Archiv ALPIN TRAVEL GmbH, Switzerland

new zealand

The main bases for heliboarding in New Zealand are Queenstown and Wanaka. Unlike many heliboarding locations, both towns have the fantastic advantage of offering day trips. There is no need to sign up for an expensive week, and more importantly if the weather is bad you can just choose another day. The season runs from early July to early October and, conditions permitting, heliboarding starts up with the season. www.nzadventure.com offer some great day trip options for around NZ$800 in the Harris Mountains, Clarke Glacier and Mount Cook areas. Methven near Christchurch offers some varied terrain with an area of 1000 square kilometres.

Mount Potts, the highest resort in New Zealand at 2200m, consists of three huge basins and has some fine slopes which are accessed with cats after you're flown up by helicopter. Also check out BCH www.heliskinz.com who are based out of Wanaka and fly daily into Mount Aspiring National Park. They sell 3 runs for NZ$660, 4 runs for $710 and 7 runs for $880. In good weather you could get up to 11 runs for the price of 7.

Russia

There are many options for Heli boarding in Russia. You can board on peaks like Mount Elbrus in the east, to Kamchatka in the very far west of the country. There truly are loads of possibilities and **www.snowboarding.in-russia.com** is a good site to check out where you can go. The helicopters are normally huge ex-Russian military beasts and can land as high as 5300m, carrying groups of 10 riders plus a guide.

Mount Elbrus in the Caucasus mountains, which are almost 1500km long, offers some great boarding. Operations are run from the resort of Dombai which is close to the Georgian Boarder and only a 15min flight from Elbrus where it's possible to board from its very summit, 5670 metres. There are numerous mountains over 4000 meters in the area with some great and varied terrain as well as some good tree runs. It's also possible to acess the area from the Black Sea resort of Sochi see **www.eaheliskiing.com** Week long trips run for around £2500.

Kamchatka the land of Reindeer, volcanoes and nomadic shepherds also offers some heliboarding on some very varied terrain. Many peaks reach over 4,000 metres and offer runs in excess of 3000 vertical metres. A 7 night, 6 day trip costs €4200 / £2838 and can be organised through www.eaheliskiing.com You will have to fly to **Petropavlosk** and when you get there don't expect luxury.

- $1800 depending on the type of helicopter. There are several agencies which provide heliboarding tours, but you need to book it at least a few months before, otherwise it will be hard to find an available helicopter. To hire the helicopter you can contact **www.krechet.com**. It's the only company which owns its own helicopters. **www.helipro.ru** also organise and run tours across Russia, Chile, Canada

Things here are basic but that's Russia for you. Most boarders prefer to ride at **Viluchinskiy** (2173 m), **Mutnovskiy** (2323 m), **Avachinskiy** (2741 m), **Goreliy** (1826 m), and **Opala** (2460 m) volcanoes. The average route length is 6 km, and the average vertical drop is 1500 m. The helicopters can be paid on a flight time basis. The price per flight hour is $500

Sweden

Out of **Riksgraensen** it's possible to fly north to some unvisited areas. Although the peaks are low, its position so far north in Lapland makes it a great destination for Spring boarding. Departures run until late April. Another option is to fly south to the area around the highest mountain massif of Sweden the Kebnekaise where there are some real wild spots.
www.aeroski.com

Switzerland

Schweiz has many companies offering packages from 1 day to a week so do your research before you book an over priced trip.

Situated in **Valais**, Helicopter Service sell trips through agencies in resorts such as **Zermatt**. They'll fly you to glaciers and peaks on mountains between Zermatt and **Chamonix**. Every area offers a variety of descents ranging from 1300 to 2500 metres, suitable for all abilities. Flights operate every fair weather day from December to May. The helicopters seat 4 to 6 passengers so groups are small with all guides being UIAGM certified. **www.heliservice.ch**

usa

Alaska

Valdez is the main town of Alaska, the Main Man, the Big Daddy, the Queen of all, and the Goddess of powder faces (no trees here). Whatever you want to call it Alaska is steep and deep personified. The seaport of Valdez is located in the **Chugach Mountains**, an 8 hour drive from Anchorage. Lots of companies run trips out of Valdez with day trips to week long holidays on offer. Blade Runner Adventures **www.heliskiworld.com** have some great prices with lower end accommodation keeping the cost down. 7 night and 5 days with the helicopter start at $3300 with 6 drops /day. A day with 6000 metres of vertical decent is $600. **www.valdezhelicamps.com** offer day trips at around $700, up to $4900 for a 6 day, 7 night package, with 80,000 vertical feet per six-day package guaranteed. It's lots of cash but it's not actually that expensive in the grand scheme of things. If cash is short you can mix the helicopter in with some snowcat boarding at $200/day and if the weather is bad at least there are snowcats to get you up the hill. If you're in the UK you can book similar deals through **www.eaheliskiing.com** ensuring you can talk to someone on the phone who knows their stuff before departure. Trips run from Feb to April.

Colorado

Helitraxs run trips out of **Telluride** and claim the highest mountain access in North America. This winter, Telluride Helitrax are offering a One-Run Heli Ticket. Early each morning snowboarders can start their day with a helicopter flight to an area outside the boundary of the Telluride ski area. For a run of approximately 1,100 vertical feet, the price is $250 per person. $895 will get you six drops in one day and if you're in Vail, Aspen or Crested Butte $1045 will get you a fixed winged flight to Telluride and a six drop heliboard day. **www.helitrax. net**

Photo credits. Photographer Ehren Wiener, Valdez Heli Camps
Location: Wortman's Glacier - run "Proud Mary"

Photo credits. Photographer Ehren Wiener, Valdez Heli Camps
Location: "The Tusk" via A-Star Helicopter

Learn to Snowboard

R™ are the first all British board instruction operation in Europe. Based in Courchevel and with hundreds of British boarders sliding away as satisfied customers, we at WSG thought it a good place to seek some advice on lessons.

So, you're heading off snowboarding. May be you've never done it before or perhaps you can rip up the slopes. So why take lessons?

For first timers it's pretty obvious why you need a lesson. You haven't got a clue how to do it but for intermediates or advanced boarders it might not be so clear. In reality a lesson for the intermediate is highly beneficial as it could be the difference from taking on steep terrain with confidence, stomping landings or riding off piste with ease.

Some people hear how easy it is to snowboard, and think "it can't be too hard, can it?" Maybe you've skied before and think it's the same thing. After all, it's all about sliding down a slope, isn't it?

It can be easy to pick up, especially if there is good snow and no ice. There are other factors to also consider like how sporty you are, and whether you have done any other board sports (skating, wakeboarding, surfing, kitesurfing or windsurfing), which all rely on balance. Even if you have all these skills, you still need to know how to actually make a snowboard turn and how to control your speed and most importantly: stop.

Anybody can learn to snowboard. How well you pick it up depends to some extent on the above but also on your motivation for being there, your attitude and how good your instructor is.

The classic beginner's lessons are in a group and normally run for a week. These should get you to the point where you are happy riding down green, possibly blue, or even red runs. Group lessons provide the best value for money but you are sharing that instructor's time with everyone else in the group so you don't always get their full attention.

If you are finding it hard to keep balance, for example, while others in the group are moving along by themselves it can feel frustrating. Don't get too disheartened. Everyone learns at different rates and at some point it will 'click'. An alternative is to take a private lesson, where you have the full attention of the instructor. You'll get the hands-on help needed to get you through these difficult stages but of course this will cost more cash.

Questions you need to ask yourself before booking are: Are you looking forward to the experience? Are you of a sporty disposition? Do you have good balance? Do you have a get up and go attitude? If the answers are 'yes', then group lessons should work well.

If you feel nervous and apprehensive, are you just doing this to please a friend, aren't really sport, or don't think your

balance is too great, then maybe private lessons would be more beneficial. That is not to say that you won't learn in a group but this private lesson would give you the best possible chance for success.

What to expect in those first few days

To start with, your instructor should give you a lot of help, both technically and with encouragement. It is true that you will fall over a lot but lessons will minimise this. It is normally during the time away from the instructor when you fall more. Many past beginners will tell you they felt like they had been run over. To help get around this think about protecting yourself. Impact shorts are especially padded to help reduce the pain of falls on the derriere and aren't too expensive. Cheaper alternatives are a rolled up hand towel stuffed down the trousers, a piece of foam or even a cushion / pillow. Just remember to take it out when you're having that post boarding pint in the bar. Knee pads and wrist guards can also help. Nowadays more people, especially kids, are wearing helmets too and they can be hired from most rental shops.

Getting the right equipment

The correct equipment and set-up tailored for you will also aid the learning process. Many hire shops will try to palm you off with any size of board and binding position, so hire your kit from a snowboard specialist.

Boots

Boots must fit your feet! Your heels shouldn't lift inside the boot. If they do, the boots are either not laced up properly, are too big or are the wrong width for your foot shape. People who've skied before will find more movement than in a pair of ski boots. That is normal and part of the joy of boarding! Try boots on that are your actual shoe size or even try a half size smaller. Do not take boots a size bigger because your snowboard socks are thicker - they are not that thick!

When lacing them up make sure all of your trousers are out

pic: RTM taking a heel edge turn

Skiers, don't you just love 'em?

pic: RTM showing some toe edge carving turns

of the boots. The inner snow gaiter should be outside the boot as well as the outer section of the trousers. If not then you may get pressure points on your legs along with snow melting down your leg into the boot.

Bindings

Just as important are bindings. Your booted foot should be held snugly in the binding and there should be no heel lift of the boot. Make sure you can do up the bindings with ease, ensuring they fit right over the boots. Quite often rental bindings need adjusting to fit smaller or larger feet, so get them to do this in the hire shop. It's a right pain to realise your kit doesn't fit when you're standing on the top of a mountain.

For all levels of rider the traditional strap binding system is still the best. For beginners they allow you to bend at the ankle joint easily when doing manoeuvres on the toe edge. Other systems can block this movement. You will also feel more from the board so movements you are making to try to turn the board actually have an effect, rather than the foot moving and the board not.

Stances

The correct angles and stance width for the bindings are equally important. Everyone is different, so their set up needs to be individually tailored. If set incorrectly movements made by the body will feel hindered and uncomfortable, thus reducing the effectiveness of your riding. Seek advice in the hire shop if you think this is happening.

Board

Choosing the right board is also important. Decide what kind of riding you are going to be doing and be honest about your ability and body weight. All boards have a weight range which you should fall in to. At the lower end of the scale the board may feel stiffer when riding and softer if you are at the higher end of the scale. For example, the same board ridden by a 9 stone person will feel stiffer compared to someone of the same riding ability

weighing 13 stones.

If you are a strong rider who likes to ride fast, the stiffer board will aid edge grip and will not bend as much as a softer board (which has a higher chance of losing edge grip). If you want to do a lot of freestyle then use a board designed for this purpose, and once again look at the weight range. Freestyle boards are shorter than freeride boards. Also, look at the width of the board.

Feet

Your feet when booted up should be centred so the toes and heels are just over the edge. If not, then it's too wide. If your feet hang well over the edges then it's too narrow, so look for a board that is wider or see if a riser plate underneath the bindings will reduce toe and heel drag while riding.

So you arrive, fully armoured up, feeling like an extra from some Sci-Fi film for the first lesson. Now you will learn how to stand correctly on the board, how to control your speed, how to change direction and maybe even how to link turns down the slope. Gradually, through the week you start to move away from the beginner's slope onto easy greens

pic: BASI showing some basic heel edge control

whilst developing your turns, speed and control. As you get more proficient, you learn to deal with the steeper blue runs. By the end of the week you'll hopefully be happy cruising around the same slopes that initially felt intimidating and taking in the scenery from the chairlifts, rather than feeling knackered and worrying about the next run down. You are now a snowboarder.

Yeh but, I can board already

For those of you who can already ride around the mountain the question often asked is "why do I need lessons? I can do it".

Well, do you want to feel more relaxed and in control riding steep slopes? Can you carve? Do you want to learn techniques for riding off-piste? What about learning some tricks in the park or how to ride a pipe? Lessons are still going to help you achieve these goals.

When choosing a group be honest about your ability: what pistes are you turning on? Green, blue, red or black? Doing falling leaf (swinging side to side when coming down a slope on one edge) is not turning! Also, your confidence when coming down these slopes is important. Being a little slow or nervous on the decent can alter which group you should aim to join.

Once signed up, things to expect in the lesson are: working on improving edge grip to reducing skidding in a turn which works towards carve turns on easier slopes and control speed on steep slopes. Other techniques covered are how to improve the steering of the board on steeps, and how to develop the techniques originally learnt to ride confidently down harder pistes. If you only do one week a year you

will never develop these skills properly without a lesson.

You may also want to look at the changes needed to ride off piste, in powder or chopped up snow. These skills will enable you to get away from the crowds and truly explore the mountains. Those of you looking for the perfect holiday photo may want to try freestyle. Learning how to make those first grabs and hold them for longer, how to start spinning, or get air out of a pipe or do rails will vary your whole outlook. Of course you can try and work it out for yourself but with guidance it is often an easier, quicker and less painful process.

Another alternative for freestylers is to book into a specialist camp (see Summer Boarding). A lot of these have pro-riders on hand to help with the coaching. Their competition background provides a massive repertoire of tricks for you to aim towards. These camps are often run in the summer months so allow you to keep getting your snowboard fix and reduce the wait for next season's first snowfall.

If you do decide to have lessons please do a little homework. Check out the different schools in the resort, see what they have to offer and try and get some recommendations.

Get out on the mountain and take the falls with the good turns. If you're not falling you're not trying hard enough! Most of all - enjoy it.
The **RTM team**.

Photo credits. top, left, first page by PaulColeman © BASI
page2 top by Patrick Leclerc © Oxbow Avoriaz, bottom left © Obergurgl Resort. All other photos © RTM

How to build a terrain park ...

The progression of parks

10 years ago when you arrived in a resort and looked for the terrain park there would all to often not be one to be found. In many resorts people are still looking. When resorts finally got round to building a park it was often in a totally unsuitable place, nowhere near a lift or where the landings were flat. Half-pipes were rarely shaped and often placed where one side of the pipe got sun all day while the other just saw shade, leading to one rock hard wall and one misshaped pile of slush. But don't be down heartened things are on the up. Ski executives were seeing their bonuses disappear as everyone was buying snowboards and turning their backs on the dark side. So they reinvented twin tips ski, with much success. This lead to skiers entering the parks and incorporating boarding moves into their aerials, and don't they look more stylish? So the people in power within the resorts had to keep not just that passing trend of boarders, who just wouldn't go away, happy but the future generations of skier's content to. So parks moved from an after thought, to high up on the list of a resort development. They moved form the furthest most inaccessible spots to smack bang in the middle of resorts central station and are now a major draw to resorts. Often cheap lift tickets are sold for park only access, with many lit for night riding, with tunes blearing out all day and night.

So with many resorts building bigger and better parks we at WSG hope park users will follow some basic advice on safety and etiquette in the park. More importantly is that resorts design parks that allow for natural progression from beginners to pro. Flynn Seddon has seen resorts turn full circle, when he started riding, boarders in Big White weren't allowed on the lifts and had to walk up the mountain to catch freshes. Last year Big White handed him a large suitcase of money and told him build us a park that's a world beater and we think he's done it. It truly a park for everyone there's hits, rails and pipes of all sizes, with a fantastic signage system allowing for that all important progression, how you ever going to go big, and avoid the hospital, without hitting a few small hits first.

The following article is Flynn's take on what's needed in a park, how you should use a park and what it takes to run one.

Park Design

When designing a park you must look at the following issues.

Build a park for all abilities.

It's important to Design a park with the progression system in mind. Every one needs features that suit there ability, if we design a park with features for only advanced riders up to 70 % of resort visitors are left out. The main reason terrain parks are seeing a huge increase in beginner traffic is at last park designers are finally starting to build features that are suitable for the novice rider to learn on.

Run size and natural terrain shape.

It's vital to lessen the environmental impact of a park on the mountain, so I aim to use the natural shape of the terrain to help design a park. Working with the shape of the land not against it.

Availability of snow.

Make sure that the area for your park has enough snow. Many resorts rely solely on natural snow fall, so you need to consider the area surrounding the park. Is it possible to easily move snow into the park area if snow fall is light?

Flow of the park traffic.

A resorts Traffic is hard to control, so design your park with areas for people to stop and watch riders, without being in the way. Do not place the features to close together, as people need room to land and set up for the next hit, or wipe out without hitting anything.

Building features that can be easily maintained and viewed.

When you build a feature make sure that it can be easily maintained. Do not build something that will be difficult for the cat or crew to access and keep in good shape. Some features take a long time to build and can get worn out really fast.

Have a good crew to maintain the park.

When you have a park it is only as good as the crew that maintains it. At Big White we have a crew of 16 full time staff. We also have two full time groomers with two pipe grinding machines. It takes a lot of commitment, money and energy to have a world class park.

Riders need to understand that many resorts do not have the ability to build and maintain a park to a world class level. Make sure you take all these things into consideration when you travel the world and ride different resorts. Each area is unique, and it is up to you to make the most of your experience. It helps to appreciate all the time and effort that goes into the making of a park and the natural restraints a resort has to cope with.

Progression System

Parks are being designed so riders have a progressive system of features to learn and develop their skills. It's imperative that people can learn safely on jumps and rails that fit their ability level. In recent years the resort industry has noticed a dramatic increase of park use. Beginners are flocking to areas that provide easy to intermediate park lanes, parks are now not only for the elite.

My crew and I designed the Big White park using a new progression and rating system, which was developed in Canada along with input from the Burton Smart Style program and a Canadian terrain park panel from Blackcomb, Seymour and Grouse mountains. Together we have created a progression system based on a Small, Medium, Large and Extra Large rating scale. The concept is that we build easily recognised features for all abilities of rider. By creating this rating system we enable riders to start on short and wide rails progressing to longer and larger rails with ride on, to air on, access, the same approach and sign system is applied to jumps. **This is no substitute for inspecting the terrain park before using it.** You should always inspect the park as snow conditions, visibility and feature design can vary from resort to resort and conditions do change throughout the day.

Below is a chart that shows an example of the small to extra large progression level for Rails.

LEVEL	HEIGHT	LENGTH	WIDTH	PITCH	RAIL	RAMP
S	Up to 1.5'	Up to 16'	At least 1'	flat	flat	ride-on
M	Up to 2'	Up to 24'	At least 1'	flat / slope	flat/kink	ride-on
L	Up to 3.5'	24' +	Less than 1'	flat/slope	flat/kink/curve	combo
XL	3.5' +	30' +	Less than 1'	flat/slope	flat/kink/curve	air-on

As you travel the world in search of the ultimate park you'll notice resorts are developing more parks that have a progression system approach. The designers are offering the riders smaller boxes and wider rails and a progressive selection of jumps that start off small and get larger as person's skills get more advanced. We hope that one day all parks will use our progressive approach and our signing system.

This Park contains the following features

LOOK BEFORE YOU LEAP!

Freestyle Terrain has four levels of progression and designation for size. Start small and work your way up. It is your responsibility to familiarize yourself with the terrain before attempting any of the features.

Designations Are Relative To This Resort

Freestyle Terrain **S** — Introductory freestyle terrain
- Small features, surface-level rails & boxes
- Less Difficult features

Know It. Respect It. Ride It.

Freestyle Terrain **M** — Small to medium size features
- Ride-on rails & small to medium half pipe
- Difficult features

Know It. Respect It. Ride It.

Freestyle Terrain **L** — Medium to large size features
- Introduction to jump-on rails
- Rail's with gaps & narrow surfaces
- Large half pipe
- More Difficult features

Know It. Respect It. Ride It.

Freestyle Terrain **XL** — Largest size features & jumps
- Jump-on rails with gaps & narrow surfaces
- Advanced and Experts only
- Most Difficult features

Know It. Respect It. Ride It.

Park Lanes

Parks are now being designed with different lane entrances, accessing only a selected and uniformed sizes of features. We at Big White have a Small and medium lanes as well as other lanes that contain Medium, large and extra large features.

These lanes have entrance signs that educate the user as to the size of features they will encounter in that particular zone. Allowing for compete use of a lines features, no longer do you have to hit only a few of the features on the way down, you can relax knowing your not about to fly of anything beyond your standard.
Once in a lane all features are marked with an ability marker showing the size of the feature that you are approaching.

Some resorts have enough room to build a lane of each size. Most resorts face a space issue. The nice thing about the progression system is that you can design a single lane that incorporates all of the different sized features and clearly mark each individual feature, allowing riders a safer decent. With the progression system all you need is a main entrance sign informing the user what ability level features are and the rider can decide which features they are best suited for.

Park Rules

When you visit a new terrain park for the first time, take a moment to read the signs and information provided in the park. Some areas or countries may have a slightly different program so the information provided could make a massive difference in how you enjoy the ride.

Some simple rules to follow that apply to all resort terrain parks round the world.

1) You must inspect and check out all the features that you will be using in the park before you start making runs. Some parks do not build features the same way as other park builders do. What you rode on in Switzerland may not be the same type of design as the terrain park in Canada.

2) Always ride with in your ability and limit. Do not take unnecessary chances that can leave you hurt and seriously injured. Work your way up on the features. Learn easier tricks that help you develop your skills.

3) Respect others riders and skiers in the park. Call you drop in. Don't stop on the landing area. One person at a time on the features. Always watch were you are going and plan your route through the park.

Burton is promoting a program called Smart style through out the resort world.

Visit www.freestyleterrain.com to get educated on the Burton program. This type of industry campaign is something you will see more of as you travel the world in search of that powder Mecca or ultimate park. Many resorts in Canada are adopting this system of rating the size and difficulty of their terrain park features. We have a program that combines the Burton Smart Style signs and safety messages. Visit www.bigwhite.com and check out our park tour for a sample of the program.

The Cost ?

The continued advancement of terrain parks and the development of safety and features require a large commitment, of energy and money. I think you'll be surprised by just how much it actually costs.

Grooming and Equipment.

To keep a good and consistent park you need to groom every night. Generally we have one machine dedicated to the maintenance of our half pipes and another machine dedicated to the maintenance of the jumps and rails.
The pipe's need a specialized pipe grooming machine which is attached to its own snow cat. These two bits of kit cost $400,000 if not more depending on the equipment you buy. The snow cat needed to groom the jumps and rails costs another $350,000

The snow cats then of course need fuel, and they break down so there are repairs and parts. You also need drivers, who need wages.
The total number of grooming hours for just two machines to maintain our park is approximately 2160 hours. This translates to about $216,000 per season. That's $1,000 an hour.

Add the cost of signs, educational material fences , bamboo, shovels, Rakes and all the other materials need that's another $15,000 per season.

If your resort has a chair lift that just services the park, you have to add the cost of running, maintaining and staffing the lift. At Big White we had a chair built specifically to run in the park which operates 12 hours a day, 7 days a week. The cost to run the chair for the season is approximately $150,000

Park Staff

Building a park is one thing but once its built you need a full time team of staff to run it. A large park, like here at Big White employees a team of 17 people.
Each day we have between 7 to 10 people spotting features, hand grooming take offs, fixing fencing and working with the public to ensure every one is educated in how to safely use the terrain park. This relates to Just over $140,000 in staff wages alone each season.

Totals

As you can see the commitment, energy and financial resources that are required to maintain, build and keep up a world class terrain park is tremendous.
Our park costs over $1/2 Million Canadian a year to run.

Add the cost of buying the pipe grinder and the two snow cats it comes to $1.27 Million Canadian. That's without the initial cost of building the park, or buying/installing the new chair lift which services it.

Have fun, be safe and make sure you stick around and enjoy the ride.

Flynn Seddon.

Holidays & Accommodation

Chamonix, Val d'Isere, Meribel, Courchevel/3 Valleys, Les Arcs, Portes du Soleil, Verbier, St Anton & More

Catered Chalets
Self-Catering Apartments & Chalets
Hotels

Flexible options & durations
Weekends/Short Breaks
Tailor Made Holidays
Groups, families & singles
Resorts throughout Europe & North America

www.ski-links.com

Tel: 0870 747 9121
info@ski-links.com

Independent Ski Links

Health on the Hill

Y ou're off for a game of football with your mates. When you arrive, you spend five minutes stretching and warming up. Or maybe you're watching some competition footage from a snowboarding DVD, and in the background the other competitors are touching their toes, or swinging their arms - basically warming up. So now it's your turn, first run of the season. You get off the chair lift, and what do you do? You put your board on, as fast as you can, and set off down the slope at full speed, reminding yourself of why you love this sport so much. Three days later you can hardly walk, and you feel like you've been struck by a freight train. The rest of your holiday is spent walking like a man who dropped the soap in the shower on his first day in prison.

The following article is some advice on how to pre-empt the funny walks and torn muscles. There are many ways to do this: spend the summer surfing, skating, wakeboarding or windsurfing. But if they don't tickle your fancy, then another great thing to do is use a Balance Board. This is a skateboard deck, with a runner underneath which sits on a free moving roller, the size of a beer can. They are easy to store, and can be used at any time, even in your lunch hour. Great for improving your balance and keeping muscles toned! If you use public transport, another way to improve balance is to see how much of your journey on the bus/tube you can stand for, without holding on to anything. This uses the muscles in your legs, feet and trunk to keep you balanced. Sounds daft, but with practice your co-ordination will improve! (just don't sit in too many peoples laps!)

We at WSG asked Claire Hickman, a registered osteopath and keen snowboarder, what it is that we should do, both over the summer months and in resort, to help make our boarding holiday/season injury free. Whilst these exercises won't stop you from injuring yourself, they will tone the right muscle groups and help your improve your strength and stamina. We hope that they will help you to ride longer and harder, but remember - no lycra, not even when you're alone.

Exercises for improving fitness:

Wall squat
strengthens the thighs in a static position

Stand with your back to a wall and lower your body down as if you are sitting on a chair. Your hips should be level with your knees, and your knees should be directly above your ankles. Keep back straight against the wall. Try to hold for 30-60 seconds. Repeat 3-5 times. Stretch the front thigh muscles afterwards. (see quadriceps stretch below) (n.b. can also be done as a time challenge when having a beer, after boarding, see who lasts longest – try slightly raising one foot off floor and trying to balance for extra interest)

Walking lunge
strengthens the thighs whilst moving

Take a medium-sized step with one foot in front of you, lower the back knee towards the floor, as your front leg also bends to 90 degrees at the knee. Make sure the front knee is directly over the ankle, not beyond it, and that your back is straight. Push up and step forward to repeat with the other leg. Walk-lunge for 10 steps then turn around and walk-lunge to your start position.

Calf strength

These muscles help control the ankle and strength here is useful during toeside traverses.

Stand facing a step with just your toes on the step and your heels off the back, slightly below the level of the step. (Hold something nearby for balance if necessary, or do one foot at a time). Slowly press down on your toes and raise the heels up to stand on tip-toe, keeping your back straight. Slowly lower to start position and repeat 10 times. You can easily do this one in the queue waiting for the lifts as well – just push up both feet on tip toes. For added interest and balance training, try it with your eyes shut.

Abdominal strength

Helps keep your upper body strong and stable, as the upper body plays a big part in keeping your balance whilst boarding

Lie on your back on the floor, knees bent, feet on floor, hands resting behind head for support. Breathe in, and as you exhale, 'pull' your belly button in towards your spine then slowly raise your shoulders from the floor. Breathe in as you relax back to staring position. Do not pull on the neck, make the work happen at belly-button level. Repeat 10-15 times.

Abdominal twists

as above, but as you raise the shoulders, slowly rotate the upper body one way, then return to centre and then the start position, and the next time rotate the other way. Repeat 10 times each side. Good for helping with both traverses and turns.

Stretches (banish that morning stiffness (!))

Ideally these stretches should be done, at the start of your day's boarding (after the above exercises) and again when you finish, before hitting the local eateries and nightlife. Stretching daily will help to reduce that familiar nasty feeling of stiffness and aching in the joints and muscles:

Double knee hugs

lying on your back, pull both knees up to your chest. Hold 10 seconds. Repeat 5 times.

Low back rotations

lying on your back with knees bent, drop both knees over to the left and your arms over to the right. Hold 10 seconds and slowly return to centre. Repeat other side. Both sides 5 times.

Hamstring stretch
(back of thigh)

lying on your back with one knee bent, foot on floor. Bend up the other knee and, taking a hold behind the thigh, start to straighten the leg upwards. You should feel the stretch at the back of the leg. Try to keep your pelvis flat on the floor, and relax your head, neck and shoulders as well. Pulling your toes down towards you will increase the stretch. Hold 20-30 sec, repeat other leg.

Quadriceps stretch
(front of thigh)

standing up, hold a chair or wall (or your board) for balance if necessary. Lift one heel towards your bottom and hold the ankle. Try to keep both knees together, and slightly bend the leg you are standing on – do not over-arch your low back. Hold 20-30 sec, repeat other side.

Calf stretch
(back of lower leg)

this muscle works hard whilst boarding, so do stretch it well. Stand with your arms against a wall (tree/pillar/post will all do too) then step one foot back far behind you and keeping the leg straight, really push the heel down towards the floor, feeling the stretch below the back of the knee, down towards the ankle. Hold 30 sec, repeat other side.

The last two stretches shown here are really easy to do during the day as well, whilst waiting in the lift queue etc.

Claire Hickman is a registered osteopath based in London and Kent with an interest in sports injury and prevention. For queries regarding the exercises or other aspects of fitness for the slopes, please contact Claire at osteosynergy@hotmail.com www.osteosynergy.co.uk

Doing a Season

It's been snowing non-stop all week, now when you look outside there's not a cloud in the sky. All you can see, as you stumble back from the pub, is a moon lit untouched powder field stretching as far as the eye can see. Great, or is it? The next thing you know its 4:30 in the morning and some holiday rep is rapping on your door, telling you your holiday is over, and shift your arse on to that coach. "Bollocks" you grunt from under the duvet. So, what are you going to do? Get a job, which pays much cash and gives you loads of free time? Well if you find it let me know.

To avoid such terrible moments in one's life, there is only one realistic thing to do: a season. Doing a season is the only real way for most of us to improve our boarding, and also never miss out on all those fresh powder days.

So how are you going to do this season? Work or be a bum? Do it in Europe or North America, Argentina or New Zealand? There are loads of things to think about before doing a season. Just taking any old job, could see you stuck pouring pints all day or counting yellow gondolas while holding a four year old's hand, whilst thinking of everyone else in the powder. "Oh look, another yellow one". So before you take a job, find out what your hours are.

There are two main channels open for you: you either get a job for a tour operator or in North America the resort i.e. hotel work-chalet person, chef, bar work, dish pig (washing up), or you get a job on the slopes as a lifty or instructor.

There is a third option, boarding. This is only open to those lucky ones who are sponsored by the like of Burton, or Ride and spend their time jumping out of helicopters with their mates who are filming them. Becoming a sponsored rider is done by competing and getting yourself noticed, and the only way to do that is to be a child prodigy, or do seasons, get good and enter those comps. As for taking pictures or making films, well it's the same deal as the riders, be talented, do seasons, and put a good portfolio together.

Tour Operators

Working for a tour operator is a good first time step into working seasons. They will get you to the resort, give you accommodation, feed you, supply you with a snowboard, give you enough money to get drunk once a week, and most importantly give you that expensive Lift Pass.

This all sounds great,

but what they will do is squeeze you into accommodation tighter than beans in a tin, send you to a hire shop that will try to palm you off with kit that was out of date in the 90's, work you hard and long for your beer money. Often they will even ask you for a deposit for your lift pass, which is returned at the end of the season. Having said all that, it's still good starting off point. Contact all the Tour Operators in the summer as they normally start hiring around September. They'll ship you out to the resort in the beginning of December, and expect you to work until the end of April with one day off a week.

Working For A Resort

Unlike Europe where resorts were built on land once owned by peasant farmers who suddenly became very rich when the snow sports industry was born, the resorts of North America are owned by one company. So there are no complications with someone owning the land while some

else owns the lifts and someone else owns the hotel etc. Big White in Canada for instance rents the land from the Government and owns everything that's been developed there. Therefore the job options are great, from bar to bin man, from catering to cat driver. Again, contact resorts in the summer if looking for work the next season.

Resort Bum

Many people just turn up in a resort and look for work. This can be good but of course you either need a friend with a place for you to sleep or some money to keep you going. The best thing to do is go there in November or very early December if you want to rent accommodation for the season. If you're looking for work with a Tour Operator in the Northern Hemisphere, it's best to leave it until after the New Year as most operators start the season fully staffed.

By the New Year some people start to realise a season away is not for them, and run home to Mummy, leaving you a sweet job to take, having missed out on the hardest part of the season-getting set up. If you do have your own pad, then companies are always looking for Transfer Reps on change over days. You just have to take people to the airport at the end of their holiday and pick up the new lot. If you have your own car, then there's cash to be had offering private airport transfers, but just watch out for angry local taxi drivers. There's also often random part time bar or kitchen jobs and you can always rely on other friendly resort workers to help you out with the odd meal here and

Before you take a course find out where your resulting qualification will be valid. Instructing can be well paid, although not always. It's great to see people progress on their boards, and it can give you a real buzz introducing our great sport to new people.

The down side is that if you have a lesson booked, you have to work: whether its -20, pissing with rain, or worst of all you may find yourself watching your mates getting fresh tracks while you are picking a beginner up off their arse on a green slope, but at least there's no toilets to clean.

Whatever job option you decide upon, "Doing a Season" will be one of the best things you've ever done. Loads of boarding, loads of partying, and loads of likeminded people. But remember loads of work too.

Photo credits. This page: Karin @ marco's photo Woody, tother WSG. **first page** shadow photo by Woody, group shot (c) big white.

there. The biggest draw back of going it alone is you'll have to buy your own lift pass and pay for accommodation. Also it doesn't matter how skint you are, anyone out there mine sweeping (stealing beers) in the bars is low, and I hope you get some nasty mouth scabs.

On The Piste

For almost all jobs on the slopes you'll need to be well qualified. One which is achievable for most of us is an Instructor Qualification. Courses are run by many organisations and you should check with governing bodies for affiliated members. UK www.basi.org.uk. Canada www.casi-bc.com USA www.aasi.org New Zealand www.nzsia.net .

FRENCH
LANGUAGE GUIDE

BASIC WORDS

Yes - Oui
No - Non
Please - Sil vous plait
Thank you - Merci
Hello - Bonjour

Call - Appeler
Carry - Porter
Change - Changer
Close - fermer
Come - Venir
Drink - Boire
Eat - Manger
Exhausted - Epuise
Fall - Tomber
Get - Recevoir
Give - Donner
Help - Aider
Here - Ici
Hold - Tenir

How - Comment
Lift - Soulever
Look - Regarder
Meet - Rencontrer
None - Aucun
Open - Ouvrir
Pull - Tier
Push - Pousser
Rain - Pluie
Release - Lacher
Slide - Deraper
Snow - Neiger
Speak - Parler
Take - Prendre
There- La
To - A
Turn - Tourner
Wait - Attendre
Wear - Porter
Week - La semaine

When - Quand
Why - Pourquoi

NUMBER - NOMBRE
Zero - Zero
One - Un
Two - Deux
Three - Trois
Four - Quatre
Five - Cinq
Six - Six
Seven - Sept
Eight - Huit
Nine - Neuf
Ten - Dix
Eleven - Onze
Twelve - Douze
Thirteen - Treize
Fourteen - Quatorze
Fifteen - Quinze

Sixteen - Seize
Seventeen - Dix-sept
Eighteen - Dix-huit
Nineteen - Dix-neuf
Twenty - Vingt

Day: - Jour:

Sunday - Dimanche
Monday - Lundi
Tuesday - Mardi
Wednesday - Mercredi
Thursday - Jeudi
Friday - Vendredi
Saturday - Samedi

Time - Temps

COMMON PHRASES

Do you speak English? - Vous parlez anglais?
I don't speak French - Je ne parle pas francais
I don't understand - Je ne comprends pas
Please speak slowly - Veuillez parler lentement
I hope you understand my English - J'espere que vos comprenez mon anglais
Where do you come from? - D'ou venez-vos?
I come from..... - Je viens de.......
I live in London - J'habite a London
My name is - Je m'appelle
I am _ _ years old - J'ai-__ans
I am marred and I have children - Je suis marie et j'ai enfant
What's your name? - Comment vous appelez-vous?
What time is it? - Quelle heure est-il?
It is eight o'clock -Il est huit heures
Good Morning - Bonjour

Good Afternoon - Bonjour
Good Evening - Bonsoir
Good Night - Bonne nuit
I would like to make a telephone call/reverse the charges to....- Je voudrais telephoneren/telephoner en PCV a....
The number is - Le numero est
I would like to change these travellers cheques/this currancy/this Eurocheque - J'aimerais changer ces cheques de voyage/ces devises/cet Eurocheque
Can I obtain money with my? creditcard? - Puis-je avoir de L'argent avec ma carte de credit
How much is this? - C'est combien
Money - Argent
Credit card - Carte de credit
Bank - Bank
Change - Changement

TRAVEL TERMS

Flying - Volant
Passport - Passeport
Airport - Aeroport
Customs - Douane
Passports please - Les passeports, s'il vous plait
I have nothing to declare - Ja n'ai rien a declarer
Excuse me, where is the check-in for? - Excusez-moi, ou est le comptoir d'enregistrement de....?
What is the boarding gate? - Quelle est la porte d'embarquement?
Which way is the baggage reclaim? - Ou se trouve l'aire de reception des bagages?
How long is the delay likely to be? - Le retard est de combien?
Driving - Conduite
No parking - Stationnement interdit
Car - Voiture
Stop - Stop
One way - Sens unique
Give way - Cedez la
No Entry - Sens interdit

How much dose it cost to hire a car for one day? - Quel est le prix de location d'une voiture pour un jour?
I have ordered a car in the name of - J'ai reserve une voiture au nom de
Is insurance and tax included? - Est-ce que l'assurance et les taxes sont comprises?
By what time must I return the car? - A quelle heure dois-je ramener la voiture?
I've had a breakdown at......... - Je suis tombe en panne a........
I am on the road from.......... - Ju suis sur la route de........
Please call the police - Vous pouvez appeler la police
There has been an accident - Il y a eu un accident
Train - Train
Railway Station - Gare
Where is the ticket office - Ou se trouvre le guichet?
May I have a single/return ticket? - Puis-je avoir un aller/un aller retour ticket?
Does this train go to? - Est-ce que cet autobus va a....?

SPANISH
LANGUAGE GUIDE

NUMBERS & DAYS

Zero Cero	Four Cuatro	Eight Ocho	Day:	Wednesday Miercoles
One Uno	Five Cinco	Nine Nueve	Sunday Domingo	Thursday Jueves
Two Dos	Six Seis	Ten Diez	Monday Manana	Friday Viernes
Three Tres	Seven Siete		Tuesday Martes	Saturday Sabado

BASIC WORDS

Yes - Si
No - No
Please - Por favor

Thank you - Gracias
How? - Como?
Hello – Hola

COMMON PHRASES

Do you speak English? - Habla usted ingles?
I don't speak Italian. - No hablo espanol
I don't understand. - No entiendo

My name is - Me llamo
What time is it? - Que hora es?
It is eight o'clock - Son las ocho
Good Morning - Buenos dias
Good Afternoon - Buenas tardes
Good Evening - Buenas noches

Good Night - Buona notte
I would like to change these travellers cheques/this currancy/this Eurocheque - Quisiera cambiar estos cheques de viaje/dinero/este Eurocheque
How much is this? - Cuanto es?
Can you please write it down - Lo puede escribir, por favor
I come from....- Soy de.....
Control your speed - Controla la velocidad
How are you today? - Que tal estas hoy?
Where are you from? - De donde eres?

FOOD & DRINK

Cheers - Salud
Waiter - Camarero
Can you recommend a restaurant? - Puede recomendarme un buen restaurante?
I'd like a table for...... - Quisiera una mesa para.....
May I please have the menu? - Puedo ver la carta, por favor?
Do you have a set menu? - Tienen menu del Dia
Main Courses - Platos principales
Fish dishes - Pescados
Meat dishes - Carnes
Vegetarian dishes - Platos vegetarianos
Do you have any vegetarinan dishes? - Dan

comidas vegetarians, por favor?
The food is cold - L comida esta fria
I would like a cup of tea - Quisiera una taza de te
I would like a beer please - Quisiera una cerveza, por favor

Red wine - Tinto vino
White wine - Blanco vino

Bread - Pan
Cheese - Queso
Chips - Patatas fritas
Coffee - Cafe
Dessert - Postre

Fruit - Frutas
Ketchup - Salsa de tomate
Lemon - Limon
Milk - Leche
Potatoes - Patatas
Rice - Arroz
Salt - Ensalada
Seafood - Mariscos
Vegetables - Legumbres
Vinegar - Vinagre
Gallina - Chicken
Salchicha - Sausage
Seta - Mushroom

TRAVEL TERMS

Passport please - Los oassaportes por favor
I have nothing to declare - No tengo nada que declarar
What is the boarding gate? - Por que puerta?
One way Sentido unico - No Entry Prohibido el paso
I've had a breakdown at....... - El coche se ha averiado en.
I am on the road from.......... - Estoy en la carretera de......
Please call the police - Llame a la policia
There has been an accident - Ha habido un accidente

How much does it cost to hire a car for one day? - Cuanto cuesta alquilar un coche por un dia?
Is insurance and tax included? - Esta incluido en el precio los impuestos y el seguro?
Does this train go to? - Quest' treno va a....?
Where is the ticket office?- Donde esta la taquilla de billetes?
When is the next train to? - A que hora sale el proximo tren para....?

ON THE SLOPES

Avalanche - El alud
Danger - El peligro
Rescue - Salvar
First Aid Kit - El botiquin

Chairlift - El telesillas
Cable Car - El teleferico
Gondola - La cabina

Powder Snow - Nieve polvo
Old Snow - Nieve asentada

Sticky Snow - Nieve primavera
Wet Snow - Nieve pesada
Glacier - El glaciar
Slope - La pendiente
Piste - La pista
Run - La bajada
Mogul - La banera

Beginner - El principiante
Intermediate- El esquiador de nivel intermedio

Advanced - Avanzado

Traverse - La Traversa
Off Piste - Fuera de la pista

Lift Ticket - El billete
Ski Instructor - El monitor de esqui
Lesson - La leccion

It's been a long journey, with many miles of pistes descended, thousands of miles of motorways and dirt tracks driven, new contributions from many different nationalities from many different continents, hours on computers, and not to mention the litres of beer drunk, but we've got there. The 2006 World Snowboard Guide covers more countries and more resorts than ever before. Stuffed full of reviews, articles, informative tips, and language guides, the 2006 World Snowboard Guide is a must for any open minded snowboarder looking to broaden their mountainous horizons.

This is the 10th edition of the World Snowboard Guide, it's fully updated and revised for the 2005/6 season. There's around 600 resorts listed, with over 300 in detail, including any new resort improvements. There's also information on Summer Riding, Heliboarding, Designing Terrain Parks, Back Country Riding, Instruction, Summer Camps, and our well received Far Flung section, with countries as diverse as China and Lebanon included.

We pride ourselves on informing you of every aspect of a resort from an unbiased snowboarder's perspective. From piste to pub, from hidden spots to kicking night club, from Canada to Kazakhstan. When you pick up this guide, you pick up the inside knowledge of our Worldwide Team of snowboards. The pistes have been boarded and the bars have been drunk in. This is categorically the best snowboard guide you can buy, written by boarders for boarders.

Where ever you go boarding this year, be it France or Morocco, make sure you stick our book in your bag and enjoy the ride. The WSG Team

We've split the resort information into sections covering mountain, snow, facilities/prices. terrain, and location and contact.

LINKED AREAS

We don't see any point in displaying the stats for an entire linked area. We'll tell you that its linked and how big the area is, but we try and keep things local. There's little point telling you of a park that will take you half a day on lifts to get to, so we usually try and keep the stats and reviews local. So you're often find we cover lots of resorts separatley that make up the linked area.

MOUNTAIN STATS

The total ride area is either given in KM's as the length of the combined length of the pistes, or in acres as the whole boardable area. Generally the Europeans like the piste lengths, and the US go for mountain size.

Pistes are broken down into easy, intermediate and advance slopes. To standardise between US and European styles, combine Green and Blue slopes and call them easy. Red's are intermediate, and black slopes advanced. Again, the US like to break things into blacks and double blacks, but we lump them together to standardise. The percentage of slope each distinction indicates the proportion of slopes designed for that purpose.

PRICES

All lift pass prices unless stated are for an adult, and for peak season. You can expect to pay up to 25% less for lift passes during the early and late season, when not all the slopes will be open. They also tend to ramp up prices during holidays, so watch out for that one. Lessons and hire generally stay the same throughout the season

TERRAIN

We split the reviews intp Freeride, Freestyle, Pistes and Beginners. We have also included this year a little graph showing how good we think a resort lends itself to a particular style (shown to your right). The higher the Freestyle bar the better the terrain park or the more the opportunity to find good natural terrain.

SNOW

Where possible we give the average annual snowfall that a resort receives. This is a very vague figure, as it depends where on the mountain you measure it, so it is only useful as a guide. Artificial snowmaking allows resorts to open earlier and stay open for longer. Resorts employ snow cannons and other machinary to achieve this, but rather than give numbers we show how many pistes snowmaking can cover.

THE RATING

Overall ratings are very subjective, but the most important thing to consider is snowfall. No snow turns a 10 resort into just a hill. Aside from that we think a resort that earns a 10 is able to satisfy ever boarder with a combination of the mountain and the resorts services. All resorts have something new to offer, and while a a rating of 6 may not sound very good, it will offer something for most riders except the more

advanced, but please take them with a pinch of salt!

COUNTRIES

There's some pretty self-explanatory information on each of the country pages. We've included some very rough currency conversion information, it was correct at the time of going to press, but will change.

This year we've also included web links and phone numbers for transport services and airports.

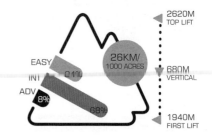

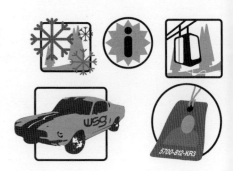

Pic - Andorra Tourism

Andorra is a self-governing principality under the joint sovereignty of France and Spain, and has become known as the cheap snow-package tour centre of Europe - a reputation richly deserved. Over the years it's also been steadily climbing the leader board and now is the 4th most popular destination for British snow hounds, behind France, Austria and Italy. Nestled high in the Pyrenees, Andorra is a very friendly, laid back place which is constantly improving the on-slope facilities, how ever this place has not always had a great snow record.

Andorra has a number of very small resorts that are ideal for total beginners and just okay for intermediates on a three day visit. As has happened across much of Europe, the big thing is to offer a combined lift pass that covers many resorts, stick a few more euros onto the bill, and hey presto you now have a resort with a beast lift system offering hundreds of kilometres of pistes. Sure they're only connected by bus, and you'll spend all day on it if you want to see the whole area, but the marketteers love it. Andorra now has 2 such super areas, **Vallnord** and **Grand Valira**.

Vallnord (89km pistes) covers the resorts of Pal, Arinsal, Ordino and Arcalis. The Grand Valira (193km of pistes) covers the resorts of Pas de la Casa, Soldeu, El Tarter, Grau Roig, Canillo and Encamp.

In general, though, there's no challenging terrain for expert riders, or at least nothing that won't take more than a few hours to tackle. A week here will bore the tits off any rider who likes to ride steep, fast and challenging terrain.

All the areas are located within a short distance of each other and can be reached via France or Spain. The nearest international airport is in **Barcelona**, but transfer is not easy if you don't have a car. The resorts offer basic local services, with lots of apartments available.

Duty free Andorra is well known for its very boozy nightlife, helping to make it a party-style hangout. Its reputation for a bargain is not quite what is was, but overall it's not a bad country to visit as long as it's for no more than a week.

Capital City: Andorra La Vella
Population: 69,865
Highest Peak: Coma Pedrosa 2946m
Language: Catalan-Spanish-French
Legal Drink Age: 18
Drug Laws: Cannabis is illegal and frowned upon
Age of consent: 16
Electricity: 240 Volts AC 2-pin
International Dialing Code: +376

Time Zone
UTC/GMT +1 hr
Daylight saving time: +1 hour

Office de Tourisme de la Principauté d'Andorre
Director: Sr. Enric Riba
26, avenue de l'Opéra - 75001 Paris
Tel.: (01) 42 61 50 55
E-mail: OT_ANDORRA@wanadoo.fr
Web: www.tourisme-andorre.net

Driving Guide
All vehicles drive on the right hand side of the road
Speed limits:
In towns 40kph
In rural areas 70kph
Emergency
Police/Ambulance Service - 17
Fire Service - 18
Tolls
None
Documentation
Driving license, insurance and vehicle registration, along with your passport.

Currency: euro
Exchange Rate:
UK£1 = 1.45 euro
US$1 = 0.8 euro

wsg ARCALIS/ORDINO

5 OUT OF 10

Ok for a few easy days

	POOR	FAIR	GOOD	TOP
FREERIDE Trees and some off-piste				
FREESTYLE A terrain park				
PISTES Okay intermediate trails				

Pic - Ordino Tourism

Arcalis is the least known, least visited, and most remote of all Andorra's resorts. It has recently joined with **Pal/Arinsal** forming the **VallNord** area, the shared lift pass giving you access to 60km of pistes. An undeveloped area, Arcalis doesn't come with the immediate resort facilities demanded by tour operators and skiers. The 18 miles of snow-sure terrain is perched much above the tree line, and offers some of the best terrain in the whole principality, with a small number of modest but quite difficult trails. All styles will find that a day or two here is not a waste of money, but hardcore riders will soon get bored.

FREERIDERS
There are some nice spots for intermediate freeriders to check out, and a special marked freeride area within the resort boundary.

FREESTYLERS
Theres been improvements to the resort and since 2003 they've added a small park with a few kickers and rails in, but it's not always kept in top notch condition. You'll find it between the La Portella and La Portella del medio pistes. You'll find a better park and halfpipe over at Pal

BEGINNERS
One thing the slopes do offer, is excellent areas for beginners, with easy to reach trails, that make up some 55% of the snowboard area.

THE TOWN
Local facilities can be found in **Ordino** which is about 10 miles or 16 km away. What you get is very dull, but there's a reasonable selection of restaurants. There's a bit more life in nearby **La Massana**

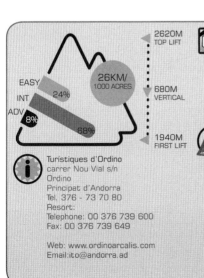

2620M TOP LIFT

26KM/ 1000 ACRES

EASY
INT 24%
ADV
8%
68%

680M VERTICAL

1940M FIRST LIFT

Turístiques d'Ordino
carrer Nou Vial s/n
Ordino
Principat d'Andorra
Tel. 376 - 73 70 80
Resort:
Telephone: 00 376 739 600
Fax: 00 376 739 649

Web: www.ordinoarcalis.com
Email:ito@andorra.ad

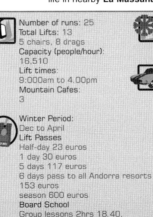

Number of runs: 25
Total Lifts: 13
5 chairs, 8 drags
Capacity (people/hour):
16,510
Lift times:
9:000am to 4.00pm
Mountain Cafes:
3

Winter Period:
Dec to April
Lift Passes
Half-day 23 euros
1 day 30 euros
5 days 117 euros
6 days pass to all Andorra resorts
153 euros
season 600 euros
Board School
Group lessons 2hrs 18.40,
4hrs 33.50 euros
Snowmobiles
28/42.50 euros for 15/30 minutes
Evening trips 80euros for 1hr

Annual Snowfall:
Unkown
Snowmaking:
30% of slopes

Fly
Barcelona 220km, Tolouse 210km
Bus
9 services daily from Andorra la Vella to Ordino. 0.90 euros. Various daily coach services from Barcelona (ALSINA GRAELLS) and Toulouse (AUTOCARS NADAL) to Andorra la Vella
Train
L'Hospitalet près l'Andorre in France is 8km away. Puigcerdà in Spain is 60km away.
Car
From Andorra la Vella drive to Ordino via La Massana or Canillo.

101

POOR FAIR GOOD TOP

FREERIDE
A few trees and some of off-piste
FREESTYLE
A park & a half-pipe
PISTES
What there is is good

5
OUT OF 10

Great for beginners

A

ANDORRA

rowdy both on and off the slopes. The area is, however, a place for total novices and slow learning intermediates with 90% of the terrain graded blue and red.

There's absolutely nothing of note for advanced riders, no matter your style of riding. Only 10% of marked-out trails are black, and even some of these are over-rated, especially if you can ride at a competent level. Most riders will have the whole joint licked in the time it takes to smoke a good joint.

FREERIDERS
Easy-going freeriders will find some wooded areas around Comellada that on a good day allow for some off-piste through the trees

FREESTYLERS
Freestylers may find the odd log to grind, but that's about all unless you head over to the park in Arinsal

BEGINNERS
have nearly the whole place to roam around with a degree of total ease.

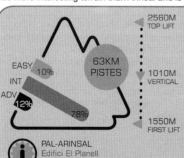

Pal and Arinsal are two villages linked via the Teleferic Arinsal-Pal Gondola. Nearby village La Massana is now also linked to the area via gondola. Pal/Arinsal have joined with Ordino/Arcalis to form the VallNord Ski area.

THE TOWN
Pal has very basic local services a few miles away.

PAL
Pal is a slightly bigger and better resort than that of its near neighbour Arinsal, with which it shares a lift pass. It also has more interesting terrain than Arinsal and is not quite as

2560M
TOP LIFT

EASY 10%

63KM
PISTES

INT

1010M
VERTICAL

ADV
12%

78%

1550M
FIRST LIFT

PAL-ARINSAL
Edifici El Planell
Pal Sector – Principality of Andorra
Tel. 00 376 737 000
Fax.00 376 835 904
Web: www.palarinsal.com
email: palarinsal@palarinsal.com

Number of runs: 41
Total Lifts: 29
1 Gondola, 1 Cable-car, 12 chairs, 15 drags, 1 Magic carpet
Capacity (people/hour): 31,700
Lift times:
9am to 4.00pm
Mountain Cafes:
11

Winter Period:
Dec to April
Lift Passes
Half-day 23 euros
1 day 30 euros
5 days 117 euros
6 days pass to all Andorra resorts 153 euros
season 600 euros
Board School
Group lessons 2hrs 18.40,
4hrs 33.50 euros
Snowmobiles
28/42.50 euros for 15/30 minutes
Evening trips 80euros for 1hr

Annual Snowfall:
Unknown
Snowmaking:
30% of slopes

Car
From Barcelona take the C-58 motorway to Terrassa - E-09 motorway to Manresa - C-16 to the Cadí Tunnel (toll)- N-260 road through Bellver de Cerdanya as far as La Seu d'Urgell- Take the N-145 towards Andorra to the border-Andorra La Vella-Escaldes-La Massana. Take the Arinsal turn off through Erts
Fly
Closest airport Toloda (150km), Barcelona (200km)
Bus
Bus services available from most towns in France and Spain.
Eurolines, tel (34) 93 490 40 00, run 4 services daily from Barcelona
Daily service from Toulouse (33) 562 151 809

Pics - Pal-Arinsal Tourism

ARINSAL

Arinsal is a small resort with very basic terrain, perfect for a group of beginners on their first snowboard holiday, but nothing much for the advanced freerider. There is a terrain park and a halfpipe in its favour, and it links with the resort of Pal enabling you to escape the place with ease.

FREESTYLE

Theres a 10 acre terrain park serviced by the Les Fonts chair lift. The terrain park has a number of boxes, rails, kickers, spines and a good size booter. Its also home to a 110m halfpipe and a boardercross circuit.

FREERIDE

The resort has a small specialised freeride area at the Alt de la Capa

THE TOWN

Small compact, and everything you need especially if its booze you're after. There are a number of rowdy bars, free pouring the spirits, and a disco. Its not exactly international 5* cuisine, but there is a Mexican and Chinese restaurant. You can also stay in La Massana which has a few good bars to pick from.

wsg PAS DE LA CASA

Great for beginners & partying

FREERIDE
A few trees but poor off-piste
FREESTYLE
A dodgy park & a half-pipe
PISTES
Good for beginners

POOR FAIR GOOD TOP

4 OUT OF 10

A

A N D O R R A

Pas de La Casa is the second largest snowboard resort in Andorra, lying in the eastern section of the country along Route N2, close to the French border. It forms part of the area called **Grand Valira**, linking to **El Tarter, Ooldeu, Grau Roig, Canillo,** and **Encamp** . 63 lifts provide access to 192km of pistes, and there's talk of linking to Porte Puymorens in France at some stage.

Each year, the resort attracts more and more riders in groups of lively revellers at novice stage, looking for an easy resort to sample a few beginner bruises. Pas de La Casa takes ones side of the mountain and **Grau Roig** (pronounced 'grau rosh') the other. Both are lift-linked, offering a collective area of easy-to-master intermediate terrain, with an excellent walk to beginner slopes and a few advanced black runs which can be ridden over a day or two. Three days or more will bore adventurous riders, but a week for beginners is ideal. The mountain is well serviced by some 30 lifts, but there have been complaints on the speed of some of the lifts, and there's quite a few drag lifts to contend with.

FREERIDERS should be advised that this is not a freeriding metropolis. However, the area can offer some good powder stashes after a recent dump. The best riding is on the Grau Roig, up on the main slope and down the other side. Once in the Grau Roig,

a whole new area, and if you take the main run down the hill and across the top of the black run, you will find some okay powder fields.

FREESTYLERS will find a number of natural hits on the Grau Roig area. However, you will need to plan your route using the piste map if you want to avoid a long walk back to the lift station. Overall, this is not a hot freestyle resort. There is a terrain park and pipe off the Coma 111 trail, but its usually not very well maintained. You'll find the park by taking the Number 1 chair.

BEGINNERS can take most advantage here, with good novice areas reached by foot from the village. The flats are perfect for novices and it won't be too long before you can tackle the rest.

THE TOWN
Local services at the foot of the slopes are cheap and cheerful, offering a host of duty-free shops, supermarkets, restaurants and bars that stay open very late, and see a fair share of hardcore partying. Shops and night-life are within walking distance, doing away with the need for a car or public transport in the evenings. Cool hangouts are *Kamikaze Surf Bar* for happy hour and *Billboard* for a late night dance, beer and holiday talent spotting.

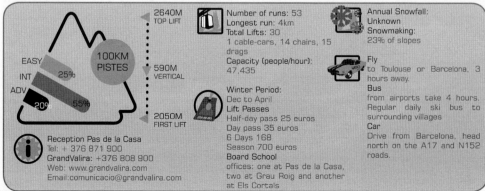

2640M TOP LIFT

100KM PISTES

EASY
INT 25%
ADV
20% 55%

590M VERTICAL

2050M FIRST LIFT

Number of runs: 53
Longest run: 4km
Total Lifts: 30
1 cable-cars, 14 chairs, 15 drags
Capacity (people/hour): 47,435

Winter Period:
Dec to April
Lift Passes
Half-day pass 25 euros
Day pass 35 euros
6 Days 168
Season 700 euros
Board School
offices: one at Pas de la Casa, two at Grau Roig and another at Els Cortals

Annual Snowfall:
Unknown
Snowmaking:
23% of slopes

Fly
to Toulouse or Barcelona, 3 hours away.
Bus
from airports take 4 hours. Regular daily ski bus to surrounding villages
Car
Drive from Barcelona, head north on the A17 and N152 roads.

Reception Pas de la Casa
Tel: + 376 871 900
GrandValira: +376 808 900
Web: www.grandvalira.com
Email:comunicacio@grandvalira.com

	POOR	FAIR	GOOD	TOP
FREERIDE Trees and some off-piste				
FREESTYLE A terrain park and pipe				
PISTES Good intermediate trails				

6 OUT OF 10

Best terrain in Andorra

Pic - Andorra Tourism

Soldeu - El Tarter makes up the biggest rideable area in Andorra, with some 92km of linked terrain. Its also linked to **Pas** creating the **Grand Valira** area totalling 192km of pistes. This the country's most popular resort which makes the place hellishly busy, with clogged up lifts and slopes. Budget-conscious skiers have been flocking here for years, and it is now also becoming a popular snowboard destination. Cheap and tacky maybe, but it is still okay for your first snowboard holiday. Although this is the largest area in Andorra, there is still not much to brag about. The terrain is not adventurous and basically poor for riders with ability. There are only a couple of black runs to choose from. However, Soldeu has a good snowboard scene and plays host to a number of locally organised snowboard events, which include boardercross competitions that attract the odd pro.

FREERIDERS will find that Soldeau has the best terrain in Andorra, especially for off-piste. The unpisted runs graded black and red, running down from the summit area of **Pic D'enc Ampadana**, are good freeriding areas. The trail starts off in a fast open section before dropping through a thick tree-lined area. For something to suit a novice rider, the red run that descends from the main summit, through the open expanse of the **Riba Escorxada**, is cool.

FREESTYLERS are offered a park and halfpipe next door

pipe, ridges, various jumps, rails and boxes and a 110m half-pipe. However its not always well maintained. There are also plenty of cool natural hits to catch air, but nothing is really big so there's no need to call air traffic control. Look out for locals spotting hits to know where to ride

PISTES. Riders have plenty of flats, with the option to ride hard and fast down a number of blacks, or the more sedate, pisted red and blue trails off the Tosa Espiolets chair.

BEGINNERS have a great little mountain to explore with lots of easy, green nursery slopes to learn on, even if they do get clogged. Unfortunately, the easy runs are serviced by T-bars. Novices can ride down a series of open green trails, which will take you through trees and back to Soldeu.

THE TOWN
An overload of apartments are available at the base of the slopes, with some very cheap lodging options. Like the rest of Andorra, local facilities are basic, but perfectly adequate for a week's stay. Night-life is fast, raunchy, with booze, booze and more booze - the streets are pebble-dashed with diced carrots on a nightly basis. Lively bars to check out are the *Piccadilly*, *Pub Iceberg* or *Fat Alberts*.

2560M TOP LIFT

92KM PISTES

EASY
INT 20%
ADV
20% 60%

850M VERTICAL

1800M FIRST LIFT

Soldeau/ El Tarter
Tel - +376 890 500
Web: www.grandvalira.com
Email:comunicacio@grandvalira.com

Number of runs: 52
Longest run: 8km
Total Lifts: 32
2 cable-cars, 13 chairs, 12 drags, 5 Magic Carpets
Capacity (people/hour):
38,100
Mountain Cafes:
5

Winter Period:
Dec to April
Lift Passes
Half-day pass 25 euros
Day pass 35 euros
6 Days 168
Season 700 euros

Annual Snowfall:
Unknown
Snowmaking:
36% of slopes

Fly
to Toulouse or Barcelona, both 3 hrs away.
Bus
Bus services from airports take 4 hours.
Car
Drive from Barcelona, head north on the A17 and N152 roads.

A

Argentina is a country that is split by the awesome **Andes Mountain range** which is home to a vast array of ski resorts, from large 'internationally acclaimed' chic areas to small and humble 'local hills'. Take your pick: they're relatively easy to get to and can be pretty cheap when you're there.

Argentinean resorts are mainly located in two regions along the Andes; the High Andes between Santiago (Chile) and **Mendoza** (Argentina), and the Lake District/**Patagonia** further south. The regions differ in many aspects; the High Andes region contains a bunch of resorts in the area around South America's highest peak, Aconcagua, close to areas such as Los Penitentes and Las Lenas. The resorts are high, much above the tree line, and receive good light snow due to their high altitude. They are also considered to be 'top notch' resorts and this is reflected in their prices of accommodation and other resort services.

Flights from London to either Buenos Aries cost from £600 return, and take about 14 hours. The airport is well out of town so a taxi back into the city centre costs around £20, but try bargaining as it works. Car hire is expensive; from AR$120 a day plus mileage. Argentina has an exhaustive network of long distance buses which aren't your stereotype 'latin America' affair. Distances are long but the buses are comfy, and due to the heavy competition are often half empty. If you can spare the extra few dollars go for a "coche cama" which means 'bed coach' or reclining seat.

Traveller's cheques may be cashed at banks and large hotels but with dire rates of commission being taken in. It's better to bring plastic and use the common placed cash machines to withdraw money when you need to, you get a better rate and less commission charged. The peso is more stable these days, but many hotels still quote in US$, and you can still often pay for things in US$.

Night clubs in Argentina usually do not start until midnight. All common drugs (dope etc) are illegal with heavy penalties if caught. Paperwork, if you are rumbled, takes forever to sort out and you can bank on being inside for a long time before it's sorted. The people are among the friendliest and welcoming in the World and Spanish (castillano) is the main language. It's worth having a few phrases of Spanish up your sleeve, though many people in the tourism industry and local boarders can often speak some English.

Map labels:
Cordoba
Tacuarer
Rosario
Pay
alparaiso
Mendo a
Santiago
San Rafael
Buenos Aires
LAS LENAS
Bahia Blanca
M
Neuquen
CHAPELCO
CERRO BAYO
CATEDRAL
PERITO MORENO
LA HOYA
Valdes Penninsula
Rawson
Coihaique
Comuduro Rivadavia
Puerto Santa Cruz
Puerto Nariles
Rio Gallegos
VALDELEN
Port Stanl

Capital City: Buenos Aries
Population: 39 million
Highest Peak: Cerro Aconcagua 6962 m
Language: Spanish
Legal Drink Age: 18
Drug Laws: Cannabis is illegal and frowned upon
Age of consent: 16
Electricity: 220 Volts AC 2-pin
International Dialing Code: +54

Currency: Peso (AR$)
Exchange Rate:
UK£1 = 5.4 peso
US$1 = 2.9 peso
1EURO = 3.6 peso

Argentina Snowboard Association
Doblas 14 - 1st floor
Buenos Aires
ARG-1425
Tel: +54 1 490 29209

Time Zone
GMT/UTC -3 hours

Driving Guide
All vehicles drive on the right hand side of the road
Speed limits:
40kph cities
60kph other built-up areas
80kph highways
120kph motorways
Emergency
Ambulance - 107
Fire - 100
Police - 10
Tolls
Toll booths on motorways.
Documentation
Must have an international drivers licence & passport if hiring a car

	POOR	FAIR	GOOD	TOP

FREERIDE
A some trees and off-piste

FREESTYLE
A park & a half-pipe

PISTES
Usually bumpy

Okay basic resort

5 OUT OF 10

Pic - Chapelco resort

Just above the town of **San Martin De Los Andes** lies the resort of **Chapelco** which despite being a small resort still offers a big variety of terrain for all types and levels of rider. The arrival of a new resort director has led to the development of a number of snowboard friendly policies on the mountain, including the construction of a permanent halfpipe accessed from the Palito drag lift, and a programme of snowboard demos and freestyle classes. A low elevation means unreliable snow cover at the base area but up at the mid station things are usually fine. The resort has a good reputation among Argentine boarders, but due to its North facing aspect suffers unreliable snow conditions at times. The slopes are equipped with a modern lift system and a number of mountain cafes. But note, food and drink on the mountain is expensive.

FREERIDERS will find, that when the lower section has snow cover, it offers a rolling terrain of fast cruising dotted with cat track hits. The moss shrouded Lenga trees are well spaced for excellent tree riding off the sides of the mid and lower pistes, but lack pitch in places. Steeps are found on the faces of **Cerro Teta** and the **La Pala face** (40 degree) which remain unpisted and are fed by a speedy quad and poma drag respectively. Although short these faces provide the buzz that the freerider is looking for with 3-10m cliff bands laying down the gauntlet between the Teta and the **La Puma** areas. The back bowl offers superb powder if you're willing to do the one hour hike back out.

FREESTYLERS have a permanent halfpipe accessed from the Palito drag lift which the locals session all day long. On a good day the **Perímetro terrain park** has 3 kicker lines of various grades and a rail line.

PISTES A lack of good piste grooming means the runs are bumpy and rutted, making this place not so ideal for beginners and speed freaks alike.

BEGINNERS have an mountain with 40% of the terrain graded to suite their needs, but its not all ideal or super easy.

THE TOWN is small enough to be able to walk everywhere. **Accommodation** can be found in **San Martin** 18 miles from the base. The *Poste del Caminero Hostel* has bunks from $10 a night and there is a helpful tourist office to get you sorted. Check out the '*Deli*' by the lake for cheap snacks and the best priced beer in town. There are also a couple nighclubs and laid back bars.

A

ARGENTINA

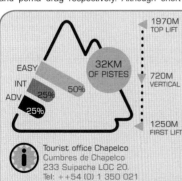

EASY
INT 50%
ADV 25%
25%

32KM OF PISTES

1970M TOP LIFT

720M VERTICAL

1250M FIRST LIFT

Tourist office Chapelco
Cumbres de Chapelco
233 Suipacha LOC 20.
Tel: ++54 (0) 1 350 021

Web: www.cerrochapelco.com
Email: info@cerrochapelco.com

Number of runs: 22
Longest run: 5.3km
Total Lifts: 10
1 Gondolas/cable, 5 chairs, 4 t-bars
Capacity (people/hour): 11,600
Lift times: 9.00am to 4.00pm
Mountain Cafes: 8

Winter Period:
July to Sept
Lift Passes
1 Day pass - 96 pesos
5 Day pass - 447 pesos
Season 2510 pesos
Board School
Morning/Afternoon 2.5hr lessons 3 days 165 peso
Private lesson 77/439 for 1/6hrs
Rental
Hire shop at the foot of the Hill
Board & Boots 51 peso per day, 5 days 207 peso

Annual Snowfall:
Unknown
Snowmaking:
none

FLY
to Buenos Aires and then inland to Bariloche and then take a bus or taxi to Chapelco
TRAIN
to Bariloche with a two hour transfer time to the resort with onward travel by bus or taxi to Chapelco.
CAR
Via Bariloche, head north to San Martin de Los Andes on highway 234 and then take the bumpy dirt road Hwy 19 to reach the resort.

POOR FAIR GOOD TOP

FREERIDE
No trees but huge off-piste

FREESTYLE
A terrain park

PISTES
Good pistes

7 OUT OF 10

Very good resort - when it snows

Pic (c) laslenasski.com

A

ARGENTINA

Las Lenas is the largest resort in **Argentina** and has become a major destination for pro-riders, be they a sponsored rider doing some race training, or an air head getting the latest action with a film crew for a new video we've all seen before. It's no wonder that those in the know, and those with the money, come here when you look at what the resort has to offer. It's steep, offers the rider big mountain terrain and it's high elevation should ensure good deep fluff, while the 14 lifts access 40 miles of piste and an abundance of challenging off piste terrain. Although this is easily the most challenging area in S.America, Las Lenas also has its bad points. Its high altitude renders it totally above tree line and the snowfall can be very sporadic, but when it dumps you get feet of it (annual snowfall can vary from less than 1m to over 10m). The lift system is also extremely slow, and when theres wind storms (which there often are) the lifts can be shutdown until they pass, which is fine, but usually you're still sat on them shivering away. The later the season the worse things tend to get.

Although more overseas visitors are trying Las Lenas, its still very much the resort for the seriously minted and famous Argentinians. Afraid to lose their designer shades, you can often find off-piste areas untracked for days, weeks if you're lucky enough to get on the snowcat. You'll also find the nightlife different, clubs don't get going until midnight and stay open to 5am and people are

remarkably sober, but the ladies are truly to die for. The exchange rate means that whilst its extremely expensive for Argentinians, you'll be able to enjoy yourselves no matter what budget.

FREERIDERS willing to do the short hikes can get to 50 degree faces and big ball cliff drops making this place a freerider's dream. When its open, the Marte chair delivers you to terrain that is possibly the best that the Southern Hemisphere has to offer. Ask in the wine bar about a guide and examine the off-piste maps on the walls for all the runs you'll need. From the top of the Marte head down toward the Iris t-bar, once the patrol have made you sign your life away, you can drop into one of the many chutes that will end up at the top of the Vulcano lift. For AR$25 peso you can take a ride in the snowcat, where you'll be almost guaranteed in getting fresh tracks for the next couple of hours. You'll find it next to the first aid hut on the Apolo run.

FREESTYLERS will find a park at the base which is the setting for the Reef big air comps. Its very snow dependant, but when theres snow theres a good variety of jumps and some rails.

PISTES. Theres some well groomed fast trails and some great steep un-groomed runs. The Vulcano and Apolo runs have good long wide pistes.

BEGINNERS may struggle a little here with most of the slopes geared towards intermediates. Venus is one of the few beginner runs but due to its flatness, people coming from the Marte will try and fly down it, and you can find your self skating if you take a tumble. There are lessons available, and some of the instructors do speak english but often not fluent.

THE TOWN
The village is small but has a number of plush hotels and some cheaper apartments available. There is a supermarket selling most things, but if you want any thing fresh then bring it with you. Theres a cash machine, a couple of board shops, restaurants and the usual tourist trappings in the

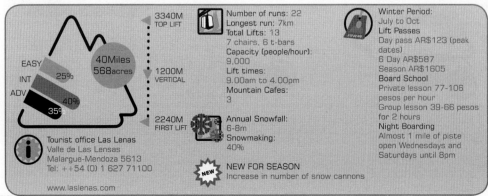

EASY
INT 25%
ADV 40%
35%

40Miles
568acres

3340M
TOP LIFT

1200M
VERTICAL

2240M
FIRST LIFT

Number of runs: 22
Longest run: 7km
Total Lifts: 13
7 chairs, 6 t-bars
Capacity (people/hour):
9,000
Lift times:
9.00am to 4.00pm
Mountain Cafes:
3

Annual Snowfall:
6-8m
Snowmaking:
40%

NEW FOR SEASON
Increase in number of snow cannons

Winter Period:
July to Oct
Lift Passes
Day pass AR$123 (peak dates)
6 Day AR$587
Season AR$1605
Board School
Private lesson 77-106 pesos per hour
Group lesson 39-66 pesos for 2 hours
Night Boarding
Almost 1 mile of piste open Wednesdays and Saturdays until 8pm

Tourist office Las Lenas
Valle de Las Lensas
Malargue-Mendoza 5613
Tel: ++54 (0) 1 627 71100

www.laslenas.com

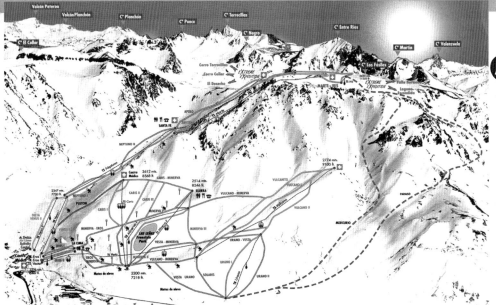

A

ARGENTINA

mall, but thats about it. The nearest town is Malargue about an hours drive away.

ACCOMODATION in Las Lenas is pricey (4 star hotels), though it is often easy to get a bed in the 'workers' dormitory for US$10 per night. There are a number of apartments available if you can't quite stretch to the *Piscis* or Otherwise the nearest 'affordable' beds are in **Malargue**, a small town down the valley, where you'll find hotel rooms from US$20 a night.

FOOD wise the 5* Piscies do a good AR$50 peso 3 course meal at one of their 2 restaurants and the food at the Aries can be very good. Apart from hotels, *El Refugio* do a reasonable fondue and *Huaco* some good steaks. If its burgers then *the Innsbruck* is ok, and the UFO Point do great pizzas. A good way to end the day is a meal at *La Cima*, situated at the top of the Eros lift. They serve authentic Argentinian grills including a parrillada, a mixed grill or rat on stick depending on your viewpoint. The place really kicks off once the eatings finished and the band start playing. If you're eating on a budget then you'll find a restaurant in the workers accomodation, open to all its AR$15 peso for a 3 course meal including wine. The local supermarket stocks everything you'll need if you're self catering, however fresh vegtables are rare so make sure you stock up before arriving.

NIGHTLIFE starts late and finishes early, so its just as well the lifts don't close till 5pm. Do what the locals do and grab a beer or a chocolate, sit outside or in the Innsbruck or *UFO point* until about 6pm then take a break. Around 9pm the restaurants will start to open up, grab some food then head to one of the late bars. The *BU bar* above the *Corona Club* is a good place to hang, and they often have bands playing. UFO Point and Corona Club take alternate nights, things don't start getting lively until its past midnight and theres usually a cover charge to get in. They certainly know how to party, but you wont find many people drinking so at least you'll always get served quickly. For a change in atmosphere the tiny wine bar's a good place to chat to locals whilst you sup a good Malbec.

FLY: to Buenos Aires and then inland to Mendozas, transfer to resort takes 5hrs. One flight a week to Malargue airport from Jorge Newbury Airport (Buenos Aires), transfer to resort takes 1 hr
COACH: Overnight coach services available from Buenos Aires. Resort buses free and operate 24hrs
TRAIN: to Malargue, 40 miles from Las Lenas and will take 1 hour to reach Las Lenas.
CAR: 450 km away from Mendozas, head south on highway 40, and Provincial 222 to Las Leñas, 20 km after the city of Los Molles

Pic Cran Catedral Tourism

CERRO BAYO

Cerro Bayo is a resort with a local hill feel and some wicked scenery across the lakes of **Patagonia**. The area has 10 lifts giving access to an assortment of treelined pistes with an upper T-bar extending the last 300m above the trees to the summit. Freeriders can ride a 720m vertical off piste bowl before heading back into the trees to pick up a chair or continue to the base. Lodging and eating can be found in the village of **Villa La Angostura**, which is a small and very friendly place. Services are limited and not really geared towards winter holiday makers. However, it's a cool place with a few restaurants and places to kip in. Access to and from the slopes is made easy by either driving up yourself or taking the shuttle bus or taxi (pricey).

La Hoyita

Resort size: 12miles of pistes 200hectares
Runs: 21 Longest: 5km
Easy runs: 20%
Intermediate runs: 50%
Advanced runs: 30%
Top Lift: 1782m
Bottom Lift: 1050m
Total Vertical: 720m
Total Lifts: 10 - 5 chairs, 5 drags
Lift Capacity PH: 5,700
Av Snowfall: unknown
Snowmaking: 10%

Open June to Sep
Lift Passes Day AR$42, 3 Days AR$133, Week AR$300,
Season AR$1450
WEB: WWW.CERROBAYOWEB.COM
EMAIL: INFORMES@CERROBAYOWEB.COM

CRAN CATEDRAL

lies west of San Carlos de Bariloche. The resort is spread across three peaks and gives rise to the second most extensive resort in S.America. Although a low elevation prevents snow cover to the base for the whole season, cover is usually good higher up with a variety of terrain. Best freeriding areas include the off piste from the Piedra del Condor peak. Accommodation is available at the base, but expensive. Its cheaper and better for nightlife and food, to stay in Bariloche.
In total $23million is being invested over the next few years. in 2004 there was 5 new babylifts,
new for 2005 season: Amancay cablecar, 2 new chair lifts, 2 drags, and a special drag lift giving access to off-piste in

Resort size: 70km of pistes 600 hectares
Runs: 53
Easy runs: 25%
Intermediate runs: 25%
Advanced runs: 50%
Top Lift: 2388M
Bottom Lift: 1030M
Total Vertical: 1358M
Total Lifts: 29 - 1 cablecar, 10 chairs, 18 drags
Mountain Restaurants: 14
Terrain Park: yes
Open June to Oct
Av Snowfall: 2m
Snowmaking: 6%

Fly to Buenos Aires and then Bariloche 20 miles away.
WEB: WWW.CATEDRALALTAPATAGONIA.COM
EMAIL: INFO@CATEDRALALTAPATAGONIA.COM

CERRO CASTOR

Only in its 5th season. 2 new runs added this year. Lessons available from the base, private expect to pay between 63-70 pesos an hour, group lessons 35-42 pesos (2 hours). Board & boots available to hire at 42 pesos per day.

Top: 1057m
Bottom: 195m
Vert: 772m
Runs: 19 Total Lifts: 3 chairs, 3 drags

Easy: 30%
Intermediate: 30%
Advanced: 40%

Fly
to Ushuaia 26km away
Main town is Tierra del Fuego

Web: WWW.CERROCASTOR.COM
Email: CONTACTO@CERROCASTOR.COM

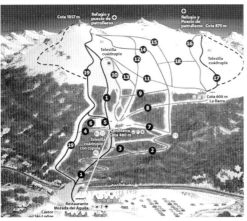

LA HOYA

La Hoya is decent size resort by South American standards, located a short distance from the town of **Esquel**. The notable point about this place is the amount of **advanced level terrain** on offer that will suite hard core freeriders 100%. Some of which will entail hiking and a few thigh burning traverse sections. Theres no halfpipe for freestylers. The area has good intermediate trails as well as okay novice runs at the lower sections. **Accommodation** and other facilities are available at the base area.

Resort size:**22KM of pistes**
Runs: 24 Longest: 5.1km
Easy runs: 15%
Intermediate runs: 60%
Advanced runs: 25%

Top Lift: 2150M
Bottom Lift:1350M
Total Vertical:800M
Total Lifts: 8 - 4 chairs, 4 t-bars
Lift Capacity PH: 4,400
Lift Passes
Day Pass 34 peso, 6 Day pass 168 peso
Av Snowfall: 2-4m (base-top)
Snowmaking: some
Location
Esquel - 13 Km, Bariloche - 300 Km, Buenos Aires - 2000 km
Route
Fly to Buenos Aires and then to Bariloche

Web: WWW.CAMLAHOYA.COM.AR
Email: CAMLAHOYA@CAMLAHOYA.COM.AR

PERITO MORENO

is a tiny resort with more lifts than runs. This tiny outpost is located about 16 miles from the town **El Bolson**. You have a mountain area covered with densely spaced trees, with the piste cut out in a straight trail and a thin stretch of wood in the centre of the main Pista de Mario. **Freeriders** will find that although the piste is limited there is good backcountry with great powder, but be prepared to hike. Basic lodging at the base, and down in El Bolson.

Top: 1450m Bottom: 1000m Vert: 450m
Runs: 2 Total Lifts: 5 drags
Easy: 20% Intermediate: 60% Advanced: 20%
Fly to Buenos Aires and then Bariloche 2 1/2 hours away

PRIMEROS PINOS

is not really a resort as such. What you have here is a mountain area operated by a local company, with a few portable lifts, placed wherever the best snow is, which on occasions is non existant. However, when the place is able to tow punters up, the decents are for one style and one level of ride only. Beginners, nothing else. Truly, if you can ride and have two hours experience don't bother with this place. Some beds at the base, but main services down in Zapala.

Top: 1870m Bottom: 1600m Vert: 270m
Runs: 5 Total Lifts: 3
Easy: 90% Intermediate: 10%
Fly to Buenos Aires and then Bariloche 1 1/2 hours away.

VALDELEN

is located way down in the southern tip of the country and the bottom of the Andes. As well as being Argentina's smallest resort, it is also one of the busiest ,attracting large numbers of skiers on a regular basis. It's a bit hard to see why because there is naff all here, no decent piste or off-piste just a few intermediate and beginner areas. There is little else here to please, especially if you're an advanced rider or freestyler. All local services are found down in the town of Rio Turbio.

Top: 1450m Bottom: 1000m Vert: 450m
Runs: 5 Total Lifts: 5 drags
Easy: 20% Intermediate: 60% Advanced: 20%
Fly to Buenos Aires and then Rio Gallegos 1 1/2 hours away

A

ARGENTINA

Pic Mt.Buller Tourism

Australia has some nine resorts located on the eastern mountain ranges on the state borders of **New South Wales** and **Victoria**. There are also places to ride on the separate southern island of **Tasmania**. All the main resorts are easy to reach from the two major ports of entry, Melbourne and Sydney.Overall Australian snowboarding opportunities are no where near as good as what is available in Europe, North America or at nearby New Zealand. Still to make up for dull mountains with below average slopes, the aussies have a reputation for being party animals.

Road travel in Australia is good but with the draw back of having to pay high toll charges at the entry gates to some mountain ski areas. Once through the entrance gate, snow chains must be carried at all times. It is illegal not to have them and could result in a A$200 fine. There are internal **flights** from Melbourne and Sydney to airports closer to the resorts, but prices are pretty steep. If a **train** ride through the countryside is what you seek enroute to a resort, then central station in Sydney or Spencer Street in Melbourne is where to head for. Melbourne doesn't have any direct train line going to any of the apline regions, however theres a train service direct from Sydney to Jindabyne, the major station for NSW resorts. **Bus**

companies run daily trips from the major cities to the bigger resorts. Costs vary, but for around you A$55 you can kick back and watch a video while some one else does the driving.

Accomodation will vary depending on your budget. Five star chalet lodges, club lodges and hostels can be found above the snowline but it may be cheaper if a bed is sought in a nearby town.

If you want to spend a season in Australia, it would be best to get here in late April, as this is when resorts start advertising job vacancies. The normal Australian winter season is between June and mid September.

Capital City: Canberra
Population: 19.9million
Highest Peak: Mount Kosciuszko 2229 m
Language: English
Legal Drink Age: 18
Drug Laws: Cannabis is illegal
Age of consent: 16
Electricity: 240 Volts AC 3-pin
International Dialing Code: +61

Currency: Australian Dollar (A$)
Exchange Rate:
UK£1 = A$2.6
1 EURO = A$1.7
US$1 = A$1.4

Ski & Snowboard Australia (SSA)
Level 1, 1 Cobden Street
Sth Melbourne, 3205
Tel: (03) 9696 2344
Fax: (03) 9696 2399
Email: info@skiandsnowboard.org.au
Web:www.skiingaustralia.org.au

Driving Guide
All vehicles drive on the left hand side of the road
Speed limits:
110km/h Motorways
100km/h normal
60km/h built up areas
Emergency
For police,fire and ambulances dial 000
Tolls
A few, on some motorways . more info www.hillsmotor-way.com.au
Some resorts have toll roads to acess them.
Documentation
Driving licences and permits must be carried at all times
Seatbelts
It is illegal to travel without a seat belt on

Time Zone
Victoria & New South Wales
UTC/GMT +10 hours

	POOR	FAIR	GOOD	TOP
FREERIDE few trees and some good off-piste				
FREESTYLE A park & a half-pipe				
PISTES Can be bumpy				

Pic - Mt Buller Tourism

sometime, with an even spread between all levels.

FREERIDERS who like their terrain with a side serve of steeps, should head for the summit and try to tame **Fannys Finnish** or **Fast One** which are Bullers most notorious black diamond runs. If you have conquered Fannys then it must be time to head backcountry with the best reached by hiking out past the fire hut on the summit to a place known as **Buller Bowls**. The bowl is serious terrain that will avalanche if given the chance, so it is best to check conditions with the ski patrol. If tree runs take your fancy then slip off the side of Standard and make tracks between the snowguns. If you are early it is possible to get fresh tracks in the powder stashes in this area.

FREESTYLERS have an abundance of natural hits which makes the trails resemble a spread out fun-park. Theres a terrain park located at **skyline**, the halfpipes over at **Boggy Creek** and a separate rail park at **BB2**

PSISTES .The runs can often be a bit rutted, but with some good early morning grooming, speed freaks can cut some nice fast tracks down a number of well spaced trails to suit all levels.

BEGINNERS will manage perfectly well at Buller, with a good selection of easy slopes that are crowd free on weekdays but crowd drenched on weekends. Rookies should go and get a lesson from one of the professional instructors at the ski school, which also offers a 'Discover Boarding' lift ticket.

THE TOWN
Off the slopes Mt Buller is a equipped resort with great options for doorstep riding. Buller has the most on-mountain **accommodation** in Victoria, so guests can stay above the snowline and take full advantage of the fact that Buller has the largest number of alpine restaurants and night-spots in the state with partying up here going on until day light hours. But note this is an expensive resort that attracts Aussie's finest.

A

A U S T R A L I A

Mt. Buller is 400 hectares of riding pleasure, with 26 lifts that would, in a perfect world, whisk 39,500 snowboarders per hour up the 400m vertical rise so they could make the best of Victoria's largest trail system. '**Buller**' as it is affectionately known is the closest major resort to **Melbourne** so weekend riding is not recommended, unless you enjoy lift lines and busy slopes. The terrain mix at Buller will keep all levels of rider amused for

---

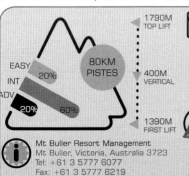

1790M
TOP LIFT

80KM
PISTES

400M
VERTICAL

1390M
FIRST LIFT

EASY
INT
ADV
20%
20%
60%

Number of runs: 19
Longest run: 2.5km
Total Lifts: 25
14 chairs, 8 drags, 3 Magic carpets
Capacity (people/hour):
40,000
Lift times:
8.30am to 5.00pm

Winter Period:
June to October
Lift Passes
Day pass $85
3 Day pass - $234
5 Day pass - $375
Season pass $1150
Night Boarding
Bourke Street on Wednesdays and Saturdays from 7pm until 10pm.

Annual Snowfall:
1.5m
Snowmaking:
15% of slopes

Fly
Fly to Melbourne international airport which is 248 miles away and will take 5 hours by bus to reach
Car
Via Melbourne, take the Maroondah highway route 153 north to Mansfield and then follow signs for Mt Buller

new 05 season:
$2million spent on new quad-chairlift.
04 season: earth-shaped FIS spec 100m halfpipe, and $750k of new snow cannons

NEW

i Mt Buller Resort Management
Mt Buller, Victoria, Australia 3723
Tel: +61 3 5777 6077
Fax: +61 3 5777 6219

Web: www.mtbuller.com.au
Email:info@mtbuller.com.au

usg PERISHER BLUE

FREERIDE
Trees and good off-piste
FREESTYLE
4 terrain parks & 2 pipes
PISTES
Masses of trails

6
OUT OF 10

Good freeriding

accessible by T-bar only and it really is a drag.

FREERIDERS should check out the **Guthega** and **Blue Cow** areas. There are winding creek beds and some nice little rock drop offs. For powder try out the **Burnum, Eyre** and **Leichhardt** runs, thought don't bother in September as it's all gone.

FREESTYLERS have 3 parks for different abilities and a dedicated rail park. They've made big improvements over the last few years, and theres even a snowskate park. The superpipe often play host to events, running alongside is a beginners pipe. The parks run the full gammet of toys from a boardercross style series of quarter pipes to plastic picnic tables, barrels and rails.

BEGINNERS will find plenty of open easy slopes. However, although there are 50 lifts most of these are T-bars and J-bars which are slow and not very snowboarder friendly.

Perisher Blue is in the **Kosciusko National park** in the Snowy Mountains. **Mt Kosciusko**, the highest point in the country is called Australia's 'Super Resort' as it has come about through the amalgamation of a number of resorts including, Perisher, Blue Cow, Guthega and Smiggins. There are 1250 hectares of rideable terrain with an elevation to 2054m. However the vertical descent is only about 350m. Nevertheless they have installed 50 lifts and the Australians make the most of the terrain available. Another plus is the huge amount of encouragement for snowboarders. There is a fun-park, a separate Board Riders school a woman's snowboard programme, a Board rider's guide and the Addiction Snowboard store where they will tune and groom your stuff. In September 2005 during the resorts 10th anniversary, it hosted Australias first **Burton Snowboarding Open**. The mountain itself has a good range of difficulties but unfortunately the black runs are few and far between. Also if you stick too much to pisted areas you will find little to challenge riders above intermediate standard. Most of the black runs are

THE TOWN

Hotels in the resort cost at least $130-A a night. However you can stay just outside the resort for around $65 for bed, brekie and a huge supper. Don't worry about getting around because there is a free bus service between Perisher and **Smiggins** every ten minutes. There are no hostels or lodges for riders on a tight budget but if you ask around you could secure some floor space with a local rider. **Night life** here comes as standard grade Australian, very boozy and very basic with Ozzy girls flashing their tits.

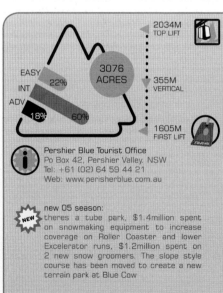

EASY
22%
INT
ADV
18%
60%

**3076
ACRES**

2034M
TOP LIFT

355M
VERTICAL

1605M
FIRST LIFT

Pershier Blue Tourist Office
Po Box 42, Pershier Valley. NSW
Tel: +61 (02) 64 59 44 21
Web: www. perisherblue.com.au

new 05 season:
theres a tube park, $1.4million spent on snowmaking equipment to increase coverage on Roller Coaster and lower Excelerator runs, $1.2million spent on 2 new snow groomers. The slope style course has been moved to create a new terrain park at Blue Cow

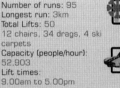

Number of runs: 95
Longest run: 3km
Total Lifts: 50
12 chairs, 34 drags, 4 ski carpets
Capacity (people/hour): 52,903
Lift times:
9.00am to 5.00pm

Winter Period:
June to October
Lift Passes
Half-day $AU70
1 Day pass - 87
3 Day pass - 248
5 Day pass - 376
Board School
2hr lesson + day lift pass $117
5 days of 2hrs lessons + pass $477
Just 2hr lesson $45
Private lesson $98 for 1hr
Rental
Board & Boots $70 for day
Night Boarding
Tuesdays and Saturdays 6:30 to 9:30 on the front valley. Halfpipe is floodlit on saturdays. Pass price $21

Annual Snowfall:
2.5m
Snowmaking:
Covers 95 acres

Fly
Snowy Mountain Airport (Cooma) 1hr from sydney, and 1hr from resort. Fly to Sydney airport with a 6 hour transfer time.
Car
From Sydney, head south to Jindabyne and then take the Kosciuszko road to reach Perisher Blue (about 6hrs). Jindabyne to Perisher is 20miles (33km).
Bus
SnoBus Snowscene Express from Brisbane/Gold Coast Tel. 07 3392 1722. Valley Bus and Coach Services operate from Sydney and Canberra Tel. 02 6297 6300.
Train
to Jindabyne station, 45 minutes away.

wsg MOUNT HOTHAM

POOR FAIR GOOD TOP

FREERIDE
Trees and some good steeps
FREESTYLE
A park & a half-pipe
PISTES
Some goof trails

5 OUT OF 10

Australias most snow sure resort

OTHAM.COM.AU

Mount Hotham is Australia's highest resort and thus is the most snow sure area. The slopes area is a mixture of easy to negotiate beginners runs to tricky fast steeps that often cross between the more gentle slopes, so novice beware, one minute you could be riding down a simple blue and the next minute hurtling down a steep black trail (study your piste map). Generally this is a resort that will suit intermediate freeriders with a number of very good trails that take you off the piste and in and out of open bowls and wide snow fields.

FREERIDERS. Some of the best freeride trails can be found off the **Heavenly Valley** chair lift which will give you access to some short but steep blacks that although may not take too long to do, they will however, test you to the limits. Over the last few years the resort has expanded its terrain cover which now includes some double diamond runs that are seriously steep and not for wimps. They are reached by the **Gotcha chair** lift which also takes you over to some nice blue out back trails.

FREESTYLERS who like fly high off natural hits will find

from. There is also a cool halfpipe and okay terrain park to check out.

CARVERS will love this place as it will suite your style of riding with twisting fast trails that take you over the whole area.

BEGINNERS only have a couple of green trails which are located right up at the top of the Summit chair, however quick learners will soon be able to tackle the array of blue trails with some of the most interesting to be found off the Village quad chair lift.

THE TOWN
Generally this is an expensive resort but it offers lots of things to do, all of which are well appointed for both on the slopes and the slope side village. **Off the slopes** visitors will find an abundance of resort facilities with a large selection of well placed hotels, lodges and other **accommodation** outlets that collectively can sleep over 4000 holiday makers. The village has a good selection of places to get a meal in and a number of good late night drinking outlets.

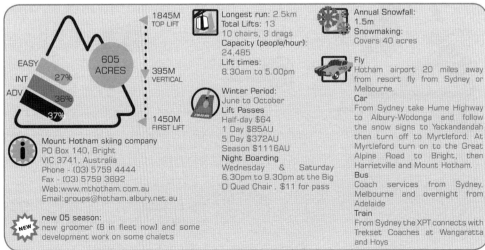

1845M
TOP LIFT

605 ACRES

EASY
INT 27%
ADV 36%
37%

395M
VERTICAL

1450M
FIRST LIFT

Mount Hotham skiing company
PO Box 140, Bright
VIC 3741, Australia
Phone - (03) 5759 4444
Fax - (03) 5759 3692
Web:www.mthotham.com.au
Email:groups@hotham.albury.net.au

new 05 season:
new groomer (8 in fleet now) and some development work on some chalets

Longest run: 2.5km
Total Lifts: 13
10 chairs, 3 drags
Capacity (people/hour):
24,485
Lift times:
8.30am to 5.00pm

Winter Period:
June to October
Lift Passes
Half-day $64
1 Day $85AU
5 Day $372AU
Season $1116AU
Night Boarding
Wednesday & Saturday
6.30pm to 9.30pm at the Big
D Quad Chair . $11 for pass

Annual Snowfall:
1.5m
Snowmaking:
Covers 40 acres

Fly
Hotham airport 20 miles away from resort fly from Sydney or Melbourne.
Car
From Sydney take Hume Highway to Albury-Wodonga and follow the snow signs to Yackandandah then turn off to Myrtleford. At Myrtleford turn on to the Great Alpine Road to Bright, then Harrietville and Mount Hotham.
Bus
Coach services from Sydney, Melbourne and overnight from Adelaide
Train
From Sydney the XPT connects with Trekset Coaches at Wangaratta and Hoys

One of the best overall resorts in Oz

	POOR	FAIR	GOOD	TOP
FREERIDE Trees and some off-piste				
FREESTYLE A terrain parks & 2 pipes				
PISTES Some good long trails				

Thredbo is a large resort that has the highest lift access slopes and longest trail in **Australia**. Extensive use of snowmaking and good piste grooming make this a cool place for a weeks stay. The terrain here is equally matched for all levels and styles of riding with much of the mountain suited to intermediates. Although there are a number of steep advanced runs to keep hardcore freeriders happy for a good few days.

FREESTYLERS will also be pleased to find that there are a number of places to gain air from some big natural hits. There is also a good halfpipe and terrain park which has a series of man made jumps.

CARVERS have some really nice runs to excel on including a rather long trail that measures almost 6km (the longest trail in Australia).

BEGINNERS. The beginner slopes here are ideal for first timers with easy runs on the upper sections as well as on the lower areas making the whole mountain accessible.

THE TOWN
The nearest accommodation and local facilities are located at the base of the slopes with a selection of hotels restaurants, sporting attractions and shopping.Nightlife is very lively but basic.

2037M TOP LIFT

43 MILES PISTES

EASY 16%
INT
ADV 17%
67%

672M VERTICAL

1365M FIRST LIFT

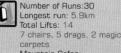

Kosciusko Thredbo Pty Limited
P.O Box 92, Thredbo Village, NSW 2625
Tel: (02) 6459 4100
Fax: (02) 6459 4101

Web:www.thredbo.com.au
Email:reservations@thredbo.com.au

Number of Runs:30
Longest run: 5.9km
Total Lifts: 14
7 chairs, 5 drags, 2 magic carpets
Mountain Cafes:
7

Winter Period:
June to October
Lift Passes
Half-day $54
Day Pass - $87
6 Day Pass - $330
Night Boarding
Friday flat every Thursday night and Crackenback Supertrail on saturday. 6:30 – 9:30pm through July and August. Free with standard pass otherwise $21
Rental
Board and boots $71 per day
Board Schools
1day, 2hr group lesson $115
6 days $564
Private lesson $109 per hour

Annual Snowfall:
2m
Snowmaking:
25% of pistes

Fly
daily flights into the Snowy Mountains Airport (Cooma) from Sydney - 1.5 hours transfer. Cooma from Sydney
Car
Sydney CBD to Thredbo – Once on the M5 there are only 3 sets of traffic lights to Thredbo – the Kosciuszko Alpine Way is now fully sealed.
Bus
Most major cities are linked by daily service to Thredbo. Greyhound operated a Sydney service, Suimmit Coaches from Canberra, Clipper coaches operate a regular service from and to Sydney (Prices start from $134 per adult return).

CHARLOTTE PASS

Charlotte Pass is located some 310 miles (500 km) south of Sydney. The resort is the highest in New South Wales and provides a rather small amount of rideable terrain with only five access lifts. Overall the area will suit slow learning beginners and carvers without a brain. Still the slopes are crowd free and will do for an afternoons fun. But forget about staying for more than a day or two (dull is the word).

Accommodation is conveniently located near the slopes at the *Kosciusko Chalet*, which offers mid priced beds, eating and a bar.

Ride Area: 50 hectares
Number of Runs: 19
Top Lift: 1954m
Bottom Lift: 1760m
Vertical Drop: 189m
Total Lifts: 5 - 1 Chair, 3 Drags, 1 portable tow
Lift Capacity (People per Hour): 2600

FALLS CREEK

Falls Creek is a well developed modern resort that will make a weeks stay well worth it, but any longer a bit tedious. The 90 or so marked out trails are evenly split between beginner and advanced level, but although there are a lot of runs none are that long. Still the terrain is good and expert riders will find a selection of steep runs off the Ruined Castle chairlift which also gives access to some open sections and a route down to the terrain park. The terrain park has a 120m superpipe, the first in Australia. Carvers who like to go fast, will be able to down the fast blacks of the Internation t-bar, while beginners will find the Eagle chair gives access to good nursery slopes.

Lots of **accomodation** exists at the base of the slopes in Falls Creek village where you will find shops, bars and restaurants.

Pic - Falls Creek Tourism

Ride Area: 75km
Number of Runs: 92
Easy 17%
Intermediate 16%
Advanced 23%
Top Lift: 1780m
Bottom Lift: 1600m
Vertical Drop: 360m
Total Lifts: 15
Lift Capacity (People per Hour): 20,000

MOUNT BAW BAW

Mt Baw Baw is a small resort and the closest to the city of Melbourne. Overall nothing grabs you about this place unless you are a total beginner with a few hours to kill. The eight lifts cover a mixture of uneven terrain with a splattering of trees and gentle pistes that will suite carvers.

Local facilities are basic but very good with a choice of lodges and holiday apartments although not all that affordable apart from the Youth Hostel ++64 (0) 65 1129.

Ride Area: 30 hectares
Number of Runs: 14
Easy 25%
Intermediate 64%
Advanced 11%
Top Lift: 1564m
Bottom Lift: 1460m
Total Lifts: 5 - all drags

MOUNT BUFFALO

Mount Buffalo is not only a well established resort with a long history as a ski resort, but also a dull boring novices hangout that will bore the tits off any advanced freerider within an hour of being here

Ride Area: 15km
Number of Runs: 14
Easy 50%
Intermediate 40%
Advanced 10%
Top Lift: 1695m
Total Lifts: 5 - 2 Chairs, 3 Drags
Lift Capacity (People per Hour): 20,000

MOUNT SELWYN

Mount Selwyn is a small resort that is the ideal family ski resort, but is totally dull for any advanced snowboarder. The small amount of terrain on offer is best suited to piste loving, slow going carvers. The nearest accomodation and local facilities are to be found in the town of Adaminaby

Ride Area: 45hectares
Number of Runs: 10
Easy 40%
Intermediate 48%
Advanced 12%
Top Lift: 1614m
Bottom Lift: 1492m
Vertical Drop: 122m
Total Lifts: 12 - 1 chair, 7 drags, 4 tows
Lift Capacity (People per Hour): 9.500

A

AUSTRALIA

TRAIL MAP

117

is their après-ski. This will work in one of two ways, you will either fall in love with it and congo around the bars until you fall on your face, or you will never come back. Its pretty much the norm to see people taking a beer before the first gondola in the morning. Lunch will obviously involve a schnapps or two, and then at 4pm the umbrella bars will fill up on the slopes and hoards of party goers will sing their heads off to the worst Euro pop whilst getting absolutely blind drunk. Oh yeah, and then at 7pm you have to board back down to the resort, probably collapse and wake up ready for the first lift, to do it all again.

ACCOMMODATION

The Austrian's don't go in for the purpose-built style resorts so common in other parts of Europe. Here there are old traditional villages adapted to accommodate modern tourists. Standards for accommodation are extremely high, and family run pensions are popular, and cost upwards for 30 euros per night. Most bookings work from Saturday to Saturday, so it can be tricky to arrange a weekend as many operators will be reluctant to split weeks. If you arrive in a resort without accommodation and the tourist information is closed, then take a wander around and look out for "Zimmer" signs outside pensions which indicate if there are any rooms available.

FOOD

Austrian cuisine is pretty basic, stodgy and rarely involves vegetables. You'll find dishes like Tafelspitz (boiled beef), schnitzel (Veal in breadcrumbs) or various cured hams and German-style sausages. The Tyrolean's go in for sweet and savoury dumplings in a major way. Goulash soup in this part of the world is wicked, but not so hot if you're sharing a room. A Tyrolean Gröstl is a great hangover cure (fried potato, bacon, herbs, and cheese with a fried egg on top) but can severely limit your afternoons boarding. One thing you will find is that Austria does lack is fast

A ustria is known as the snowboard capital of Europe with great resorts and a cool attitude. Their resorts aren't stretched out like the mega-sized places found in the French Alps and apart from being far more affordable than France, the slopes here are far better laid out with excellent mountain facilities, modern lift systems, easy access to the slopes, coupled with great traditional local services.

Of all the areas in Austria the most famed and the largest winter destination is the Tirol, which apart from being at 'the heart of the Alps' is also an area of outstanding beauty and home to some fantastic snowboard resorts that offer something for everyone. The Tirol resorts are spread across huge valleys, so you'll find Oetz, Solden, Obergurgl in the Otzal valley, and Zell am Ziller, Mayrhofen and Hintertux in the Zillertal Valley. So although you can see Pitzal quite clearly from Solden, getting to it will involve driving 60km into the next valley.

What really sets Austria apart from its neighbours though

Capital City: Vienna
Population: 8.2million
Highest Peak:
Grossglockner 3797m
Language: German
Legal Drink Age: 18
Drug Laws: Cannabis is
illegal and frowned upon
Age of consent: 16
Electricity:
240 Volts AC 2-pin
International Dialing Code:
+43

Currency: Euro
Exchange Rate:
UK£1 = 1.5
US$1 = 0.8
AU$1 = 0.6
CAN$1=0.6

Driving Guide
All vehicles drive on the right hand side of the road
Speed limits:
Motorways-130kph (81mph
Highways-100kph (62mph
Towns-50kph (31mph)
Emergency
Fire - 122
Police - 133
Ambulance - 144
Tolls
Payable on motorways and some bridges. Austrian vignette for driving on the motorways costs 7.6 euros for 10 days, available from most garages.
Documentation
carry driving licence, vehicle registration document and certificate of motor insurance. Photo ID needed
Seatbelts
Seatbelts front & back must be worn.

Time Zone
UTC/GMT +1 hour
Daylight saving time: +1 hour
(March - December)

AUSTRIAN SNOWBOARD ASSOCIATION
POSTFACH 57
6025 INNSBRUCK
fax. 0043 512 34 38 48 / 31
Email: info@powdern.com
Web:w ww.powdern.com

The Austrian National Tourist Office
Vienna, Margaretenstr. 1
A-1040 Wien
Phone: +43 (0)1 / 588 66-0
Fax: +43 (0)1 / 588 66-20
www.austria-tourism.at

Useful Web links
www.tiscover.com
www.innsbruck-tourismus.com

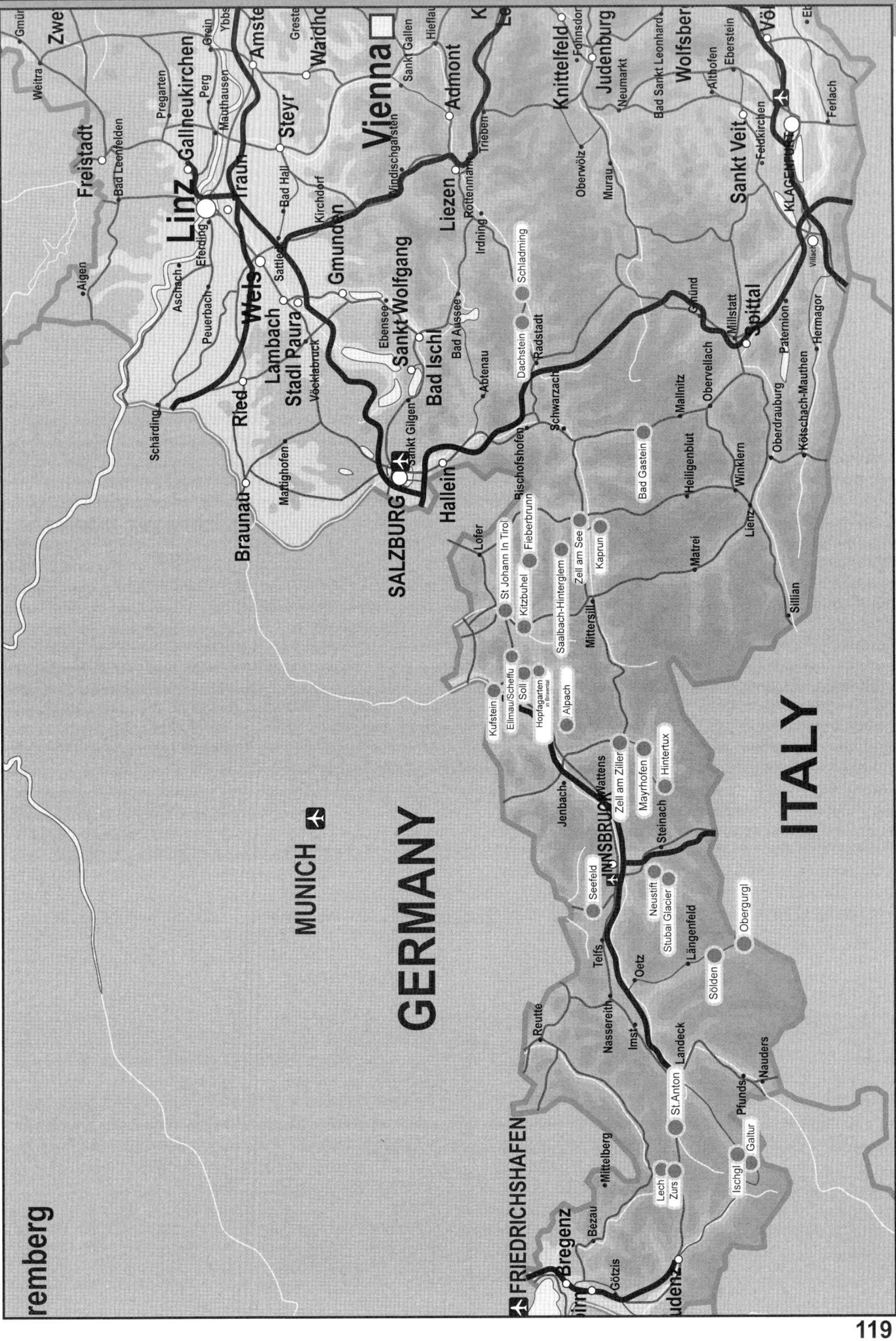
GERMANY
ITALY
MUNICH
Vienna
Linz
SALZBURG
INNSBRUCK
FRIEDRICHSHAFEN
KLAGENFURT
Freistadt
Bad Leonfelden
Gallneukirchen
Pregarten
Perg
Mauthausen
Weitra
Steyr
Traun
Wels
Lambach
Stadl Paura
Ried
Schärding
Braunau
Mattighofen
Vöcklabruck
Gmunden
Kirchdorf
Bad Hall
Sattledt
Eferding
Aschach
Peuerbach
Aigen
Ebensee
Sankt Wolfgang
Bad Ischl
Sankt Gilgen
Bad Aussee
Abtenau
Hallein
Windischgarsten
Admont
Liezen
Rottenmann
Trieben
Irdning
Schladming
Dachstein
Radstadt
Schwarzach
Bischofshofen
Lofer
St Johann In Tirol
Fieberbrunn
Kitzbuhel
Saalbach-Hinterglem
Zell am See
Kaprun
Mittersill
Kufstein
Ellmau/Scheffu
Soll
Hopfgarten in Brixental
Alpach
Jenbach
Wattens
Zell am Ziller
Mayrhofen
Hintertux
Steinach
Seefeld
Neustift
Stubai Glacier
Telfs
Oetz
Längenfeld
Sölden
Obergurgl
Reutte
Nassereith
Imst
Landeck
St.Anton
Pfunds
Nauders
Galtur
Ischgl
Lech
Zurs
Mittelberg
Bezau
Bregenz
Götzis
Bad Gastein
Heiligenblut
Mallnitz
Obervellach
Winklern
Lienz
Matrei
Sillian
Oberdrauburg
Kötschach-Mauthen
Hermagor
Paternion
Millstatt
Spittal
Gmünd
Villach
Sankt Veit
Feldkirchen
Ferlach
Althofen
Eberstein
Wolfsberg
Bad Sankt Leonhard
Neumarkt
Judenburg
Fohnsdorf
Knittelfeld
Oberwölz
Murau
Hieflau
Sankt Gallen
Waidhofen
Gresten
Ybbs
Grein
Weitra

Pic - Austrian Tourist Board

food joints. The major towns with have the golden arches, but while most resorts will have a take-away you'll be pressed to find one open when you stumble out of the clubs after 2am.

MONEY

It's bizarre that Austria still isn't comfortable with credit cards. Large hotels and some restaurants will take cards, but have a wad of euros or travellers cheques with you as it's certainly not the norm. There are increasing numbers of ATM machines in most resorts which will accept most foreign cards.

TRAVELLING

Innsbruck and Salzburg are the major air gateways into the country, Klagenfurt is the budget offering. However it's often a lot easier and cheaper to get a flight to Germany (Munich or Friedrichshafen) or Switzerland (Zurich) and use the excellent road, bus or train services to your destination. Most resorts are within a short distance from a train station and first-class local bus services can connect you to the resort.

Driving in Austria is convenient and easy, with the roads and resorts being well sign-posted. In some parts, snow-chains are required. Austria has a motorway tax called the Vignette which can be purchased at petrol stations near the borders. If you are caught without the tax, you'll be liable to a costly on-the-spot fine, it costs 7euros for 10 days use. If you're driving from Germany, watch your speed as you cross into Austria as attitudes change and fines add up!

WORKING

If you are planning to do a working season in Austria, then EU nationals don't need either a visa or work permit and can stay for as long as they want. But if you want to teach snowboarding, you may need to have the relevant Austrian snowboard instructors teaching qualifications, and speaking fluent German is a given. There's 3 month courses teaching German and Instructing starting October in Kitzbuhel

INNSBRUCK

Innsbruck is the capital of the Tyrol region, and comes with quite a pedigree. Its twice hosted the Winter Olympics, has 8 resorts within 45 minutes drive including NordPark that you access via funicular from town, and is home to the likes of Burton and Method Mag. Innsbruck is home to 128,000 people and is a tourist attraction in its own right. Wander into the old town, the narrow winding streets lead into the plaza where you'll see the Gothic 15th century three-story

balcony called the Golden Roof. Burton Snowboards set up their first non-American headquarters in Innsbruck in 1992. Theres a shop selling some of their old gear and seconds, next to their factory at 111 Haller Strasse, on the outskirts of town.

Accommodation is well located: you can bed down cheaply within walking distance of the city centre and prices are extremely reasonable. Pension Paula the local backpacker's place, is only five minutes from the town centre and is without doubt the best place to stay in the city, with rates from 25 euros a night. There is also a hostel and numerous hotels. Hotel Central is a budget place that also has a bar, and is only two minutes from the city centre.

Innsbruck has a huge number of restaurants, from international cuisine to local dishes, avoiding some of the tourist traps you can eat well and fairly cheap. There's a McDonald's which pumps out its cardboard crap, and a Wiener Wald, a version of Kentucky Fried Chicken.

The Innsbruck Glacier Ski Pass gets you access to 6 local resorts including NordPark, Axamer and Stubai including transport, 3 days will cost 90 euros. Theres an extended pass that also gives you access to Zillertal area (Mayrofen) or Arlberg region (St.Anton)

GETTING THERE
FLY: to Innsbruck International airport which is 10 minutes from the city centre.
TRAIN. Theres a train station in the centre of the town, with direct connections to Munich and Salzburg amongst others.
BUS: The bus station is next to the train station. Ski buses go from various parts of the city but all go via the bus station.
DRIVING: from Munich, head south on the A8 and A12 Autobahn routes direct to Innsbruck, journey time about 2 hours. The drive time from Calais is 11 1/2 hours

A nice place, just a bit bland.

	POOR	FAIR	GOOD	TOP
FREERIDE A few trees and some of off-piste				
FREESTYLE A park & a half-pipe				
PISTES What there is is good				

7 OUT OF 10

Pic - Alpbach Tourism

Alpbach is a cool, all-Austrian alternative to some of its more famous nearby cousins. This perfect picture postcard resort, decked out with traditional chalets dotted in and around a gently rising mountain, is one of those places beloved by skiers in one-piece ski-suits who seem to spend more time sunning themselves outside mountain restaurants than checking out the slopes. Alpbach is without doubt, an intermediate's resort and one that won't take too long to conquer; you wouldn't spend more than a week here, and certainly not a whole season, unless you're easily pleased and like an unadventurous mountain.

FREERIDERS have a small area to explore, with some interesting terrain to ride. On the upper sections, you can check out some wide, open powder fields that eventually descend through trees en route to the base area. Advanced riders will find that the few black runs are not to be treated with arrogance. Unpisted routes from **Loderstein** back to the gondola station, give freeriders in soft boots a great time, as do the runs around the **Wiedersbergerhorn**, which often have excellent powder.

FREESTYLERS fed up with looking for natural hits, should make their way to the halfpipe and fun-park, located on **Gahmkopf**, where grommets can take their frustrations out in this average play area.

PISTES
Boarders with a pair of hard boots will love Alpbach. It's a full-on carver's resort, with wide pistes devoid of any trouble spots. Although there isn't an abundance of pisted runs, what is available is well looked after, and easily negotiated.

BEGINNERS have a great learner's mountain. There are some perfect flats around the base areas to start out on, with excellent wide, open novice trails up in the **Skiweg** area.

THE TOWN
Alpbach offers some slope side **accommodation** with the bulk of beds available within easy reach of the village a two minute bus ride from the base lifts. Being a resort used by package tour operators means that on the one hand, the place can become very busy, but on the other, some cheap package deals are available. The village is a relaxed affair offering a number of restaurants, swimming and skating. As for **night-life**, apart from a few bars, you won't find much to shout about.

A U S T R I A

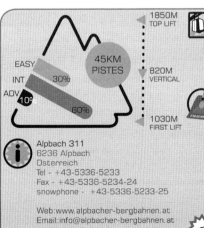

1850M TOP LIFT

45KM PISTES

EASY
INT 30%
ADV 10%
60%

820M VERTICAL

1030M FIRST LIFT

Longest run: 8km
Total Lifts: 19
2 Gondolas, 7 chairs, 10 drags
Capacity (people/hour):
19,000
Lift times:
8.30am to 4.00pm

Winter Period:
Dec to April
Lift Passes
1 Day 26,50 euros
6 Days Peak 122 euros
6 Days Off-Peak 108 euros
Season Ticket 262 euros
Hire
Schischule Alpbach charge 44 euros for a day lesson (4hr) or 5 days for 120. Private lessons 145 euros for 4hrs

Annual Snowfall:
6m
Snowmaking:
70% of slopes

Fly
to Innsbruck (60km), 50 minutes transfer time. Munich 170km, Salzburg 150km
Car
From Innsbruck head east along the A12 and exit at junction 32 for via Brixlegg and on to Alpbach
Drive time from Calais is 11 1/2 hours, 676 miles (1088 km).
Bus
direct from Innsbruck airport.
Train
fast trains to Wörgl or Jenbach then change to local railway for Brixlegg

Alpbach 311
6236 Alpbach
Osterreich
Tel - +43-5336-5233
Fax - +43-5336-5234-24
snowphone - +43-5336-5233-25

Web:www.alpbacher-bergbahnen.at
Email:info@alpbacher-bergbahnen.at

NEW NEW 05/06
new 8-seat gondola replaces 2 chairs from Inneralpbach to the Wiedersbergerhorn. New 4-person chair replaces drag lift on racing piste at Inneralpbach

ꞃꞅꞡ AXAMER LIZUM

POOR FAIR GOOD TO

FREERIDE
Some trees & a bit of good off-piste
FREESTYLE
A park
PISTES
Limited, but what theres is good

Small, but some great terrain

8
OUT OF 10

and on certain days snowboarders actually out-number skiers, especially when competitions are on.

FREERIDERS wanting off-piste and trees won't be disappointed, although it should be pointed out that the resort management frowns upon shredding through the spruce since it kills off the trees. Off-piste terrain is limited, but if you get the conditions, great powder can be ridden without a trek. There's a great area if you go right at the exit point off the funicular train, and follow the line of reds, Trail 4 and 3. Theres also a cool powder run back under the funicular. Riders already past the novice stage and with a few bruises under their belts will be able to collect a few more down Trails 5 and 5a. Experienced riders can go for it down the blacks on Piste 10 where the trail is on a bumpy, steep run, and is not the greatest descent in the world.

FREESTYLERS looking for the best hits should take the funicular train to the top, then follow the Number 1 blue run off to the left, which will bring you out onto a really cool mixture of red runs, with the best hits on Run 2. The terrain park is located at the base area and reached from the beginner's T-bars or by hiking up. The terrain parks been upgraded but still not huge, there's a couple of decent

Axamer Lizum may not be the biggest of resorts, nor is it the chosen resort for holiday package tour operators, and yes the ski press may slag the place off, but then what would that clueless lot know. Built in 1964 for the winter Olympics, Axams is a full-on no nonsense great natural freeride-freestyle snowboarder's paradise. The resort has everything you could possible ask for and although not extensive, the terrain in places is as natural as it gets with top-to-bottom riding from Axams to Gotzens possible when snow permits. Axams may be a small place but don't be fooled Axamer Lizum, is the playground for the Innsbruck crowd that includes Max Plotzeneder and top racer Christine Rauter - and it's easy to see why. Axams is a quiet place, free of holiday ski crowds (although weekends are very busy), big on air and short on lift queues. Having twice hosted Olympic disciplines, the runs are obviously a decent standard, with something to suit all. Freeriders and freestylers are going to get the best out of the slopes, with loads of great hits, big banks, and gullies that form natural pipes to drop in and out of and tight trees to weave through. The atmosphere on the slopes is really cool,

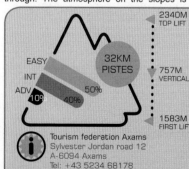

2340M
TOP LIFT

Longest run: 4.3km
Total Lifts: 10
1 Funicular train, 5 chairs,
4 drags
Capacity (people/hour):
12,042
Lift times:
8.30am to 4.00pm

Winter Period:
Nov to April
Lift Passes
1 Day pass - 27.50 euros
4 Day pass - 99 euros
5 Day pass - 118 euros
Night Boarding
Yes, pipe floodlit (when built)

EASY

32KM
PISTES

INT

ADV

50%

10% 40%

757M
VERTICAL

Annual Snowfall:
1.7m
Snowmaking:
none

1583M
FIRST LIFT

Tourism federation Axams
Sylvester Jordan road 12
A-6094 Axams
Tel: +43 5234 68178
Web:www.axamer-lizum.at
Email:verkauf@axamer-lizum.at

sized kickers and some rails and boxes, but with such good natural terrain, you don't need man-made hits.

PISTES . Carvers will look and feel a little out of place here, as this is not long, wide autobahn territory. Saying that, there is room to crank some big carves, especially on piste Numbers 1 and 2.

BEGINNERS having their first go at snowboarding can loosen up and get to grips with the basics, on easy trails located at the base area just up from the ticket booths. The only drawback is that the easy slope is serviced by two T-bars, which may cause shy ones a few problems at first, but not for long.

THE TOWN
Off the slopes, this is one of those places where you will have to put yourself out, and having a car may also be a preferred option. There is some accommodation at the base of the slopes consisting of a couple of B&B pensions and hotels, but that's it. Staying slopeside is not recommended, unless you're a hermit. The village of Axams is only a few miles away and has a decent selection of local services, which include a few shops and a sports centre. However, the best option is to stay down in Innsbruck, (the biggest and best snowboard resort-city in Europe). There are regular transfer buses to get you there, and once there you are bombarded with services, shops galore, an Olympic ice ring, swimming pools, concert halls, the list is endless. What's more, Innsbruck is an inexpensive and friendly place.

Food. Innsbruck is the place for food with loads of cafes and restaurants at budget to suit all. Theres a good number of restaurants in the old town; obvious tourist traps but still pretty good. Around the same area are a couple

of take away kebab and pizza places, and the standard McD's.You'll find a few Chinese and Indian restaurants and loads of Austrian restaurants serving dishes such as Tafelspitz (boiled beef).

Pics - Axamer Lizum tourism

Night-life in Axams is dull, without much happening. Off Limits is Axam's main hangout. Innsbruck, on the other hand, is a different story with simply loads going on and a large choice of cafe bars. There's an Irish bar called Limerick Bills and a club under Jimmy's Bar that rocks until very late.

SUMMARY. A great resort that will appeal to freestylers and intermediate freeriders spoilt only by the weekends queues. Some might find a full week stay too long

FLY: to Innsbruck International transfer time 25 mins. Munich 2 1/2 hrs away
BUS: Ski buses from Innsbruck train station hourly for Axams and back again (45min journey). Bus services also from Munich to Innsbruck.
TRAIN: to Innsbruck International transfer time 25 mins. Munich 2 1/2 hrs away
CAR: Drive to Innsbruck via motorway A12. Axamer Lizum = 15 miles (24Km). Drive time is about 20 minutes
*From Calais, 646 miles (1039 Km) Drive time is around 11 1/2 hours.

123

A few trees and a bit of off-piste

FREERIDE

FREESTYLE

A park & a half-pipe

PISTES

Vast but areas spread out

POOR FAIR GOOD TOP

Not a bad group of mountains

6
OUT OF 10

Pic - GASTEINERTAL TOURISMUS

Bad Gastein is an old Austrian spa town that is located in the middle of the **Salzburg** region along the **Gastein Valley** and perched up at a height of some 1080 metres a short distance from the village of **Bad Hofgastein**. What you have here is a relatively unknown but large ridable area which is basically split into four resorts that although each are similar, they never the less offer something different. Collectively you have over 200km of marked out piste to ride though it should be pointed out that not all the areas or pistes are linked up by lifts. So study the local piste maps to ensure that you don't have any problems finding slopes and lifts. Overall this is an area that predominantly favours intermediate riders with an excellent choice of cruising runs to enjoy. Bad Gastein gives direct access to the slopes on the **Stubnerkogel**, **Sportgastein** and higher up to the summit of **Kreuzkogel**. You can also gain access via Bad Gastein to the half dozen or so runs on the **Gravkoel** where you will find some decent trees to shred. Bad Hofgastein and the area known as **Dorfgastein** are two other locations where you can do some cool riding.

FREERIDERS can basically pick and choose from any one of the areas in order to have a good time. The collection of slopes on the **Dorfgastein** are okay for freeriding.

FREESTYLERS might not embrace this place with its rather dull freestyle appeal. However, you will still be able to find some good hits and be able to catch some big air. There is also a pipe and terrain park up on the **Dorfgastein** slopes. The FIS hold boardercross competitions here in February

PISTES. Carvers will possibly like this place the most no matter which area you select. The whole area is littered with good pisted cruising runs, especially the runs up on the **Stubnerkogel** area.

BEGINNERS should think about choosing another resort as this is not really a hot place for learning snowboarding.

THE TOWN
Off the slopes, Bad Gastein is a glamorous joint with okay services but dull night-life. **Off the slopes**, hotels chalets and other local facilities are in abundance but not very convenient to all the slopes and other areas. Having a car around Bad Gastein may be a good idea, local transport is not hot. **Accommodations** options within the area are not overpriced and cheap budget priced lodgings are easy to find. **Eating** out options are not mega in terms of the types of places, what you have is a lot of hotel restaurants selling much the same style of food. As for a good lively night out, forget it.

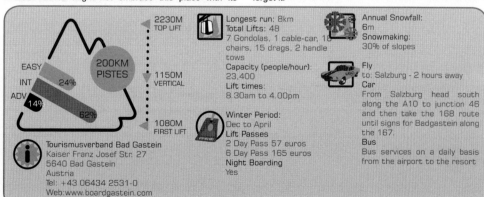

2230M TOP LIFT

1150M VERTICAL

1080M FIRST LIFT

EASY

INT 24%

ADV 14%

62%

200KM PISTES

Longest run: 8km
Total Lifts: 48
7 Gondolas, 1 cable-car, 18 chairs, 15 drags, 2 handle tows
Capacity (people/hour): 23,400
Lift times:
8.30am to 4.00pm

Winter Period:
Dec to April
Lift Passes
2 Day Pass 57 euros
6 Day Pass 165 euros
Night Boarding
Yes

Annual Snowfall:
6m
Snowmaking:
30% of slopes

Fly
to: Salzburg - 2 hours away
Car
From Salzburg head south along the A10 to junction 46 and then take the 168 route until signs for Badgastein along the 167.
Bus
Bus services on a daily basis from the airport to the resort

Tourismusverband Bad Gastein
Kaiser Franz Josef Str. 27
5640 Bad Gastein
Austria
Tel: +43 06434 2531-0
Web: www. boardgastein.com
Email: info@skigastein.com

	POOR	FAIR	GOOD	TOP
FREERIDE — A few trees and some of off-piste				
FREESTYLE — A park & a half-pipe				
PISTES — Vast area				

7 OUT OF 10

Pic -Hoffagarten tourism

A

AUSTRIA

Hopfagarten in Brixental is a resort that forms part of Austria's largest linked area known as the **'Ski Welt'** and is located just 50 miles (80km) from **Innsbruck**. Collectively the resorts that make up Ski Welt have over 250km of marked out pistes and lots more off-piste terrain. The area is linked across a series of mountain slopes by a staggering array of over 93 lifts which are mainly chair lifts. Getting around all the areas will take some careful piste map reading, as you can easily get lost around here. Thankfully though the local piste map is well laid out and shows what is actually on the ground. The piste are also well marked, so you should have no excuse for ending up miles from where you started. Like all the resorts of the Ski Welt, Brixental, which sits across the valley floor from **Westendorf**, is a low laying resort with a high point of 1674m. In the past there has been a problem with a lack of real snow, however, the area has over 135km of snow-making facilities which helps to keep the runs open when the real stuff is in short supply. Brixental is a spread out affair and depending on where you stay, it may mean having to catch the ski bus to reach the slopes, not all the accommodation is close the runs.

FREERIDERS who plan to take a weeks holiday in the Ski Welt could do a lot worst than this area, and although Brixen on its own would be a bit tedious after a few days if you are a competent rider, but the fact that you have easy access to a lot more of well connected terrain, means a 7 days stay will not be wasted time. The expanse of this area means that provided the snow is good and plentiful, you will be able to ride each day on a new selection of pisted slopes aided by the fact that lift queues are never that long meaning you will be able to roam freely with ease.

FREESTYLERS have a number of options for getting air. Most of the resorts in the Ski Welt have either a halfpipe or fun park; some even have both, as does Brixental. However, it should be pointed out that not all the resorts maintain the pipes and parks unless there is an event being staged, which is often the case around here.

PISTES. Boarders should feel at ease here, the area offers a vast number of well groomed pistes to suite all levels making this a cool place for laying out turns on or simply a place for improving your technique.

BEGINNERS will find the slopes of Brixental are easy to get to grips with. There are some nice low down nursery slopes and once you have mastered Brixental the Ski Welt offers lots of easy opportunities to learn on.

THE TOWN
Off the slopes Brixental offers a good choice of accommodation, restaurants, and bars and what's more this is not an expensive resort.

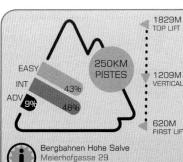

1829M TOP LIFT

250KM PISTES

EASY
INT 43%
ADV 9% 48%

1209M VERTICAL

620M FIRST LIFT

Number of Runs: 120
Total Lifts: 91
11 Gondolas, 35 chairs, 45 drags
Capacity (people/hour): 130,000
Lift times: 8.30am to 4.00pm

Winter Period: Dec to April
Lift Passes
Day pass 32 euros
6 Days 157.50 euros
Season 475 euros

Annual Snowfall: Unknown
Snowmaking: 70% of slopes

Fly
1 1/2 hours from Salzburg (100km) airport. Munich 150km, Innsbruck 70km
Car
via Munich (100 km) - exit Kufstein Süd towards Innsbruck, via Innsbruck (70 km) - exit Wörgl Ost - to Brixental
Train
via Munich, Kufstein and Wörgl to Hopfgarten main station or Hopfgarten Berglift

Bergbahnen Hohe Salve
Meierhofgasse 29
6361 Hopfgarten im Brixental, Austria
Tel +43(5335)2238
Fax +43(5335)3085
Web:www.skiwelt.at
Email:bergbahnen.hopfgarten@skiwelt.at

WSG ELLMAU/SCHEFFU

Poor freestylers resort

6 OUT OF 10

FREERIDE
A few trees and some of off-piste
FREESTYLE
A park & a half-pipe (in Soll)
PISTES
Plenty of groomed slopes

POOR FAIR GOOD TO

Pic - Scheffu Resort

A AUSTRIA

place. This is a very popular ski resort which on the one hand means long lift queues but on the other hand, and in the resorts defence, this is also an affordable destination.

FREERIDERS who know their stuff, won't find the offerings here to their general liking. You can have a good time but nothing is that testing or to prolonged in terms of long runs and although the Ski Welt offers a lot of riding opportunities, a weeks trip would be better spent at a more adventurous resort. However, an okay to check out is the trail down from **Brandstadl** to **Scheffau**.

FREESTYLERS should make the trip back down to the resort of **Soll**, to check out their halfpipe and terrain park because it's about the best place to get any big air from as this is not a freestylers resort whether you want natural hits of man mad offerings. But like any resort, if you look hard enough, you will find something to leap off.

PISTES. Riders of limited experience can have a great time at **Ellmau** or at any of the nearby linked resorts. The area boasts a lot of wide and well groomed runs that will let you cruise with ease for hours on end. Check out the Hohe Salve for some fun.

BEGINNERS are the one group who should have no problems with this resort even if the place is a bit fragmented. There are plenty of easy to reach nursery slopes to seek out.

THE TOWN
Ellmau may be a quaint Austrian village, but it is also a bit of a mishmash of a place. **Off the slopes**, there's plenty of good Austrian hospitality on, or close to the slopes, with affordable pensions. Getting around can be a real pain in the arse and local transport services are poor. **Accommodation** is affordable and there are lots of hotel restaurants to get a meal in. **Night life** is super dull, unless you're in to après ski games.

Ellmau forms part of the massive **Ski Welt** which is said to be Austria's largest linked ridable area located in the **Tirol** and only 90 minutes from **Salzburg**. 250km of linked piste covered by 92 lifts should mean utopia, but unfortunately this place is not that hot. The resorts low altitude means that good annual snow is not a feature of this place although to be fair the place has a good snowmaking set up to help when the real stuff is lacking. As for the slopes this is mountain that tends to suffer from a good selection of advanced freeriding areas, come to that, it lacks good natural freestyle terrain as well. The biggest let down here or the most annoying thing are the hordes of novice ski groups clogging up the place and littering the slopes with ski and poles as they fall over all over the

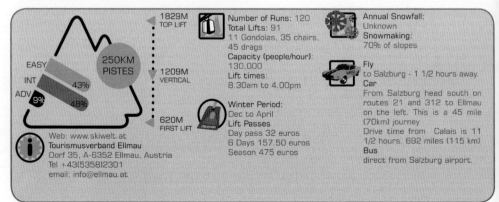

1829M TOP LIFT
250KM PISTES
EASY
INT 43%
ADV 9% 48%
1209M VERTICAL
620M FIRST LIFT

Web: www.skiwelt.at
Tourismusverband Ellmau
Dorf 35, A-6352 Ellmau, Austria
Tel +43(5358)2301
email: info@ellmau.at

Number of Runs: 120
Total Lifts: 91
11 Gondolas, 35 chairs, 45 drags
Capacity (people/hour): 130,000
Lift times: 8.30am to 4.00pm

Winter Period:
Dec to April
Lift Passes
Day pass 32 euros
6 Days 157.50 euros
Season 475 euros

Annual Snowfall:
Unknown
Snowmaking:
70% of slopes

Fly
to Salzburg - 1 1/2 hours away.
Car
From Salzburg head south on routes 21 and 312 to Ellmau on the left. This is a 45 mile (70km) journey
Drive time from Calais is 11 1/2 hours. 692 miles (115 km)
Bus
direct from Salzburg airport.

wsg FIEBERBRUNN

POOR FAIR GOOD TOP

FREERIDE
A few trees and fair bit of off-piste
FREESTYLE
Just a few natural hits
PISTES
Nice easy and maintained slopes

Up and coming resort

6
OUT OF 10

system that arrives at two levels: the first of which will bring you out on easy terrain around trees, whilst the second takes you to open reds and a black run.

FREESTYLERS looking for an endless supply of natural hits will be disappointed with Fieberbrunn. This is not the place to seek big air.

PISTES. Riders will find that the slopes appeal if you like well pisted and easy flats.

BEGINNERS have a very good choice of beginner-friendly areas for learning the basics. As a decent novice's resort, you can avoid the drag lifts by riding the runs down off the first gondola station.

Pic - Fieberbrun Resort

Fieberbrunn is a rather strange tale in terms of its popularity with snowboarding. It's not a high resort, nor is Fieberbrunn an adventurous place, and most good riders will have had enough after three or four days. Its snowboard status must be something to do with either the fantastic halfpipe, or else someone at the International Snowboard Federation has got a thing going with a local chick. The area lies in a natural snow pocket receiving 50% more snow than nearby **Kitzbuhel** over a course of a season. Sandwiched either side of the night illuminated half-pipe are the **Doischberg** and **Streuboden** gondolas which whisk you up from the car park to mid station. Fieberbrunn has never really attracted tour operators, the result being that the slopes are mainly inhabited by either locals or their cousins from Germany. Like most resorts, the well-prepared slopes do have busy periods (mainly at weekends and holidays), but don't be put off as this is a cool snowboard-friendly place.

FREERIDERS will find that the terrain is not the most testing, with only a couple of black runs that offer nothing much for advanced riders. The main runs on **Streuboden** are reached via a short journey on an unusual gondola

THE TOWN. **Fieberbrunn** is a small village. Hotels, pensions and rooms in private houses are the main form of accommodation. Some of which are very close to the slopes. Prices vary, but in general the place is affordable. **Night-life** is definitely not one of Fieberbrunn's strong points. Night action is very quite compared to more commercial resorts but the town centre (Dorfplatz) with its new 'village-square' is cool. The *Rivershouse* is a good place for beers, guinness and snacks. There is a pool table and live music most weekends. The *Londoner* became the *Cheers* pub many years ago and stripped out all the tat that was on the walls, its the most expensive place for a beer in town but cheaper than most resorts. *Biwak* is a at the bottom of the slopes which looks out onto the halfpipe and plays more up to date sounds than the oompah band in nearby *Enzianhutte*. *Tenne* nightclub is the place for a late beer or dance, but avoid until 1 am when the under 16s are booted out (unless this is your sort of thing). **All in all** - a rapidly up and coming resort with great snow and off piste but lacking the nightlife in low season. Still if you're with a good crowd of people, who cares and **St Johann in Tirol** is only a ten minute taxi ride away which is home to the legendary *Bunny's Pub*.

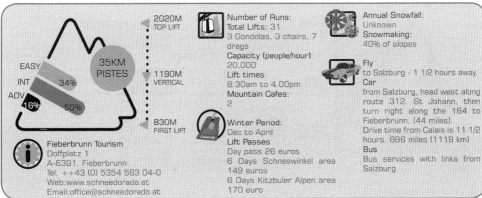

EASY
INT 34%
ADV 16%
50%

35KM
PISTES

2020M
TOP LIFT

1190M
VERTICAL

830M
FIRST LIFT

Number of Runs:
Total Lifts: 31
3 Gondolas, 3 chairs, 7 drags
Capacity (people/hour):
20,000
Lift times:
8.30am to 4.00pm
Mountain Cafes:
2

Winter Period:
Dec to April
Lift Passes
Day pass 26 euros
6 Days Schneewinkel area
149 euros
6 Days Kitzbuler Alpen area
170 euro

Annual Snowfall:
Unknown
Snowmaking:
40% of slopes

Fly
to Salzburg - 1 1/2 hours away.
Car
from Salzburg, head west along route 312. St Johann, then turn right along the 164 to Fieberbrunn. (44 miles). Drive time from Calais is 11 1/2 hours. 696 miles (1119 km)
Bus
Bus services with links from Salzburg

Fieberbrunn Tourism
Doffplatz 1
A-6391. Fieberbrunn
Tel. ++43 (0) 5354 563 04-0
Web:www.schneedorado.at
Email:office@schneedorado.at

	POOR	FAIR	GOOD	TOP
FREERIDE Some good pockets but limited				
FREESTYLE A few natural hits maybe				
PISTES Nice easy slopes				

7 OUT OF 10

Good freeriding resort

Galtur is the less famous cousin of **Ischgl**, 20 minutes away at the head of the **Paznaun Valley**. Although a small resort, Galtur proves that size doesn't always matter. Whilst Ischgl gets all the attention Galtur is left relatively alone, making it a far quieter place to ride. Galtur is a very Austrian resort, with all the usual trappings. The terrain doesn't measure to mega status and pistes are fairly ordinary. However, it is possible to buy a lift ticket for the **Silvretta** area (of which Galtur is a part), that includes Ischgl, opening up some 155 miles of terrain. You can also do night riding here, which is not a common thing in Austria.

FREERIDERS in softs looking for interesting terrain should check out the Innere **Kopsalpe** area. It won't test advanced riders too much, but should keep intermediates happy for a few days.

FREESTYLERS won't love Galtur as it doesn't offer any real big air opportunities - though like any resort there are hits to be found if you look. The best thing to do is either take the 20 minute bus journey to Ischgl to ride their amazing fun-park, or check out the halfpipe at **Samnaun**, a small neighbouring Swiss resort.

PISTES. PISTES. The well-pisted runs allow carvers to progress with ease, and the red and black runs on the **Saggrat** should give you a rush.

BEGINNERS are the one group of riders who will really like Galtur. The flats are easy to reach from the village and riders should have no real problems, unless they are scared of using the drag lifts that serve many of the runs (including the easy ones). Still, as the lift lines are non-existent and quiet, you'll be able to keep trying without too much hassle from irate skiers. The local ski-school, which caters mainly for beginners, will help you out.

THE TOWN
Everything is within easy access of the slopes and for such a small resort, there are plenty of things to do. Galtur is a typical Austrian village with normal **accommodation** offerings, from pricey hotels to well priced pensions. **Eating out** is all Austrian, which is average but bland. There is, however, way too much après-ski which will appeal to some sad types, but not the hardcore rider who likes to party hard.

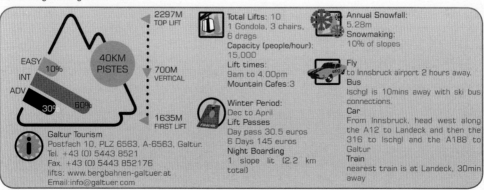

40KM PISTES

EASY
INT
ADV
10%
30%
60%

2297M TOP LIFT

700M VERTICAL

1635M FIRST LIFT

Total Lifts: 10
1 Gondola, 3 chairs, 6 drags
Capacity (people/hour): 15,000
Lift times:
9am to 4.00pm
Mountain Cafes: 3

Winter Period:
Dec to April
Lift Passes
Day pass 30.5 euros
6 Days 145 euros
Night Boarding
1 slope lit (2.2 km total)

Annual Snowfall:
5.28m
Snowmaking:
10% of slopes

Fly
to Innsbruck airport 2 hours away.
Bus
Ischgl is 10mins away with ski bus connections.
Car
From Innsbruck, head west along the A12 to Landeck and then the 316 to Ischgl and the A188 to Galtur
Train
nearest train is at Landeck, 30min away

Galtur Tourism
Postfach 10, PLZ 6563, A-6563, Galtur.
Tel. +43 (0) 5443 8521
Fax. +43 (0) 5443 852176
lifts: www.bergbahnen-galtuer.at
Email:info@galtuer.com

Great open pistes

7 OUT OF 10

	POOR	FAIR	GOOD	TOP
FREERIDE				
No trees but fair bit of off-piste				
FREESTYLE				
A park & a half-pipe				
PISTES				
Huge motorway pistes				

A
AUSTRIA

Pic - Summer Park , (c) Hintertux Tourism

The base of Hintertux sits at a height of 1,500m at the far end of the **Zillertal valley**, which is also home to the resorts of **Mayrhofen** and **Eggalm**. It now forms part of the **Zillertal 3000** area offering 230km of pistes. Hintertux has a number of advantages and disadvantages: on the plus side, it's a glacial resort, and apart from being one of the best summer snowboard resorts in Europe, it also has an enviable snow record in winter. However, in winter the same pluses mean that when the lower altitude resorts of the valley are suffering from a lack of snow, Hintertux can become very busy. Still, the open expanse of freeride terrain provides some excellent powder fields that are seldom tracked out by the morning ski masses. In summer the extent of snow cover over the length of the runs is often more than many resorts get during the winter season. Slopes are always crowd-free and riding in a t-shirt is the norm

FREERIDERS have the pick of the slopes with various terrain on and off-piste. There are huge open expanses and loads of gullies and natural walls to ride. There's no tree riding as the altitude deters their growth, but it's no big loss as the terrain is more than sufficient, especially if you take a look at what's available to ride off Number 3 chair.
FREESTYLERS have loads of hits to check out, which

include a few cliff drops and a number of wide, natural gap jumps. If you're still not content, there's a fun-park and two halfpipes which they maintain all year round, although it's not always possible in July and August.

THE PISTES are really good for laying out big turns, and tend to be long with a few sharp turns here and there.

BEGINNERS may find Hintertux a bit too daunting, especially if you're a total novice. There are some easy runs, but in truth you may be better off at another resort.

THE TOWN
Hintertux has a lot going for it on the slopes, but off the mountain, the place is totally crap with little or no real local services. . It's not that cheap either, with only a few restaurants and decent drinking holes. If its après-ski you're after though, you must check out the bar at the bottom of the gondola called *Hohenhaus Tenne*. Its full on, and has got the most bonkers toilets you've ever seen. The best thing is to stay down the valley at Mayrhofen, which is about a forty minute bus ride away. **Mayrhofen** is a cool place with loads of places to stay, lots of restaurants and heaps of other things going on.

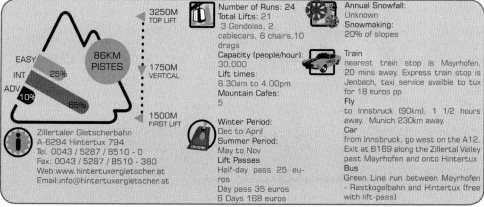

3250M TOP LIFT

EASY

86KM PISTES

INT 25%

ADV 10%

65%

1750M VERTICAL

1500M FIRST LIFT

Zillertaler Gletscherbahn
A-6294 Hintertux 794
Tel. 0043 / 5287 / 8510 - 0
Fax: 0043 / 5287 / 8510 - 380
Web:www. hintertuxergletscher.at
Email:info@hintertuxergletscher.at

Number of Runs: 24
Total Lifts: 21
3 Gondolas, 2 cablecars, 6 chairs,10 drags
Capacity (people/hour): 30,000
Lift times: 8.30am to 4.00pm
Mountain Cafes: 5

Winter Period: Dec to April
Summer Period: May to Nov
Lift Passes
Half-day pass 25 euros
Day pass 35 euros
6 Days 168 euros

Annual Snowfall: Unknown
Snowmaking: 20% of slopes

Train
nearest train stop is Mayrhofen, 20 mins away. Express train stop is Jenbach, taxi service availble to tux for 18 euros pp
Fly
to Innsbruck (90km), 1 1/2 hours away. Munich 230km away.
Car
from Innsbruck, go west on the A12. Exit at B169 along the Zillertal Valley past Mayrhofen and onto Hintertux
Bus
Green Line run between Mayrhofen - Rastkogelbahn and Hintertux (free with lift-pass)

129

One of the greatest fun-parks in Europe

	POOR	FAIR	GOOD	TOP
FREERIDE Trees & some good off-piste				
FREESTYLE Great Park & floodlit pipe				
PISTES Nice wide, well maintained				

9 OUT OF 10

Pics - Ischgl Tourism

Ischgl has gained a reputation as being one of Austria's best resorts - and it's a worthy reputation at that. Mind you, it's also one of Austria's more snobbish areas and can be very expensive. Ischgl may not be the most testing place, but it offers something for everyone, with well groomed slopes serviced by fast modern lifts. Snowboarders have been coming here for years to sample the excellent selection of wide, open, long runs which suit all standards and styles of rider. The FIS regularly stage slalom and halfpipe events here, so it must have something to offer. If what you find at Ischgl is not enough, then you can ride into the neighbouring Swiss duty-free resort of **Samnaun**. It can be reached by connecting lifts and is covered by the **Silvretta** lift pass, which can be used at three other resorts, **Galtur, Kappl** and **See**.

FREERIDERS have a high altitude mountain that ensures a good annual snow record, providing excellent wide open powder fields. For some easy freeriding, check out the stuff in the **Idjoch** area, which has a good mixture of blues and reds to play around on. Advanced riders will find plenty of stuff to keep them busy, although you won't be tested too often. **Pardatschgrat**, a black run leading back into the village (with the lower section cutting through some trees), is well worth a go, and you'll also find good off-piste freeriding down the runs off **Palinkopf**.

FREESTYLERS are probably going to be the most pleased with Ischgl for one reason, and one reason only - the

Boarder's Paradise fun-park is the dog's bollocks. It is without doubt, one of the best parks in Europe and is equipped with all sorts of interesting obstacles with marked areas such as Freeride, New School, and Mogul, which starts at the top. At the bottom there is a well-shaped halfpipe. The whole area is designed with the intention of satisfying air heads of all levels (there's also a halfpipe at **Samnaun**). However, freestylers who are still not content will find plenty of natural hits to get that extra air fix off, with big drop ins, banks and gullies all over the mountain.

PISTES. Boarders, especially hard boot riders, will love this resort, with its wide, motorway pistes where you can put down big arcs and easily make those 360° snow turns. Ischgl often hosts top slalom and giant slalom events so there must be good quality, fast carving terrain. The runs are so well-marked and pisted, that carving up Ischgl is a total pleasure, no matter what is on your feet.

BEGINNERS will soon see the benefits of learning here. The novice-marked runs are just that, being well located and offering some long, easy-to-negotiate trails. The only drawback is the amount of drag lifts that beginners need to use, but you've got to learn some time. The local ski school has a lot of snowboard instruction and lesson programmes

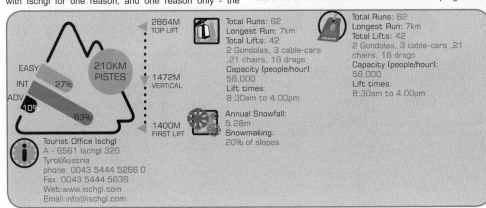

EASY
INT 27%
ADV 10%
63%

210KM PISTES

2864M TOP LIFT

1472M VERTICAL

1400M FIRST LIFT

Total Runs: 62
Longest Run: 7km
Total Lifts: 42
2 Gondolas, 3 cable-cars ,21 chairs, 16 drags
Capacity (people/hour): 58,000
Lift times: 8:30am to 4.00pm

Total Runs: 62
Longest Run: 7km
Total Lifts: 42
2 Gondolas, 3 cable-cars ,21 chairs, 16 drags
Capacity (people/hour): 58,000
Lift times: 8:30am to 4.00pm

Annual Snowfall: 5.28m
Snowmaking: 20% of slopes

Tourist Office Ischgl
A - 6561 Ischgl 320
Tyrol/Austria
phone: 0043 5444 5266 0
Fax: 0043 5444 5636
Web:www.ischgl.com
Email:info@ischgl.com

are very reasonable.

THE TOWN

Ischgl is a modern resort, rather than an old traditional Austrian hamlet. However, this is a resort popular with the ski tour groups who come here by the coachload, so it can get very busy both on and off the slopes. Ischgl is also not the cheapest of places, so skint or budget-conscious riders will need to do some serious scamming to see a seven day trip through. Around the village there are a number of attractions from the adventure swimming pool, squash courts and a number of shops (selling tack mostly). There is a few snowboard hire outlets, with prices much the same from where ever you go.

Food. Depending on what you're into may have a lot do with how you eat here. There are quite a lot of restaurants in Ischgl, mostly hotel restaurants. However, they are nearly all Austrian style, offering a lot of bland menus. Fast food around here is a shop-lifter running out of the supermarket with a packet of biscuits. The Pizzeria is good, so it's not all bad news.

Night-life in Ischgl is dire and really lets the place down. There is a number of bars and late night hangouts. But the problem is that most places are full of sickly aprés-ski bores, wearing silly coloured lipsticks and face paints.

Accommodation is of a very high standard but with high rates to match. There are plenty of typical Austrian hotels, pensions and a number of Austrian-style apartment suites, with self-catering sleeping 6 or more. Nothing is more than a few minutes from the base lifts, with many of the places located in areas where cars are banned. Many tour operators come here offering package deals for weekly and two week stays.

SUMMARY

Ischgl has one of the best fun-parks in Europe and offers some excellent all-round terrain for all levels. However, off the slopes things are a bit poncy.

FLY: Fly to Innsbruck (100km) International transfer time to resort is 2 hours. Munich/Salzburg 300km**BUS:** Buses from Innsbruck, can be taken via Landeck to Ischgl on a daily basis. Landeck is 55 mins.**TRAIN:**Trains go to Landeck , then take bus to resort (55 mins), buses typically run every hour in the winter
CAR: Drive to Innsbruck via motorway A12 to Ischgul, 178miles (286km). Drive time is about 2 hours
*From Calais = 639 miles (1028Km, Drive time is around 11 1/2 hours.

wsg KAPRUN

Good riding to be had

FREERIDE
No trees but some off-piste
FREESTYLE
Year round park and usually pipe
PISTES
Good slopes

7
OUT OF 10

Pic -San Tang

A
U
S
T
R
I
A

PISTES. Any carvers will be at ease whether they ride at Kaprun or Zell am See, as both resorts have some great, open carving runs. At Kaprun you can access some excellent carving spots from the **Alpencentre**.

BEGINNERS can get going on a number of easy runs on the **Maiskogel mountain**, which is reached by a drag lift from the centre of the village. If you can't handle a drag lift, take the cable car at the north end of the village to reach the east slopes. Beginners are spoilt when it comes to snowboard instruction; Kaprun was the first Austrian resort to have an independent snowboard school. If you get bored with Kaprun, Zell am See is a good 20 minute bus ride away, which gives you access to an extra 50 miles of piste covered by the same pass.

THE TOWN.
Kaprun is a fairly large and stretched out affair. Having a car may save a lot of walking but there is also a good and regular local bus service. Around town, you get a mixture of the old and new with a typical Austrian flavour. **Accommodation** options are excellent and Kaprun will satisfy both rich and skint snowboarders alike.**Evenings** in Kaprun are laid back - check out the *Austrian* Pub, *Bauber's*, or the *Fountain bar*. Nothing great about any of them, but there are worse places.

Winter or summer, Kaprun cuts it big style. The ride area is located on one of Austria's best glaciers, the **Kitzsteinhorn Glacier,** which reaches an altitude of 3,203 metres, making it a perfect place to ride. Being a glacier resort, you can ride here all year and no matter what month you visit, riders of all levels will find something to shred. It has to be said however, that much of what is here (or at nearby **Zell am See**), is best suited to intermediate freeriders and carvers

FREERIDERS wanting to gain access to Kaprun's best terrain and main runs, should head to the **Kitzsteinhorn**. Further up, you can reach good off-piste powder stashes, which can often still be found in the summer months of June and July.

FREESTYLERS are provided with a halfpipe at Kaprun all year round, and there's another one down in Zell am See during the winter. Kaprun's pipe is not the world's best but it still allows for some okay riding. The fun-park has an array of hits, but really freestylers should search out Kaprun's natural hits.

Kitzsteinhorn – Maiskogel

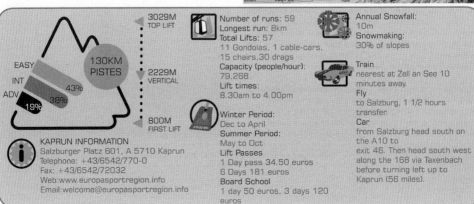

3029M
TOP LIFT

2229M
VERTICAL

800M
FIRST LIFT

EASY
INT
ADV
43%
38%
19%

130KM
PISTES

Number of runs: 59
Longest run: 8km
Total Lifts: 57
11 Gondolas, 1 cable-cars,
15 chairs,30 drags
Capacity (people/hour):
79,268
Lift times:
8.30am to 4.00pm

Winter Period:
Dec to April
Summer Period:
May to Oct
Lift Passes
1 Day pass 34.50 euros
6 Days 181 euros
Board School
1 day 50 euros, 3 days 120 euros

Annual Snowfall:
10m
Snowmaking:
30% of slopes

Train
nearest at Zell an See 10 minutes away.
Fly
to Salzburg, 1 1/2 hours transfer.
Car
from Salzburg head south on the A10 to exit 46. Then head south west along the 168 via Taxenbach before turning left up to Kaprun (56 miles).

KAPRUN INFORMATION
Salzburger Platz 601, A 5710 Kaprun
Telephone: +43/6542/770-0
Fax: +43/6542/72032
Web:www.europasportregion.info
Email:welcome@europasportregion.info

ᗯᔕᎫ KITZBUHEL

FREERIDE
A few trees and some off-piste
FREESTYLE
A park & a half-pipe
PISTES
Good variety when covered

6
OUT OF 10

Way overated and cheesy

A

A
U
S
T
R
I
A

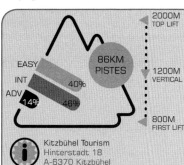

Rk- Kitzbuhel Tourism

The chances are that if you know **Austria**, you'll know about **Kitzbuhel**, famed for the **Hahnenkamm** (a World Cup ski downhill course), and noted for the billions of ski-package tour groups. Yep, Kitzbuhel is Austria's Benidorm, due to the hoards of skiers cluttering up the slopes and making fools of themselves in the bars and around town. A shame really, for apart from the long lift queues and the fact that it is a low-level resort, which doesn't guarantee snow cover on the bottom runs, it is a cool place to ride. Still, when the snow has dumped, no rider should get bored as there is enough room to ride without constantly bumping into skiers.

FREERIDERS should look under **Bichlam** in order to ride some cool powder, while advanced riders will find the more testing runs on **Ehrenbach** (part of the Hahnenkamm) & down the steeps of Ehrenbachgraben. The **Jochberg** area has some easy bowls to hunt out. The best way to cut the off-piste is to seek out the assistance of a local guide at the off-piste school.

FREESTYLERS are attracted to Kitzbuhel for its extensive amounts of natural hits, like the stuff found on **Pegelstein**, or those hits dotted around Safari, which starts at Pegelstein. The park and pipe also provide plenty of air time, even if they're not that well looked after.

PISTES. Advanced riders are primarily drawn to Kitzbuhel by the thought of tackling the **Hahnenkamm**. The rest of the area has plenty of good advanced and intermediate terrain that also allows for some fast carving descents.

BEGINNERS in particular are well suited to these slopes, as there's the chance of riding some long, easy runs serviced by chair lifts, and not just drags, offering the nervous T-bar virgin good, alternative options for getting around. The long **Hagstein** run is ideal for first timers; the only problem with this area is that it is often littered with fallen down skiers.

THE TOWN.
Lodging in a town like **Kitzbuhel** is no problem, with heaps of beds at average prices in pensions and apartments. Mercifully, it has loads of cheap eating joints. **Boozing** goes off in a number of places, allowing drinking into the early hours of the morning. But beware, skiers apres all over the place, although most are in bed by 9pm having had their two glasses of gluhwein. Popular hangouts are *Take 5* & the *Londoner* bar (no points for names). A cheaper option is to head to **Kirchberg**, about 10km away. Its got less glitz but some good bars, and a good range of facilities.

2000M
TOP LIFT

EASY
INT 40%
ADV 14% 46%

86KM
PISTES

1200M
VERTICAL

800M
FIRST LIFT

Number of Runs: 58
Longest Run: 10km
Total Lifts: 53
6 Gondolas, 27 chairs, 18 drags
Capacity (people/hour): 77,589
Lift times:
8.30am to 4.00pm

Winter Period:
Dec to April
Lift Passes
Day 36.5 euros,
6 Days 170 euros
Season pass 455 euros
Board School
Many companies to choose from.
Day lesson 60 euros, half-day 35, 6 days 135. Private lesson half-day 140 euros
Night Boarding
Thursday & Friday 6:30pm to 9:30pm Gaisberg quad chairlift open in Kirchberg. 13 euros

Annual Snowfall:
1.8m
Snowmaking:
45% of slopes

Train
Kitzbuhel has its own train station
Fly
Fly to Salzburg/Innsbruck airport, 1 3/4 hours transfer time. Transfers from Innsbruck call 0043 (0)512 584157 (4 seasons)
Car
From Insbruck take the A12 towards Kufstein, exit Wörgl Ost, then B178 (st. Johan), then 161 to Kitz

From Salzburg, take Federal highway to Walserberg, highway 21 towards Unken, then B178 towards St. Johann, finally the 161 Paß-Thurn to Kitzbühel (82km total)

Kitzbühel Tourism
Hinterstadt 18
A-6370 Kitzbühel
Tel.: +43 (0) 5356 777
Fax: +43 (0) 5356 777-77

Web:www.kitzbuehel.com
Email:info@kitzbuehel.com

POOR FAIR GOOD TOP

FREERIDE
A few trees and fantastic off-piste
FREESTYLE
A park & an okay half-pipe
PISTES
Very well maintained

Slopes Yes - Village No

8
OUT OF 10

A

A U S T R I A

Pic -Woody

The Arlberg, in the far eastern section of Austria, is home to all the top classy resorts that the country has to offer. Lech is just one of them, along with its close neighbours **Zürs, Stuben, St Christoph** and **St Anton**. Lech is linked via lifts with Zürs, and is without doubt Austria's number one poncy retreat. Year in, year out, this high altitude resort attracts numerous royals along with the finest from the film and pop world - and all the arse-lickers they can muster to join them. Skiers come here to be seen, not to ski, so while they pose you can ruin their immaculate slopes, and tackle some great freeriding terrain.

Fresh from the latest Bridget Jones film, the face of Lech doesn't do anything to dispel its posh image. You'll see poodles dressed in tartan, Ferraris and sit on utterly pointless heated lift seats. However away from that, you'll release why Robot Food and Absinthe films come here to do the filming for their latest films, and it's the only place in Austria you can try heliboarding.

FREERIDERS will love this place, with large amounts of steeps and deep powder. The runs off **Kriegerhorn** are the total dog's

'B's, as are the powder trails down from **Zuger Hochlicht,** which can take you from top to bottom free of any piste-loving pop star. On the other side of the valley, you can take the cable car to the peak of the **Rüfikopf** for some good steep terrain. From the restaurant you can take a short run, and then a 40 minute hike to access a long continuous off-piste descent back in Lech, you'll need a guide though. For an easier run take the red 38a, which you can drop off and board down to the **Schafalplift t-bar,** take that, and from there are various routes into the valley eventually joining up to with a trail back to Lech.

FREESTYLERS have a pretty decent fun-park area, located under the **Schlegelkopf** lifts. The park is loaded with gaps, quarter-pipes, a good selection of boxes and rails, and a halfpipe. The halfpipe's not always well maintained, but like all the best areas here, its free of posing image junkies.

PISTES here are immaculate and groomed to perfection. You'll rarely have to queue for long for lifts, and theres a great variety of long pistes to choose from. From the top of the **Rüfikopf** you can board all the way over the Zürs.

BEGINNERS have a perfectly acceptable series of novice runs and good trails to progress on, making Lech a good first timer's resort. The only drawback is sharing the easy slopes with moaning no-hopers from the pop world, or a public school kid who thinks he's street wise (stick a finger in his eye and see what he thinks then).

THE TOWN
The town at the base of the slopes is expensive and dripping with sad people in fur coats and gold, so expect to pay highly for everything. Even the pensions cost an arm and a leg; you may find that a stay here is beyond the reach of most. Try lodging in one of the nearby hamlets. If you do give Lech the one night treatment, remember that night-life is pretty dull and super poncy.

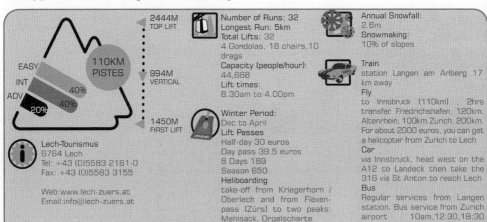

2444M TOP LIFT	Number of Runs: 32	Annual Snowfall: 2.6m
	Longest Run: 5km	Snowmaking:
	Total Lifts: 32	10% of slopes
110KM PISTES	4 Gondolas, 18 chairs,10 drags	
EASY	Capacity (people/hour): 44,668	Train station Langen am Arlberg 17 km away
INT	Lift times:	Fly
ADV 40%	8.30am to 4.00pm	to Innsbruck (110km) , 2hrs
40%		transfer Friedrichshafen, 120km.
20%		Altenrhein, 100km. Zurich, 200km.
994M VERTICAL	Winter Period: Dec to April	For about 2000 euros, you can get a helicopter from Zurich to Lech
	Lift Passes	Car
1450M FIRST LIFT	Half-day 30 euros	via Innsbruck, head west on the A12 to Landeck then take the 316 via St Anton to reach Lech
	Day pass 39.5 euros	
	6 Days 189	
	Season 650	Bus
Lech-Tourismus 6764 Lech Tel: +43 (0)5583 2161-0 Fax: +43 (0)5583 3155	Heliboarding take-off from Kriegerhorn / Oberlech and from Flexen- pass (Zürs) to two peaks: Mehlsack, Orgelscharte	Regular services from Langen station. Bus service from Zurich airport 10am,12:30,18:30 fri-sun (75 euros return) with Arlberg Express
Web:www.lech-zuers.at Email:info@lech-zuers.at		

wsg MAYRHOFEN

FREERIDE
A couple of trees and some off-piste
FREESTYLE
Excellent Park and good pipe
PISTES
Good but busy slopes

Good all-round resort

8
OUT OF 10

Pic -Mayrhofen Tourism

This quaint Tyrolean village, framed by beautiful mountains, is located just 43 miles from **Innsbruck** and welcomes many British package holiday makers every year. It offers the largest ski area in the **Ziller valley** now it is linked with **Hippach, Finkenberg** and **Eggalm/Rastkogel**. Although it is picturesque, the highest peak is only 2500 metres, and thus the snow conditions can sometimes suffer. In order to counter this, many snow making machines have been installed, covering 96 hectares of the terrain. The 146km of pistes are split into 40 km of blues, 86 km of red runs and 20 km of blacks.

For those staying in the centre of Mayrhofen, the only way up and down is the **Penken bahn gondola** as it is not possible to board back into Mayrhofen. Even though the lift is high speed, there can still be big queues early in the day. To avoid the crowds you can take the free ski bus to the **Finkenberg** or **Ahorn** lifts, which are popular with locals or the new Horbergbahn which is to the east.

Once you exit the Penken, there is a short stroll and a drop off down to a learner t-bar or the Penken Express. The red runs on this side are good fun and have a few short tree runs, but can get quite crowded.

Drop down into the other valley for some more testing runs like the Black 14 which is fairly steep and icy but good fun. For here you can access the **Burton terrain park** which has been used for the British Championships and has some BIG jumps! The park also incorporates a halfpipe, rails and a chill out area. It is serviced by the Sun Jet chairlift so no walking is required.

Nearby the new 150 person cable car, the 150er-Tux, whips you up to the **Horberg peak**. From here you can turn right off the lift and take the Blue 6 piste then drop off the edge into the **Horbergtal** and go off-piste back to the terrain park. Work out where you are going to cross the river before dropping into the valley!

In this area this is also a nice wide blue learner slope next to the **Tappenalm lift**, which leads to the **Schneekar lift**. Ascend this and visit the Schneekarhütte restaurant at the top of a nice black run (Route 17). It stilll has a big log fire and good food which can be washed down with all sorts of organic schnapps. Take Black 17 or Red 7 down which is also pleasant.

After a few days you may have seen most of these mountains so it is well worth buying the Super Zillertal lift pass as it costs only slightly more than the standard pass and includes other resorts in the valley. With this pass you can take the old rickety Zillertalbahn mountain train or the bus for free to other resorts from the station at the bottom of town.

From here the **Hintertux Glacier** is only half an hour. This is an amazing place but at 3250 metres the conditions can be extreme, with wind chill factor down to -30 so make sure you wrap up! White outs can occur suddenly too. On a sunny day though, this place is very close to heaven. It is

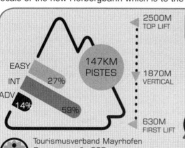

EASY
INT — 27%
ADV — 14%
59%

147KM
PISTES

2500M
TOP LIFT

1870M
VERTICAL

630M
FIRST LIFT

Number of runs: 109
Longest run: 9km
Total Lifts: 46
4 Gondolas, 1 cable-cars,
16 chairs,19 drags
Capacity (people/hour):
67,520
Lift times:
8.30am to 4.00pm

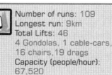

Winter Period:
Dec to April
Summer Period:
May to Nov (Hintertux Gla-
cier)
Lift Passes
Day pass 33.5 euros
Zillertal Super Ski Pass
(589km pistes):
6 Day 168 euros

Annual Snowfall:
10m
Snowmaking:
50% of slopes

Night Boarding
Yes
Board Schools
Snowboardschule Mayrhofen
Total charge 34 euros for a
2hr lesson, private lesson 101
euros for 2hrs (for 1-2 people),
4hrs 175

Tourismusverband Mayrhofen
Dursterstraße 225
6290 Mayrhofen
Tel: +43 5285 67600
Fax: +43 5285 676033

Web:www.mayrhofen.com
Email:info@mayrhofen.at

not often that busy, and there is lots of off-piste available but beware of crevasses and blue ice. After a day ripping it up, you must visit the *Hohenhauste* and go to the toilets. They cannot be explained, just make sure you drink a beer then nip to the loo!

Another nice place for a day trip is the small resort of **Kaltenbach**. This place often has lots of untracked powder after a dump because no one goes there! You can also take the same train to **Zell am Ziller**, and then a bus or taxi to their lift. Unfortunately your Super Zillertal pass isn't valid here, but it is still worth a visit as it is a large area linked to **Gerlos** and **Konigsleiten**, which is famous for its tree runs.

THE TOWN
There is an old tradition in Mayrhofen which states after a day's boarding you must visit the *Ice Bar* as soon as you step off the Penken and drink a Grolsch. This bar sells the most Grolsch is Europe and is only open 4 hours a day! It gets heaving but can be great fun. In 2003 they also build a Kebab shop in the bar, so you don't even have to stumble outside for refreshment.

After après boarding, late beers can be drunk at the chilled and friendly *Scotland Yard* pub, and then you can dance til dawn at *Arena*. *Moe's Bar* serves decent food and good cocktails too. Other tips are the restaurant under *Sport*

Garni Strauss Hotel which serves nice Austrian food, or there is a good Chinese near Scotland Yard.

In brief, visit Mayrhofen, have a great party but be sure to shred Hintertux too.

Pic -Mayrhofen Tourism

FLY: Fly to Innsbruck (65km), 1 1/4 hours transfer. Salzburg airport (170km) about 2 1/2 hr transfer. Munich airport 190km

TRAIN: Jenbach railway station is about 35 km away. Take the Zillertalbahn train or bus to Mayrhofen.

CAR: Drive from Innsbruck and go west on the A12, take the Zillertal exit onto B169 along the Zillertal Valley to 30km to Mayrhofen.
° Drive time from Calais is 12 hours, 692 miles (1113 km).

Good sedate carvers & wrinkleys resort

	POOR	FAIR	GOOD	TOP
FREERIDE No trees but some off-piste				
FREESTYLE No park or pipe				
PISTE MERCHANTS Wide, smooth & plentiful				

6 OUT OF 10

A
A
U
S
T
R
I
A

If you've ever wondered what you'll find if you keep driving further down the valley past Sölden then the answer is Obergurgl. Just 20 minutes from Sölden and 90 minutes from Innsbruck, Obergurgl is traditionally a popular haunt for more elderly skiers; its slopes perfect for sedate snowploughing. Obergurgl is linked, with its slightly higher neighbour Hochgurgl, and is the first resort to open in Austria in mid November, and has one of the longest season, closing at the end of April.

At 3080m the resort is one of the highest in Austria, and most of its terrain is completely devoid of trees. Obergurgl and Hochgurgl are linked via a gondola, theres not a huge amount to choose between the two, but you'll find the more advanced terrain at Hochgurgl. The resort shines and gets top marks is as a carver's resort, where you area treated to huge wide open

intermediate slopes. The resort's high altitude scores highly in its snow record with heaps of the stuff falling every year, and to keep the lower slopes open early the resort boasts snow cannons covering 90% of its pistes. Most of the 110km of runs are of an intermediate level with a series of reds, a few easy blues and only a couple of advanced black trails to check out. There's good off-piste potential, but almost no interest for the freestyler. 99% of visitors are skiers, and the resort removed the half-pipe and terrain park last season as they said no one used it.

FREERIDERS
who like jagged and rough mountain slopes with big chutes and long gullies may find things around here a little on the tame side. There are no tree runs but there are some good off-piste and powder areas that can be ridden at speed.

FREESTYLERS
will largely be wasting their time up here, this is not an air head's retreat. There are of course a few natural hits as with most mountains covered in snow, but they are few and far between. The resort removing their park & pipe gives a clear indication where they see their clientele.

PISTES
Piste lovers and carvers are the ones in for a treat. Obergurgl is dream for those who want to arc over in style on well groomed runs that are wide and free of obstacles.

BEGINNERS should have no real problems with this place. The mountain is nicely laid out and novices can ride from the mid point all the way to the base via the number 5 and 6 trails.

THE TOWN
Off the slopes Obergurgls local services are excellent and very convenient for the slopes. There is a good choice of hotels and guest house along with shops and sporting facilities. A number of the big hotels have indoor swimming pools and gyms. Night life is a tad tame with only a handful of bars to choose from.

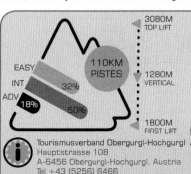

EASY
INT 32%
ADV 18% 50%

110KM PISTES

3080M TOP LIFT

1280M VERTICAL

1800M FIRST LIFT

i Tourismusverband Obergurgl-Hochgurgl
Hauptstrasse 108
A-6456 Obergurgl-Hochgurgl, Austria
Tel +43 (5256) 6466
Fax +43 (5256) 6353
Web: www.obergurgl.com
Email: info@obergurgl.com

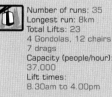

Number of runs: 35
Longest run: 8km
Total Lifts: 23
4 Gondolas, 12 chairs,
7 drags
Capacity (people/hour):
37,000
Lift times:
8.30am to 4.00pm

Winter Period:
Nov 15th to end April
Lift Passes
Day pass 38 euros
6 day pass 187 euros
Night Boarding
8km of pistes open on
tuesdays till 10pm (10
euros)

Annual Snowfall:
7m
Snowmaking:
90%

Train
train to Innsbruck or to Ötztal
Bahnhof
Bus
bus from Innsbruck (4 times a
day) or Ötztal-Bahnhof (8 times
a day)
Fly
25 minutes from Innsbruck
airport.
Car
From Innsbruck head along
the A12 and turn off on to the
B186 down the Ötztal Valley to
Obergurgl.

137

POOR FAIR GOOD TOP

FREERIDE
No trees and untracked
FREESTYLE
A park & a small half-pipe
PISTES
Well maintained

Snowsure resort with a good park

6
OUT OF 10

A

A U S T R I A

ama
er Gletscher

Ausgezeichnet
mit dem Snowboard
und Pistengütesiegel
des Landes Tirol

stentfläche:
76 Hektar
stenlänge:
20 km

1	= Mittagskogel	9	= Pitz Panorama
1a	= Gletschersee	9a	= Witwenmaker
1b	= WISBI-Rennstrecke	9b	= Teamrun
2	= WISBI RUN	12	= Macho Macho
3	= Longline		= Bergstation Pilzexpress
4	= Wildspitze		Restaurants, Souvenir-Shop,
5	= DSV Pitz		Ski- u. Snowboardservice,

Pitztal is another of Austria's glacier resorts, but this little gem season is a little shorter than the others with the lifts stopping at the end of May for snow sports. With an area of 185 acres its not great in size but the terrain is ideal for a trip for beginners to intermediates and family's. Most of the area can be bagged in two days, but don't be put off as Pitztal sister mountain, **Hochzeiger** is right next door with another 45km of pistes on offer, and a dual lift pass is only a few euros more.

The **Pitztal Glacier** is accessed through a 3.7km tunnel, which brings you out at the restaurant and rental shop. After a quick walk you're at the lifts, jump on the gondola to get to the highest point and take in the amazing views. One point to note is that the lifts are long and boring, so if you like a rest after each run you are laughing. Plans are in place to link the resort with **Sölden** but at present the Green party aren't too keen.

FREERIDING
You don't find many freeriders in Pitztal so you'll be almost guaranteed to ride powder every day and most of it untracked. The best option is to jump on the 4 x cable cars which take you to the highest point follow the 9a and head for the middle station, then cut onto the black 10 cutting through to the chair lift 1a. This run cuts out the long T bars.

FREESTYLE is where Pitztal pulls it out of the bag. They have a number of parks, a rail park with a large selection on offer and they are well maintained. There's also a short half pipe, and a boarder cross track will some nice banks. You'll also discover a number of sets of rollers dotted around the mountain.

BEGINNERS
The designated areas are very small and a waste of time, use 1a if your planning to use Pitztal as your training ground as its longer than the recognised areas and its serviced by a chair lift.. Pitztal is definitely an area perfect to log your first turns.

TOWN
The beauty of the Pitztal valley is it's at altitude so there's no need to sit on a packed bus for the 20 min journey to the base station, getting taken out by ski poles. The lifts are on your door step or at least just a few stops. The main night time hang out is at the *Hexenkessl* which is good for food and often has live music. Other than that it's a quite night in. Eating options are good but are a little pricey. The nearest large supermarket is a 15 min drive down the valley. In the summer month's there's lots to do in the valley, a vast amount of mountain biking routes, a large climbing wall and a small skate park further down the valley.

ACCOMMODATION. *Haus Berghein* is a nice B&B just a short ride/walk to the base station 0043 541 386226. *Landhaus Edelwiess* is ideal if you want to stay in an apartment which offers friendly service and great meals 0043 541 38320 www.edelweiss-pitzal.at

Pic -Ted Land

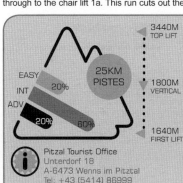

EASY
INT 20%
ADV
20% 60%

25KM
PISTES

3440M
TOP LIFT

1800M
VERTICAL

1640M
FIRST LIFT

Number of Runs: 16
Longest Run: 6km
Total Lifts: 6
1 Funicular, 1 Gondola, 1 chair, 2 drags, 1 learner tow
Lift times:
0830-1630hrs

Winter Period:
Sep to mid May
Lift Passes
Half-day pass 22 euros
Day pass 33.50 euros
6 Days 159 euros

Annual Snowfall:
Unknow
Snowmaking:
Unknown

Train
nearest station is 38 km away in Imst, which have frequent runs from Innsbruck and to Pitzal.
Fly
Innsbruck is 55 km, 1hr 20 min.
Car
From Munich go either via Garmisch and the Fernpass route and Imst or via take the autobahn towards Salzburg then take the A12 via Kufstein, Innsbruck and Imst

Pitzal Tourist Office
Unterdorf 18
A-6473 Wenns im Pitzal
Tel: +43 (5414) 86999
Web:www.pitztaler-gletscher.at
town: www.pitztal.com
Email:info@pitztal.com

SAALBACH/
HINTERGLEMM

Good easy freeriding & apres

POOR FAIR GOOD TOP

FREERIDE
Some good tree runs and off-piste
FREESTYLE
Leogang park okay, no pipe
PISTES
Wide, well maintained

8
OUT OF 10

Pic -James Woodward

Saalbach and Hinterglemm are two villages at the end of the **Glemm Valley**, and combined with Leogang create the **Saalbach ski circus** giving you access to 120miles of pistes. The cul-de-sac layout means no matter where you start you can loop in either direction back to the start.

The area is perfect for beginners to good intermediates with mile upon mile of well groomed and wide pistes. The pistes are very spread out giving you a huge area to roam on and off the pistes, picking out powder staches to throw spray turns in. You can literally pick lines from the lifts, pushing yourself as far as you want to, great for wannabe freeriders.

Advanced riders may find things a little tame with only a few black runs. The run under the **Schattberg x-press** in Saalbach is long and steep, but the other under the

Zwölfer-Nordbahn in Hinterglem can be a windswept icy mogul nightmare. The black/red from the top of the **Zwölferkogel** is good for opening things up and speeding down and plenty wide enough to find a clear path.

The last few seasons have seen huge investments in the lift system and a series of new gondolas have replaced many of the rickety old chairs. There are still a few bottlenecks for the 3-seater Sesselbahn and Mitteregg lifts. T-bars tend to service a lot of the short beginner runs and the park in Hinterglemm, avoid that area and you can get to most other parts via chairs. The **Bergeralm lift** provides a shortcut to Leogang from Saalbach but the t-bar's 1.3km long and 52° in places, and it feels even worse.

The resorts lie at quite a low elevation and rise to a modest

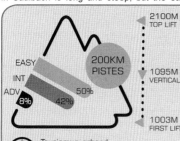

EASY
INT
ADV
8%
42%
50%

200KM
PISTES

2100M
TOP LIFT

1095M
VERTICAL

1003M
FIRST LIFT

Number of Runs: 61
Longest Run: 7km
Total Lifts: 55
13 Gondolas, 14 chairs, 28 drags
Capacity (people/hour): 87,000
Lift times: 8.30am to 4.00pm

New for 05/06
The Hochalm-chairlift will be replaced by 8-person-cable-car. Kohlmaisgipfel lift and Bergeralm lift will be replaced by 6-person-chair lifts with heated seats and bubbles

Annual Snowfall:
Unknown
Snowmaking:
20% of slopes

Winter Period:
Dec to April
Lift Passes
Half-day 29.4 euros
Day pass 36 euros
6 days 173 euros
Board Schools
Snowboardschule Saalbach. Beginners 1/2 day lesson 54 euros, week 244. Freestyle/freeride 163 for 3 day course. Backcountry & private lessons available. www.board.at for more info
Hire
Board & Boots from 29 euros a day
Night Boarding
Small park and beginners area lit in Hinterglemm

Tourismusverband
Glemmtaler Landstraße 550
A-5753 Saalbach
Tel.: +43(0)6541/6800-68
Fax: +43(0)6541/6800-69

Web:www.saalbach.com
Email:contact@saalbach.com

THE TOWN & GETTING THERE

Pic Dine rider: Woody

2020m, but due to its position in the valley it gets plenty of snow, with regular snow throughout the season. All of the main slopes have snowmaking facilities to cover any shortfall. There is a regular ski-bus service between the two villages and a taxi will cost around 10€. Do give yourself plenty of time to get back from Leogang, if you miss the last lift you'll be looking at a 40€ taxi back. For a change of scenery **Zell am See** is only 30 minutes away by bus (from the bottom of the Schattberg lift), and the high altitude resort of **Kaprun** about 45 minutes.

FREESTYLERS

There are two terrain parks; one in **Hinterglemm** the other in **Leogang**. The Hinterglemm park is aimed more towards beginners and is served by its own t-bar. There are a couple of kickers and rails, and at such a low elevation it usually doesn't get going until later in the season. The park at Leogang is much better and aimed much more toward the advanced airhead. The lines are always changing, but there's usually a couple of rollers and boxes to get you started, and an advanced rail and kicker line. The parks are designed and maintained by Austrian X-gamer **Mario Fuchs**. The halfpipes are being removed, but the resort does insist the effort is switching to improving the parks. There is talk of replacing the t-bar at the Hinterglemm park with a chair, and building a boarder cross circuit above where the park is.

Away from the parks you'll find a good number of lumps you can throw yourself off, but there's not much in the way of cliff drops.

FREERIDERS

The layout of the lifts and mountains ensures that theres a huge amount of accessible off-piste, albeit between pistes, and not too steep and taxing. There's a couple of nice small runs down to the bottom of the **WetterKreuz lift** from the top of the **Reiterkogel** and **Bernkogel** peaks, you'll need to duck under the ropes to watch yourself. Towards Leogang the area under the **Polten lift** is always good fun with a mixture of trees and dips that can be taken at speed.

BEGINNERS

Beginners will find things pretty much perfect. The blue run under the **Berkogel Sesselbahn** gets busy but is rarely moguled even at the end of the day. The area from the top of the Kohlmaiskopf back down into Saalbach is huge and open and great for progressing. The blue down from the Schattberg to Vorderglemm can be a little narrow at times but it meanders for 7km and its gradual pitch shouldn't present any problems. You will also find this an easier way to reach Leogang. The beginner's areas at the bottom of Hinterglemm and in Saalbach can get very icy, so it's recommended to get higher up the mountain as none of the slopes are too intimidating to tackle.

ACCOMMODATION

There's a good range of accommodation to suit most budgets. Unlike other resorts, location isn't too important in so far as you'll never be too far away from a lift. You can find Pensions from 20€ per night. For a full listing take a look at their website, or if you're already there then you'll find the tourist information in Saalbach on Glemmtaler Landesstrasse who should be able to find you something

EATING

You certainly won't starve here, but as with any resort if you have the cash you can eat like a king. There's many restaurants serving mainly Austrian cuisine, but you'll also find Italian and French restaurants. Both villages have a supermarket for take-outs and some very late night kebab and burger houses. On the slopes it's the usual expensive story, however the Alte Schmiede in Leogang serves fantastic made to order pizzas, and the Goasstal a mean gröstl

NIGHTLIFE

If you're not a fan of après ski then this place may be best avoided. If you're still reading then there's a choice of 32 après ski bars to pick from. Without question the Hinterhag Alm is the pick of the bunch, located at the top of the turmlift t-bar in Saalbach. You'll struggle to get in after 4:30 and the live band ensures everyone's dancing on the tables. At 7pm you'll stumble out and remember the only way back is to board back down the piste, and funnily enough, waiting at the bottom is the famous Bauer's Ski Alm which is open till 3am. Over in Hinterglemm the Goasstal kicks off with strippers and live goats (no kidding), its also a good place for lunch. Away from the après ski scene the Londoners open till 4am and the Alm bars pretty good (yes there's a tree inside the bar). In Saalbach you can get your pool/darts/skittles and football fix at Bobby's pub, and theres a few clubs open till the early hours around the main square.

FLY: to Salzburg International (90km) transfer time to resort is 1 1/2 hours
TRAIN: Trains: to Zell am See (12 miles), then taxi or local buses run every 1-2hrs daily.
BUS: from Salzburg, can be taken to Zell am See, then transfer by local bus to Saalbach.
CAR: From Salzburg take Tauern Autobahn A10 towards Villach, at Bischofshofen interchange take the B311 towards Zell-am-see. Follow signs for Maishofen, then heads towards Glemmtal follow for 14km

POOR FAIR GOOD TOP

FREERIDE
A few trees and limited off-piste
FREESTYLE
A park & an all year half-pipe
PISTES
Very well maintained

Good all-round resort

7
OUT OF 10

Pic -Sshladming Tourism

A
U
S
T
R
I
A

although it has a bigger riding area, it's less convenient for Schladming. Snow cover is pretty good with snowmaking facilities 90% of the Planai and Hochwurzen pistes. The lift pass covers the entire **Ski Amade** region, 865km of pistes altogether including **Flachau** that has an impressive park and many others around the Salzburg region.

FREERIDERS will find that any of the areas listed above can suit their needs, with some cool tree runs to be found on the **Planai**, and favourable powder to be found at **Hauser Kaibling**.

FREESTYLERS will find natural hits in most areas, with the Planai and the **Dachstein Glacier** having the best spots. There are also two halfpipes and fun-parks in the area to catch air on. One of the pipes is also well maintained during the summer months. The park on the Dachstein Glacier really comes to life in Autumn and Spring when the park season kicks off. The Home to the Pleasure Jam and the Superstar Session are held here every year.

BEGINNERS will find the **Rohrmoss** area at 869m is flat and boring, but should still appeal to novices. Snowboard instruction is very good, and they even have a children's snowboard school. **Blue tomato** run a snowboard school on the Planai

Schladming is fast becoming a magnet for snowboarders, providing a lively base for visiting the connected local mountains. Dachstein is an all year-round resort, with summer riding on the **Dachstein Glacier**, and is home to the **Burton Superpark**. The riding is spread out over a number of areas which offer basic intermediate terrain, and perfect beginner stuff. Schladming is not a hardcore or advanced rider's destination, but that's not to say there aren't any testing runs.

The four mountains **Planai, Hauser Kaibling, Hochwurzen** and **Reiteralm** make up the local area. The **Hauser Kaibling** mountain has lots of intermediate terrain, with a series of long reds that are ideal for carvers. There are excellent novice trails, with the option to ride a long blue all the way down to the base at the village of Haus, just up the road from Schladming. **Hochwurzen**, which rises up to 1,850m, has lots of trees for freeriders to drop through, and a number of reds at the top that base out into simple blues, with easy runs back to base. Theres also there's a small well shaped park from Christmas time onwards which is floodlit at night. The **Planai Mountain** holds the main trails and is reached from the edge of Schladming by gondola. Planai's runs offer something for everyone, with some interesting intermediate freeriding terrain. The **Reiteralm area** is much the same as Hochwurzen and

THE TOWN

Accommodation is spread out around a large area, but the old town of Schladming has the biggest selection and offers the best facilities. Prices vary throughout the area, but as there is a youth hostel with cheap bunks, life is made easy for riders on a budget.

Food wise, Schladming offers everything from typical meaty Austrian faire in the *Vorstadtstube*, Italian in *Giorgios*, and a quick yet very filling snack in the form of Schnitzel burgers and Sausages at the take away *Ums Eck*. **Nightlife** is improving every year. *Marias Mexican Bar, La Porta cocktail bar* are good and finish the night off in the *Sonderbar disco* which is always rammed at weekends. The area offers a vast amount of sporting facilities.

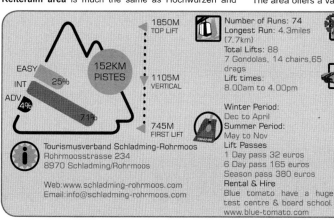

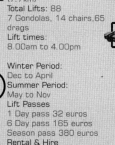

1850M
TOP LIFT

1105M
VERTICAL

745M
FIRST LIFT

EASY

INT 25%

ADV 4%

71%

152KM
PISTES

Number of Runs: 74
Longest Run: 4.3miles (7.7km)
Total Lifts: 88
7 Gondolas, 14 chairs,65 drags
Lift times:
8.00am to 4.00pm

Winter Period:
Dec to April
Summer Period:
May to Nov
Lift Passes
1 Day pass 32 euros
6 Day pass 165 euros
Season pass 380 euros
Rental & Hire
Blue tomato have a huge test centre & board school.
www.blue-tomato.com

Annual Snowfall:
5m
Snowmaking:
30% of slopes

Train
The nearest train stop is Schladming
Fly
Fly to Salzburg, 90km away. Munich 290km, Graz 190, Innsbruck 320km
Car
From Salzburg go to Radstadt on highway A10, then on federal road (B 320) 18 km to Schladming.

From Graz to Liezen on highway A9, federal road B 320 to Schladming

Tourismusverband Schladming-Rohrmoos
Rohrmoosstrasse 234
8970 Schladming/Rohrmoos

Web:www.schladming-rohrmoos.com
Email:info@schladming-rohrmoos.com

141

Pretty, but nothing too pulse racing

6
OUT OF 10

Pic -Seefeld Tourism

A

AUSTRIA

back down to the village outskirts. The ride area is split across two separate areas that of the **Gschwandtkopf** and the **Rosshutte**. The smaller of the two, being the Gschwandtkopf, is rather limited with only a few easy slopes for novices to try out. However, its still easy to get around and is a good spot for beginners to spend a few days learning on. The Rosshutte is a little more extensive with longer trails and wider slopes, but nothing that adventurous.

FREERIDERS will find riding here is done at sedate pace. Nothing is going to take you to long to conquer and good intermediate and expert riders will have this place licked within a day or two at the most. Still, there is a few spots to make a visit here a worth the while. The top section of the **Seefelder Joch** gives access to a few interesting spots which includes a few trees that line the lower parts of the main run down to the base area and the village.

FREESTYLERS are offered the delights of a fun park located on the Rosshutte area and reached by taking the funicular train that takes you up to 1800m. Theres a well maintained assortment of jumps, quarter pipes, rails & boxes. However, out of the park, good natural hits are hard to come by.

PISTES. The open wide runs of the **Rosshutte** area are superb for laying out fast turns on.

BEGINNERS have a resort that is in the main all theirs. Very little of the place is out of bounds to novices.

THE TOWN
Off the slopes Seefeld is quaint village with superb local facilities. Five star hotels and well appointed guest houses make up this almost car free hamlet. There are also good sporting attractions aš well as decent restaurants and okay bars.

Seefeld is a tiny picture post card resort and every thing you imagined an Austrian village to be. This low key retreat is only 20 kilometres from **Innsbruck** and can be reached with ease along the A12 Autobahn via **Zirl**. Seefeld is noted more in the winter for being a cross country ski retreat and in the summer a popular holiday destination attracting visitors to sample the beauty and the tranquillity of the area. The German resort of **Garmisch** is only a short distance away across the Austrian German boarder and both resorts can be ridden with the one ski pass called the 'Happy Card', which can be used in other resorts in various countries. On its own Seefeld is not noted for its hard-core down hill skiing or snowboarding, but nevertheless this is still a fun mountain with riding possible up to an altitude of 2100 metres and descends

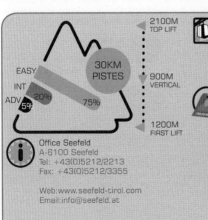

2100M TOP LIFT
900M VERTICAL
1200M FIRST LIFT

EASY
INT
ADV 5% 20%
75%

30KM PISTES

Office Seefeld
A-6100 Seefeld
Tel: +43(0)5212/2213
Fax: +43(0)5212/3355

Web:www.seefeld-tirol.com
Email:info@seefeld.at

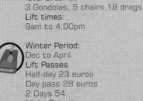

Number of runs: 36
Longest run: 6km
Total Lifts: 25
3 Gondolas, 5 chairs,18 drags
Lift times:
9am to 4.00pm

Winter Period:
Dec to April
Lift Passes
Half-day 23 euros
Day pass 28 euros
2 Days 54
Night Boarding
mon,tue,wed & friday on Rosshütte from 6:30 until 10pm. The lower Härmele slope is floodlit
Board School
1 day (2hr) lesson 46 euros, 5 days 135. Private lesson 40 euros per hour
Hire
Board & Boots 34 euros a day

Annual Snowfall:
3m
Snowmaking:
90%

Train
take the Karwendelbahn from Innsbruck to Garmisch
Fly
Innsbruck 21km away, Munich 138, Zurich 300
Car
East: Highway A12 / Exit Zirl east, head 12km in a northerly direction following the signs for Garmisch Partenkirchen
West: Highway A12 / Exit Telfs east + 12 kms

wsg SOLDEN

One of Austria's best all round resorts

9
OUT OF 10

FREERIDE
Some trees and some off-piste
FREESTYLE
All year park, boardercross, pipe
PISTES
Good variety of intermediate runs

POOR FAIR GOOD TOP

A

A
U
S
T
R
I
A

This World Class Resort is located 90 km (56 miles) from **Innsbruck** and 40 km (25 miles) from **Ötztal**, and is just down the road from the better known resort of **Obergurgl**. The area consists of "The Big 3" mountains, **Schwarze Schneide, Gaislachkogel** and **Tiefenbachkogel**, which are all over 3000 metres and serviced by high speed lifts with stunning views into Italy from their summits. At the top are 2 glaciers offering Austria's biggest glacial ski area and the mountains offer 147km of pistes, which are all perfectly groomed when the lifts open at 8am. More importantly, there is least double this distance in easily accessible off-piste terrain. One night a week the **Gaislakogel** opens in the evening and you can go nightboarding on a few of the slopes. There is also a big ski / snowboard and firework show on the same night which is worth a look. The **Giggijoch** gondola serves the other end of town and both are linked with a frequent bus service. Every Friday there is a big party at the top of the gondola with bands playing. **Rettenbach** also hosts the Hannibal outdoor musical in April which is a re-enactment of his mission to cross the Alps with an elephant, incorporating 500 actors, a 20 metre snow pyramid, lasers and fireworks. At the bottom of the piste there is the **Salomon station** with a really cool bar upstairs.

FREERIDERS. The **Gaislakogel** mountain is quite limited in terms of high altitude pistes, but there is a large area of off-piste right underneath the gondola in the **Wasserkar valley**. However, this is avalanche prone, so check the risk level before you shred it. There are also routes off the side of this peak down to the **Ski Route**, but it is easy to end up at the top of some very big cliffs so it is advisable to go with a guide ! Off piste under the **Giggijoch** gondola through trees, come to road, walk for 20 minutes, or you can stop short and join back to the piste at the *Sonnblick bar* and drink a beer before descending. On the way to the glacier from the Giggijoch, be sure to try the **Schwartzseekogl** and make some tracks in the powder on either side. It can be a great run as it is steep and fast but look out for rocks. There is also a large mountain restaurant at the bottom of the run which gets the sun on its huge terrace all afternoon. The red run on the **Rettenbach Glacier** is used every year for the opening event of the World Cup Skiing Championship. At the top it is quite steep, which makes it a great place to duck the ropes for overhead powder

3250M
TOP LIFT

1900M
VERTICAL

1350M
FIRST LIFT

EASY
INT
ADV
16%

147KM
PISTES

32%
52%

Winter Period:
Dec to End April
Summer Period:
June to Oct
Lift Passes
Half-day 30.5 euros
Day pass 39.5, 6 Days 193.5
Season pass 501 euros
1 Day (summer) 35.5 euros
Board Schools
various board schools in town.
Schischule Sölden, Yellow
Power,Aktiv, Vacancia all run english
speaking group and private lessons
for all abilities.
Night Boarding
Wednesday evenings theres a night
ski show and night skiing on the
4km no.10 run

Solden Tourism
Otztal Arean, Postfach 80
Solden A-6450. Tirol
General info: +43 (0) 5254 2120
Web: www.soelden.com
Email: info@soelden.com

Longest Run:
12.8km
Total Lifts: 34
7 Gondolas, 19
chairs, 8 drags
Lift times:
9am to 4.00pm
Mountain Cafes:
20

Annual Snowfall:
5m
Snowmaking:
27% of slopes

POOR FAIR GOOD TOP

FREERIDE
Trees and awesome off-piste
FREESTYLE
Plenty of natural hits
PISTE MERCHANTS
Wide & some testing slopes

Best resort in Austria, but very snobby

10
OUT OF 10

A

A U S T R I A

Pic: James Woodward

Those who know about where to ride would have to agree that **St Anton** has the best terrain in Austria, making this place an absolute must. This is a resort that has it all and will suit all styles of riding, though favouring freeriders the most. Whether you're a freestyle freak, a piste carving poser, a freeride speed king or simply a nappy-wearing new kid, you will love this place.

The area does have the reputation for being expensive and attracting the fur-clad, Ferrari-owning skiers, but whilst they sip pink gins in mountain bars, snowboarders can roam freely over miles of excellent terrain. With steeps, deep powder, air, and trees on all sides of the mountain slopes, it's hard to beat. The **Arlberg ski pass** allows you to ride the linked areas of **St Christoph** and **Stuben**, and via bus the resorts **Lech** and **Zürs** which all offer great snowboarding terrain, with amazing amounts of powder.

FREERIDERS
Freeriders are best suited to St Anton as it's the perfect playground, with a little of everything: steeps, powder, trees and big drop offs. Riders who know what they're doing should worm their way up to Kapall where they'll find loads of great freeriding terrain, with good natural hits. Alternatively, head to the summit of **Valluga Grat** via the Galzig cable car to reach some major off-piste, with long runs back down to St Anton and St Christoph. Intermediates just getting it together will find loads to ride, especially on **Gampen** and **Kapall**. The runs on Galzig are easier, but tend to get busy with skiers. Advanced riders will love **Rendl**, a separate mountain on the opposite side of St Anton across to the Gampen runs. Whenever there's a fresh dump, expect to find the locals and ski-bums cramming into Rendlbahn for first tracks. This area is absolutely amazing for full-on freeriding terrain with tight and open trees and

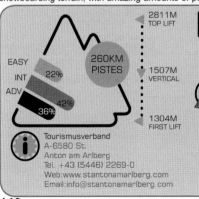

EASY
INT   22%
ADV
36%   42%

260KM
PISTES

2811M
TOP LIFT

1507M
VERTICAL

1304M
FIRST LIFT

Number of runs: 134
Longest run: 10.2km
Total Lifts: 83
10 Gondolas, 36 chairs, 37 drags
Lift times:
8.30am to 4.00pm

Winter Period:
Dec to April
Lift Passes
1/2 day 30 euros
1 Day pass 39.5 euros
6 Day pass 189 euros
Season pass 650 euros
Board School
4hr group lesson 53 euros
Private 4hr lesson 209 euros
Hire
Board & Boots around 35 euros a day

Annual Snowfall:
7m
Snowmaking:
30%

NEW New for 05/06 season:
the slow 3-man chair from Alpe Rauz to Ulmerhütte (run 17) being replaced by 6-person chair. Some improvement in snow making facilities.

Tourismusverband
A-6580 St.
Anton am Arlberg
Tel. +43 (5446) 2269-0
Web: www.stantonamarlberg.com
Email: info@stantonamarlberg.com

crowd-free slopes.

Within a few days of a good dump, you'll be amazed to find much of the off-piste area to be completely tracked out. This is a serious Freeriders resort, with the right conditions and definitely with a guide, its possible to board from the top of the **Valluga** into **Zürs**, and off the back of **Rendl** from the top of the **Riffelscharte**, but do not underestimate the risks.

FREESTYLERS spending a month or two here will never find every natural hit - the resort is simply littered with great take off points and drop ins. Theres a good area running parallel to run 17 to St.Christoph that's packed with drops offs and several natural half-pipes. It's a great freestyler's place, but lovers of man made obstacles will be disappointed. The park at **Rendl** feels cramped, but has some large kickers and rails. A better park and a half-pipe is located in **Lech**.

PISTES.Everynight the pistes are bashed to perfection, but the mass of skiers make sure they're moguled by the end of the day. The variety of pistes is fantastic; from the Mach 5 runs down from the **Valluga** to the gentle runs off the **Gampen** and **Galzig**. Fast carvers will enjoy the black **Kandahar** run down from the Galzig, and beginners will love the pitch of run 5.

BEGINNERS with a little adventure will be able to handle St Anton, but wimps may have trouble if they stray too far from the easy runs. A learner's slope at Nasserein provides a good starting point for a number of easy blue trails. Runs 4 & 5 from the Galzig are great for beginners, but theres a few flat bits at the bottom of run 4; stick your thumb out and try and hitch a pole from the passing skiers. If you're after lessons then its worth hunting around to find a specialist boarding instructor.

THE TOWN
St Anton is without doubt one of Europe's most prestigious resorts with a reputation for attracting the rich and famous. Unlike nearby Lech though, the snobbery of the place won't prevent you from enjoying yourself off the slopes, but you'll need a big fat wallet to get the most out of the place. Theres plenty of fancy shops, but luckily also some supermarkets, banks, internet cafes and numerous other sporting facilities.

ACCOMMODATION. There's plenty of lodging but nothing's cheap and anyone on a low budget will find it hard going. B&B's are available in the hamlets of Bach, St Jakob and Nasserein, all are less expensive than St Anton, there's also a free regular ski-bus linking them and taxi to the outskirts shouldn't cost more than 10€

AUSTRIA

FOOD. As you would expect there are some seriously expensive places to eat, but look around and you'll find places for mortals as well. The **Funky Chicken** is reasonable, **Pizzeria Pomodora** as well as serving excellent cheap food, is the only place that'll let you in after 8pm with your board boots on. There's a serious lack of late night takeways around, so make a bee line for **Snack-attack** on the main high street which is the only take-away open until 2am

NIGHT-LIFE is lively. You can kick off the evenings entertainment descending on run 1 (the Zammermoos). The **Krazy Kangaroo** is the first stop, as the name suggests its an Ozzy bar and always loud and rammed with boarders. Next door is the more chilled **Taps**, then take the slope further down and you'll find the rammed **Mooserwirt** don't forget you've still got a kilometre or so before you can take your board off. Back into town and **Piccadilly**, and the **Post-Keller** are good options, the **Kandahar's** open till 6am. **Bar Cuba** is a little soulless, **Funky Chicken's** okay as long as the bar staff don't catch you on the tables. For a chilled beer and a chat, the small and friendly **Bar 37** makes a pleasant change.

FLY
to Innsbruck International, transfer time to resort is 1 1/2 hours (100km). Friedrichshafen 140km, Munich 250km, Zurich 200km

BUS
from Innsbruck go direct to St Anton with daily return services from Innsbruck. A service runs from Friedrichshafen to St.Anton visit www.airport-bus.at for more details

TRAIN
various express trains direct to St Anton center, including the Orient Express

CAR
From Innsbruck take A12 motorway for 70km take Landeck (E60) turnoff for 15km, picking up the B197 straight to St Anton. Drive time is about 1 1/4 hours, 100km total

	POOR	FAIR	GOOD	TOP
FREERIDE Trees but no decent off-piste				
FREESTYLE A park & pipe				
PISTE MERCHANTS Some good trails to burn				

7 OUT OF 10

Pic -St.Johan Tourism

A AUSTRIA

periods and from mid January through to the end of March. Although this is not a high altitude resort, St Johann can still boast a decent annual snow record of over 780cm a season and should the real stuff not fall, the resort has snowmaking facilities that cover over 47% of the marked out slopes. In terms of terrain, an advanced rider will have this place licked within a matter of two days, intermediates four days while beginners will enjoy a full week exploring the slopes, which are collection of reds, a handful of blacks and a load of easy blues. Still slope facilities are very good and the unusually for a place of this size, there are some 15 mountain cafes and bars. Another plus side for St Johann is that this is a cheap resort and very affordable resort.

FREERIDERS, if you are a basic intermediate freerider then this mountain will suit you and should provided you wil a number of intresting options that should easily take a week to muster. The best thing for advanced riders to do is check out the offerings at the nearby resorts of **Kitzbuhel** or **Saalbach-Hinterglem**.

FREESTYLERS have fairly decent halfpipe and terrain park to play in. Whilst around the slopes riders will be able to find plenty of good natural hits to get air from. But by any stretch of the imagination this is not an adventrious freestylers place.

PISTES. There are a number of well pisted trails on which some fast carving can be had.

BEGINNERS who holiday with their parents and don't plan to do a lot of riding in their lives will love this place as its perfect for novices.

THE TOWN
Around the town you will find lots of hotels, Pensions (B&B's) and other local services close to the slopes and at affordable prices. **Nightlife** options are excellent with a good choice of bars and restaurants to choose from.

St Johann in Tirol is **Austrian** through and through, read any one of the numerous ski guides and see how this place is often described as 'quaint, charming, traditional, lovely and picturesque. And while these points are true, the important factor is, what has this traditional village to offer visiting snowboarders?. Well St Johann has some 60km of well groomed and well marked out pistes to ride serviced by a modern lift system comprising of 3 gondolas, 4 chair lifts and 10 drag lifts. The **Schneewinkel** lift pass gives you access to 170km of pistes around the local area, including the resorts of **Oberndorf** and **Fieberbrunn** but they are only connected via ski-bus.

An important point to note about St Johann is that this is a very popular resort with a large number of British and German visitors. The resort is usually buzzing through the winter months especially over the Christmas and new year

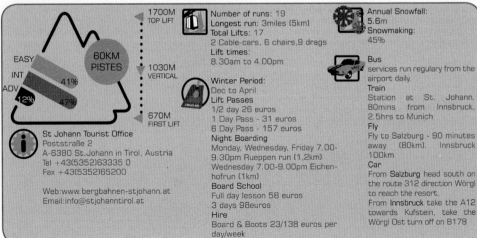

EASY
INT 41%
ADV 12% 47%

60KM PISTES

1700M TOP LIFT

1030M VERTICAL

670M FIRST LIFT

St Johann Tourist Office
Poststraße 2
A-6380 St.Johann in Tirol, Austria
Tel +43(5352)63335 0
Fax +43(5352)65200

Web:www.bergbahnen-stjohann.at
Email:info@stjohanntirol.at

Number of runs: 19
Longest run: 3miles (5km)
Total Lifts: 17
2 Cable-cars, 6 chairs,9 drags
Lift times:
8.30am to 4.00pm

Winter Period:
Dec to April
Lift Passes
1/2 day 26 euros
1 Day Pass - 31 euros
6 Day Pass - 157 euros
Night Boarding
Monday, Wednesday, Friday 7.00-
9.30pm Rueppen run (1,2km)
Wednesday 7.00-9.00pm Eichen-
hofrun (1km)
Board School
Full day lesson 58 euros
3 days 98euros
Hire
Board & Boots 23/138 euros per
day/week

Annual Snowfall:
5.6m
Snowmaking:
45%

Bus
services run regulary from the airport daily.
Train
Station at St. Johann. 80mins from Innsbruck, 2.5hrs to Munich
Fly
Fly to Salzburg - 90 minutes away (80km). Innsbruck 100km
Car
From **Salzburg** head south on the route 312 direction Wörgl to reach the resort.
From **Innsbruck** take the A12 towards Kufstein, take the Wörgl Ost turn off on B178

WSG STUBAI GLACIER

A couple of trees and limited off-piste

Good open flat runs, but weekend crowds

	POOR	FAIR	GOOD	TOP
FREERIDE				
A couple of trees and limited off-piste				
FREESTYLE				
Small park & occasional pipe				
PISTES				
Motorways				

7 OUT OF 10

A
U
S
T
R
I
A

FREERIDERS will find an abundance of trails to ride, but none of them are too demanding and lack a bit of variety. The 4 black runs on offer are pretty short, but trail 8 should keep you on your toes. The majority of the resort is above tree level, the only trees are below the **Mittelstation**, just watch out for crevaces and avalanches. From the gondolas you should be able to pick a few nice decents and drops without hiking. The **Wilde Grubn** is a 10k run back to the base, its not always properly marked so make sure you know where you're heading.

FREESTYLERS have a park & halfpipe but its not particularly well maintained and a little hit and miss. You'll find some natural hits over the place though.

Stubai Glacier is the biggest resort under the Innsbruck area. It's also the only **Innsbruck** resort that has summer snowboarding. Stubai is a great mountain to try and offers the chance to ride fast on wide, open runs that are well groomed and serviced by a set of efficient, modern lifts. The only drawbacks are that, being a high glacier resort, it can be stupidly cold in the winter where the temperature can make it almost impossible to ride, and there's very little tree cover. The other problem is that because Stubai nearly always guarantees snow when lower areas are short on the stuff, the masses head here, making the place very busy, especially at weekends. Munich is only two and a half hours away and so the place also gets a regular German overload. Access to the slopes involves a twenty minute cable car ride, but once up, you're presented with a great selection of runs. There's 2 rental & service centres at the top of the eisgrat and gamsgarten gondolas, they promise a 20 minute service while you take a beer.

PISTES. The management take great care in preparing the slopes; they don't just piste bash at night, but throughout the day, so there's plenty of opportunity to cut the corduroy. There's plenty of nice wide, well maintained pistes available.

BEGINNERS are well taken care of with a number of perfectly well-appointed, easy, flat blue runs. But watch out for the drag lifts. For the tots and the seriously bad, they've added a number of magic carpet lifts, and they're even covered.

THE TOWN

Theres many small villages on the road to Stubai, the main one of note being **Neusift**, a 20 minute drive from the glacier. There you'll find a good selection of hotels and pensions, some bars and restaurants. Probably the best place to stay is in Innsbruck, although it takes about an hour by car to get there.

EASY
INT
ADV 23% 54%
23%

110KM PISTES

3200M TOP LIFT

1500M VERTICAL

1721M FIRST LIFT

Number of Runs: 22
Longest Run: 10km
Total Lifts: 19
5 Gondolas, 8 chairs,9 drags,3 Magic carpets
Lift times:
8.00am to 4.45pm

Winter Period:
Dec to April
Summer Period:
May to Nov
Lift Passes
Half-day pass 28.5 euros
1 Day pass - 35 euros
6 Day pass - 178 euros
Summer day 27.8 euros
Board Schools:
1 day 60 euros,4 days 139 euros
Rental:
board & boots 24-37 euros for 1 day

Annual Snowfall:
Unknown
Snowmaking:
10% of slopes

Train
The nearest train station is Innsbruck.
Fly
to Innsbruck airport, 40 mins away.
Car
Drive Via Innsbruck, head south on the A13 toll road until the Staubi turn off at Mieders. Then head up the B183 to Staubi.
Bus
Free buses daily between Schönberg & Stubai

NEW 05/06:
new 2-seater chair replaces t-bar on Schaufelspitz-peak

i Staubi Gletsvherbahn
A-6167 Neustiff im Stubaital
Tel. +43 (0) 52 26 81 41

Web:www.stubai-gletscher.com
Email:info@stubai-gletscher.com

149

WILDSCHONA VALLEY

FREERIDE
Scattered trees & bit off-piste
FREESTYLE
A park & pipe
PISTE MERCHANTS
Short, quiet easy slopes

Beginner and intermediate area

6
OUT OF 10

A
U
S
T
R
I
A

Pic -Wildschona Tourism

One point to note about Auffach is that 99% of the lifts are drag lifts, so be warned novices.

The Wildschonau Valley, which is located in the **Kitzbuheler Alps**, is home to a number of tiny and traditional Austrian resorts. **Niederau, Oberau, Thierbach** and **Auffach** may all seem on the surface to be to small to bother with, but first impressions are often deceptive. Okay none of the resorts that make up this part of the **Tirol** are extensive or in any way adventurous. However, what this collection of novice and intermediate mountain retreats do provide, is an area that's relaxed, void of any crowds, very laid back and with out any of the hustle and bustle of the bigger and more popular destinations favoured by the tour operators and ski crowds. This collection of resorts would be idea for a family group on a weeks holiday, but would not appeal to hard-core riders in terms of the mountain or larger louts looking for an action packed resort bustling with night life. The majority of visitors here are either cross country skiers or middle aged downhill skiers. But with most things, there's always something that will appeal to most and although there are only a couple of black graded runs, proficient riders will be able to take advantage of the reds that are open planed and free of crowds. No one queues up long around here, and although none of the resorts link up on the slopes, getting around them is easy.

AUFFACH is the larger of the four resorts with around 20km of marked piste set out on the **Schatzberg** mountain slopes. Auffach offers the highest altitude riding in the area with a nice series of red runs set out over a wide open plateau. This is also the home to the areas main halfpipe and fun park, which are located up on the upper regions.

NIEDERAU is the second largest with just 14km of piste and is the first resort you come to along the valley floor. The slopes have one black run and some okay reds and all in all this place can be ridden with ease in day.

OBERAU is basically a place for total beginners with only 10km of piste and just 8 runs. There is simply nothing here for intermediates of advanced riders to really try out.

THIERBACH is much the same as Oberau, and really only of interest to first time skiing grannies and grand dads. Even novices may even have this place licked after a few hours.

THE TOWN
Off the slopes you are presented with typical Tyrolean hospitality. All the resorts have accommodation close to slopes and offer good quality hotels, chalets, farm accommodation and pensions. Everything about this area is laid back and basic, so don't expect a large amount of facilities. There are a few restaurants, but night life is extremely tame, although still very good and affordable.

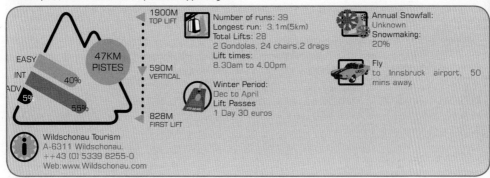

EASY
INT
ADV 5%
40%
55%

47KM
PISTES

1900M
TOP LIFT

590M
VERTICAL

828M
FIRST LIFT

Number of runs: 39
Longest run: 3.1m(5km)
Total Lifts: 28
2 Gondolas, 24 chairs,2 drags
Lift times:
8.30am to 4.00pm

Winter Period:
Dec to April
Lift Passes
1 Day 30 euros

Annual Snowfall:
Unknown
Snowmaking:
20%

Fly
to Innsbruck airport, 50 mins away.

Wildschonau Tourism
A-6311 Wildschonau.
++43 (0) 5339 8255-0
Web:www.Wildschonau.com

150

	POOR	FAIR	GOOD	TOP
FREERIDE Trees but limited off-piste				
FREESTYLE Park & Pipe				
PISTES Good untaxing slopes				

Not a bad resort but too busy

6 OUT OF 10

Pic -Ride Snowboards

A

A U S T R I A

cool runs down the **Sonnkogel**. If you are looking for deep powder and open bowl riding, then head on up to the glacier at **Kaprun**.

FREESTYLERS can choose to ride the pipe and park at Zell or try out the same at Kaprun, which has a pipe all year round. Around Zell locals often build their own hits but if you can't be bothered, you will be able to find lots of stuff to fly from.

PISTES. Riders have an ordinary mountain to cut up with plenty of well groomed trails to try out, more so at Zell than at Kaprun.

BEGINNERS have lots of nursery areas as well as spots that allow for easy progression making this a good novice resorts.

THE TOWN

Zell am See is a busy village with a lot going on and plenty of accommodation at all price ranges. The village is a lively one and as well as having loads of restaurants, mainly hotel ones. **Night- life** here is also quite good with some okay bars to check out. , including the *Resi Dutch bar*, and the friendly *Crazy Daisy's*

Zell am See is located close to a large lake and not far from the glacier resort of **Kaprun**. Zell offers over 130km of marked out piste, much of which is treelined. A third of the runs are covered by snowmaking facilities, which is a good thing, as this resort doesn't have the greatest annual snow record. This resort has long been popular with snowboarders in Austria and has always been welcoming. The management do frown when it comes to riding in the trees, as you are not allowed to snowboard through the wooded sections. In general this is a pretty good snowboarders resort with the added advantage of a glacier at Kaprun 30 mins down the road should the snow here turn out to be crap or you simply fancy a change. Zell's main disadvantage is its own popularity as it's high on tour operators lists and therefore very crowded. Each Saturday the resort sees a fresh intake of thousands of tour plankers in their new holiday clothes ready to make a mess of the overnight grooming of the pistes. Whatever level of a rider you are or whatever style of riding you do, this place will give you the opportunity to practice your skills, and most people will be able to make a 5 day trip well worthwhile

FREERIDERS have a varying selection of runs to choose from. Advanced riders may want to take the cable car up to the **Berghotel** where you will be able to gain access to a couple of good steep sections. There are also a number of

Zell am See

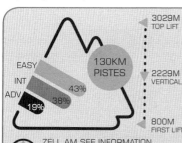

3029M TOP LIFT	Number of runs: 59 Longest run: 8km Total Lifts: 57 11 Gondolas, 1 cable-cars, 15 chairs,30 drags Capacity (people/hour): 79,268 Lift times: 8.30am to 4.00pm	Annual Snowfall: 10m Snowmaking: 30% of slopes
130KM PISTES		
EASY INT ADV 43% 38% 19%	2229M VERTICAL	Train Station at Zell an See Fly Fly to Salzburg - 1 1/2 hours away (80km). Munich 180km
	800M FIRST LIFT	Winter Period: Dec to April Summer Period: May to Oct (Kaprun) Lift Passes 1 Day pass 34.50 euros 6 Days 181 euros Board School 1 day 50 euros, 3 days 120 euros	Car from Salzburg head south on the A10 to exit 46. Then head south west along the 168 via Taxenbach

 ZELL AM SEE INFORMATION
Brucker Bundesstrasse 1a,
A-5700 Zell am See
Telephone: +43/6542/770-0
Fax: +43/6542/72032
web: www.zellamsee.com
Email:welcome@europasportregion.info

Okay beginners & intermediates area

7
OUT OF 10

POOR FAIR GOOD TOP

FREERIDE
Some trees & off-piste
FREESTYLE
2 parks & 2pipes nearby
PISTE MERCHANTS
Some good varied trails

A

A U S T R I A

Pic Zell Tourism

FREERIDERS can spend a week here and still not ride half of what is available through out the Zillertal Arena. With much of the terrain best suited to intermediates, what freeriders can achieve is a fun easy time that will allow them to explore some cool off-piste areas that on occasions has some deep powder stashes. You will also be able to shred down some decent gullies and through some open tree sections. The **Krimml Express** chair gives access to a really cool long red trail that can be ridden either back to **Zell** or down into the connecting resort of **Gerlos.**

FREESTYLERS are best provided with facilities at **Gerlos** under the name of **'Boarders Town'**. **Gerlos** has a good large fun park which is packed with various jumps, spines, waves and 100m half-pipe pipe draggon shaped halfpipe . In **Krimml**, a fair distance along from Zell, theres a 700m park with numereous toys and a 80m halfpipe.

Zell im Zillertal is situated in the spectacular **Zell Valley** which is a mere 40 miles from **Innsbruck.** What you have here is a traditional Austrian village set out over the valley floor with ridable slopes that rise to a respectable high point of 2480m. Zell am Ziller forms part of what is known as the **Zillertal Arena** which along with resorts such as **Gerlos, Krimml** and **Konigsleiten/Wald** offers some 215km of terrain, and although the 65 plus lifts are not all linked on the slopes, they are linked by a single lift ticket which costs from E120 for 5 days. All the resorts that form part of the arena have something different to offer but in general this area can best be described as suiting intermediate freeriders and piste loving carvers. Zell and its neighbouring resorts are all well designed and spread out giving a nice sense of open space but note, this open space attracts quite a lot of weekend skiers, although in general lift lines are not very big apart from the early morning first gondola ride up from the village. Zell's terrain is spread out above the tree line offering some wide open runs and some nice off-piste powder areas. Most of the upper runs are graded red, but some of them are a bit over rated and there's not a great deal for expert riders to ride down.

PISTES. Carvers have mountain that should keep then happy for the duration of their stay be it a week or two. The pistes are well maintained and there are some nice long trails.

BEGINNERS are the ones who should appreciate this area the most because this is a first class beginners resort and any novice spending a week here will leave a competent intermediate rider.

THE TOWN
Off the slopes Zell has good local services with affordable accommodation, shops, restaurants, a post office and sporting facilities all next to the slopes. Nightlife is very quiet but there is a disco should you want to strut your stuff.

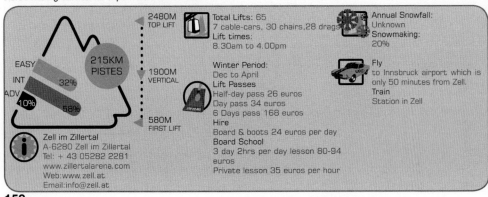

2480M
TOP LIFT

1900M
VERTICAL

580M
FIRST LIFT

EASY
INT
ADV

215KM PISTES

32%
10%
58%

Total Lifts: 65
7 cable-cars, 30 chairs,28 drags
Lift times:
8.30am to 4.00pm

Winter Period:
Dec to April
Lift Passes
Half-day pass 26 euros
Day pass 34 euros
6 Days pass 168 euros
Hire
Board & boots 24 euros per day
Board School
3 day 2hrs per day lesson 80-94 euros
Private lesson 35 euros per hour

Annual Snowfall:
Unknown
Snowmaking:
20%

Fly
to Innsbruck airport which is only 50 minutes from Zell.
Train
Station in Zell

i Zell im Zillertal
A-6280 Zell im Zillertal
Tel: + 43 05282 2281
www.zillertalarena.com
Web:www.zell.at
Email:info@zell.at

POOR FAIR GOOD TOP

FREERIDE
Awesome off-piste
FREESTYLE
Park & Pipe in nearby Lech
PISTES
Good untaxing slopes

8
OUT OF 10

Great freeriding resort

Pic Lech/Zurs Tourism

A

A
U
S
T
R
I
A

There are so many ways down that there aren't really any no-go areas; just be careful and pay attention to the avalanche warnings. Alternatively, the other side of the valley which makes up the resort, has plenty of long, steep pistes, gullies and chutes - take a piste map with you.

FREESTYLERS would do well to check out the pipe and park area on Lech's slopes. However, Zürs has a lot of good natural terrain for grabbing big air. There are loads of cliff drops of various sizes, and plenty of banked walls to pull off tricks.

PISTES. The marked-out slopes are groomed to perfection, and perfect corduroy tracks are left just waiting to be sliced up at Mach 6.

Who knows or cares what Zürs means in Austrian; what we can tell you is that in plain English, Zürs stands for super-sad, super-rich, super ponces, and the worst level of stuck-up skiers known to man. This relatively small resort is in the same locality as that other fur-dripping hangout, **Lech**. However, on a more positive side, the slopes are surprisingly free of champagne-drinking 'wa wa's', which means that riders can roam freely over some excellent slopes. Zürs is without doubt, one of Austria's most spectacular resorts and could rival any in Europe when it comes to the type of terrain it has to offer. Its diverse and interesting slopes make it a great place to snowboard, offering powder fields and miles of pistes

FREERIDERS will literally be able to pick a line as they travel on a chair lift over vast areas of untracked mountain. You're never far away from marked areas and the lifts, so no hiking is involved with this side of the mountain.

BEGINNERS
Although Zürs is primarily an intermediate/advanced freeriding area, some of the lower slopes offer perfect conditions for learning. The lifts are slow, but redeemed by the generally patient and friendly lift attendants (yes, they do exist!).

THE TOWN
Lodging, eating and drinking in **Zürs** is classicly Austrian, and will burn a big hole in your wallet. You can stay out of Zürs in neighbouring villages that are far cheaper and have a better local feel to them, offering a more relaxed atmosphere. In Zürs, the streets are littered with poodle-carrying idiots in search of posh hangouts, but you'll be surprised at how many snowboarders you'll come across, so don't be too put off by the hideous reputation. Zürs is definitely worth a visit.

EASY
INT
ADV
110KM PISTES
40%
40%
20%

2444M
TOP LIFT

994M
VERTICAL

1450M
FIRST LIFT

Office Zürs
6763 Zürs
Tel: +43 (0)5583 2245
Fax: +43 (0)5583 2982

Web:www.lech-zuers.at
Email:info@lech-zuers.at

Number of Runs: 32
Longest Run: 5km
Total Lifts: 32
4 Gondolas, 18 chairs,10 drags
Capacity (people/hour):
44,668
Lift times:
8.30am to 4.00pm

Winter Period:
Dec to April
Lift Passes
Half-day 30 euros
Day pass 39.5 euros
6 Days 189
Season 650
Heliboarding
take-off from Kriegerhorn / Oberlech and from Flexen-pass (Zürs) to two peaks: Mehlsack, Orgelscharte

Annual Snowfall:
2.6m
Snowmaking:
10% of slopes

Train
station Langen am Arlberg 17 km away, also one at St.Anton 20 minutes away.
Fly
to Innsbruck (110km), 2hrs transfer: Friedrichshafen, 120km. Altenrhein, 100km. Zurich, 200km. For about 2000 euros, you can get a helicopter from Zurich
Car
via Innsbruck, head west on the A12 to Landeck then take the 316 via St Anton to reach Lech
Bus
Regular services from Langen station. Bus service from Zurich airport 10am,12:30,18:30 fri-sun (75 euros return) with Arlberg Express

153

A

A
U
S
T
R
I
A

BAD HOFGASTEIN

Bad Hofgastein is located centrally in the Salzburg region, and forms part of one of Austria's largest rideable areas. Intermediate carvers are well suited to these slopes, with a nice long seven mile run to practice some wide carves. Total beginners will love it, and its not bad for freestylers with a good pipe. There is plenty of slopeside lodging and good local services

BAD MITTENDORF

Bad Mittendorf is a spa town that likes to shroud itself in strange old tales. What isn't fiction is that this is not the greatest of snowboard destinations. The 15 miles of piste rarely allows an adrenalin rush, although there are a couple of okay black trails and the odd red that's worth a look. Crap for freestylers but perfect for beginners.
Off the slopes you will find simple and affordable slopeside accommodation and services.

Ride Area: 16miles of pistes
Total Lifts: 20

IGLS

Igls is perched high above Innsbruck, 3 miles from the city centre. There's nothing here, especially for competent riders. This is a beginner's area with half a dozen trails easily accessed by a cable car.

Ride Area: 120miles
Easy 20%
Intermediate 50%
Advanced 30%
Top Lift: 2247m
Total Lifts: 35
Contact:
Iglis Tourist Office
Hilberstra'e 15
Postfach Igls, PLZ 6080
A-6080 Igls, Austria
Tel: ++43 512 377101
Fax: ++43 512 3771017

KAUNERTAL

Kaunertal is a glacial resort open all year round. Overall, the terrain is great for novices but a bit dull for advanced riders. What you get is a mixture of easy freeriding with powder areas and excellent carving terrain. Freestylers

have one of the most perfectly shaped halfpipes on the planet.

Lodging and local services can be found at Feichten, 16 miles down the valley, so a car is a must
Ride Area: 12miles
Easy 20%
Intermediate 50%
Advanced 30%
Top Lift: 3160m
Total Lifts: 7
Contact:
Kaunertal-Kauns-Kaunerberg tourist information office
Feichten 134
A-6524 Kaunertal,Austria
Tel: +43 5475 2920
Fax: +43 5475 2929

KUHTAI

At 2020m Kühtai is Austria highest resort town, and as such its open from December to May
Ride area: 35km of pistes
Number runs: 20
Easy 22% Intermediate 68% Advanced 10%
Top Lift: 2520m **Bottom Lift:** 2020m **Vert:** 500m
Total Lifts:12 - 4 chairs, 7 drags, 1 magic carpets
Lift pass:Day pass 27 euros
Half-day 24.5 euros
6 Days 142 euros
Night boarding 9 euros
Night Boarding: Wednesday & Saturdays 7:30 till 10pm. The Hochalter 4-seater chairlift is open
Contact: Tourismusbüro Kühtai
A-6183 Kühtai, Tirol
Tel. 0 5239 5222
Fax 0 5239 5255
www.schneegarantie.at
How to get there: From Innsbruck head towards Bregenz, take the exit Kematen-Sellrain, and drive for another 25km. If you end up in Oetz, you've gone too far

MUTTERS

Mutters is a small rideable area nestled between Innsbruck and Axamer Lizum. But this is no match for Axams, which can be reached with a backcountry hike. There are only a few runs, mainly suited to beginners and intermediates. Mutters attracts a lot of cross-country skiers. Great local facilities in Innsbruck, 20 mins.

Ride Area: 6miles
Top Lift: 1800m

Total Lifts: 8
Contact:
Mutters Tourist Board
Kirchplatz 11
A-6162 Mutters,
Austria
Tel: +43 512 548410
Fax: +43 512 5484107

OBERTAUREN

Just when you thought that Austria was all the same, along comes Obertauren, noted for its excellent snow records. Obertauern is also a freeride Mecca, attracting many early local risers after a dump of snow, with lots of areas to check. Advanced riders have plenty of good, testing blacks where **carvers** can leave some nice lines. Atomic Snowboards sponsor the Longplay terrain park (www.longplaypark.com) . A huge park offering plenty for beginners to intermediates.
Excellent lodging and local facilities are at the base of the slopes.Its also home to a large Blue Tomato test centre and school

Contact:
Obertauern Tourist Board
A-5562
Obertauern,
Austria
Tel: ++ 43/6456/7252 or 7320
Fax: ++ 43/6456/7515
www.obertauern.com
Getting there:
Fly to: Salzburg - 1 1/4 hours away

SCHRUNS

Schruns is a tiny resort close to the Swiss boarder. The slopes make for an okay one day visit if you can ride or a week if you can't. The place only has one noted black trail but it also has a long 8 mile run which will keep an intermediate **freerider** happy. Great place for **begiunners** but crap for freestylers.
Very basic but good local facilities at the base of the slopes.

Ride Area: 13miles
Top Lift: 2400m
Total Lifts: 13
Contact:
Tel - ++43 (0) 556 721 660
Fax - 0043 (0)5556/72554
Getting there:
Fly to: Innsbruck - 2 hours away

SCHLICK 2000

Schlick 2000 is an area which is unknown to many apart from the local boys. Schlick is found just a short drive from Innsbruck on the valley to Stubai Glacier. So why the secret! Its simple it's a large bowl which attracts lots of powder and keeps the weather out, when the rest are closed. The area isn't great in size but you'll have lots of fun. Schlick isn't an area you'll head for a holiday; a day is more than enough

Freeriding. The best free ride terrain is under the chair lift.

It nice an open at the start then you hit the trees and take in the small rock drops. While you are having your fun the mobile audience are cheering you on. Once finished its back on the chair ready for the next run
Freestylers. Has a fun park but it isn't on the top of the lift companies priorities
Beginners. the terrain isn't too taxing but don't expect a nursery slope once you jump from the gondola. I'm afraid it's a bit of a hike to a suitable area. The bottom of the chair lift is idea but is a long hike.
The town. the village at the base Fulmples is small but does have a few bars and restaurants. Staying in Neustift or Innsbruck would be a wise choice

Number runs: 9
Easy 33% Intermediate 56% Advanced 11%
Total Lifts:10 - 2 Gondolas, 1 chairs, 7 drags
Lift pass:Day pass 28.7 euros
Half-day 20 euros
Contact: TSki center mud 2000
Village center
A-6166 Fulpmes/Stubaital
Tirol - Austria
Telephone +43 (0) 5225 62270
Fax +43 (0) 5225 64243
www.schlick2000.at

SERFUS

Serfus is a cool place with a decent mountain. Overall, the area provides good all-round snowboarding, no matter your style or standard. Well appointed and affordable local services.

Ride Area: 50miles
Top Lift: 1427m
Total Lifts: 21
Contact:
Serfus Tourist Board
Untere Dorfstra'e 13
A-6534 Serfaus,
Austria
Tel: +43 (0) 5476 / 62390
Fax: +43 (0) 5476 / 6813
Getting there:
Fly to: Zurich - 120 minutes away

ST WOLFGANG

St Wolfgang put simply, is not a good snowboarding resort. There is nothing much here, not even for beginners. Granny may manage a few turns, but others will soon tire of it. Freestylers do have a small park and pipe, but don't blink or you'll miss it. In truth, this is a family-orientated, beginner's ski resort. On the slopes theres lots of close by accommodation

Ride Area: 24km
Top Lift: 1600m
Bottom Lift: 1200m
Total Lifts: 9
Contact:
St Wolfgang Tourist Office
Postfach 20
A-5360 St. Wolfgang
Austria
Tel: +43 6138 2239

A

AUSTRIA

Fax: +43 6138 2239 81
Getting there:
Fly to: Salzburg - 45 minutes away

Westendorf

A WAGRAIN

As a base to reach any one of a dozen other ride areas, offering over 200 miles of linked cool, freeriding terrain, with a number of good parks and pipes, then this is a great place to be. Piste-hugging **carvers**, are also spoilt for choice here with dozens of well groomed trails. **Beginners** are spoilt for choice. **Off the slopes**, it's Austrian picture postcard stuff, but dull.

Top Lift: 2109m
Bottom Lift: 850m
Total Lifts: 9
Contact:
Bergbahnen AG Wagrain
Markt 59,
A-5602 Wagrain
Tel - ++43 6413 8238
Fax - ++43 6413 8238 11
Getting there:
Fly to: Salzburg - 60 minutes away

WALDRING

Waldring is a dull, geriatric heaven, and of interest only to those who are brain-dead. Its only saving grace is that the place is close to other resorts so you can at least escape the tedium of the place. Anyone planning more than an hour's stay here needs to see a shrink.
Local services consist of a few old people's homes and a morgue.

Ride Area: 16 miles
Top Lift: 1900m
Total Lifts: 12
Contact:
Ferienwohnungen & Komfortzimmer Mitterer
Pillerseestra_e 33
A-6384 Waidring
Tel: ++43 (0) 5353 5616
Getting there:
Fly to: Salzburg - 60 minutes away

WESTENDORF

Westendorf is all but the same as its nearby neighbours, Soll and Ellmau.7 There are a couple of black trails for advanced riders._ Unlike Ellmau, however, there is at least a decent halfpipe and park for air heads to try out. e Carvers also have a good choice of trails on which to practice the art of signing snow with an edge. There are a couple of black trails for **advanced** riders. Good **beginner's** areas.
Local services at the base of the slopes are cheap and cheerful.

Ride Area: 25 miles
Top Lift: 1865m
Total Lifts: 14
Contact:
Michaela Zass/Christl Beihammer
Pfarrgasse 1
PLZ A-6363
A-6363 Westendorf
Austria

Tel: +43 5334 6230
Fax: +43 5334 2390
Getting there:
Fly to: Salzburg - 120 minutes away

WINDISCHGARSTEN

Forget it totally. This place is crap

Ride Area: 4 runs
Getting there:
Fly to: Salzburg - 120 minutes away

ZAMS

Zams is a relatively unknown and small resort. There's a grand total of eight runs, all suited to beginners going backwards. The best thing to do is pass by and check out the **Kaunertal Glacier** which is far better. **Off the slopes** forget it, the place may be traditionally Austrian, but it is dull.

Ride Area: 26km
Runs: 16
Top Lift: 2212m
Bottom Lift: 780m
Total Lifts: 8
Easy 50%
Intermediate 40%
Advanced 10%
Contact:
Zams Tourist Board
Hauptplatz 6
A-6511 ZAMS
Tel - +43-(5442)633 95
Fax - +43-(5442)633 95 15
Getting there:
Fly to: Salzburg - 90 minutes away.

Bulgaria is ahead of its neighbours in attracting westerners to sample its winter hospitality with a number of resorts which provide a good and a far cheaper alternative to many of the resorts in the Western Europe. Travelling to Bulgaria should pose no real problems with international flights arriving at the capital of Sofia. Note for entering Bulgaria visitors from EU member countries don't need a visa Another point, forget about credit cards, although there are not widely accepted, you're better off with hard cash, US Dollars are the best currency for changing into Lev's. On the slopes, piste preparation is not hot and mountain facilities are primitive but prices are very low and the pistes are un-crowded. A number of tour operators offer package tours to Bulgaria with great budget deals available.

Freeriders will enjoy the unpredictable and uneven terrain features found in most rideable places but freestylers will be left a little disappointed if big pipes and man made terrain parks are your thing. Such things are almost none existent however lots of natural freestyle terrain is available along with some very big cliff jump areas.

The best way of travelling in Eastern Europe, is to hire a car or bring your own reliable vehicle. Always check with the national embassy to get the latest facts about travel in Bulgaria or any other part of Eastern Europe. Overall, resort's services are very basic with low key primitive accommodation, restaurants and amenities. Locals on the whole are very friendly and will look after you, especially if you flash a few dollars.

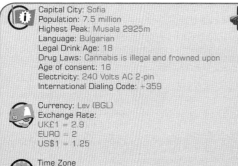

Capital City: Sofia
Population: 7.5 million
Highest Peak: Musala 2925m
Language: Bulgarian
Legal Drink Age: 18
Drug Laws: Cannabis is illegal and frowned upon
Age of consent: 16
Electricity: 240 Volts AC 2-pin
International Dialing Code: +359

Currency: Lev (BGL)
Exchange Rate:
UKE1 = 2.9
EURO = 2
US$1 = 1.25

Time Zone
UTC/GMT +2 hours
Daylight saving time: +1 hour

Driving Guide
All vehicles drive on the right hand side of the road
Speed limits:
60 kph - towns
80kph - main roads
120kph - motorways
Emergency
Police - 166
Fire - 160
Ambulance - 150
Tolls
All 4 lane motorways have tolls of 2 leva per km
Documentation
Driving license, insurance and vehicle registration, along with your passport.

Bulgaria Snowboard Federation
Sofia 1606
51 Skobelev blvd.
Phone / Fax: ++359 2 9522 015
Web: http://bgsf.dir.bg/dynamic.html
Email: bgsf@mail.orbitel.bg

	POOR	FAIR	GOOD	TOP
FREERIDE Few trees and no good off-piste				
FREESTYLE A half-pipe				
PISTES Variety but be patient				

Basic but cheap resort

5 OUT OF 10

B
BULGARIA

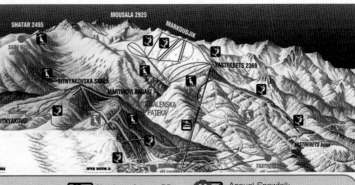

Pics -Bulgaria Tourism

Borovets is the best known of the Bulgarian Resorts, with a wide range of facilities on one of the highest rideable areas in Eastern Europe. Locals say that the season comes late in Borovets: mid-February often sees only half the runs open, but riders in the know say that April has the best snow. The terrain is mainly suited to intermediate carvers, with nothing too challenging for the experienced. The 23 miles of piste is split into three areas, offering open runs and lines through trees. Hard packed snow and ice frequently make the runs tough work and with small rocks sticking out when there's poor snow cover; a little vigilance is essential. Some of the best riding can be found on the runs above the 2500m point. The 6 person gondola ride to the top station takes about 25 minutes and to avoid queues avoid the period between 9am and 11am. A tip for those on a package trip is to buy your lift ticket before you arrive, it could save you $20.

FREERIDER'S favourite spot is an off-piste run down under the gondola pylons. The small cluster of trails off the Sitnyakovska chairlift are

ideal for intermediate riders but they are a bit short.
FREESTYLERS will be glad to know that it's not frowned upon if you want to build kickers. The Rotata halfpipe is located off the Martinovi Baraki 4 chairlift, there is a portable drag lift that sometimes services the area.

PISTES. Carvers will find enough wide areas to put in a few turns, but overall this is not a very good carving resort.

BEGINNERS have only one official blue marked run, but you should soon master some of the reds. Take note, the French designed lift system caters well for skiers, but it's not hot for novice boarders. The main problem is some of the lift take-offs are quick with deep rutted tracks that will throw you off with ease. One particular lift is so bad that it's not uncommon to see bodies dropping like flies.

THE TOWN
Borovets is a is a small place set around 1400 metres. The main hotels are the Rila, Samokov and the Olympic. Everything here is cheap. Evenings can be very boozy, with cheap beer available every where. It's worth noting that most places don't accept credit cards or travellers cheques. Food is basic, filling and mainly based on pork and chicken. Evenings are okay and go on until the early hours of the morning and with booze so cheap be prepared for serious drinking and wicked hangovers.

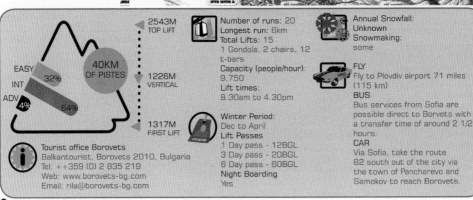

2543M TOP LIFT

1226M VERTICAL

1317M FIRST LIFT

EASY 32%
INT
ADV 4% 64%

40KM OF PISTES

Number of runs: 20
Longest run: 6km
Total Lifts: 15
1 Gondola, 2 chairs, 12 t-bars
Capacity (people/hour): 9,750
Lift times: 8.30am to 4.30pm

Winter Period:
Dec to April
Lift Passes
1 Day pass - 12BGL
3 Day pass - 20BGL
6 Day pass - 60BGL
Night Boarding
Yes

Annual Snowfall:
Unknown
Snowmaking:
some

FLY
Fly to Plovdiv airport 71 miles (115 km)
BUS
Bus services from Sofia are possible direct to Borvets with a transfer time of around 2 1/2 hours.
CAR
Via Sofia, take the route 82 south out of the city via the town of Pancharevo and Samokov to reach Borovets.

Tourist office Borovets
Balkantourist, Borovets 2010, Bulgaria
Tel: ++359 (0) 2 835 219
Web: www.borovets-bg.com
Email: rila@borovets-bg.com

	POOR	FAIR	GOOD	TOP
FREERIDE Trees and some off-piste				
FREESTYLE Occasional half-pipe				
PISTES Some good runs but rutted				

Small and basic

4
OUT OF 10

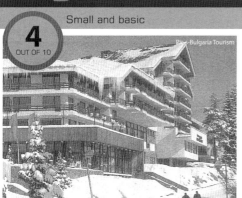

Pic - Bulgaria Tourism

Pamporovo is a small un-assuming resort that is set amongst the **Rhodope Mountains** which are located in the south of Bulgaria. This is also a resort that claims to be the sunniest in Europe and the home to the mythical singer 'Orpheus'. Pamporovo is only an hour or so away from Bulgaria's second city Plovdiv which makes this a popular destination for weekend city dwellers. The mild winters in this part of the country give rise to two distinctions, great sunny mountain but not always great snow capped slopes, due mainly to the weather patterns coming from the nearby Aegean sea. However when the mountain is covered in snow Pamporovo becomes the ideal place for beginners with a nice selection of easy slopes, along with a number okay trails to please intermediate riders. But this is not a resort for hard-core freestylers or riders of an advanced level, although fast carvers will find a number of cool runs to take at speed, notably the area of The Wall which is often used for major ski events. But the dominating feature at this the 500 ft giant TV tower and restaurant which sits on the summit of Snezhanka at 1926m.

FREERIDERS have a mountain that doesn't offer a great deal in terms of exciting or varied terrain if you like to ride hard and fast. But that said there are some tight trees to check out and a few natural uneven spots to hit.

FREESTYLERS who crave natural wind lips and big cliff jumps will be disappointed, however, the guys from the Smolyan snowboard club regularly build and maintain a decent halfpipe which measures over 100 metres.

PISTES. There's a couple of good carving runs to check out but note, piste grooming is not hot here, resulting in runs being left rutted and often uneven.

BEGINNERS are the ones who will like Pamporovo the most. The terrain is ideally suited to novices with a selection of easy to reach green and blue runs serviced by drag and chair lifts. Snowboard hire and instruction is available on the slopes.

B

BULGARIA

THE TOWN
Off the slopes Pamporovo is a purpose built but relaxed resort with a good level of resort facilities located close to the slopes. There is a shopping complex, hotel swimming pool, sauna, a number of bars and the odd disco all within easy reach of the slopes and all with a common theme, cheap. Every thing is affordable and booze is almost a give away. Around the resort there are a number of well appointed hotels offering cheap nightly room rates and good weekly packages. Hotels Perelik and Mourgavets are both popular place to stay and have pools, bars, restaurants and even a bowling alley. For those wanting self catering then the Malina Village is the place to stay with a number of well equipped chalets for hire.

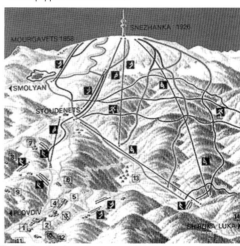

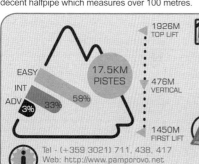

1926M TOP LIFT	Number of runs: 25 Longest run: 4km Total Lifts: 18 5 chairs, 13 drags Capacity (people/hour): 8,500 Lift times: 8.30am to 4.00pm	Annual Snowfall: 1.5m Snowmaking: unknown
17.5KM PISTES		
476M VERTICAL		FLY Fly to Plovdiv airport which is around 52 miles (83 km) away with a 2 hour transfer time. Sofia airport is 260km away. BUS Bus services from either Plovdiv or Sofia are possible.
EASY INT ADV 3% 33% 58%	Winter Period: Dec to April Heli Boarding No Hire/Board Schools Yes/Yes Night Boarding: No	
1450M FIRST LIFT		

Tel - (+359 3021) 711, 438, 417
Web: http://www.pamporovo.net
Email:info@pamporovo.net

159

ᴡꜱɢ VITOSHA

Okay for a few days

POOR FAIR GOOD TOP

FREERIDE
Few trees and a bit of off-piste
FREESTYLE
Bring a shovel
PISTES
Nothing too tricky

3
OUT OF 10

Pic - Bulgaria Tourism

Черни връх
2290

Стената

МОРЕНИ

ЩАСТЛИВЕЦА

ПРОСТОР

АГЛИКА

СОФИЯ

СИМЕОНОВО

ДРАГАЛЕВЦИ

slopes especially if you head up the highest point of the **Cherni Vrah peak**. From here you will be able to gain access to a number of challenging runs which includes the **Vitoshko Lale area** which has a mixture of un-even red and black runs but one thing this place is not noted for is off-piste or backcountry riding. Although there are some trees to check out, there's no back bowls of deep powder spots.

FREESTYLERS won't fall in love with Vitosha as this is not a place for getting big natural airs. Yes there are a few natural hits, and local are always building kickers, but there isn't any big launch pads or permanent terrain parks

Vitosha is Bulgaria's highest resort and one that boasts a long season, is located just half an hour from the capital of city **Sofia** and set amid the **Vitosha National Park.** This is a small resort that attracts hordes of punters form the nearby capital especially at weekends. The village is perched high up at a level of 1800 metres with lifts travelling up to a top station of over 2290 metres. The season here generally runs from December to mid April with the mountain best described as suiting beginners and slow learning intermediates. The 20 or so marked out trails are serviced by 11 lifts, which is almost one lift to two runs, thus helping to keep lift lines to a minimum. Overall Vitosha is a simple place resort that should keep you amused for a couple of days if you are an advanced rider or entertained for a week should you be a novice. The mountain boasts a number of interesting slopes, a long 5km run and some nice wooded areas. But if you are the sort of rider who looks for something different at every turn and doesn't like riding the same runs more that twice, then you won't enjoy this place.

FREERIDERS will be pleasantly surprised with some of the

or halfpipes to ride.

PISTES. Riders have a mountain that on one hand provides some decent fast spots, but on the other hand the choice of good wide carving sections are limited to just a few runs.

BEGINNERS have the best of things here with 10 out of the 20 runs graded as easy, with the largest cluster of novice runs found around the **Stenata** area. The long green off the **Romanski** chair is a nice easy run.

THE TOWN
Off the slopes you will find that Vitosha is a bit low key with not a lot going on. The resort has a number of convenient hotels with cheap rates. Around the resort you will find a few night spots, but in truth this sleepy place is not a hot spot. The best night spot is the Hotel Prostor. For a far greater selection of locals services you should visit the city of Sofia which is 23 km away reach.

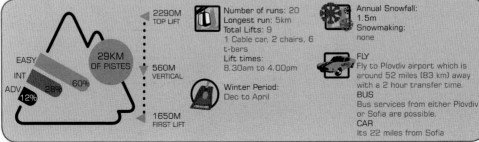

2290M
TOP LIFT

29KM
OF PISTES

EASY
INT
ADV 12%   28%   60%

560M
VERTICAL

1650M
FIRST LIFT

Number of runs: 20
Longest run: 5km
Total Lifts: 9
1 Cable car, 2 chairs, 6 t-bars
Lift times:
8.30am to 4.00pm

Winter Period:
Dec to April

Annual Snowfall:
1.5m
Snowmaking:
none

FLY
Fly to Plovdiv airport which is around 52 miles (83 km) away with a 2 hour transfer time.
BUS
Bus services from either Plovdiv or Sofia are possible.
CAR
Its 22 miles from Sofia

Canada has around 270 resorts, located on either the west or east coast of the country with a few resorts in the central provinces. There is even a snowboard only resort known as 'The Snowboard Ranch' which is located 18 miles from the town of Peterborough in the province of Ontario.

The western provinces boast Canada's best mountainous areas, Alberta and British Columbia (BC). Both regions have resorts that are a match for any in Europe. The gateway cities for flights to the west coast areas are Calgary in Alberta, and Vancouver in BC.

On the east coast there are a number of areas to ride, the majority being in the French speaking province of Quebec. The 100+ resorts on the east coast of Canada resemble much of what is found on the east coast of America - low level, wooded, and often windswept terrain. Canadians treat their visitors with respect and provide a very high level of resort services to meet customer requirements. There are good slope facilities in most places, along with an abundance of places to eat and sleep close to the slopes. Prices are generally higher than those in the US but lower than in Europe. Canadians also like a beer and a good night out, so expect to party hard.

Accommodation facilities in Canada include condos and high quality hotels, as well as B&B's, lodges, hostels or dorms. Prices vary from place to place and are generally quite high wherever you go, (unless you can bunk on a floor and overload with people).

 Capital City: Ottawa
Population: 32.5 million
Highest Peak: Mt Logan 6050m
Language: English & French
Legal Drink Age: 18/19
Drug Laws: Cannabis is illegal but attitudes are changing
Age of consent: 16
Electricity: 110 Volts AC 2-pin
International Dialing Code: +1

Currency: Canadian Dollar (CAD)
Exchange Rate:
UK£1 = 2.4
EURO = 1.6
US$1 = 1.3

Canadian Ski and Snowboard Association
Suite 200, 505 8th Avenue S.W.
Calgary, AB T2P 1G2
Tel: (403) 265-8615
Fax: (403) 777-3213
www.canadaskiandsnowboard.net

 Driving Guide
All vehicles drive on the right hand side of the road
Speed limits:
Motorways-100kph (62mph)
Highways-90kph (55mph)
Towns-50kph (31mph)
Emergency
911 for police/ambulance/fire
Tolls
Some tunnels & a few roads
Documentation
Must carry drivers license
Info
Driver & Passengers must wear seatbelts. Frequent drink driving checks in place, and its illegal to have an opened alcohol container in your vehicle.

 Time Zone
6 time zones in Canada
GMT +4 to +8

C
A
N
A
D
A

Getting around Canada by train is easy on VIA Rail, the Canadian national rail network, or Amtrak which runs across the Canadian/US border. Greyhound buses are another cheap option. Entry into Canada is liberal but you will need a passport and be advised, you can't work in Canada without a work permit as rules are strict. If you get caught scrubbing dishes in a hotel without the correct paper work, you'll soon be on your way home.

If you wish to teach snowboarding in Canada, you will need the Canadian Association of Snowboard Instructors (C.A.S.I.) Level 1 certificate. For details on the course, which costs from C$294, contact C.A.S.I. on 001-514 748 2648 or visit www.casi-bc.com

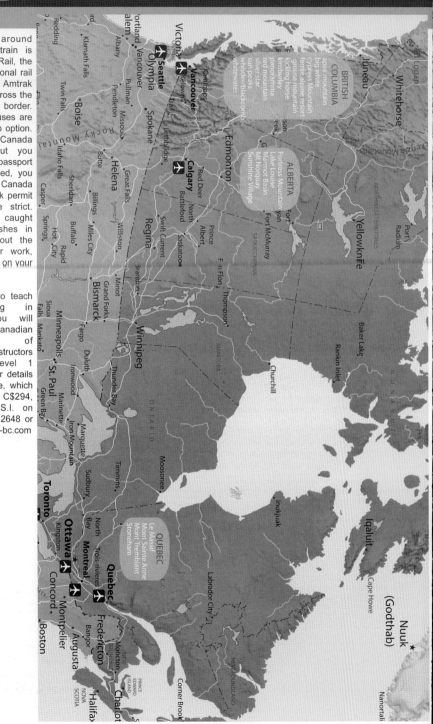

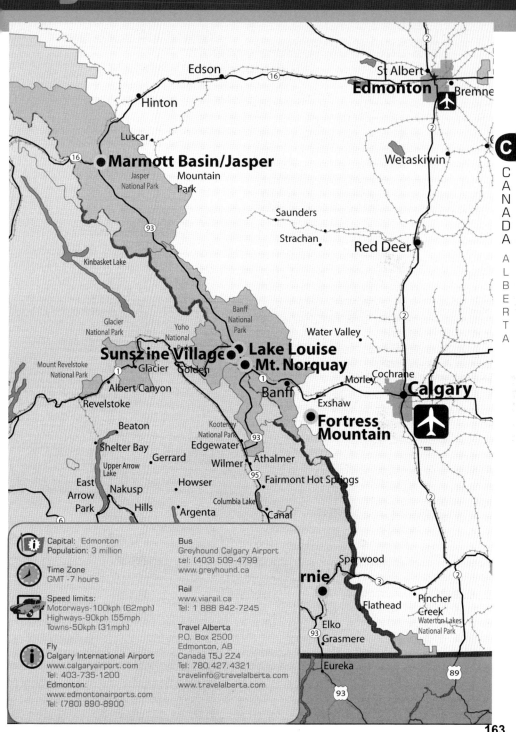

Capital: Edmonton
Population: 3 million

Time Zone
GMT -7 hours

Speed limits:
Motorways-100kph (62mph)
Highways-90kph (55mph)
Towns-50kph (31mph)

Fly
Calgary International Airport
www.calgaryairport.com
Tel: 403-735-1200
Edmonton:
www.edmontonairports.com
Tel: (780) 890-8900

Bus
Greyhound Calgary Airport
tel: (403) 509-4799
www.greyhound.ca

Rail
www.viarail.ca
Tel: 1 888 842-7245

Travel Alberta
P.O. Box 2500
Edmonton, AB
Canada T5J 2Z4
Tel: 780.427.4321
travelinfo@travelalberta.com
www.travelalberta.com

wsg CASTLE MOUNTAIN

FREERIDE
More chutes than a Panda
FREESTYLE
A natural terrain park
PISTES
Not really what its about

POOR FAIR GOOD TOP

What it's all about

8
OUT OF 10

Pic - Pistemap - Castle Mountain resort

C
A
N
A
D
A

A
L
B
E
R
T
A

Castle Mountain was saved from bankruptcy by a group of local families, and if I knew where they all lived I'd pop round and give them all a pat on the back. This tiny resort, only 2 ½ hours from **Calgary**, is rough. The car parks pothole the chair lifts will snap your legs in half if you don't time it right, there's only one pub, only one place to stay and there's only one thing to do, Snowboard. Castle is the kind of place where snowboarders who are pissed off with overcrowded and overpriced resorts dream of. If you're in the area and it's just snowed get in your car and head to Castle.

FREERIDE
Castle has two main lifts which slowly take you to the **Skyline Traverse**; from here it's up to you. Right or left as far as you fancy then just drop into the powder. To the right you will find mostly steep tree areas with a few open easier descents like **North Bowl**. To the left is more of the same although the trees are wider spaced. Keep going left as far as you can and you pass through a wooden gate adorned with a hangman's noose. Beyond the gate is an area of Chutes with names like **Desperado** and **Lone Star**, all the chutes are steep and great for flying down at full speed, you have to take the **Cinch Traverse** back to the lifts, but the descents worth every meter of the traverse.

FREESTYLE. There's no park here and nor should there be. This is a freeride resort with enough natural hits to keep even the most park bound rider happy. In the Chutes there are loads of rock drops and if you look in the trees you'll find plenty of logs to side on.

PISTES. Some of the pistes are groomed but Castles not really about groomed runs. If you want to lay it over on hard packed pistes then head for Panorama and leave Castle to the powder hounds.

BEGINNERS. Complete beginners will save money on an expensive pass but may find the resort a little short on easy slopes. Second and third weekers will love it as it will push their riding to the limit. Watch you don't head too far into the trees or you may find yourself looking a little closer at the pines than you would have hoped.

TOWN. What town? The nearest town is **Pitcher Creek** which does has a few guest houses but no real life. The resort has a hostel which is fine; it has dorm and private rooms and is cheap at $25/night www. castlemountainskilodge.com . There's a day centre offering great breakfasts and lunches, and there's the **T-bar pub** offering beer and pizza. It's a well laid back place, just like the whole resort.

Pic - The Chutes Pistemap - Castle Mountain resort

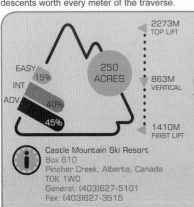

EASY
15%
INT
ADV
40%
45%

250
ACRES

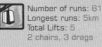
2273M
TOP LIFT

863M
VERTICAL

1410M
FIRST LIFT

Number of runs: 61
Longest runs: 5km
Total Lifts: 5
2 chairs, 3 drags

Winter Period:
Dec to April
Lift Passes
1/2 Day Pass - $37.5
Day Pass - $48
5 days pass $215
Season $674
Board School
Private lesson $45 per hour
Group lesson $30 2hrs
Full day inc rental, lift pass & 2hr lesson $91
Rental
Board & Boots $35 per day

Annual Snowfall:
Unknown
Snowmaking:
none

Car
From Calgary take the Highway 22 towards Burmis, pick up the 774 to Beaver Mines then onto Castle
Fly
Calgary - 2-1/2 hours away.

Castle Mountain Ski Resort
Box 610
Pincher Creek, Alberta, Canada
TOK 1WO
General: (403)627-5101
Fax: (403)627-3515

Email: info@castlemountainresort.com
Web: www.castlemountainresort.com

wsg LAKE LOUISE

Excellent freeriding on four mountain faces

	POOR	FAIR	GOOD	TOP
FREERIDE Trees and good off-piste				
FREESTYLE A terrain park and pipe				
PISTES Well pisted and long				

9 OUT OF 10

Pic - Henry Georgi

Lake Louise is widely rated as one of Canada's best resorts and feels more like a European resort than most in Canada. Being a popular place and only 2 hours from Calgary has led to an area that is often unbearably busy, both on the slopes and around town. In the past year or two, the resort has endeavoured to address this with a lot off changes on the slopes including the inclusion of the new Glacier Triple Chair and New in 2005 the 6 person Grizzly Express Gondola which both start at the base area. The resort has also done much to improve the slopes with new piste groomers and a new Super Pipe Grinder.

The terrain on offer here is spread out over four mountain faces, Front Side/South Face, the Ptarmigan, Paradise and Back Bowls and the Larch area that collectively provide slopes to suit all levels and styles of rider. The well-connected lift system includes a high speed quad that can whisk you to The Top of the World in under ten minutes, from where you can access the Back Bowls with unlimited long tree-lined powder runs lying in wait at every turn, and with new

runs and lifts planned for the Wolvern and Richardsons Ridge areas, there's always new ground to explore. Lake Louise is also located close to the smaller resorts of Sunshine and Mt Norquay with all three sharing a joint lift pass.

FREERIDERS should note that it is illegal to ride in the marked out avalanche danger areas. If you're caught expect to be ejected from the hill with your pass confiscated, and even prosecuted. However, if you have the balls and fancy some out of bounds, the Purple Bowl in the Larch Area is a mega place to check out, offering a mixture of extreme and easy terrain. If you don't mind a knee-deep hike, trek up to the double black at Elevator Shaft where you'll find a host of black runs, cornice drops and rock jumps to try out. For those looking for easy to access powder, drop into the back bowls of the Summit Plater lift, the steep blacks here will test the best, but be warned: don't go outside the marked boundary into the West Bowl unless you know what you are doing.

C

CANADA

ALBERTA

FREESTYLERS have a superb fun park known as the 'The Jungle' and reached off the Olympic chair. First you hit the pipe and then ride through some well spaced rails before entering the jump area which has loads of options, some huge hits, a little closely placed together, which leads you back to the base area. For the complete freestyle novice there is a baby park above the magic carpet to the right of the base area. It's hidden enough that not to many people will laugh at you fall flat on your face.

PISTES. Corduroy lovers can opt to weave down a large number of well groomed pistes or try out. For a long easy run on the front side of the South facing slopes, turn a hard right off number 14 onto number 39 and have it down a well quite piste which, at 8 kms, is the longest run in the area. Alternatively, for less crowded riding, check out the Larch area.

BEGINNERS will find Louise a particularly good place to start out, with a host of easy to reach runs starting at

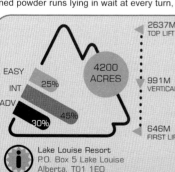

EASY
INT **25%**
ADV
30% **45%**

4200 ACRES

2637M TOP LIFT

991M VERTICAL

646M FIRST LIFT

Number of runs: 51
Longest runs: 8km
Total Lifts: 10
1 Gondola, 8 chairs, 1 drag
Capacity (people/hour): 19,000
Mountain Cafes: 3

Annual Snowfall: 3.8m
Snowmaking: 40%

Winter Period:
Nov to May
Lift Passes
1 day lift pass: $60 CDN
5-day lift pass: $290 CDN
7-day lift pass: $406
Season Pass: $729
Board Schools
2.5 hours group $59
5.5 hours group $89
Hire
board and boots $39/day
Night Boarding
No
Heliboarding
full day 3 to 5 drops $700
20 Dec- 15 Apr

i Lake Louise Resort
P.O. Box 5 Lake Louise
Alberta. T01 1E0
General info: 001 (800) 258 7669
Reservations: 001 (800) 258 7669
Snowphone: 001 (403) 244 6665
Web:www. skilouise.com
Email:info@skilouise.com

NEW 6-passenger "Grizzly Express Gondola" opened in February 2005 replacing the old 2 person chairlift

Pic - Lake Louise Tourism

C

C
A
N
A
D
A

A
L
B
E
R
T
A

the base area. The runs off Eagle chair are the best and allow you to have a long cruise home down trails such as 14 and 1, which are also in a speed restricted area. The Lake Louise Snowboard School is excellent and offers loads of beginner to advanced programmes. As learning at all big resorts if it's your first week you may find that you are paying top $ for a large resort and only seeing a small part of it.

THE TOWN
Lake Louise's holiday complex is located a five minutes drive from the slopes and can be reached by local shuttle bus. The village, which is dominated by the Chateau Lake Louise has a good selection of local facilities and caters well for dot.com millionaires but not for budget conscious snowboarders. The truth is, Lake Louise has become far too overcrowded with holiday punters and charges excessive prices for everything. Many visitors prefer to stay in Banff which is 45min drive from Louise and offers a far greater choice of services and much lower prices. The bus free bus can be mobbed and can take over an hour. The one affordable option is the excellent Hostel with dorm rooms from $30/night www.hihostels.ca tel 403 522 2200.

Evenings in Louise are simply lame although Charlie's or The Grill are good for a beer and a game of pool. Banff offers more street-wise entertainment and goes on well into the early hours. The Irish pub is popular as is the Rose and Crown.

Accommodation in Lake Louise is very expensive with a number of classy hotels and lodges to choose from. Self catering is also possible with some reasonable deals available for groups. If you have the cash, the Post Hotel is excellent. However, Banff offers the best selection of affordable places. The Blue Mountain has nightly rates from $55 for B&B. The High Country Inn has rooms from $75 a night while the Youth Hostel has bunks from $30 per night per person.

Around Lake Louise the choice of restaurants is excellent, but very pricey; The Chateau is criminally so. The licensed cafe at the youth hostel has the best value food.

CAR
Calgary via Canmore/Banff. Lake Louise is 115 miles (185km). Drive time is about 2 1/4 hours.
FLY
Fly to Calgary International. Transfer time to resort is 2 1/4 hours.
BUS
A bus from Calgary takes 2 1/4 hours. Info: (403) 762 6700, a return is $99, and buses run every other hour. A local shuttle bus runs daily to Lake Louise from Banff.

166

ωsg MARMOT BASIN

FREERIDE
Trees and good backcountry
FREESTYLE
A terrain park and good natural
PISTES
Well prepared slopes

Great freeriding mountain

8
OUT OF 10

Pic - Hugh Lecky/Marmot Basin

Marmot Basin, sometimes incorrectly called **Jasper** which is actually the local town, is an absolute gem of a resort and highly rated by those in the know. Just driving to this place through **Jasper National Park** in the Rockies is a pleasure in itself with some stunning scenery en-route. Marmot is a resort that attracts snowboarders and skiers who like their slopes hassle-free and despite being a popular haunt, no one spends more than a few minutes queuing in lift lines, the lifts here can shift over 10,000 people an hour uphill.

Recently Marmot, has opened up even more terrain with two new mountain faces known as the **Eagle Ridge** which provide a further 20 runs of steep double black diamond slopes and intermediate trails. Overall the terrain here is evenly split between all levels and styles of riding, with good backcountry areas to explore, nice bowls and trees to dip into and fast carving slopes.

FREERIDERS looking for powder should check out **Eagle East** where the bowls are full on. This area is avoided by the vast majority of punters, so the snow stays for days after a storm. The area is covered in trees but they are well spaced so you can let rip. Take the **Kiefer T-Bar** or the **Paradise Chair** to check out **Caribou Ridge** which offers

an abundance of testing terrain with bumps and hits for both the freerider and freestyler. Intermediates who know what they are doing will also like this area and can ride most of the mountain one way or another. If you have the energy, advanced freeriders can hike up to **Marmot Peak** which yields an amazing ride down through powder bowls. The trees in the lower sections are pretty cool, but if you have the balls, check out **Knob Bowl** off Knob Chair for a taste of heaven.

FREESTYLERS have plenty of good natural terrain for catching air, but check out **Rock Garden** for some of the best hits. There are lots of trees here and if you look out, you will find the odd log to slide. You wouldn't come to Marmot just to ride the Terrain Park, however it's still fun. There's a couple of table tops, rails and a quarter pipe but nothing too scary. Here, grommets can catch air all day without bothering anyone else.

PISTE lovers have some good opportunities to lay out nice, big arcs on the kind of prepared piste that carvers delight in. For some demanding riding, **Exhibition** is the place to visit, while the more sedate rider will like **Dromedary trail**.

BEGINNERS will note one clear thing about Marmot Basin and that is how good it is for cutting their first tracks. The slopes are accessible with the easy stuff at the bottom and some good progression runs found higher up, which allows for long and gentle riding back to base. What's more, novices can get around the slopes without having to use any T-bars thanks to the way the chair lifts have been set out. Snowboard instruction services are good with a number of tuition packages available for all levels and styles of riding. There are even lessons available with video analysis to quicken your progression. A two hour group lesson costs from C\$50 with lift pass and full equipment hire.

THE TOWN
Marmot Basin doesn't offer any slopeside accommodation or full local services other than the new *Caribou Chalet*

C

C
A
N
A
D
A

A
L
B
E
R
T
A

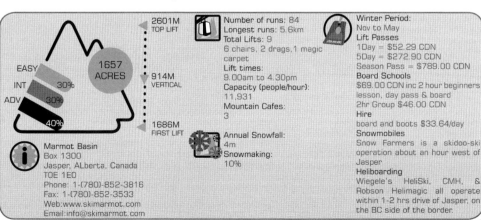

2601M
TOP LIFT

914M
VERTICAL

1686M
FIRST LIFT

EASY
INT 30%
ADV 30%
40%

1657
ACRES

Marmot Basin
Box 1300
Jasper, ALberta, Canada
TOE 1EO
Phone: 1-(780)-852-3816
Fax: 1-(780)-852-3533
Web:www.skimarmot.com
Email:info@skimarmot.com

Number of runs: 84
Longest runs: 5.6km
Total Lifts: 9
6 chairs, 2 drags,1 magic carpet
Lift times:
9.00am to 4.30pm
Capacity (people/hour):
11,931
Mountain Cafes:
3

Annual Snowfall:
4m
Snowmaking:
10%

Winter Period:
Nov to May
Lift Passes
1Day = \$52.29 CDN
5Day = \$272.90 CDN
Season Pass = \$789.00 CDN
Board Schools
\$69.00 CDN inc 2 hour beginners lesson, day pass & board
2hr Group \$46.00 CDN
Hire
board and boots \$33.64/day
Snowmobiles
Snow Farmers is a skidoo-ski operation about an hour west of Jasper
Heliboarding
Wiegele's HeliSki, CMH, & Robson Helimagic all operate within 1-2 hrs drive of Jasper, on the BC side of the border.

167

Pic - Hugh Lecky/Marmot Basin

at the base of the slopes. However, the town of Jasper is only 10 miles away and although it isn't as big as its more famous cousin Banff, Jasper is less crowded and you shouldn't have any problem finding good quality lodging at prices to suit all. There is a regular ski bus that runs all day stopping at many of the hotels en-route from Jasper to the slopes.

Night-life in Jasper is best described as very low key and a bit boring. Pete's Bar seems to be the in-place to check out, where you can mix with a lively crowd boozing and playing pool. The Whistle Stop is also a cool hang out with pool and on screen sports action. O'Shea's is a typical Irish pub, while the Atha-Bar is the place for live music and a dance

Accommodation in Jasper ranges from the usual selection of lodge-style hotels to B&B's or hostels which are widely spread out. Places like The Amethyst Lodge offer a selection of well equipped rooms with rates from C$75/night per room, while The Astoria, located in central Jasper, has winter rates from C$104/night per room. The Marmot Lodge, also centrally located, offers self catering style accommodation for groups or couples as well as having an indoor swimming pool and fitness centre.

Eating options in Jasper are much the same as in any

of Alberta's towns. If you want a slap up feast, then dine at the expensive Edith Cavell, or the Tonquin Rib Village where you can get a damn fine steak. If you like pizza, then visit Papa George's or Jasper Pizza Place. If you are in need of a fast food fix there's also a Pizza Hut, McDonald's and KFC.

SUMMARY
Great freeriding mountain with excellent challenging runs on crowed free slopes. However, the resort is let down by the lack of slope side facilities, although what is on offer in Jasper is first class.

Pic - Hugh Lecky/Marmot Basin

CAR
Edmonton via Jasper Marmot Basin is 270 miles. Drive time is about 4 1/2 hours.
FLY
to Edmonton International, transfer time to resort is 4 1/2 hours. Local airport is Hinton 38 miles.
BUS
A daily bus service run by Greyhound, operates 4 times a day from Edmonton to Jasper and takes around 5 hours.
TRAIN
run direct into Jasper

POOR FAIR GOOD TOP

FREERIDE
Trees but no backcountry
FREESTYLE
A terrain park and halfpipe
PISTES
Short but well groomed

Uncrowded varied slopes

6 OUT OF 10

C
A
N
A
D
A

A
L
B
E
R
T
A

more time in Banff then on the hill.

FREESTYLERS have a good halfpipe and fun-park, both of which are shaped by the Rockies first magician Pipe Grinder. Next to the pipe is a full on fun-park with all types of hits, including a massive quarter-pipe, gap jumps and table-tops. The great thing is that it's nearly always deserted. A discounted lift pass is available for riders using the park via the Cascade lift at just $33.

PISTES. Most of the pistes of Norquay are well groomed, and although not particularly long, they are great for having it down at high speed and as the rest of the resort often empty. The easy flats of the **Spirit Quad** chair is the place to head first before cranking it down **Excalibur**, a decent black run off the M**ystic Quad**.

Mount Norquay is the nearest boarding area to Banff and offers some great riding, including good night riding and flexible ticket options, such as hourly rates and a terrain park ticket. Norquay is a ten minute bus ride from **Banff**. With only 5 lifts it is the smallest resort in the area, but it's not without a lot of varied terrain to ride in fact some of the steepest in the area. Locals claim the terrain either side of the North American chair is superb after a heavy dump. Norquay often has the quietest slopes for miles around, people always head straight to the crowded slopes of **Lake Louise** and **Sunshine Village** and pass this great little resort by. Norquay's night riding is on Fridays 5pm till 11pm a night ride ticket costs $24

FREERIDERS should take the high speed **Mystic Express** lift to ride the best boarding area on the mountain. It gives you access to six long blue runs through the trees, with **Imp** and **Knight Flight** being favourites. There are some steeper options from this lift, like **Black Magic**, and the interestingly named **Ka-Poof**, which can either be great after a heavy fall of snow, or awful with icy hardpack late in the season. For the real steep stuff take the **North American chair** and have it down the **Gun Run**, but make sure you know what you're doing or you maybe spending

BEGINNERS have very easy access to tame pistes from the base station. The green runs next to the **Cascade chair** are a great place to learn some linked turns. There's also a great little fenced area for complete beginners with a long magic carpet right at the base area.

THE TOWN

There are no local facilities at **Norquay** apart from Timberline Inn at the bottom of the ride-out (tel: (403) 762 2281). The *Timberline Inn* has a bar and restaurant with nightly rates from $88 for a single. **Banff** is the better option; here you'll find all the local services that you could possibly want. Banff is only ten minutes away and is served by a regular bus that runs seven days a week to and from the slopes.

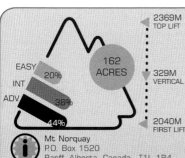

2369M
TOP LIFT

329M
VERTICAL

2040M
FIRST LIFT

EASY
20%
INT
ADV
36%
44%

162
ACRES

Number of runs: 26
Longest runs: 1.16miles
Total Lifts: 5
4 chairs, 1 magic carpet
Winter Period:
Dec to April
Lift Passes
1/2 Day $37
1 Day pass $49
Night $24
Night Boarding
fridays 5pm till 11pm
Hire
Board & Boots
1 Day $32
5 Days $150

Annual Snowfall:
3m
Snowmaking:
90% of pistes

Bus
services direct from Calgary & Edmonton via Banff.
Fly
to Calgary 1 1/2 hours transfer to Mount Norquay.
Drive
From Calgary, via Highway 1 head towards Banff via Canmore. Mt Norquay lies north of Banff and south of Lake Louise alongthe Norquay road. Calgary to resort is 68 miles.

Mt Norquay
P.O. Box 1520
Banff, Alberta, Canada, T1L 1B4
Tel: (403) 762-4421
Fax: (403) 762-8133
Web: www.banffnorquay.com
Email:info@banffnorquay.com

ωsg SUNSHINE VILLAGE

FREERIDE
Trees and backcountry
FREESTYLE
A terrain park & halfpipe
PISTES
Huge number

8
OUT OF 10

Excellent terrain

Pic - mike moynihan/Sunshine Resort

**C
A
N
A
D
A**

**A
L
B
E
R
T
A**

Sunshine and **Goat's Eye Mountain** are amongst the oldest resorts in Alberta and are the best places in the **Banff** area for deep snow. The area receives serious amounts of snowfall every year and is a good alternative to its neighbour, Lake Louise. From the car park the high speed 8 man Gondola takes you up to the Sunshine Village base area and offers you the chance to get out at Goat's Eye Mountain, which is where most of the hard core riding is, including some severely steep, double black diamond runs such as **The Wild Side**, **Hell's Kitchen** and **Freefall**. Two areas are accessed form Sunshine Village; **Mt Standish** and **Lookout Mountain** most of the runs on Mt Standish are annoyingly short especially when the resorts busy. Lookout Mountain has longer runs, the park and also the resorts highlight Delirium Dive great but for nutters only.

FREERIDERS with experience will head straight for Delirium Dive a short walk off the **Continental Divide chair**, this area is roped off and you access it through a little gate which only opens if you're wearing a Transceiver. What a great idea it keeps all those twats who know shit all about backcountry boarding out. **The Dive** is a steep open powder face with some insane shoots and drop offs at the top, it's a must. Away from the Dive, the best and most challenging areas can be found on **Goat's Eye Mountain**. On Lookout steep runs through the trees to check out include Little Angel, Ecstasy and Horot's Revenge where you may find

powder.
From the Wawa chair you can ride down a frozen waterfall on the aptly named **Waterfall run**.

FREESTYLERS have the usual offerings, but those who don't dig freeride and just want to ride the park should head to Lake Louise. There's a cool halfpipe under the **Strawberry chair** and a sizeable terrain park reached from the Continental Divide chair. You can also pull some big air and spin until you're dizzy, on the natural hits dotted all over the place. For a great drop off hit the entrance to the **Head Wall** run with speed.

PISTES. There's an array of pistes to have it down at speed, you will find lots of groomed runs to tackle all over resort, the best of which are on **Lookout Mountain**. With a chose of lazy green down to the day lodge or some well maintained steeper blacks under the **Angel Quad**. You can also find some okay cruising trails on Sunshine Coast and Wild Fire, but make sure you have plenty of speed for the long traverse back to the lift station.

BEGINNERS and intermediate riders are well catered for on runs that include The Red 90, South Divide and Green Run. The Wawa chair gives access to some excellent novice freeriding, although short. The Dell Valley run off the Strawberry chair has some great banks to slow you down when trying to link those first few turns.

THE TOWN
You can stay in **Sunshine Village**, at the *Sunshine Inn* which is accessed only by the Gondola, offering the only ride-in, ride-out accommodation in the Banff area. The hotel has a great fire place to relax at, but there's no real night life although the *Old Sunshine Lodge* can kick off if it's the staff's payday. It's not cheap, although they do offer some good midweek deals, but remember you do get first tracks everyday while everyone else is waiting for the Gondola down at the car park.
The cheaper option is to stay in **Banff**. It's only 15 minutes away along Route 93 and a regular local bus services operates between Banff and Sunshine.

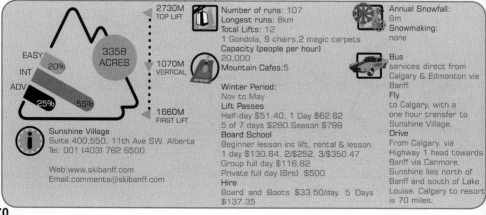

2730M TOP LIFT
1070M VERTICAL
1660M FIRST LIFT

EASY
INT 20%
ADV
25% 55%

3358 ACRES

Sunshine Village
Suite 400,550, 11th Ave SW, Alberta
Tel: 001 (403) 762 6500

Web:www.skibanff.com
Email:comments@skibanff.com

Number of runs: 107
Longest runs: 8km
Total Lifts: 12
1 Gondola, 9 chairs,2 magic carpets
Capacity (people per hour)
20,000
Mountain Cafes:5

Winter Period:
Nov to May
Lift Passes
Half-day $51.40, 1 Day $62.62
5 of 7 days $280.Season $799
Board School
Beginner lesson inc lift, rental & lesson.
1 day $130.84, 2/$252, 3/$350.47
Group full day $116.82
Private full day (6rs) $500
Hire
Board and Boots $33.50/day. 5 Days $137.35

Annual Snowfall:
9m
Snowmaking:
none

Bus
services direct from
Calgary & Edmonton via
Banff.
Fly
to Calgary, with a
one hour transfer to
Sunshine Village.
Drive
From Calgary, via
Highway 1 head towards
Banff via Canmore.
Sunshine lies north of
Banff and south of Lake
Louise. Calgary to resort
is 70 miles.

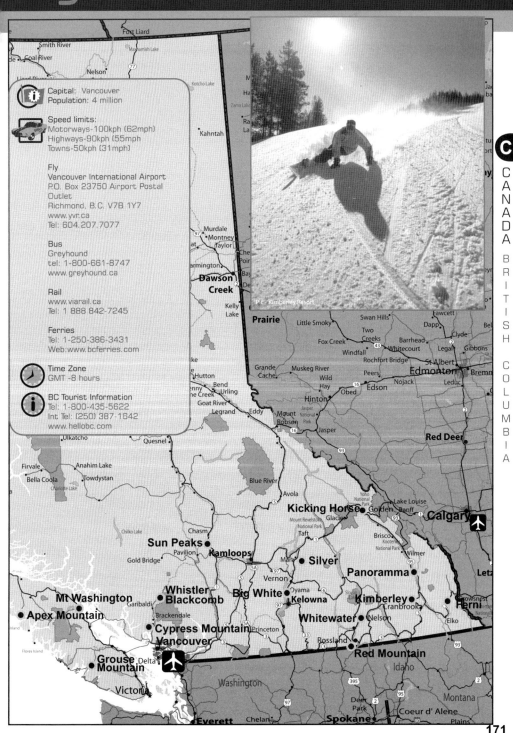

Pic - Kimberley Resort

Capital: Vancouver
Population: 4 million

Speed limits:
Motorways-100kph (62mph)
Highways-90kph (55mph)
Towns-50kph (31mph)

Fly
Vancouver International Airport
P.O. Box 23750 Airport Postal
Outlet
Richmond, B.C. V7B 1Y7
www.yvr.ca
Tel: 604.207.7077

Bus
Greyhound
tel: 1-800-661-8747
www.greyhound.ca

Rail
www.viarail.ca
Tel: 1 888 842-7245

Ferries
Tel: 1-250-386-3431
Web:www.bcferries.com

Time Zone
GMT -8 hours

BC Tourist Information
Tel: 1-800-435-5622
Int Tel: (250) 387-1642
www.hellobc.com

C

CANADA BRITISH COLUMBIA

ωsg APEX MOUNTAIN

POOR FAIR GOOD TOP

FREERIDE
Trees and some off-piste

FREESTYLE
A terrain park

PISTES
Good gladed runs

Great riding

7
OUT OF 10

Pic - Apex Mountain

FREESTYLERS. There is a terrain park with a quarter-pipe and various rails on the Claim Jumperrun. With a bit of hunting you'll find some good natural gullies and hits on **Mt Beaconsfield**.

PISTES. Riders will fair well on Apex's short, but challenging trails. There are enough steep blacks for the advanced alpine rider to carve, while the novice can practice on some nice, flat blues.

C

C A N A D A

B R I T I S H

C O L U M B I A

Apex Mountain may be a small resort, but with it's down-to-earth atmosphere and great riding opportunities, it's no wonder that Apex is a popular place. Located in the sunny **Okanagan Valley**, Apex is known for its great natural terrain: bowls, gullies, glades and groomed cruising runs radiate from the rounded top of the resort's main peak, **Mt Beaconsfield**. If you're a novice or intermediate, head for the wide boulevards off the Stocks Triple chair, where you'll find half a dozen nicely graded, rolling descents. Notice how the trail names evoke the area's mining history - **Motherlode, Gambit** and **Sluice Box**.

FREERIDERS looking for some decidedly 'darker blue' cruising should head on up to **Mt Beaconsfield** and try **Ridge Run** and **Juniper** where a search for more challenging terrain won't take long. Alternatively, check out the whole series of wicked runs plunging down Apex's North Side. Wind your way through the woods and, if you dare, peer down **Gunbarrel**, a chute that's just 'one turn wide', and drops straight down the fall-line for 366 double black diamond vertical metres (1,200 ft).

BEGINNERS should find that Apex allows for an easy time, as in general, this is a good mountain to learn on and allows for quick progression. **Grandfather's** Trail is a nice green that allows you to ride from the summit to the base with ease. The local snowboard school offers various learn to ride packages with a one day lesson, lift and full hire costing form C$57 per person.

THE TOWN
The *New Inn* at **Apex** offers ride-in accommodation and some good value bed and lift ticket deals, from C$60/night mid-week. If you're planning on staying a while there are apartments available to rent, otherwise there are plenty of beds in the town of Penticton, forty minutes away. When the sun goes down on Apex Mountain, The *Gunbarrel Saloon* is the main place to eat and enjoy all sorts of entertainment. Other good food haunts are *The Rusty Spur* and *Longshot Bar*.

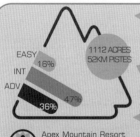

EASY 16%
INT
ADV
47%
36%

1112 ACRES
52KM PISTES

2180M
TOP LIFT

605M
VERTICAL

1575M
FIRST LIFT

Apex Mountain Resort
PO Box 1060
Penticton BC
V2A 6J9
Phone (250) 292-8222
Fax (250) 292-8100
Web: www.apexresort.com
Email: info@apexresort.com

Number of runs: 67
Longest runs: 5km
Total Lifts: 5
2 chairs,1 t-bar, 1 platter tow,
1 tube tow
Capacity (people per hour)
8700
Lift times:
9:00am to 3:30pm

Winter Period:
Dec to April
Lift Passes
1 Day pass - $52
5 Day pass - $240
Season pass - $649
Board School
Group $60 for 3 hours
Private $65 for 1hr, all day (4rs)
$165
Hire
$38/day additional days $29
Night boarding
4:30pm to 9:00pm, Fridays &
Saturdays. Price $12

Annual Snowfall:
6m
Snowmaking:
40% of pistes

Bus
Bus services direct from
Vancouver takes around 5
hours. Bus Transfers from
Penticton & Kelowna airports
available tel: (250) 492 5555
Fly
to Vancouver, 4 1/2hrs away.
Domestic transfers possible to
Penticon airport, 35min drive
away. Kelowna airport 90mins
from resort.
Drive
From Vancouver, take highway
1 at Hope join Highway 3 to
Keremeos, take highway 3A for
11.5 km take Green Mountain
Rd for another 14km
and take Apex Mountain Rd for
further 11km to Apex village.
About 4 1/2hrs drive

172

POOR FAIR GOOD TOP

FREERIDE
Trees and good backcountry
FREESTYLE
Impressive parks & pipes
PISTES
Well prepared slopes

Excellent freeriding on crowd free slopes

9
OUT OF 10

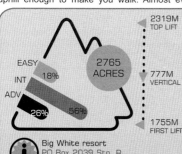

Pic: Big White ski Resort, BC, Canada/Klaus Gretzmacher

littered with hits, allowing for you to take air numerous times on every decent. The lift system allows the crowd to disperse around the mountain making for crowd free slopes even on the busiest of days. Big White is an ideal resort for mixed abilities groups, there are miles of easy slopes which can be enjoyed by the advanced rider hitting the rollers, while the beginner can learns to link there turns on the same pistes. The only thing missing here is wide open powder faces, with a max elevation of 2319 meters the trees cover most of the mountain leaving only small powder faces.

FREERIDERS get the chance to ride through trees, trees and more trees. From the **Gem Lake Express** chair you can access the **Sun-Rype bowl** area, one of the only powder faces, before dropping through the trees or onto the deserted rolling pistes below. Riders with balls (or equivalent) should take the **Alpine T-bar** and test their extreme riding on one of the double black diamond runs that are found on the Cliff, but only if you can ride and ride well. Likewise, the black runs off the **Powder chair** are not for the squeamish. For those not quite up to the same standard, the blue runs off the **Ride Rocket chair** are worth a blast, as is the **Blue Ribbon** over in the West Ridge area.

Big White! Where? Big White is the worlds best big unknown resort; it's a giant skate park covered in snow and trees. Recently bought by an Australian family along with Silver Star, they don't seem to be afraid to spend some cash. $125 million last year with $4 million on the Telus terrain park alone. Snowboarders in search of good mountains have been cruelly misled by the world's slack ski press for years and Big White is a prime example. Knowledgeable Canadians have had a freeride paradise with an annual 7.5 meters of champagne powder largely to themselves. Big White is located in the **Okanagan Valley**, 45 min from the large town of **Kelowna**.

The recent large investment has resulted in an excellent lift system, good off slope facilities and a lot of marketing. The secret of Big White won't last much longer. Most of the mountain is covered in trees with rolling pistes, but never uphill enough to make you walk. Almost every piste is

FREESTYLERS have one of the best parks anywhere. Flynn Seddon has designed a fantastic park which is permanently managed and repaired by a dedicated team. All the rails and hits are clearly graded allowing for the perfect progression form hopping of small hits all the way through to flying off huge ones. The park has its own lift going diagonally over the park, so you can check out other people's moves on the way up, it's also lit up during night riding night. There's a great Board cross and two well maintained pipes, often used for national events. Outside the park the mountain is full of natural hits. If you like rollers check out Black Jack and Black magic, if you want some small rock drops kickers and banks to turn on check out under the **Rocket Ridge** Express.

BEGINNERS will dig Big White, as it is totally accessible from top to bottom with a good selection of easy trails. If you can link your turns then you can explore the mountain,

C

C
A
N
A
D
A

B
R
I
T
I
S
H

C
O
L
U
M
B
I
A

2319M
TOP LIFT

777M
VERTICAL

1755M
FIRST LIFT

EASY
18%
INT
ADV
26%   56%

2765
ACRES

Number of runs: 118
Longest runs: 7.2km
Total Lifts: 15
1 Gondola, 9 chairs, 2 drags,1 Magic carpet, 1 beginners tow, 2 Tube Lifts
Lift times:
8.45am to 8.00pm
Capacity (people/hour):
25,400
Mountain Cafes:7

Annual Snowfall:
7.5m
Snowmaking:
none

Winter Period:
Nov to April
Lift Passes
Half-day $49
Day pass $64
Day pass inc nightboarding $69
5 of 6 Days $292
Season pass $859
Board Schools
2 Hour Group $42
Private 2 Hours $157
Hire
Board & Boots, 1 day $36 additional days $27
Snowmobiles
1 to 4 hour tours
Night riding
5:00 pm - 8:00 pm Tuesday to Saturday free with any multi-day pass otherwise $24

Big White resort
PO Box 2039 Stn. R
Kelowna B.C.
Canada, V1X4K5
Tel: (250) 765-3101
Web:www.bigwhite.com
Email:bigwhite@bigwhite.com

173

Pic teluspark2 Big White Ski Resort, BC, Canada /Quick Pics

but study your lift map first. Instruction is good and well priced, with a one day lesson, equipment hire and lift pass costing from C$55.

PISTE lovers will enjoy Big White as the terrain is perfect for laying out some big turns, although none of the runs are overly wide. By taking any of the main lifts, such as Ridge Rocket or Bullet, you gain access to some fast slopes. Cougar Alley is full on and for a long carve you should crank it from the summit of the Alpine T-Bar, down to the base.

THE TOWN

Off the slopes, **Big White** is a friendly and affordable place, with lots of staff from around the world. Weekends usually see an influx of extra punters from surrounding towns and cities, but the place is never so busy as to be annoying - there is room for all. Local amenities are growing, offering everything you may need during your stay, with shops and other services being well located and within walking distance of each other. Riders with too much money can throw it away at the casino, whilst families can prance around on the 7500 sq,ft, ice rink. If that's not enough, then blow some cash on a snowmobile tour.

Eating choices are numerous and of an extremely good standard. For a hearty breakfast, check out the *Ridge Day Lodge* which opens from 8.30am daily. *Snowshoe Sam's* is good for a beer and a game of pool, it also shows football and is good for a burger. Soup and a sandwich lunch is best in the Village Centre.

Night-life: By no means mad cap or hardcore drinking, but you can make it lively. The *Loose Moose* is the place to get on the dance floor, while *Raakels* is the place to chill and listen to some live music. For a bigger selection of night-life, check out the action in **Kelowna**. It is only 45 minutes away but you will need your own transport at night.

Accommodation in Big White is very good with much of it on, or close to the base slope areas, which allows you to ride straight to your door. There are a couple of classy hotels to choose from and a few chalets. For groups, there is a choice of condominiums with prices to suit most budgets. The *White Crystal Inn* is a quality hotel located close to the slopes. It has a bar, restaurant, and fitness room, but note, it's not cheap. For a hostel *Same Sun Backpacker* Ski Lodge is best.

TELUS Park - Rider Phil Wright (c) Big White Ski Resort, BC, Canada pic Mark Fisher.psd

CAR
Vancouver via Merrit & Kelowna. Big White is 278 miles (447km), drive time is about 5 hours.
FLY
to Vancouver International. Transfer time to resort is 5 hours. Local airport is Kelowna 45 mins.
BUS
A bus from Vancouver takes around 5 hours. Local buses run daily from Kelowna to Big White and take just 45 minutes.

Pic -MArk Gunter

	POOR	FAIR	GOOD	TOP
FREERIDE Trees & small off-piste				
FREESTYLE A terrain park and halfpipe				
PISTES Busy short slopes				

5 OUT OF 10

Okay for a few days

C

C
A
N
A
D
A

B
R
I
T
I
S
H

C
O
L
U
M
B
I
A

also more snow.

There are some truly top class off-piste tree runs to contend with (although a little short by European standards), and some challenging black runs too.

FREESTYLERS have a snowboard park sponsored by 'Bell' one of the local mobile phone companies. It is well maintained by the owners, the instructors and a few local riders who are constantly changing the set-up. There is also a big halfpipe and if that's not enough, there are two awesome 12 foot quarter-pipes (snow permitting!)

PISTES. Carvers in search of loads of fast and extreme slopes will be a little disappointed but head for Horizon or Fork when the slopes are nicely groomed or Upper & Lower Collins when it's less busy.

BEGINNERS have it best at Cypress Mountain. The Eagle chair on Black Mountain gives access to some easy/intermediate winding runs; alternatively, the flats on Mt Strachan and the Sunrise chair are ideal for learning the basics. Cypress Mountain Snowboard School offers courses to suit all, with a one week course that includes full equipment hire, costing from C$290.

THE AREA

There is no accommodation on the mountain as the city of Vancouver is so close. In downtown Vancouver, there is an excellent hostel which has friendly staff, awesome facilities and runs daytrips to the mountain. Alternatively there are all the normal types of hotels that any large city can offer down town and on the North Shore itself.

There is plenty happening in **Vancouver** at night, on the North Shore head for the 'Rusty Gull' on 2nd or 'The Shore' on 3rd just off Lonsdale. Downtown on Granville Street, watch out for 'Fred's Tavern' or 'Roxys'. For incredibly rich but incredibly fit women head for the 'SkyBar' downtown, but make sure you got the cash to keep the ladies in bubbly!

Cypress Mountain is one of three local mountains in the **Vancouver** area (the other two being Grouse Mountain and Mt Seymour). Situated 30 minutes drive from Vancouver, Cypress Mountain caters largely for people living in the city. It's a relatively small resort with five chair lifts, 2 high speed quads, 1 quad and 2 doubles. The terrain on offer is very much beginner to intermediate level, but that doesn't deter the large number of 'Vancouverites' who flock here. Night-boarding is one of the biggest draws at Cypress, offering uncrowded riding for the true enthusiasts until 10pm every night.

FREERIDERS may find the best riding to be had on **Mt Strachan** in the east, which has two main chair lifts, Sunrise and Sky (plus Midway and Easy Rider for the beginners) that take you to the top of the best black runs. On a clear day, the view is absolutely stunning, with the enormous Mt Baker dominating the horizon down to Washington, USA. Snowboarding on this side of Cypress Mountain is better than anywhere else in the resort due to the steep and variable terrain, and because of the altitude, there is

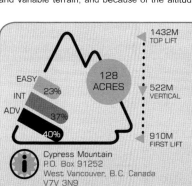

EASY

INT 23%

ADV 37%

40%

128 ACRES

1432M TOP LIFT

522M VERTICAL

910M FIRST LIFT

Cypress Mountain
P.O. Box 91252
West Vancouver, B.C. Canada
V7V 3N9
Tel: 604-926-5612
Web: www.cypressmountain.com
Email: contact@cypressmountain.com

Number of runs: 38
Longest runs: 2.1km
Total Lifts: 7
5 chairs, 1 magic carpet,
1 tube tow

Winter Period:
Dec to April
Lift Passes
1 Day pass $42
Night $34
Night Boarding
15 Dec to 28 Mar till
10pm on all main runs
Hire
Board and Boots $37/41
Day

Annual Snowfall:
6.22m
Snowmaking:
85% of pistes

Bus
Bus services direct from
Vancouver takes around 30
minutes. $15 return, $8 one
way
Fly
to Vancouver 30 minutes
transfer to Cypress Bowl
Drive
From Vancouver, use highway 1
westbound, direction Horseshoe
Bay. Leave at exit 8 for Cypress
Bowl (13km)

175

POOR FAIR GOOD TOP

FREERIDE
Trees and some off-piste
FREESTYLE
3 terrain parks
PISTES
Some good runs

A nice day out

5 OUT OF 10

FREERIDERS will find that much of what is on offer here at will suit them so long as they are not looking for major long steeps covered in knee deep powder. There are however, some areas where the average rider can show off on runs such as the Devil's Advocate. This is a short but fast steep trail that winds its way down through some tress before linking up with a long intermediate run known as the Inferno. With all or most of the runs carved out of trees, there are ample opportunities to slice through the trees and grind the odd fallen log.

FREESTYLERS. There are 3 terrain parks at Grouse. The Rookie Park, below the Screaming Eagle lift, the Advanced Park on Side Cut and the Paradise Jib Park in Paradise Bowl. On a good day there's up to 30 rails and boxes in the parks and a number of jumps for all abilities. There's no pipe anymore though.

C

CANADA

BRITISH COLUMBIA

Grouse Mountain is the smallest resort out of the three (Cypress, Grouse, Seymour) located on the North Shore of BC's capital Vancouver. Along with a mountain top multi-media theatre, Grouse Mountain has a good selection of trails that will keep the average grade snowboarder content for a day or two, amuse an expert rider for an afternoon and totally please a beginner for a 5 day period. Regular night riding on Grouse's flood lit slopes is very popular with townies from Vancouver, who take to the slopes in the evenings after a day in the office. However, Grouse doesn't attract mass crowds due largely to the poor and unreliable snow conditions. Still, when the 25 well marked trails are covered in snow then this is a mountain that provides some good fun riding with a little for everyone. Apart from a couple of double black diamond extreme runs, however, much of the terrain is rated intermediate and overall is tame. Grouse Mountain is best known for its truly amazing views of the North Shore and downtown Vancouver, the guide will tell you this in the cable car, along with many other 'interesting' facts about Vancouver.

PISTES. Carvers have a reasonable selection of trails to choose from with some excellent wide carving to found off the Peak Patio and Peak chair lifts. Both lifts give access to some basic runs.

BEGINNERS may not have dozens of novice trails to choose from, but nevertheless, the easy runs are well appointed and most first timers should have no bother negotiating the nursery areas before progressing on up to more challenging terrain. The local ski school offers a number of snowboard programmes.

THE TOWN
Off the slopes the place to stay is in **Vancouver**, where you will be able to find just about anything to suite you're fancy. Vancouver is a fantastic city loaded with tourist attractions. Vancouver Tourist Office tel: 001 (604) 683 2000.

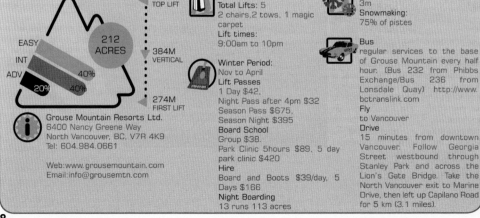

EASY
INT
ADV
212 ACRES
40%
20% 40%

1250M TOP LIFT
384M VERTICAL
274M FIRST LIFT

Grouse Mountain Resorts Ltd.
6400 Nancy Greene Way
North Vancouver, BC, V7R 4K9
Tel: 604.984.0661

Web:www.grousemountain.com
Email:info@grousemtn.com

Number of runs: 25
Total Lifts: 5
2 chairs, 2 tows, 1 magic carpet
Lift times:
9:00am to 10pm

Winter Period:
Nov to April
Lift Passes
1 Day $42,
Night Pass after 4pm $32
Season Pass $675,
Season Night $395
Board School
Group $38.
Park Clinic 5hours $89, 5 day park clinic $420
Hire
Board and Boots $39/day, 5 Days $166
Night Boarding
13 runs 113 acres

Annual Snowfall:
3m
Snowmaking:
75% of pistes

Bus
regular services to the base of Grouse Mountain every half hour. (Bus 232 from Phibbs Exchange/Bus 236 from Lonsdale Quay) http://www.bctranslink.com
Fly
to Vancouver
Drive
15 minutes from downtown Vancouver. Follow Georgia Street westbound through Stanley Park and across the Lion's Gate Bridge. Take the North Vancouver exit to Marine Drive, then left up Capilano Road for 5 km (3.1 miles).

ʊଌଌ KICKING HORSE

	POOR	FAIR	GOOD	TOP
FREERIDE Trees & some off-piste				
FREESTYLE No park or pipe				
PISTES Huge array of slopes				

Freeride paradise

7
OUT OF 10

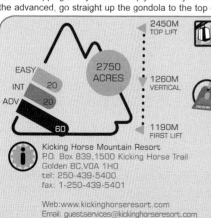

Rider: Ryan J/Photo:Mike McPhee

mountain and drop into either of the bowls off the ridge. If you fancy some hard core riding then take the **Stairway to Heaven chair** and take a short walk up to your left into the **Feuz Bowl**, or stay high and keep walking above Feuz Bowl leaving resort and access another huge bowl. If you've got a spare $4000 then take a 3 day Heliboarding trip, www.canadianheli-skiing.com based in Golden. Or $600 for a 3 decent day trip Purcellhelicopterskiing.com

FREESTYLERS may be forgiven for thinking that kicking horse is not for them. Freestyles not what Kicking Horse is about. It's splattering of natural hits and the occasional log won't keep your attention for long. There's no park although there's talk of one in the future.

PISTES. People who love the piste will enjoy the tree-lined trails which run in a straight line down to the base area. **Pioneer** and **Grizzly** are notable carvers' trails where you can lay out some fast lines at speed, but this is an advanced rated run so be warned.

BEGINNERS might look at the piste map and think that the place is made up of runs not suited to their ability, but on the ground it's a different story. You should head up **Catamount chair** where you'll be able to choose a number of well groomed very wide runs. If you can handle a short path then head up to the top and check out the **Crystal bowl** area.

THE TOWN
Off the slopes there is little to offer. At the base there is a small hire shop and a few places to get a bite to eat. There's new condo development going up with good position next to the base area but there not cheap. *Vagabond lodge* is the cheapest and has rooms from $160pppn and offer a good menu. Lodging and other local facilities can be found 2 miles away in the town of **Golden**. Although not the most happening place, it's free of marauding crowds, very affordable and is still okay. The *Kicking Horse Hostel* (www.kickinghorsehostel.com) Station Avenue, tel (250) 344-5071 has beds for $25.

Three hours west of **Calgary** and close to the town of **Golden** lies the resort of Kicking Horse. With large sums of dollars being spent on development, the resort is staking its claim as one of the biggest resorts around trying to be a match for the likes of Fernie and Lake Louise. A swift new gondola which takes you up to the very flash Eagle's eye Restaurant and a whole load of boarding options, is certainly helping to stake this claim. They are also hoping to open up some new extreme terrain in the Super Bowl area below Terminator ridge, and some new gladded beginners terrain near the base area; positions been granted so it should be soon. All the lower trails are hacked out between thick lines of ferns and suit novices, although there are a couple of notable advanced runs such as Pioneer and Grizzly. The top half of the mountain is of more interest to the better boarder with some decent black runs and a couple of double-diamonds to get your ticker going.

FREERIDERS Will love it; it's one of a few BC resorts with wide open powder faces. The trail marked out as **Porcupine** is a cool run that can be done at speed, but only if you know what you're doing. For the intermediate freerider, check out Kicking Horse, which starts out fairly mellow before dropping away more steeply mid-way down. For the advanced, go straight up the gondola to the top of the

---

2450M TOP LIFT	**Number of runs:** 106 Longest runs: 10km Total Lifts: 5 1 Gondola, 3 chairs, 1 drags Mountain Cafes: 2		Annual Snowfall: 7.6m Snowmaking: none
EASY **2750 ACRES**			Bus services to Golden from Calgary, takes around 3 hours. Snow shuttles run from Golden to Kicking Horse (15mins)
INT 20 **1260M** VERTICAL	Winter Period: Dec to April Lift Passes		
ADV 20	Half-day pass $42 1 Day pass - $57 6 Day pass - $309 Season pass - $735		Fly to Calgary, transfer time to is 3 hours.
60 **1190M** FIRST LIFT	Board School Private lesson $459 (6rs), Group $50 (2hrs). Beginner package $80 full day inc equipment, lesson & lift pass		Drive From Calgary take Trans-Canada Highway 1 west to Golden, 9 miles from highway,Goldens 15 mins.164 miles, 3 3/4 hours.
Kicking Horse Mountain Resort P.O. Box 839,1500 Kicking Horse Trail Golden BC,V0A 1H0 tel: 250-439-5400 fax: 1-250-439-5401 Web:www.kickinghorseresort.com Email: guestservices@kickinghorseresort.com	Hire Board & Boots $31 per day, performance stuff $47 Heliboarding See client services at the base lodge		1.5 hours west of Banff via the Trans Canada Highway

	POOR	FAIR	GOOD	TOP
FREERIDE Trees and some off-piste				
FREESTYLE A terrain park				
PISTES Good wide tree runs				

Good family resort

8 OUT OF 10

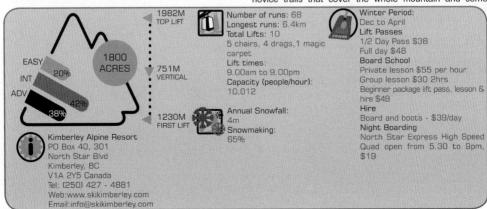

Pic. Kimberley Resort

C

C
A
N
A
D
A

B
R
I
T
I
S
H

C
O
L
U
M
B
I
A

owned by the same company that owns Lake Louise in Alberta, but that's about the only connection between two. Located 3 hours from Lake Louise, Kimberley is a resort that will appeal to everybody with a good selection of all level trails. The large percentage of easy and intermediate runs may be one reason that the slopes here attract a lot of skiers, however, snowboarders in the know are not left short changed with a good choice of fast black runs.

The runs are spread out over two faces and cut through a lot of thick spruce trees providing some great tree-riding. Although advanced riders are not going to be pushed much here, there are a couple of notable double black diamond runs that deserve full attention in order to avoid a broken collar bone.

FREERIDERS will find that Kimberley offers them some really cool tree-riding and some fairly good powder days. The runs off Buckhorn chair take you to some nice terrain, while the Easter triple chair lends access to the double black Flush run, which descends through trees that will either make or break you.

FREESTYLERS will be please to know that the park, the **Mambo Terrain Park** and the halfpipe have improved greatly since we last reviewed the resort. There are quiet a few unusual but really cool rails for all abilities. There are also a few good natural hits located off the Rosa chair, which also gives access to some gentle terrain interspersed with wooded sections where you can practice some grinding skills on downed logs.

PISTE lovers get the best look-in on Kimberley's slopes with some decent wide open runs allowing for big arcs. The run marked Main is a fast long burner which brings you out at the main base area, while Flapper is a shorter but faster pleaser.

BEGINNERS who plan to spend a week here should leave far more competent than when they arrived. This is a particularly good resort for beginners with some excellent novice trails that cover the whole mountain and some

Kimberley Alpine Resort, to give the place its full title, is on the up and up and is currently in the middle of a multi million dollar expansion plan that has incorporated new mountain facilities as well as a new slope side village. Kimberley's history, like many old Canadian towns, stems from the days of mining. However, you would be forgiven for not knowing this when you arrive as the area has been developed into an all year round quality outdoor recreation centre. First impressions of the place are not one of a sleepy old mining town; instead you are left feeling like you've just landed in a sausage-munching Bavarian town. Still, this strange fusion of Canada and Germany seems to work well as Kimberley is growing rapidly and is presently the fourth largest resort in British Columbia. Kimberley is

EASY **INT** 20% **ADV** **42%** 38%

1800 **ACRES**

1982M TOP LIFT

751M VERTICAL

1230M FIRST LIFT

Number of runs: 68
Longest runs: 6.4km
Total Lifts: 10
5 chairs, 4 drags, 1 magic carpet
Lift times:
9.00am to 9.00pm
Capacity (people/hour):
10,012

Annual Snowfall:
4m
Snowmaking:
65%

Winter Period:
Dec to April
Lift Passes
1/2 Day Pass $38
Full day $48
Board School
Private lesson $55 per hour
Group lesson $30 2hrs
Beginner package lift pass, lesson & hire $49
Hire
Board and boots - $39/day
Night Boarding
North Star Express High Speed Quad open from 5.30 to 9pm, $19

Kimberley Alpine Resort
PO Box 40, 301
North Star Blvd
Kimberley, BC
V1A 2Y5 Canada
Tel: (250) 427 - 4881
Web:www.skikimberley.com
Email:info@skikimberley.com

Pic - Kimberley Resort

nice long green runs that allow easy riding from the top to bottom.

THE TOWN

Downtown Kimberley is only five minutes from the slopes and offers a very good selection of facilities as well as what is said to be Canada's biggest cuckoo clock. Overall Kimberley is not a cheap resort in terms of accommodation and general local services. However, what is not in question is the way you are looked after; the locals are very friendly. Kimberley is also an all year round holiday destination offering a host of sporting attractions form golf to white-water rafting and water skiing.

Night wise, Kimberley is a bit dull and definitely not a hot action town. Nothing really stands out or captures your attention. The place has a number of bland bars that all seem to go in for far too much stupid après ski rubbish. Still, you can get very messy and drink on until the early morning hours.

Accommodation in Kimberley is very good with easy access slope side lodging in condo units or chalets. The *Rocky Mountain Condo* and Hotel centre is located at the very base of the slopes just a short walk from the North Star Express chair lit. The hotel offers everything you could want during your stay with units sleeping up to 14 people. Downtown Kimberley has the biggest selection of lodging with cheap B&B's and motels.

Food. Around Kimberley you will find a good mix of eateries with something for everyone to sample whether on the mountain or in the village. The Day Lodge Cafeteria serves up a good breakfast while *Mingles' Grill* specialise in killer grills. *Kelsey's* Restaurant and the *Steamwinder Pub* offer a good selection of bar food, although both are a bit cheesy going in for après ski.

Pic - Kimberley Resort

CAR
From Calgary, travel via Memoral Drive and the P2 / P3 and P95A routes all the way to Kimberley. Calgary to resort is 281 miles, 8 hours drive time.
FLY
to Calgary/Vancouver with daily domestic flights to Cranbrook (15 mins away).
BUS
Greyhound bus leaves Calgary at 6:15 pm and arrives 12:15 am, tel 1-800-661-8747

POOR FAIR GOOD TOP

FREERIDE
Trees and some steep stuff
FREESTYLE
A terrain park & pipe
PISTES
Some good runs

5 OUT OF 10

Basic but still cool

Pic Mt Washington

C
CANADA

BRITISH COLUMBIA

powder, trees and well groomed runs. As Mt Washington grows, so do the crowds, therefore be warned that the slopes can get busy at peak times.

FREERIDERS up to advanced status have a good selection of steep blacks reachable off the top of the **Eagle Express** chair. Here you can head down trails like Hawk, a fast run that starts out wide before dropping down through trees. Less adventurous but still as good is the cluster of runs off **The Gully**, such as **Scum's Delight.**

FREESTYLERS head here en-masse to ride some great natural terrain and take advantage of the clean hits in the park. Located by the **Coaster run** off the **Whiskey Jack** chair, the park is loaded with table-tops, gaps, hits and a good halfpipe.

PISTES. Carvers who only want a series of straight, fast slopes to cut up, will not be disappointed. If you're up to the grade, check out **Chimney** - it will prove whether you are a man or a mouse. Alternatively, **Whisky Jack** is a gentle but excellent carver's run, especially if you are still mastering the art.

BEGINNERS will have to do introductory courses on how to cope with bruises on the lower slopes, before heading up higher. Based at the lower sections, the **Green chair** and **Discovery** lift gives rise to some easy novice terrain.

THE TOWN
In resorts that are constantly growing and developing, one is bound to find differences each time you visit.
Local facilities are a bit sparse but what is on offer is good. If you can't find what you're after, then check out the offerings in **Courtney**, 25 minutes away. This is where you will also get the best night-life. **Accommodation** options are fairly extensive with 4,000 tourist beds available in a variety of condos and chalets, many of which are on, or very close to, the slopes. Lodging is not overpriced here - you can get a decent condo for C$70/night or a chalet from C$100.

Just off the west coast of Canada and floating in the Pacific Ocean is **Vancouver Island**, which is home to a number of resorts. The most notable and indeed the biggest is Mt Washington, which is located in the middle of the island. Over recent years large amounts of money has been spent on upgrading the whole area to make it modern and more fashionable. The amount of terrain available here is pretty cool offering a good mixture of off-piste,

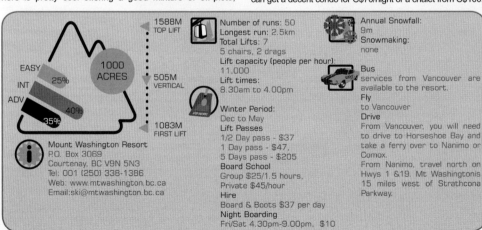

EASY
INT
ADV
25%
40%
35%
1000 ACRES

1588M TOP LIFT
505M VERTICAL
1083M FIRST LIFT

Number of runs: 50
Longest run: 2.5km
Total Lifts: 7
5 chairs, 2 drags
Lift capacity (people per hour):
11,000
Lift times:
8.30am to 4.00pm

Winter Period:
Dec to May
Lift Passes
1/2 Day pass - $37
1 Day pass - $47,
5 Days pass - $205
Board School
Group $25/1.5 hours,
Private $45/hour
Hire
Board & Boots $37 per day
Night Boarding
Fri/Sat 4.30pm-9.00pm, $10

Mount Washington Resort
P.O. Box 3069
Courtenay, BC V9N 5N3
Tel: 001 (250) 338-1386
Web: www.mtwashington.bc.ca
Email:ski@mtwashington.bc.ca

Annual Snowfall:
9m
Snowmaking:
none

Bus
services from Vancouver are available to the resort.
Fly
to Vancouver
Drive
From Vancouver, you will need to drive to Horseshoe Bay and take a ferry over to Nanimo or Comox.
From Nanimo, travel north on Hwys 1 &19. Mt Washingtonis 15 miles west of Strathcona Parkway.

wsg PANORAMMA

Great heli-boarding

FREERIDE
Trees & some bowls
FREESTYLE
park & pipe
PISTES
Some good wide pistes

POOR FAIR GOOD TOP

8 OUT OF 10

Pic - Taynton Bowl (c) Panoramma resort

P anorama has some cash and is spending it. In the last few years they've replaced 2 drag lifts with high speed quads, built some new accommodation, beefed up their snowmaking capabilities and opened up a great double diamond area called **Taynton Bowl**. Snowmaking! Snowmaking? Panorama has more sunshine days than any other resort in western Canada, great for the goggle marks, but not so good for the white stuff. The marketing team of Panorama has aimed at the family market, which if you are single or don't have kids is a real shame. If you do have kids then the short transfer time (3 hours/Calgary), the occasional fire work display, the hot pools and the kids party's make it a good chose. But and it's a big but, be prepared to pay through the nose for accommodation, it isn't cheap and there isn't a lot of choice. One of the other draws to Panorama is the Heliboarding in the **Bugaboos** area, which boasts over 2,000sq KM to ride so you'll always find freshies, but once again in true scamarama style, be ready to pay for it, call R.K. Heli-ski 1 888 7767730.

FREERIDING. Trees, trees and more trees. There's a limitless amount of tree riding here; steep, shallow, wide, tight, long short you name it, they've got a tree run for

you. For the advanced rider a short walk from the summit quad will lead you to **Taynton Bowl** which has a lot of steep treed shoots, but has a leg burning exit path. The **Extreme Dream Zone** has some shorter but still steep runs, with an easy out. Don't take your inexperienced mates into the Dream Zone as the trees are really tight and it'll be more of a nightmare zone.

FREESTYLE. The park is situated in the base area and has an ok pipe, a few hits and lots of rails. The park is fine but compared to some Canadian resorts Panoramas park is small and limited. The pistes don't offer too much in the way of hits or rollers but in Taynton Bowl there's loads of rock drops to fling yourself off.

PISTES. If you like it wide, well maintained and empty then this is the place. Most of the runs from the **Champagne Express chair** are well set up for you to crank out some full speed turns but with all that fake snow make sure you're edges are sharp.

BEGINNERS have lots of good blues and greens straight off the base chair. The designated beginner's area has a surface lift and there's a magic carpet for the complete novice. For those getting around the mountains who don't mind a pathway check out the **Sun Bowl Trail**.

THE TOWN
There's loads of slope side accommodation, but none cheap. If you're on a budget and have your own transport stay in **Invermere**, a 15 min drive away. The best place to rent a board or get your's serviced is *Lusti's*. Not much happens in Panorama at night unless you want to dress as a sailor and jump around on a bouncy castle and if that's your thing then get yourself off to the doctors, weirdo.

C

C A N A D A

B R I T I S H

C O L U M B I A

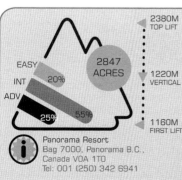

EASY
INT 20%
ADV
25% 55%

2847 ACRES

2380M TOP LIFT

1220M VERTICAL

1160M FIRST LIFT

Panorama Resort
Bag 7000, Panorama B.C.,
Canada V0A 1T0
Tel: 001 (250) 342 6941

Web:www.panoramaresort.com
Email:paninfo@intrawest.com

Number of runs: 100
Longest runs: 5.5km
Total Lifts: 9
1 Gondola, 5 chairs, 3 drags
Lift Capacity (people per hour): 8,500

Winter Period:
Dec to May
Lift Passes
1 Day pass $59, 5 days $249
Season $799
Board School
Group $49/1.5hr, Private $109/1.5hr
Hire
Board & Boots $35 per day, 5 days $140
Snowmobiles:2 hours $110
Heliboarding: Yes
Night Boarding
Thu-Sun Till 9.00pm inc Terrain parks

Annual Snowfall:
4.8m
Snowmaking:
40% of slopes

Bus
direct from Calgary
takes around 2 hrs.
Fly
to Calgary, 2 hours transfer
Drive
From Calgary, use highway 1 and P93 to Radium Hot Springs, then Hwy 95 to Invermere, which is 11 miles from Panorama. Calgary to resort is 184 miles. 4 3/4 hours drive

WSG RED

	POOR	FAIR	GOOD	TOP
FREERIDE Trees and good off-piste				
FREESTYLE A terrain park				
PISTES Good testing runs				

Great terrain, lots of new development

8 OUT OF 10

Pic -Red Resort

nevertheless has a lot going for it with excellent, crowd-free runs and early powder untrashed by morning masses. This could change as the resort's growing off the slope annually, with the new owners planning to build 1,400 dwellings and 70,000 sq feet of commercial space in the next 15 years. Having said that it's one of the only resorts in Canada to develop with style, taking full advantage of the abundant natural building materials, let's hope that keep to that philosophy.

Granite Mountain and Red make up 1,585 acres of terrain, but are serviced by only three very slow chair lifts and a short drag which at weekends can lead to a bit of a wait. There are plans over the next two years to install new lifts and open up more terrain. Both mountains offer a variety of runs that mainly suit snowboarders who ride well. First timers are going to have their work cut out. The trail map lists many of its runs with a star to mean extreme, and that's exactly what the runs live up to. Grante is the bigger of the two areas and is easily accessed from the base lodge. Once at the top you can head off in a variety of directions, but note that most of the runs at the top are for advanced riders, although Ridge Road will take novices off to easier slopes.

FREERIDERS should check out **Buffalo Ridge** which takes you down one side of Grante into bowls, natural hits and lots of trees. **Sara's Chute**, a double black, takes you down steeps, through trees and eventually brings you out onto **Long Squaw**, a green trail that leads back to the base area.

FREESTYLERS will find Red's new 6 acre park next to the drag lift at the base station. It's full of kickers and rails but no pipe. The local geeky kids will show you how to do it, watching an 8 year old in specs and all tucked in by his mother getting massive air is a regular occurrence. Alternatively, there are plenty of natural hits, especially on Grante Mountain.

PISTES huggers will find loads of good runs although not all are regularly groomed. On the Paradise side of the mountain, the terrain will suit those wanting tamer stuff

C
A
N
A
D
A

B
R
I
T
I
S
H

C
O
L
U
M
B
I
A

Red and the town of **Rossland**, which is a cool little town, go back in history to the days of the Canadian gold-rush of 1896. Founded by Scandinavian's looking for gold, Red is one of the oldest resorts in Canada. It's been operating as a ski resort since 1947 when its first chair lift was installed. As time has passed, so has Red's reputation, known for it's powder and some of the best extreme riding in Canada, Red has earned it's new found fame.

Freeriders will be stoked when they see what awaits them. Although this may not be in the super league of resorts, it

2073M
TOP LIFT

Number of runs: 83
Longest runs: 7km
Total Lifts: 6
5 chairs, 1 drag
Lift times:
8.45am to 3.30pm
Mountain Cafes:
2

EASY 10%
INT
ADV 45%
45%

1585 ACRES

813M
VERTICAL

Annual Snowfall:
7.6m
Snowmaking:
none

1185M
FIRST LIFT

Winter Period:
Dec to April
Lift Passes
Half-day £39
1 Day pass $52
6 of 7 Days pass - $288
Season Pass - $789
Board School
Private lesson $55 per hour
Group lesson $30 2hrs
Beginner package lift pass, lesson & hire $49
Hire
Board and boots - $39/day
Night Boarding
North Star Express High Speed Quad open from 5.30 to 9pm, $19

Red Mountain
P.O. Box 670,
Rossland, VOG 1YO, BC
General info: 001 (250) 362 7384
Web:www.ski-red.com
Email:info@ski-red.com

wsg RED

Pic - San Tan

have some cash and want to live it up, check out the Lofts, there fantastic high spec chalets with hot tubs, TV's bigger than a car and great views of the mountains. Red Robs are a good bet if you don't have the cash for the Lofts, Mountain Gypsy restaurant underneath serves great food. The base lodge does a good burger at lunch time.

Rossland is an old town that offers a variety of good local services from cheap eating haunts to boozy late night hangouts. Board and boot hire is available next to the slopes or in Rossland, check out Powder Hounds for all your needs.

Night-life in Rossland is not exactly the most happening, but it's still cool. It offers a number of good night-time hangouts where you can drink to jazz music or boogie to pop. Most bars play decent tunes and have pool tables. The Flying Steamshovel is bar, as are The Powder Keg and Rafter's.

Accommodation is as you'd expect from any resort. At the slopes there is a selection of Lodges, Chalets and Condo's. Places such as the Red Mountain Cabins, a short walk from the slopes, is pricey but very good as are the lofts. However, the best option is to stay in the town of Rossland which is only 2 miles from the slopes. The options include cheap B&B's and a hostel which are all close to the night-time action. Check the web site for accommodation and the latest prices.

Food. Rossland is not noted for its restaurants, but what you find is very good, and at prices to suit all pockets. Sunshine Cafe has a good menu while Elmer's serves great veggie food. The Flying Shovel dishes up good pub grub. Mountain Gypsy is the spot for pizzas and pasta.

and carvers can lay out big lines on runs such as Southern Comfort. Other notable trails to check out are **Doug's Run** and **Maggie's Farm.**

BEGINNERS may be a bit put off when they first see the terrain level ratings and although the slopes are rated intermediate/advanced, it doesn't mean novices can't ride here. There is ample terrain to play on at the Upper and Lower Back trails, before riding the Long Squaw trail that runs back to the base lodge. The local snowboard school caters well for all your first time needs by offering a number of tuition program's that will soon have you shredding Red Mountain with ease. They have a very helpful new 225 foot Magic Carpet lift at the base for first timers.

THE TOWN
Red Mountain has a good selection of lodging properties and facilities at the base of the slopes. Prices vary but staying close to the slopes is generally more expensive than staying down the road in the town of Rossland. If you

CAR
From Vancouver take TRANSCANADA 1 eastbound to Hope. Then Hwy 3 through to Grand Forks. Continue another 45mins to Nancy Greene Lake, turn right onto Hwy 3B. Follow Hwy 3B until you reach Red Mountain
TRAIN
to Spokane in the US
FLY
Fly to Vancouver International is 7hrs drive away. Spokane Airport is 2.5hrs drive away.
Castlegar airport is 30 mins.
BUS
A bus from Vancouver takes around 7 hours. A Local bus runs daily from Rossland to Red Mountain. Airport transfer available from Spokane airport $C90 each way.

wsg SILVER STAR

FREERIDE
Trees and good off-piste
FREESTYLE
A terrain park
PISTES
Some good testing runs

POOR FAIR GOOD TOP

Good all-round resort

7
OUT OF 10

Pic - Silver Star Mountain Resort BC, Canada/Don Weixl.psd

Take a trip to Silver Star and you'll feel like you've taken a trip. When you walk down the high street, which is part of a piste, you walk through a purpose built fake mining village. The shops are painted bright colours and have a raised wooden walkway outside. If you look up you expect to see a mock cowboy shootout around each corner you expect to bump into Mickey Mouse. That said Silver Star has an average snow fall of over 6 meters, a front side of well groomed pistes, and a backside of hard core shoots. Silver Star won't disappoint riders, and you won't see Mickey. Beginners will also appreciate Silver Star with its well connected green and blue runs. The local snowboard school runs daily programmes as well as weekly camps which offer video analysis.

FREERIDERS who start in the town and should head down to the 6 man **Comet Express** which takes you to the top of the

Vance Creek area, from here you can head down Big Dipper over a few rollers to the park or back down one of the many groomed pistes to the chair. After warming up, take the flat Bergerstrasse green run to the hard core **Putnam Creek Area**. The double diamonds in this area are steep tree lined shoots which will test the best. Check out **Where's Bob** and after 50 meters drop left into a hidden shoot which will join up with the bottom of **Stardust**. All the runs on the **Putnam creek** area are only serviced by the **Powder Gulch Express** chair, so on a fresh snow day get there early.

FREESTYLERS looking for air will be pleasantly surprised with the natural hits. However, with a two acre fun-park, you don't need to look far to find places to hit. The park is located below **Big Dipper** trail.

PISTE lovers will find this a challenging resort. The **Milky Way** is an excellent open area where big arcs can be accomplished with ease. However, the steepest carvable pistes are on the North Face slopes where you'll be put to the test. Most of the **Vance Creek** area is well maintained but is always the busiest part of the resort.

BEGINNERS will find that Silver Star has a good selection of progressive runs easily accessed by chair lifts, although you will find you'll have to negotiate some pathways to make the most of the resort.

THE TOWN

Off the slopes, Silver Star's old-fashioned Victorian theme is by far the maddest village you'll ever board from, Silver Star has a good range of accommodation and although not kicking it does have a few bars fine for a drink and a bite to eat. The best bar is *Long Johns pub*, which often has live music. Those on a budget should stay at the hostel where many of the resort staff hang out and is a good place to meet a local to show you round. The town of **Vernon** is located only a short distance from Silver Star and offers a greater selection of facilities. Vernon is the place to go for a lively Saturday night out and to eye up some local skirt.

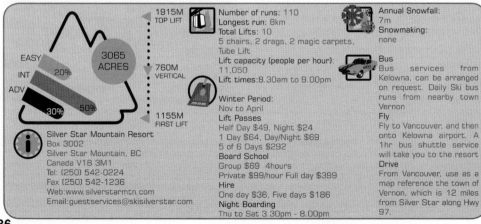

EASY
INT 20%
ADV
30% 50%

3065 ACRES

1915M
TOP LIFT

760M
VERTICAL

1155M
FIRST LIFT

Silver Star Mountain Resort
Box 3002
Silver Star Mountain, BC
Canada V1B 3M1
Tel: (250) 542-0224
Fax (250) 542-1236
Web: www.silverstarmtn.com
Email: guestservices@skisilverstar.com

Number of runs: 110
Longest run: 8km
Total Lifts: 10
5 chairs, 2 drags, 2 magic carpets, Tube Lift
Lift capacity (people per hour): 11,050
Lift times: 8.30am to 9.00pm

Winter Period:
Nov to April
Lift Passes
Half Day $49, Night $24
1 Day $64, Day/Night $69
5 of 6 Days $292
Board School
Group $69 4hours
Private $99/hour Full day $399
Hire
One day $36, Five days $186
Night Boarding
Thu to Sat 3.30pm - 8.00pm

Annual Snowfall:
7m
Snowmaking:
none

Bus
Bus services from Kelowna, can be arranged on request. Daily Ski bus runs from nearby town Vernon
Fly
Fly to Vancouver, and then onto Kelowna airport. A 1hr bus shuttle service will take you to the resort
Drive
From Vancouver, use as a map reference the town of Vernon, which is 12 miles from Silver Star along Hwy 97.

wsg SUN PEAKS

	POOR	FAIR	GOOD	TOP
FREERIDE Trees & some backcountry				
FREESTYLE park & pipe				
PISTES Something for everyone				

A really good resort

7 OUT OF 10

Pic - Sun Peaks Tourism

C
A
N
A
D
A

B
R
I
T
I
S
H

C
O
L
U
M
B
I
A

Peaks is a large resort with a large vertical descent. The marked-out terrain isn't super-varied, but what is on offer is still good and well prepared with riding to suit all levels and styles.

FREERIDERS looking for long, wide straights with trees galore will find this mountain ideal, keeping you well occupied for a week or more. Take the long **Burfield Quad** to the top and you can gain access to some great terrain. If you plan to go outside the marked boundary, you are required to register with the ski-patrol. For some cool in-boundary riding, **Head Wall** is the place to bust a gut, with a series of short but demanding double diamond blacks. For something a little less daunting, try out the long and sweeping 5 mile trail off the **Ridge**, which can be tackled by intermediate riders.

FREESTYLERS have a massive 30 acre fun park area located off the **Sunrise chair**, which is loaded with hits and a pipe. Around the slopes you also find numerous natural hits to launch off.

PISTES. Sun Peaks appeals to carvers and fast riders in a big way; some of the runs here are superb, and just right for laying the board over an edge at speed. If you have the balls, try the steep **Expo**; if not, try your luck down **Spillway**.

BEGINNERS who don't appreciate the novice slopes here or manage to progress with style should give up snowboarding and take up train spotting. This is an excellent beginner's resort with some perfect novice tracks off **Sundance**.

THE TOWN

Accommodation and all other amenities can be found in **Sun Peaks** or in the small hamlet of **Burfield**. Whichever you choose, both offer good facilities that compliment those on the slopes. Mind you, it should be pointed out that this is not a budget rider's destination as it can get expensive. There's a good choice of restaurants, bars and shops to choose from, but night-life is very tame with *Masa's* the favoured evening hangout for booze, music and meeting the locals.

Sun Peaks is a resort that hopes to knock Whistler off the top spot. Situated about 40 miles from **Kamloops**, in the interior of the Rockies, this is a resort that has come of age. Over the past few years, huge expansion plans have been put into operation with fast modern lifts and massive changes to the layout and structure of the village. The overall results mean a damn fine mountain to ride that is not overpopulated with holiday masses. Sun

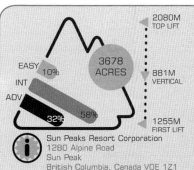

2080M TOP LIFT

881M VERTICAL

1255M FIRST LIFT

3678 ACRES

EASY 10%
INT
ADV
32% 58%

Number of runs: 117
Longest runs: 8km
Total Lifts: 11
5 chairs, 3 drags, 2 tows, 1 magic carpet
Lift Capacity (people per hour): 9,000
Lift times: 8.30am to 3.30pm

Winter Period:
Nov to April
1/2 Day pass $46
1 Day pass $56
Season pass $799
Board Schools
2Hours Group $49/69
Private $52/hr
Snowmobiles
Yes

Annual Snowfall:
5.59m
Snowmaking:
65% of slopes

Bus
Bus services from Vancouver takes 5 1/2 hours. Sun-star run a Shuttle service from Kamloops airport to resort, $34 visit www.sunstarshuttle.com

Fly
Fly to Vancouver with domestic flights to Kamloops (45 mins away).

Drive
From Vancouver, take Hwy 1 east via Kamloops, then via Hwy 5 exit to Jasper for Sun Peaks.

Sun Peaks Resort Corporation
1280 Alpine Road
Sun Peak
British Columbia, Canada V0E 1Z1
Phone: (250) 578-7222
Fax: (250) 578-7223
Web:www.sunpeaksresort.com
Email:info@sunpeaksresort.com

187

	POOR	FAIR	GOOD	TOP
FREERIDE Trees and amazing off-piste				
FREESTYLE World leader in parks & pipes				
PISTES Huge array of good runs				

10
OUT OF 10

Pic - Photographer Toshi Kawano

C

C
A
N
A
D
A

B
R
I
T
I
S
H

C
O
L
U
M
B
I
A

Whistler/Blackcomb. Where to begin? Repeatedly rated as the No. 1 resort in North America and not without reason, Whistler will host the **2010 Winter Olympics** and is without doubt one of the best resorts in the world. A combination of absolutely unbelievable terrain combined with Intrawest ownership has shunted Whistler to super-resort status, but glitz aside, experience the riding here for yourself to see why.

Two monstrous mountains cradle the purpose built village of Whistler itself - year round population 10,000, swelling to 5 times that peak season - beware school holidays. Now almost as famous for it's amazing mountain biking as it's snowboarding (freestyle adrenaline seekers checkout the downhill park if in summer camp!), Whistler is a magical encounter for all ability levels. You really can ride here for years without becoming bored. Whistler has it all - 33 lifts accessing over 7000 acres of varied and challenging terrain, amazing backcountry access, bowls, steeps, trees, 2 terrain parks and 3 pipes, 2 of them superpipes. The downside of having it all is crowding - avoid Christmas and Easter at all costs. Early Dec. or Jan. are often good for a local vibe with no crowds and lots of pow. The village throngs with restaurants, bars and clubs. Doing a season here is an excellent choice to do both the vast mountain and social scenes justice. Brits under 35 (and now non-students) can obtain a 1 year BUNAC work permit and as a result may soon be competing with droves of Aussies seeking beds in Intrawest staff housing for the winter.

Party hounds should check out the annual **World Ski and Snowboard Festival** held every April, with pipe and big air comps, live bands and DJ's. Powder hounds - go for 'Fresh Trax' tickets to access the mountain before the crowds at 7am - if any sense leave the breakfast to the skiers and go ride those pillows lines!

Blackcomb Glacier is home to a handful of snowboard camps in summer, including Camp of Champions and Whistler Summer Snowboard Camp. Open to all levels they can be pricey but what a way to parallel superkid Shaun White! The summer scene up there is spectacular with tons to do in the evenings - Whistler has it's own skatepark, dirt jumps and downhill park, a must for the still hungry adrenaline seeker.

FREERIDERS

The resort is sheer powder heaven when it dumps, which is often with its Pacific Northwest climate. Natural hits spring up all over both mountains which both have amazing tree

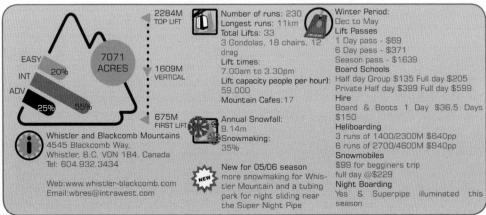

2284M
TOP LIFT

1609M
VERTICAL

675M
FIRST LIFT

EASY
20%
INT
ADV
25%   55%

7071 ACRES

Whistler and Blackcomb Mountains
4545 Blackcomb Way,
Whistler, B.C. V0N 1B4, Canada
Tel: 604.932.3434

Web:www.whistler-blackcomb.com
Email:wbres@intrawest.com

Number of runs: 230
Longest runs: 11km
Total Lifts: 33
3 Gondolas, 18 chairs, 12 drag
Lift times:
7.00am to 3.30pm
Lift capacity people per hour):
59,000
Mountain Cafes: 17

Annual Snowfall:
9.14m
Snowmaking:
35%

NEW New for 05/06 season
more snowmaking for Whis-tler Mountain and a tubing park for night sliding near the Super Night Pipe

Winter Period:
Dec to May
Lift Passes
1 Day pass - $69
6 Day pass - $371
Season pass - $1639
Board Schools
Half day Group $135 Full day $205
Private Half day $399 Full day $599
Hire
Board & Boots 1 Day $36,5 Days $150
Heliboarding
3 runs of 1400/2300M $640pp
6 runs of 2700/4600M $940pp
Snowmobiles
$99 for begginers trip
full day @$229
Night Boarding
Yes & Superpipe illuminated this season

runs, both marked and unmarked. On Whistler try **Peak to Creek** via the Peak Chair and Bagel or West Bowl. Even better, get a local to point you to **CBC trees** and **Khybers** for a 'Clearcut' BC forest experience. The whole **Harmony area** is awesome, with open bowls, cornices, shutes and pillow lines galore. Blackcomb Glacier is a must - access it via Spanky's Ladder to drop into **Ruby, Diamond, Sapphire** and **Garnet bowls** or the Showcase T Bar to encounter the infamous wind-lip. Seventh Heaven and Crystal Chair offer pillows, cliffs, tight trees and more. Remember, if it's raining in the village it's often puking up top - don't let the sometimes damp village conditions put you off.

FREESTYLERS

Both mountains have pristine terrain parks, with Blackcmb's beauty continually rated no. 1 in Transworld Snowboarding alongside Mammoth, CA (also Intrawest owned). The park is split into 3 levels - pay an extra $15 for unlimited use of the Advanced park and remember the mandatory helmet - most of the booters are an average of 40-60 ft. DJ's blast an eclectic mixture of tunes from a booth on the legendary shack booter, the first in a series of similar monstrosities which take you either to **Catskinner Chair** or continue through the superpiupe to **Solar Coaster.** The park also features a wide variety of technical rails, spine jumps, a gap jump and quarterpipe with alterations throughout the season. 90% of Canada's pro-riders reside in Whistler so watch out for cutting edge action and lots of filming. The Intermediate park on skiers right has the same features on a smaller scale and beginners can try the **Terrain Garden** (off Easy Out) or **Habitat Park** on Whistler. Newly opened last season as part of the **FIS Snowboard World Championships** was the Night Superpipe located at Base 2, in conjunction with the 'King of the Rail' competition held weekly under Magic Chair lights.

PISTES

Carvers and speed freaks will love the deliciously long, wide open groomers of both mountains. On **Blackcomb, Springboard, Rock and Roll** and **Ridgerunner** are a must and Panorama on 7th Heaven features a set of natural, groomed rollers that will boot you to the gods. On Whistler, cruise down to Creekside via the **Dave Murray downhill**. The **Saddle, Tokum** and **Bear Paw** are also immaculate groomers, ripe for early morning ripping but always check the grooming maps to avoid running into mogul fields!

BEGINNERS

The enormous and expertly staffed Snowboard School caters for riders from 6 upwards - Super Sliders (6-8), Super Riders (9-12), Ride Tribe (13-17) and Adult. Group (up to 8 people), private and other tailored lessons leave from all 3 bases, Whistler, Blackcomb and Creekside, and cater for every level. Beginners are well looked after on the Magic Chair (Blackcomb base) or Olympic Chair (Whistler mid-station). Whistler has the most green (novice) trails so it is best for practising riders. Freestyle programmes focusing purely on park and pipe are also available. Contact www.whistler-blackcomb.com

THE TOWN

Whistler is a paradoxical paradise with extreme being the word, attracting anything from the likes of Timberlake and Diaz to hoards of Kokanee swigging Aussies living the dream and 'doing a season'. On the surface it appears hellishly expensive, and can be so, but dig deeper and the friendly locals will point you to the good spots to ride, eat, party and purchase. There are dozens of high profile shops and some cool local establishments, Showcase, Evolution and the Circle are thriving snowboard shops with knowledgeable, easy going staff. Whistler is also home to dozens of bars and restaurants, 2 movie theatres, ice skating and swimming at Meadow Park, and an indoor climbing wall and tennis courts. All amenities are within easy walking distance including the lifts accessing both mountains.

C

C
A
N
A
D
A

B
R
I
T
I
S
H

C
O
L
U
M
B
I
A

Pic - Photographer Toshi Kawano

NIGHTLIFE

Nightlife begins at Apres. Worth checking out in the village are *GLC* featuring chilled live DJ's, vaulted windows overlooking the slopes and a huge log fire. *Amsterdam Cafe* caters for a funky young crowd and *Citta* and *Crystal Lounge* are cool places to chill back with some Nachos and the odd Hockey game. The *Longhorn* and *Merlins* can be a laugh, often housing fur clad skiers in ridiculous head-gear playing party games under instruction of local character and musician 'Guitar Doug'. In the Creek, *Dusty's* is the place to go. After dark the options are varied: again GLC rates highly, with local and international DJ's spinning music such as hip hop and drum 'n' bass. Local hip hop legend Mat the Alien (from Bury no less!) plays weekly at *Moe Joe's*, a locals favourite night. Try Thursday's at *Garfinkels* for an evening of cheesy drunken debauchery or *Tommy's* for a young, clubby dance crowd or hideous 80's night on a Monday. *Buffalo Bills* is where the over 30's head, a notorious cougar hangout, watch out boys!

ACCOMODATION

Accommodation in general is expensive but top quality, with outdoor pools and hot tubs the norm even at mid price places. Whistler has the most ski in-ski out accommodation of any resort in North America, ranging from the royally expensive Chateau Whistler and recently opened 5 star *Four Seasons*, to *Hostelling International* on Alta Lake and the *Shoestring Lodge* at Nesters. With over 2 million annual visitors a year, rooms in all areas fill early so book early to avoid disappointment. Decent mid price hotels include the *Coast Whistler* and *Blackcomb Lodge*. Most places offer deals late and early season - take advantage of this to experience the World Ski and Snowboard Festival in April and often surprisingly good snow conditions.

FOOD

Locals frequent cafes such as *Ingrid's*, *Gone Bakery* and *Behind the Grind* for hearty, homemade soups and snacks. *Java* and *Samaurai Sushi* at Nesters Mall are great local hangouts if you have wheels (or are staying at the Shoestring Lodge). On the cheap but nasty side, Whistler hides McDonald's and KFC in its Marketplace, alternatively, meat eaters should pop around the corner to *Splitz Grill* for the best burger in town. Higher on the price ladder do not leave Whistler without a visit to *Sushi Village*, eternal local favourite and as famous for it's strawberry sake margs as scrumptious menu. *La Bocca* is funky and fresh with a great patio and expensive but amazing extremes are *Araxi* and *Bearfoot Bistro*. When riding, avoid the ludicrously overpriced junk on-mountain and ride to the village for lower cost and way better quality.

CAR Vancouver via Squamish on Hwy 99. Whistler is 115km , drive time is about 2 1/4 hours.
TRAIN direct to Whistler
FLY Fly to Vancouver International. Transfer time to resort is 2 hours. If you have the cash, you can take a HeliJet straight to the resort in 30mins
BUS A bus from Vancouver takes around 2 hours.
Take the Perimeters Whistler express from the airport straight to Whistler, its $65 each way, $130 return and leaves every couple of hours. Geryhound and Snowbus run daily services from Vancouver city.
A local bus runs daily around Whistler and Blackcomb.

FREERIDE
Trees & awesome bowls
FREESTYLE
Just natural features
PISTES
Some moderatly tricky slopes

7
OUT OF 10

It's all about the powder!

Pic -Whitewater

and lay down one powder track next to another. Get up early to challenge **Blast**, a steep fall-line under the chair lift. There are many, many awesome areas filled with powder at Whitewater, however, we think they should remain secret...sorry! But if you are up for a walk and you have a look around you'll find them.

FREESTYLERS need to roam over the whole area to find places to get air, as there is no permanent pipe or park. However, there is plenty of great natural freestyle terrain.

PISTES. Carvers wanting fast groomed terrain will enjoy Whitewater's trails which offer every level of hard booter something to tackle. But, c'mon, you are at Whitewater...enjoy the pow!

C

C A N A D A   B R I T I S H   C O L U M B I A

Whitewater is located close to the town of **Nelson** and is a very good bet for riding even when other resorts are begging for snow. Whitewater receives 1,200cm of snow each winter and due to the areas stable winter temperatures, the snow lasts and lasts. The lifts access some of the best high altitude in-bounds terrain in Canada. Whitewater is a huge bowl, contained by two ridges that join at the apex to form the 2,440m (800 ft) **Ymir Peak**. Ymir (pronounced 'why-mur') is named after a Norse legend and traps any westerly storm. Water vapour sucked off nearby **Kootenay Lake** is turned into consistently dry champagne powder that fills the bowl. Admittedly a 'high end' resort, with a majority of expert and intermediate terrain, Whitewater still has a lot of room for those lovers of groomed run cruising with long, easy beginner runs off the **Silver King lift**.

FREERIDERS should take the Summit chair to access the opposite ridge which offers steeper, groomed, intermediate runs and the most challenging off-piste through bowls and trees. Try **Dynamite, Catch Basin** and **Glory Basin**,

BEGINNERS will find that Whitewater is the kind of area that doesn't really have beginners - just learners who progress in powder by riding steeper and deeper lines. A beginner park called **The Hunter** has been created near the day lodge. However most people who have mastered the basics choose to head for the hills and carve up snow where groomers never reach.

THE TOWN
There is no in-resort **accommodation** available at present, but there is a wide range of places to sleep in the town of Nelson. **Nelson** has good local facilities and is very affordable, if only a bit dull and basic. *Coal Oil Jonny's* offers Nelson brewed beer on tap. *The Dancing Bear Inn* and *Flying Squirrel International Hostel* have Stay and Ride specials from C$53 (04/05 prices). During the day there is great food in *Shucky's Eatery* (even the soups are made with wine), and offers everything from fries to a full course lunch. This is NOT your standard resort food; it's more like that cosy, quaint little mom and pops type food. Yum!

EASY	20%
INT	
ADV	40%
	40%

2040M TOP LIFT
396M VERTICAL
1640M FIRST LIFT

Number of runs: 24
Longest runs: 8km
Total Lifts: 3
2 chairs,1 drag magic carpet
Lift times: 9.00am to 3.30pm

Winter Period:
Nov to April
Lift Passes
1/2 Day pass $32
Full day $44
Season $630
Board Schools
$49 2 hour lesson, pass, board hire
Halof day $29
Full day $45

Annual Snowfall:
12m
Snowmaking:
none

Bus
services from Vancouver, go to the town of Nelson.
Fly
Fly to Vancouver, with a transfer time of around 12 hours.
Castlegar Airport is 41km from the resort
Drive
From Vancouver, use as a map reference the town of Nelson along Hwy3 of Hwy 6, 394 miles. From Nelson head south on Highway 6 towards Salmo for 12km until you see the turn off for resort.
Calgary to resort is 374 miles

Whitewater Ski and Winter Resort
PO Box 60. Nelson, BC
Canada. V1L 5P7
Phone: (250) 354-4944
Fax: (250) 354-4988

Web:www.skiwhitewater.com
Email: info@skiwhitewater.com

191

FAIRMONT SPRINGS

Small family resort, about 40 miles from Banf
Number of Runs: 13
Longest run: 1 mile (1.6km)
Info: Has a terrain park (nothing big) & beginners pipe
Top Lift: 1585m

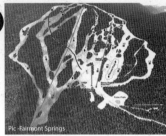
Pic - Fairmont Springs

Bottom Lift: 1280m
Vertical: 304m
Total Lifts: 2 - 1 chairs, 1 drags
Lift pass: 1/2 Day Pass - $25
Day Pass - $34
Lift times: 4.00pm to 10.00pm
Hire: Board & Boots $20
School: 1 Hour lesson - $44
Contact:
Fairmont Hot Springs Resort
Box 10, Fairmont Hot Springs,
British Columbia, Canada, V0B 1L0
Phone: 1-800-663-4979 or
Tel: 250-345-6311
www.fairmontresort.com
info@fairmonthotsprings.com
Location: Hwy. 93/95, 3 hours west of Calgary

HARPER MOUNTAIN

A decent size family resort, near Kamloops.

Ride Area: 400 acres
Number of Runs: 15
Easy 25%
Intermediate 50%
Advanced 25%
Info: Has a terrain park
Top Lift: 1524m
Bottom Lift: 1097m
Vertical: 427m
Total Lifts: 3 - 1 chairs, 2 drags
Lift pass: 1/2 Day Pass - $21
Day Pass - $29
Lift times: 9.30am to 10.00pm
Hire: Board & Boots $34 a day
School: Full day inc hire, lift pass & lessons $215
Contact:
Snow Phone 250-573-4616
Office 250-372-2119
Lodge 250-573-5115
www.harpermountain.com
info@harpermountain.com

HEMLOCK VALLEY

Number of Runs: 34
Info: Has a terrain park
Top Lift: 1524m
Bottom Lift: 975m
Vertical: 397m
Total Lifts: 4 - 3 chairs, 1 drags
Lift pass: 1/2 Day Pass - $32
Day Pass - $39
  Night Pass - $15
Lift times: 9.30am to 10.00pm
Hire: Board & Boots $36 a day
School: Beginners all in day lesson, lift, hire $59.00
Private lesson $56 per hour
Contact:
20955 Hemlock valley road.
Agassiz B.C. Canada V0M-1A1
Phone: (604) 797-4411
Fax: (604) 797-4440
www.hemlockvalleyresort.com
info@hemlockvalleyresort.com

Pic -Hemlock Valley

MOUNT SEYMOUR RESORT

30 minutes from Vancouver with 3 terrain parks & a halfpipe

Ride Area: 60 acres
Number of Runs: 21
Longest run: 1.6km
Info: Well setup up for freestylers with 3 terrain parks and a halfpipe
Snowfall: 17m
Top Lift: 1265m
Bottom Lift: 1020m
Vertical: 330m
Total Lifts: 5 - 2 chairs, 2 magic carpets
Lift pass: Day pass $34
Lift times: 8.30am to 10.00pm
Night Boarding: 11 slopes lit, pass $15
Hire: Board & Boots $37 a day
School: Day lesson, lift & hire $45
Contact:
Mount Seymour Resort
1700 Mt Seymour Rd
North Vancouver, BC
V7G 1L3
General Information 604.986.2261
24-Hour Snow Phone 604.718.7771
Resort Fax 604.986.2267
www.mountseymour.com
guestservices@mountseymour.com
Location: 30 minutes from downtown Vancouver. Heading west on Hwy #1, cross the Second Narrows Bridge, take the 3rd exit (#22) on to Mount

Seymour Parkway and follow the signs to the Provincial Park. Turn left at Mount Seymour Road (at MohawkStation) and arrive at the base area in 15 minutes.

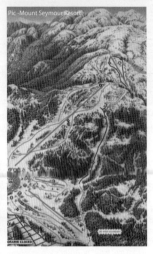
Pic -Mount Seymour Resort

POWDER KING

Number of Runs: 24
Easy 34%
Intermediate 33%
Advanced 33%
Average snowfall: 12.52m

Top Lift: 1829m
Bottom Lift: 935m
Vertical: 640m
Total Lifts: 3 - 1 chairs, 2 drags
Lift pass: Day pass $40, half day $33
Adult Season passes $574-804 depending on when bought.
Lift times: Thursday to Sunday.
Usually 9 or 9:30AM till 3 or 3:30PM
Hire: Board & Boots $25 per day, half-day $20. Demo boards $30 per day
School: Group lesson, 2hrs $16.05
Private lessson $23.99 first hour, then $14.99 ph
Contact:
Powder King Mountain Resort Inc.
P.O. Box 22023
Pine Centre Postal Station
Prince George, B.C.
V2N 4Z8
Tel/Fax: (250) 962-5899
Web: www.powderking.com
Fly to Prince George, 195 km from resort
Drive: From Vancouver, head north on Highway 97 to Prince George, then head north 195 km (122mi) to the mountain.
From Edmonton head north to Dawson Creek, and then come south to Powder King approximately 210km (131mi)

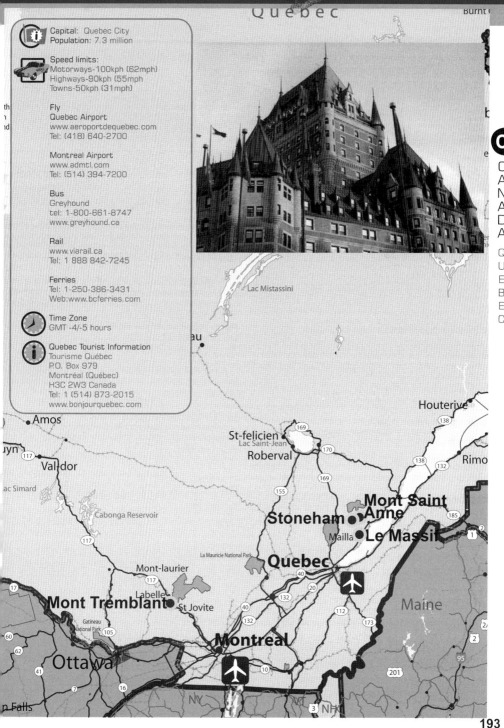

Capital: Quebec City
Population: 7.3 million

Speed limits:
Motorways-100kph (62mph)
Highways-90kph (55mph)
Towns-50kph (31mph)

Fly
Quebec Airport
www.aeroportdequebec.com
Tel: (418) 640-2700

Montreal Airport
www.admtl.com
Tel: (514) 394-7200

Bus
Greyhound
tel: 1-800-661-8747
www.greyhound.ca

Rail
www.viarail.ca
Tel: 1 888 842-7245

Ferries
Tel: 1-250-386-3431
Web:www.bcferries.com

Time Zone
GMT -4/-5 hours

Quebec Tourist Information
Tourisme Québec
P.O. Box 979
Montréal (Québec)
H3C 2W3 Canada
Tel: 1 (514) 873-2015
www.bonjourquebec.com

Quebec

Burnt

C

CANADA QUEBEC

Lac Mistassini

Houterive

Amos

St-felicien
Lac Saint-Jean
Roberval

138

138   132   Rimo

Val-dor   117

Lac Simard

Cabonga Reservoir

155

169

170

169

185

Mont Saint Anne

Stoneham

Mailla

Le Massif   1   2

117

La Mauricie National Park

Mont-laurier

Quebec

Maine

17

Mont Tremblant   Labelle   St Jovite

40   132

132

112

173

40   20

Gatineau National Park   105

60

62

Montreal

Ottawa

41

7   16

10

201

2

95

n Falls   NY   3   NH

FREERIDE
Trees but very limited off-piste
FREESTYLE
A terrain park
PISTES
Some well groomed slopes

POOR FAIR GOOD TOP

4
OUT OF 10

Le Massif is an unassuming and rather un-adventurous small mountain resort that lies just 45 minutes north of **Quebec City**. In recent years the resort has undergone a number of major re-developments spending in excess of 25 million dollars on facilities that will greatly improve not only the number and type of mountain runs, but also access to the resort and local facilities. It was also taken over in 2004 and its new owners spent a further $5million on improvements.You can now travel from Quebec City along route 138 to the top of the slopes, as well as the base. What you will find on your arrival is a mountain that offers most grades something to try out although it has to be said that a week here would become very boring after a few days. Still the resort can now boast up to 36 marked out trails which are tree lined up to the summit which is also the location of the new Day Lodge. All 36 runs are serviced by just 5 lifts including a new fast quad chair, which Le Massif boasts at being the longest high speed chair lift in **Quebec Province**. And that's not the only boast they make around here, as they also claim to have the most extensive snowmaking facilities on the east coast. What ever the legitimacy of such claims, Le Massif can claim to be an okay place to ride if you are a total beginner or basic intermediate rider.

FREERIDERS have a fairly ordinary mountain to ride that allows for some basic freeriding down mixed ability slopes which are sandwiched between lots of dense wooded sections. However, this place is not hard-core and forget about any decent back-country terrain or powder bowls.

FREESTYLERS should be able to have fun here. There are plenty of spots where you can pull some natural air with banks of snow lining many of the tree lined slopes. You will also find the odd log to grind over, (should you not mind wrecking your boards base). There is a terrain park under the Camp Boule Express .

PISTES. Riders who come to a resort looking for loads of super fast steeps, should go else where. That said Le Massif does have a number of nicely groomed carving trails to ride along.

BEGINNERS have the best chance to shine here with a good selection of easy runs to choose from which can all be reached with ease and with out needing to use drag lifts all the time.

THE TOWN. Off the slopes Le Massif's local facilities are basic to the extreme. All your accommodation and eating needs can be found down in Quebec City which is 45 minutes away.

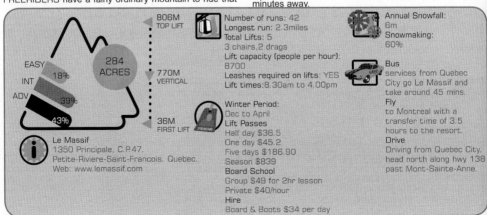

284 ACRES

EASY 18%
INT
ADV 39%
43%

806M TOP LIFT

770M VERTICAL

36M FIRST LIFT

Le Massif
1350 Principale, C.P.47,
Petite-Riviere-Saint-Francois, Quebec.
Web: www.lemassif.com

Number of runs: 42
Longest run: 2.3miles
Total Lifts: 5
3 chairs,2 drags
Lift capacity (people per hour):
8700
Leashes required on lifts: YES
Lift times:8.30am to 4.00pm

Winter Period:
Dec to April
Lift Passes
Half day $36.5
One day $45.2
Five days $186.90
Season $839
Board School
Group $49 for 2hr lesson
Private $40/hour
Hire
Board & Boots $34 per day

Annual Snowfall:
6m
Snowmaking:
60%

Bus
services from Quebec
City go Le Massif and
take around 45 mins.
Fly
to Montreal with a
transfer time of 3.5
hours to the resort.
Drive
Driving from Quebec City,
head north along hwy 138
past Mont-Sainte-Anne.

POOR FAIR GOOD TOP

FREERIDE
Trees & bit of off-piste
FREESTYLE
2 terrain parks & halfpipe
PISTES
Some okay slopes

A bit tedious, but okay for a few days

6
OUT OF 10

Pic Mt Saint Anne Resort

C

C
A
N
A
D
A

Q
U
E
B
E
C

Mont Sainte-Anne is a decent resort and will certainly keep an intermediate rider content for a few days and a beginner satisified for a week with ease. With its proximity to Quebec City, the tree lined slopes here attract hoards of city dwellers at weekends, making this a busy place to ride and while the resort can boast lots of rideable terrain, this is not the highest of resorts. Any resort close to a large city is often busy and suffers long lift queues, but thanks to the fast, high-tech lift system, these are greatly eliminated. Spread out on three facing slopes, **South, North** and **West**, the trails cut through thick trees that stretch to the summit. The **South Face** offers the most challenging terrain, with a number of decent black and extreme runs, which will test both freeriders and carvers alike.

FREERIDERS of all levels should like **Mont Saint-Anne,** however, if you like to ride fast, you could get round this place in a day or two. All the slopes are carved out of closely knitted trees providing for some bumpy trails, but lacking in wide, open powder bowls. The south side slopes offer the most challenging runs with a cluster of fast double black diamond runs down the middle, one of which runs from the top all the way to the base and will burn up your thighs or make your eyes water if you bail. They've recently opened up the Black Forest area proving access to 20 acres of steep terrain.

FREESTYLERS are free to roam the whole mountain, but may wish occupy any of the 2 terrain parks or the halfpipe. The main park is on **La Grande Allee** trail where there is a good series of man made hits and a well shaped 75 metre halfpipe with walls cut by Quebec's first *Pipe Dragon*. You'll find the other park located under the **La Tourmente** chair.

PISTES. The pisted runs are well-suited to cranking over at speed. The most testing trails, including double black diamond runs, can be found on **South Face**.

BEGINNERS are provided with gentle green runs that allow riding from top to bottom on some very tame descents. If you stay here for a week, you should be very competent by the time you leave (a two-week trip might be a bit much, even for a novice).

THE TOWN
Mont Sainte Anne offers a very good selection of local services both at the base of the slopes or 25 miles away in down town Quebec City. Local lodging options are extensive with some 3000 visitor beds within a 3 mile stretch of the slopes. The main village is well set out and pleseant place to stay. There are a number of shops to serve your needs from boutiques to basic snowboard shops all mainly geared towards the casual visitor. The area also offers loads of other sporting attractions.

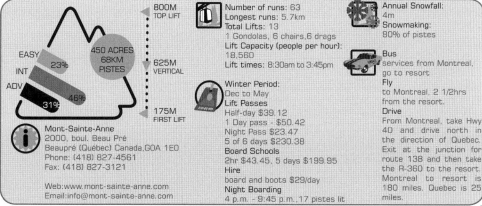

800M
TOP LIFT

625M
VERTICAL

175M
FIRST LIFT

EASY
INT
ADV
23%
450 ACRES
68KM
PISTES
46%
31%

Mont-Sainte-Anne
2000, boul. Beau Pré
Beaupré (Québec) Canada, G0A 1E0
Phone: (418) 827-4561
Fax: (418) 827-3121

Web: www.mont-sainte-anne.com
Email: info@mont-sainte-anne.com

Number of runs: 63
Longest runs: 5.7km
Total Lifts: 13
1 Gondolas, 6 chairs, 6 drags
Lift Capacity (people per hour):
18,560
Lift times: 8:30am to 3:45pm

Winter Period:
Dec to May
Lift Passes
Half-day $39.12
1 Day pass - $50.42
Night Pass $23.47
5 of 6 days $230.38
Board Schools
2hr $43.45, 5 days $199.95
Hire
board and boots $29/day
Night Boarding
4 p.m. - 9:45 p.m., 17 pistes lit

Annual Snowfall:
4m
Snowmaking:
80% of pistes

Bus
services from Montreal,
go to resort.
Fly
to Montreal, 2 1/2hrs
from the resort.
Drive
From Montreal, take Hwy
40 and drive north in
the direction of Quebec.
Exit at the junction for
route 138 and then take
the R-360 to the resort.
Montreal to resort is
180 miles. Quebec is 25
miles.

195

wsg STONEHAM

Okay resort all round

	POOR	FAIR	GOOD	TOP
FREERIDE Trees & some off-piste				
FREESTYLE 4 terrain parks & a superpipe				
PISTES Okay slopes for all				

6 OUT OF 10

C

C A N A D A

Q U E B E C

Pic -Stoneham Resort

Stoneham is one of the largest resorts in **Quebec** which forms part of the 'Resorts of the Canadian Rockies Group' who also own the likes of Lake Louse, Fernie and Kimberley amongst others. With such a pedigree one would expect Stoneham to have something good to offer, and indeed it does, as well as playing host to the **FIS Snowboard World Cup**. The 30 plus trails are spread out over a group of mountain faces with the slopes carved out of tightly knitted trees that grow over the whole area form the base up to the summits of each mountain area. Initial access to **Stoneham** is via route 73 from **Quebec City**, which is only 20 minutes away. As you drive into the resort you are presented with a series of mountains peaks set out in a horse shoe like fashion that all base out together. In general Stoneham offers mostly simple slopes to suite beginners and intermediates. However, expert and advanced riders will find some okay terrain with a least six double diamond black trails to ride down. The 326 acres of terrain is serviced by 9 lifts with the highest area achieved by a quad chair up to 630 metres. The mountain faces are not exactly lift linked but you can easily travel

around all the areas by the series of interconnecting trails. 183 acres of terrain, which equals 16 runs, is also used for night riding.

FREERIDERS will find that Stoneham offers a number of decent challenges making a weekend stay worth while. There are a series of double black runs that will provided a few white knuckle rides with trees and other obstacles to negotiate en-route down. However, Stoneham is not a powder mountain.

FREESTYLERS should note that Stoneham is not a mountain paved with loads of natural freestyle terrain however, the management have decided to address the balance by building a host of features which includes four large terrain parks loaded with all sorts of toys, including a boarder-cross run. The resort also has a Super-Pipe with 17 foot walls, located down a steep black slope on mountain 4.

PISTES. Riders have a resort that should appeal with a good selection of well groomed trails to choose from.

BEGINNERS will find that this is a good place to learn the basics of snowboarding. There are a number of novice runs that run from the highest points down to the base area.

THE TOWN. Stoneham offers a choice of condos and hotels beds at the base of the slopes. The *Stoneham Hotel* has double bed rooms from $83 per night and comes with a bar and restaurant. As for **night life**, forget it. Although there are half a dozen good restaurants and a couple of okay bars, none are that hot and nothing rocks. For a full range of services you will need to stay down in **Quebec City**.

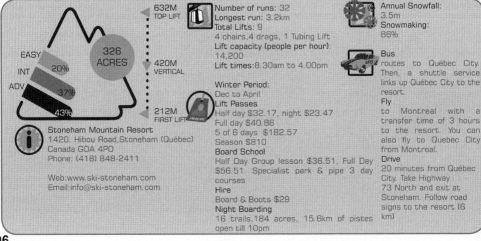

632M TOP LIFT

420M VERTICAL

212M FIRST LIFT

EASY
INT 20%
ADV 37%
43%

326 ACRES

Stoneham Mountain Resort
1420, Hibou Road,Stoneham (Québec)
Canada G0A 4P0
Phone: (418) 848-2411

Web:www.ski-stoneham.com
Email:info@ski-stoneham.com

Number of runs: 32
Longest run: 3.2km
Total Lifts: 9
4 chairs,4 drags, 1 Tubing Lift
Lift capacity (people per hour): 14,200
Lift times:8.30am to 4.00pm

Winter Period:
Dec to April
Lift Passes
Half day $32.17, night $23.47
Full day $40.86
5 of 6 days $182.57
Season $810
Board School
Half Day Group lesson $36.51, Full Day $56.51. Specialist park & pipe 3 day courses
Hire
Board & Boots $29
Night Boarding
16 trails,184 acres, 15.6km of pistes open till 10pm

Annual Snowfall: 3.5m
Snowmaking: 86%

Bus
routes to Québec City. Then, a shuttle service links up Québec City to the resort.
Fly
to Montreal with a transfer time of 3 hours to the resort. You can also fly to Quebec City from Montreal.
Drive
20 minutes from Québec City. Take Highway 73 North and exit at Stoneham. Follow road signs to the resort (6 km)

196

POOR FAIR GOOD TOP

FREERIDE
Trees & some off-piste
FREESTYLE
A terrain park & halfpipe
PISTES
Good mix of slopes

6
OUT OF 10

Okay but not hot

C

C
A
N
A
D
A

Q
U
E
B
E
C

Tremblant is one of the largest boarding areas in east Canada and forms part of what is believed to be one of the oldest mountain ranges on the planet. Tremblant's organisational connections with Blackcomb, Panorama and also mighty Stratton in the US, helps them lay on a good time. The mountain's layout is excellent and extremely well planned, covering two sides, the South and the North which also has a new beginner slope running from the top to the bottom. The **South side** gives initial access to the runs which are all carved out of thick forest. The **North side** is a little smaller, but offers the same degree of cool riding. Both sides make up an area suited to carvers and freeriders, especially intermediate and advanced riders.

FREERIDERS have a really good mountain to explore, with plenty of white knuckle trails with drop offs, trees and powder. For some excellent tree-riding, go to **Emotion**. This area is graded a double black diamond trail, so it's not for the weak-kneed.

FREESTYLERS have a decent size halfpipe and park,

located under the **Express Flying Mile** chair on the South side, and only takes a few minutes to reach. The park is well looked after and you also get to listen to some tunes blasting out of the P.A.

PISTES. Buckle up tight as you'll be able to show off in style on well-pisted trails with 'carve me up' written all over them. **Geant**, a long wide black run on the North side, is really fun, while **Zag-Zag o**n the South side is a killer double black that tames out lower down.

BEGINNERS Tremblant offers more than enough for first timers, with easy green and blue runs on the South side. Take the **Express Tremblant chair** and novices can ride from top to bottom, via **La Crette** and Nansen green trails. If you're a late (in the day) starter then you may wish to have a late lesson; for around C$20 you can have an evening instruction session.

THE TOWN
The village of Tremblant is only a few minutes from the slopes, although there are some slopeside facilities with a good selection of condos and hotels to choose from. Getting around is easy on foot, alternatively there is a daily local bus service. **Food** and drinking options are okay and night-time can be pretty rowdy, rocking 'til the late hours. But note this is not the cheapest of places, so expect to notch up some credits on your card.

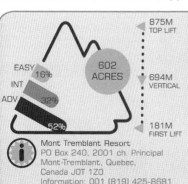

EASY	16%	
INT		
ADV	32%	
	52%	

602 ACRES

875M TOP LIFT

694M VERTICAL

181M FIRST LIFT

Number of runs: 94
Longest runs:6km
Total Lifts: 12
2 Gondolas, 9 chairs,1 drags
Lift Capacity (people per hour): 27,230
Lift times: 8.30am to 4.00pm

Winter Period:
Nov to April
Lift Passes
6 Days peak season $343
low season $250
Board Schools
90 minute group lesson, morning lesson $50, afternoon $57
Hire
Board & Boots $32 per day, $45 for top stuff
Snowmobiles
3 hour tour $149+$49 for passenger

Annual Snowfall:
3.82m
Snowmaking:
70% of pistes

Bus
services from Montreal, go to the town of Tremblant.
Fly
to Montreal, with a transfer time of around 2 hours.
Drive
From Montreal, travel north along Hwys 15 &117, direction Ste Jovite, turning of at signs for Mont Tremblant. Montreal to resort is 91 miles, 2 hours drive time.

Mont Tremblant Resort
PO Box 240, 2001 ch. Principal
Mont-Tremblant, Quebec,
Canada J0T 1Z0
Information: 001 (819) 425-8681
Fax: 001 (819) 425-9604

Web:www.tremblant.com
Email:info@tremblant.com

ROUND-UP

BELLE NEIGE
Number of Runs: 19
Easy 29%
Intermediate 28%
Advanced 43%
Top Lift: 305m
Bottom Lift: 150m
Vertical: 115m
Total Lifts:4 - 2 chairs, 2 drags
Lift pass: Day pass $28

CARTE DES PISTES
TRAIL MAP

Contact:
Nos coordonnées
6820, Route 117
Val-Morin (Qc) J0T 2R0
Tel: (819) 322-3311
www.belleneige.com
info@belleneige.com

BROMONT
Ride Area: 202 acres
Number of Runs: 52
Easy 25%
Intermediate 23%
Advanced 23%
Expert 20%
Info: Has 3 terrain parks
Top Lift: 565m
Bottom Lift: 180m
Vertical: 385m
Total Lifts:5 - 4 chairs, 1 magic carpet
Lift pass: 1/2 Day Pass - $36
Day Pass - $44
Night Boarding: 30 trails open
Hire: Board & Boots $33 per day

Ski Bromont

Contact:
150, Champlain
Bromont (Québec)
1 866 BROMONT • (450) 534-2200
www.skibromont.com
operations@skibromont.com
Location: From Montreal. On Highway
10, take Exit 78 towards bromont.

Cross the traffic light on Boulevard
Bromont and turn right on Champlain
to SkiBromon, takes 45 minutes

CAMP FORTUNE
Number of Runs: 17
Total Lifts:5
Contact:
Camp Fortune
300 ch. Dunlop,
Chelsea, QC J9B 2N3
Tel - 819.827.1717
Fax - 819.827.3893

CLUB TOBO
Number of Runs: 6
Total Lifts:2
Contact:
Tel: (418) 679 5243

COTES 40-80
Number of Runs: 6
Total Lifts:2
Contact:
Tel: (514) 229 2921

EDELWEISS VALLEY
Has a terrain park & night boarding
Ride Area: 150 acres piste, 1300
acres total
Number of Runs: 18
Easy 33%
Intermediate 48%
Advanced 17%
Expert 2%
Longest run: 1mile (1.6km)
Night Borading: 12 out of 18 trails
Top Lift: 343m
Bottom Lift: 152m
Vertical: 191m
Total Lifts:5 - 4 chairs, 2 drags,1
Magic carpet
Lift pass: Weekday Pass - $32
Weekend Pass - $34 Night $23
Lift times: 8.00am to 10.00pm
Board School: Private lesson (1hr), lift
pass & rental $65 for day
Hire: Board & Boots $28 per day

Ski Edelweiss

Contact:
Mont Saint-Sauveur 350 Saint-Denis
Saint-Sauveur,
Québec, J0R 1R3
Telephone - (450)227-4671
www.edelweissvalley.com
Directions:
From Ottawa-Hull - 5-15 miles via routes
105, 307, & 366 to Edelweiss Valley.

GRAY ROCKS
Number of Runs: 22
Easy 19%
Intermediate 45%
Advanced 36%
Vertical: 189m
Annual Snowfall: 4.2m
Total Lifts:5 - 4 chairs, 1 Magic carpet
Lift pass: 1/2 Weekday Pass - $20
Weekday Pass - $25 1/2 Day Weekend
Pass - $25 Weekend Pass - $35
Lift times: 8.00am to 10.00pm
Board School: weekend lessons $105
for 2 days inc 6hrs lessons, lift & hire
1/2-day (2hrs) lesson $40, full day
(4hrs) $60
Hire: Board & Boots $30 per day
Contact:
Gray Rocks Resort & Convention
Center
Mont Tremblant, Quibec.
Tel - 1-800-567-6767
www.grayrocks.com
Directions:
FLY: Fly to Montreal 1 1/2hrs away
BUS: Shuttles from Montreal Airport,
tel: 1-800-471-1155
DRIVING:
From Montreal (by car : 90 minutes /
120km / 75 miles) Take Autoroute 15
North until it merges with route 117
North at Ste-Agathe. Continue along
route 117 and take the first exit for
St-Jovite. At the first traffic light in
St-Jovite, turn right on route 327
North for 5 km to Gray Rocks (on your
right).

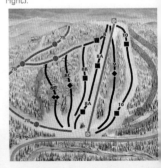

BLACKSTRAP

Blackstrap has just 8 runs with only 88 metres of vert with the longest run just making 450m. , This small mountain is best for novices and slow intermediates. The resort also, provides a cool fun park with a few table tops and a halfpipe. . No slope side lodgings exist, the nearest accommodation and services can be found at Dundurn, Hanly and Saskatoon.

Location: DRIVING: Located 32km south of Saskatoon via Hwy 11 and Hwy 211
Contact:
Blackstrap Winter Sports Park
Blackstrap Provincial Park
Box 612 Mailing Address:
Dundurn,
Phone: (306) 492-2400
Fax: (306) 492-2401

BLUE MOUNTAIN

Located 32km south of Battleford, Blue; Mountain is a very small retreat that offers a host of sporting activities including some limited snowboarding. There is some basic accommodation on site as well as other basic amenities.

Location: DRIVING: 1 1/2 hours west from Saskatoon via Highway #16 and Grid # 687 north at the town of Denholm (which eventually turns into Highway # 378).
Contact:
Blue Mountain Outdoor Adventure Center R.R.
#1 North Battleford
Saskatchewan CANADA S9A 2X3 Phone (306) 445-4941

CUDWORTH SKI AREA

Located south on 6th Ave, Cudworth consists of just one 230 metre trail with just 24 metres of vertical with one tow. Accommodation and other facilities are available in Cudworth.

Contact:
tel- (306) 256 3281

LITTLE RED RIVER PARK

Located 3km east of Prince Albert via Hwy 5, Little Red River Park consists of just two runs and two lifts. One slope is of beginner level while the other is an intermediate trail. The are also ski patrol, snowboard Instruction and a halfpipe. Accommodation and other facilities are available in Prince

Albert

Contact:
1084 Central Ave, Prince Albert SK
tel- (306) 953

MISSION RIDGE SKI AREA

Located 2km south east of downtown Fort Qu'Appelie Mission Ridge, is a mountain with 8 runs, 92 metres of vert and 4 lifts. This small resort is a popular destination and can get busy. The area boasts a funpark and also provides night riding with special rates. **Freestylers** will find a 3.5 acre park featuring hip jumps, rails. Accommodation and other facilities are available close by in Fort Qu'Appelie
Number of Runs: 35
Easy 10%
Intermediate 60%
Advanced 30%
Top Lift: 6,770 ft
Bottom Lift: 4,570 ft
Vertical: 2,200 ft
Annual Snowfall: 4.2m
Total Lifts:6 - 4 chairs, 2 drags
Lift pass: Day pass $40 Night Pass $10
Lift times: 9 AM to 4 PM (4PM to -9PM select days in Jan & feb)
Location: FLY: Fly to seatle (140 miles away), local airport is Pangborn Memorial Airport
TRAIN: Amtrak serves Wenatchee, 12 miles away
DRIVING: From Seattle, Take U.S. Hwy. 2 east to Wenatchee and follow the signs to Mission Ridge, 138 miles.

Contact:
Mission Ridge P.O. 1668, Wenatchee, WA 98807-1668 Phone (509) 663-6543

PASQUIA SKI SLOPE

Located 12km south east of Zenon. Pasquia is a tiny hangout with 4 slopes, 1 tow and only opens for afternoon riding with private bookings. Accommodation and other facilities are available in Zenon.

Contact:
RR Tisdaie, SK tel- (306) 767 2682

SKI TIMBER RIDGE

Located 5km south of Big River on Hwy 55, Ski Timber Ridge provides 5 trails, with the longest run at 800 metres and the max vert at 90 metres. You can also get snowboard hire and instruction at the slope with daily lessons and privates. Main accommodation and other local facilities are available in Big River which is only 2 km away and has a number of okay lodging options, good places to eat as well as a host of sporting activities
Number of Runs: 6
Top Lift: 2600ft
Bottom Lift: 1400ft
Total Lifts:2
Hire:Boards available from rental shop on slopes
Board School:Board instruction available
Location: DRIVING: Located 32km south of Saskatoon via Hwy 11 and Hwy 211
Contact:
Ski Timber Ridge
Box 741 Big River,
Saskatchewan (Canada) SOJ 0E0
Phone: 469-4545

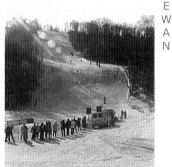

C
A
N
A
D
A

S
A
S
K
A
T
C
H
E
W
A
N

STURGIS ASSINIBOINE

Located 1km south of Sturgis off Hwy 49, Tiny area offers five trails with a maximum vert of 36 metres and one drag lift.Very basic and limited local facilities are available in Sturgis 1 km away

TABLE MOUNTAIN PARK

Located 29km west of Battleford off Hwy 40. Eight trails, 107 metres of vert and 4 lifts make up this small hangout that also has night riding and a fun park. Local services and lodging available in North Battleford and Cut Knife

Contact:
Box 343, North Battleford, SK
tel. (306) 937 2920

TWIN TOWERS SKI AREA

Only 3km south of Stranraer off Hwy 31, Twin Towers has six slopes, the longest being 853 metres, 91 metres of vertical and 2 lifts with a snowboard area and rentals on site. All local services availible in Herschel, Rosetown (58km), Kindersley and Plenty.

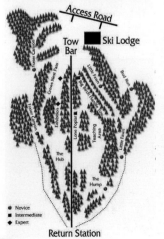

Verical Drop: 90m
Total Lifts:3 - 1 chair, 2 drags
Lift times: 9:00 am - 4:30
Lift Pass:Day Pass - $20 1/2 Day Pass - $15 Season $199
Hire:Board & Boots $25 per day
Board School:Private lesson 1hr $25
Group lesson 1hr $12-16
Location: DRIVING: Wapiti Valley is located 47 kms north of the City of Melfort and 24 kms south of Choiceland on Highway #6 to Codette Lake and the Saskatchewan River Valley.
Contact:
Wapiti Valley Regional Park
P.O. Box 181 Gronlid,
Saskatchewan, Canada, S0E 0W0
Telephone: (306) 862-5621
Fax: (306) 862-5621

WHITE TRACK

Located 27km from Moose Jaw in

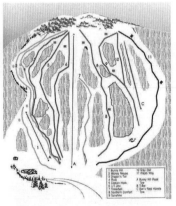

Buffalo. Its nine slopes are evenly split between 3 drag lifts and a maximum vert of 70m. All local services available in Moose Jaw, Chamberlain and Regina

Contact:

Box 702, Moose Jaw, SK
Tel (306) 691 0100

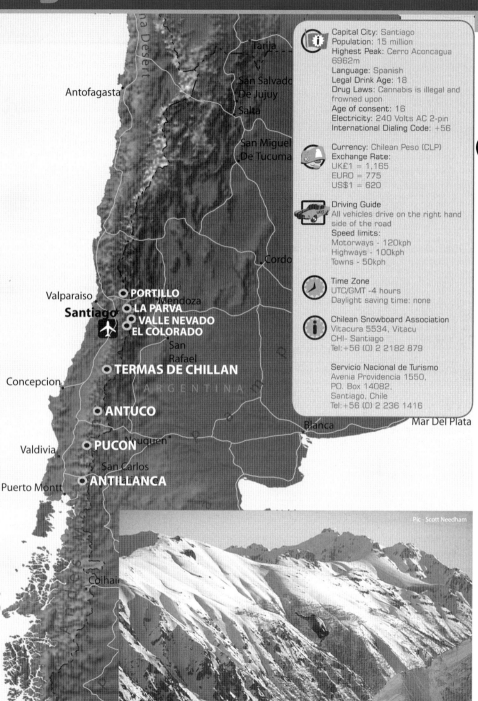

Tarija

Antofagasta

San Salvado
De Jujuy

Salta

San Miguel
De Tucuma

Cordo

Valparaiso

Santiago

○ **PORTILLO**
Mendoza
○ **LA PARVA**
○ **VALLE NEVADO**
EL COLORADO

San
Rafael

○ **TERMAS DE CHILLAN**

Concepcion

ARGENTINA

○ **ANTUCO**

○ **PUCON** Neuquen

San Carlos
○ **ANTILLANCA**

Valdivia

Puerto Montt

Blanca   Mar Del Plata

Coihai

ao
ula

Puerto
Natales

Capital City: Santiago
Population: 15 million
Highest Peak: Cerro Aconcagua
6962m
Language: Spanish
Legal Drink Age: 18
Drug Laws: Cannabis is illegal and
frowned upon
Age of consent: 16
Electricity: 240 Volts AC 2-pin
International Dialing Code: +56

Currency: Chilean Peso (CLP)
Exchange Rate:
UK£1 = 1,165
EURO = 775
US$1 = 620

Driving Guide
All vehicles drive on the right hand
side of the road
Speed limits:
Motorways - 120kph
Highways - 100kph
Towns - 50kph

Time Zone
UTC/GMT -4 hours
Daylight saving time: none

Chilean Snowboard Association
Vitacura 5534, Vitacu
CHI- Santiago
Tel:+56 (0) 2 2182 879

Servicio Nacional de Turismo
Avenia Providencia 1550,
PO. Box 14082,
Santiago, Chile
Tel:+56 (0) 2 236 1416

C

C
H
I
L
E

Pic - Scott Needham

wsgARPA

Deep powder, extreme & great views of the Andes

	POOR	FAIR	GOOD	TOP
FREERIDE No trees just 100% off-piste				
FREESTYLE Natural pipes, cliffs				
PISTES Not a piste in sight				

8 OUT OF 10

C

CHILE

FREERIDERS can feel in paradise. During the snowcat ride up it's possible to check the many possibilities that El Arpa offers. Cliffs, steep terrain, vast, quiet and untracked slopes, cornice drops, etc. So it's easy to plan your way down. On the first run, skiarpa's host, Toni Sponar will go up with the group, and give a brief speech at the top, about the different runs and their level of skill required.

"**La Ratonera**" is an avalanche path so it will be available if it's possible or under your own risk. It also gives access to more steep runs like "**Tarapacá**" and "**Sacacorchos**". Far to the west, you can access "**Avalanchas**" (the name says it all) and "**Concha y Toro**". Both end up in "**Exhibición**" just in front of the meeting point to start your way up. If you're after a leg-warm up ride then ride down through "**Valle Alto**", the longest run to the meeting point, where you can "surf" the mountain widely from side to side.

Ski Arpa has gained publicity for the past 2-3 years, becoming an exclusive valley for those who have heard about the valley and its great natural conditions and those who want to experience the unique snowcat experience in Chile. Ski Arpa is about unbelievable views, unbelievable amounts of vertical in one day and unbelievable snow. The two valleys of Ski Arpa, "**Valle el Arpa**" and "**Valle la Honda**", make a unique experience to anybody around the World. At the summit you can see east to "Cerro Aconcagua", the highest peak of the Americas, and on clear days, west to the Pacific. From there, there are 3,000 of vertical feet of untracked snow to enjoy. Ski Arpa is strictly on natural snow, no snow-making and no prepared slopes. It's just the mountain and yourself.

Toni the host will welcome you to his Valley with warm arms and several languages. He speaks German, English and Spanish. Before climbing up the snowcat, it's required to sign a responsibility release form where you declare riding at your own risk. BRING YOUR HELMET. ALWAYS USE IT.

FREESTYLERS: options are endless. Bring your equipment and build up a kicker or shape a natural quarter pipe. If you're not feeling so, then look for a cliff, a rock or a nice looking cornice and let you style flow. No park, rail or pipe here. There is a natural pipe where "**la Ratonera**" meets "**La Quebrada**". Frequently, avalanches leave a path that gives form to natural and soft landing jumps.

CARVERS: Speed is guaranteed, steep is guaranteed…if you got the guts, go for it!!

BEGINNERS: not really a place for start riding.

THE TOWN
There is no accommodation on-site, but the web site recommends two options. It's possible to find more in the town of **Los Andes** .

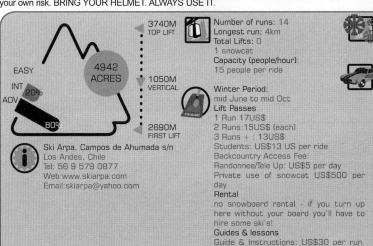

EASY
INT
ADV
20%
80%

4942 ACRES

3740M TOP LIFT

1050M VERTICAL

2690M FIRST LIFT

Ski Arpa, Campos de Ahumada s/n
Los Andes, Chile
Tel: 56 9 579 0877
Web:www.skiarpa.com
Email:skiarpa@yahoo.com

Number of runs: 14
Longest run: 4km
Total Lifts: 0
1 snowcat
Capacity (people/hour):
15 people per ride

Winter Period:
mid June to mid Oct
Lift Passes
1 Run 17US$
2 Runs:15US$ (each)
3 Runs + : 13US$
Students: US$13 US per ride
Backcountry Access Fee:
Randonnee/Tele Up: US$5 per day
Private use of snowcat US$500 per day
Rental
no snowboard rental - if you turn up here without your board you'll have to hire some ski's!
Guides & lessons
Guide & Instructions: US$30 per run.
No formal ski instruction given, but tips on how to handle difficult terrain will be provided when asked

Annual Snowfall:
3-4m
Snowmaking:
none

Fly
Comodoro Arturo Merino Benitez Internacional Airport in Santiago; 108 km away, 2 hours drive approx.
Drive
From **Santiago** head North,73km to Los Andes
From **Los Andes** drive to San Esteban then Lo Calvo. Just before Lo Calvo turn right to El Cobre and finally Campos de Ahumada. Continue until you see the snowcat. Its then a further 16km along a dodgy unsealed dirt track, 4wd recommened.

wsg PUCON

	POOR	FAIR	GOOD	TOP
FREERIDE Some nice backcountry				
FREESTYLE A terrain park				
PISTES Bumpy				

5 OUT OF 10

Okay resort

Pics Pucon Tourism

Pucon is a friendly and laid back place situated on the slopes of the **Villarica Volcano** in the **Lake District** region. It provides the rider with a perfect natural funpark for freestylers and cool freeriding destination. It should keep all snowboarders no matter what your ability, busy and content for a good seven days or more, although the volcano is still live and smoking. The resort is made up of four old creaking chairlifts and three drags, all but one of which are above tree line. Plans are afoot to install a further lift above the long left hand chair to access the steeper higher terrain. The feeling of riding the mountain is unique. The previous volcanic eruptions and lava flows have left behind a terrain of rollers and deep gullies. While the lift-accessed area is not particularly large and the lift positioning unimaginative, it contains some excellent freeriding/freestyle terrain with never ending hits, cornices and huge natural halfpipes that easily compensate for the lack of steeps. In short it's a playground. Snow quality varies due to the lower elevation and local climate factors. Storms roll in from the Pacific and drop their load, or the mountain may become fogged in. Winds quite often affect the operation of the old lifts.

FREERIDERS should check out the gullies on the left, and the cliff banks on the far right of the area. Steeper freeriding can be found by hiking from the tops of lifts, and guides (essential) can be hired in town to hike to the crater if you long to stare into the fiery bowels of the Earth

before riding back to the base for a coco.

FREESTYLERS are now presented with an okay halfpipe, when conditions permit. However, whether there is a pipe or not, the area has so much natural terrain for getting air, that it's not really needed. There are some major cliff jumps and big banks here.

PISTES. Piste bashing it's not the thing here.

BEGINNERS will manage here but in truth there are better places.

THE TOWN

Access to the resort is by hitching at the foot of the access road or by minibus taxi ($6 per person return) from agencies in town. Adventure tourism is big in Pucon. Rafting ($20-35) is a buzz; take the upper trip as the lower one is for wusses. The nearest **accommodation** is found in Pucon 1 mile away where you can get a cheap bed from as low as $8 a night. Good **night time** hangouts include *Mamas and Tapas* where local girls strut their stuff, and *Piscola*.

C
H
I
L
E

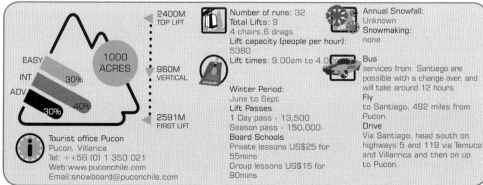

2400M TOP LIFT	Number of runs: 32 Total Lifts: 9 4 chairs,6 drags Lift capacity (people per hour): 5380 Lift times: 9.00am to 4.00	Annual Snowfall: Unknown Snowmaking: none
EASY **1000 ACRES** INT 30% ADV 40% 30%	Winter Period: June to Sept Lift Passes 1 Day pass - 13,500 Season pass - 150,000 Board Schools Private lessons US$25 for 55mins Group lessons US$15 for 90mins	Bus services from Santiago are possible with a change over, and will take around 12 hours. Fly to Santiago, 492 miles from Pucon. Drive Via Santiago, head south on highways 5 and 119 via Temuco and Villarrica and then on up to Pucon.
960M VERTICAL 2591M FIRST LIFT		

Tourist office Pucon
Pucon. Villarica
Tel: ++56 (0) 1 350 021
Web:www.puconchile.com
Email:snowboard@puconchile.com

POOR FAIR GOOD TOP

FREERIDE
Some trees & good off-piste

FREESTYLE
A terrain park and pipe

PISTES
Bumpy & not best laid out

7 OUT OF 10

Very good resort

FREERIDERS will find what is regarded by locals as the best on offer, is accessed via a 10 minute hike from the top of the temperamental **Don Otto** chair. Hiking right from the top of this the rider is rewarded with 890 vertical meters of open bowls that exit into a series of 35-45 degree chutes back into the base. With pisting operations seemingly unheard of here the area is a freeriders dream. Beware though, avalanche control is also almost unknown of and you'd be lucky to ever see the ski patrol.

FREESTYLERS have a well constructed snowboard park and pipe reached off the middle poma.

PISTES. Riders who require pisted corduroy tracks may want to stay away

BEGINNERS, if it were not for the way the lifts are laid out, then this would be an ideal novices haunt, but it's not.

THE TOWN

Without your own transport access to the base is dependant on either hitching (relatively easy) or if you're staying in Chillan, taking the early bus.

With the nearest 'town' being 50 miles away the resort has developed a complex of hotel and condo's below the base, mainly catering for affluent Chilean and visiting westerner. This accommodation is far out of reach of the average boarders pocket making finding somewhere to sleep nearby a problem. Four bed apartments ($25 per-person) can be rented at **Las Tranoas** 10 km from the base.

Termas De Chillan is a small resort positioned on the south facing slopes of a dormant volcano and boasts the longest season of any of the S. American resorts. Despite a good snow record the resort has done little to make the most of it and offers only three ageing chairlifts and three drags. Most of the terrain is above treeline with the lower chair retrieving adventurous boarders from the trees and depositing them back at the base. The upper chair, **Don Otto**, not only accesses the best freeriding terrain on the mountain, but also holds the record for being the longest chairlift in S. America (2.5 Km). It is also one of the oldest and slowest and its frequent closure whenever the wind blows, means it's long overdue for replacement. The alternative when this chair is down is to ride a succession of three drags, (the middle poma holding the record for 'most blokes rendered infertile') to access some neat gullies with big banks. Plans have been made to extend the top drag further into the higher terrain which otherwise is rewarding but the hike-to country.

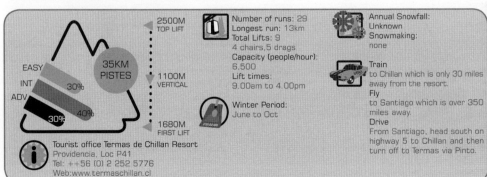

EASY
INT 30%
ADV
30% 40%

35KM PISTES

2500M TOP LIFT

1100M VERTICAL

1680M FIRST LIFT

Number of runs: 29
Longest run: 13km
Total Lifts: 9
4 chairs, 5 drags
Capacity (people/hour):
6,500
Lift times:
9.00am to 4.00pm

Winter Period:
June to Oct

Annual Snowfall:
Unknown
Snowmaking:
none

Train
to Chillan which is only 30 miles away from the resort.
Fly
to Santiago which is over 350 miles away.
Drive
From Santiago, head south on highway 5 to Chillan and then turn off to Termas via Pinto.

Tourist office Termas de Chillan Resort
Providencia, Loc P41
Tel: ++56 (0) 2 252 5776
Web: www.termaschillan.cl

ROUND-UP

ANTILLANCA

Antillanca is yet another volcano based resort. However, unlike similar hangouts there is at least some good backcountry tours you can take and without too much hiking or traversing, though you'd better be tooled up incase you get lost on one of the many other volcanos in the area. The pisted areas provide some basic freeriding above and amid trees. Nothing is laid on for freestylers but there are rocks to get air from. Good facilities are available at Antillanca's base area

Number of Runs: 13
Easy 20%,Intermediate 30%
Advanced 30%,Expert 20%
Top Lift: 1534m
Bottom Lift: 1070m
Total Lifts:5 - 1 chairs, 4 drags
How to get there: Fly to Santiago, then bus which will take over 10 hours

ANTUCO

Antuco is one of Chile's resorts that can easily be over looked, simply because there is not much to look at. Located on a volcano (like so many other resorts in this part of the world), Antuco is a place best left to locals in the area. It's certainly not worth going out of you're way to visit. The two runs wouldn't hold the attention of a nat beyond 30 seconds. Beginners can have fun, but freestylers forget it as should piste loving carvers.
Best lodging are local and local services can be found at Los Angeles (not the US city), 40 minutes away
Number of Runs: 2
Easy 20%,Intermediate 50%
Advanced 30%
Top Lift: 1850m
Vertical Drop: 450m
Total Lifts:2
How to get there: Fly to Santiago, then bus via Los Angeles 40 mins away

EL COLORADO

30 miles, or 40 minutes from the capital is El Colorado, Chile's biggest resort. Being so close to Santiago has its draw backs as the slopes can often get very busy with Chile's high earning city dwellers who have been coming to the resort for skiing, since the thirties.u The 25 marked out trails cater for everyone's needs especially advanced riders although the off-piste is a bit naff. However, this is a good resort for piste carvers and novices.
Expensive lodging, restaurants and bars are all slopeside
Number of Runs: 25
Easy 40%,Intermediate 20%
Advanced 30% ,Expert 10%
Top Lift: 3333m
Bottom Lift: 2430m
Vertical Drop: 903m
Total Lifts:18 - 4 chairs, 14 drags
Lift pass:Day Pass - $29
How to get there:
FLY: Fly to Santiago, then bus, which will take 40 minutes.
BUS: Bus service from Santiago, US$13 round trip.
DRIVING: 39km east of Santiago

LA PARVA

La Parva is another resort in the throws of Santiago, and another popular modern affair loaded with all the razzmatazz and trappings found at many big foreign resorts. However,

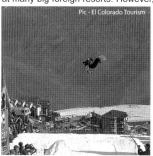
Pic - El Colorado Tourism

this is not big resort, but rather a good two days and its an all done sort of place . Still what is available is extensive, well set out and caters well for piste lovers and fast riding freeriders with some nice blacks and expert trails to try out. Lots of good local facilities are provided at the base area of the slopes, but nothing comes cheaply.

Number of Runs: 20
Easy 15% ,Intermediate 55%
Advanced 30%
Top Lift: 3630m
Vertical Drop: 960m
Total Lifts:14
How to get there: Fly to Santiago, then bus, which will take 50 minutes

LLIAMA

Visitors could be excused for getting a bit confused when they arrive here. Nothing to do with the slopes, but more to the fact that there are to Lliamas here with both using the same name and both similar in character,
with much the same terrain, number of runs and lifts that serve them. Another common feature about this place is that for any fast riding thrill seekers, pick somewhere else, as this place is very flat and basically boring. Best lodging and local facilities are in Temco, 5 minutes away.

Number of Runs: 7
Easy 20%,Intermediate 60%
Advanced 20%
Top Lift: 1800m
Total Lifts:5
How to get there: Fly to Santiago and then to Ladeco 55 minutes away

PORTILLO

in 2004 new $1.4 million quad chairlift to access the Plateau side of the resort quickly
Portillo is a world renowned American run resort located at the foot of Aconcagua. Its high elevation provides it with plenty of dry snow making for good powder. 12 lifts access some 22 pistes and an abundance of steep off piste faces._ Heli operations will take those with flexible enough plastic to higher elevations and descents. Heli operations will take those with flexible enough plastic to higher elevations and descents. The resort is distinctly up-market offering expensive accommodation and eating in its ugly complex of posh hotels, condos and slightly cheaper 'dormitories'

Ride area: 800 acres
Number of Runs: 22
Easy 10%,Intermediate 70%
Advanced 20%
Top Lift: 3348m
Total Lifts:12 - 7 chairs, 5 drags
How to get there:
Fly to Santiago and then bus 2 hours away.
DRIVING: Access Portillo by hitching from Los Andes, via the access road. 100 miles northeast of Santiago

Pic -Jonathan Selkowitz

also have lessons available in English. The season seems to be from early December to late March for southern Finland (south of Tampere). Central Finland keeps going until the end of April and northern Finland can be open until early June. At the start of the season, there is generally little natural snow but most resorts have snow cannons and they do a good job. From early March (in southern Finland), the snow starts to melt and the conditions are not particularly reliable. The easy runs tend to be closed first with most resorts only half open by the end of March.

Temperatures vary quite a lot. In the south, -5 to -10 is the typical winter daytime temperature but -15 to -20 is not uncommon.

Travelling: Fuel is actually cheap (around 1 euro/litre or 60p/litre). If you are based in Helsinki, there are buses to most of the local resorts. Language: Although the official languages are Finnish and Swedish, almost everyone speaks very good English. Finns are also friendly and very reserved (except when drunk, which is quite often).

Crowds: The Finns are fair-weather skiers and boarders. If it's a nice sunny afternoon, they flock to the resorts and it gets rather busy (although nowhere near as bad as the Alps). If it's a bit too cold or dull or it's late in the day, some of the places are practically empty.

Finland produces some of the best young freestylers in the world. You may ask how such a small country, with a small population, can do this, well the answer must lie in the fact that Finnish resorts offer so little in terms of terrain that the main challenge is the halfpipes. Finlands resorts are small. Max drop of runs is 50-120m (for southern Finland) depending on the resort. There are usually 5-6 runs per resort (although they claim more - if there's a tree on the piste, that makes it 2 runs)

All resorts have ski/snowboard hire and a restaurant. Many

Resorts are usually open from around 10am to 8 or 9pm. Since it's dark by 4pm in the winter, most runs are floodlit although some places only keep a few runs open, particularly if it's not busy.

Costs do vary a bit but in general 4 hours equipment hire cost 30 euros. A lift pass will set you back 25 euros.

Capital City: Helsinki
Population: 5.2 million
Highest Peak: Haltia 1328m
Language: Finnish and Swedish
Legal Drink Age: 18
Drug Laws: Cannabis is illegal and frowned upon
Age of consent: 16
Electricity: 240 Volts AC 2-pin
International Dialing Code: +358

Currency: Euro
Exchange Rate:
UK£1 = 1.5
US$1 = 0.8
AU$1 = 0.6
CAN$1 = 0.6

Time Zone
UTC/GMT +2 hour
Daylight saving time: +1 hour

Finnish Snowboard Federation
Radiokatu 20
00240 Helsinki.
Finland
tel- ++358 400 414 587
www.fsa.fi

Finnish Tourist Board
Head Office: P.O. Box 625,
Töölönkatu 11,
00101 HELSINKI, FINLAND
Tel.: +358 (0)9 4176 911
www.visitfinland.com

Driving Guide
All vehicles drive on the right hand side of the road
Speed limits:
Motorways-120kph (74mph)
Highways-100kph (80mph)
Towns-50kph (31mph)
Emergency
Police - 10022
Fire and Ambulance - 112
Tolls
None
Documentation
carry driving license, insurance certificate and vehicle registration, along with your passport

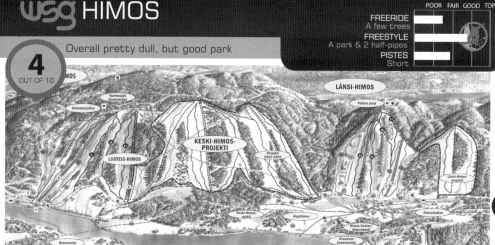

wsg HIMOS

Overall pretty dull, but good park

4 OUT OF 10

LÄNSI-HIMOS

KESKI-HIMOS PROJEKTI

LUOTEIS-HIMOS

Projekti 2002-2005

Keski-Himos-mäkit

Alppihimos

Himos-Center/Himoslomat

Himoksen Vuokramökit

Himoslaakso

Himosranta

F
FINLAND

Most resorts in **Finland** are tiny blips spread over rolling hills and although Himos is small, it is by no means the smallest resort in the country. Located in the southern part of the country and three hours by road from the Finnish capital of Helsinki, Himos is a very popular resort with a large number of Finnish snowboarders, especially freestylers. The resort opened in 1984 and first impressions will have you wondering what the hell you are doing there. The tiny hill that rises above the shores of the frozen lake is split into two slope areas, both offering the same terrain: a mixture of flat, unadventurous trails. For the new season the two sides of the resort will be joined by a lift for the first time and with an additonal 3 pistes.

FREERIDERS are not going to find this place up to much as there's nothing really to excite. The longest trails are on the north slopes, with one black and a couple of red runs on offer. The runs on the west slope offer a few more challenges, with some blacks that weave through the trees, but don't expect powder.

FREESTYLERS will get the most out of this place. You're provided with two half-pipes and a fun park, which they call '**The Street**', comprising of hits and rails which at

least make up for the boring terrain. Locals often build the odd hit and you may even find a few logs to session in the trees.

PISTES. The longest trail only just manages about 1000m, the slopes on the west hill give you the chance to shred at speed down some well prepared black trails and the short red runs are good for carvers who want progress.

BEGINNERS have only a few, very short green trails to get started, but as the blue trails and even the reds are overrated difficulty-wise, novices have more on offer than it first seems. To help total first timers, there is a slope with a free lift. Most novices should have this place sorted in three days, if not, take up cross country skiing as you'll be more in tune with that.

THE TOWN
Accommodation, which is spread out but within easy reach of the slopes, is offered mainly in chalet form with a number of hotels, but nothing is cheap!
Don't expect any happening **night life**: the main place is the *Himos Hotel* which is dull to the extreme. The place isn't totally crap, it just doesn't offer very much.

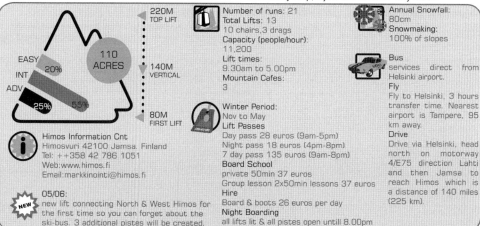

EASY 20%
INT
ADV 25% 55%

110 ACRES

220M TOP LIFT
140M VERTICAL
80M FIRST LIFT

Number of runs: 21
Total Lifts: 13
10 chairs,3 drags
Capacity (people/hour): 11,200
Lift times: 9.30am to 5.00pm
Mountain Cafes: 3

Winter Period:
Nov to May
Lift Passes
Day pass 28 euros (9am-5pm)
Night pass 18 euros (4pm-8pm)
7 day pass 135 euros (9am-8pm)
Board School
private 50min 37 euros
Group lesson 2x50min lessons 37 euros
Hire
Board & boots 26 euros per day
Night Boarding
all lifts lit & all pistes open untill 8.00pm

Annual Snowfall: 80cm
Snowmaking: 100% of slopes

Bus
services direct from Helsinki airport.
Fly
Fly to Helsinki, 3 hours transfer time. Nearest airport is Tampere, 95 km away.
Drive
Drive via Helsinki, head north on motorway 4/E75 direction Lahti and then Jamsa to reach Himos which is a distance of 140 miles (225 km).

i Himos Information Cnt
Himosvuri 42100 Jamsa. Finland
Tel: ++358 42 786 1051
Web:www. himos.fi
Email:markkinointi@himos.fi

NEW 05/06:
new lift connecting North & West Himos for the first time so you can forget about the ski-bus. 3 additional pistes will be created.

	POOR	FAIR	GOOD	TOP
FREERIDE Good for Finland				
FREESTYLE 2 terrain parks and 2 pipes				
PISTES Some good runs				

6 OUT OF 10

Terrain that allows some freeriding

Pic - Ruka Tourism

F

FINLAND

Finland is generally a flat country with lots of lakes and the Kusamo region, where this typical Finnish resort is located, is no exception. The journey to **Ruka** involves no great uphill climbs or winding mountain passes, you simply arrive to see the hill popping out of the landscape like a volcano. Ruka is just about Finland's largest resort and has hosted some major snowboard championships, indicating that the place has something to offer. Don't get too excited though as this is not hardcore freeriding territory and you can explore the whole area in half a day. However, the mainly intermediate slopes do offer carvers some nice flats to carve up and the slopes can be accessed with ease from any of the 5 car-parks dotted along the road that circles most of the hill. Trees cover much of the mountain, so all the trails are cut through the forest giving you the

feeling you are on a different run every time, rather than just riding 100 metres across from where you were originally. All the slopes are well groomed and pisted constantly, so bumps don't get a chance to build up. Most of the area has blue and easy red runs, with only a couple of blacks down the front side.

FREERIDERS will find some interesting terrain to explore, although it won't take too long. There are some nice areas to ride including open and tight tree sections, especially round the side of the ski jump. Ruka is also known for having some good powder stashes. Although it's never super deep, it's still good fluffy stuff.

FREESTYLERS have two fun park areas and three halfpipes, all serviced by T-bars. Both parks have a good range of gaps and table tops of all sizes and are groomed daily, so you won't need to hike up with your own shovel to shape hits. One of the parks and pipes are located up off lift number 17, where it gets cold but you will find a shelter with a wood fire burning to warm you up between runs. Don't leave your gloves drying above the fire though, as a pair of $200 smoked Fishpaws are not as trendy as you may think.

PISTES. Carvers are provided with flats and well spaced out trails, allowing for some interesting carving, most of which needs to be done on a series of red runs. The runs off the 7 lift are nice, long descents which allow novice carvers the option to move across from some tamer blue trails. Lift 15 also gives access to a good tree-lined carving trail that can be taken at speed.

BEGINNERS are presented with plenty of gentle runs that allow for long descents from the summit, making Ruka a good place to learn the basics. Lifts stay open with the help of flood-lights until 8 pm most nights, so you can get loads of riding in if early mornings aren't your thing. Instruction facilities are very good here and you can get tuition for riding the flats or the halfpipe.

THE TOWN

Ruka is an all year round tourist destination, so add that to the fact that Finland is an expensive country, and what you

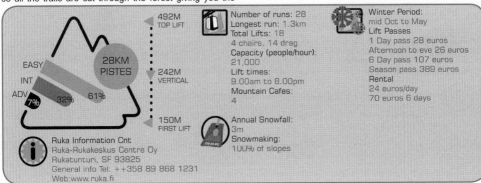

EASY
INT
ADV
7% 32% 61%

28KM PISTES

492M TOP LIFT

242M VERTICAL

150M FIRST LIFT

Ruka Information Cnt
Ruka-Rukakeskus Centre Oy
Rukatunturi, SF 93825
General info Tel: ++358 89 868 1231
Web: www.ruka.fi

Number of runs: 28
Longest run: 1.3km
Total Lifts: 18
4 chairs, 14 drag
Capacity (people/hour): 21,000
Lift times: 9.00am to 8.00pm
Mountain Cafes: 4

Annual Snowfall: 3m
Snowmaking: 100% of slopes

Winter Period: mid Oct to May
Lift Passes
1 Day pass 28 euros
Afternoon to eve 26 euros
6 Day pass 107 euros
Season pass 389 euros
Rental
24 euros/day
70 euros 6 days

Pic - San Tang

get is a super expensive but good resort. Ruka, which is only half hour bus ride from **Kuusamo** airport, has a good selection of well appointed local facilities which include a damn fine sports centre and a number of shops. If Ruka is not your thing, Kuusamo is the nearest big town with a far greater selection of everything with slightly lower prices, which will help the budget conscious rider.

Accomodation. The choice of accommodation is extremely good, both at the slopes and back along in Ruka. Options range from very expensive hotels to very expensive shared chalets. If you find staying in Ruka or at the slopes is just too expensive then the town of Kuusamo is only 20 miles away and offers a greater selection of places to stay with a wider price. You will have to commute to the slopes however.

Food. The options for eating out are fairly good, with a choice of restaurants around town and near the slopes, but it hurts having to pay so much money even for a burger. Still The *Ampan* is well known for serving up a good pizza, while *Ali-Baba* does great grills to order, burnt or rare, it's your call.

Night life in Ruka is tame and not bright lights and disco style. However, things are very lively and the Fins know how to party hard (mind you how they manage to get drunk

with the cost of booze in this place is a mystery). The only main night time hang out is *Ruka Mesta Club*, forgetting how much things costs, will initially take a while and it won't be until you're drunk that you can loosen up.

SUMMARY
Not a bad place with terrain that allows for freeriding and some really good carving. Great for novices. Good but expensive slope side facilities.

CAR
Drive to Helsinki via Kuusamo, its 800km Drive time is about 14 hours.
TRAIN
Helsinki to Oulu, from which the 217 km coach trip to Kuusamo takes only approximately three hours. Contact www.matkahuolto.fi for bus details
FLY
Fly to Helsinki international then onto Local airport Kuusamo, 20 miles from resort. Shuttle bus from Kuusamo to resort always available and takes 30mins
BUS
Buses from Helsinki can be taken via a change over at Kuusamo with a journey time of around 14 hours.

ᴡꜱꞬ TAHKO

FREERIDE
Poor trees & tiny off-piste
FREESTYLE
A terrain park and 2 pipes
PISTES
Short and easy but well pisted

POOR FAIR GOOD TOP

4
OUT OF 10

Not up to much

ON RINTEET   >> Uusi rinnealue   >> Lumilaakso

Tahko is regarded by many Finnish snowboarders as their premier resort, which when compared with what else is on offer in the country, is easy to see why: even the ISF liked Tahko enough to sanction snowboard events here. Tahko is a resort that attracts many cross-country skiers, but these strange creatures that dress in spray-on clothing set off into the trees and thankfully aren't seen again until the later hours of the day. Lucky, as the terrain is not very extensive and can easily become clogged up with two plankers of all types. The riding on the **Tahkovuori** hill is not going to excite you for very long: a few hours and you have done the lot. Still, the terrain is not bad and the pistes are well looked after, with full snowmaking facilities to help when the real stuff is in short supply. All the runs are cut through trees, offering slopes to suit intermediate and novice riders, but absolutely nothing for advanced riders to get their teeth into.

FREERIDERS have nothing to write home about. There are some tree areas which most of the runs are carved out of, but most are unrideable. However, on a good day there are some okay powder spots , but don't get up late they're all gone within an hour.

FREESTYLERS have a well shaped halfpipe located at the lower section alongside the tree line. Apart from the pipe, locals like to build their own hits, but as for big natural hits, forget it. There are a number of banks to ride up, however.

PISTES. Carvers who dare to be seen in hard boots here will find some decent trails, with a couple of good red pistes to cut big wide turns on. But you won't be putting in too many before you hit the bottom and are being stared at again by everyone else in the lift queue who will be in soft boots for certain.

BEGINNERS have an ideal resort with half of the runs suited to novices, even if all the lifts are drags. Snow Valley is an area set aside for kids and first timers, but if you're a 300 pound, hairy arsed learner with no sense of control, stick to the main beginner runs as wiping out three year olds is not funny, and not on.

THE TOWN
Tahko has a small, but good selection of **accommodation** options near the slopes. You can opt to sleep in a hotel, chalets or a bungalow. Alternatively if you're driving here, and on a tight budget, you could park up in a caravan spot, but it will be freezing in mid winter. **Night life** is quite sad and expensive, but there are worse haunts

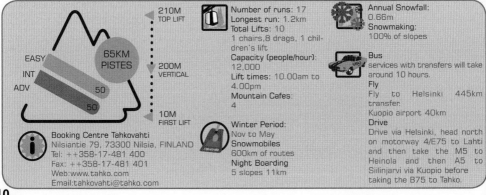

EASY
INT
ADV

65KM
PISTES

50
50

210M
TOP LIFT

200M
VERTICAL

10M
FIRST LIFT

Number of runs: 17
Longest run: 1.2km
Total Lifts: 10
1 chairs,8 drags, 1 children's lift
Capacity (people/hour):
12,000
Lift times: 10.00am to
4.00pm
Mountain Cafes:
4

Winter Period:
Nov to May
Snowmobiles
600km of routes
Night Boarding
5 slopes 11km

Annual Snowfall:
0.66m
Snowmaking:
100% of slopes

Bus
services with transfers will take around 10 hours.
Fly
Fly to Helsinki 445km transfer.
Kuopio airport 40km
Drive
Drive via Helsinki, head north on motorway 4/E75 to Lahti and then take the M5 to Heinola and then A5 to Siilinjarvi via Kuopio before taking the B75 to Tahko.

Booking Centre Tahkovahti
Nilsiantie 79, 73300 Nilsia, FINLAND
Tel: ++358-17-481 400
Fax: ++358-17-481 401
Web:www.tahko.com
Email:tahkovahti@tahko.com

ROUND-UP

ISO-SYOTE
Iso-Syote is one of Finlands biggest resorts with a total of 21 runs. What you have here are two small mountains, offering you an area of gentle snowboard terrain that allows for some okay freeriding with some fantastic novice trails from top to bottom. There is a good halfpipe and some of the trails are flood lit for late riding! Lots of very basic lodging is available near the slopes in cabins and chalets. You can also party late but not hard.

Runs: 21, Total Lifts:5
Top Lift: 432m How to get there: Fly to: Helsinki- 14 hours away by car

KALLI
Ultra boring ride area
Runs: 1, Total Lifts:1

KALPALINNA
Okay ride area located 2 hours from Helsinki
Number of Runs: 18

KASURILA
Very boring ride area located 9 hours from Helsinki
Runs: 8,Total Lifts:3

KAUSTINEN
Small halfpipe, Located 10 hours from Helsinki
Runs: 5 ,Total Lifts:4

KOLIN HIIHTOKESKUS
Flat and very dull. Located 7 hours from Helsinki
Runs: 6 ,Total Lifts:4

LAKIS
Not worth the effort. Located 10 hours from Helsinki.
Runs: 3 ,Total Lifts:3

LEVI
Levi is a small resort that boasts 140 miles of trails although 125 of them are for oldies on cross country skis. The terrain is set out over a stump of a hill

and offers freeriders a little bit of uneven rough to ride, including some trees. **Freestylers** have a natural halfpipe and a 100 metre man made version. **Carvers** have a few good trails.Levi is also ideal for **beginners**. Local facilities are well located

Ride area: 29km
Number of Runs: 45
Easy 41%,Intermediate 51% ,Advanced 8%
Top Lift: 530m
Bottom Lift: 200m
Vertical Drop: 325m
Total Lifts:26 - 1 Gondola, 25 drags
Night Boarding:13 slopes and halfpipes illuminated
How to get there:
FLY: Fly to Kittila airport Transfer time to resort = 20 minutes Buses from Helsinki can be taken via Rovaniemi to Levi on a daily basis. Rovaniemi is 1h 45 mins. Trains go to Rovaniemi – 1h 45 min and to Kolari – 1h.. DRIVING: From Helsinki via Rovaniemi to Levi its a 20 hours drive by car (1028km)

MERI - TEIJO
Small halfpipe, 8 hours from Helsinki
Runs: 8   ,Total Lifts:3

MESSILA
Ok slopes & halfpipe, 7 hours from Helsinki
Runs: 9, Total Lifts:9

MIELAKKA
Very flat ride area,2 hours from Helsinki
Runs: 3,Total Lifts:2

MUSTAVAARA

Small halfpipe,6 hours from Helsinki
Runs: 4,Total Lifts:3

MYLLYMAKI
Small halfpipe,7 hours from Helsinki
Runs: 5,Total Lifts:4

OLOS
Flat area with a pipe, 1 hour from Rovanemi
Runs: 6,Total Lifts:4

OUNASVAARA
Tiny area with a pipe, Located 1hour from Kittila
Runs: 5,Total Lifts:4

PAASKYVOURI
Flat dull area, 8 hours from Helsinki
Runs: 4,Total Lifts:2

PALLS
Very boring ride area, Located 20 hours from Helsinki
Runs: 9, Total Lifts:2

PARNAVAARA
Small halfpipe, 8 hours from Helsinki
Runs: 3, Total Lifts:1

PEURAMAA
Good for carvers, 10 hours from Helsinki
Runs: 5,Total Lifts:6

PUKKIVUORI
Small halfpipe,8 hours from Helsinki
Runs: 15,Total Lifts:2

PYHA
Phya is as small as they can possible get, with just eight or so runs and nothing longer than two turns on a long carving board. However, it is a snowcovered hill that has a half-pipe and a couple of fairly steep runs. A good intermediate will manage quite easily, but an advanced rider really shouldn't bother with this place. Actually, only novices should give it a go, if you live locally because its not worth trekking up other-wise.

SALLA
Salla seems a rather remote resort but it's no more remote than any other Finnish outback. This place is located in the mid to northern section of the country and on the Russian border, infact you can take a snowcat trip in to the Russian side to ride back down.Y The 9 runs on the Finnish side are basic but an easilypleased freerider may find it okay. At the base are there is a hotel and not much more

SAPPEE
Sappee is one of the closest resorts to Helsinki and a place that attracts a few weekend city dwelling snowboarders. However never to the point of bursting, which is surprising because this place is small, half a dozen riders giving it shit at mach 6 would crowd the slopes as well as clear them. Great for novices and ideal for freestyles who like man made hits, crap for any one else. Expensive but okay lodging and local services are in easy reach

YLLAS
Yllas is much in keeping with what is found at most Finnish resorts and while it is bigger than many places, it's not mega. It is also linked with Levi. What you get is a hill rising above the tree line, which allows for some okay intermediate freeriding, as well as some powder spots and decent carving terrain. Freestylers are usually found in the halfpipe, or pulling air off one of the many natural hits. Ideal for novices. Local facilities can be found in two small villages nearby

usgFRANCE

Mont Blanc

Sixty million French people are the lucky owners of some of the best snowboard resorts in the world, (Chamonix and Serre Chevalier should be on the calling card of all snowboarders) and without doubt, have the most extreme and largest areas in Europe.

Resorts vary from the old to the new, but what makes them stand out is the variety of resorts themselves. Some are ugly, semi-modern dumps, whilst others are olde worlde hamlets. What is common however, are the facilities on offer. Fast-food and good bars are plentiful and all help to create a good snowboard scene.

Getting to French resorts is no problem; most are reached by road, although please note that motorways have expensive tolls. Flying to France offers a number of routes, with the principal airports to resorts being Grenoble, Lyon, Chambery and Geneva in Switzerland.

Train services in France are affordable, excellent and fast. Furthermore, during the winter months there is a direct train service from London's Waterloo station to Bourg St Maurice station, a short five minute walk to the funicular that serves the resort of Les Arcs. Most resorts can be reached indirectly by train and bus. EU nationals won't need a visa to work in France; however, France is the worst country in the world to get a job as a snowboard instructor. The authorities are very protective of their own. If you're caught teaching on the slopes and don't hold the French ski instructor's certificate. You will be arrested and jailed. However, more mundane forms of work such as bar work are permitted. Many opportunities do exist, especially at the bigger resorts.

Accommodation in most places consists of apartment blocks sleeping any number from 1-21, which are usually quite easy to overload with floor scammers, provided they pay up with some beers.

On the money side, France is expensive, but you can get by if you eat fast-food or buy in supermarkets (where alcohol is really cheap). Avoid the overpriced discos as late night bars are just as good.

Capital City: Paris
Population: 60 million
Highest Peak: Mont Blanc 4808m
Language: French
Legal Drink Age: 18
Drug Laws: Cannabis is illegal and frowned upon
Age of consent: 16
Electricity: 240 Volts AC 2-pin
International Dialing Code: +33

Currency: Euro
Exchange Rate:
UK£1 = 1.5
US$1 = 0.8
AU$1 = 0.6
CAN$1 = 0.6

Driving Guide
All vehicles drive on the right hand side of the road
Speed limits:
Toll Motorways - 130 kph
Motorways - 110kph
Main Roads - 90kph, Towns - 50kph
Emergency
Fire 18 / Police 17 / Ambulance 15
Tolls
Payable on motorways & some bridges
Documentation
Driving licence must be carried along with motor insurance.

Time Zone
UTC/GMT +1 hour
Daylight saving time: +1 hour

French Tourist Board
178 Piccadilly, W1J 9AL, London
Tel : 09068 244 123 (60p/min)
Fax : (020) 7493 6594
E-mail : info.uk@franceguide.com
Web: www.franceguide.com

French Snowboard Association
Route du Parc du Souvenir
06500 Menton, France
tel+33 492418000
web:www.afs-fr.com
Email:afs@afs-fr.com

Trains
www.sncf.com - National Service
www.eurostar.com - Eurostar
www.autocars-martin.com - run bus transfers from Bourg St.Maurice to Les Arcs, Tignes, Val d'isire

Airport transfers/Buses
www.vfd.fr - provide transfers from Grenoble to Deux Alps & Alp d'huez amongst others.
www.satobus-alps.com - provide transfers from Lyon to Alp d'huez, Courcheval, Tignes, val Thorens etc
www.intercars.fr - provide transfers from Geneva

Airports
www.lyonairport.com - Lyon Airport
www.gva.ch - Geneva airport
www.grenoble-airport.com - Grenoble Airport
www.annecy.aeroport.fr - Annecy

Really good slopes

7 OUT OF 10

FREERIDE
No tree runs but good off-piste
FREESTYLE
Terrain park and halfpipe
PISTES
Huge number of busy but good runs

F

F R A N C E

Anyone planning a two-week trip to **Alpe d'Huez**, will not have enough time to ride all the amazing and varied terrain that this place has to offer. Each year, this high altitude resort offers amazing amounts of great powder days covering some fantastic backcountry and wide open plateaus. The terrain is as much for the advanced rider as it is for the novice. Due to its location and mostly south-facing slopes, the runs here get a lot of annual sunshine. This has the benefit of letting you ride in great sunny conditions and also helps to soften up certain areas early on in the day. There's heaps of snow here so don't be worrying if the odd bit thins out early. The resort has a well-equipped and fast lift system that can shunt almost 100,000 punters up the mountains per hour. Unfortunately, its popularity with overseas holiday crowds means that Alpe d'Huez can get a bit clogged up, especially at weekends. Holiday periods are absolutely crazy, so avoid this time at all costs if you want to escape millions of day-glow two-plankers. However, during normal periods you can ride freely all week long from top to bottom, on and off-piste, without having to cross-track your own path or that of another skier.

FREERIDERS can be forgiven for thinking that they are in heaven. Alpe d'Huez is a backcountry freeride gem with miles of off-piste powder, in areas such as **Gorges de Sarenne** and **Glacier de Sarenne**. Please note that, riding without a guide is total folly. For assistance seek out the services of a local guide through one of the ski-schools or via Planet Surf snowboard shop.

FREESTYLERS are provided with a fun-park under the **Lac Blanc** chairlift. There's a half-pipe, boardercross, and the park has a number of jumps and rails. Away from the park there are loads of natural air spots you'll feel spoilt for choice.

PISTES. Riders are teased with so many well groomed trails, that picking one as a favourite is just not possible.

BEGINNERS are bombarded with a easy green runs at the lower areas, the only bug being that these areas are usually very busy.

THE TOWN
the whole place is cheesy and very tacky. On the other hand it provides great all-round affordable local services close to the slopes.You can dine very affordably with cheap pizza restaurants in abundance. Night-life ranges from a cinema to loud partying which is brash and full-on, although this place does go in for a lot of apres crap.

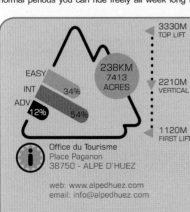

EASY
INT 34%
ADV 12%
54%

238KM
7413
ACRES

3330M
TOP LIFT

2210M
VERTICAL

1120M
FIRST LIFT

Office du Tourisme
Place Paganon
38750 - ALPE D'HUEZ

web: www.alpedhuez.com
email: info@alpedhuez.com

Number of runs: 117
Longest run: 16km
Total Lifts: 84
10 Gondolas, 6 cable-cars, 24 chairs, 41 drags, 3 magic carpets
Capacity (people/hour):
98,000
Lift times:
8.30am to 4.30pm

Winter Period:
early Dec to end April
Lift Passes
Half-day 27.3 euros
1 Day 36.20, 6 days 187
Board Schools
ESF do a 2 1/2 hr/day over 6 days freestyle and freeride courses for 115 euros
Night Boarding
Tues & Thurs, Signal Slalom Stadium piste. 8.5 euros/free if 2 day pass+

Annual Snowfall:
unknown
Snowmaking:
20% of slopes

Bus
services go direct from Lyon airport to the resort. Transfers from Grenoble visit www.vfd.fr
Fly
to Lyon with a transfer time of around 2 hours.
Drive
From Grenoble take the motorway A480. Take the No.8 exit (Vizille - Stations de l'Oisans) onto the N91 until you reach Bourg d'Oisans. Alpe d'heuz a further 13km. 163km from Lyon
Train
To Grenoble or Lyon

Great all round boarders resort

	POOR	FAIR	GOOD	TOP
FREERIDE Tree runs & some good off-piste				
FREESTYLE Park & half-pipe				
PISTES Plenty of good slopes				

8 OUT OF 10

Pic -Affif Bellakdar - Tourist Office of Avoriaz

F

F
R
A
N
C
E

Avoriaz, for a number of years.

153km of piste in Avoriaz links up with **Les Portes du Soleil**, a group of resorts straddling the French/Swiss border, creating one of the largest circuits in Europe with some major off-piste to shred. The terrain on offer in Avoriaz is more than amazing and will suit every level and style of rider: trees, big cliff drops, powder bowls and easy, wide flats - it's all here. And as everybody gets the odd off day and fancies doing something other than riding, Avoriaz puts on a choice of services that are normally found only in US resorts: quad-bike riding, snowmobiling and climbing are all an alternative buzz.

Lindaret is accessible for any level and offers fun runs off piste when there is fresh snow. **Mossets bowls** in Avoriaz is another fun adventure for intermediates and up. When there is new snow this is unbeatable. There are also some mellow spots for building jumps around this area.

Overall this mountain is worth exploring, with a few tips and pointers in the right direction you can find a little bit of everything. And if there is no new snow you can head to the park and jib all day instead. If this isn't enough Chamonix is one and a half hours drive away and Flaine, Les Cluzas, Samoens and Morillion are all just a short drive.

FREERIDERS with bottle will find the steep blacks on **Hautes Forts** well worth the effort, where you can cut some nice unspoilt terrain at speed and in style. However, riders who really want to explore the major off-piste terrain can do so by going heli-boarding, since Avoriaz is one of the few resorts in France that allows this pursuit.

A voriaz is easily one of the top French snowboard resorts and is seen by many as the snowboard capital of Europe. The management have been very positive in promoting snowboarding here since day one. For instance, Avoriaz was one of the first areas to have a snowboard-only section, including a pipe, a park-and-ride area and its own lift. Furthermore, the resort has been producing a snowboarder's passport, covering all aspects of

FREESTYLERS flock here for the natural hits and big air opportunities, of which some of the best are found around the tree-lined **Linderets** area. Avoriaz's fun-park has been established for years now and is located at the top of the main chair lift in the centre of the resort and is easily accessible. It features jumps of all sizes and is well groomed, most of the time. There is also a selection of rails and

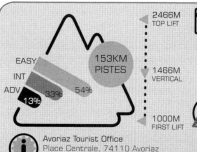

EASY

INT

ADV 33% 54%

13%

153KM PISTES

2466M TOP LIFT

1466M VERTICAL

1000M FIRST LIFT

Number of runs: 50
Longest run: 5km
Total Lifts: 37
2 Gondolas, 1 cable-cars, 18 chairs, 16 drags
Capacity (people/hour): 47,000
Lift times: 8.30am to 4.00pm
Mountain Cafes: 20

Annual Snowfall: 9m
Snowmaking: 17% of slopes

Winter Period:
mid Dec to end April
Lift Passes
Day pass to snowboard park area 15.7
Day pass 30 euros
Day pass to Ports du Soleil area 36euro, 6 days 176 euros
Heli Boarding
minimum of 4 people, from 230 euros/pp excluding guide (nearby in Italy)
Board Schools
lessons from 35euros/hr
6 days from 150 euros

Avoriaz Tourist Office
Place Centrale, 74110 Avoriaz
Tel: + 33 (0)4 50 74 02 11
Web:www.avoriaz.com
Email:info@avoriaz.com

NEW new for 05/06 season
5million euros spent on a new 6 seater chairlift 'The Fornet'

215

F

F
R
A
N
C
E

boxes of varying difficulty.

A drag lift runs along side the park so access is convenient and tunes are blasting all day so there is usually a relaxed vibe. There is also a pipe located in the centre of Avoriaz just down from the piste side cafes. It is built to international specifications and is kept in good shape although unfortunately in France they do not normally shape their pipes everyday so it can sometimes be disappointing, especially towards the end of the season. Another option is the park in **Les Crosets** which is accessible just across the boarder in Switzerland. It takes about half an hour to ride there from Avoriaz and is easy to find as long as you get directions. This park includes jumps and rails for all abilities with the small course running down the side of the park layout. There are several decent size kickers of approx 8m-12m with nice smooth raised take-offs. They are well maintained and have decent landings. On a good day this is easily the best park in the area. A drag lift allows maximum use of the park. There is also a short pipe set in between the drag lift and the park, it is smaller than the Avoriaz pipe and not generally in a good condition.

PISTE hounds will love it here, the resort is as much suited to you as any other rider, with plenty of wide, open slopes for the French hard booters to lay out a lot of Euro's carves. The reds down **Chavanette** and **Arare** are good for cranking it over.

BEGINNERS. There are plenty of easy flats around the base area to try out your first falls, before progressing up to the higher blues and reds reachable by chairs (which will help those who can't get to grips with T-bars and the Poma button lifts). One note of caution is that a lot of ski classes use the easy runs, which means they can be very busy at times, so expect congestion.

THE TOWN
As for the local services, what you get is a wonder of contemporary architecture - a purely purpose-built resort

perched way up the mountain with most of the buildings being made of wood. However, whatever your opinion on the looks, the resort provides excellent access from all accommodation to the slopes, with riding to your door the norm. Overall Avoriaz caters well for snowboarders and is not too fancy (in fact it's pretty damn cheesy and down market). There are heaps of local attractions with a number of sporting complexes and cinemas to help while away your evenings, although most people just party the night away.

Accomodation. There are loads of wooden apartment blocks, with self-catering being the main choice. Prices vary but you can get great deals. Chalet Snowboards ++44 (0)1235 767 575 or Snowboard Lodge ++44 (0) 01562 743 888 offer good holiday packages and are based close to the slopes.

Food. Cheese Cheese Cheese. Yes as in the rest of France it's Pizza's, Fondue, and Over priced pieces of meat. Some of the bars do simple pub grub but if your hear for the food your in the wrong resort.

Nightlife here is self comntained as your way up in the mountains, but there are several bars with good tunes and plenty of beer flowing throughout night. Best to ask a local if anythings going on while your there, as there's often guest DJ's in town.

CAR
From Geneva, drive to Avoriaz is 52 miles (80km)Drive time is about 120 minutes
FLY
Fly to Geneva international, transfer time to resort is 2 hours (80km away). Annecy Airport is 96km away, Lyon 200km
TRAIN
TGV's stop at Clues (20 mins) and Thonon-les-Bains
BUS
Bus services from Geneva airport in Switzerland, are available on a daily basis to Avoriaz via Clues

FREERIDE
Tree runs & amazing off-piste
FREESTYLE
Half-pipe but great natural
PISTES
Spread out & ungroomed slopes

A rough diamond, and a freeriders Mecca

10 OUT OF 10

F
FRANCE

As you drive into the Chamonix valley on a two lane elevated road your stomach empties, not from the bad food on the plane or the tight bends of the road, but from that tingle of anticipation the very name Chamonix excites even the most hardened of pro's and it doesn't disappoint. On your right towers above Europe's highest mountain, **Mont Blanc**, (don't tell the French about **Mt Elbrus**) the blue ice from a brimming glacier tumbles towards the road threatening to break off and take you out. Once in the town you pick up on the hardcore vibe of the place. Early morning there's skiers and boarders stuffing a pastry into their mouths whilst rushing to get first lift, a rope over one shoulder a transceiver over the other and a waist full of carabineers. Chamonix was a town long before anyone thought of making purpose built ski resorts and unlike most French resorts it's an all year round destination, with climbers flocking here when the snow melts like migrating geese. The place benefits from this with loads of bars, cheep eats and all kinds of shops. The lift system is antiquated and should have been sold to the Hungarians years ago. The pistes are unkempt and the queues for the bus home can be a joke, but that's the Chamonix experience it's not polished like some of it's neighbours it's infrastructure is rough and so are it's slopes, great. The valley is really a collection of ski areas Le Brevent out of Chamonix town. **La Flegere** out of **Les Praz** and at the head of the valley are Argentiere and Le Tour, both with great terrain. The best way to deal with Chamonix is to have a car if not there is a bus service and a train.

FREERIDERS Chamonix can be heaven and hell. With good snow it's the big one when it come to hard core riding. You've got it all steep faces, glacial runs, trees and couloirs. With little snow you may find yourself spending more time on the lifts and in the pub than on the slopes. With a 6 day

pass you get 2 rides on the **Grands Montets** cable car (after that you've got to get your hands in those pockets) from it's top there are two black pistes **Point de Vue** and **Pylones**, with heaps of off-piste alternatives, including skirting the impressive **Glacier d'Argentiere**. From the top of the Bochard bubble you can head into the **Combe de la Pendant bowl** for 1000m of unpisted descent. The runs down are amazing with loads of cliffs, hits and chutes, but the area can be avalanche prone. Out of **La Tour** are some fun tree runs towards the Les Esserts chair with small drop offs just big enough to make you keep your wits about you, don't get carried away and head down to far as you'll end up walking back up to the lift. The world renowned Vallee Blanche is great it takes 4/6hrs, involves a cable car ride, a few uphill sections and sphincter testing ridge walk. Although the 20km decent isn't the most challenging of terrain, the surrounding ice and scenery are fantastic. You'll need to stump up for a guide as there's crevasses to fall into and it's best to do it early on a week day as it's less crowded.

FREESTYLERS don't need a fun-park here as there's lots of natural hits and drop off's. **La Tours** is a good place to head. It seems that the attitude is to build a pipe for competitions and then leave it to melt, and after 2005's late cancellation and future move of the chamjam to the Pyrenees who knows when the next comp will be. Anyway Chamonix is a freeride mountain resort if you want some man made things go else where. Having said that there is now a permanent pipe on the grands montets but it's not the best.

PISTES. Lovers of perfect courdroy slopes will be out of luck as the pisters here spend more time drinking pastis

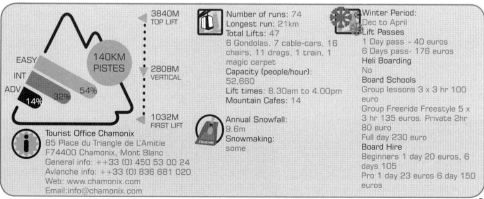

3840M TOP LIFT

140KM PISTES

EASY
INT
ADV

54%
32%
14%

2808M VERTICAL

1032M FIRST LIFT

Tourist Office Chamonix
85 Place du Triangle de L'Amitie
F74400 Chamonix, Mont Blanc
General info: ++33 (0) 450 53 00 24
Avlanche info: ++33 (0) 836 681 020
Web: www.chamonix.com
Email:info@chamonix.com

Number of runs: 74
Longest run: 21km
Total Lifts: 47
6 Gondolas, 7 cable-cars, 16 chairs, 11 drags, 1 train, 1 magic carpet
Capacity (people/hour): 52,660
Lift times: 8.30am to 4.00pm
Mountain Cafes: 14

Annual Snowfall: 9.6m
Snowmaking: some

Winter Period:
Dec to April
Lift Passes
1 Day pass - 40 euros
6 Days pass- 176 euros
Heli Boarding
No
Board Schools
Group lessons 3 x 3 hr 100 euro
Group Freeride Freestyle 5 x 3 hr 135 euros. Private 2hr 80 euro
Full day 230 euro
Board Hire
Beginners 1 day 20 euros, 6 days 105
Pro 1 day 23 euros 6 day 150 euros

and smoking gauloises than grooming the slopes.

BEGINNERS will find Chamonix's slopes a little sporadic, there are greens and blues but they are so spaced out that it's best to learn to ride elsewhere and then come here when you've got it nailed.

THE TOWN
One of the plus sides of Chamonix being a real town is the fact that there's no attitude. The locals are used to visitors all year round and know that's where the cash comes from. You'll see people skateboarding to work something you'd never see in the more stuck up French resorts. There are also plenty of things to do in Chamonix with a large sports centre, swimming pool, climbing wall, arcades and a bowling alley. Argentiere at the head of the valley has a good choice of bars and restaurants and is a great place to stay as it's close to the two best board areas. Le Praz is very quite with little on offer, if you are going to walk into Chamonix town take a torch as the French drive like white van man.

Accommodation is varied you can get a bed in a bunk house for £10 or get yourself a nice hotel room. The tourist office are really helpful if you arrive needing a bed. Go to www.chamonix.net for a good range of accommodation. There's lots of self-catering apartments particularly in Chamonix sud. For an all inclusive snowboard centred chalet

holiday and also training weeks go to www.mcnab.co.uk. If you've got a car there's a great bunk house at the head of the valley on the road towards Italy near Le Tour.

Food choice is good here, there's the French norm

Pic -Chamonix Tourism

F
R
A
N
C
E

of pizzas and melted cheese but there's also a whole choice of pub food and cellar restaurants. In the main pedestrian area is a great hole in the wall fast food joint, which always has a fast moving queue outside try their Americana sandwich.

Nightlife. It can be a real party town with lots of **bars** having happy hours and cheep jugs of beer. The centre of town has a bar for most and a few late night clubs like *Dicks Tea Bar* and the *Jeckyl and Hyde*. There's lots of English bars, some popular with the Swede's there's even a *Queen Vic* a good night can be had at the Cantina. The *Office bar* in Argentiere is good for a beer and has a tex-mex menu which is reasonably priced. There are also a few French bars which are a little cheaper. Le Praz has a couple of very local bars.

Pic.-Chamonix Tourism

SUMMARY

Chamonix offers some truly excellent freeriding and great natural freestyle terrain. It's not great for beginners and can suffer if there's not much snow. It's rough round the edges but that's its charm. If you can wait till there's fresh snow then jump in your car.

CAR
from Calais drive to Geneva. From Geneva, Chamonix is 50 miles away, approx 1 hour drive.
FLY
Fly to Geneva international, 85km away. Grenoble 153km. Lyon 220km
TRAIN
Trains stop in Chamonix. TGV sometimes available to nearby Saint-Gervais Le Fayet station.
BUS
Bus services from Geneva airport in Switzerland, are available on a daily basis to the centre of Chamonix.

POOR FAIR GOOD TOP

FREERIDE
Look hard to find some good off-piste
FREESTYLE
Terrain park and halfpipe
PISTES
Access to a huge number of runs

6
OUT OF 10

Good for families or day board from Geneva.

F

F
R
A
N
C
E

Chatel, part of the **Portes du Soleil** area, has the heart of a traditional village and is surrounded by new flats and chalets, all of which have the compulsory wood cladding to give it that alpine feel. While other resorts suffer from lack of snow Chatel can get more than it's fare share. Due to it's proximity to **lac Leman** (the French for lake Geneva). The water of the lake evaporates and if the wind is favourable falls on the nearest mountain as snow Chatel. You get some great view over the lake when you're up on the slopes of **Super Chatel** the main pisted area. It's accessed by an over crowded gondola which then gives way to a series of lifts allowing you easy access to Morgins and with a short walk through **Morgins** town to **Champoussin**, remember your passport as both are in Switzerland. It's been known for customs officers on skis to stop people and search their backpacks. A drive up the valley from Chatel leads you to Linga and Pres la Joux there's a free bus. From **Pres la Joux** it's a couple of chairs to **Avoriaz** or **Les Crosets**. It's not the best placed resort within the Portes du Soleil to explore the 680km of piste but you almost feel like your in a traditional French alpine village, well almost.

FREERIDERS could find it hard to get the most from Chatel but if you take a real close look and don't mind a bit of a walk in or out you may just find some truly great off piste runs. There are some easy pitch tree runs from **Tour de Don** towards Barbossine. From the top of Col-des-Portes you can take a long sometimes tricky route down the Morgins Valley into Morgins village and if you're up for a walk try Pointe de Chesery and head down to Les Lindarettes. Head to **Pre-la-Joux** if you fancy some steep blacks.

FREESTYLERS are in for a treat as in amongst the trees of Super Chatel and accessed by a gondola and the new ski-tow **Les Bossons** is the new snowpark which has a large half pipe 120meters, 3 different graded slope style runs and an 800 meter board cross track. At last Chatel is trying to rival it more prestigious neighbour Avoriaz. Also avalable is a Special "smooth park" pass @ €18.30 a day or €13.70 for half a day

PISTES. Riders will enjoy Chatel with its groomed intermediate piste and access to the miles of Portes du Soleil. You can get off on trying to get as much done before racing the lifts home.

BEGINNERS will find Chatel ok. The draw backs are not the runs as there are plenty of blues and greens, although some are a bit flat which leads to a bit of hopping. The main problem is the drag lifts up high, there's loads of them and the runs down into resort are often over crowded. Having said that it's possible to board from near the top all the way into resort on a blue, snow permitting.

THE TOWN
Off the slopes, Chatel's fairly chilled with a few bars such as the *Avalanche,* which is the main place to hang out ,along with the *Tunnel bar. The Avalanche Bar* features wide screen TV's showing English Premership Matches and internet access. *La Tunnel* bar is busy and has a regular DJ. Bars stay open late until 4am. **Accommodation** is mainly chalets, a lot of which have been brought by the Swiss as property is cheaper in France than Switzerland. For hotels there's a limited choice but a lot of British tour operators sell holidays here so it's best to book before you arrive, there's also 3 and 4 star hotels with and without board. **Food** wise, we're talking pizzas, pizzas, pizzas. The best place for a pizza with a friendly group of staff and a vibe of Ben Harper music washing your food down along with the wine is *Basse Cour* on the lower road of the main village. There's also plenty of cheap eats to suit all budgets. Crepes, Burgers and Pizza to a full-on three course meals.

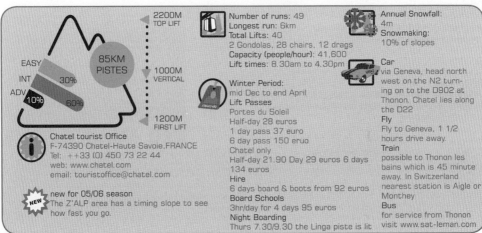

EASY
INT   **30%**
ADV
10%   **60%**

85KM PISTES

2200M
TOP LIFT

1000M
VERTICAL

1200M
FIRST LIFT

Chatel tourist Office
F-74390 Chatel-Haute Savoie,FRANCE
Tel: ++33 (0) 450 73 22 44
web: www.chatel.com
email: touristoffice@chatel.com

NEW new for 05/06 season
The Z'ALP area has a timing slope to see how fast you go.

Number of runs: 49
Longest run: 6km
Total Lifts: 40
2 Gondolas, 28 chairs, 12 drags
Capacity (people/hour): 41,600
Lift times: 8.30am to 4.30pm

Winter Period:
mid Dec to end April
Lift Passes
Portes du Soleil
Half-day 28 euros
1 day pass 37 euro
6 day pass 150 eruo
Chatel only
Half-day 21.90 Day 29 euros 6 days 134 euros
Hire
6 days board & boots from 92 euros
Board Schools
3hr/day for 4 days 95 euros
Night Boarding
Thurs 7.30/9.30 the Linga piste is lit

Annual Snowfall:
4m
Snowmaking:
10% of slopes

Car
via Geneva, head north west on the N2 turn-ing on to the D902 at Thonon. Chatel lies along the D22
Fly
Fly to Geneva, 1 1/2 hours drive away.
Train
possible to Thonon les bains which is 45 minute away. In Switzerland nearest station is Aigle or Monthey
Bus
for service from Thonon visit www.sat-leman.com

Fantastic but pricey playground for intermediates

9 OUT OF 10

Pic -Patrick Pachod/Courcheval Tourism

F
F
R
A
N
C
E

late season. There's two bubble lifts one going direct to the fun park, there's also an Olympic ski jump if you fancy breaking your legs. If you've got loads of the green or manage to get a cheep chalet deal then Courchevel can be a fantastic resort, but don't go during school holidays as the place is mobbed.

FREERIDERS will love this place; there's everything from wide rolling pistes of 1650 to steep rock shoots under the saulire cable car. Theres so much piste that it doesn't get chopped up and they have a huge fleet of piste bashers to flatten it out

Courchevel is one of France's premier resorts, and part of the world renowned Trois Vallees ski area. It offers a complete range of terrain, a fantastic modern lift system, an ok park and a reasonable snow record. All that comes at a cost; it's one of the most expensive resorts in Europe, full of very rich French in Versace ski suit and furry boots closely followed by wannabe Brit snob. At the end of the week you won't think twice about paying £1.50 for a bag of crisps and washing it down with a £5 pint of euro fizz. There are four stations all named after their altitude. 1850 home to flash hotels, luxury chalets and Michelin star restaurants with a good connection over to Meribel. 1650 has had a lot of money spent replacing most of the drag lifts, which means all those hidden spots have been opened up. It's almost a resort to itself with a new very slow second hand chair added to a couple of old chairs linking it to 1850. 1550 with direct access to 1850 has lots of chalets, which can be a long walk from the lifts. 1300 (le praz) the only alpine style village is good if you want to chill out at night but is sometimes short of snow early and

each night. There's some good off-Piste straight off the lifts, under the Vizelle bubble and Dou des Lanche chair, besides the Chanrossa chair and down through the trees to Le Praz a must in bad visibility. If you don't mind a walk check out the back of the Creux Noirs.One great spot which must be treated with the utmost respect in the Vallee des Avals which is prone to a

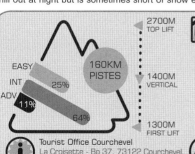

2700M TOP LIFT

160KM PISTES

EASY
INT — 25%
ADV — 11%
64%

1400M VERTICAL

1300M FIRST LIFT

Number of runs: 117
Longest run: 5km
Total Lifts: 65
10 Gondolas, 1 cable-cars, 16 chairs, 36 drags
Capacity (people/hour): 68,000
Lift times: 8.30am to 4.00pm
Mountain Cafes: 10

Annual Snowfall: 6m
Snowmaking: 26% of slopes

Winter Period:
early Dec to end April
Lift Passes
3 Vallees
1 Day 42 euros, 6 Days 210
just courchevel
1 day 35.5, 6 days 170 euros
Heli Boarding
In Monta Rosa area, Italy
Night Riding
In 1650
Board Schools
Group lessons 15 hr 195 euros
12 hr 165 euros
private 2 hr 120 euros, 3 hr 165 euros
Board Hire
Board & Boots 6 days 150 euros

Tourist Office Courchevel
La Croisette - Bp 37, 73122 Courcheval.
General info Tel: ++33 (0) 4 79 08 00 29
Web: www. courchevel.com
Email: pro@courchevel.com

NEW new for 05/06 season
in 1650, Signal and Bel Air drag lifts replaced with a new 6-person chairlift. in 1550 16-person lift connecting road to the main gondola. Overall, new Hands-free lift pass system, more snowmaking, improvement to piste signing

Pic -J Kelagopian/Courcheval Tourism

plenty to do with ice rink, climbing wall cinema, bowling and gyms. If you've got strong pants you can organise a tandem freefall, flying out of the tiny airport (March only). But remember to bring those Euros in Courchevel as cash is king.

Accommodation. If cash is short the best thing to do is get a half board chalet, so you don't do all your cash on food. You can get some great last minute deals on the web. If your wallet is fat then there are some great French hotels and some amazing chalets with under ground swimming pools and huge fire places. All the big tour operators have chalets/hotels. If you've got kids try Le Praz.

slide but has a great refuge and is stunningly beautiful, access is from the Chanrossa chair and a short walk.

FREESTYLERS will find the big snow-park under the Plantrey chair, there's some good hits and two pipes. If the suns out get there early as by afternoon one walls slush and the others bullet, there's a free drag. The top of the Verdon's got some man made dunes and some good kickers. A small drop off can be found by the Bel air and Signal drags 1650. Go to the top of the Suisses if your looking for some big drop offs.

PISTE lovers will be in heaven. They reputedly spend £20,000 a night grooming the pistes, so get up for first lift and you can carve your way down the Saulire racing the cable car. When everyone else gets up, head over 1650 for motorway wide runs.

BEGINNERS should head for the Biollay and Bellecote both have a good sustained pitch, the Biollay even has a travelator at the bottom for total beginners. 1650 has some great wide runs but still a lot of drag lifts so watch out. If looking for a lesson, check out rtmsnowboarding. com a British board school who hold beginners, freestyle and carving clinics.

Food. If you are catering for yourself then it's pizza, melted cheese in various guises or raw meat cooked at the table on a hot stone. If you've loads of dough then get out your Michelin guide. The D'Arbeilo in Le Praz is good rustic place.

Night-life has been slowly dieing as the French reclaim the resort, leaving people with little choice, there are a few English bars or some rip off French clubs. 1850 it's the Jump bar and the tiny TJ's. Both hot and packed with bad rugby tops and chalet girls with pearl earings. In 1650 the Bubble, which looks like an airport departure lounge, is cool and run by attitude free staff. If you're staying in 1550 the Tavernas a good place for a pint.

Vallée de COURCHEVEL

THE TOWN
Everything but Le Praz is a purpose built 70's nightmare, although they've stuck up some wood to try to add some charm it's still an ugly place. The lift access from most accommodation is great, and there's

CAR
from Lyon take the A43 to Chambery, then A430 to Albertville, then RN90 to Moutiers , finally the D91
FLY
Fly to Lyon international, transfer time to resort = 2 1/4 hours or 3hr transfer from Geneva
TRAIN
snow train and euro star to Moutiers, 15 miles on from station by road.
BUS
Bus services from Lyon or Geneva airport in Switzerland, are available on a daily basis to the centre of Courchevel.

	POOR	FAIR	GOOD	TOP
FREERIDE Tree runs & some good off-piste				
FREESTYLE Terrain park & small pipe				
PISTES Some good fast slopes				

Okay slopes, dire off

6
OUT OF 10

Pic - Flaine Tourism

F

F
R
A
N
C
E

FREESTYLERS may at first feel they are invading a Euro-carver's hangout, but air heads have a good two mile long fun-park area. The **Jampark** is set up on the Calcédoine run over the Aujon ski area it's loaded with big hits to get high. There's even a kid's halfpipe called the **Fantasurf**. The park is supported by a reduced lift pass, so check at the ticket office for the latest deals.

THE PISTES are well maintained and hard booters are certainly at home here: Flaine was one of the first carving capitals in France and France as we all know is home to the hard booter. Like most of the country, there are many good areas for Alpiners to show off, which makes for some real fast areas.

Flaine is a purpose-built, 1960's mess, whose architects must have designed the resort in the space of five minutes, then built it with five million tonnes of waste concrete. Ugly? Yep, and designed purely for hordes of skiers. However, as far as snowboarding is concerned, Flaine offers some great and varied terrain for different abilities. Flaine sits in a big bowl and forms part of **Le Grand Massif** area, which includes the linked resorts of **Samoens, Morillon**, and **Les Carroz**, offering good off-piste.

FREERIDERS have some great opportunities for off-piste riding, with long, interesting runs to tackle. The area above the Samoens lift is pretty good, but alternatively, you should check out the trees in **Les Carroz**, where you will get a good lesson on how to treat wood at speed. Advanced riders should check out **Combe de Gers**, which is a steep back bowl that drops away with 700 metres of vert (don't bail this one). To get the best off-piste riding, hire a guide, which will cost about 60 euros for two hours. Heli-boarding is also possible here.

BEGINNERS have a number of very easy flat runs which are serviced by a free lift located a short walk from the village area. However, to progress, you will need to buy a pass and head up to the more interesting runs. There are a couple of long blues leading away from the top of **Les Grandes Platieres** cable car, that will allow novices to find out what linking turns are like.

THE TOWN
Flaine is not a massive or happening village, nor is it the most expensive, but it's hell on earth in terms of the way it is presented as a holiday camp on a mountain. The Brits that have come here over the years have done a good job in turning it into a tacky hole. Lodging is basic, and apartments are the main accommodation with most either next to the slopes, or within a short walk. Evenings are noisy with Brits and lots of apres-ski

EASY 7%
INT
ADV 13%
80%

140KM PISTES

2500M
TOP LIFT

900M
VERTICAL

1600M
FIRST LIFT

Flaine Tourist office
Galerie des Marchants, 74300 Flaine
Tel: ++33 (0) 450 90 80 01

web: www.flaine.com
www.grand-massif.com
email: welcome@flaine.com

Number of runs: 52
Longest run: 14km
Total Lifts: 28
1 Gondola, 1 cable, 9 chairs, 17 drags
Capacity (people/hour): 28,000
Lift times: 8.30am to 4.30pm

Winter Period:
mid Dec to end April
Lift Passes
Flaine area:
Half-day 21.50 euros, Day pass 29.8
GRAND MASSIF:
1 day 35 euros, 6 days 173.50
Night Riding:No
Heli Boarding
Yes, email info@mdh.fr min 4 people
Snow mobiles
Check out flainesnowski.com
Board Schools
private lesson 1hr 32 euros
group 3hr/6 days 118 euros
Board Hire
Board & Boots 100-150 euros for
6 days

Annual Snowfall:
5m
Snowmaking:
5% of slopes

Car
Via Geneva, head south
on the A40 to Cluses and
then take the B road on
the left up to Flaine.
Fly
to Geneva 90km, about
1hrs transfer to Flaine.
Also Annecy 80km & lyon
190km
Train
services go to Cluses
which is 30km away
Bus
Alpbus runs between
Cluses and Flaine 22euros
return tel: +33 (0)4 50
03 70 09. Contact +33
(0)4 50 34 74 08 for
other options.

POOR FAIR GOOD TOP

FREERIDE
Some easy to get to off-piste
FREESTYLE
Terrain park
PISTES
Well groomed runs

4 OUT OF 10

Okay but a little bit cheesy

Pic - Isola 2000 Tourism

F
R
A
N
C
E

FREESTYLERS Isola 2000 is home to the Back to Back Snowboard Club, and a dedicated and maintained snowboard park. They don't have a residential Pipe Dragon yet, but with the experienced locals, you can be sure of a park with table-tops, spined tombstones and gaps. The locals are good to watch and know how to take a good line

PISTES. The whole area was planned to make runs long, well groomed and easy to return to base, with good cruising

Isola 2000, situated in the south of France, has more to offer than you'd expect. A calculated and very purpose-built resort, the French seem to have got their sums a bit wrong in the early days when they built this rather cheesy and tacky mess, whose original plan was to pack in hordes of cheap package tour groups. However, things have changed a little, and the place is losing its poor reputation and gaining a lot of respect. The resort has easy access to lifts, and the area offers plenty of varied terrain to keep even the most adventurous rider busy for a week or two, a season here would be pushing it.

FREERIDERS scoping the land will touch the piste only to hop between tree runs, or to get back on the lift. Isola has ample tree coverage over the mid to lower areas. Natural gullies can be hit near Melezes, plus look out for the drop offs in the trees as you're going up the chair lift - they're all over the place. Turn to the north-facing slope when conditions are good, above Grand Tour, as it is well worth hiking the ridge for freshies. Do watch your run out though as you come to a severe drop off onto a flat piste below.

and smooth pistes on both sides of the mountain. You can pick up some good speed and lay over your turns.

BEGINNERS have a massive designated area near the base lift station. This keeps them out of trouble on a good area for progression, before they take on the higher grade runs, allowing quick learners the chance to ride the whole resort.

THE TOWN
The easiest option with accommodation would be to stay in one of the apartment blocks - comfortable, unfussy and just a stone's throw away from the lift station and amenities. If you're after a bit more style and want to impress your other half, take up space in one of the chalets available. For food, why not try the Crocodile Bar, which serves up some decent Tex-Mex. It's also a good local snowboard hangout and stays open long into the early hours, with good measures and good sounds.

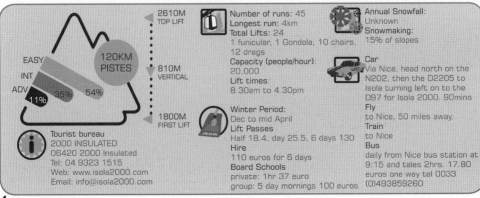

2610M TOP LIFT

810M VERTICAL

1800M FIRST LIFT

EASY
INT
ADV
11% 35% 54%

120KM PISTES

Number of runs: 45
Longest run: 4km
Total Lifts: 24
1 funicular, 1 Gondola, 10 chairs, 12 drags
Capacity (people/hour): 20,000
Lift times: 8.30am to 4.30pm

Winter Period:
Dec to mid April
Lift Passes
Half 18.4, day 25.5, 6 days 130
Hire
110 euros for 6 days
Board Schools
private: 1hr 37 euro
group: 5 day mornings 100 euros

Annual Snowfall:
Unknown
Snowmaking:
15% of slopes

Car
Via Nice, head north on the N202, then the D2205 to Isola turning left on to the D97 for Isola 2000. 90mins
Fly
to Nice, 50 miles away.
Train
to Nice
Bus
daily from Nice bus station at 9:15 and tales 2hrs. 17.80 euros one way tel 0033 (0)493859260

Tourist bureau
2000 INSULATED
06420 2000 Insulated
Tel: 04 9323 1515
Web: www.isola2000.com
Email: info@isola2000.com

wsg LA CLUSAZ

5 OUT OF 10

Limited terrain and can get very busy

Pic - La Clusaz Tourism

La Clusaz is located in the distant shadow of Mont Blanc and is only an hour-and-a-half from **Geneva**. La Clusaz is a cluster of five low-level rideable areas, linked by a series of lifts. The two very noticeable problems with La Clusaz are a) the low altitude, which can mean poor snow levels, and b) the French disease of overpopulation by ski-tour groups. Collectively, snowboarding can be described as poor. It lacks anything of great interest, unless you're a carver who likes to pose alongside lift lines on blue runs. Advanced riders will have this place licked in a few days, with the only decent challenge being a long black on the **Massif de Balme area**. You can ride four of the five areas via a network of connecting lifts, while the fifth, the Massif de Balme, can be reached by road or chair lift. Here you ride down a red or black before taking the gondola back up.

FREERIDERS will like the less crowded area of the Massif de Balme, where a series of red runs and a long black lead to open slopes which allow you to ride off-piste, hitting some powder stashes. The **Combe du Fernuy** is the area that descends a red section, down a tree line onto a cool run, en route to the **Massif de Balme** area. There are lots of trees, but no great challenges.

FREESTYLERS have a halfpipe and park on the

Massif de Balme slopes, but neither are shit hot or particularly big. The way the area is spread out means that there is a lot of okay natural terrain for catching air, but this is not a great freestyle place.

THE PISTE'S are very well maintained in all five areas. The slopes allow for some good wide arcs on intermediate terrain; the longest run is on the Balme slopes, whilst on Massif de Beauregard, there's an interesting long run to tackle at speed.

BEGINNERS can achieve a lot here, with slopes that are excellent for finding out what snowboarding is like at the early stages. The **Beauregard** and **L'Etale areas** have good, easy slopes; the only potential problem is that they are mostly serviced by drag lifts.

OFF THE SLOPES, the village has everything you would expect from a tourist trap. There's a good selection of beds ranging from expensive chalets to cheap, shared apartments, set in a traditional French-style village. Accommodation, shops, and restaurants are located within easy reach of the slopes, with many slope side hangouts. Evenings are dull and uneventful, unless you're a brain-dead apres fan

F

F R A N C E

la Clusaz

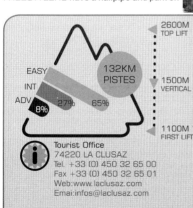

2600M TOP LIFT

1500M VERTICAL

1100M FIRST LIFT

EASY
INT
ADV
8% 27% 65%

132KM PISTES

Tourist Office
74220 LA CLUSAZ
Tel. +33 (0) 450 32 65 00
Fax +33 (0) 450 32 65 01
Web:www.laclusaz.com
Emai:infos@laclusaz.com

Number of runs: 83
Longest run: 3km
Total Lifts: 55
4 Gondola, 2 cable-cars, 14 chairs, 35 drags
Capacity (people/hour): 53,000
Lift times: 8.30am to 4.00pm

Winter Period:
Dec to April
Lift Passes
Half-day 21.50 euros
1 Day pass 27 euros
6 Days 140.5 euros
Season 560
Board Schools
Group lessons, 1 day 30 euros, 5 days 125 euros
Board Hire
Board & Boots 22-26 euros for 1 day
115-140 euros for 6 days

Annual Snowfall: 5m
Snowmaking: 10% of slopes

Car
Via Geneva 50 km, head south on the A40 and exit at Bonneville on to the D12 via Borne to La Clusaz
Fly
to Geneva (50km), then 1.5 hour transfer time. Lyon airport 150km away, nearest is Annecy 30km away.
Train
Train services go to Annecy which is 30km away.
Bus
3 coaches /day from Geneva airport (8am, 1pm, 5pm). Takes 1hr 45, 50 euros return.

With the right conditions, awesome

8 OUT OF 10

Pic - La Grave Tourism

F

F
R
A
N
C
E

snow in weeks, this mountain gets mogul madness. Therefore, the 15 minute hike over the top to **Les Deux Alpes** should entice the pipe and park enthusiast. If it does dump snow, cruise down the glacier, but be pre-warned of the numerous, unmarked crevasses. Have a chat with the patrouilleur sat in the hut next to the cable-car station, who will give you the current whats what. **Guides are essential** to get the most out of the place, or even sometimes, just to get out of the place.

Further down Glacier de la Girose, lies many steep cliffs and unavoidable gullies. Once past these gullies, stay on the traverse to the skier's right and keep an eye out for the gondola station at **P1**. Do not become bewitched by the untracked powder through the trees and river beds, or you will find yourself plummeting off 100m cliffs. Ruillans, spread out like curtains, are four couloirs to be explored. This gives you the chance to ride top to bottom. Further down, are some great natural quarter pipes and tree runs. Take warning of the cliffs and the river near the bottom.

This side of **La Meije** has held the legendary **Derby** for the past 17 years. In the world of snow racing, The Derby has the largest vertical drop of 2,150 metres on snowboard, ski, monoski or telemark and is held at the end of March and lasts for 5 days. For details visit **www.derbydelameije.com**

La Grave is secretly stashed away in the **Oisans**, behind the back of **Les Deux Alps**. When the snow falls, this mountain has 7,100 continuous vertical feet of drops, couloirs, cliffs, gullies, chutes, steeps, trees and crevices. This mountain isn't child's play so never ride alone. This is basically home to only die-hard extremists, with a few snowboarders who can hold their own. Still, the lack of skiing tourists simply guarantees 'no battle of the freshies' with untracked powder for days

THE TOWN
Local facilities at **La Grave** are pretty basic. There are a few shops, 5 hotels and a couple of campsites. Riders spending a season here will find that rent and a season's lift pass is cheap. On the social scene its not exactly kicking. The *pub le Bois des fees* runs some DJ nights, but party animals should head over to **Les Deux Alps**.

Freeriders will find above the only gondola, two T-bars that lead to the **Glacier de la Girose**. If La Grave hasn't seen

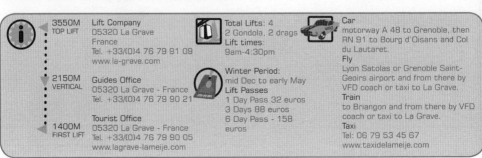

3550M TOP LIFT	**Lift Company** 05320 La Grave France Tel. +33/(0)4 76 79 91 09 www.la-grave.com
2150M VERTICAL	**Guides Office** 05320 La Grave - France Tel. +33/(0)4 76 79 90 21
1400M FIRST LIFT	**Tourist Office** 05320 La Grave - France Tel. +33/(0)4 76 79 90 05 www.lagrave-lameije.com

Total Lifts: 4
2 Gondola, 2 drags
Lift times:
9am-4:30pm

Winter Period:
mid Dec to early May
Lift Passes
1 Day Pass 32 euros
3 Days 88 euros
6 Day Pass - 158 euros

Car
motorway A 48 to Grenoble, then RN 91 to Bourg d'Oisans and Col du Lautaret.
Fly
Lyon Satolas or Grenoble Saint-Geoirs airport and from there by VFD coach or taxi to La Grave.
Train
to Briancon and from there by VFD coach or taxi to La Grave.
Taxi
Tel: 06 79 53 45 67
www.taxidelameije.com

POOR FAIR GOOD TOP

FREERIDE
A few tree & some good off-piste
FREESTYLE
4 Terrain parks & half- pipe
PISTES
Some wide easy slopes

Okay slopes but cheesy town

6
OUT OF 10

Pic - La Plagne Tourism

F
F
R
A
N
C
E

people, with 380m between you and the ground, so keep your eyes closed for the 4 minutes it takes.

FREERIDERS there are some great advanced runs down from the *Bellecote glacier*, which goes up to 3250m, so there shouldnt be a shortage of snow here even at the end of the season. You can also head off piste down to *Peisey- Nancroix* to link up to the Les Arcs area. Another great long piste run runs from the top of Les Verdons down to Champagny en Vanoise, with a vertical drop of 1250m. It has some sweet trees to cruise through at the bottom, but you will have to catch it on a good day to get the best snow. Whenever you get bored, just jump on the Vanoise Express and head over to Les Arcs.

FREESTYLERS won't find many natural hits in La Plagne, but there are now 4 terrain parks to keep you happy, including the new Pro-park in the centre of town. One in Plagne Bellecôte under the Blanchets chairlift, with a 120m halfpipe. A second at Montchavin-Les Coches, accessed from the Dos Rond chairlift. The Champagny en Vanoise's park is accessed from the la Rossa chairlift. Full of kickers, spines, tabletops, rails, and benches with lines for all levels.

PISTES. The slopes allow for some good, wide arcs on intermediate terrain; the longest run is on the Balme slopes, whilst on Massif de Beauregard, there's an interesting long run to tackle at speed.

BEGINNERS can achieve a lot here, with slopes that are excellent for finding out what snowboarding is like at the early stages. The Beauregard and L'Etale areas have good, easy slopes; but they are mostly serviced by drag lifts.

OFF THE SLOPES
the village has everything you would expect from a tourist trap. Accommodation, shops, and restaurants are located within easy reach of the slopes, with many slope side hangouts. There's a good selection of beds, from expensive chalets to cheap shared apartments. Evenings are dull and uneventful, unless you're a brain-dead apres fan.

There are 10 resorts that compose the **La Plagne** boarding area, ranging from traditional villages to modern purpose high altitude resorts built resorts, some of which are horrible such as Aime la Plagne, a single great apartment block. La Plagne is mainly suited to intermediate boarders as theres not much steep terrain and few challenging runs. There are some good wooded areas which can be a blessing in white outs, especially around the areas of *Les Coches* and *Champagny en Vanoise*. This resort is ideally suited to the Euro carver with mile after mile of motorway cruising. In 2003 the **Vanoise Express** opened which links La Plagne with **Les Arcs**, creating the **Paradski** area with access to 238 runs totally 425km. Vertigo sufferers be aware its 2km long, holds 200

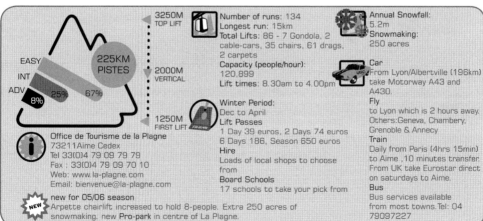

EASY
INT
ADV
8%   25%   67%

225KM
PISTES

3250M
TOP LIFT

2000M
VERTICAL

1250M
FIRST LIFT

Number of runs: 134
Longest run: 15km
Total Lifts: 86 - 7 Gondola, 2 cable-cars, 35 chairs, 61 drags, 2 carpets
Capacity (people/hour): 120,899
Lift times: 8.30am to 4.00pm

Winter Period:
Dec to April
Lift Passes
1 Day 39 euros, 2 Days 74 euros
6 Days 186, Season 650 euros
Hire
Loads of local shops to choose from
Board Schools
17 schools to take your pick from

Annual Snowfall:
5.2m
Snowmaking:
250 acres

Car
From Lyon/Albertville (196km) take Motorway A43 and A430.
Fly
to Lyon which is 2 hours away.
Others:Geneva, Chambery, Grenoble & Annecy
Train
Daily from Paris (4hrs 15min) to Aime ,10 minutes transfer.
From UK take Eurostar direct on saturdays to Aime.
Bus
Bus services available from most towns.Tel: 04 79097227

Office de Tourisme de la Plagne
73211Aime Cedex
Tel 33(0)4 79 09 79 79
Fax : 33(0)4 79 09 70 10
Web: www.la-plagne.com
Email: bienvenue@la-plagne.com

NEW new for 05/06 season
Arpette chairlift increased to hold 8-people. Extra 250 acres of snowmaking. new Pro-park in centre of La Plagne.

usg LA TANIA

FREERIDE
Tree runs & some good off-piste
FREESTYLE
Just natural hits
PISTES
Big open pistes

POOR FAIR GOOD TOP

Cheaper option for accessing the 3 Valleys

6
OUT OF 10

F
R
A
N
C
E

Pics - La Tania Tourism

La Tania is an off shoot of the **Albertville Olympics** built to house the spectators, it's steadily grown ever since, popular with the Dutch and Brits. The resort built in between **Courchevel** and **Meribel** has good access to the Trois Vallees. It's got a couple of drags, one just for total beginners and a big bubble with bench seats that aren't big enough to get half your arse on. At the top of the bubble you've got two choices, take the **Praz Juget** drag to access Courchevel or the **Dou Des Lanches** chair for Meribel, if you don't do drags you can get to Courchevel off the Dou Des Lanches but the runs flat and you'll be walking. If heading for Meribel make sure you've got a Trois Vallees pass, and best to endure the flattish path to reach Meribel proper as if you drop down to soon you'll end up at the altiport and the only way out is a flat track or a slow drag.

FREERIDERS have got two great runs down, the blue Folyeres a rolling run through the trees with some great drop off hits or the red **Moretta Blanche** good for a full speed hack. Off Piste access is good the trees are ok at the top but they get real tight as you near the resort. Under the **Dou Des Lanches** can be fantastic but don't go near it without a transceiver as it's prone to sliding. Also good is between **Loze** and **Dent de Burgin** chairs.

FREESTYLERS will find lots of natural hits and loads of areas up high to build a big kicker. If you want pre made then head for **Courchevel** or **Meribels** fun parks.

PISTES. For those who want just the piste, will enjoy the two main rolling runs into resort or you could head down towards the altiport in **Meribel** as the pitch is good and the width wide

BEGINNERS will find a short drag lift out of resort, but not the best place to learn. Beginners will find the best slopes link with Courchevel.

THE TOWN
basically a collection of chalets and a couple of blocks of flats, in typical French purpose built style, but its a good place to sit, look up the hill and have a beer. Other than a few French bars *Le Pub* gives all there is to give, affordable filling lunches on a big sun terrace, live music a few times a week and doesn't mind a loud piss up. Which is a good job as it's all there is to do, and the Dutch do it all. Food wise its Pizza, cheese and meat, savoie style.

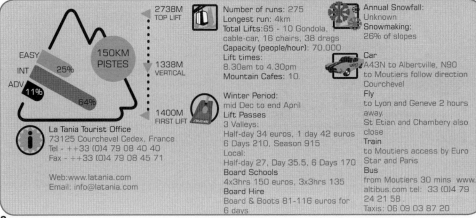

2738M
TOP LIFT

1338M
VERTICAL

1400M
FIRST LIFT

EASY
INT   25%
ADV
     11%
          64%

150KM
PISTES

La Tania Tourist Office
73125 Courchevel Cedex, France
Tel - ++33 (0)4 79 08 40 40
Fax - ++33 (0)4 79 08 45 71

Web:www.latania.com
Email: info@latania.com

Number of runs: 275
Longest run: 4km
Total Lifts:65 - 10 Gondola, cable-car, 16 chairs, 38 drags
Capacity (people/hour): 70,000
Lift times:
8.30am to 4.30pm
Mountain Cafes: 10.

Winter Period:
mid Dec to end April
Lift Passes
3 Valleys:
Half-day 34 euros, 1 day 42 euros
6 Days 210, Season 915
Local:
Half-day 27, Day 35.5, 6 Days 170
Board Schools
4x3hrs 150 euros, 3x3hrs 135
Board Hire
Board & Boots 81-116 euros for 6 days

Annual Snowfall:
Unknown
Snowmaking:
26% of slopes

Car
A43N to Albertville, N90 to Moutiers follow direction Courchevel
Fly
to Lyon and Geneve 2 hours away.
St Etian and Chambery also close
Train
to Moutiers access by Euro Star and Paris
Bus
from Moutiers 30 mins www.altibus.com tel: 33 (0)4 79 24 21 58 .
Taxis: 06 09 03 87 20

POOR FAIR GOOD TOP

FREERIDE
Tree runs & excellent off-piste
FREESTYLE
Park & half-pipe
PISTES
Pisted to perfection

Lots of off-piste, powder & natural hits

9
OUT OF 10

Pic - A - Snowboards

F

R
A
N
C
E

isolated, but has good access to some amazing terrain. The latest village is **1950**, next to a 60m waterfall which opened in 2003 and has been created by those Intrawest people. Despite having a huge riding area, Les Arcs has managed to retain a cosy feel as its dead easy to get from one area to another and you are only likely to run into heavy lift queues during the height of the French holidays. On the mountain, Les Arcs has it all, from mellow beginner slopes to some of the most challenging runs anywhere in France, with hardly any moguls. What Les Arcs does have however, is a lot of punters as this is a very popular resort, but with such a vast expanse of snow to explore, the slopes are left fairly quite. The **Vanoise Express** opened in Dec 2003 and now links the resort up with **La Plagne** creating the **Paradiski** area.

FREERIDERS it's all here and it's all good! If there is fresh snow on the ground, you can be guaranteed an amazing day through trees in **Peisey** or above 1600, off cornices in 2000, or just straight lining anything all day long. The area off the **Trans Arc** cable car gives access to some great off-piste riding

FREESTYLERS might not see a lot of jumps on first arrival, and in truth, there aren't many natural jumps, but the best area is in **Peisey**, 2000 and high above 1800. The hits on an area known as **Les Clocherets** are also worth a visit. If you're into man-made jumps, then you should head to the **Apocalypse Park** which has green, red or black runs. It also has a good selection of rails and a strange boardcross thing called the boarder gliss. However, it's true to say that the park is not well maintained, but things are getting better.

PISTES. If you like to stick to the piste then you're in luck. Les Arcs is blessed with amazingly well groomed, wide open pistes. There generally crowd free, well most of the time, especially the higher grade runs. Les Arcs piste lends itself perfectly for big slashing turns. The **Mont Blanc** piste on 1600 is ideal for intermediate carvers, and the **Belette** and **Myrtille** runs are good for advanced riders who can handle a board at speed.

BEGINNERS are sorted here and it shouldn't be long before

Most people delight in telling you that Les Arcs is a massive, concrete carbuncle on the arse of the **French Alps** - but these people probably haven't been here, let alone spent any sort of time in the place. Ignore such comments, come with an open mind, and ride one of the best sets of mountains in the world. Les Arcs itself is split into five distinctive resorts - 1600, 1800, 1950, 2000 and **Bourg-St-Maurice**. Each place has a different feel to it, so choose wisely. **1600**, where most of the chalets are situated, is quite chilled out with loads of trees. **1800** is the party place, while **2000** is a bit hideous and

3226M
TOP LIFT

241KM
PISTES

EASY
INT
ADV
50%
17% 33%

2026M
VERTICAL

1200M
FIRST LIFT

Tourist Office Courchevel
La Croisette - Bp 37, 73122 Courchevel.
Tel: ++33 (0) 4 79 08 00 9
Web: www.courchevel.com
Email: pro@courchevel.com

Number of runs: 121
Longest run: 7km
Total Lifts: 76
1 Funicular, 3 Gondolas,
1 cable-car, 30 chairs,
40 drags, 1 Telebenne
Capacity (people/hour):
68,000
Lift times:
8.30am to 4.30pm
Mountain Cafes: 14

Annual Snowfall:
5m
Snowmaking:
25% of slopes

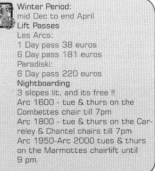

Winter Period:
mid Dec to end April
Lift Passes
Les Arcs:
1 Day pass 38 euros
6 Day pass 181 euros
Paradiski:
6 Day pass 220 euros
Nightboarding
3 slopes lit, and its free !!
Arc 1600 - tue & thurs on the Combettes chair till 7pm
Arc 1800 - tue & thurs on the Car-reley & Chantel chairs till 7pm
Arc 1950-Arc 2000 tues & thurs on the Marmottes chairlift until 9 pm.

ᴜꜱ⫶LES ARCS

Pic -**Piste map for Arc 1600/ Arc 1800/ Peisey-Vallandry (c)** Les Arcs Tourism

F

F
R
A
N
C
E

you're riding all over the place aided by the quality of the piste and the fact that most areas are connected by fairly easy trails and lifts. There are a lot of drag lifts, so expect a bit of embarrassment as you fall off after the first two yards.

THE TOWN

The five areas of **Les Arcs** are somewhat spread out, although they link up by both lift and road. Each area has quick access to the slopes, making riding back to your **accommodation** the norm at the end of the day. 1800 is the most popular place to stay, where there is a good selection of apartment blocks and hotels. The best thing about all the areas is that prices for accommodation, eating out and partying are largely the same throughout, with something to appeal to everyone. The general feel to the whole area is one of a gigantic, spread-out holiday camp that rocks 'til late, looks tacky, but has heaps going on with all manner of sporting facilities and shopping.

Many operators run package holidays using chalets, hotels and apartments throughout the resort. Prices vary however - you can rent an apartment for four people for a week from 400 euros, loading in at least four more bodies, and then split the cost. Most lodging is next to the slopes, with nothing involving a long trek. No matter what area you base yourself in, you will be able to find somewhere that serves up food to your liking. The place is littered with **restaurants** with cheap and chearful offerings being the favoured selection. 1800 has the best offerings with places like *Mountain Cafe,* where they serve huge portions of everything including Tex-Mex. The *Red Rock Bar* is also noted for grills etc.

CAR
via Lyon to Les Arcs, 210 km (130 miles), approx 2 hours. Take motorway to Albertville, dual carriageway to Moûtiers then the RN 90 to Bourg Saint Maurice
FLY
to Lyon international Transfer time to resort is 2 hours. Contact Satobus Alpes on +33 (0)4 37 255 255 to arrange transfer. Chambéry-Aix & Geneva airports available.
TRAIN
to Bourg-St-Maurice, then funicular or bus to Les Arcs. Eurostar snowtrain takes 8hrs from London Waterloo.
BUS
from Lyon airport, are available on a daily basis via Bourg St Maurice to Les Arcs. Bus from Bourg to resort tel: +33 (0)4 79 07 04 49

	POOR	FAIR	GOOD	TOP
FREERIDE Few trees but some good off-piste				
FREESTYLE Park & half-pipe				
PISTES Wide motorway pistes				

7 OUT OF 10

Decent all-year, all-style resort

Pic - Bruno Longo/2 Alpes Toursim

F
F R A N C E

programmes mainly aimed at freestylers. The excellent park has been put to good use hosting various competitons including the finals of the Orange Brits a couple of years back.

FREERIDERS While skiers with poor imagination brand it a motorway resort, the same is not true for boarders. When there is a fresh dump, you can ride almost everywhere you can see - the off-piste is huge and challenging. The only terrain missing is that of trees, but with a free day on the lift

Les Deux Alpes ranks amongst France's biggest and most friendly resorts. Not just friendly, but snowboard-friendly. The resort has plenty of testing and rider-friendly terrain, and and a very good park. The pistes are big and wide, pretty featureless, but great for beginners and intermediates. As a glacial resort, when other areas are suffering from a lack of the white stuff, Les Deux Alpes has no such problem. Once freeriders have exhausted the local area, and if you've got the guts, you can hike or snowcat and drop into neigbouring resort **La Grave**.

The end of October sees the now legendary **Mondial**, a huge event that attracts most of the world's snowboard equipment manufacturers, holding a 'come and try it' session of next season's kit. Hand in your passport, and ride off on next year's board! Five thousand boarders, a Big Air jump comp, a boardercross and full-on night-life, makes it a wild time. A great time to vist this place is summer, as the glacier allows for some fine summer riding in T-shirts. A lot of camps are held here in June and July, with camp

pass in nearby Serre Chevalier, tree huggers should feel catered for. Check out the Dome for a powdergasm, and routes off the new 6-man chair, La Fee, for steep, deep and testing riding. The resort of **La Grave** is connected via the Dôme de la Lauze ski tow, and its a renowned freeride wilderness.

FREESTYLERS can pipe and park ride all year round. Winter sees the park located at the mid-station with a well prepared earth shaped pipe, which is is 120 m long, and a permanent boardercross course which has moved to the Toura piste (between the Lac Noir TSF and the new Toura TSF) and completely redesigned, the new boardercross run offers a 185 m drop over more than 1,000 m. The Slopestyle is made of a gap jump, Big Airs, 2 tables tops, several handrails and a huge hip and if thats not enough it's shaped every day. In the summer, the park is on the glacier, which features in virtually every European snowboard video, such is its reputation. In summer the Soreiller green run on the glacier becomes a big park

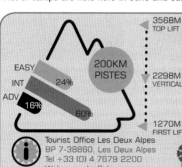

EASY	200KM PISTES	24%
INT		
ADV	16%	60%

3568M TOP LIFT

2298M VERTICAL

1270M FIRST LIFT

Number of runs: 75
Longest run: 12km
Total Lifts: 58
1 Funicular,
4 Gondolas,
2 cable-cars,
20 chairs, 30 drags
Capacity (people/ hour): 61,000
Lift times:
8.30am to 4.30pm
Mountain Cafes: 6

Annual Snowfall:
Unkown
Snowmaking:
20% of slopes

Winter Period:
end Oct to mid Dec/mid Dec to end April
Summer Period:
Mid June to end of August
Lift Passes
Super Ski 51 lifts
Day 34.7, 6 Days 165 + free la Grave access. Season 750 euros
Ski Sympa (21 lifts) day pass 16.90
2 Alps + La Grave day 45
Board School
120 euro 5 days for 3hrs
Guides
The Maison des 2 Alpes offer off-piste guiding days, 60 euros per person, inc bleepers. Contact guides2alpes@yahoo.fr tel: 04 7611 3629
Hire
Atelier du Snowboard charge Board & Boots 28 euros per day, 108 for 6 days.

Tourist Office Les Deux Alpes
BP 7-38860, Les Deux Alpes
Tel +33 (0) 4 7679 2200
Web: www.les2alpes.com
Email:les2alp@les2alpes.com

with huge pro-jumps, a huge array of rails, 2 halfpipes and plenty of smaller kickers for mere morttals.

PISTES. This is an piste lovers dream retreat, with nicely pisted runs like the Roch-Mantel and the Signal for a warm up. The glacier itself is great for ballistic speed. The Sandri run at the foot of the glacier to the mid-station is a warp factor 9, if you adhere to the essential turn only rule. So, for those of you who think turning is to admit defeat, tuck 'em away and go for it.

F

FRANCE

BEGINNERS starting out couldn't ask for a better place to make steady progress. The only problem is that the home runs down the front face are amongst the steepest in the resort, but there is a winding green run as an alternative. A real bonus is that the gentlest terrain is at the very top of the resort, where you can find the best snow.

Due to the layout of the lift system, other than your first morning on the beginner's slope, you need never take a drag for the remainder of your stay. The chairlifts, gondolas and other lifts make the whole uplift problem easier to sort out than a wonderbra, which should please the wimps.

THE TOWN
Off the slopes and at the base of the runs, Les Deux Alpes sits conveniently for most local services, but being a large town, not everything is within walking distance. The resort is a mix of old school and purpose-building. There are loads of off-slope services, including a cinema, bowling alley, sports complex and an outdoor climbing wall. It is a busy package tour destination so expect a lot of tourist junk shops, but there are a couple of decent boarders shops.

Accommodation: Standard grade apartment blocks, and a number of traditional-style chalets and modern hotels at prices that won't always hurt.

Food-wise, this place caters well for people on a budget, as well as those who want to splash out. There are some reasonably priced pizza and burger bars that are very good indeed. The Thai takeaway is much better than the disappointing Chinese. For a Tex-Mex, visit Smokey Joes or Saxo - also home to some of France's loveliest bar staff (top french tottie).

Night-life goes off seven nights a week, and it's common to see apres-ski idiots throwing up all over the place early on, having had a glass of gluwein at a poxy teatime bonding session. Bars to get wasted in are *Smokey Joes* , *Yeti bar, Mikes* and the *Dutch Bar,* followed by a drunken fumble/stumble in *L'Avalanche.*

CAR
From Lyon take the E70/A48 motorway to Grenoble. Take Exit 8 (Briançon) onto the RN91 , take the D213, exit at Chambon dam to Deux Alps. Drive time is about 2 1/2 hours. 170km
FLY
Lyon international 160km away, transfer time roughly 2 1/2hrs. Grenoble is 120km away, Geneva 220km
TRAIN to Grenoble an hour away.
BUS
Satobus runs from Lyon airport via Grenoble to 2 alps, tel: + 33 (0)4 7687 9031. Taxis: +33 (0)4 7680 0697

FREERIDE
Some trees & some good off-piste

FREESTYLE
2 Parks & sometimes 4 half-pipes

PISTES
Plenty of varied pistes

Over hyped resort. Good park though.

6
OUT OF 10

Pic - San Tang

M eribel at 1450m is a favourite for the Brits. Set in the middle of the Trio Vallees it's a good base to explore this massive area. So good in fact the French want it back. The Brit's have been slowly buying this resort and you can spend a week here without the need to speak a word of French, which is a good job as most of the bar staff wouldn't understand you anyway. This resort has enough varied terrain to keep everyone in a mixed ability group happy. Because of it's altitude the runs into resort can suffer from lack of snow and are often rock hard ice. They do have good snow making capabilities but as we all know its no replacement for the real thing. Meribel can be busy it's over priced and full of British skiers but has some great boarding.

FREERIDERS have a massive area to explore with well maintained pistes and lots of powder faces. From the **Saulire** are some long reds down to **Mottaret** which it turn will allow you to gain access to the **Mont Vallon** area the highest point in the Meribel Valley. Under the **Plan de Homme** chair are some well spaced trees with an easy pitch but a lot of rocks. Get off the **Olympic Express** chair and keep going straight and you drop into a 845 meter decent towards **St Martin de Belleville**, keep left as you may run out of snow early or late season. A short walk between two peaks off the **Mont Vallon** bubble will lead you to a huge bowl with some big drop offs, **take care** avalanche is a real possibility here. If you do leave the valley don't miss the last lift home as taxis are ridiculously expensive.

FREESTYLERS have a good fun park which is reached by the **Plattieres** bubble get of at the second stage. There are 2 pipes one of which was used one year for the British championships, following the pipe are a number of graded hits which could do with steeper and longer run outs but are fine. Serviced by the **Arpasson** chair is the **Moonpark** (www.moonpark.ne) which has a good wide Pipe, and a new boardercross. A pass just for the Moonpark are available at €50 for 3 days which don't have to be consecutive.

PISTES. On the piste there's some really sweet runs. The pistes are not as well maintained as in Courchevel but are plentiful and wide. Meribel has red runs with a vertical drop of almost 1300m if you cant find somewhere to crank it over on a run that long give up.

BEGINNERS have lots of opportunities to master those linked turns around the Altiport area, although some of the lifts are very old and slow. If heading for the **Mont Vallon** area be prepared for some flat spots on the way home.

THE TOWN
Meribel is tainted by the Brit's, the bars have imaginative names like *Le Pub*. It's a big spread out resort as they sensibly won't allow high rise developments so its grown

F

F R A N C E

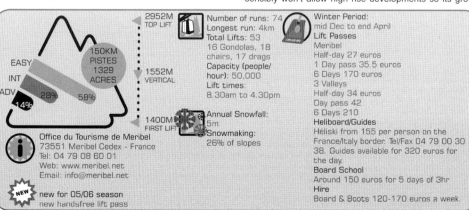

2952M
TOP LIFT

1552M
VERTICAL

1400M
FIRST LIFT

EASY

INT

ADV
14%

28%

58%

150KM
PISTES
1329
ACRES

Office du Tourisme de Meribel
73551 Meribel Cedex - France
Tel: 04 79 08 60 01
Web: www.meribel.net
Email: info@meribel.net

new for 05/06 season
new handsfree lift pass

Number of runs: 74
Longest run: 4km
Total Lifts: 53
16 Gondolas, 18 chairs, 17 drags
Capacity (people/hour): 50,000
Lift times:
8.30am to 4.30pm

Annual Snowfall:
5m
Snowmaking:
26% of slopes

Winter Period:
mid Dec to end April
Lift Passes
Meribel
Half-day 27 euros
1 Day pass 35.5 euros
6 Days 170 euros
3 Valleys
Half-day 34 euros
Day pass 42
6 Days 210
Heliboard/Guides
Héliski from 155 per person on the France/Italy border. Tel/Fax 04 79 00 30 38. Guides available for 320 euros for the day.
Board School
Around 150 euros for 5 days of 3hr
Hire
Board & Boots 120-170 euros a week.

233

uSg MERIBEL

Pic - Meribel Resort

out rather than up. The two main streets are full of bad clothes shops, board/ski hire, bars and restaurants. On the slopes away from the board you can take a tandem paraglide or ride a snow-mobile. Just up from **Meribel** is the village of **Mottaret** which is more of a purpose built village but is better placed for access to Mont Vallon the main fun park and Val Thorens.

Meribel is package deal central, and as such the bars are full of pissed Brit's in silly hats waiting for dinner, or later on really pissed Brit's after buckets full of cheep wine they got free with their chalet dinner. Before the days board is over you can sink a few in the lively *Rond Point*. *The Pub* has pool and a few tv's, opposite is *La Taverne* which is often mobbed and of course where there's Brit's there's a *Dicks Tea Bar*. All the bars are way over priced so if you are in a chalet ask them to chill the red wine so you don't have to hold your nose to get it down your throat.

All the big tour operators come here. You should be able to get a deal as there's chalet after chalet to choose from. Don't stay in **Brides-les-Bains** however cheep it is (see trio vallees)

Tex-mex, pizza and burgers to be had in the pubs. As for the restaurants *The Tremplins* good and if you want it there's a Michelin star at the *Cassiopee*.

CAR
From Lyon, go south via A432, A43 to Albertville, RN90 to Moûtiers and then D90, 18km to Meribel. 200km total
FLY
Lyon 185km, Geneva 135km. Nearest airport is in Chambéry 95km away.
TRAIN
Train services go to Moutiers which is 20 minutes away, 18km away.
BUS
Alp-ski bus from Geneva takes 3hrs Tel: 04 5043 6002, 111 euros return. Satobus from Lyon takes 2 1/2hrs and costs 86 euros return.

234

FREERIDE
A few tree runs & some off-piste

FREESTYLE
a dodgy park & pipe

PISTES
Links to a huge area

POOR FAIR GOOD TOP

Okay but basic

4
OUT OF 10

tends to be the quietest area to ride, give access to some cool freeride terrain and has a nice big powder bowl. There are some good value heliboarding options that drop you in nearby Italy once you've exhausted everything locally.

FREESTYLERS are presented with what they call a fun-park, but in truth it is a dire park, with only a few man-made hits. The best options for air are to seek out the natural terrain features.

PISTES. On the pistes you can't escape that French phenomenon the all in one wearing hard booter. There a common sight here, with boy wonders in hards posing on Les Anges and Le Querelay, which are both popular and easy. The two blacks down the Pian del Sole en route to the village of Claviere, are a little more interesting and worth a blast.

BEGINNERS are well catered for here, with a host of easy trails that can be reached (having first studied the piste map), without needing to ride a drag lift. Fast learners will soon be able to ride from the summit of Les Anges to the base, via a mixture of blue and green trails.

THE TOWN. Services are based conveniently for the slopes with a mixture of apartment blocks, chalets, shops, sporting facilities and restaurants, styled in a sober manner but aimed at the package tour ski groups. The village is okay, although there isn't a great deal to get excited about. Lodging is very affordable. Evenings can be very lively, with a number of bars that have young crowds partying every night all night.

Montgenevre forms the only French part of a circuit known as the **Milky Way**: a collection of resorts that extends along a number of valley floors and criss-crosses over into Italy. Montgenevre is basically at the opposite end to its more famous relation, the Italian resort of **Sauze d 'Oulx**. Collectively, the circuit offers over 250 miles of rideable terrain on slopes that have a good, reliable snow record, thanks to the average height of each area. Montgenevre's own 50km of marked out trails are an interesting mixture of mainly intermediate trails and some poor advanced terrain, rising from the village which is at an altitude of 1850m. Although this is a popular tourist resort, it is not as tainted with package tours as some other resorts in the region. Easy access to the slopes is made possible by a number of base lifts that will take you up to the main slopes of the **Les Anges** and **Le Querelay** areas, or in the opposite direction to **Le Chalvet**.

FREERIDERS can cut decent off-piste powder and ride some nice tree lines, although you won't find much of it a great challenge. The trails on Le Chalvet, located in what

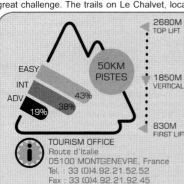

2680M
TOP LIFT

1850M
VERTICAL

830M
FIRST LIFT

EASY

INT

ADV

50KM
PISTES

43%

38%

19%

Number of runs: 21
Longest run: 7km
Total Lifts: 13
6 chairs, 7 drags
Capacity (people/hour): 6,500
Lift times: 8.30am to 4.30pm
Mountain Cafes: 5

Winter Period:
partial opening end Oct
early Dec to end April
Lift Passes
Just local area, Day pass 23.5 euros
Montgenevre/La Lune
Day pass 26.5, 6 days 126 euros
Heliboard/Guides
Many shops offer Heliski trips that leave
from town and head for Italy and the
Dormillouse, Terra Nera and Clausi peaks
Board Schools
Private lesson 35 euros per hour visit
www.a-peak.com

Annual Snowfall:
unknown
Snowmaking:
20% of slopes

Car
From Turin head west
along the A21 and the
E70, turning off at signs
for Oulx and precede
down the B24 to Mont-
genevre.
Fly
Fly to Turin in Italy which is
1 hour away.
Grenoble is 145km away
Train
Train services are
possible all the way to
Briancon, which is a 20
minutes transfer (12km)
or taxi 06 0706 7998

TOURISM OFFICE
Route d'Italie
05100 MONTGENEVRE, France
Tel. : 33 (0)4.92.21.52.52
Fax : 33 (0)4.92.21.92.45
Web: www.montgenevre.com
Email:office.tourisme.
montgenevre@wanadoo.fr

wsg MORZINE

POOR FAIR GOOD TOP

FREERIDE
Tree runs & some good off-piste
FREESTYLE
2 parks
PISTES
Well maintained but bland

Low, lively & part of the huge Portes du Soleil

6
OUT OF 10

F

F R A N C E

Morzine is a long established Alpine town witch is surrounded by tall mountains on all sides. Morzine is directly below the popular resort of **Avoriaz**. Unlike many purpose built French resorts it still holds an alpine charm, unlike Avoriaz. Its location at 1,000 metres (3,300 feet) can turn snow to rain fairly quickly, so temperature is crucial to this resort. With a good snow fall, however, Morzine and the nearby resort of Les Gets, can suffice for the snowboarder. The terrain varies from the long, tree lined, wide slopes of Morzine, to a board park in **Les Gets**, to the more challenging slopes of **Mont Cherry** and **Chammossiere**.

FREERIDERS.These mountains can be less busy than the slopes on the Avoriaz and Swiss side. Hence, beginners and intermediates will find more room to get the confidence up before heading for the **Portes du soleil** more challenging areas. There are plenty of tree-lined slopes, and many gentle pistes. Most riders particularly advanced riders will find their way up to the slopes above Avoriaz.

FREESTYLERS. Off the main chair in Morzine there is a small park with beginner level jumps and a rail or two. There is another beginner to intermediate park located at the top of **Super Morzine Gondola** and chair. It features a row of 5-7m kickers which are great for learning on. There is also a beginner box and an easy rail. There is a short drag lift that services this park so it's ideal for getting lots of runs in without having to take long chair lift rides.

THE PISTES are well maintained but a little dull. Fine for beginners and intermediates but advanced riders will soon be looking outside of the immediate Morzine area.

BEGINNERS will be glad to hear that it's mainly chair lifts on these slopes, so the dreaded poma or t-bars don't have to be tackled. The green slopes will be too flat for the snowboarder, but there are some easy blues and reds in Morzine for the beginner. The **Pleney slope**, which heads back to the town, is a steep red.

THE TOWN
For those who need to take a break from the slopes there is plenty of shopping available in the town ranging from equipment to fashion. There is a swimming pool, bowling alley, pool tables, cinema, ice skating and ice hockey games.

Accommodation. There is plenty of accommodation in Morzine in every price bracket. *Chalet Nantegue* offer dorms with communal breakfast, tv rooms etc. They regularly have backyard jams in the garden with small rails, a quarter pipe and a bbq. This place is wicked for those on a budget. *Chill Chalet* also offer good value for money, £35 gets you a cosy room in a traditional chalet with breakfast and dinner. *Rude Chalets* offer a very comfortable accommodation option for a little extra, holidays are fully catered and include hot tubs and plasma screens as well as wireless connection for laptops. The *Farmhouse Hotel* inside the oldest building in Morzine offer fine dining, roll top baths and four poster beds.

Food. Providing you are not allergic to cheese, Morzine has plenty of restaurants at reasonable prices. *The Panini hut* in the centre of town offers a variety of snacks and is an ideal stop on the way home. *L'Etal* is a very reasonably priced restaurant also in the centre, with a sun terrace for daytime dining and a cosy atmosphere inside in the evening.

Nightlife. The town has a good selection of bars with everything on offer. The *Dixie Bar* is good to go and watch the football & open until 2am. The *Cavern* is another central bar, which also has a mainly English cliental. It's open until 2am and there's live music or DJs most nights. A trendy hangout is the new English run bar and hotel '*The Ridge*' just outside the centre, it has gone for the more minimalist, contemporary look and is a refreshing change in the resort. They also have wireless internet connection which is handy to use while sipping a cappuccino. For a quieter option chill in the low lit *Buddha Bar. The Opera* is located just next door so if things liven up there is a big dance floor and a dancers cage! It's open until 4am . *The Paradis* is also open until 4am and takes you straight back to the 8o's with it's red and black tiger striped couches and disco balls.

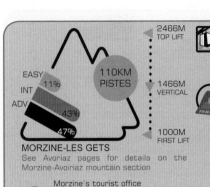

EASY — 11%
INT
ADV — 43%
47%

110KM PISTES

2466M TOP LIFT

1466M VERTICAL

1000M FIRST LIFT

MORZINE-LES GETS
See Avoriaz pages for details on the Morzine-Avoriaz mountain section

Morzine's tourist office
B.P. 23 - 74110 Morzine - France
Tel: 00 33(0) 450 74 72 72
Web:www.morzine-avoriaz.com
Email:info@morzine-avoriaz.com

Number of runs: 66
Longest run: 6km
Total Lifts48
2 funiculars, 3 cable-cars, 22 chairs, 18 drags

Winter Period:
Dec to April
Lift Passes
Morzine-Les Gets:
1/2 Day Pass 20.20 euros
Day Pass 26.8 euros
6 Day Pass - 134.4 euros
Portes du Soleil:
Day 37, 6 days 179
Board Schools
ESPA charge 40 euros for 2hrs lesson, 6x2hrs 115 euros. Visit www.morzineski.fr
Night Boarding
On Boule de Gomme & Stade slopes

Annual Snowfall:
9m
Snowmaking:
some

Car
Head towards Cluses (A40),
35 km from Morzine
Fly
Geneva 1 hour away, 80km
Train
Stations of Cluses (35km away) or Thonon-les-Bains
- Daily TGV links with Cluses, Saturday and Sunday with Thonon
Bus
SAT buses go from the airport to Morzine and take about 2 and ½ hours. Tel: 0033 (0) 450 791569

wsg RISOUL

POOR FAIR GOOD TOP

FREERIDE
Some tree runs & good off-piste

FREESTYLE
150m pipe

PISTES
Some good well pisted runs

Cool place & largest half-pipe in France

6
OUT OF 10

F R A N C E

Risoul is located between **Gap** and **Briancon**, and combined with the neighbouring resort **Vars**, the whole area offers about 160 km of terrain. The big men of the resort are more than happy to have snowboarders here, since the image of non-conformity fits in nicely with the way the resort is run - clearly with the young in mind. Risoul 1850 offers everything from easy slopes for beginners, to double black diamond runs for extreme freaks.

FREERIDERS tend to show up here around New Year in search of decent terrain, which they can find on **Pic de Razies, Melezet and Platte De La Nonne**, or **Pic De La Mayt**. Ride in these big powder bowl areas, and you can forget about sex being the best thing in the world. One warning - you won't decide on which is your favourite run for days or even weeks, as there are so many damn good ones.

FREESTYLERS should take De Cezier chair to reach **Surfland**, where the jibbing begins. This playground (which is akin to paradise), offers a complete boardercross run, rails, several quarter-pipes, small practice kickers, a pro-jump over a bus, and one of the longest, and reputedly the longest halfpipe in France. 150m long, 20m wide and with 5m walls, this pipe will probably offer you more air-time than you

actually want. Every Thursday night there's a high-jump contest, with local riders & holiday makers out to impress. There's also DJ's and a barbecue .

PISTES. All the slopes are designed and prepared for hardcore edge-to-edge activities, and there are even special slopes for race practice (poles available at the ski school).

BEGINNERS If you take the cabin lift named Accueil, you'll find the area that Risoul has set aside for its snowboard kindergarten - the short and easy run is perfect for your first try on a board. There are also two small, slow drag lifts to practice on, before going up into the real snowboard world.

THE TOWN
Risoul is a small village where the inhabitants still treat you as a guest. There is a good selection of slope side **accommodation**, with seven nights in an apartment costing around 120euros per rider. **Eating out** is cool at places like *Snack Attack*. For **night-life**, head to the *Yeti* (little Holland), where you must drink more booze than the Dutch dude, then leave him on the floor and take off with his girlfriend.

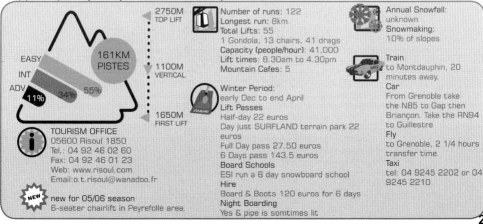

EASY

161KM PISTES

INT

ADV

11%   34%   55%

TOURISM OFFICE
05600 Risoul 1850
Tel.: 04 92 46 02 60
Fax: 04 92 46 01 23
Web: www.risoul.com
Email:o.t.risoul@wanadoo.fr

NEW new for 05/06 season
6-seater chairlift in Peyrefolle area.

2750M
TOP LIFT

1100M
VERTICAL

1650M
FIRST LIFT

Number of runs: 122
Longest run: 8km
Total Lifts: 55
1 Gondola, 13 chairs, 41 drags
Capacity (people/hour): 41,000
Lift times: 8.30am to 4.30pm
Mountain Cafes: 5

Winter Period:
early Dec to end April
Lift Passes
Half-day 22 euros
Day just SURFLAND terrain park 22 euros
Full Day pass 27.50 euros
6 Days pass 143.5 euros
Board Schools
ESI run a 6 day snowboard school
Hire
Board & Boots 120 euros for 6 days
Night Boarding
Yes & pipe is somtimes lit

Annual Snowfall:
unknown
Snowmaking:
10% of slopes

Train
to Montdauphin, 20 minutes away.
Car
From Grenoble take the N85 to Gap then Briancon. Take the RN94 to Guillestre
Fly
to Grenoble, 2 1/4 hours transfer time.
Taxi
tel: 04 9245 2202 or 04 9245 2210

237

POOR FAIR GOOD TOP

FREERIDE
A few tree runs & excellent off-piste

FREESTYLE
good natural

PISTES
Forget it

Fantastic freeriding when theres fresh snow.

8 OUT OF 10

Pic - Sainte Foy Tourism

F

FRANCE

Sainte-Foy who told them? The word is out, but there's still time. Ten years ago if you asked someone about Sainte-Foy a blank look would greet you. If you'd driven there you would've missed it, if it hadn't of been for the fact the road ended. The home of mushroom loving David Vincent has changed, ask now and a gleam will light up the eyes of those who've been and the answer of no but I'd love to from those unlucky others. Towards Val d'Isere and Tignes from Bourg St Maurice there's a small turning to the left. Up it's 8km of once potholed tarmac lies the hamlet of Saint Foy. Not a place to spend a weeks holiday but if you're nearby, have use of a car and it's just dumped GO. This place with good snow has a hallucinatory feel, you won't be asking your mates to pinch you, you're going to need a twat round the head with their board to believe what you're seeing. A boarders dream, but who knows for how much longer? The road in is smooth, the building of chalets is changing the vibe from ramshackle farm house to modern resort. Gone are the days of being greeted by goats looking at you from their barns, lets hope they leave the slopes alone.

FREERIDERS, its what snowboards were invented for. There are basically 3 slow lifts, they run one after the other to take you from 1550m to the *Col de L'Aiguille* at 2612m. From here you have a myriad of choices but be careful each brow you come over leads to another untouched field and the next thing you know your ollieing your way over fences and the bottom lift will be a hitch hike away. On the way up you can look for the line you want to take. Be it wide open face, rock shoots or into the trees this place is a wide open mountain with only a few runs winding their way down under the lifts. If you can handle a walk and a long flattish path then you can drop down over the back side of Rocher d'Arbine. **WARNING** to get the best of this place get a guide; not just to show you the way, but to advise about safe routes and snow conditions.

FREESTYLERS need to discover how to seek out natural hits, since that's all you're going to get - but that's all you're going to need! Why bother making pipes in a natural heaven - they're better left to the tourist traps. Riding will never be as free or as natural as in this place. There's loads of drop offs and plenty of banked walls just waiting to be hit, but novice air heads must take care and ride only with a competent rider who can pre-spot for you, as who knows what may lie under that flat blanket of soft looking snow.

PISTE lovers will soon whish they'd headed for Val d'Isere or Tignes, with only 25km of marked pistes.

BEGINNERS have some fine rolling runs under the first 2 chairs and won't have the crowds of bigger resorts to contend, and cheaper lift passes.

THE TOWN
On the slopes are some great little mountain restaurants, off the slopes, you will find a resort with little to offer. There are chalets, but they are spread out with no connections to night-life or eateries. But then, if you stay here it's for the riding not for anything else. Nightlife is a beer in the British run pub or a glass of wine in your chalet. Sainte-Foy is small and let's hope it stays that way.

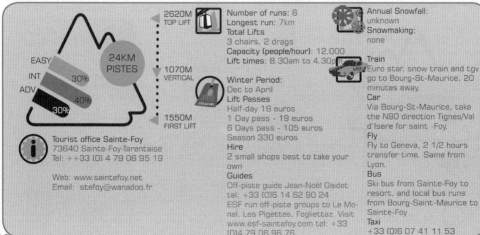

Tourist office Sainte-Foy
73640 Sainte-Foy-Tarentaise
Tel: ++33 (0) 4 79 06 95 19

Web: www.saintefoy.net
Email: stefoy@wanadoo.fr

EASY
INT 30%
ADV 40%
30%

24KM PISTES

2620M TOP LIFT
1070M VERTICAL
1550M FIRST LIFT

Number of runs: 6
Longest run: 7km
Total Lifts
3 chairs, 2 drags
Capacity (people/hour): 12,000
Lift times: 8.30am to 4.30pm

Winter Period:
Dec to April
Lift Passes
Half-day 16 euros
1 Day pass - 19 euros
6 Days pass - 105 euros
Season 330 euros
Hire
2 small shops best to take your own
Guides
Off-piste guide Jean-Noël Gaidet tel: +33 (0)6 14 62 90 24
ESF run off-piste groups to Le Monal, Les Pigettes, Fogliettaz. Visit www.esf-saintefoy.com tel: +33 (0)4 79 06 96 76

Annual Snowfall:
unknown
Snowmaking:
none

Train
Euro star, snow train and tgv go to Bourg-St-Maurice, 20 minutes away.
Car
Via Bourg-St-Maurice, take the N90 direction Tignes/Val d'Isere for saint -Foy.
Fly
Fly to Geneva, 2 1/2 hours transfer time. Same from Lyon.
Bus
Ski bus from Sainte-Foy to resort, and local bus runs from Bourg-Saint-Maurice to Sainte-Foy
Taxi
+33 (0)6 07 41 11 53

wsg SAINT LARY

POOR FAIR GOOD TOP

FREERIDE
Tree runs but little off-piste
FREESTYLE
Park & pipe
PISTES
Busy but easy cruiser terrain

6
OUT OF 10

Ye olde village, with some good learner terrain

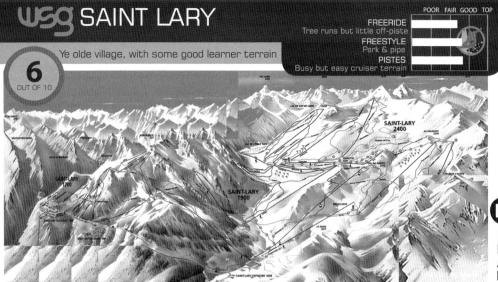

SAINT-LARY
2400

SAINT-LARY
1700

SAINT-LARY
1900

The main village of Saint Lary lies at 630 metres in the Aure Valley; above here there are two small villages, **Saint Lary La Cabane** at 1,600 metres, and **Saint Lary Pla D'Adret** at 1,700 metres. All three are connected by a series of lifts, with the upper villages reachable by road, or from Saint Lary by the cable car which takes you to the slopes. This relatively small resort lies in the **French Pyranees** and goes back to the 1950's. If you think that French ski resorts are massive purpose-built shams, this place will make you think again. What you get is a resort that is very snowboard-friendly, with good terrain that can be tackled by novices and riders with only a few days under their belts. However, this is also a popular resort which results in a number of long lift queues, especially at weekends.

FREERIDERS looking for vast powder bowls are not going to get them here. Advanced and hardcore riders wanting major long steeps are going to find this place a bit easy without too many challenges. The cluster of black runs off the Tortes chair offers some opportunities for freeriders to excel on fairly featureless terrain. Alternatively, the area known as Bassia is pretty cool, and will suit riders looking for trees to shred.

FREESTYLERS will find the **Quicksilver Snowpark** interesting, with its long boardercross circuit, an improved pipe, and a series of decent hits. The parks split into 3 definite areas the family park, which is great for beginners the slide park which is full of rails and the snowskatepark which is a slope style run

PISTES. Riders looking for fast, wide piste to lay out big turns on will find the few reds that are basic but okay. They should also provide novices who are getting to grips with steeper terrain some early learning opportunities

BEGINNERS will certainly find the easy blues spread out across the resort perfect for learning, with a mixture of chair lifts and drags to ferry you around. The short easy stuff reached from Saint Lary Pla D'Adret will sort you out, before taking the runs over on Vallon Du Portet. The Corniche is a long, easy blue that freeriding novices will soon be able to handle.

THE TOWN
An old Pyrenean village, St Lary is laid out along a main street where you'll find chalets and hotels. Services are extremely good here, without the hustle and bustle of tourist traps. Although somewhat limited, most facilities are found in Saint Lary, rather than the other two villages. Eating and night-time hangouts are okay: quiet and tame, and inexpensive.

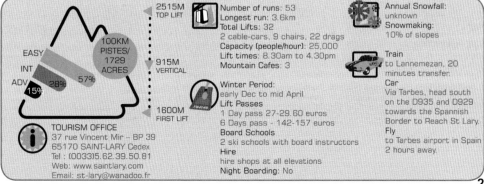

EASY
INT
ADV 15%
28%
57%

100KM
PISTES/
1729
ACRES

2515M
TOP LIFT

915M
VERTICAL

1600M
FIRST LIFT

TOURISM OFFICE
37 rue Vincent Mir – BP 39
65170 SAINT-LARY Cedex
Tel : (0033)5.62.39.50.81
Web: www.saintlary.com
Email: st-lary@wanadoo.fr

Number of runs: 53
Longest run: 3.6km
Total Lifts: 32
2 cable-cars, 9 chairs, 22 drags
Capacity (people/hour): 25,000
Lift times: 8.30am to 4.30pm
Mountain Cafes: 3

Winter Period:
early Dec to mid April
Lift Passes
1 Day pass 27-29.60 euros
6 Days pass - 142-157 euros
Board Schools
2 ski schools with board instructors
Hire
hire shops at all elevations
Night Boarding: No

Annual Snowfall:
unknown
Snowmaking:
10% of slopes

Train
to Lannemezan, 20
minutes transfer
Car
Via Tarbes, head south
on the D935 and D929
towards the Spannish
Border to Reach St Lary.
Fly
to Tarbes airport in Spain
2 hours away.

239

POOR FAIR GOOD TOP

FREERIDE
few tree runs & some good off-piste
FREESTYLE
Park & Pipe
PISTES
Some good wide slopes

Some good freeriding from this Chamonix cousin.

6
OUT OF 10

F

**F
R
A
N
C
E**

© Pic - St Gervais Tourism

FREESTYLERS have a fun park at Mont Joux, although it is not very impressive and seems to be rather neglected, particularly the halfpipe. The few jumps range from a small table top to a 30ft gap jump. It also gets very busy at times, especially weekends.

PISTES. Riders will find plenty of wide pistes, although some of them do tend to get chopped up by the end of the day. There are slalom courses at Mont Joux and across Megeve at Rochebrune.

BEGINNERS can save money by getting a lift pass for just the Bettex area, which has a few nursery slopes, including

Despite its proximity to Mont Blanc and the ever popular Chamonix, St Gervais is not a very well known resort, probably due to the fact that no major tour operators go there. St Gervais itself is fairly small, but the lift pass (Evasion Mont-Blanc) covers 6 ski areas comprising of over 450km of slopes and some easily accessible off piste areas. It is also one of the areas covered on the Ski Pass Mont Blanc which allows access to the whole of the Mont Blanc region, (12 areas).

FREERIDERS should check out the huge wide open bowls at Les Contamines, where there is varied off piste riding almost everywhere you look. It's best when visibility and snow are good though, as if it is cloudy you will just get frustrated that you are missing all the best lines and hitting all the hidden cat-tracks. Mont-Joy has some good steep off-piste riding. It is possible to ride right down to Les Contamines, but taking a guide to avoid accidental cliff drops is highly recommended.

one chairlift. However, the slopes on the other side of the mountain tend to get more sun and are less icy. The areas around the Mont d'Arbois and Ideal lifts are recommended as there are a variety of easy runs as well as some easily reached harder ones for when you start feeling brave. The low points for beginners are the flat bits on the runs back down to Bettex.

THE TOWN
Local services are good and include ice skating, ice climbing, a cinema, loads of shops and a large number of restaurants. Around the mountain there is a good choice of accommodation in St. Gervais, with over 30 hotels, chalets, lodges and apartments. A lot of these are located below the St. Gervais-Bettex gondola, so theoretically you can ride to your door, snow permitting. Night life, however, is tame and limited to one club which is crap, plays dull French music and is expensive.

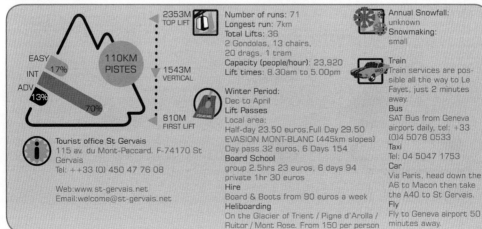

EASY
INT 17%
ADV
13%
70%

110KM PISTES

2353M
TOP LIFT

1543M
VERTICAL

810M
FIRST LIFT

Number of runs: 71
Longest run: 7km
Total Lifts: 36
2 Gondolas, 13 chairs,
20 drags, 1 tram
Capacity (people/hour): 23,920
Lift times: 8.30am to 5.00pm

Winter Period:
Dec to April
Lift Passes
Local area:
Half-day 23.50 euros, Full Day 29.50
EVASION MONT-BLANC (445km slopes)
Day pass 32 euros, 6 Days 154
Board School
group 2.5hrs 23 euros, 6 days 94
private 1hr 30 euros
Hire
Board & Boots from 90 euros a week
Heliboarding
On the Glacier of Trient / Pigne d'Arolla / Ruitor / Mont Rose. From 150 per person

Annual Snowfall:
unknown
Snowmaking:
small

Train
Train services are possible all the way to Le Fayet, just 2 minutes away.
Bus
SAT Bus from Geneva airport daily, tel: +33 (0)4 5078 0533
Taxi
Tel: 04 5047 1753
Car
Via Paris, head down the A6 to Macon then take the A40 to St Gervais.
Fly
Fly to Geneva airport 50 minutes away.

Tourist office St Gervais
115 av. du Mont-Paccard. F-74170 St Gervais
Tel: ++33 (0) 450 47 76 08

Web:www.st-gervais.net
Email:welcome@st-gervais.net

wsg SERRE CHEVALIER

One of the best resorts in France, but pricey

10 OUT OF 10

	POOR	FAIR	GOOD	TOP
FREERIDE Great tree runs & good off-piste				
FREESTYLE Parks & 2 half-pipes				
PISTES Lots of tree & open pistes				

Pic - Agence Zoom/Serre Chevalier Tourism

Serre Chevalier is one of the best places to ride in France. This great resort has heaps of major terrain, tight, open trees to weave, extreme drop offs to get the adrenaline going, big bowls with silly amounts of good powder, countless banks and gullies, super-fast flats to push the hair back, hits everywhere, and a giant, natural fun-park - all located next to an unassuming, old-fashioned French village (with a hint of the new here and there). As one local rider once put it 'who needs fun-parks, when this place is a complete fun-park at every level and distinction!' Serre Chevalier is suitable for everyone, with an area that links up with **Briancon** and **Le Monetier**, to provide 230km of terrain. **Chantemerle** is the largest of the three areas, and also the place for the best terrain and action. However, being a great resort does have its drawbacks as this is a major destination for package tour operators. This has the result of causing some long lift lines first thing in the morning, but once up, things become a lot better.

FREERIDERS get to shred plenty of open, tight trees, gullies and deep bowls, as well as some long steeps, where advanced riders can busy themselves for weeks on end. Serre Chevalier is perfect soft boot territory, and those riders wanting wide expanses of powder without having to hike, should check out the stuff off the Balme chair lift.

FREESTYLERS should basically session the whole mountain as there are too many hits to mention - it will take most riders at least a season to hit each jump only once. The place is a super-big, natural fun-park, with lots of logs to grind, and loads of big jumps everywhere

There's also a man-made park on the in Serre Chevalier 1500 slopes should you need it. It's open from 10.00 till 21.00 there's also two Boarder Cross, at Combe du Grand Serre Che and Clausas and a beginners and full size set of pipes. Not to forget the huge Table tops in **Pré Chabert** 1500.

PISTES. Riders are presented with as much alpine terrain as they could possibly need. If you have the bottle, the Olympique trail is a fast, black race run that bases out in the village of Chantemerle, and will certainly get the adrenaline pumping. You can get some serious speed down the **Olympique trail**, and although advanced riders and competent intermediate boarders will manage, novices should give this run a miss (unless they have a death wish).

EASY
INT 42%
ADV 46%
12%

249KM PISTES

3850M TOP LIFT

1630M VERTICAL

1200M FIRST LIFT

Number of runs: 115
Longest run: 10km
Total Lifts: 77
3 cable-cars, 6 Gondolas,
20 chairs, 39 drags
Capacity (people/hour):
68,000
Lift times:
8.30am to 4.30pm

Annual Snowfall:
Unknown
Snowmaking:
18% of slopes

Winter Period:
early Dec to end April
Lift Passes
Grand Serre Che linked area:
1 Day 35 euros, 6 Days 170
Just Serre Chevalier:
1 Day 31 euros, 6 days 150
Night skiing free from Serre Chevalier
1200 and 1400 (with a 6 days Grand
Serre Che pass)
Nightboarding
on Serre Chevalier 1200 and 1400
Board School
A number of board schools. Private
lessons from 31 euros an hour. Group
4hrs for 6 days 102 euros.

Tourist Office Serre Chevalier
BP 20-05240 La Salle Les Alpes
Tel: +33 (0) 4 92 24 74 43
Web: www.serre-chevalier.com
Email: contact@ot-serrechevalier.fr

NEW new for 05/06 season
3 new 6-seater chairlifts; Grand Serre in Serre Chevalier 1350, Forêt in Serre Chevalier 1400, Clot Gauthier in Serre Chevalier 1400. Extention of snowmaking coverage.

Pic - Agence Zoom/Serre Chevalier Tourism

Food. Your dietary needs are well sorted here, with a vast selection of restaurants and fast-food outlets to choose from, including a number of creperies. Le Frog (please), is known for its French cuisine, as is the *Yeti*, *Nocthambule* and *Le Refuge*. For a decent fish meal, *La Bidulle* is highly recommended and is located in Villeneuve. *L'Amphore* is the place for a slab of pizza

Night life is somewhat mixed here, with some happening and lively bars but also a few sad and very expensive disco's, Night life rocks until late in most bars so you don't need the clubs. Check out the likes of the Iceberg or Yeti Bar, where they often have live music. The *White Hare* is a cool hangout.

BEGINNERS should find the runs around Frejus more suited to their needs, with a number of long, easy runs that bring you back down the mountain into the village of Villeneuve, via some tree-lined trails. Serre Chevalier has a lot of drag lifts - some of which can be a nightmare, often travelling a long way at speeds suited to riding down, not up. Watch out for the sharp turns that some of the drag lifts make through the trees. If you can master Serre Chevalier's drag lifts, you shouldn't have any trouble in the rest of the world.

THE TOWN

Serre Chevalier provides a number of options for lodging and other local services. These are situated along a stretched-out valley road, set back from the base lifts. Briancon is the largest place to stay, but is not so convenient for the main slopes, whereas the villages of Chantemerle and Villeneuve (a few miles apart, linked on the slopes and by road), offer the best facilities nearer the slopes. There are plenty of shops as well as good watering holes, but there is one small blip on Serre Chevalier's otherwise shining record: it's a tourist trap that attracts a number of British and Italian tour companies, who bring in far too many package groups.

Accommodation: 30,000 visitors can be bedded around here. The choices range from a bunk house and modern apartment blocks for groups on the cheap, to classy hotels.

Pic - Serre Chevalier Tourism

CAR
From Grenoble, Lyon or Paris take Motorway A51, exit Pont de Claix at 80 km from the resort via Lautaret Pass.
FLY
Fly to Lyon (200km) airport 3 hour transfer. Nearest airport is Turin (108km), Marseille (250km) has a free bus saturdays 2pm to the resort.
TRAIN
The nearest train station is in Briancon, 10 minutes away. Daily night trains from Paris gare Austerlitz to Briançon dep 10.05pm arr 8.37am
BUS
available from Lyon airport. Shuttles run from Briancon train station to Serre Chev every 20mins from 8.30-6 pm

	POOR	FAIR	GOOD	TOP
FREERIDE No tree runs but huge off-piste				
FREESTYLE All year parks & half-pipe				
PISTES Open motorway cruisers				

Snow sure, true boarders moonscape

9 OUT OF 10

© A-Snowboards

F
R
A
N
C
E

satisfied. You drive up to the resort on the same road towards Val D'Isere from Bourg Saint Maurice accessible by euro star and the snow train. A painting of Hercules holding back the water greets you as you cross over the high dam, and as you pass a church on your right you can see Jesus, who has freed his arms from the crucifix pointing towards the old submerged village, eerie man eerie. Tignes is one of the major resorts in France, and has long been hosting national and international events, their web site even has a Japanese translation. BASI runs some of it's snowboard instructors courses here. Snowboard teams and manufacturers also use Tignes to host training camps and events. The main lifts open early September and close late May and with summer boarding on the Grande Motte Glacier from mid June to September you can almost board every day of the year. This year they even had a summer fun park. If you are up for it you can dive under the ice of Tignes-Le-Lac and look up at the ice distorted mountains.

FREERIDERS have loads of choice, there are some really long off piste runs some great reds and blacks and the wide Grande Motte Glacier. If you are lucky with the snow there's the 1200 meter decent in the Aiguille Percee to Tignes Les Brevieres on a choice of runs, with help you can find a very long off piste route. To the sides of Les Lanches you can find good little rock shoots and bowls. Tignes is set in a wide open valley so you can see all the lines you'd love to take, it's just working out how to get to them. From the Toviere area there's some great spots of snow between the runs and two long blues into Val Claret. The Funiculaire and Cabel Car take you to the Glacier at 3456 meters for more or less guaranteed good snow. From the top a choice of Reds and off piste routes await you, but watch out for crevasses. Always a good side trip is the Vallee Perdue in the Val D'Isere valley just make sure you have a espace killy lift pass and you make the last lift home. Take it easy in Tignes especially after a fresh dump, as it doesn't take much to trigger off avalanches and it's no fun stuck in an upside down world of blue light. If you

Tignes is very snowboard friendly; long before the other French resorts welcomed snowboarders, Tignes opened it's arms wide and said come here and slide down that, jump over that, and listen to this while your at it. If Carlsberg made snowboard resorts they would have made Tignes. Set at 2100 meters and part of the 290km of pistes that is the Espace Killy, it has a very good snow record, a glacier, a lake and a lot of varying terrain; Tignes can almost guarantee everyone leaves

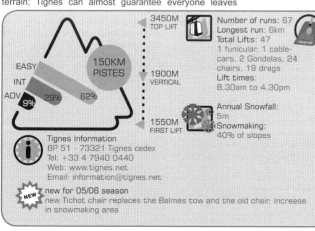

3450M
TOP LIFT

EASY

150KM
PISTES

1900M
VERTICAL

INT

ADV 9% 29% 62%

1550M
FIRST LIFT

Tignes Information
BP 51 - 73321 Tignes cedex
Tel: +33 4 7940 0440
Web: www.tignes.net
Email: information@tignes.net

NEW new for 05/06 season
new Tichot chair replaces the Balmes tow and the old chair. Increase in snowmaking area

Number of runs: 67
Longest run: 6km
Total Lifts: 47
1 funicular, 1 cable-cars, 2 Gondolas, 24 chairs, 19 drags
Lift times:
8.30am to 4.30pm

Annual Snowfall:
5m
Snowmaking:
40% of slopes

Autum Period: early Oct to end Nov
Winter Period: end Nov to May
Summer Period: June Nov to Sept
Lift Passes
Early Autumn glacier only, day 25.50
Autumn day pass 33 euros
Espace Killy:
1 day pass 40, 6 days 192.5
Tignes only:
Half-day 26, day 34, 6 days 165
Board Schools
Huge (too many) number of ski & board schools in the resort
Hire
loads of hire shops, all over priced. Board and boots start around 150 euros for 6 days.
Heliboarding
from nearby Italian resort; 2 drops Miravidi-Ruitor (3300 vertical drop) 225 euros. Contact Snocool.com, tel: 06 1534 5463

want to go off piste take a guide, Snocool offer freeride and freestyle lessons. If you've got the cash and a group of four they'll drop you and a guide out of a Helicopter in Italy, 2 drops cost around 200 Euros.

FREESTYLERS will love the newly moved fun park which has two pipes some rails, a boardcross, and a number of hits ranging from spines to kickers and of course the grosse table pro, a big mother off a table top. There's always a bit of French hip-hop blasting from the bottom of the pipe and when the locals are there it realy goes off. Tignes has a very high standard of freestyle boarders, even the purest Freerider will be impressed, but don't be put off just get down there check out the small hits and move on up in size as your confidence improves. Don't go to the park and wipe out on a huge kicker probably chopping up the hit at the same time as putting an end to your holiday. If you've never jumped before build a small hit somewhere soft before hitting the park, or find a natural hit and session it, and remember no silly hats ever they just aren't funny. The new park is next to the Les Lanches chair lift and walkable from Val Claret.

PISTES. Riders of all abilities are provided with slopes of all widths and pitch. The **Grande Motte Glacier** although sometime wind swept and cold is normally pisted flat. It's great for cranking it over at full speed it's long enough to give even the hardest boarder leg burn.

BEGINNERS have plenty of blue runs and loads of schools to choose from. Although not as good for the complete novice as Val D'Isere for someone on week 2 or 3 it's fine and you can always head out of the valley to ride the runs under the Marmottes chair. **Kebra Surfing** in Le Lac, which is Tignes oldest snowboard shop and school, and **Surf Feeling** in Val Claret offer a number of teaching programmes for freestyle or freeriding. It's around 150 euros for a weeks lesson.

THE TOWN

tignes is a relatively ugly place it consists of two main areas Le Lac which is the main hub and Val Claret a split level town joined by a urine stinking lift, both joined by a free bus. Le Lac is strangely enough next to a lake which is normally frozen over. The areas mobbed with apartment blocks, hotels, and an array of bars, restaurants and shops all of which are expensive. At the head of the valley within an easy walk of the funicular is Val Claret smaller than Le Lac but of a similar ilk. It has better slope access and good parking next to the slopes, if you're on a day trip and has a few piste side cheep eats. Wherever you choose to stay, prices are much the same in both high. Tignes is an expensive resort whether you visit in winter, or come for summer snowboarding. Summer is actually a great time to visit as so much goes on, from snowboarding to water sports on the lake there's even a skate park.

Pic - J. Mitchell

ACCOMODATION

With over 28,000 visitor beds, this place has something for everyone, although there is not a wide selection of cheap accommodation. However, there are plenty of apartments for self-catering groups. The Tignes web site has a good listing of accommodation. Tour companies use this place big style, which means last minute package deals are always available at budget prices. www.tignes.net

EATING

French food is full fat all butter croissants followed by melted cheese. If you're on a diet when you arrive, then this place will kill it dead and you'll go home fatter than ever. Every type of fast-food is available along with a large selection of restaurants serving expensive French dishes with heaps of garlic. None of it comes cheep so it's probably best to sort out catered accommodation before arriving.

NIGHTLIFE

Night-life starts early and ends late - in fact, for some it never ends. This is a major party resort, with a wide choice of English and French bars, but you will never have enough funds to keep going in the bars or clubs as beer prices are shocking, at around 6 euros a pint. The best thing to do is tank up on supermarket carry-outs or the cheep plonk they give out with your chalet dinner. Minesweepers will be able to compare their pint nicking skills with some of the best in the industry. Le loop and the Angel bar in Le Lac are pretty good bars to get you started.

CAR
Drive via Lyon to Tignes, about 102 miles (165 km). Drive time is about 2 hours.
FLY
Fly to Lyon or Geneva international, 2 1/2 hour transfer to resort. Local airport is Chambery.
TRAIN
Trains to Bourg-St-maurice, 30 min drive away
BUS
Bus services from Lyon airport, are available on a daily basis direct to Tignes.
TAXI: +33(0)6 07 05 84 85

	POOR	FAIR	GOOD	TOP
FREERIDE Some tree runs & good off-piste				
FREESTYLE Park & Pipe				
PISTES Plenty of good wide slopes				

Great mountain, crap town.

8
OUT OF 10

Pic - Val D'Isere Tourism

F

FRANCE

along one road starting with La Daille a few ugly blocks of flats, mostly full of resort staff, time shares and self catering apartments. You may find you'll start or finish your day here as it's only a short free bus ride from the resort proper and home of the Funival funicular which will whip you to the top of the mountain faster than Bush could invade any oil producing state. The main village has been tastefully developed using a lot of the local stone. The main streets full of designer shops, restaurants and British bars, set back from the road are loads of hotels and chalets ranging from affordable to ridiculous.

FREERIDERS will want to come back again and again, there are miles of piste, 200 in fact (inc Tignes) and more off piste than you'll be able to do in a week. There's terrain here for all, from motorways like Ok and Orange to the steep and tight of piste S. After a dump it's an off piste playground with fresh tracks to be had all day on the les Marmottes face or try the Vallee Perdue which is a mad track only a few feet wide in places with blind bends and a couple of board off scrambles. In bad visibility head for the trees of Le Fornet. Warning you want to be on that flight home so follow resort advice on Avalanche risk and if you are not sure don't do it.

FREESTYLERS can find endless natural hits. The terrain park's is over at **Bellevarde**, there's an FSF approved half-pipe, numerous jumps and rails and a boarder cross.

BEGINNERS on their first ever day will find the two free slopes, located in the centre of the village, perfect. Once confident of putting together a few turns, there are plenty of easy slopes and you can always get the bubble down at the end of the day. As most of the runs into resort are steep and at the end of the day packed.

THE TOWN
Off the board, there's husky dog sledging, ice climbing, ice karting, Snowmobiles, paragliding, cinemas and loads of

Val d'Isere would be the best resort in France if it wasn't for all the stuck up twats. It's got a great lift system a reliable snow depth and some fantastic riding with loads of off piste only a short hop from the lifts. They are trying a little harder to make snowboarders welcome, holding events like The Big Day Out, but are way behind Tignes which together make up Espace Killy. The resort is set

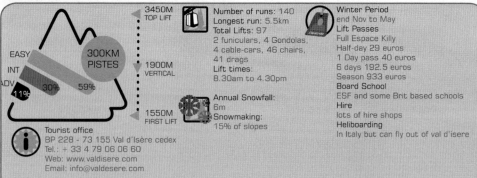

3450M
TOP LIFT

1900M
VERTICAL

1550M
FIRST LIFT

EASY
INT
ADV
11%   30%   59%

300KM
PISTES

Number of runs: 140
Longest run: 5.5km
Total Lifts: 97
2 funiculars, 4 Gondolas,
4 cable-cars, 46 chairs,
41 drags
Lift times:
8.30am to 4.30pm

Annual Snowfall:
6m
Snowmaking:
15% of slopes

Winter Period
end Nov to May
Lift Passes
Full Espace Killy
Half-day 29 euros
1 Day pass 40 euros
6 days 192.5 euros
Season 933 euros
Board School
ESF and some Brit based schools
Hire
lots of hire shops
Heliboarding
In Italy but can fly out of val d'isere

Tourist office
BP 228 - 73 155 Val d'Isère cedex
Tel.: + 33 4 79 06 06 60
Web: www.valdisere.com
Email: info@valdesere.com

NEW new for 05/06 season
new 6-seater chair in the Laisinant area linking to Fornet and Solaise. Installation of snow cannons on the glacier for summer/autumn, and more cannons on winter area. Replacement of Montets drag lift

Pic - Val D'Isere Tourism

bars full of merchant bankers and red faced blonde haired Swedes and maybe a few French. Like Courchevel the main draw back is the cost.

ACCOMODATION

Watch out for where your accommodation, most is close to the slopes. If your not then there's the free buses which are sometimes quicker than going by board if you want to get somewhere specific, but at night after a skin full you may be in for a cold wait for that bus home.

EATING & NIGHTLIFE

The Pacific bar is good to watch English football, Cafe Face is a cool place but has that bull shit French thing about putting your coat in the cloakroom at a fee. Bananas has a good vibe but can get packed and the Moris pub

has live music. For a fry up breakfast go to the Billabong café, if you want a meal in the evening take a stroll with the fur clad poseurs along the main street and choose from sausage to sushi.

SUMMARY

Overall, Val d'Isere has something for everyone there's varying terrain for all abilities some great off piste and a good snow record but be ready to pay for it, they take card and cash don't you worry.

CAR
From Lyon take the A43 to Albertville, then onto Moutiers, then the D902 to Bourg-St-Maurice continue to Tignes and then on to Val d'Isere
FLY
Fly to Geneva, 2½ hours transfer time.
TRAIN
TGV & Eurostar train services go to Bourg-St-Maurice, 40minutes away.
BUS
Autocars Martin run a bus service from Bourg-St-Maurice to Val d'isire about 10 times a day and costs 11.70 euros. Tel: 04.7907.0449 www.autocars-martin.com. Taxi: +33 6 0951 9099

wsg VALMOREL

Dull, crap, and a dodgy snow record

3
OUT OF 10

	POOR	FAIR	GOOD	TOP
FREERIDE A few tree runs & some ok off-piste				
FREESTYLE Park & Pipe				
PISTES Plenty of easy if dull slopes				

F

F
R
A
N
C
E

Pic - Valmorel Tourism

As a relatively new resort, established around 25 years ago, **Valmorel** has grown into a family/group ski-centre. This is by no means an adventurous place - indeed it's best described as dull. Nevertheless, it is a well planned and well set out resort, with slopes that are ideal for simple piste-riding. Valmorel, on its own, boasts 50 or so pistes which are not always that well maintained. When linked to *St Francois Longchamp*, the ride able terrain increases to a respectable 100 miles (152km). Getting around the slopes should pose no problems, although you might have to queue for lengthy periods of time with skiers who sing nursery rhymes to their offspring. Valmorel is not noted for having the best snow record, especially on the lower slopes. Still, once you do get away from the idiots in the lift lines and hit the slopes, things only get better. Keep an eye open, however, for ski-classes cluttering up certain slopes

FREERIDERS are not going to get too excited with what's on offer here, but there is some alright off-piste riding around the *Mottet* area. Although Valmorel is a tame resort, some challenging riding is possible on a couple of black trails, though a good rider would rate them more as red runs.

FREESTYLERS are going to be most disappointed. There is a so-called fun-park and a halfpipe, but it's not often shaped properly. Any resort of any worth should have some natural freestyle terrain, but this place doesn't not even a sniff of a jump. The best thing to do is take a shovel and build your own kicker.

PISTES. Snowboarders who don't manage to hold an edge here, should give it up immediately and become a skier. Valmorel is a perfect resort for edging a board over at speed, or for general riding on intermediate trails it a good resort for first times but anyone else will soon be bored.

BEGINNERS, this area is littered with easy trails, but novices need to learn quickly to avoid sharing the same slopes with so many novice skiers.

THE TOWN
Valmorel's village is dull, boring, expensive and full of some of the worst ski groups around (families). Accommodation options are good, but evenings aren't. Nothing happens, and there aren't any good bars of note, or come to that, places to eat. Well, there is *Pizzaria du Bourg* which serves up great slices.

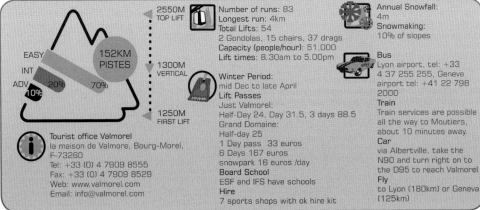

EASY
INT
ADV
10% 20% 70%

152KM PISTES

2550M TOP LIFT
1300M VERTICAL
1250M FIRST LIFT

Number of runs: 83
Longest run: 4km
Total Lifts: 54
2 Gondolas, 15 chairs, 37 drags
Capacity (people/hour): 51,000
Lift times: 8.30am to 5.00pm

Winter Period:
mid Dec to late April
Lift Passes
Just Valmorel:
Half-Day 24, Day 31.5, 3 days 88.5
Grand Domaine:
Half-day 25
1 Day pass 33 euros
6 Days 167 euros
snowpark 16 euros /day
Board School
ESF and IFS have schools
Hire
7 sports shops with ok hire kit

Annual Snowfall:
4m
Snowmaking:
10% of slopes

Bus
Lyon airport, tel: +33
4 37 255 255, Geneva
airport tel: +41 22 798
2000
Train
Train services are possible
all the way to Moutiers,
about 10 minutes away.
Car
via Albertville, take the
N90 and turn right on to
the D95 to reach Valmorel
Fly
to Lyon (180km) or Geneva
(125km)

Tourist office Valmorel
la maison de Valmore, Bourg-Morel,
F-73260
Tel: +33 (0) 4 7909 8555
Fax: +33 (0) 4 7909 8529
Web: www.valmorel.com
Email: info@valmorel.com

	POOR	FAIR	GOOD	TOP
FREERIDE No tree runs but good off-piste				
FREESTYLE Terrain park & half-pipe				
PISTES Busy but decent slopes				

Tacky with lots of skiers, but access great terrain

7 OUT OF 10

Pic - Val Thorens Tourism

F

F R A N C E

High, high, high; Val Thorens is the highest resort in Europe, it's a load of purpose built block of ugly flats, a few shops and a line of bars with nothing to do at night but drink and at a height of 2300m it's painfully cold when walking for that drink. Who cares with a lift system that whisks you up to 3200m, north facing slopes, a 900cm average snow fall and a connection to the Trois Vallees you can stick the bad points where the sun don't shine. Furthermore, although not noted as a summer resort, you can still ride here right up until early August. Like the rest of the Trois Vallees it's full of package deal holiday makers. Lots of Brit's but not as many as Meribel or Couchevel, it's also popular with the Dutch and Swedes. Many of the apartments will give you instant slope access; some have a high rise chair going past your window so keep an eye out when leaving the shower. They've made Val Thornes a car free zone so at least you don't have to look out for motors when running for the pub, but you will have to make

parking arrangements if driving. It's a rip off 53 Euros a week if you book on the tinternet otherwise its 62.5 if you just turn up. It's a board friendly place with a Fun Park and without the stuck up attitude of some of the Trois Vallees resorts.

FREERIDERS have much choice, take a trip up to the Cime de Caron for the best view in the Trois Vallees and then drop down the back side or follow the long sweeping red or black down. Intermediates should try the long, wide red runs around Fond 1, Boismint or the Peclet Glacier. The expert will relish the sheer volume of challenges on offer, from powder snow on the glaciers of Peclet and Chaviere, to world class, mogul-bashing on the long, steep Cime de Caron black run. If you have a head for heights, then visit Le Plein Sud, where you can cut some nice couloir descents. If you can handle a walk get a guide and head up left from the top of the Col Chair, over the col de Gebroulaz and ride the Glacier de Gebroulaz down into the Meribel Valley a truly amazing run. The resort height gives good snow but no trees so if you want to pretend to be James Bond head for Meribel.

FREESTYLERS have a dedicated snowboard park serviced by the **2 Lac lift**, which has a boardercross circuit and a 110 meter long halfpipe. However, these are only kept in tip-top condition during a competition, rather than on a regular basis. There are some good natural hits but mainly drop offs. Look out for the Val Thorens board week in early December

PISTES. Riders have a stupid amount of pistes to fly down. The **Cime de Caron** is a well-established black run that tests the best speed-freaks and race heads, it's also possible to have snowboard slalom training with poles ask at the tourist info.

BEGINNERS have a variety of easy runs leading into the resort, which allow for easy access and steady progression. You don't have to travel far from the resort base before getting to a novice trail, but be advised there are heaps of little kids in bash hats that take up space while snaking down behind their all in one red suited ESF instructor. If you want lessons try one of the independent

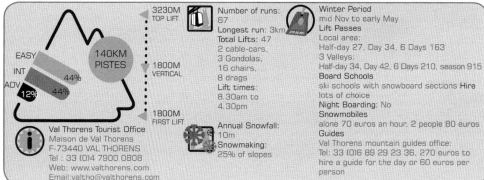

3230M TOP LIFT

1800M VERTICAL

1800M FIRST LIFT

EASY
INT
ADV
12% **44%** **44%**

140KM PISTES

Number of runs: 67
Longest run: 3km
Total Lifts: 47
2 cable-cars,
3 Gondolas,
16 chairs,
8 drags
Lift times:
8.30am to
4.30pm

Annual Snowfall: 10m
Snowmaking: 25% of slopes

Winter Period mid Nov to early May
Lift Passes
Local area:
Half-day 27, Day 34, 6 Days 163
3 Valleys:
Half-day 34, Day 42, 6 Days 210, season 915
Board Schools
ski schools with snowboard sections Hire lots of choice
Night Boarding: No
Snowmobiles
alone 70 euros an hour, 2 people 80 euros
Guides
Val Thorens mountain guides office:
Tel: 33 (0)6 89 29 23 36, 270 euros to hire a guide for the day or 60 euros per person

Val Thorens Tourist Office
Maison de Val Thorens
F-73440 VAL THORENS
Tel : 33 (0)4 7900 0808
Web: www.valthorens.com
Email:valtho@valthorens.com

ski schools which should have a board specialist if they don't go elsewhere.

THE TOWN
Val Thorens is the archetypical purpose built resort. No one would have built a thing here if it wasn't for alpine sports, not even a cow shed. A sheltered valley and an almost flattish spot have turned into high rise central. The obvious remit when planning this place was, 'get them in, pile them high, and don't worry about how the place looks or feels'. The outcome is a place that looks dire, but serves its purpose which is beer shelter and food in that order. Around the resort, you'll find a number of shopping complexes and places to eat. There is also a comprehensive sports centre, with a swimming pool and artificial climbing wall.

Accommodation: 20,000 visitors can sleep soundly here, all within spitting distance of the slopes. There are loads of self-catering apartment blocks, sleeping up to eight people, and a number of good hotels and serviced chalets, many actually on the slopes and next to a lift.

Food is plentiful here with a selection of restaurants more than 45 ranging from the normal selection of resort-style, expensive French restaurants, dodgy fast-food stands, to the normal offerings of a supermarket. For a cheap slap-up meal, try *El Gringo's*, or for something more classy, *Chalet Glaciers*. The *Scapin Pub* is also noted for its quick and affordable dishes which include pizza and garlic overdose food.

Night-life comes in the form of drunken Dutch après skiers. There are some ok bars at the top of town. Check out The Frog, The Malaysia, or The Underground. It's a great place for New Years Eve with fire works and music in the streets, even the firemen get in on it.

Pics - Val Thorens Tourism

CAR
From Lyon drive via Albertville. Val Thorens is 130 miles (209 km). Drive time is about 2 hours. There is no street parking at the resort, you must use one of the dedicated car-parks, then a shuttle
FLY
Lyon 193km away, Geneva 159km, Chambery 112km away. Bus services available to resort.
TRAIN
TGV run services from Lyon, Geneva, Paris to Moutiers. Resort 37km from station.
BUS
Altibus run services from Lyon, Geneva, Chambery airport, on a daily basis direct to Val Thorens. Altibus run service from Moutiers to resort, tel: +33(0) 820 320 368
TAXIS Tel: 04 7900 6954

wsg FRANCE

ALPE DU GRAND SERRE
Good riding here, 2 hours from Lyon airport
Runs: 35. Total Lifts:20

AURON

Some thick wood, 1 hour from Nice airport
Runs: 70, Total Lifts:21

BAREGES
Okay for novices, 45 minutes from Lourdes airport. Has a terrain park
Number of Runs: 18

GOURETTE

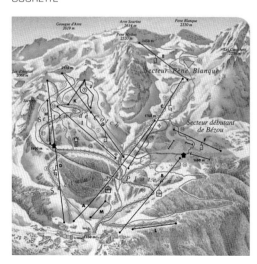

Ride area: 30.5km/716 acres
Runs: 25 Easy 48% Intermediate 48% Advanced 4%
Total Lifts:16 - 6 chairs, 7 drags, 3 Magic carpets
Freestyle: terrain park
Contact: www.gourette.com
How to get there: Fly or get train to Pau-Pyrénées 60km away, then get a bus, Tel: 33 15 5927 2222.
Drive: From Bayonne take the A64 Motorway, Exit no 9 Artix then follow directions to Pau
Taxi: 33 15 5905 4114

LA FOUX D'ALLOS
La Foux d'Allos, a purpose-built resort, is located way down in the southern section of the French Alps, 50 miles from the village of Digne. On its own, La Foux d'Allos offers a ride area of 70 miles, but linked with nearby resorts, the combined range gives freeriders of all levels 150 miles of terrain, with a good selection of advanced and novice runs. Local services are slopeside and very affordable, if only a tad dull
Ride area: 12km
Top Lift: 2600m
Bottom Lift: 1800m
Total Lifts:22
How to get there:
Fly to: Nice 2 hours away
Contact: www.valdallos.com

LA JOUE DU LOUP
South of Grenoble and a stone's throw for the Veynes, lies the almost unheard of resort of La Joue du Loup, a tiny place place providing a mere half dozen trails. However, when linked with the resort of Superdevoluy, there's a more respectable 60+ miles to ride and explore. If you're an adventure seeker, nothing here is really that daunting. Great for first timers on a family outing

Ride area: 97km
Top Lift: 2750m
Vertical Drop: 1040m
Total Lifts:32
Night Boarding:13 slopes and halfpipes illuminated
How to get there: By air: 126 km from the airport of Grenoble-Saint Geoirs. By train: 28 km from the train station of Veynes-Divoluy. By car: Superdivolue is located 640 km from Paris, 216 km from Marseille and 190 km from Lyon

LA NORMA
La Norma is yet another unspolit tourist spot, although it does get its fair share of weekenders. They who are attracted to the open trails that offer some steep and fast, although rather limited, riding with only a couple of black graded trails and

251

F

F R A N C E

nothing that will require many turns before you're back in a lift line. In truth this is a novices retreat where first timers can learn to ride without all the hassles associated with the big tourist resorts.

Affordable slopeside services are available but are best described as dull

Ride area: 97km
Runs: 27
Top Lift: 2750m
Bottom Lift: 1350m
Total Lifts: 18
How to get there: Air: Lyon or Geneva Airports - 2 hrs 30 mins transfer by hire car . Train: Modane station (overnight train from Paris), then 6km by bus or taxi to resort. Car: To Chambery (A43) and on to St Jean de Maurienne, then take the N6 to Modane (direction of Torino - Tunnel of Frejus).
Contact: www.la-norma.com

LA ROSIERE

On its own, La Rosiere is a tiny outpost, with an even balance of terrain that any rider worth their salt will have licked in a day or two. However, as La Rosiere crosses the border with Italy and is lift linked to La Thuile, the 80+ miles poses a different question. Add the 900+ miles of the Aosta Valley, and suddenly we are into a whole new ball game, which will take the best of the best years to conquer.

Ride area: 55km
Runs: 32
Top Lift: 2642m
Bottom Lift: 1850m
Total Lifts: 19
How to get there: Fly to: Geneva 2 hours away.

LES ANGLES

Les Angles is definitely not one of your normal ski tourist traps. Located in the Pyrenees, it shares a non-lift linked pass with a few neighbouring resorts, with 200 miles of average rideable terrain for all styles. It is, however, crowd-free, and an alternative to the massly populated areas further north. There's a pipe for air heads, but in truth most runs are for novices. There are plenty of slopeside services but most things around here are boring and dull and not the cheapest.

Ride area: 40km
Top Lift: 2400m
Total Lifts: 20
How to get there: Fly to: Perpigan 1 1/2 hours away.

Contact: www.les-angles.com

LES GETS

Linked to the 450kms of the Port du Soleil, Les Gets sits at 1172 meters to the south of Morzine. It's a small Savoyard village escaping the all too typical high rise developments that blight Avoriaz across the valley. It's possible to buy a Les Gets/Morzine pass which includes Le Mont-Chery, les Chavannes, Nyon and Le Pleney this adds up to 110km of red and blue pistes, which is fine for a weekend but if you're here for a week you should stump up the cash for the Port du Soleil Pass. It's an annoying walk across Morzine Village or a ridiculous mini train ride to access the lifts up to Avoriaz, but well worth it to both freeriders and freestylers as it opens up not only a great fun park but also another 340km of piste. Les Gets has spent more than 24 million Euros over the last two summers upgrading the lift system and creating a new access point outside the village, with a huge car park so as to keep the traditional vide to the village. **Freeriders** will enjoy the slopes around Chamossiere and Le Ranfolly as they lead to some little gullies and tree runs. **Freestylers** will be best off heading for Avoriaz although there's a good little park on Mount-Chery's with hits and rails, accessible with the Les Gets/Morzine pass. **Carvers** have a lot of well suited terrain if fact almost all of it. **Off the slopes** there's not much in the way of lively night life with only a few bars. There is Bowling and a Cinema

METABIEF

Metabief is slap bang on the border with Switzerland, which is probably why it is a cool and very friendly snowboard hangout. Although there are only 26 miles of piste and just a couple of black runs to entice hardcore freeriders, the place is still worth a visit. Laid back, unpopulated, with good slopes for all, and plenty of lodging and night-time action, although hangouts are some distance from the slopes.

Ride area: 40km
Runs: 23
Top Lift: 1430m
Bottom Lift: 880m
Total Lifts: 22
How to get there: Fly to: Geneva 1 hour away

MONTCHAVIN

Linked to the tourist trap of La Plagne, this small resort

suddenly seems a better option.On its own slopes, Montchavin has nothing to offer advanced riders, but plenty to entertain intermediate carvers and total beginners - they will find the place seemingly designed for them by Mother Nature. **Freestylers** are also presented with a park and pipe, but they are crap.Slopeside **lodging** is plentiful and okay

Ride area: 200km
Runs: 16
Top Lift: 3250m
Vertical Drop: 2000m
Total Lifts:22
How to get there: Fly to: Geneva 2 hours away
Contact:www.montchavin-lescoches.com

PRA LOUP

Spread over two areas, Pra Loup and Molanes are not that bad to try, although being popular with weekenders and package tours, means clogged-up blues and busy lift lines. Par Loup is more or less a beginner's and intermediate piste-lover's hangout. Advanced riders will want more than what's on offer. **Accommodation** is provided in a selection of affordable, tacky apartment blocks
Ride area: 80km

Top Lift: 2500m
Total Lifts:31
How to get there: Fly to: Toulouse 2 1/2 hours away.
Contact www.praloup.com

SAMOENS
Good fun park
Runs: 38
Total Lifts:16
How to get there: 30 minutes from Geneva airport
Contact: www.samoens.com

VARS
Ok advanced runs
Runs: 60
Total Lifts:30
How to get there: 140 minutes from Marseille airport.

VILLARD DE LANS
Linked resort with Correncon en Vencours. Okay advanced runs.

Ride area: 130km
Runs: 32 Total Lifts:27
How to get there: 40 minutes from Grenoble airport.

pic - Bayerische Zugspitzbahn Tourism

Not many people think of Germany as a snowboard destination and although it's no match for its close alpine neighbours, Germany can still boast plenty of rideable terrain. The dozen or so resorts are all located in the southernmost parts of the country, with some crossing over into Austria. The thing that seems to be consistent amongst about German resorts is the efficient way things are set out and how you're looked after. Most places are expensive and often stupidly overcrowded at weekends.

Travelling by car is a good idea, with resorts reached on one of the best road systems in the world. Unlike many other European destinations, there are no road tolls so you aren't hit with extra costs **Munich** is the most convenient gateway airport for all the resorts with good onward travel facilities. It is possible to take a train across Austrian, Swiss and French borders direct to many resorts making train travel a good option.

For those thinking about doing a season in Germany, work is possible but you will need to speak the language (or have a good grasp of it). EU nationals can stay as long as they want without a work permit.

Accommodation is similar to that in Austria, from affordable pensions to way overpriced hotels. It's often cheaper to stay in a nearby town. **Night life** in Germany is pretty cool, Germans like to party hard and the beer is pure nectar. Clubs and discos are not bad, although far too many bars allow Euro pop. Overall, Germany is not the cheapest place, but is highly recommended.

Capital City: Berlin
Population: 82.4 million
Highest Peak: Zugspitze 2963m
Language: German
Legal Drink Age: 16 beer, 18 spirits
Drug Laws: Cannabis is illegal and frowned upon
Age of consent: 16
Electricity: 240 Volts AC 2-pin
International Dialing Code: +49

Currency: Euro
Exchange Rate:
UK£1 = 1.5
US$1 = 0.8
AU$1 = 0.6
CAN$1 = 0.6

Time Zone
UTC/GMT +1 hours
Daylight saving time: +1 hour

German Snowboard Association
Zizelsbergerstrasse 3.
81476 Munchen
Tel - ++49 (0) 89 7544 7320
Web: www.gsahome.de

Driving Guide
All vehicles drive on the right hand side of the road
Speed limits:
50kph (31mph) Towns
81kph (62mph) Highways
130kph (recommended) Autobahns
Emergency
Fire - 112
Police and Ambulance - 110
Tolls
None
Documentation
A driving lisence must be carried as well as insurance.

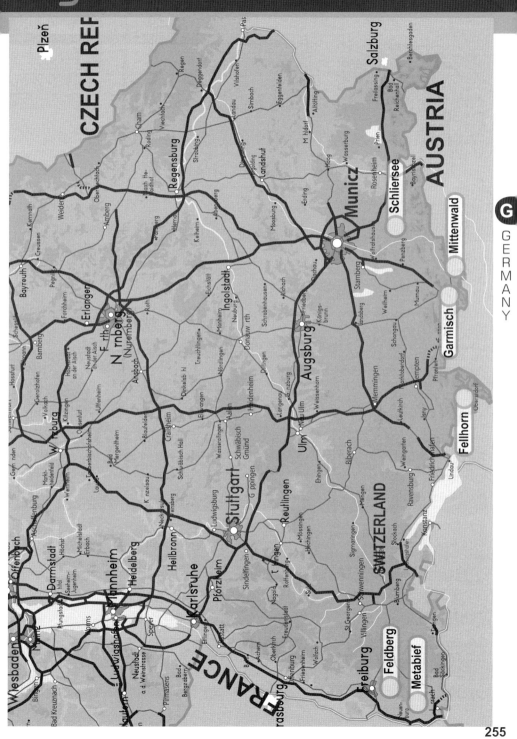

wsg FELDBERG

POOR FAIR GOOD TOP

FREERIDE
A few trees & some off-piste

FREESTYLE
A terrain park

PISTES
Very easy & well pisted slopes

Okay beginners resort

4 OUT OF 10

pic - feldberg tourism

G

GERMANY

Feldberg is located in the south west of Germany In the Black Forest and a stones throw from the French and Swiss borders. The town of Feldberg is a sprawling affair and offers its visitors a mass of attractions all year round. As a winter destination, this adequate resort is regarded by many in Germany as the countries number one resort even though in terms of terrain its 50 kms of piste are half of what is available over in Garmisch, which is south of Munich and Germany's most famous resort. Feldberg's location means that if you are planning to visit by air then the easiest way to get here is to fly into Zurich in Switzerland and then hire a car and drive up or catch a bus. In terms of skiing and snowboarding, Feldberg is a resort that attracts a lot of families as the two main mountain areas are made up largely of novice trails with a few intermediate slopes. All the runs are laid out over wide open spaces with a splattering of trees here and there namely on the Grafenmatt-Hochst mountain. This mountain is the one and only area that has anything difficult to ride with a few interesting black trails to check out. The runs on the Seebuck mountain are mostly intermediate trails while the Gafenmatte is home to the best novice slopes. Overall this is not a place that you would want to spend more than a few days at. The size and pace of what is going on here will make it a bore after three days, unless you are brain dead or a child in nappies.

FREERIDERS who want for a simple day's riding and are not too adventurous, will find Feldberg an ideal place to spend some time at. There is an okay mixture of terrain with the best and most challenging freeriding to be found off the letter K drag lift.

FREESTYLERS should stick to riding in the terrain park located under the 6-seater chair on **Seebuck**. This is the only place to get any air time. Theres usually 2 kickers and 3 rails there.

PISTES. Riders have a good resort for just cruising around with a number of well groomed trails to check out, especially those on the Seebuck.
BEGINNERS have a mountain that is perfect for learning on with a number of easy blue trails that cover all the areas, but note that all the easy runs are served by drag lifts.

THE TOWN
Feldberg is a large town with a very good choice of local services that include hotels, pension homes and chalets. There is also a good choice of bars and restaurants, the only draw back being that this is an expensive resort.

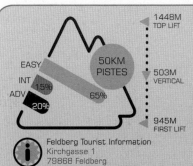

1448M
TOP LIFT

50KM
PISTES

EASY

INT 15%

ADV 20%

65%

503M
VERTICAL

945M
FIRST LIFT

Number of runs: 36
Longest run: 2.8km
Total Lifts: 29
4 chairs, 25 drags
Capacity (people/hour):
24,000
Lift times: 8.30am to
4.00pm

Winter Period:
Dec to April
Lift Passes:
1 Day 22 euros,
2 Days 42,
6 days 99

NEW

New for 05/06 season:
additional chairlift

Annual Snowfall:
unknown
Snowmaking:
10% of slopes

Train
Train services go direct to
Feldberg.
Car
From Zurich head north
along the B315 and travel via
Schaffhausen.
Fly
Stuttgart, Basel and Zurich
airports approx 1hr drive
away.

Feldberg Tourist Information
Kirchgasse 1
79868 Feldberg
Tel - ++49 (0) 7655 / 8019
Fax - ++49 (0) 7655 / 80143
Web:www.liftverbund-feldberg.de
Email:info@liftverbund-feldberg.de

Projekt Skibruck
2005/2006

wsg GARMISCH

6 OUT OF 10

Average resort, some decent intermediate terrain.

pic - Garmish Tourism

POOR FAIR GOOD TOP

FREERIDE
Some tree runs

FREESTYLE
A park & half-pipe

PISTES
Scattered Intermediate slopes

G

GERMANY

thousands of visitors. The area offers loads of out-door sporting attractions as well as putting on lots of top sporting competitions. The ski world hosts all sorts of world ranking ski events here which includes ski jumping. Garmisch even played host to the 1936 Winter Olympics, although to be fair, the world was a bit messed up during that period of time, so anyone boasting about such a role should be viewed with a bit of contempt. All said and done, this is a resort where you can have a good time, located beneath Germany's highest mountain, the **Zugspitze**, where a cable car goes to the rocky 2964m summit (no rideable descent is possible). The five resort centres dotted around the village are all connected by buses and trains. Five mountains make up the area. Zugspitze opens in November until May/June. The other mountains, **Alpspitze**, **Kreuzeck**, **Hausberg**, and the unfortunately named **Wank**, open later in December until April. The pistes will appeal mostly to intermediate riders looking for easy descents but expert riders will soon get bored.

FREERIDERS coming here for the first time may be a bit disappointed if they arrive thinking that they will find a mountain blessed with loads of hardcore freeride terrain. They will find a big mountain with a number of steep sheer unrideable faces, and a number of okay rideable slopes that will allow advanced riders to blast around at speed for at least two days, but bore them after three. Snowboarders in general favour the Zugspitzplatt slopes, which is the only area not directly linked on snow with the other sections. Although this is not an adventurous place, there are opportunities to ride through trees and on a good day a few stashes of powder can be cut.

FREESTYLERS will find quite a few good natural hits as well as those built by local grommets. You'll also be able to grind a few downed logs around the tree areas, but in the main, this is not a great place for getting any serious air. ,There is a good terrain park and a halfpipe on the Zugspitze plateau, and during May and June GAP 1328 run a summer camp from here.

PISTES. Boarders who want to carve around on gentle,

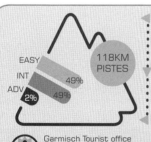

Garmisch is Germany's most popular resort, although some say the resort of Feldburg has more claim to the favourite title award. What ever the merits of this, Garmisch certainly the countries biggest resort which is located in the southernmost part of the country a short distance from Munich and Innsbruck in Austria. This very German of German places is in fact an extremely popular all year round holiday destination that attracts

---

EASY
INT 49%
ADV 49%
2%

118KM PISTES

2830M TOP LIFT

830M VERTICAL

2000M FIRST LIFT

Number of runs: 60
Longest run: 3km
Total Lifts: 36
1 Track Railway, 6 cable-cars, 1 Gondolas, 5 chairs, 24 drags
Capacity (people/hour): 50,000
Lift times: 8.30am to 4.30pm
Mountain Cafes: 12

Annual Snowfall: unknown
Snowmaking: 15% of slopes

Winter Period: Dec to April
Summer Period: May to June
Lift Passes: Happy Ski Card pass covers all local resorts including Seefeld in Austria
3 Days 85 euros
6 days 159 euros
Board Schools
6 days with 3 hour lessons from 110 euros
Hire
Board & boots 20 euros a day

Garmisch Tourist office
Verkehrsamt, Richard Strauss-Platz 2
D-82467 Garmisch-Partenkirchen
Tel - +49 (0) 8821-180-700
Web: www.garmisch-partenkirchen.de
Mountains: www.zugspitze.de
Email: tourist-info@garmisch-partenkirchen.de

G

GERMANY

centres.

Restaurants are plentiful and cater for all tastes, if not all budgets. Most places serve up a variety of disgusting sausages and potato dishes. However, you can get some decent chicken and fish meals. Veggies should pay a visit to the Grand Cafe. If you do want to taste a local dish and don't mind sucking on bland pieces of horse meat, then check out the Max Cafe.

Nightlife here is pretty good and very lively set to a Bavarian theme. An excellent choice of German beers are available in a number of okay bars where the booze flows fast and well into the early morning hours, mind you, the music in most places is enough to make you want to leave. Check out the *Irish Bar* or the *Rose and Crown*.

short slopes will favour the areas off the Alpspitzbahn cable car, but there is other carving to be found up on the Zugspitz slopes. Whatever area you ride, you'll have fun spotting how many mullets with head bands there are riding around with ski-boot set ups.

BEGINNERS are well catered for with a number of spots ideally suited to novices. There is a number of easy options for riding up high and back down through the trees to the village and car parks.

THE TOWN

Garmisch is an all year-round holiday destination which caters extremely well for it's visitors. There is a huge selection of places to stay with services spread out over a wide area. Numerous events are held in the town all year round, so not only is this place a very expensive town, it can also be very busy. The area also has loads of sporting attractions and if you are feeling lucky there is even a casino to try your hand in.

The area can **accommodate** over 20,000 visitors with a number of places in the main town area or spread out into the countryside. Prices are not cheap and no real budget options exist even though there is a large number of pension's and self catering places. Still one thing is for sure, most places are of a very high standard and hotels come loaded with restaurants, bars, pools, and sporting

pic: Garmish Tourism

CAR
From Munich, head south on the A95 Autobahn and then route 23 direct to Garmisch (140km)
*From Calais 575 miles (925 Km), drive time is around 10 hours.
FLY
Fly to Munich airport about 120km (1 1/2 hours) away or Innsbruck (Tyrol) 60km.
TRAIN
Train services are possible all the way to the centre of Garmisch.
BUS
Bus services from Munich airport are available on a daily basis direct to Garmisch

SCHLIERSEE

FREERIDE
With the right conditions
FREESTYLE
An occasional park
PISTES
Some nice slopes

POOR FAIR GOOD TOP

5 OUT OF 10

Rather basic but okay

pic - Schliersee Tour

G

G E R M A N Y

Frequented by Munich's high-society kiddies and some cool riders, Schliersee is also home to the living snowboard legend Peter Bauer (you still meet him riding here). What you get are two areas, interconnected by a free shuttle-bus: the Taubenstein is less crowded and is the place to be on a fresh powder day but you'll get bored pretty quickly in the days in-between! Most of the runs are intermediate and nothing will keep you excited for long. At the parking lot you jump on the shuttle that takes you to the Stumpfling-an-Sutten area at the other side of the Spitzingsee, where the whole area lies in front of you, waiting to be ridden

FREERIDERS if there's enough snow, take the Brecherspitz lift, opposite the Firstam, to gain access to a freerider's paradise: long, steep tree-runs that remind you of Canada. On this mission you should follow the locals because there's a 25 metre cliff, with a flat and rocky landing hidden in the trees.

FREESTYLERS have a good mountain to practice getting air at various points around the slopes. The Osthanglift T-bar takes you to a good freestyle area. If you stay on the slope-side of the lift on the way down, you'll find some good natural hits and spines decorated with some nice rollers. The Firstalm is where the funpark is but it doesn't get

shaped too often.

PISTES. Riders have a very good mountain to ride, with well groomed runs that will intrigue the hopeless novice, but bore the tits off most advanced riders. However, the pistes are open enough to allow for some wide carves and to be fair, a decent amount of speed can be achieved. The longest run is the 3200m Sutten, which is good for screaming down in under 3 minutes.

BEGINNERS have a cool first timer's resort, although there's a limited amount of slopes and a lot of weekend ski crowds cluttering up the place. Easy access is possible to all the beginner trails.

THE TOWN
Local facilities are located in two areas, Schliersee in the east and Rottach-Egern in the west which has the best night-life and some cheap B & B's. Both places offer good local services but be prepared to pay for it because this is not a cheap hangout, no matter what you're after.
Eating spots are good and evenings begin at the Braustuberl Bar, but watch out for the big waitresses who eat snowboarders for supper. Later, head for the Moon-Club where you are bound to find a nice fraulein.

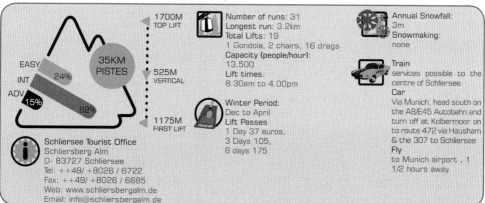

1700M TOP LIFT

525M VERTICAL

1175M FIRST LIFT

35KM PISTES

EASY
INT 24%
ADV 15%
62%

Number of runs: 31
Longest run: 3.2km
Total Lifts: 19
1 Gondola, 2 chairs, 16 drags
Capacity (people/hour):
13,500
Lift times:
8.30am to 4.00pm

Winter Period:
Dec to April
Lift Passes
1 Day 37 euros,
3 Days 105,
6 days 175

Annual Snowfall:
3m
Snowmaking:
none

Train
services possible to the centre of Schliersee.
Car
Via Munich, head south on the A8/E45 Autobahn and turn off at Kolbermoor on to route 472 via Hausham & the 307 to Schliersee
Fly
to Munich airport, 1 1/2 hours away.

Schliersee Tourist Office
Schliersberg Alm
D- 83727 Schliersee
Tel: ++49/ +8026 / 6722
Fax: ++49/ +8026 / 6685
Web: www.schliersbergalm.de
Email: info@schliersbergalm.de

ROUND-UP

G
G E R M A N Y

BALDERSCHWANG
Intermediate's place. Overall this is a boring place with a small and badly kept halfpipe.

How to get there:120 minutes from Munich airport

FELLHORN
Fellhorn is the mountain, Obersdorf is the town that serves it and together they are rated by many nationals as the best on offer in Germany. What you get is a mountain area that has a series of open trails with a few tree lines and a couple of decent steeps. They regularly stage top events in the competition standard halfpipe. Whereever you ride here, expect to bump into a lot of skiers as it's a popular hang out.; **Freeriders**, check out the Kanzelwand trail for a good ride. **Freestylers** have a well maintained fun-park to play in. **Carvers**, have a good series of pisted trails from top to bottom.4 **Beginners** this place is perfect for all your needs. There are good **facilities** 10 minutes from the slopes.

Ride area: 44km
Top Lift: 1967m
Total Lifts:30
www.fellhorn.de
How to get there: Fly to: Munich 1 1/2 hours away.

MITTENWALD
Mittenwald is located in the Isar Valley and is an okay freeriders destination. It is famous for its steep

Dammkar run which is served by a cable car that climbs 1311 vertical metres with only one tower (sufferers of vertigo take note). **Freestylers** have a halfpipe. **Beginners** have plenty of easy slopes. Local **services** are convenient but not cheap

Ride area: 22km
Top Lift:2244m
Total Lifts:8
How to get there: Fly to: Munich 1 1/2 hours away

METABIEF
Metabief is slap bang on the border with Switzerland, which is probably why it is a cool and very friendly snowboard hangout. Although there are only 26 miles of piste and just a couple of black runs to entice hardcore freeriders, the place is still worth a visit. Laid back, unpopulated, with good slopes for all, and plenty of lodging and night-time action, although hangouts are some distance from the slopes.

Ride area: 40km
Runs: 23
Top Lift: 1430m
Bottom Lift: 880m
Total Lifts:22
How to get there: Fly to: Geneva 1 hour away

OBERAMMERGAU
Oberammergau is a happy go lucky sort of place but certainly not the most adventurous of resorts. On the Laberjoch area the runs offer more testing and challenging terrain. For those freestylers wanting to get big air, the halfpipe is

your best option, but it's not the best nor well kept. The west side of the valley, on the Kolben, is the place for novices and intermediate riders looking for gentle and simple terrain to shred. Okay expensive local services exist, but not near the slopes

Ride area: 10km
Top Lift:1700m
Total Lifts:10
How to get there: Fly to: Munich 1 1/2 hours away

OBERSTAUFEN
Oberstaufen is a collection of seven small rideable areas. The main offerings are to be found on the Hochgrat mountain which offers some good off-piste and challenging runs. Intermediate carvers will also find the slopes worth the effort while beginners have access to some okay areas. **Off the slopes**, this place is by no means cheap as it is a very popular German tourists town.

Ride area: 20km
Top Lift: 1340m
Total Lifts:12
How to get there: Fly to: Munich 2 hours away

WILLINGEN
Willingen is a northern low key resort which is virtually unheard of. The area is spread over two large hills with mainly nursery slopes. The main hill has some decent runs with the option of cutting through the trees but lacks any great length. Note also that this place inhabited by lots of skiers (the older generation) and sledgers, so the few slopes that there are, are often very, very crowded, especially at weekends. Freeriders have very little to keep them interested beyond an hour, but there are a few trees to drop through.Freestylers haven't got a chance here unless you dig your own hit.

Carvers will find the number 11 trail about the only thing of worth. Beginners aged 1 or 100 will love it here as the slopes are so slow and easy you'll be able to change your nappy as you ride.
There are lots of small villages close by but they're all pricey

Top Lift: 830m
Total Lifts:14
How to get there: Fly to: Munich 1 hour away

WINTERBERG
Winterberg, is situated southwest of Dortmond in the Sauerland mountain range which not many snowusers have heard of. The runs are spread over 5 hills with 25 slopes, but nothing too testing, the longest barely making 2 miles.**Freeriders** have lots of trees to weave through and with many runs interlinking, there are a few nice freeride spots to check out.**Freestylers** don't have a pipe or park but many of the runs have natural hits formed en route at the sides and there's also a number of ski jumps that you can air off. **Carvers** could do worse, but if you know how to carve at speed then you won't want a week here. **Beginners**, this place is great for you, however, only for a one off trip before going to Austria for your next snowboard holiday. Very good and lively local **facilities** slope side or close by

Ride area: 40km
Top Lift: 809m
Total Lifts:11
How to get there: Fly to: Dortmund 1 hour away

normal public transport routes, driving is often the only option. Italian resorts are not always well located for airports as most places require an average of three hours transfer.

Train services are not too convenient, but you can get fairly close to many places. Rail fares are cheap and so it's a good option. Bus fares are also cheap,

Italy is somewhat different from the rest of Europe; a little more temperamental it might be said. Rather sad mountain dress sense is quite obvious, with a love for the all in one day-glow colour ski suits. That said, Italy is a great place to snowboard and one of the cheapest European countries to visit. Italian resorts (which vary more off the slopes than on) are stretched across the northern part of the country, with many linking with neighbouring countries.

If you're intending to drive in Italy, remember: Italians can't drive; the term 'giving way' refers more to bowel movements than it does to other road users! But due to the fact that Italy has loads of small, remote resorts tucked away off

but services are not very reliable and understanding the time tables is an art form in itself.

Riders looking to work should have no real problems, lots of winter tour operators include Italy in their programmes and are always hiring catering staff and the normal array of tour reps etc. Italy is a member of the EU so normal visa rules apply.

Accommodation is on the whole basic and cheap. Around resorts, facilities are not as intense as in France, but the over indulgence in après ski behaviour and stupid face painting is still the same. That aside, however, Italy is well worth a visit.

Capital City: Rome
Population: 58 Million
Highest Peak: Mont Blanc de Courmayeur 4,748m
Language: Italian
Legal Drink Age: 18
Drug Laws: Cannabis is illegal and frowned upon
Age of consent: 16
Electricity: 240 Volts AC 2-pin
International Dialing Code: +39

Currency: Euro
Exchange Rate:
UK£1 = 1.5
US$1 = 0.8
AU$1 = 0.6

Torino Airport - www.aeroportoditorino.it
Airport transfers - www.savda.it
Trains - www.trenitalia.com

Italian Snowboard Association
Piazza Regina Elena,
12 – 38027 MALE
Tel 045 8303277
Web: www.fsi.it
Email: fsi@iol.it

Driving Guide
All vehicles drive on the right hand side of the road
Speed limits:
50kph (31mph) Towns
90kph (55mph) Highways
130kph (80mph) Motorways
Emergency
Fire - 115
Police - 113
Ambulance - 118
Tolls
Payable on motorways using the Autostrada system
Mont Blanc tunnel charges approx 20 euros each way
Documentation
A driving lisence must be carried as well as insurance.

Time Zone
UTC/GMT +1 hours
Daylight saving time: +1 hour

wsgANDALO

POOR FAIR GOOD TOP

FREERIDE
Trees & some off-piste

FREESTYLE
A terrain park

PISTES
Some good wide slopes

No hype, just a relaxed place to ride

5 OUT OF 10

pic - Andalo Tourism

Andalo lies at the base of the **Brenta Dolomite** mountain range just north of the city of Verona, which is also the gateway city for air transfer being only an hour and a half away. The towns of **Andalo**, **Fai della Paganella** and **Molveno**, form the **Paganella ski area** with over the 60 kilometres of marked out runs. It may not have the greatest annual snow record when the snow does fall; it provides a mountain that allows for some fine off-piste riding which includes lots of tight tree runs. Should the real snow not fall, then the resort boasts at least 90% snowmaking coverage on its pistes. The fact that this place is not the most famous resort may be its saving grace, because while some of the bigger and more popular destinations attract hordes of piste lovers, Andalo is left relatively crowd free and un-spoilt. The resorts history dates back many years yet this place is not an old fashioned out dated dump, on the contrary, the resorts management are constantly spending large sums of money keeping the mountain facilities up to date. In general the resort is split between being good for novices and intermediate riders. Advanced riders are not blessed with to many steep sections but that said, there are a number of hair raising descents to test the best. All the slopes are easily reached from the village via the main gondola. Once up the slopes you will be able to get around with ease, and for those who hate drag lifts, you'll find most of the runs are reached by chair lifts with a chair possible to the top section at 2125m.

FREERIDERS will be pleased to find that Andalo is actually a good place to ride with a number of riding options on offer. There are lots of tight trees to shred as well as a number of scary drops and fast steeps.

FREESTYLERS will also find Andalo a cool place. There is a halfpipe on occasions but its not always maintained. Local riders often construct their own hits and session them before moving on to try out some of the natural air terrain which is in abundance all over the mountain.

PISTES. Riders have lots of wide open spots where it is possible to lay out some big turns on runs that are well pisted on a daily basis.

BEGINNERS can start out on the easy slopes around the village area before heading up the mountain where you will find some excellent novice trails from the top station down to the mid section. The local ski school offer snowboard lessons and board hire is available in the village.

THE TOWN. **Andalo** is a basic and simple village that offers its visitors a high standard of good facilities. There are a number of good hotels with **accommodation** available next to the slopes. Around the village you will find shops, a sports centre, an ice ring and a swimming pool. There is a **night-club** and a couple of bars but don't expect a lot of action as night times are relaxed and basic.

ITALY

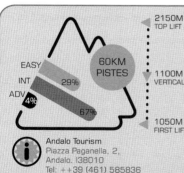

2150M
TOP LIFT

EASY

INT 29%

ADV 4%

67%

60KM
PISTES

1100M
VERTICAL

1050M
FIRST LIFT

Number of runs: 24
Longest run: 5km
Total Lifts: 18
2 Gondola, 15 chairs, 1 drags
Capacity (people/hour): 25,000
Lift times: 8.30am to 4.00pm
Mountain Cafes: 10

Winter Period:
Dec to April
Lift Passes:
Skipass for Paganella-Brenta area:
Day pass 30 euros
2 Day pass 53.5 euros
6 Days 141 euros
Board Schools
Altopiano ski schools has snowboard lessons

Annual Snowfall:
1m
Snowmaking:
95% of slopes

Bus
Trento (32 km) or
Mezzocorona (17 km)
Train
Take the Brennero line to Trento (40 km) or Mezzocorona (17 km)
Car
Highway A 22 - Brennero Modena, take San Michele All'Adige exit. Take SS43 to Mezzolombardo, then SP64 21km to Andalo
Fly
90 minutes (130km) from Verona airport. 170km from Brescia airport

Andalo Tourism
Piazza Paganella, 2,
Andalo. I38010
Tel: ++39 (461) 585836
Web: www.paganella.net
Email: info@paganella.net

NEW New for 05/06
8 person gondola, Andalo to Dos Pelà
4 person chairlift at Sant'Antonio
New piste at Paganella summit

wsg BARDONECCHIA

Location for Olympic snowboarding events

POOR FAIR GOOD TOP

FREERIDE
A few trees & some off-piste

FREESTYLE
A park & half-pipe

PISTES
Well pisted moderate slopes

6
OUT OF 10

pic Torino Olympic Org

I T A L Y

Bardonecchia is not only a small fashionable mountain town or a popular all year round holiday destination, but also rated in the top ten of Italy's resorts. Skiers have been flocking to these slopes for many years bringing with them all the razzle dazzle of the Italian ski world, indeed one of Italy's past Kings was said to be a regular visitor to this part of the Susa valley. This season Bardonecchia plays host to all the snowboard competitions during the **Turin Winter Olympics**. The 12th-23rd February is going to be a busy time, so if you're not planning on watching then it may be best avoided. These are the competition dates; 12-13th for the halfpipe, 16th-17th for boardercross, and 22nd-23rd for Giant Slalom for tickets visit **www. torino2006.org.** As a town, this place has been around since the time of the Romans and although a lot of what you find here is old, clapped out and in need of immediate repair, the place can still cut the mustard with a well set out series of mountain slopes that are connected by some twenty nine lifts. The 140 kilometres of marked out pistes cover a series of mountain faces that are split either side of the valley floor, and take in the hamlets of **Campo Smith, Melezet** and **Jafferau**. The main runs on the slopes of Bardonecchia will suit all levels but in the main are best for intermediates. Campo Smith and Melezet are pretty evenly split between beginners and intermediates, but one thing that is common with all the areas are the lift queues, which at weekends and over holidays can be stupidly long.

FREERIDERS will find that this is a fairly ordinary place to ride with nothing much to entice you back. However, up on the Jafferau area, which is only five minutes bus shuttle bus from Bardonecchia, you will find a nice big snow bowl and some cool backcountry spots along with some fast steeps.

FREESTYLERS. First impressions of the terrain and the opportunities for getting air, will not be good. There is a pipe and park at the base which will be the location for all the games snowboarding events, but outside of competition dates it's not well particularly well maintained.

PISTES. Carvers are the ones who should be most at home here, especially if you are only looking for gently descents on which to lay out some easy lines. Most of the slopes are well pisted and make for good carving, some of which can be done at speed.

BEGINNERS have a resort that is well suited to their needs. At Campo Smith and Melezet there are two large nursery areas but be warned, they do get very busy with novice skiers. Note also that this area operates a lot of old drag lifts.

THE TOWN
Bardonecchia is a mountain town that provides a high level of good services although not a cheap place. There is a good choice of hotels, apartments, chalets and B&B's to choose from with rates that are mostly on the high side. Around the town, or within close proximity, there are varying attractions from skating to bowling; the town also has a good selection of shops and banks. Restaurants are also plentiful but night life is some what lame.

2750M
TOP LIFT

EASY
INT
ADV
11%
43%
46%
140KM
PISTES

1460M
VERTICAL

1290M
FIRST LIFT

Number of runs: 49
Longest run: 6km
Total Lifts: 23
9 chairs, 14 drags
Capacity (people/hour): 23,850
Lift times:
8.30am to 4.30pm

Winter Period:
Dec to April
Lift Passes
1 Day 28 euros
2 Days 48.5 euros
5 Days 123 euros

Piazza Europa 15.
Bardonecchia
Tel - ++39 (0) 122 99137
Web: www.bardonecchiaski.com
Email: colomion@bardonecchiaski.com

Annual Snowfall:
Unknown
Snowmaking:
15% of slopes

Train
Take the Torino-Bardonecchia-Modane line straight to Bardonecchia station
Car
From Torino take the A32 via the Frejus tunnel. Take the Oulx exit, follow directions to Bardonecchia.
Fly
Turin 1 1/4 hours away 90km.

POOR FAIR GOOD TOP

FREERIDE
Lots of trees & some off-piste
FREESTYLE
No local park or pipe
PISTES
Busy but some good slopes

5
OUT OF 10

Basic but okay

pic - Bormio Tourism

Bormio dates back hundreds of years and it's quite possible that the Romans who built an ancient spa town near here could have actually been the first to shred the slopes in their tin hats. However, Bormio as we know it today is rated very highly in Italy, with it's modern roots going back to the early sixties when the resort started dragging punters up its mainly intermediate all-round terrain. Bormio is a fairly busy place, with overkill in some very sad all in one ski suits. The ski world does a lot of racing on the slopes here; Bormio hosted the 2005 World Championships which suggests that there must be something on offer. Italian skiers like this place a lot, as do Germans and quite a lot of Brits. This means the slopes do become very clogged up at weekends and over holiday

periods. Lift passes also provide access to the resorts of Santa Caterina (40km pistes) and San Colombano (30km pistes) creating the Alta Valtellina ski area, but the areas are only linked via ski-buses.

FREERIDERS have a mountain that is not extensive especially for advanced riders. There is some good off piste freeriding with powder bowls and trees to check out. The best stuff reached from the Cima Bianca, where the runs start off steep and mellow out to test the best. Don't bother hitting this stuff in hards, you'll regret it as this section is soft boot only terrain.

FREESTYLERS wanting to get big air will not find a great deal, but there are plenty of natural hits. The resort doesn't have a pipe or park, the nearest is 10 minutes away at Passo Dello Stelvio (linked by a shuttle bus). The Stelvio glacier, the largest in Europe, offers the opportunity to snowboard during the summer.

PISTES. Carvers will find that Bormio is an excellent place for any level and the 6km run from the top station down to the village provides plenty of time to get those big carves in. It's perfect for riders who want to see what it's like linking turns and by the time you hit the bottom, you'll know for sure.

BEGINNERS will find the slopes at Bormio ideal for basics and excellent for progression. What's more, all the easy stuff can be reached without tackling a drag lift.

THE TOWN
Bormio is a rather strange affair, but nevertheless a very rustic and Italian place. **Accommodation** is offered in a range of locations, with the choice of staying on or near the slopes. **Around town**, you soon notice how glitzy things are however, staying here can be done on a tight budget if you leave out dining in fancy restaurants: seek out one of the cheap pizza joints. Night-life is nothing to get excited about; in fact it's pretty dull but still boozy.

ITALY

EASY
INT 37%
ADV 45%
18%

50KM PISTES

3012M TOP LIFT

1787M VERTICAL

1225M FIRST LIFT

Number of runs: 11
Longest run: 6km
Total Lifts: 14
1 Cable-car, 7 chairs, 4 drags, 2 Magic carpet
Capacity (people/hour): 13,500
Lift times: 8.30am to 4.30pm

Winter Period:
Dec to April
Lift Passes:
Lift passes for Alta Valtellina ski area, comprising of Bormio, Santa Caterina and San Colombano areas
Day pass 32 euros
2 Day pass 61 euros
5 Day pass 146.5 euros
Season pass 505 euros

Annual Snowfall:
3m
Snowmaking:
40% of slopes

Bus
From Millan take the A801 bus operate by Società Trasporti Pubblici Sondrio, tel: 0342/511212. Takes 4 hours.
Train
services are possible to Tirano which is 20 minutes away.
Car
via Milan, head north via the towns of Lecco, Sondrio and Tirano, along the A38 to Bormio.
Fly
to Milan airport, 4 hours away. Ryanair have flights to Bergamo, 170km away (its 50km from Milan, but its sold as Milan)

Tourist Office Bormio
Via Roma 131-B. Bormio 123032
Tel: ++39 (0) 349 903 300

Web: www.bormioonline.com
Email: info@bormioonline.com

FREERIDE
A few trees & good off-piste
FREESTYLE
A park & occasional half-pipe
PISTES
Well pisted slopes

POOR FAIR GOOD TOP

Big linked area in Fassa Valley.

8 OUT OF 10

pic - Canazei Tourism

Canazei forms part of what is know as the **Dolomiti Superski**, which is said to the largest ski area in the world providing over 1200 kilometres of ridable terrain. What ever the merits of this claim one thing is for sure, and that is this place has got a lot going for it and will make a two weeks stay well worth the effort. Located along the **Fassa Valley**, of the Sella Ronda, Canazei is the largest of the cluster of villages that make up this area, with lifts that link it to **Campitello, Mazzin, Alba** to name but a few. Canazei, which is a sizeable town, sits at the base of the mountain with access up to the slopes having to be made by gondola and then on up by a large cable car. The first gondola ride up is often only possible after a long wait, as it's the only lift out of the town up to the slopes, unless you are in Campitello where they have a cable car to take you up. Generally this is a place that suits intermediate riders but, with such a vast area to explore, every level of rider should find something to test them. The terrain features are a mixture of rugged gullies to wide berth carving slopes on a mountain that has a fairly average annual snow record and at a resort the operates between December and April, which is a tad short when one thinks of the vast size of the area in general.

FREERIDERS are in for a bit of a treat here simply by the very fact that there is so much terrain to explore. If you can't have a good time here you should think about becoming a monk. The area is riddled with interesting terrain from chutes to trees to powder stashes. However, one major disappointment is the lack of challenging steeps for expert riders to perform on.

FREESYLERS should be able to enjoy this place as much as any other style of rider. There a lots of big drop off's and plenty of natural hits for gaining maximum air. The resort also builds a halfpipe, but it's not very well maintained nor is there a decent terrain park to play in.

PISTES. Boarders have acres and acres of well groomed tracks to speed down with some sizeable runs that allow for carving from the top to the bottom. The longest run in the area is over six and a half miles long (11km) which will get the thighs pumping.

BEGINNERS can't fail here, the place has lots of good nursery slopes and plenty of easy to negotiate intermediate runs to try out once you have mastered the basics. Note though that Canazei may only have a few drag lifts, but the Dolomiti Superski area has over a 130.

THE TOWN

Canazei is town that has over 10,000 tourist beds with loads of hotels and apartments to choose from, and although there is plenty of lodging close to the slopes, this is not a cheap place. However, the town has loads of restaurants and bars offering some very lively nightlife.

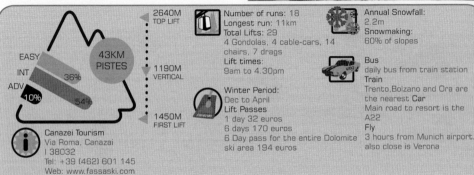

2640M TOP LIFT
1190M VERTICAL
1450M FIRST LIFT

43KM PISTES

EASY
INT 36%
ADV 10%
54%

Canazei Tourism
Via Roma, Canazei
I 38032
Tel: +39 (462) 601 145
Web: www.fassaski.com
Email: info@fassaski.com

Number of runs: 18
Longest run: 11km
Total Lifts: 29
4 Gondolas, 4 cable-cars, 14 chairs, 7 drags
Lift times:
9am to 4.30pm

Winter Period:
Dec to April
Lift Passes
1 day 32 euros
6 days 170 euros
6 Day pass for the entire Dolomite ski area 194 euros

Annual Snowfall:
2.2m
Snowmaking:
60% of slopes

Bus
daily bus from train station
Train
Trento,Bolzano and Ora are the nearest Car
Main road to resort is the A22
Fly
3 hours from Munich airport. also close is Verona

wsg CERVINIA

	POOR	FAIR	GOOD	TOP
FREERIDE Trees & some off-piste				
FREESTYLE A park & pipe				
PISTES Some very flat bits				

6
OUT OF 10

Amazing views but can frustrate

pic - Cervinia Tourism

Cervinia is set under the 4478 meters that is the **Matterhorn**. Truly one off the worlds most beautiful mountains, and if you can handle a walk you can board on its flanks. The town has a pleasant feel with a few poseurs mincing up a down the main street but nothing too bad. The resort is placed near the top of the **Aosta Valley**, and links up with the extortionate resort of **Zermatt**, so if you want to board an exclusive resort without the cost then Cervinia's for you. One thing which is a real pain is the first run into Zermatt from Cervinia. It's flat, full of skiers poling along trying to take each others eyes out, and if the wind gets up the only way back is two long t-bar drag lifts. Although it's never been anti board it has been slow in making boarders feel at home, two year ago they opened a new park designed by Daniele Milano, and even sell a cheaper day pass just to access the park area 21 euros.

FREERIDERS. Cervinia is a fine place to board for the intermediate, it's a little flat in places to get the heart thumping of an advanced rider, and the novice may find themselves hopping along the flat a little to much to put up with. Seeing your mates disappear over that rise while you come to a halt is a quick way to piss off even the calmest of beginners. The pistes are well maintained and are easily viewed, so you can see the best spots from the,

sometimes slow lifts. If you want off-piste then get your thinking head on and you can find some good routes. There's some great little spots and if you can't find them ask a local. If you get bored head over to Zermatt, or if you have the cash get a Helicopter.

FREESTYLERS will find the new **Indian Park** good for some big hits, the pipes ok and there's a few small hits to learn on. If you have a good look round you will find some good rock drops, find the right one and you could get a photo of you flying across the Matterhorn.

PISTES. Euro carvers will be get a little moist when they sit in their first chair over these slopes. There mostly wide and well groomed. The 22 km red run, Valtournenche, is the place to carve long and hard, while the blacks down into the village are cool. The pistes are never packed although they are busy during holidays.

BEGINNERS. The place to get your first bruises is up at the Plan Maison, which is reached by a cable-car. Once up be prepared to tackle some drag lifts in order to get to the easy flats, which also come with a heavy dose of ski schools. The runs rise up from the village at three main points and apart from a few areas, the lower sections are not beginner friendly, although there is a blue that leads down giving novices the chance to ride home.

TOWN. With fresh snow it almost feels like a real alpine town but as the snow melts so does its charm. There are some really uninspired concrete blobs which they call hotels but on the whole is a pleasant enough place to stay.
The resort has some lively bars and a few reasonable piste side café bars, check out the *Dragon* for a beer or the dodge *L'Etoile* disco to check out the rich Italian skirt. Large tour groups do stay here, and are getting more common, but it has a good mix of nationalities so never feels mobbed.

ITALY

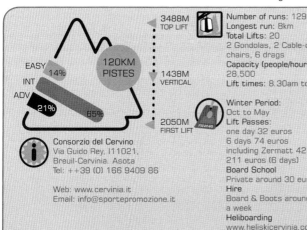

EASY 14%
INT
ADV 21%
65%

120KM PISTES

3488M TOP LIFT
1438M VERTICAL
2050M FIRST LIFT

Consorzio del Cervino
Via Guido Rey, I11021,
Breuil-Cervinia. Asota
Tel: ++39 (0) 166 9409 86

Web: www.cervinia.it
Email: info@sportepromozione.it

Number of runs: 129
Longest run: 8km
Total Lifts: 20
2 Gondolas, 2 Cable-cars, 10 chairs, 6 drags
Capacity (people/hour): 28,500
Lift times: 8.30am to 4.30pm

Winter Period:
Oct to May
Lift Passes:
one day 32 euros
6 days 74 euros
including Zermatt 42 (day) and 211 euros (6 days)
Board School
Private around 30 euros hour
Hire
Board & Boots around 150 euros a week
Heliboarding
www.heliskicervinia.com run trips for 360 euros for 3 drops. They also do 1 drop tasters for 100 euros.

Annual Snowfall:
10m
Snowmaking:
25% of slopes

Train
to Chatillon, which is 20 minutes away.
Bus
Bus service from Milan Malpensa airport to Cervinia. www.savda.it run services from Turin aiport to Aosta twice a day, 6.3 euros.
Car
via Geneva, head south on the A40, via the Mont Blanc Tunnel. Then take the A5 for 27km and turn off at Chatillon on to 406 for 28km up to the resort
Fly
to Geneva airport, 2 1/2 hours away. Milan Linate is 180 km. Turin Casselle is 118km away. Taxi services available from all airports.

267

wsg CLAVIERE

FREERIDE
Some tight trees & good off-piste
FREESTYLE
No park or pipe
PISTES
Lots of wide slopes

POOR FAIR GOOD TOP

7
OUT OF 10

Okay linked area.

pic - Claviere Tourism

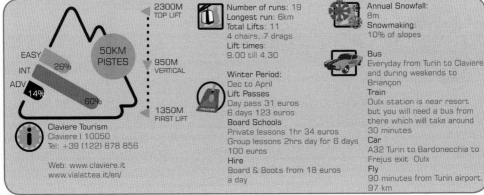

because once you get up on to the slopes, time spent in lift queues are generally minimal. Claviere, and its French neighbour **Montgenevre**, are just minutes apart and you can easily board between the two resorts on the same lift pass, which can also be used for the rest of the Milky Way circuit. The type of terrain is much the same where ever you choose to ride and in the main will favour intermediate freeriders the most.

FREERIDERS would be hard pushed to ride all of the terrain on offer here during a weeks visit. The slopes offer a good mixture of trees, off-piste powder and pisted runs. Advanced riders may only find a few decent black runs at Claviere, however, within the Milky Way circuit, there is an abundance of expert level terrain to try out.

FREESTYLERS Theres no park or pipe, so you'll need to head over the Sansicario. The area boast lots of good natural freestyle terrain where air heads can go high off banks and rollers dotted all over the place.

PISTES. Riders looking for long and wide open slopes will be happy to find that this place has lots of them. With the vast majority of the runs graded red or blue, carvers who like to glide around at a leisurely pace will love both Claviere and the rest of the Milky Way. But note, there are a lot of flat spots and some traversing is called for between runs, so expect some thigh burning moments.

Claviere is said to be Italy's oldest resort, and judging by its appearance its easy to see why, not that is look is a mark of what is on offer here. Because this happens to be a decent and popular resort that is just ten minutes away from the French resort of Montgenevre. Both resorts also form part of the ski circuit known as the **Milky Way** which offers over 400km of marked out pistes and takes in the resorts of **Sauze D'Oulx, Sansicario, Sestriere** and **Cesana** all of which are linked by an array of lifts totalling some 91, with a lift access height of over 2820 metres possible at Sestriere. Claviere has long been a popular resort and one that attracts a large number of skiers from all over Italy and from neighbouring France. This often makes the place very busy, especially at weekends, however, don't let that put you off,

BEGINNERS will have no problem coping with this place. Blue runs stretch from the summit's to the base areas allowing for some fine easy riding. But with seven drag lifts to contend with, getting around can be a bit tricky for drag lift virgins.

THE TOWN
Off the slopes the resort is full of character and duty free shops. The village is not big and getting around the place is easy. The choice of lodgings is rather small, but options to sleep near the slopes are plentiful. Nightlife is very tame with only a few restaurants and bars to chose from.

I
T
A
L
Y

2300M
TOP LIFT

950M
VERTICAL

1350M
FIRST LIFT

EASY
INT 26%
ADV 14%
60%

50KM
PISTES

Claviere Tourism
Claviere I 10050
Tel: +39 (122) 878 856

Web: www.claviere.it
www.vialattea.it/en/

Number of runs: 19
Longest run: 6km
Total Lifts: 11
4 chairs, 7 drags
Lift times:
9.00 till 4.30

Winter Period:
Dec to April
Lift Passes
Day pass 31 euros
6 days 123 euros
Board Schools
Private lessons 1hr 34 euros
Group lessons 2hrs day for 6 days
100 euros
Hire
Board & Boots from 18 euros
a day

Annual Snowfall:
8m
Snowmaking:
10% of slopes

Bus
Everyday from Turin to Claviere
and during weekends to
Briançon
Train
Oulx station is near resort
but you will need a bus from
there which will take around
30 minutes
Car
A32 Turin to Bardonecchia to
Frejus exit Oulx
Fly
90 minutes from Turin airport.
97 km

268

POOR FAIR GOOD TOP

FREERIDE
Trees & some off-piste

FREESTYLE
no park or pipe

PISTES
Some okay slopes

Okay but dull village

5
OUT OF 10

pic - Cortina Tourism

Every country has a place that the rich, famous and Royals head for, just to be seen 'on the piste' and to get a picture wearing sad clothing for the cover of Hello! Magazine. Enter Cortina, for this is one of those places, with so many balcony posers lying around outside restaurants that the slopes are left quiet. This allows snowboarders space to roam and explore the terrain. Cortina, located in the northern reaches of the Italian **Dolomites**, is an ex-Olympic resort, whose area is made up of two large mountain plateaus that rise up around the village. On one side you have an area called

Faloria, which connects up to Forcella, and rises to a height of 2950m. On the other side of the village lies the slopes of Tofana. **Tofana** is not connected by lift to the other areas, but can be reached via a cable car from the town or by the local bus to **Pocol**. The terrain here is pretty good and will suit all. Advanced riders get a mountain to challenge them to the limit and keep them interested for a week or even two, while intermediates will have ample opportunity to brush up on their skills and to progress nicely on a series of good slopes.

FREERIDERS will find that the most challenging runs are located down from the Tofana, which rises to 3243m and is accessed by cable car. From the summit you'll find plenty of stuff to check out, offering some good powder riding.

FREESTYLERS may not get man-made hits, but not to worry as there are plenty of natural ones with some cool drop offs and big banks to catch air from on both mountain sections. The Tofana area has the best stuff though.

PISTES; the Sella Ronda trail is definitely worth a visit, as is the Canellone which is a two planker's race run and the area to cut the snow in style, but not for wimps.

BEGINNERS can progress here on good easy slopes, with the best stuff around the mid section of the Tofana. These can be reached by chair (rather than drag) lifts.

THE TOWN
Cortina is a large place, with silly priced hotels and apartment style accommodation located mostly near or on the slopes. You can always try the Bobsleigh ride for 75mph fun. Around the village are various food joints offering the usual Italian fare. The evenings are pretty boring here and the rich only make it very glitzy. However, it's not all gloom as you can spend the evening mocking the rich and mine sweeping their drinks: they won't even notice because they're too busy posing.

I
T
A
L
Y

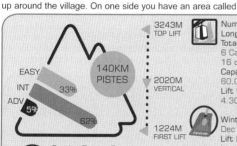

EASY

INT 33%

ADV 5%

62%

140KM PISTES

3243M TOP LIFT

2020M VERTICAL

1224M FIRST LIFT

Number of runs: 52
Longest run: 9km
Total Lifts: 51
6 Cable-cars, 29 chairs, 16 drags
Capacity (people/hour): 60,000
Lift times: 8.30am to 4.30pm

Winter Period:
Dec to April
Lift Passes:
Local area:
1 Day pass 35 euros
6 Days 180 euros
Dolomite Superpass
1 Day pass 38 euros
6 Days 194 euros
Board School
private from 36 euros/hr
6 morning lessons from 300 euros

Annual Snowfall:
4m
Snowmaking:
90% of slopes

Train
Train to Calalzo di Cadore, which is 20 minutes away and served by a bus or taxi (041 936222)
Bus
Service from Venice Airport to Cortina run by www.atvo.it costs 10 euros and takes about 3hrs
Car
From the South take the A27 from Mestre to Pian di Vedoja (Belluno), take National Road 51 via Alemagna to resort
From the north, from A22 Exit at Bressanone, take the road to Dobbiaco. From Bressanone exit to Cortina it takes about 1 hour.
Fly
Fly to Venice airport 2 hours away 162km. 35min Helicopter to resort available www.heliair.it

Cortina Tourist Board
Pizza San Francesco,
8 Cortina d'Ampezzo
Tel: +39 (0) 436 3231

Web: www.dolomitisuperski.com/cortina
www.dolomiti.org/dengl/cortina/
Email: cortina@dolomiti.org

FREERIDE
Some tight trees & good off-piste

FREESTYLE
No park or pipe

PISTES
Lots of wide slopes

POOR FAIR GOOD TOP

7 OUT OF 10

although many don't know what to pose in (ski boots are a no-no people). Top Italian female pro Martina Magenta hails from Courmayeur and can often be seen carving up the slopes.

FREERIDING here is pretty damn good, with some cool terrain to hit and the possibility of some trees to cut at the lower section. If it's powder and off piste riding you want, then Courmayeur is not the mega outlet like it's close French neighbour, but there is some good stuff to be had on steeps and trees down from the Cresta D'Arp. If you take the Mont Blanc cable car, you can gain access to the Vallee Blanche and ride into Chamonix. Although you will need to get the bus back, it'll be worth it.

FREESTYLERS here make do with the natural hits as there is no park or pipe to ride. You can however, get big air and find enough to jib off, eg snow cannons, logs, stair rails, ski instructors, there's plenty. You'll also find plenty snow built up in lumps pushed to the side of runs or covering small trees and small mounts etc.

PISTES. Boarders who like to stay on the pistes will find loads of well pisted runs to content themselves with, especially the areas under the Bertolini chair lift.

BEGINNERS who decide to give Courmayeur a try won't be disappointed; it's a perfect place to learn, although the slopes can often be far too busy, leading to a few collisions. Novices should head for the runs off the Checrouit cable car, where you'll find some nice easy slopes to try out your first toe and heel side turns amongst the ski crowds, taking out the stragglers as you go.

THE TOWN
Off the slopes, Courmayeur is a busy, stretched out place, with a lot going on. Most of the time the village plays host to package tour groups and although this helps to keep prices realistic, it does mean you have to rub shoulders with a lot of idiots. The village has a host of sporting attractions with the usual resort style swimming pools, ice rinks and fitness outlets. There is also an overdose of Italian style

Courmayeur lies on the opposite side of the Mont Blanc valley and only a stone's throw away from the top French resort of Chamonix which is a short drive back up through the Mont Blanc Tunnel. Courmayeur, a high level resort gives access to slopes that can be ridden by all and generally, this is a good place to spend a week or two. However, with its mixture of traditional Italian architecture and its modern resort offerings, Courmayeur is a destination that attracts millions of British skiers and other foreign nationals every year. They then copy their Italian counterparts by cladding themselves in horrid expensive ski wear and clogging up the slopes to often bursting point. The village is well spread out, but there is no real chance of leaping out of the nest, ollieing over a balcony and landing in a lift queue: you are going to have to do a bit of walking in order to take the cable car up to the slopes. The terrain will please intermediate carvers, but bore advanced freeriders. Be warned, every man and his dog hits the slopes at weekends and holidays. The main thing you notice is the amount of plate bindings and ski boots that there are about, as this is a carver's pose place,

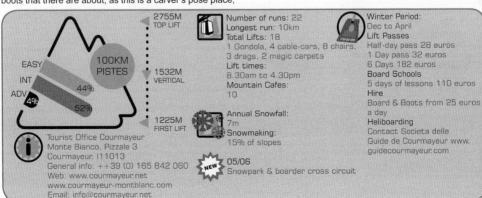

EASY
INT
ADV
4%
44%
52%

100KM
PISTES

2755M
TOP LIFT

1532M
VERTICAL

1225M
FIRST LIFT

Number of runs: 22
Longest run: 10km
Total Lifts: 18
1 Gondola, 4 cable-cars, 8 chairs, 3 drags, 2 magic carpets
Lift times:
8.30am to 4.30pm
Mountain Cafes:
10

Annual Snowfall:
7m
Snowmaking:
15% of slopes

05/06
Snowpark & boarder cross circuit

Winter Period:
Dec to April
Lift Passes
Half-day pass 28 euros
1 Day pass 32 euros
6 Days 182 euros
Board Schools
5 days of lessons 110 euros
Hire
Board & Boots from 25 euros a day
Heliboarding
Contact Societa delle Guide de Courmayeur www.guidecourmayeur.com

Tourist Office Courmayeur
Monte Bianco, Pizzale 3
Courmayeur. I11013
General info: ++39 (0) 165 842 060
Web: www.courmayeur.net
www.courmayeur-montblanc.com
Email: info@courmayeur.net

pic -Vallee Blanche la seraccata Jacquemod Attilio

boutiques, selling expensive designer wear, but alas, there are no decent snowboard shops.

Accommodation is very good here. The town can sleep 20,000 visitors with lodging close to the slopes and in the town centre. You can choose to bed down in one of the hotels, or stay in one of the self catering apartment blocks which can accommodate large groups of riders. There is also a number of reasonably priced bed and breakfast homes to choose from.

Food wise, Courmayeur does a good job fattening up its visitors with the usual option to pig out in a few pizza restaurants. There are also a number of basic holiday tourist style eateries offering funny sounding traditional Italian dishes. However, you can eat reasonably if you stick to the lower end pizza joints such as La Boite, but if you're feeling flush and want to dine, check out Pierre Alexis.

Night life in Courmayeur is late, loud and very boozy. Italians party hard here, but unfortunately so do a lot of apres skiers, who give the place a rowdy and low life feel to it. Popular places to check out are the Popas Pup, Bar Roma or The Red Lion, all of which are lively watering holes with a young party style crowd.

SUMMARY
Not a bad place, with some good carving but basic freeriding. Great for beginners apart from over crowded novice slopes. Good local services. Overall this is an expensive resort but also a good value one.

Courmayeur Tourism

CAR
Drive to Geneva via Mont Blanc Tunnel. Courmayeur 65 miles (104 km). Drive time is about 2 hours. *From Calais 563 miles (905 Km). Drive time is around 9 1/2 hours.
FLY
Fly to Geneva international or Turin which is also close.
TRAIN
Trains to Aosta then bus
BUS
Bus services from Geneva airport are available on a daily basis as well as from Milan and Turin.

wsg FOLGARIDA

FREERIDE
Some tight trees & off-piste
FREESTYLE
halfpipe
PISTES
Lots of easy slopes

Okay alpine style resort

5 OUT OF 10

pic -Folgarida Tourism

FREERIDERS don't have a great deal of adventurous terrain to explore directly at Folgarida, however, close by there is plenty of scope for shredding in and out trees or for riding across good off-piste powder fields and down some bumpy slopes. Unfortunately expert riders are the ones who are mostly let down the most here with only a few of the slopes graded as black or difficult. Intermediates on the other hand have the largest share of runs to ride, with an array of red runs that crisscross all over the slopes of Folgarida and Madonna di Campiglio and a couple of long ones on Marilleva area.

FREESTYLERS. There's a pretty good half-pipe over at Marilleva in the Val Panciana area, otherwise you'll have to content with just natural hits dotted around the place.

BEGINNERS can come here knowing that they won't be disappointed. The resort is ideal for novices with an excellent selection of easy runs to try out, including good nursery areas that can be easily reached but are serviced by drag lifts.

THE TOWN

Folgarida is low key alpine resort with a good choice of local facilities all within walking distance of the slopes. There are affordable hotels, apartment blocks and chalets as well a few shops and an outdoor ice rink. Eating out and night life are both very low key but enjoyable none the less.

Folgarida is a fairly ordinary purpose built resort that links closely with the more famous resort of **Madonna di Campiglio** and the less famous resort of **Marilleva**. Collectively the area boasts 120 kilometres of lift linked piste, however, on its own Folgarida accounts for a small portion of the total area. Unlike many purpose built resorts in France and Italy, this place is not an ugly sham crammed with mountain tower blocks. What you get here is a well balanced alpine style retreat nestled between trees and great scenery. This is also a place that attracts riders who like things easy and with out the hustle and bustle of the rather more stuck up neighbour of Madonna di Campiglio. Folgarida doesn't have a great choice of runs with only a few north facing easy slopes and almost nothing for expert riders apart from one black trail that runs down from the main gondola at the mid section. However, what this resort does have is a very good modern lift system that is able to whisk thousands of visitors up to its slopes and onto the neighbouring areas, all of which share a joint lift pass. This resort on its own, would only take two days of your time, but as the place links nicely with its neighbours, a two week stay would be well worth it.

TRENTINO **Val di Sole**

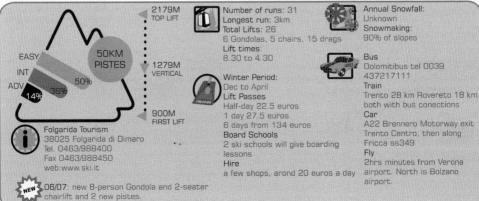

2179M
TOP LIFT

EASY
INT
ADV 14% 36%
50%

50KM
PISTES

1279M
VERTICAL

900M
FIRST LIFT

Number of runs: 31
Longest run: 3km
Total Lifts: 26
6 Gondolas, 5 chairs, 15 drags
Lift times:
8.30 to 4.30

Winter Period:
Dec to April
Lift Passes
Half-day 22.5 euros
1 day 27.5 euros
6 days from 134 euros
Board Schools
2 ski schools will give boarding lessons
Hire
a few shops, arond 20 euros a day

Annual Snowfall:
Unknown
Snowmaking:
90% of slopes

Bus
Dolomitibus tel 0039 437217111
Train
Trento 28 km Rovereto 18 km both with bus conections
Car
A22 Brennero Motorway exit Trento Centro, then along Fricca ss349
Fly
2hrs minutes from Verona airport. North is Bolzano airport.

Folgarida Tourism
38025 Folgarida di Dimaro
Tel. 0463/988400
Fax 0463/988450
web:www.ski.it

NEW 06/07: new 8-person Gondola and 2-seater chairlift and 2 new pistes.

ITALY

	POOR	FAIR	GOOD	TOP
FREERIDE A few trees & some off-piste				
FREESTYLE no park or pipe				
PISTES Some easy slopes				

Small and straight forward resort

5 OUT OF 10

pic -Foto Gimmy www.valbremanaweb.com

Foppolo is a simple resort that will appeal to visitors who like crowd free slopes but slopes with good annual snow fall. Like many purpose built resorts, Foppolo, which dates back as a ski resort many many years, is located at the foot of the mountain. As a purpose built resort, access to the slopes is easy and convenient with riding spread out over a number of connecting mountain areas with riding up to the summit of Montebello at 2100m and down to the small hamlet of Carona at 1100m. Much of the terrain on offer here is rated evenly between beginners and intermediates with only small amount of black advanced grade slopes. Despite the lack of challenging terrain, this is still a cool Italian hangout with out too many ski crowds messing up the slopes. Foppolo, has some 20 pisted runs serviced by a dozen lifts which are mainly drag lifts. The resort also links up with that of San Simone, but you need to take the 15 minute shuttle bus to reach its slopes as it doesn't link directly on snow. However, all the areas share a lift pass. Where ever you ride, what you will notice is the simplicity of the place and the ease in which to get around. You will also notice that the resort staff work hard at keeping the slopes well pisted and covered in artificial snow, when its needed, which is quite often.

FREERIDERS should be advised that this is not the most interesting place in terms of the diversity of terrain features. Much of the riding is set well above the tree line, however, there are some really nice bowls to shred through and a few okay off-piste spots to try out. From the summit point of Montebello, which is reached after a long drag lift ride, you can ride down a number of fast black trails that wind down a steep mountain face and are not to be taken lightly or you will end up in pain. At the bottom you can either elect to go back towards Montebello, or head on up in the opposite direction to the slopes of Carona where you will be able to try out a few more black runs.

FREESTYLERS won't enjoy this place that much. With no park or pipe air heads are left to either make their own hits or finding natural ones.

PISTES. Riders who like long and wide open runs will find a number to keep them occupied with a few nice reds to check out and some long easy blues.

BEGINNERS have lots of easy runs to learn on starting with the nursery slopes which rise up directly from the resort centre. The first main cluster of blue runs are reached via a long chair lift which can be used to reach most of Foppolo easy runs. Access to Carona on snow is not possible for total novices.

THE TOWN
Accommodation in the resort is basic but convenient with lodging close to the slopes. The resort has a few shops, an ice rink, a few restaurants and a splattering of bars, but don't expect any happening nightlife.

ITALY

EASY	47KM	
INT	PISTES	48%
ADV	27%	
	25%	

| Top Lift | 2200M | First Lift | 1600M | Vertical | 600M |

Number of runs: 23
Longest run: 2km
Total Lifts: 12
4 chairs, 8 drags
Capacity (people/hour):
10,000
Lift times:
8.30am to 4.30pm

Winter Period:
Dec to April
Lift Passes:
1 day 23 euros
2 days 37 euros
6 days 95 euros
Board Schools
4 ski schools in town
Hire
Available in town

Annual Snowfall:
Unknown
Snowmaking:
25% of slopes

Bus
Services available from Bergamo and Milan.
Car
From Bergamo (58Km) head to Valle Brembana, then head towards Piazza Brembana untill you reach a crossroad. Turn right and follow to Foppolo.
108km from Milano
Fly
2hrs from Verona or Milan airport.

Foppolo Tourism
Tel +39 345 74315
web: www.foppoloski.it
Email: info@bremboski.it

273

POOR FAIR GOOD TOP

FREERIDE
Some trees & good off-piste
FREESTYLE
No park or pipe
PISTES
Some flat bits

Okay freeriders resort with some nice powder spots

7
OUT OF 10

pics - La Thuile Tourism

I
T
A
L
Y

La Thuile links up with the French resort of **La Rosiere** to create the **espace San Bernardo**, which together make up 150km of piste. The town of La Thuile sits at the head of the **Aosta valley** just down the road from its more famous cousin **Courmayeur**, but unlike its neighbour it's a far quieter resort. The most annoying thing about La Thuile is its piste grading; reds should be blues and blue really means uphill. The longest run in resort is No 7 which is graded red and starts at **Chaz Dura** 2579M. The run winds it's way down a secluded picturesque valley and is great if you want to get away from everyone, the last half of the run is on a road and you end up boarding past crossing cow signs, but a red you've having a laugh, you have to walk a good 2 of it's 11KM.

The village is a mix of old and new, the old part straddles a small river and has a few good bars and some cheep eats, while the new part is a bit soulless, the locals are friendly and really welcoming and there's also one or two hotels open to the public with their own sporting facilities, such as a swimming pool, gym and saunas.

Although La Thuile is only at 1441m, a fast cable car takes you up to the **Les Sucres** area at 2200m. From here down to the resort are some very steep blacks, while above are a number of runs which mostly lead back to the same place, via a long flat run out, which will infuriate people with only a few weeks under their belts. La Thuile

looks after its pistes well, which are wide and flat, often too flat. The lift system is modern and efficient which makes waiting in line extremely rare. La Thulie is fine for a cheap week with a group of friends of mixed abilities, but don't head here if you want a week of hard core boarding.

FREERIDERS have some good black runs to try out: the **Diretta** (which runs through the trees) is full on and will test those who think they know it all. There's also some cool freeriding to be had on the La Rosiere side, while those looking for off-piste will find it off the **San Bernardo chair**. However the real off-piste is best tackled by going heli-boarding so dig deep into those pockets and take to the skies.

FREESTYLERS will find an abundance of natural hits dotted around both La Thuile and La Rosiere, but you will have to look for them. There's also plenty of space to build jumps so take a shovel. There's no park nor pipe, so if that's your thing you maybe best off holidaying else where.

PISTES. There are some great pisted slopes for laying out big carves on and most can be tackled at speed without having to negotiate too many sightseeing skiers.

BEGINNERS need to know that apart from a couple of small nursery slopes at the base, the main easy runs are located above the **Les Suches area**, which is served by

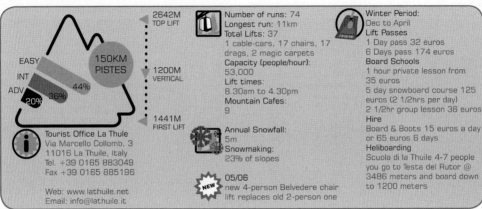

EASY
INT
ADV
20% 36% 44%

150KM
PISTES

2642M
TOP LIFT

1200M
VERTICAL

1441M
FIRST LIFT

Tourist Office La Thule
Via Marcello Collomb, 3
11016 La Thuile, Italy
Tel. +39 0165 883049
Fax +39 0165 885196

Web: www.lathuile.net
Email: info@lathuile.it

Number of runs: 74
Longest run: 11km
Total Lifts: 37
1 cable-cars, 17 chairs, 17 drags, 2 magic carpets
Capacity (people/hour): 53,000
Lift times:
8.30am to 4.30pm
Mountain Cafes:
9

Annual Snowfall:
5m
Snowmaking:
23% of slopes

05/06
NEW new 4-person Belvedere chair lift replaces old 2-person one

Winter Period:
Dec to April
Lift Passes
1 Day pass 32 euros
6 Days pass 174 euros
Board Schools
1 hour private lesson from 35 euros
5 day snowboard course 125 euros (2 1/2hrs per day)
2 1/2hr group lesson 36 euros
Hire
Board & Boots 15 euros a day or 65 euros 6 days
Heliboarding
Scuola di la Thuile 4-7 people you go to Testa del Rutor @ 3486 meters and board down to 1200 meters

chairlifts rather than all drags. Learners will not be riding back into the village as it involves too much steep, but you can get the cable car back down. There are many board schools but try to find a BASI trained one as the local lads spend more time looking good than helping you get to grips with your first turns.

THE TOWN

La Thuile is finally reached after a short drive up twisting and winding mountain road. On arrival, you are presented with a scenic and old Italian village with a hint of the new here and there. The main happenings are conveniently at the base of the slopes and straddle a large river. Visitors are made very welcome in La Thuile and local services cater very well for all your needs. Around the village you will find a few shops, places to pig out and one or two hotels with their own sporting facilities, such as a hotel swimming pool, gym and saunas. But other than that there is nothing major going on. Snowboard hire is best done from *Ornella Sports* +39 (0) 165 844 154.

Night life in La Thuile is very tame by Italian standards, so if you're the sort that likes to party hard all night long, this is not your resort. La Thuile is a very relaxed place and there is nothing much going on. Any so called action seems to be as the lifts close. Still you can enjoy a beer in the *La Bricole* bar.

Accommodation La Thuile is a relatively small resort with around 3000 beds, bunks or other things on which to kip on. However, what there is is quite sufficient for a weeks

stay with the option to lie out horizontally in a bed on the slopes or within a short walk of the first lifts. A number of tour operators offer full holiday packages here, so some good package deals are available.

Food. As for eats, you can get all the usual Italian dishes here along with a selection of standard grade euro nosh. However, your choice of where to eat out is a bit limited on the whole. Still that said, what is offered is good and you can eat very well here on a low budget. Restaurants of note are that of *La Rascards* for a choice of local dishes, or *La Grotta* which is known for its slices of pizza and pasta, although not the cheapest of places and the Mexican's not bad.

CAR
Drive to Geneva via Mont Blanc Tunnel. La Thule is 76 miles (122 km). Drive time is about 2 1/4 hours.
FLY
Fly to Turin and take a bus. Geneva international. Transfer time to resort 2 1/4 hours.
TRAIN
Trains to Pre-St-Didier (3 miles).
BUS
Bus services from Geneva airport are available on a daily basis. Check out www.savda.it, services run twice daily to/from Milano Malpensa and take 3hrs

POOR FAIR GOOD TOP

FREERIDE
A few trees & some off-piste
FREESTYLE
small terrain park
PISTES
Not well groomed

4 OUT OF 10

pic -Limone Tourism

ITALY

Limone is located south of **Turin** and only a short distance from the French and Italian border. Limone is a traditional Italian town with a past that involves the railways. Today however, this relatively unknown holiday destination is a simple place that attracts summer and winter tourists all year round to sample its holiday attractions which include great mountains. The old sprawling town sits at the base of an impressive set of high peaks, with the 2344 metre summit of the **Cima Pepino Mountain** well within sight. The place is not widely known as a ski or snowboard destination outside of Italy which can be a bit of a blessing as the place is not tainted with mass package ski tour groups. But on the down side, not being the most popular of places can often mean a lack of on-going resort development. Still, this may not be a big fancy resort boasting loads of steep challenging slopes, but you can nevertheless have a great time riding on slopes that can fill up with weekend visitors but are empty during the mid week periods. This is a simple resort that is suited to intermediate riders with very little to offer expert riders. Advanced riders will find some interesting terrain, but it won't take more than a few days to ride-out. The one big draw back about Limone is its annual snow record. Its fairly close proximity to the Mediterranean Sea means that this is not a resort blessed with heaps of regular snow.

FREERIDERS have a cool mountain to explore and should find Limone a pleasant surprise. There is a good choice of areas to ride that offers, tree riding, lots of gullies and uneven trails to descend down. Expert riders will find the Olimpica run a pleaser.

FREESTYLERS will be pleased to hear a small park was built last season in Limonetto next to the San Lorenzo piste. On a good day and when theres enough snow you'll find a couple of kickers and some rails.

PISTES riders who usually prefer miles of perfect well groomed trails may be a bit disappointed. Most of the main runs are a bit choppy and not great cruising trails; that said you can still carve here.`

BEGINNERS might well find that this resort is not for them. There are some good novice slopes but they are very limited and serviced by a host of drag lifts.

THE TOWN

Limone is an old town located within easy reach of the slopes. The town offers basic but affordable facilities with a good choice of hotels, apartment blocks and some bed and breakfast homes.

2800M
TOP LIFT

EASY
INT 20%
ADV
10%
70%

80KM
PISTES

2614M
VERTICAL

186M
FIRST LIFT

Assessorato al Turismo
Comune di Limone Piemonte
Via Roma 30
Tel. 0171 92.95.15
Fax 0171 92.95.05
Web: www.limonepiemonte.it
Email: iat@limonepiemonte.it

Number of runs: 46
Longest run: 6km
Total Lifts: 20
9 chairs, 11 drags
Lift times:
8.30 to 4.30

Winter Period:
Dec to April
Lift Passes
Half-day 22.50 euros
1 Day 29
3 days 76
5 days 111
Season 590

Annual Snowfall:
Unknown
Snowmaking:
15% of slopes

Train
Train services are possible to Limone Piemonte on the Torino-Cuneo-Ventimiglia (Nizza) line www.trenitalia.it
Car
From Turin take the A6 towards Savona for 62km, then take the Fossano exit and continue for another 50km
Fly
Fly to Turin airport which is 1 1/2 hours away.

wsg LIVIGNO

	POOR	FAIR	GOOD	TOP
FREERIDE A few trees & some off-piste				
FREESTYLE A park & pipe				
PISTES Plenty of cruisee slopes				

Cheap & boozy with a decent park

6 OUT OF 10

Something went wrong when Livigno was given the go ahead by the local planning committee as it's a badly laid out mess. Still, it's not totally crap and unlike many other Italian resorts it rates low on the pretentious scale. As one of the cheaper resorts in Italy, the rich, sun tanning idiots are not so common, but it also has the effect of attracting lots of first time skiers, which makes it a very busy place. The height that Livigno is set at helps ensure a good snow record that lasts quite late into the season. The slopes are spread across both sides of the valley and offer loads of no-nonsense intermediate runs that will appeal to all rider styles. The way the area is set out means bussing around, with some notable bus queues. Once on the slopes, the runs are reached mainly by drag lifts which will annoy some first timers, but can be conquered.

FREERIDERS with some history are not going to be too tested here, although the black down from the Della Neve is worth a go and should appeal, unless you're a wimp. There's not much to shout about as far as off-piste is concerned. It is possible to find some, but it won't freak you out and some of the areas can be a pain in the arse for getting back to the resort. There are guiding services to help you find the best areas. The trees here are not the best either.

FREESTYLERS are in for a treat. The park used to hold the Burton open until it moved to Laax last season, and its clear to see why the place is highly regarded. There's a host of kickers and rails of various sizes including a pro line of mammoth proportions. There's also a halfpipe and a boarder cross circuit depending on the conditions. Visit www.livignopark.com for the latest

PISTES. There's opportunity to ride hard here on some OK carving runs, with the Vetta Blesaccia the slope to check out, but by and large you'll have the resort tamed within a few days.

BEGINNERS this resort is perfect for learning at with wide gentle runs located at lower sections which are easy to reach. Although slow learners will find the drags a real pain.

THE TOWN
Livigno is cheap and cheerful, with lots of duty free shops. Evenings are very boozy with a lot of throwing up in the streets. Accommodation is a mixture of hotels, B & B's and cheap apartments, which are easy to overload with extra bodies should you be visiting as a group on the cheap. There are numerous local amenities and a number of good restaurants, but the whole place has a cheesy feel to it and it can often be very crowded.

ITALY

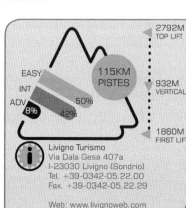

EASY	115KM PISTES	
INT		
ADV 8%	50% 42%	

2792M TOP LIFT

932M VERTICAL

1860M FIRST LIFT

Livigno Turismo
Via Dala Gesa 407a
I-23030 Livigno (Sondrio)
Tel. +39-0342-05.22.00
Fax. +39-0342-05.22.29

Web: www.livignoweb.com
Email: info@aptlivigno.it

Number of runs: 73
Longest run: 3.5km
Total Lifts: 33
3 Gondolas, 14 chairs, 16 drags
Lift Capacity (people per hour): 46,460
Lift times: 8.30 to 4.30

Winter Period:
Dec to April
Lift Passes
Half-day pass 24 euros
1 Day pass 33 euros
6 days 163 euros
Season 515 euros

Annual Snowfall:
2.5m
Snowmaking:
15% of slopes

Bus
Bus from Tirano to resort via Bormio visit www.busperego.com for more info. Can also take a bus from the train station at Zernez www.silves-tribus.it

Train
Trains from Milan to Tirano-Ferrovie dello Stato, www.trenitalia.com. From the North take the Rhätischer towards Kloisters and get off at Zurigo and take a bus

Car
Drive via Milan, head north via the towns of Lecco, Sondrio and then heading up the A29 and turning of left at La Rosa and on up to Livigno. 220km total

Fly
Fly to Milan airport 3 1/2 hours away. Bergamo Oria Al Serio Airport is 45 km from Milan

POOR FAIR GOOD TOP

FREERIDE
A few trees & some good off-piste

FREESTYLE
Terrain park & pipe

PISTES
Well groomed slopes

6 OUT OF 10

Good overall resort

Madonna Di Campiglio is one of the best resorts in the Dolomites and thankfully not tainted with too many cheap ski package tour groups, which helps to keep lift queues to almost zero. The pistes are relatively crowd free, although it should be said that Madonna does attract some of Italy's finest clientele. This well established ski haunt has now become a snowboarder's favourite, one that is trying really hard to satisfy boarders and it has to be said that it does a fairly good job. The old International Snowboard Federation used to stage a number of top events in Madonna, attracting many top riders. It's not just the snowboarding they come for, the parties go off as well, with top bands and DJ's playing at the side of the half-pipe. The ride area, which rises up around the resort, is linked with **Folgarida** and **Marillea**, giving a combined coverage of over 100 miles of extremely well groomed trails and some good off-piste. Much of the terrain will suit riders who are just getting to grips with their style and ability, but advanced riders with a few years under their belts will find it a little unchallenging in places, but still okay.

FREERIDERS should check out the areas at **Spinale**, where you'll find some good powder spots and some nice tree sections to blast through lower down. **Fortini** also offers a testing time.

FREESTYLERS like this place a lot and not just for the mega halfpipe (when an event is on) or the Ursus park located in the **Groste area**. For those who like their hits natural, there are plenty of snow walls and steep hits to get air from. Having said that though the Ursus park is usually well maintained by the crew and features a few massive kickers as well as a beginners area with some smaller jumps, rollers, and rails.

PISTES. The race run normally set aside for ski races, is the place for competent riders who want to show skiers how a mountain should be tackled at speed and with only two edges.

BEGINNERS will find Madonna is one of the best first timers resorts around, with lots of well set out easy runs, allowing for easy access and quick progression to more difficult terrain.

THE TOWN has plenty of eating and sleeping options, with affordable places to sleep close to the slopes. Around the town, there are heaps of things to do with a whole manner of attractions such as ice speedway circuit and waterfall climbs. **At night**, things can get very lively, going off big style and lasting well into the early hours of the morning. There is a good choice of bars and clubs but they are all a bit pricey.

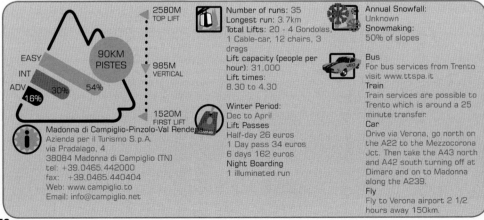

2580M
TOP LIFT

985M
VERTICAL

1520M
FIRST LIFT

EASY 90KM PISTES

INT

ADV 16% 30% 54%

Number of runs: 35
Longest run: 3.7km
Total Lifts: 20 - 4 Gondolas, 1 Cable-car, 12 chairs, 3 drags
Lift capacity (people per hour): 31,000
Lift times: 8.30 to 4.30

Winter Period:
Dec to April
Lift Passes
Half-day 26 euros
1 Day pass 34 euros
6 days 162 euros
Night Boarding
1 illuminated run

Madonna di Campiglio-Pinzolo-Val Rendena
Azienda per il Turismo S. p. A.
via Pradalago, 4
38084 Madonna di Campiglio (TN)
tel: +39.0465.442000
fax: +39.0465.440404
Web: www.campiglio.to
Email: info@campiglio.net

Annual Snowfall:
Unknown
Snowmaking:
50% of slopes

Bus
For bus services from Trento visit www.ttspa.it
Train
Train services are possible to Trento which is around a 25 minute transfer
Car
Drive via Verona, go north on the A22 to the Mezzocorona Jct. Then take the A43 north and A42 south turning off at Dimaro and on to Madonna along the A239.
Fly
Fly to Verona airport 2 1/2 hours away 150km.

I T A L Y

 PASSO TONALE

POOR FAIR GOOD TOP

FREERIDE
Some trees & good off-piste
FREESTYLE
Good natural
PISTES
Lots of wide groomed pistes

Some fine intermediate but limited expert terrain.

8 OUT OF 10

pic - Tonale Tourism

Tonale is high altitude resort perched in a wide open expanse that is both snow sure and sunny. Without doubt this a cool place to visit, a resort that is both old and new in terms of the village and its development. The resort is coming to the end of its huge improvement plan, this season will see 5 new lifts installed, and next season there'll be some additional pistes. With all the improvements the resort is becoming more and more popular. However that popularity isn't a problem, lift queues are almost non existent and the piste never become cluttered up leaving lots of wide open runs to free of crowds. During the winter months Tonale gets a good share of snow and should the real stuff be lacking then the resorts snowmaking facilities can cover over 40% of the marked out pistes. Should you want to do some summer riding then this place can also accommodate you with good riding possible up on the nearby **Presena Glacier** in the summer months. You can reach the glacier from Tonale by cable car, but the glacier only opens in the winter if the snow on the lower areas is lacking. Tonale offers great intermediate and beginner level riding with options to ride a long tree lined run between Tonale and the nearby resort of **Ponte di Legno**, although note that you can ride to Ponte di Legno, but you have to get a ski bus back. Both

resorts share a joint lift pass, which is a modern hands free system whereby you pass through the lift gates with your pass still in your pocket. The lifts them self's are equally split between being chair lifts and drag lifts along with a cable car. All the lifts link well and even novices can get around with out having to use too many drag lifts.

FREERIDERS who like wide open pistes with long sweeping runs will love this place, but for those who crave steep gullies and like tight trees you will not be so impressed, but what ever your into, this is a good freeriders resort.
FREESTYLERS will need to make do with hitting natural jumps or building there own. There are however, lots of cool jumps including a number of drop ins of rock sections and lots of cool snow banks to fly high off.
PISTES. Riders have a mountain that is simply fantastic. The wide open motorway style piste will let you ride fast and wide across runs that make carving a total joy. The 4 km trail to Ponte di Legno is a cool trail while the 3 km race runs will test the best.
BEGINNERS who can't learn how to ride here, can only be described as stupid because this place is one of the best resorts in Italy for novices. There are loads of easy to negotiate blue runs spread out over wide pisted areas with lots of nursery slopes all located close to the village centre.

THE TOWN. Tonale is a laid back resort with good hotels and apartment blocks. Around the village you will be able to get a cheap bed, a decent meal in one of the many restaurants, and have a simple but cheap night out.

ITALY

EASY	120KM PISTES	
INT	34%	
ADV	16% 50%	

3100M TOP LIFT

1216M VERTICAL

1884M FIRST LIFT

Passo Tonal Tourist Office
I-38020
Tel: 64 903 838
Web: www.passotonale.it
Ski area: www.adamelloski.com
Email: tonale@valdisole.net

NEW 05/06: 4 new quad chairs and 8 seater gondola creating new area around Casola near the town of Ponte Di Legno and Temu

Number of runs: 41
Longest run: 4.5km
Total Lifts: 30
3 Gondolas, 19 chairs, 8 drags
Lift times:
8.30 to 4.30

Winter Period:
Dec to April
Lift Passes
Adamello linked area
Half-day 24 euros
1 Day 30 euros
5 days 128 euros
Lessons
Scuola Italiana run a 5 day course (2hrs per day) 87 euros. Private lesson 30 euros per hour

Annual Snowfall:
Unknown
Snowmaking:
40% of slopes

Train
to Male of the Trento-Mali Electric Railway, Passo Tonale can be easily reached by regular bus service. The nearest station of the State Railways is Mezzocorona.
Car
A22 super highway then SS43
From Milan or Turin A4 exit at Seriate then follow signs
Fly
Verona 163km 3 hours away.
Milan 250 km 4.5 hours

Great for intermediates and mixed groups

POOR FAIR GOOD TOP

FREERIDE
Plenty of trees & good off-piste
FREESTYLE
badly maintained park & pipe
PISTES
Good wide slopes

7
OUT OF 10

pic Pila Tourism

ITALY

Set in the **Aosta valley,** Pila is a great if little place. The Aosta valley in the north of Italy has the Chamonix tunnel at its head. As you drive towards France up the valley from Turin you pass a load of resorts of which Pila is the gem, well maybe the precious stone. Pila is set at 1800 meters amongst a large pine forest, all the runs are separated by trees and most are wide, giving you the feeling of having the mountain to yourself. If you're driving your own car, on a day trip, park in Aosta town and catch a very long gondola up to the purpose built village of Pila. If you want to drive right into resort, be ready for a long slow climb, full of hairpin bends. The resort is often full of British school groups taking advantage of Italy's cheep prices (in comparison to France) and wide un-crowded piste's. The school groups can clog up the mountain cafes at lunch time with young girls trying to impress their ski instructor, but once on the slopes they soon blend in with everyone else. This resort offers fantastically varied terrain, great for intermediates and fine for both beginners and advanced riders. One problem with the resort is you keep finding yourself returning to the same **Gorraz- G Grimod** cable car area, which in high season can lead to long queues.

FREERIDERS. If you want to have it down the piste at full speed laying down some fat carves then this is the resort for you. Most of the piste's are wide and well groomed No 14 (Pre Noir) has a great pitch with a couple of drop offs

leading to a few tight bends and No2 (Du Bois) good if you like it a little steeper. From the **Couis 2** chair there are lots of places to drop in on an off piste face. If you don't mind a long walk then get your transceivers on and head off on one suggested Ski Mountaineering routes on the piste map. The trees are tightly packed but if you don't mind a few false starts you'll eventually find a route to hack it through the forests.

FREESTYLE. A short hop from the top of the **La Nouva** chair is what's described as a fun park. There's a small half pipe and a couple of rails but it's not well maintained. Pila is full of natural hits and ample space to build a kicker or two also the top right hand side of No15 (Grimod) has a natural half pipe which you can fly out of rather than back into.

BEGINNERS. After the first few bruises you pick up on the blue to the right of the cable car serviced by a comfortable chair Pila is you're oyster. With only one drag lift Pila's lift system is easy to negotiate and the runs wide and well groomed. There are many English speaking instructors.

THE TOWN
The Town has no real centre and the night life's of your own making it aint no party town. The resort is purpose built but done well and although not pretty it doesn't impose itself to much on the mountain. Accommodation is often piste-side and mostly contracted to travel firms.

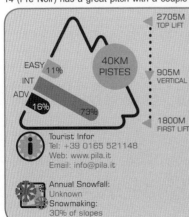

EASY 11%
INT
ADV 16%
73%

40KM
PISTES

2705M
TOP LIFT

905M
VERTICAL

1800M
FIRST LIFT

Tourist Infor
Tel: +39 0165 521148
Web: www.pila.it
Email: info@pila.it

Annual Snowfall:
Unknown
Snowmaking:
30% of slopes

Number of runs: 21
Longest run: 4.3km
Total Lifts: 14
3 Gondolas, 1 Cable-car, 9
chairs, 1 drag
Lift times:
8.30 to 4.30

Winter Period:
Dec to April
Lift Passes
Half-day 20 euros
1 day 29 euros, 6 days 162
Rental
Board & boots 18 euros per day
Lessons
Pila ski school:
5 day snowboarding lessons
(20hrs total) 145 euros
Private lessons 30 euros per hr
Guide 100 euros per day

Bus
Take the autostrada coach from Turin or Milan to Aosta. The 'Freccia delle nevi' service runs weekdays during winter from Bergamo, Milan and Genoa
Train
From Turin or Milan to Aosta via Chivasso
From the railway station: 5 minutes on foot from station to gondola in Pila (20mins)
Car
From Turin take motorway A5 towards Aosta (99km) Exit Aosta Est, then follow the regional road in the direction Pollein-Charvensod-Pila.
Fly
Turin 3 hours away. There is a small airport at Aosta

wsg PRATO NEVOSO

FREERIDE
A few trees and some off-piste
FREESTYLE
Terrain park & pipe
PISTES
Well groomed slopes

5
OUT OF 10

Good friendly resort, with a great terrain park

PRATO NEVOSO   ARTESINA   pic - Prato Nevosa Tourism

Prato Nevoso is a relatively unknown resort, yet this small and very friendly place has been operating as a ski resort since 1965, although not by any stretch of the imagination a big or adventurous hangout. Although Prato Nevoso is not a big or adventurous hangout, it is still good with some nice terrain that will please intermediate carvers and bring a smile to the face of all novices. Prato Nevoso is located close to the French border, only a stones throw from the **Mediterranean sea** in the southern part of the Alps. Despite its proximity to warm areas, this is an area with a good annual snow record with heavy snowfalls throughout the winter months. Since its birth the resort has constantly improved its facilities and is currently working on plans for new lifts which will greatly improve access and acreage of rideable snow. On its own, Prato Nevoso is tiny with only 30km of piste, however, being linked with the resort of **Aresina**, the rideable acreage rises to a respectable 100km plus. Lifts join to two resorts to form an area know as the **'Mondole Ski'** which offer a splattering of trees, some nice powder and wide open slopes.

FREERIDERS are presented with an area that will please those who like their mountains hassle free. There is option of going off piste by hiking with a pair of snow shoes and

the resort publishes a *'Free Ride'* map to help you find the best spots. You can get further advice from the local snowboard club (details available from the Surf Shop Prato Nevoso).

FREESTYLERS are well catered for with a good flood-lit terrain park of the Seggiovia lift, which packs in not only a series of killer hits, but also a halfpipe and a permanent boardercross circuit.

PISTES are well maintained, wide and sweeping, free of any rocks and uneven obstacles.

BEGINNERS have a resort that is perfect for them in every way with a good number of easy to reach novice runs.

THE TOWN

Lodging and local services are based around the mountain with a number of hotels offering direct slope access. Overall, this is not an expensive resort unless you want it to be. You can bed down in the pricey *Hotel Galassia* or flake out in one of the inexpensive apartments. The village has an array of amenities from a pharmacy, to a mini golf course. There is also a number of okay restaurants, bars and night-clubs to check out.

EASY
INT
ADV
100KM
PISTES
10%   40%   50%

2100M
TOP LIFT

730M
VERTICAL

1330M
FIRST LIFT

Number of runs: 16
Longest run: 4.5km
Total Lifts: 30
10 chairs, 20 drags
Lifts Capacity (people per hour): 9,500
Lift times:
8.30am to 4.30pm

Winter Period:
Dec to April
Lift Passes
Half-day 18.5 euros
1 Day 26 euros
6 Day pass 126 euros
Night boarding
Open until 11pm, terrain park and 2 pistes lit.
Board Schools
Private 30 euros per hour
Group 2hr/6 days 120 euros

Annual Snowfall:
6m
Snowmaking:
7 Snow Cannons

Bus
Weekends from Mondovi, 09.00 & 15.15 to Prato
Fly
to Turin airport which is 1 hour away.
Train
to Mondovi, 30 minutes from resort.
www.trenitalia.com
Car
via Turin, head south on the auto route A6 and turn off at signs for Mondovi. From here follow the signs to the resort. Total distance 62 miles (100km).

Prato Nevoso Tourism
Piazza Mirtilli 25-12083
Prato Nevoso
Tel: +39 (0) 174 334 130
Web:www.pratonevoso.com
www.pratonevososki.it
Email: associazioneturistica@pratonevo
so.com

wsg ROCCARASO

POOR FAIR GOOD TOP

FREERIDE
Lots of trees but no real off-piste

FREESTYLE
Sometimes two parks

PISTES
Some wide well pisted slopes

5
OUT OF 10

Overall okay, but basic

pic -Roccaraso Tourism

I T A L Y

East of **Rome**, in the region of **Abruzzo**, lies the mountain range of the **Apennines**. This range is home to a number of small areas collectively titled Roccaraso which was moulded into a ski resort in the 1950s and has been something of a national secret ever since. This place doesn't show up in your average travel brochure and due to this you don't find many foreigners here. In fact, during the week you might find it very quiet on the slopes, but at the weekend, expect a deluge of Romans and Neapolitans sporting the most lurid all in one ski suits and large lift queues. There is nothing really challenging here, especially if the lack of altitude results in a lack of snow. However, the pistes are well maintained, and anyone who does find themselves in a lift queue can at least have fun mocking skiers in an array of sad outfits.

FREERIDERS will find a range of terrain to cover. Pistes are varied but will suffice more for those in the beginner or intermediate category than for advanced riders. There's little in the way of natural hits or off piste powder fields, but the low altitude means there are plenty of trees around (ie;

Monte Pratello). Many of these are tightly packed though, and as such, inaccessible to many.

FREESTYLERS are blessed with two parks (off lifts 1 and 22) if there is enough snow out of which to build them or if the pisteurs can be arsed, whichever comes sooner. Otherwise take your shovel and build yourself a kicker or two.

PISTES. Speed heads will revel in the knowledge that the pistes are kept well groomed and that there's not a mogul in sight. There are a few steep runs available and many of these are pretty wide.

BEGINNERS will find this a great place to get started. Plenty of easy runs on the lower slopes mean that you don't have to take the lift to the top to find what you need. There are gentle runs down from most of the lifts, however, the majority of the reds aren't over threatening so these will be handy as you progress.

THE TOWN
The good news is that it is not over expensive here. There is lift-side accommodation at Aremogna, but the town of Roccaraso, a short drive down the hill, is where most of the visitors stay. This is also where the very limited nightlife occurs. Italians are not big drinkers and this reflects in the town's social scene. There are a couple of nightclubs, *Bilba* and *Jambo*, but most of the activity goes on within the confines of the hotels.

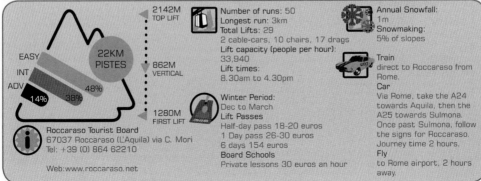

2142M
TOP LIFT

862M
VERTICAL

1280M
FIRST LIFT

EASY
INT
ADV

22KM PISTES

48%
14%   38%

Number of runs: 50
Longest run: 3km
Total Lifts: 29
2 cable-cars, 10 chairs, 17 drags
Lift capacity (people per hour):
33,940
Lift times:
8.30am to 4.30pm

Winter Period:
Dec to March
Lift Passes
Half-day pass 18-20 euros
1 Day pass 26-30 euros
6 days 154 euros
Board Schools
Private lessons 30 euros an hour

Annual Snowfall:
1m
Snowmaking:
5% of slopes

Train
direct to Roccaraso from Rome.
Car
Via Rome, take the A24 towards Aquila, then the A25 towards Sulmona. Once past Sulmona, follow the signs for Roccaraso. Journey time 2 hours.
Fly
to Rome airport, 2 hours away.

Roccaraso Tourist Board
67037 Roccaraso (L'Aquila) via C. Mori
Tel: +39 (0) 864 62210

Web:www.roccaraso.net

Modern resort with some good off-piste

POOR FAIR GOOD TOP

FREERIDE
Lots of trees and good off-piste

FREESTYLE
Nothing man made just god made

PISTES
Well groomed fast slopes

5
OUT OF 10

pic -San Sicario Tourism

Sansicario is a low level and modern purpose built resort that forms part of the vast **Vialattea** area which includes the neighbouring Italian resorts of **Sauze D'Oux, Sestriere, Cesana, Claviere** and the popular neighbouring French resort of **Montgenevre**. All these resorts link fairly well on the slopes by lifts and via the pistes, they also share a joint lift pass should you want to venture farther a field rather than staying on the local slopes. Sansicario is one of the resorts being used in the **Winter Olympics** this year, so make sure you check these dates before booking up. From the **9th January 06** the competition slopes will be closed, and from the 30th to **February 26th** all the pistes are due to be closed. After then things should be back to normal. In general what you have here is a popular resort which attracts a lot of Italians to its slopes through out the winter season period. And they are attracted to this place because of the diverse terrain, the sunny slopes good

choice of challenging runs that includes some excellent off-piste riding much of which in and out of trees and across big powder bowls. Sansicario boast some 40 marked out trails which are mainly rated as red runs for intermediate riders. However, the Vialattea has hundreds of runs for all levels, so no one is going to feel left out here. You can ride with some ease from the top station all the way back down to the resort base, although total novices won't find it an easy thing to do, as the top runs are mainly all intermediate slopes with a couple of black trails here and there.

FREERIDERS will be able to come here knowing that this place will put them to the test in many ways, with a great choice of different terrain features to choose from. They will also be able to arrive knowing that a weeks visit here and across the **Vialattea** will not be enough to see all and ride out all the terrain laid out for you. If you're into trees and off-piste terrain then you will be well satisfied here.

FREESTYLERS may find the initially offerings around Sansicario a little tame. But first impressions can be deceiving, because if you look out you will find loads of good natural spots for getting big airs. There are some cool gullies to check out and loads of hits formed by some of the un-even terrain features that make up this mountain. The nearest terrain park is in **Sestriere**

PISTES. The abundance of fast and well pisted red runs that make up Sansicario slopes are idea for laying out big turns on.

BEGINNERS are the one group that may find this place a little off putting, as only a small percentage of the runs are rated for novices, and those runs that are grade blue for beginners are limited to a few sections at the lower areas off the dreaded drag lifts.

THE TOWN
Sansicario is a good winter holiday destination with well appointed hotels and guest houses good restaurants and shops but alas rather dull night life

I
T
A
L
Y

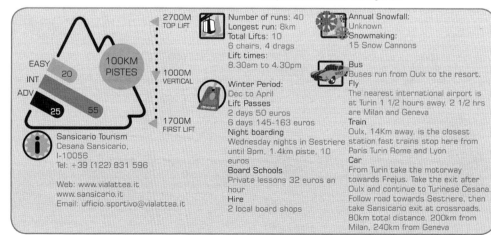

2700M TOP LIFT	Number of runs: 40 Longest run: 8km Total Lifts: 10 6 chairs, 4 drags Lift times: 8.30am to 4.30pm

EASY 20
INT
ADV
25   55

100KM PISTES

2700M TOP LIFT

1000M VERTICAL

1700M FIRST LIFT

Number of runs: 40
Longest run: 8km
Total Lifts: 10
6 chairs, 4 drags
Lift times:
8.30am to 4.30pm

Winter Period:
Dec to April
Lift Passes
2 days 50 euros
6 days 145-163 euros
Night boarding
Wednesday nights in Sestriere
until 9pm, 1.4km piste, 10
euros
Board Schools
Private lessons 32 euros an
hour
Hire
2 local board shops

Annual Snowfall:
Unknown
Snowmaking:
15 Snow Cannons

Bus
Buses run from Oulx to the resort.
Fly
The nearest international airport is
at Turin 1 1/2 hours away. 2 1/2 hrs
are Milan and Geneva
Train
Oulx, 14Km away, is the closest
station fast trains stop here from
Paris Turin Rome and Lyon
Car
From Turin take the motorway
towards Frejus. Take the exit after
Oulx and continue to Turinese Cesana.
Follow road towards Sestriere, then
take Sansicario exit at crossroads.
80km total distance, 200km from
Milan, 240km from Geneva

Sansicario Tourism
Cesana Sansicario,
I-10056
Tel: +39 (122) 831 596

Web: www.vialattea.it
www.sansicario.it
Email: ufficio.sportivo@vialattea.it

wsg SAUZE D'OULX

POOR FAIR GOOD TOP

FREERIDE
Lots of trees and some off-piste
FREESTYLE
No park, but some natural
PISTES
Some good fast slopes

Okay resort for all

6
OUT OF 10

pic - Sauze D'Oux Tourism

S auze d' Oulx is a resort that clubs together with a host of other areas to form one of the biggest rideable areas in Europe, known as the **Milky Way.** The resort plays host to the freestyle skiing competions during the **2006 Winter Olympics** between the 10th and 26th February. Check that the resort is open for regular use if you're looking to head there from January.

Located in the north west of Italy, Sauze doesn't have the greatest snow record, but does have a long history as a holiday camp style resort, the sort of place where certain low lifes come to get drunk near the snow. In truth, things aren't quite as bad as they sound and nowadays the place is inhabited by more Italians than package groups from afar. At one end of the Milky way is Sauze d' Oulx, perched at 1500m and at the other end is **Montgeneve** in France, which together offer over 285 miles of rideable terrain, linked by a hectic lift system covered by a single pass. This vast area that takes in the slopes of **Sauze, Sansicario, Borgata, Sestrieres, Claviere and Montgenevre** provides an area of mostly intermediate and beginner terrain, with enough stuff for advanced riders to take on. There are a few black graded knuckle rides up on the Borgata and Sestrieres area to test the best, particularly freeriders. The biggest cluster of runs are found on Sauze d' Oulx' own slopes, where intermediate freeriders will find loads of interconnecting red runs that weave through tight trees.

FREERIDERS looking for good off-piste won't be

disappointed, with many runs leading through dense trees. The **Rio Nero** is a long favourite off piste trail that bases out at the road between **Oulx** and **Cesana**, but does entail a bus ride back to the lifts.

FREESTYLERS have loads of natural hits to get air from, but you wouldn't call this a freestyler's hangout.

PISTES. You will find a staggering amount of good carving runs to ride in Sauze, making this a particularly good alpine resort.

BEGINNERS will get on well, but note that there are dozens of drag lifts and instruction is nothing to shout about.

THE TOWN
Resorts don't come much more basic than Sauze, although in a strange way, it all adds to the place and if you are out for a cheap time, this is where you'll get it. Lodging here is cheap in apartments and evenings are very lively, with pub upon pub and loads of good eating haunts making this place not so much a tacky hole but rather an okay place to visit. For a beer, check out the likes of *Paddy McGinty's* (full on Italian name or what!) or the *Banditos* disco for a late night drink, dance and some holiday skirt!

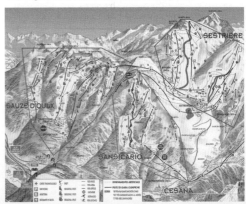

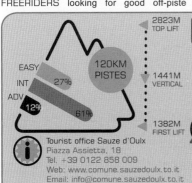

2823M
TOP LIFT

1441M
VERTICAL

1382M
FIRST LIFT

120KM
PISTES

EASY
INT 27%
ADV 12%
61%

Number of runs: 40
Longest run: 4km
Total Lifts: 22
11 chairs, 11 drags
Lift capacity (people per hour):
18,000
Lift times:
8.30am to 4.30pm

Winter Period:
Dec to April
Lift Passes
2 days 50 euros
6 days 145-163 euros

Annual Snowfall:
Unknown
Snowmaking:
40% of slopes

Train
to Oulx which is 5 minutes away.
Bus
Regular bus service from Oulx train station. Coach services on www.sapav.it
Car
via Turin, head north west on the A32 towards Bardonecchia-Frejus. At tollgate at Oulx take the road to Sauze d'Oulx
Fly
to Turin, 1hr away. Local airport is Torino

Tourist office Sauze d'Oulx
Piazza Assietta, 18
Tel. +39 0122 858 009
Web: www.comune.sauzedoulx.to.it
Email: info@comune.sauzedoulx.to.it

ITALY

usg VAL GARDENA

POOR FAIR GOOD TOP

FREERIDE
Lots of trees and good off-piste
FREESTYLE
Park & pipe
PISTES
Lots of well groomed slopes

Good mix of terrain to suit most

8 OUT OF 10

pic

Val Gardena is located in the northern area of the Dolomites and forms a collection of resorts and mountain slopes that is said to be the largest snowboarding area in the world. There is a staggering 600 miles of marked trails and are serviced by some 460 lifts of all shapes and styles these can be utilised by the **Dolomiti Superski** pass. A limited pass called the Val Gardena still covers 175km of piste with 82 lifts. Val Gardena has the unfortunate history of being the place where a particularly sad Brit with a Russian name achieved a so called top ski result (who gives a toss). However, this is not a sad place to snowboard, it's actually very good, with something for everyone. Val Gardena is a huge valley, housing three main villages and a handful of satellite hamlets. And truly, if you can't ride here and enjoy yourself, then you must be a closeted synchronised swimmer or worse, a downhill skier with a nice shiny medal! The main villages are **Ortisei** (the biggest town in the area), **Oritsei** and **Selva** .Wherever you choose to stay, you can move around the resort via a regular shuttle bus service. The well set out

mass of lifts don't connect up everywhere, but with a piste map you can get around a very large portion of it without too many problems. Try the circuit ride known as the **Sella Ronda**, which takes you around 15 miles of lift connected runs.

FREERIDERS on the whole find Val Gardena a cool place to ride, with a good mixture of terrain features from trees to banks and wind lips. The best off-piste riding can be had in areas like **Passo Pordoi**, but its best tackled with the services of a local guide.

FREESTYLERS will find that the okay fun park and half-pipe, located on **Alpe di Siusi** is the place to hang out and get some air. If you're there at the right time you could also be riding to tunes by top DJ's. Theres also 2 boardcross circuits at **Passo Sella** and **Comici/Piz Sella**

CARVERS of all levels will find millions of well pisted trails to get their fix from. Runs criss cross all over the area and no rider will see all of them in a week's trip, or even two.

BEGINNERS who can't learn to snowboard here must be clueless idiots; this place is a first timer's heaven. The runs up above **Ortisei** are full-on, perfect nappy territory.

THE TOWN
Accommodation and evenings are very Italian, with loads of good options in the main villages or at one of the smaller hamlets, which will have cheaper places to sleep and hang out. **Eating** and other local happenings are much the same wherever you are: all are laid back and okay.

ITALY

EASY
INT 30%
ADV 10% 60%

175KM PISTES

2518M TOP LIFT

1458M VERTICAL

1060M FIRST LIFT

Val Gardena Tourist Office
Tourist Office Val Gardena
Str. Dursan 80 c
I - 39047 S. Cristina
phone +39 0471 792277
fax +39 0471 792235
Web: www.val-gardena.com
www.valgardena.it
Email:info@valgardena.it

Number of runs: 75
Longest run: 10km
Total Lifts: 83
7 Gondolas, 2 cable-cars, 44 chairs, 29 drags
Lifts capacity (people per hour) :
109,300
Lift times:
8.30am to 4.30pm

Winter Period:
Dec to April
Lift Passes
1 day: 35 - 38 euros
6 days: 180 - 194 euros
Hire
board from 16 euros /day
boots from 7 euros/day

Annual Snowfall:
2.5m
Snowmaking:
95% of slopes

Fly
to Verona airport 2 hours away.
Train
to Bolzano which is 60 minutes away.
Car
From Bolzano, head north on the A22 and turn off at Bressanone taking the E66 towards Brunico and turning off on to the B244 to the resort area

NEW

New for 05/06 season
2 person chairlift between Vallunga and Danterceppies. New 4 person chairlift in nearby Mont Seura

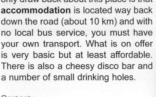

ALAGNA VALSESIA

Small resort with directly only 5 lifts but backs onto the Monterosa Ski area (see Gressony). From the top of the Punta Indren back into the village gives you access to 2000m of vertical off-piste terrain with some steep decents and couliors. A guide will set you back 240 euros for a day but is essential if you want to find some of the best areas (www. lyskammviaggi.com)

Top Lift: 3260m
List pass:
Half day pass 23 euros
Day pass 32 euros
6 days pass 170 euros
Contact:
www.alagna.it
How to get there: Fly to:
90 minutes from Milan airport, 110km
Drive:From Milan, leave motorway at Novara Ovest or the A26 junction at Biandrate for Gravellona Toce and follow the signs for Romagnano-Ghemme. Then follow the main road SS299 to Alagna.

only draw back about this place is that **accommodation** is located way back down the road (about 10 km) and with no local bus service, you must have your own transport. What is on offer is very basic but at least affordable. There is also a cheesy disco bar and a number of small drinking holes.

Contact:
Corno alle Scale Tourist Office
Pzza Marconi,
6 -40042-Lizzano in Belvedere (Bo)
Tel - 0534 50105
How to get there: Fly to: Bologna 1 hour away

GRESSONEY

Located in the Aosta Valley, Gressony is the neighbour to nearby Champoluc, with heaps of pisted terrain between the two resorts. The large amount of off-piste terrain here, offers a lot of big drop-ins, gullies and wide open bowls to please all freeriders. For carvers, there are ample wide

Alagna & Gressoney pistes

CORNO ALLE SCALE

This is not a resort that many people would have heard of, but its worth a mention and even a visit, especially if you fancy a night out in the nearby town of Bologna. Corno Alle Scale has plenty of terrain to suit all standards with some gnarly off-piste for freeriders to bury themselves in. This is not a place for novices who like everything on hand, likewise freestylers looking for a host of man made hits will be disappointed. The

spaces. Beginners have loads of easy flats to get hold of. Local facilities are very good and close to the slopes with some cheap options for lodging, eating and partying late at night.

Ride area: 200km
Top Lift: 2661m
Total Lifts:46
Contact:
Tel - +39 (125) 307113
Fax - +39 (125) 307785
Snow Phone - +39 (125) 307113
www.gressoney.com
Get there: Fly to: Turin 1 hour away

MERAN 2000
Resort in the South Tirol area of Italy, 7 lifts accessing 40km of pistes

www.meran2000.net

OBEREGGEN
20 minutes from Bozen in the South Tirol lies the resort of Obereggen. 17 modern lifts provide access to 40km of mainly intermediate pistes which forms part of the Dolmite Superski area. Theres a park next to the Pampeago piste comprising of 3 kickers and a variety of rails. Off the Toler piste is also a 80m halfpipe. Tues, thur, fri theres night boarding until 10pm. New for 2006 season is a 6 seater chair

www.obereggen.com

PINZOLO
Linked with Madonna Di Campiglio, this small resort has 9 lifts servicing 11 pistes. There is a very small terrain park. A day pass is 23 euros

www.pinzolo.it

PIANCAVALLO
Piancavallo is a tiny purpose built resort and not unsightly. There is

only a handful of runs that are split between beginner and intermediate level and nothing for advanced riders apart form a single graded black trail. Freestylers have a pipe. This is a simple piste loving carvers place through and through. Chalet accommodation and good services are slope side

Ride area: 24km
Top Lift: 1829m
Total Lifts:18
Contact:
Tourist Office
Piazzale,Della Puppa
Loc Piancavallo,33081 Aviano
Tel: 0434655191
Fax: 0434655354
www.piancavallo.com
How to get there: Fly to: Venice 3 hours away

SANTA CATERINA

Santa Caterina is a resort that will appeal to sedate riders. The resort is linked to Bormio as part of the Alta Valtellina ski area and gives you access to over 100km of pistes, 40km of them locally. The resort was improved for the 2005 season, with a new slope, Edelweiss developed especially for the FIS Alpine World Ski Championships in January. **Freeriders** may be able to find some okay backcountry riding but its very limited and will only please intermediate riders.**Freestylers** have a half-pipe, but its not always looked after. **Carvers** just out for a simple day's piste riding will be at home, even granny could have a go. Fine for **beginners** but not a great choice of runs. Slope side services are good and affordable

Ride area: 40km
Heights: 1738-2800m
Total Lifts:18
Lift pass: Day pass 29 euros, 6 days 143
Contact:
www.santacaterina.it

SELLA NEVA

Sella Neva is a small resort in the north eastern corner of Italy bordering Slovenia and Austria. This is a popular carvers resort as well as offering some excellent freeridng and natural freestyle terrain. You can shred some trees at speed, go waste deep in powder or fly off endless cliffs. The fun park contains a half-pipe and is located off the Gilberti lift. This is also a good beginners resort. Sella Nevea is a good cheap resort with basic services.

SESTRIERE

Sestriere offers the potential for some great advanced riding both on and off piste, with a vast amount of terrain to explore in this part of the Milky Way. Freeriders will find a good choice of challenging runs and some excellent off piste. Freestylers are not well catered for but you will still find some interesting natural hits. Carvers have acres of good terrain. Beginners should not want for much more than you get here. Off piste services are affordable and close to the slopes

SULDEN

This high altitude resort reaches up to 3250m from the village base at 1900m. For your 27.5 euros a day you get access to 40km of pistes including an 11km top to bottom run, when theres enough snow theres also a halfpipe

Ride area: 40km
Heights: 1900-3250m
Total Lifts:11 - 1 gondola, 5 chairs, 5 drags
Contact:
Solda Office:
Hauptstraße 72
I - 39029 Sulden (BZ)
Tel. +39 0473 737060
www.sulden.com
How to get there: 150km from Innsbruck, nearest railway station is Landeck or Merano with local buses taking you the remainder

VAL DI SOLE

Large linked area of four skiing resorts, Folgarida, Marilleva, Pejo and Passo Tonale

VAL SENALES

Val Senales is situated 20km from the town of Naturns in Italys South Tirol. The Schnals Valley Glacier guarantees snow year-round with 8km of slopes open in the summer months and a good park. In the winter the area extends to 13 lifts servicing 15 runs (35km of pistes in total). The Roter Kofel and Teufelsegg chairs provide access to some steep black runs back into the village, alternatively take the Hochjochferner gondola, and cruise back down on the 8km run. In the summer theres a good park on the top of the glacier

www.valsenales.com

How to get there: From Innsbruck take the brenner pass follow the A22 to Sterzing, continue and take the Bozen Süd exit and take the Meran turn off. Continue to Naturns then take the valley road through Schnalstal to resort.

pic -WSG , Shinjuku Tokyo

reasons for the popularity of night riding must be the lack of a party scene.

You will see a lot of riders on their knees looking up-slope in semi-pose mode while wearing the latest gear. The majority of those you meet will be ready to try out their conversational English on you and most can say a few words although whether they can understand you is a different matter.

Lift passes generally cost between 4,000 yen (£20) and 5,000 yen (£25) per day and are only slightly discounted if you purchase more than a days worth. Passes can be bought with cash at the resort, or just as easily at convenience stores all over country. (Lawson, AM-PM, 7-Eleven and Family Mart are the main ones). These stores usually produce a pamphlet listing the resorts they offer passes for. Their prices, which include 1,500 yen or so worth of lunch vouchers, are better value than buying at the resorts themselves.

TRAVELLING AROUND:

Train - Japan's train service is excellent (frequent, clean, on time) but expensive if you buy your tickets in Japan. The Rail Pass can be bought for 7, 14 or 21 day periods from your local tour operator before you travel to Japan. Prices are approximately £150, £220, £280. This is one of the best deals you will get so seriously consider this option. The pass includes unlimited travel on the world renowned bullet trains (shinkansen).

Car - If you want to hire a car you'll have to bring your International Driver's License. One difficulty will be the language, because working out the insurance terms will be a nightmare. The cheapest cars can be hired from large companies such as Toyota, Nippon and ORIX from 6000 yen a day but these are dinky toys big enough for only two.

Japan Travel: tel (03-3502-1461 (00 88 22-2800 from the

For a country the size of Japan its pretty incredible to think there are over 600 resorts dotted throughout the country, with snowboarders welcome pretty much everywhere these days. Many of the resorts are tiny with only a lift or two, but there's also some resorts to rival Europe and N.America, after all the country did hold the 1998 Winter Olympics in Nagano, Boarders are generally well taken care of with many of the resorts are building terrain parks and pipes. Snowboarding in Japan has been greatly influenced by the European scene. Most lift systems are Swiss or Austrian in make and the term 'ski area' is known as the 'Ski Gelande' (taken from German). A lot of resorts, restaurants and shops also take French or German names. Night-riding is big in Japan and almost all resorts offer some kind of flood-lit runs. One of the

Capital City: Tokyo
Population: 127.3 Million
Highest Peak: Fujiyama 3776 m
Language: Japanese
Legal Drink Age: 18
Drug Laws: Cannabis is illegal
Age of consent: 16
Electricity: 100 Volts AC 2-pin
International Dialing Code: +81

Japan Snowboard Association
Nac Shibuya Building 4F
15-10 Nanpeidai
Shibuya-ku
Tokyo 150
Tel - +81 (0) 3 5458 2661
Web: www.so-net.ne.jp/jsba

Japan Tourist Information
10 Fl., Tokyo Kotsu Kaikan Bldg.,
2-10-1, Yurakucho, Chiyoda-ku, Tokyo 100-0006
Tel:(03)3201-3331   Fax:(03)3201-3347
www.jnto.go.jp

Time Zone
UTC/GMT +9
No daylight saving changes

Currency: Yen (JPY)
Exchange Rate:
UK£1 = 196
EURO = 132
US$1 = 110

Driving Guide
All vehicles drive on the right hand side of the road
Speed limits:
40kmh towns, 80kmh Expressways
Emergency
Police 110, Fire/Ambulance 119
Tolls
Expressways charge per km. Approximate cost from Tokyo to (near) Hokkaido 14,000 yen
Documentation
International Driver's Licence not required, but must carry home driving licence.

UK) is an excellent English language phone service that can tell you anything you want to know concerning transport (fares and timetables) or accommodation. It will even help with language problems.

THE SEASON

Japan, especially the north island of **Hokkaido** gets plenty of snow. Its location puts it in the path of the cold air stream that comes off Hokkaido. Before reaching Japan, the air stream picks up its moisture over the Japan Sea then dumps when it hits the Japan Alps running up the west coast. From January through till March you can expect to have 3m base in most of the serious resorts. Several of the **Honshu** resorts boast a season from October till May, but it's only really in Hokkaido where you can expect to find any decent conditions as late as this. In fact none of the resorts are seriously running until mid-December but a few, in the name of good publicity, spend their money on creating a long strip of 'snow' on a shallow slope and declare themselves open at the end of October. At this time it's still pretty hot and humid.

Basically you have a good 3-4 month period to check things out although you are seriously advised to avoid the slopes at the beginning of January. During the first week of the year the Japanese have a long national holiday granted by most companies - it's as crowded as hell.

Riding off-piste: There are certain resorts, maybe a majority, in Japan where snowboarding is mainly a fashion statement and Tokyoites go for their one day on the slopes every year. These places tend to be pretty strict in the way they control boarding. Often some lifts are still (the number gets fewer every year) closed to boarders and any off piste will be fenced off and patrolled. On the other hand there are a few areas where the resorts really do cater for the more hardened rider and ski/board patrol will even tell you which backcountry areas are good/safe, and you may meet some locals to ride off with.

Wherever you go, those of you always looking to 'cut the fresh' will be pleased to know that you'll probably find yourself alone, carving the ivory. Japanese are very compliant, so 99% wouldn't dream of leaving the slopes for a little off-piste. There are ski-patrols of course but they are fairly inconspicuous, so the chances of you being whistled at are really slim.

ACCOMMODATION

Accommodation in Japan doesn't boast any great deals when it comes to somewhere to put your head for the night. Resort hotels are very popular with the Japanese, who will pay through the nose for a room with a view. The advise is to avoid the western style hotels and go for a traditional Japanese inn (**Ryokan**) or a family-run hotel (**Minshuku**). Both are usually reasonably priced (nice tatami-mat rooms for 7000 yen including evening meal and breakfast are possible) and you get the added feel of authenticity. Normally very small, these hotels are typically

very Japanese in style-tatami-mat floors, table heaters, futon, yukata (traditional bath robe) and slippers all make up what can be a very pleasant cultural experience when you're off the slope. The Japanese are quiet lot and for the most part you'll find the staff are extremely welcoming and helpful.

FOOD

The food in Japanese inns is great and usually traditional, but you'll sometimes even find some western foods on your plate - omelette and ham often appear at breakfast time. If you can stomach fish, rice and natto (curdled soy beans) in the morning, all power to you- it's a great way to prepare the body for the day's onslaught on the slopes.

Resort food, is usually pretty varied although there seems to be a 'standard' menu which you'll find at pretty much every resort. Meals range from western snacks like hotdogs and fries to Japanese noodle and rice dishes. Recommended is the quintessentially Japanese ski lunch of curry, pork cutlet and rice, washed down with a can of Asahi Superdry, Japan's premium beer. All for about 1500 yen, usually obtained by exchanging a ticket bought at a vending machine (jidoo hanbaiki). Look lost and forlorn if confused - someone will help you! For those you like to pig out big style, will find that some resorts offer all-you-can-eat (viking) deals for around 1500-2000 yen, which allows you to stuuf down various strange fish and traditional noodle dishes.

POOR FAIR GOOD TOP

FREERIDE
Trees & great off-piste
FREESTYLE
4 Terrain parks & pipe
PISTES
Well groomed slopes

Powder, awesome backcountry & amazing night riding

8
OUT OF 10

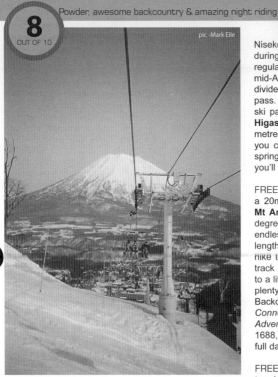

pic -Mark Eile

Niseko gets on average a good 11m of light dry powder, so during the months of January and February you can expect regular and major dumps and you can often still be riding in mid-April. Niseko is essentially one mountain although it is divided up into three linked areas covered by one mountain pass. This area does have avalanches so check with the ski patrols to get the latest info. The tops of **Annupuri**, **Higashiyama**, and **Hirafu** are all within a few hundred metres hike of the top of the mountain (1308m). From here you can ride down backcountry to **Goshiki Onsen** (hot springs) on the opposite side of the mountain. To get back you'll need a taxi or the infrequent bus.

FREERIDERS should head straight to the peak. After a 20min hike from the top chair you reach the peak of **Mt Annupuri**. From here your options are close to 360 degrees with views from volcano to sea. The terrain is endless with open powder bowls, trees and gullies. The length of your ride is governed by how far you want to hike to get back inbounds. The hike back is along a cat track however some runs off the peak can get you back to a lift without hiking. The backcountry is sensational with plenty to choose from all within easy access of the resort. Backcountry tours are available from *Niseko Powder Connection* +81-136-21-2500 or the *Niseko Outdoor Adventure Sports* Club (www.noasc.com) tel +81 136-23-1688, which has a shop and office near the Hirafu base. A full day will set you back 7000-8000 yen

FREESTYLERS are well catered for with 1 halfpipe and 4 terrain parks. The terrain parks range from pro to beginner and are well made and maintained with a good variety of hits and rails. Also if you look hard enough you will find plenty of hits built by enthusiastic locals.

Located between a volcano and the Japan Sea, Niseko is the best of the Japanese resorts and compares well with resorts in North America and Europe. **Niseko** is mostly a freeriders resort and the main attraction has to be its big mountain terrain, however it also has 4 terrain parks incredible night riding and a modern lift system; definitely a great place to ride.

PISTES. Riders can take advantage of the 900m of vertical Niseko-Hirafu has to offer. There are plenty of long wide runs especially heading towards the **Hanazono** area. The

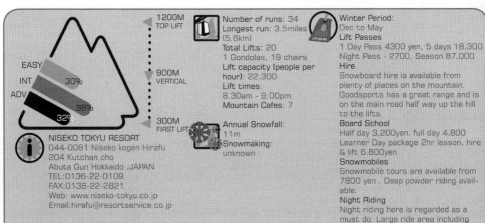

EASY

INT 30%

ADV

38%

32%

1200M
TOP LIFT

900M
VERTICAL

300M
FIRST LIFT

Number of runs: 34
Longest run: 3.5miles
(5.6km)
Total Lifts: 20
1 Gondolas, 19 chairs
Lift capacity (people per hour): 22,300
Lift times:
8.30am - 9.00pm
Mountain Cafes: 7

Annual Snowfall:
11m
Snowmaking:
unknown

NISEKO TOKYU RESORT
044-0081 Niseko kogen Hirafu
204 Kutchan cho
Abuta Gun Hokkaido ,JAPAN
TEL:0136-22-0109
FAX:0136-22-2821
Web: www.niseko-tokyu.co.jp
Email:hirafu@resortservice.co.jp

Winter Period:
Dec to May
Lift Passes
1 Day Pass 4300 yen, 5 days 18,300
Night Pass - 2700, Season 87,000
Hire
Snowboard hire is available from plenty of places on the mountain. Goodsports has a great range and is on the main road half way up the hill to the lifts.
Board School
Half day 3,200yen, full day 4,800
Learner Day package 2hr lesson, hire & lift 6,800yen
Snowmobiles
Snowmobile tours are available from 7800 yen . Deep powder riding available.
Night Riding
Night riding here is regarded as a must do. Large ride area including tree runs and terrain parks, till 9pm every day

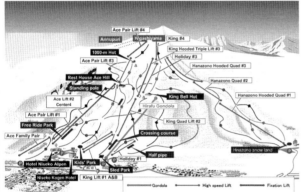

well groomed terrain provides awesome runs for everyone from beginner to experts.

BEGINNERS can start on their own slope without feeling in the way and then slowly graduate up the mountain at their own leisure. With easy runs available from top to bottom beginners can also enjoy the 900m of vertical Niseko-Hirafu has to offer.

THE TOWN

Accommodation is found in the village directly below the lifts and ranges from five star hotels to family owned

pensions. Most of the accommodation is fairly affordable, especially if you have a group of four or more.

Food in Niseko-Hirafu is excellent. There are some western style places and even a *KFC* if you feel the need. However most of the restaurants are Japanese. But the variety of local traditional places is superb with each one creating its own unique atmosphere. The bu-cha bar & restaurant is a great place to go for a meal or just to have a cheeky one off the wood. *Hank's* a cosy little cabin where Hank cooks up meals on an open fire and *Big Cliff* serves great food and is open late. There is also a couple of mini marts for groceries and alcohol. There are more options in the town of **Kutchan** (15 mins away)

Nightlife is rather laidback but can get amped up at certain times of the year if you know where the parties are. Plenty of bars to choose from and most are open to the early hours if you're feeling thirsty. *Fatty's bar* is two trucks parked together to create a unique bar.

CAR
Sapporo to resort is 102.1km, approx 2 1/2hrs drive Take nakayama pass(route230) for 66km, then Kyougoku (route276) for another 30km, then (route 343) to resort.
FLY
International flights available to and from Chitose Airport, Sapporo approx 2 1/2hrs from resort
TRAIN
To Kutchan station, 15 mins away take a bus or taxi to resort. Kutchan to Sapporo (Hakodate Line) approx 2 hours
BUS
Bus Service from Chitose Airport, Sapporo to Niseko-Hirafu. 8 times daily 38,500 yen return

ASAHIDAKE ONSEN

Other Hokkaido Hills, are Asahidake and its located in the centre of Hokkaido with one lift and you're free to make your own route down (a major draw point in regulated Japan). There are plenty of trees and with Hokkaido's excellent snow record there is usually plenty of powder

Ride area: 100acres
Runs: 4 Longest run: 2.2km
Top Lift: 660m Bottom Lift: 140m
Total Lifts:1
Contact:
Tel: 0166-68-9111
www.asahidakeropeway.com
How to get there: You can take a bus from Asahikawa Station (4 per day) take Tenninkyo/Asahidake route (no. 66) from the No. 4 bus stop outside.

FURANO

pic -Furano Resort

Furano is a major summer and winter resort. It is run by the Prince Hotels Group, which offers the largest hotel slopeside. There is also plenty of accommodation to be had in the town. It can be reached by bus from either Sapporo or Asahikawa (the nearest airport). This place is one of Japan's most famous ski areas and has hosted World Cup ski events. There's a big night skiing area, plenty of trees and natural hits for freeriders and also long groomed runs for carvers. In the centre of Hokkaido it is known to get very cold in January which means the powder usually remains fine.

Top Lift: 1209m Bottom Lift: 250m
Total Lifts:17 Runs: 12
Contact: http://www.princehotels.co.jp/furano-e

How to get there: Furano station - 10 mins away, 60 minutes from Asahikawa Airport. Buses available from Sapporo and take 3 hours

NISEKO KOKUSAI MOIWA

Niseko Kokusai Moiwa is a cheaper and much smaller resort on a lower peak just to the west of the main mountain. It is probably only worth a trip if you have more than 3 or 4 days in the area, but it is reputed to offer some great backcountry riding

Ride area: 8 runs
Top Lift: 800m Bottom Lift: 330m
Total Lifts:4
How to get there: Niseko Station - 20 mins away

SAPPORO KOKUSAI

Sapporo Kokusai is 30 minutes from Sapporo, is well set up for boarders with both a park and pipe. You can find good freeriding and some excellent riders. Japanese who decide to do a season but don't want to move to a resort itself, often take a part time job in Sapporo and spend their free time riding here. Sapporo was one of the first in Japan to actively encourage riders. The run below the gondola is fun, while a hike to the top gives access to some backcountry.

Runs: 7 Total Lifts:5
Top Lift: 630m Bottom Lift: 140m
Contact:
www.sapporo-kokusai.co.jp
How to get there: Sapporo Station - 90mins away

ARAI MOUNTAIN

Arai Mountain Resort has been running for just over 10 years and was developed by the Sony Corporation. As a result the facilities are quality, and unlike a lot of other Japanese resorts the lifts are all new and fast. It's definitely one of the best resorts on Honshu and attracts some very good riders. It often hosts rider camps in the spring and international contests. The terrain is in a bowl and even allows for a little hiking (unfortunately banned by most resorts here). There a very well kept 100m pipe but the main attraction is the powder resulting from the big dumps (04/05 season 6.5m) because of its location in the first mountain range west of the Japan Sea. This could also be seen as its main drawback as it is a long way from Tokyo. Snowboarders just edge out the number of skiers, and theres night boarding on saturday nights

Ride area: 100acres
Total runs: 11
Run difficulty: Easy 30%, Intermediate 45%, Advanced 25%
Top Lift: 1280m
Bottom Lift: 340m
Longest trail: 5.4km
Total Lifts:6
Lift passes: Day pass 4,500 yen, nightboarding 2,000 yen
Contact:
www.araimntspa.com
How to get there: To get to Arai, take the bullet train to Nagano (2 hours from Tokyo) then a local train (1hr 40mins) then a free shuttle bus (15-mins) to the slopes. All this will set you back about 90 USD in train fares, so it may be worth looking into bus tours if you don't have a rail pass

GALA YUZAWA

Conveniently located, it even has its own bullet train stop, (one along from Echigo Yuzawa) this is a modern set-up, especially popular with the younger day trippers. Here you don't have to endure a 10-minute bus journey but you will have to put up with higher prices and unfriendly staff (even a single locker costs #5).

Ride area: 126acres
Runs: 15
Top Lift: 1181m
Bottom Lift: 800m
Total Lifts:11
Contact: www.gala.co.jp
How to get there: Gala Yuzawa train

station at resort

JOETSU KOKUSAI

Joetsu Kokusai is a little further afield (30-mins by bus). It has one of the largest terrain parks (i.e. more than 4 jumps) in Japan and two good pipes. These are both in front of the Edwardian looking hotel. For freeriders the Osawa slopes are best. This is a good resort for boarders, although some of the lifts are old and slow. It is not worth visiting the peak.

MUIKAMACHI HAKKAI-SAN

Muikamachi Hakkaisan can be a powder paradise in January and February. It is an hour further west from Echigo Yuzawa (30-mins by local train to Muikamachi, then 30-mins by bus). Because of this it is usually less busy but still manageble in a day trip from Tokyo. The resort is especially popular with skiers out to enjoy the moguls, so there is usually plenty of terrain left for freeriding. Below the gondola is a 3km downhill course that will take it out of you. The No. 3 chairlift lets you enjoy a shorter workout. The Raku (easy) course allows you to cut through the thick forest and offers plenty of air points but there is no pipe or park. The area itself is one of the most famous in Japan for sake (rice wine) which you will no doubt get to taste if you stay here. In the winter 'Atsukan' (hot rice wine) is good for warming you up, it's available here and in all other resorts.

MYOKO KOHGEN

Seki Onsen is a resort, which understands the needs of the powder hounds. Near the west coast in Niigata Prefecture it has a great snow record, often with 1m plus dumps overnight in Jan/Feb. There's a decent pipe and some good natural hits and kickers. Locals or the patrol will advise you on back country riding - they'll also tell you that you have to take responsibility for yourself, although in the land of group culture it's cool to find somewhere that lets you do this. Seki Onsen is the home resort for Masanori Takeuchi, a well-known Japanese rider.

NAEBA

Naeba is perhaps the most famous resort in Honshu and more like a

western one in terms of the number of hotels and other things going on. It is a 45-mins bus journey from Echigo Yuzawa station. Snowboarding has been allowed all across the hill since the 98/99 season and they have now built their own mini park and regularly host air contests. However, there is no pipe and the resort is best for freeriders. Similarly to Niseko and Zao, you can happily enjoy three or four days here without getting bored. There are some excellent tree runs if you duck the ropes and because of the lack of Japanese who do this you're always able to make your own tracks. The best spots for doing this are below the No. 1 gondola, and of the No. 2 gondola.

Accommodation in Naeba is operated by the Prince Group, which offers a variety of modern slopeside accommodation (++81 (0) 257-89-2311). If you call in advance there are usually special deals going, including lift pass. Oji Pension (0257-89-3675) is just 5 minutes walk behind the Prince Hotel, and is run by the friendly Mr. Sakamoto. He has a stock of new rental boards and a Brazil shirt signed by Pele. A futon, breakfast and evening meal should cost around 7500 yen, and he can sort you out with lift pass discounts

http://www.princehotels.co.jp/Naeba-e/index.html

J

J
A
P
A
N

Shot: Lake Matheson pic © WSG

N
E
W

Z
E
A
L
A
N
D

New Zealand consists of two main islands, North and South. Whakapapa and Turoa are the only commercial resorts on the North Island, so most visitors will use Queenstown, Wanaka and Christchurch as a base for visiting the South Island resorts. Winter season generally lasts between June to October.

There are twelve commercially owned and operated resorts and a dozen or so 'Club Fields' run by non-profit club committees.Small, social and New Zealand made, they are a classic piece of Kiwiana and well worth while checking out. In recent years many people have rediscovered the charms and attractions of Club Fields. They are lured by the uncrowded slopes, with the spectacular setting of the Southern Alps, spread out as a back drop.

The commercial resorts have spent big over the last 5 years building parks and pipes. It is now the standard that every resort has a decent park and at least one halfpipe. This has been spured on even further with New Zealands

first dedicated terrain park resort, Snowpark, which opened a couple of seasons ago.

Taking a 'Snowboard Tour' is a good idea if you're visiting NZ for a short time, as it would help maximise your time on the mountain. There are a number of companies offering all inclusive boarding tours for New Zealand, shop around because prices are competitive.

New Zealand resorts tend to have very limited on-mountain accommodation, so you will be most likely staying in some nearby town. Naturally, these vary in size as does the night-life from the busy party towns to the quieter club fields. Queenstown has over 20 bars and clubs and is often referred to as the action and adventure capital of NZ.

NZ's international gateway airports are, Auckland and Wellington for North Island and Christchurch and Queenstowns for the South Island. The average flight time from London is 21 hours with a few stop overs.

Capital City: Wellington
Population: 4 Million
Highest Peak: Mount Cook 3764m
Language: English
Legal Drink Age: 18
Drug Laws: Cannabis is illegal and frowned upon
Age of consent: 16
Electricity: 230 Volts AC 2-pin
International Dialing Code: +64

New Zealand Snowboard Association
PO Box 18911
South New Brighton
Christchurch, New Zealand
Tel: +64 3 382 2206
Fax: +64 3 382 2106
Web: www.nzsba.co.nz
Email: nzsba@xtra.co.nz

Time Zone
UTC/GMT +12
DST +1 hr (March - Oct)

Currency: New Zealand Dollar (NZ$)
Exchange Rate:
UK£1 = 2.8
EURO = 1.9
US$1 = 1.6

Driving Guide
All vehicles drive on the left hand side of the road
Speed limits:
50kph (31mph) Towns
100kph (60mph) Motorways
Emergency
Fire/Police/Ambulance - 111
Tolls
No tolls, but check if hiring a car that its allowed on all roads
Documentation
International Driver's Licence not required, but must carry home driving licence.

Auckland

Rotorua

Wzakapapa/Turoa

Cape Farewell

Westport

★Wellington

Cape Pallister

NEW ZEALAND

Mt. Lyford

Mt. Hutt

Porter Heigzts

Ozau

mt. Dobson

Czristczurcz

Cardrona

Treble Cone

Remarkables

Snowpark Cornet Peak

Queenstown

Dunedin

N

NEW ZEALAND

Driving in NZ is an economical way to get around. If you'r e looking to drive to some resorts then you will probably need chains. A lot of the drives to the resorts are on unsealed and very dodgy dirt roads. Car hire services are available at all the airports and when hiring, ask about deals for road trips to the mountains, these can include discounts on accommodation and lift passes. Campervans are a cheap hire option with a five day hire costing from $460. As well as the usual hire companies, there are some that specialise in longer term rental for backpackers, with prices from $25 per day. More info take a look at *www. rentalz.co.nz* Do check and make sure you are allowed on certain roads with a hire care.

Bus travel in NZ is cheap and convenient, either with a local bus company or one of the majors with most resorts covered. You can travel from Queenstown to Christchurch for around $40.

Most resorts can be reached by train which is not that expensive. However, you will need to transfer by local buses, in most cases under 12 miles.

CLUB/PRIVATE FIELDS ROUND-UP

In recent years many people have rediscovered the charms and attractions of Club Fields. They are lured by the uncrowded slopes, with the spectacular setting of the Southern Alps, spread out as a back drop.

Facilities at the club fields tend to be quite modest and basic, there are no club fields with chairlifts, but some do have T- bars or platter lifts. The most common lift is the rope tow. If you contact the club offices in advance and tell them the day you wish to come, they can help arrange a ride for you by putting you in touch with someone else who is driving there. Local Ski or Snowboard Shops will sometimes have booking sheets of people who are going or want to go to a club field.

All the club fields have on-mountain lodging available. This can range from dormitory cabin style, to double rooms with en-suite. If you are planning on staying overnight on the mountain, ring ahead to check there are vacancies because often they have large groups and clubs booked in or staying and may be full up, depending on bed numbers. There are package deals available which can include accommodation, an evening meal and breakfast, and discounted day passes (and sometimes transport). There are cheaper prices staying mid-week and for a week. This is a great time to go because there is usually no one else to share the slopes with.

For day visitors, there is a cafeteria or snack shop for food. It is a good idea to bring a few of your own munchies too. There is usually a communal dining and kitchen area where you can prepare and eat food.

At some club fields you can buy alcohol (mainly beer), but supplies can run out, so if you are staying a night of more it would be rise to bring your own, if you are one of those people who need a couple of cold ones to finish the day. Check with the ski area first about their policy on alcohol.

North Island

pic: Broken River Resort

STRATFORD MOUNTAIN CLUB
Ride area: 100acres
Runs: 10
Easy 5%, Intermediate 30%,Advanced 65%
Top Lift: 1680m Bottom Lift: 1260m
Total Lifts:4 - 1 t-bar, 3 rope tows
Contact:
PO Box 3271,
New Plymouth,New Zealand
Phone: +64 027 2800 860
snow.co.nz/manganui
Location:
20km from Stratford, take the sealed access road off highway 3 for 18km, 20 min walk from carpark

South Island
All the clubfields listed below, except Erewhon, are located in the Craigieburn Mountain Range. :To get there take highway 73, which goes from Christchurch to Greymouth via Arthurs Pass. Mt Cheesman, Broken River, Temple Basin, Porter Heights (a commercial field) and Mt Olympus, have a combined sea son pass deal

HANMER SPRINGS
Easy 10%
Intermediate 60%
Advanced 30%
Hire: Available on slope
Lift passes: Day pass $5 for a member $40 otherwise
Accomodation $5 for a member, $25 otherwise. Membership $120
Total Lifts: 2
Contact:
PO Box 66
Hanmer Springs
Phone: (025) 341 806
Fax: (03) 315 7201
www.skihanmer.co.nz
Location:
Take the access road Clarence Valley road from Hamner Springs. 155km from Christchurch & Kaikoura

BROKEN RIVER
Top Lift: 1820m Bottom Lift: 1400m
Ride Area: 300 hectares
Board School: Private $42 per hour
Group lesson $20 per hour
Lift passes:Day pass $42
Overnight accomodation:
$25 - White Star Chalet
$48 - Broken River Lodge
$70 - Lyndon Lodge
Total Lifts: 5 tows
Contact:
PO Box 2718, Christchurch,New Zealand
Phone / Fax: (03) 318 7270
www.brokenriver.co.nz
Location:
1 1/2 hours west of Christchurch on State Highway 73 (the Arthur's Pass Road approx 8km past Castle Hill Village). Follow 6km access road

CRAIGIEBURN
Top Lift: 1811m Bottom Lift: 1308m
Ride Area: 101 hectares
Intermediate 55% Advanced 45%
Total Lifts: 3 rope tows
Board School: Goup lesson $20 per hour. Private lesson $30 per hour
Hire: No hire equipment available
Lift passes:Day pass $25 member, $44 non-member
Accomodation $65 non-member
$2 tow belt hire per day
Contact:
Box 2152, Christchurch
New Zealand
Tel: +64 3 365 2514
www.craigieburn.co.nz
Location:
From Christchurch take highway 73 to Craigieburn for 110Km, 1 1/2 drive time then take 6km access road

CLUB/PRIVATE FIELDS ROUND-UP

INVINCIBLE SNOWFIELDS

pics: Invincible Snowfields

Privately owned and operated area on the South Island, about 50km from Queenstown at the head of Lake Wakatipu. The resort operates on demand, and is very weather dependent, basically its run on peoples days off.

Included in the price is a helicopter to and from the area, and once there a single 700m rope tow serves the area. Overnighters can stay in the hut on the slope, theres no electricity so its candles and gas burners, and you'll need to bring your own sleeping bag.

Top: 1800m Bottom: 1500m
Total Lifts: 1 rope tow
Hire: Board & Boots $35 day
Lift passes:
Prices based on 5 people, prices drop up to 20% for larger groups
1 day $445
2 days $580 (inc overnight stay), 3 days $750
Contact:
Invincible Snowfields,
Rees Valley Station,
Glenorchy 9195, Otago,
Tel: (03) 442 9933
Email:info@invincible.co.nz
Web:www.invincible.co.nz
Location:
Glenorchy is north-west of Queenstown (50km), at the Head of Lake Wakatipu. From Glenorchy its a further 15km to the Helipad (sealed & unsealed).

MOUNT CHEESEMAN

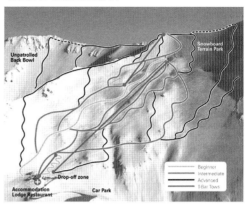

Top Lift: 1845m Bottom Lift: 1552m
Easy 15%, Intermediate 50%, Advanced 35%
Total Lifts: 3 - 2 pomos, 1 rope tows
Hire: Board & Boots $35 day
Lift passes:Group lesson $20 per hour. Private lesson $45 per hour. Beginners lesson, hire & lift pass $58 per day
Contact:
PO Box 22178
Christchurch,New Zealand
Phone: +64 3 344 3247
www.mtcheeseman.com
Location:
located in the Craigieburn Range, 112km (1.5hrs) from Christchurch on SH 73, take the 12km unsealed access road to resort sign posted 1km past Castle Hill Village

pics:Mt.Cheeseman resort

ʍsg CARDRONA

FREERIDE
No trees & some good off-piste
FREESTYLE
2 Terrain parks & 4 pipes
PISTES
Some okay slopes

7
OUT OF 10

Okay all round resort

pic: Cardrona Resort

Cardrona lies off the **Crown Range** road between **Wanaka** and **Queenstown**. Shuttle bus services operate from both towns, so it is accessible wherever you choose to base yourself. The last few seasons has seen the major NZ resorts really step up a gear in developing decent terrain parks and pipes. Cardrona being no exception with a 1000m terrain park and 4 half-pipes which for the past 2 seasons has attracted the likes of Burton to hold the NZ open there. Although this may not be in the super league of big resorts, the humble offerings here are never the less acceptable and will appeal to all levels and style of rider. If you are moved by the steep and deep then you won't be disappointed with such areas known as **Powder Keg** and **Arcadia** Chutes reached off the La Franch chair.

FREERIDERS will love it here. There is a fantastic variety of snow-gathering gullies and plenty of rocks

to throw yourself off. Keg and Arcadia are the areas where Cardrona holds it's National Extreme Championships. Records have been set by dropping down the 30 metre plus Eagle Rock in Captain's Basin, so if you're feeling suicidal this one is for you. If the runs within the boundary don't satisfy you, you could go heli-boarding in Cardrona's expansive back bowls.

FREESTYLERS are provided with a 800m boardercross course and a cool 1000m terrain park that comes loaded with a large table top, spines, jumps and rails. There are also four halfpipes including 2 superpipes, reached off the Macdougall quad chair lift. The 90m beginner's pipe has a not too intimidating 3m high wall; at the other end is the 140m Johnny Holmes Superpipe with 5m high walls.

PISTES. Riders will find either of the two main faces ideal for laying out some big turns on. The Sluge Box is a great carvers run.

BEGINNERS may find the novice slopes a bit overcrowded on weekends and during holidays. However, persevere as this is a resort that should appeal to first timers with nice beginners runs of the Macdougall quad, which allows for easy progression.

OFF THE SLOPES. life goes on in the town of **Wanaka** (20 miles), or **Queenstown** (35 miles). Wanaka is the quieter of the two and more relaxed place with a number of cool bars and plenty of cafes. Overall, prices for **accommodation** are good and affordable. If you get to know the right people you'll be able to join in on the popular past time of 'Keg' parties.

N E W Z E A L A N D

1894M
TOP LIFT

EASY
INT 25%
ADV
20% 55%

800 ACRES

390M
VERTICAL

1504M
FIRST LIFT

PO Box 117, Wanaka, New Zealand
Tel: +64 3 443 7341
Fax: +64 3 443 8818

Web: www.cardrona.co.nz
Email: info@cardrona.com

Annual Snowfall:
2.7m
Snowmaking:
none

Number of runs: 25
Longest run: 1.6km (1 mile)
Total Lifts: 7
3 chairs, 1 drag, 3 x Magic Carpets in beginners area
Lift capacity (people per hour): 7,700
Lift times:
9.00am to 4.00pm

Fly
to Christchurch 3 1/2 hours away.
Air New Zealand fly to Wanaka from Christchurch, 1 lunch time flight per day.
Queenstown is 60 minutes from Cardrona.
Wanaka is 35 minutes from Cardrona.
Bus
Pre book seats in Wanaka and Queenstown. Buses usually leave at 08:30 and return at 16:00. Prices around $25 return.
Car
From Christchurch, take routes 1,8,8A and 89. The drive time is around 3 1/2 hours. 277 miles (446km).
Queenstown is 36 miles (58km).

Winter Period:
late June to Oct
Lift Passes:
Half-day pass $52
1 Day $71, 5 Days $319
Season pass $1049
Hire:
Board & Boots NZ$46 per day
Board School
Group lessons 2hrs $37-43
Pre courses exist for those wanting to obtain NZ certification in Snowboard instruction or just improve their riding. Also pipe camps with exclusive use of one of the pipes and park technique courses. around $600-700 for a 10 day rider improvement course. Around $380 for a 5 day pipe camp (passes extra).
Heli-boarding
numerous operations in Wanaka, Queenstown and the surrounding areas. Expect to pay around $600-700 for 4 -5 drops. If you're there for the season, look out for "locals day" deals.

FREERIDE
No tree & some off-piste
FREESTYLE
Gulies, a park & 2 pipes
PISTES
Well groomed pistes

Good freeriding & park, cracking do anything town

7
OUT OF 10

pic -Coronet Peak Tourism

L ocated amid the Southern Alps and lakes of the **South Island**, Cornet Peak, on the shores of Lake Wakatipu, is only 30 minutes from the hustle and bustle of the town to **Queenstown**. Cornet which has a shared lift pass with the neighbouring resort of The Remarkables, has terrain

suitable for snowboarders of all abilities, with slopes that offer a combination of wide open pistes and well groomed trails that drop to a vert of 428 metres. The ride area is serviced by six well set out lifts and to ensure good snow cover at all times, Cornet has a multi-million dollar snowmaking system that covers from top to bottom. The low altitude here gives Cornet natural, undulating terrain with great spines and gullies for some of the best-riding available. The Cornet Express high-speed, detachable quad takes you to the summit where you gain access to some hot back bowls so loved by hard core freeriders. Check they are open though, because if you catch an avalanche and survive, it could be a long hike out when there is powder. However, it is worth it and make sure you ride the Rocky Gully T-bar.

FREERIDERS will find the runs down from the summit pretty cool, especially the M1. Advanced riders should try out the series of blacks from the summit known as the Exchange Drop, which if you don't treat with respect will make your eyes water as you do DROP. Powder hounds looking for some steep, deep, fluffy stuff need to check out the back bowls or the terrain around the Sarah Sue run, but note riding down this area does entail a hike back up to the resort to get on the lifts again.

FREESTYLERS should try out Sara Sue off Greengates for some big spine jumps, banks and natural quarter-pipes. Cornet is continually developing its terrain parks theres 2 FIS quality halfpipes and a terrain park either side of the Million Dollar run. Cornet gets pretty crowded so be careful. The patrollers, including some on snowboards, are serious about using look outs on blind jumps, especially down Exchange Drop, where you would do well to obey the No-Hit/No Jump and slow down zones to avoid any trouble.

N
N E W   Z E A L A N D

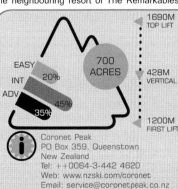

1690M
TOP LIFT

428M
VERTICAL

1200M
FIRST LIFT

700 ACRES

EASY
INT   20%
ADV
45%
35%

Number of runs: 25
Longest run: 1.8km
(1.2 miles)
Total Lifts: 6
3 chairs, 1 drag,
1 magic carpet, 1
beginner tow
Lift times:
9.00am to 4.00pm
Mountain Cafes: 3

Annual Snowfall:
Unknown
Snowmaking:
30% of slopes

Winter Period:
June to Oct
Lift Passes
Half day $51
1 Day pass - NZ$79
5 of 7 Day pass - $337
Season pass - $1699 (inc Hutt,
Oahu, Remarks)
Hire
Board & Boots NZ$51 per day, good
stuff $61
Board School
Group lessons NZ$47 1hr50. New
3hr freestyle lessons $85, starts
10:20am
Night Boarding
Mid July to mid September, Friday
and Saturday nights 4pm to 9pm
(NZ$39)
Heli-Boarding
Sweep the shops in Queenstown for
some excellent deals

Coronet Peak
PO Box 359, Queenstown
New Zealand
Tel: ++0064-3-442 4620
Web: www.nzski.com/coronet
Email: service@coronetpeak.co.nz

NEW 05: new Greengates Express six-seater chairlift, additional pistes and easier access to some off-piste. 4.5km of new snowmaking

Food. Being a big town, as one would expect, there is a massive choice of restaurants and cheap cafes in Queenstown. Every type of food is available with lots of options to eat cheaply. Notable places for a feed are; The Cow, which offers moderately priced pizza and spaghetti. Berkels Gourmet frys up a good burger, while Gourmet is good for breakfast.

Night life, in Queenstown rocks hard and late. Locals here like and know how to party hard, and if there's nothing laid on then guaranteed something will happen to set the evening off. The choice of bars is great with some good boozers, such as the Red Rock Cafe which also serves good bar food. The World Bar is also cool hangout.

PISTES. Carvers will enjoy the long blue trail known as the M1 as well as the runs known as Greengates and Million Dollar, which are pisted to perfection and great for leaving some nice long lines on.

BEGINNERS will find the best stuff is off the Meadows chair and alongside the learners poma. But there isn't a mass of novice trails here, although what is available is still good. The local ski school offers a 'Snowboard Starter' package for $60 and is well worth the money as instructors know their stuff.

N

E
W

Z
E
A
L
A
N
D

THE TOWN
After hard days riding, the next best thing is to be able to hang out in a place that offers you a good choice of accommodation, plenty of restaurants and loads of bars with varying price ranges to suite all pockets. And that is exactly what you get in **Queenstown**, a big town full of all the joys and spoils to make a week a month or even a year an eventful one. Queenstown has every possible holiday services you could want and a vast array of outdoor sport activities. You can take part in paragliding, rock climbing, go jet skiing or even have a game of golf (if you?re sad enough) or really bored.

Accomodation. The choice of lodging around here is very impressive, but forget about any beds slopeside. Queenstown is the best place to be as it has the biggest selection and best budget options, but its also close to all the off-slope action. Motels are a common form of accommodation around here as are bed and breakfast homes. Bungy Backpackers is a cheap hangout. Tel ++64 03 442 8725

SUMMARY
Good freeriding resort offering some very nice powder areas. The resort management has a healthy attitude towards snowboarding here.
On the slopes: Really good
Off the slopes: Very good
Money Wise: Overall this is an expensive resort but offers good value.

pic -Coronet Peak Tourism

CAR
From Christchurch, take routes 1,8,8A and 89. 277 miles (446km) , 3 1/2 hrs. Queenstown is 36 miles (58km).
FLY
to Christchurch 3 1/2 hours away. Flights available to Queenstown (10mins away)
BUS
A bus from Queenstown will take around 20 minutes, costs $18 return and rund 4 times every morning, tel: 03 442 8106. From Christchurch, its 6 hours by coach.

Basic and dull, but a beginners paradise.

POOR FAIR GOOD TOP

FREERIDE
No trees but some off-piste
FREESTYLE
No park but natutal halfpipe
PISTES
Fairly short pistes

4
OUT OF 10

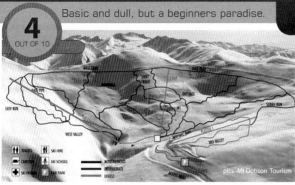

pics -Mt Dobson Tourism

Mount Dobson is a small commercial resort located in the **Southern Canterbury** region of the country on the **South Island**. With a mere nine miles or so of rideable marked piste, Dobson boasts at having the largest beginner's slopes in New Zealand. Whatever the merits of such a claim are, Mt Dobson is a laid back place and has far less hassle about it compared to some of the bigger commercial resorts. The slopes here attract family groups and those out for a simple afternoons sliding around. Even though lift prices are a lot cheaper than other resorts, the slopes are not over populated with budget minded skiers. The terrain sweeps around a main face offering a mixture of very easy gentle slopes and a number of short fast tracks which are all serviced by drag lifts.

FREERIDERS of an intermediate level will find a day riding the slopes here is not a bad way to pass some time. The best of which will be the trails on the main face of the T-bar, and runs off the **West** and **East** trails. Riders, who like something to get stuck into and need a few challenges, may find Dobson a little repetitive and lacking in general interest. However, there is some nice challenging riding in the back bowls and the series of short blacks that drop down from the West and East runs, will give you something to think about. **The Bluff** is not a bad run and has a few humps en-route to the bottom of the Platter 2 drag lift.

FREESTYLERS will find it hard pressed to find anything

man made to fling off. There is a natural half-pipe to be found off the west trail, but thats about it.

PISTES. Riders who like to do big wide turns but don't like to do them for too long, will find Mt Dobson perfectly in tune with their thinking and liking. Nothing here takes that long to carve up, with only a couple of fast pisted tracks to choose from.

BEGINNERS will find the whole place a joy and even though a number of the runs graded "Difficult and intermediate" are a bit over rated and can be challenged after a short time by most.

OFF THE SLOPES, accommodation and other local facilities are offered in the towns of **Fairlie** or **Kimbell**. What you get in either, is very basic, affordable and sufficient for a few days stay. Night life is very tame and not up to much.

N

**N
E
W**

**Z
E
A
L
A
N
D**

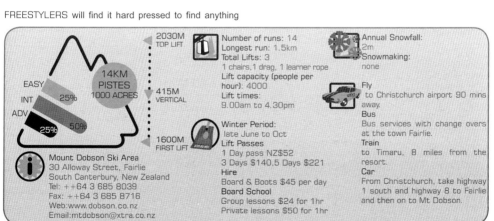

EASY	**14KM PISTES** 1000 ACRES	**2030M** TOP LIFT
INT 25%		**415M** VERTICAL
ADV 25% 50%		**1600M** FIRST LIFT

Number of runs: 14
Longest run: 1.5km
Total Lifts: 3
1 chairs,1 drag, 1 learner rope
Lift capacity (people per hour): 4000
Lift times:
9.00am to 4.30pm

Winter Period:
late June to Oct
Lift Passes
1 Day pass NZ$52
3 Days $140,5 Days $221
Hire
Board & Boots $45 per day
Board School
Group lessons $24 for 1hr
Private lessons $50 for 1hr

Annual Snowfall:
2m
Snowmaking:
none

Fly
to Christchurch airport 90 mins away.
Bus
Bus services with change overs at the town Fairlie.
Train
to Timaru, 8 miles from the resort.
Car
From Christchurch, take highway 1 south and highway 8 to Fairlie and then on to Mt Dobson.

Mount Dobson Ski Area
30 Alloway Street, Fairlie
South Canterbury, New Zealand
Tel: ++64 3 685 8039
Fax: ++64 3 685 8716
Web:www.dobson.co.nz
Email:mtdobson@xtra.co.nz

301

wsg MT. HUTT

Worth the dodgy drive up

5 OUT OF 10

	POOR	FAIR	GOOD	TOP
FREERIDE No trees but some off-piste				
FREESTYLE Terrain park & 2 halfpipes				
PISTES some ok slopes				

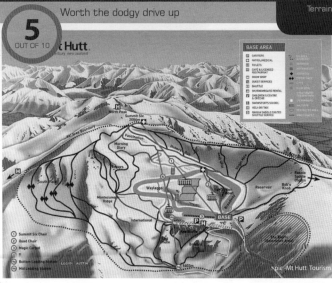

pic -Mt Hutt Tourism

runs to check out, especially for ungroomed and touched powder, are Towers and Virgin Mile. Here you can ride free of crowds but remember that Mt Hutt is a very popular resort so move fast on powder mornings to get the best uncut stuff which there is plenty off on offer with no need to hike to.

FREESTYLERS There's a large earth sculpted 10,000m2 terrain park packed with tabletops and spines. There are also 2 halfpipes. You will find plenty to jump and launch off down Exhibition Bowl, Morning Glory and through Race Hill, although exercise some caution on these blind jumps. If possible have someone spotting if possible especially if there are races or training in the area.

NEW ZEALAND

Mount Hutt is the third resort in **Mount Cook** Line's 'Big Three', located 30 minutes from **Methven**. This is an early opening resort mainly thanks to its snowmaking facilities as well as the high altitude. You can enjoy some of the best snow cover for the longest season in the **South Island**. The 9 lifts service an excellent expanse of terrain for everybody to take advantage off. Being one of NZ's biggest commercial resorts means that Mt Hutt can become very busy, attracting a lot of family ski groups. However, don't let that stop you, the resort is very snowboard friendly and there are plenty of good areas to ride with out crashing into two plankers all day. As with most of the NZ resorts access is via an ungraded road, which can be closed during snow or windy storms.

FREERIDERS who like the challenge of steep and extreme terrain, then the **South Face** is covered with double black diamond runs to test the cockiest of riders. Other great

PISTES. Any carvers gracing the slopes in hard boots will find some nice corduroy terrain around Broadway to carve up.

BEGINNERS. Mt Hutt is considered one of the best learning resorts in NZ with novice trails serviced by fixed grip tows.

OFF THE SLOPES
You can base your self in **Methven**, **Christchurch** or **Ashburton**, all offering a variety of accommodation, food and nighlife. Methven is the closest, just 30 minutes away. Budget **accommodation** is limited so try to book ahead. There are plenty of restaurants and cafes serving a variety on dishes at varying rates. **Night life** is okay in the bars but avoid the cheesy discos.

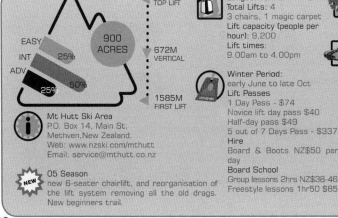

2075M TOP LIFT	Longest run: 2km (1.2 miles) Total Lifts: 4 3 chairs, 1 magic carpet Lift capacity (people per hour): 9,200 Lift times: 9.00am to 4.00pm	Annual Snowfall: 1.8m Snowmaking: 15% of slopes	
EASY **900 ACRES** INT 25% ADV 25% 50%	**672M** VERTICAL		Fly to Christchurch airport 90 mins away.
	1585M FIRST LIFT	Winter Period: early June to late Oct Lift Passes 1 Day Pass - $74 Novice lift day pass $40 Half-day pass $49 5 out of 7 Days Pass - $337 Hire Board & Boots NZ$50 per day Board School Group lessons 2hrs NZ$38-46 Freestyle lessons 1hr50 $85	Bus Bus services from Metven direct to Mt Hutt take 30 min (www.ridesnowshuttles. co.nz, tel: 03 302 1919). The Snowbus runs direct daily connections from Christchurch (tel: 0800 7669 287), also Mt Hutt Express 0800 80 80 70 Car From Christchurch, take highways 73 & 72 trrough Tardhurst and Homebush to Metven and then on up to Mt Hutt.

Mt Hutt Ski Area
P.O. Box 14, Main St,
Methven,New Zealand.
Web: www.nzski.com/mthutt
Email: service@mthutt.co.nz

NEW 05 Season
new 6-seater chairlift, and reorganisation of the lift system removing all the old drags. New beginners trail.

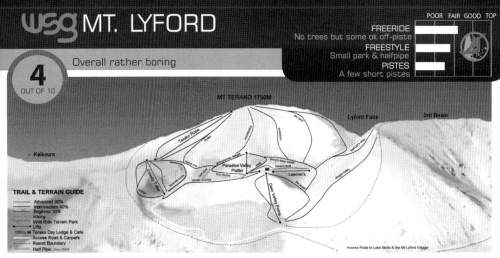

	POOR	FAIR	GOOD	TOP
FREERIDE No trees but some ok off-piste				
FREESTYLE Small park & halfpipe				
PISTES A few short pistes				

4
OUT OF 10

Overall rather boring

TRAIL & TERRAIN GUIDE
Advanced 30%
Intermediate 40%
Beginner 30%
Hiking
Wild Ride Terrain Park
Lifts
Terako Day Lodge & Cafe
Access Road & Carpark
Resort Boundary
Half Pipe

Located just hours from **Christchurch** and only 18 miles from the town of **Kailoura**, is the small and commercial resort of **Mount Lyford.** This totally privately owned mountain may not be the biggest resort in New Zealand, but by the same token it's not the smallest, and unlike some of the other commercial resorts, Mt Lyford is far more affordable and offers great value for money for any rider who can handle a few days. Mt.Lyford is a very snowboard friendly hangout and on occasions has boarders out numbering skiers. Still who ever is there, will tell you that its pretty dull for any more than a couple of days if you stick to the marked slopes but great if you go heli-boarding into the backcountry areas. The area gets good natural snow cover that is spread out over two areas which are somewhat different to each other. The **lake Stella** area a short drive around the mountain, is the advanced riders spot while beginners will find the best slopes on the **Terako** field.

FREERIDERS should make their way to the top of **Mt Terako** via the Terako lift for some uneven terrain. From the top and after a short hike, you can either ride down the series of steep blacks such as **Die Hard**, or you can elect to take the slightly easier runs such as the **Thriller**. Riders who can afford it and want to ride some backcountry powder, will be able to experience the best stuff by taking a heli-board trip with Hanmer Helicopters.

FREESTYLERS. The small Wild Ride terrain park has one kicker and a selection of rails and boxes. They've just shelled out on a pipe-cutter so you can expect a 120m halfpipe from this season. Away from the park, you will find a few rocks to leap over and one or two wind lips but nothing major.

PISTES. Piste huggers will find the least to do here if your only desire is corduroy trails. However, an hour here will allow for some fun. Only 20% of the rideable area is groomed.

BEGINNERS will love Mt Lyford because you can practice your thing on some very tame slopes, which are free of large ski groups. The only thing is that all the lifts are drags.

OFF THE SLOPES the by word is, 'very basic and dull'. There is chalet **accommodation** along the access road but little else. *Keiths Cafe* is the place for breakfast while the *Lodge Hotel* will provide some evening madness.

N

N E W

Z E A L A N D

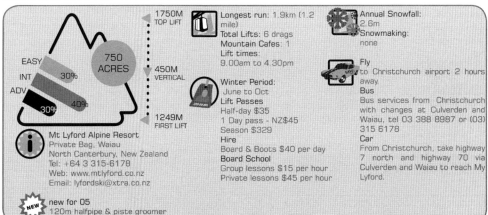

EASY
INT 30%
ADV
30% 40%

750 ACRES

1750M TOP LIFT

450M VERTICAL

1249M FIRST LIFT

Mt Lyford Alpine Resort
Private Bag, Waiau
North Canterbury, New Zealand
Tel: +64 3 315-6178
Web: www.mtlyford.co.nz
Email: lyfordski@xtra.co.nz

Longest run: 1.9km (1.2 mile)
Total Lifts: 6 drags
Mountain Cafes: 1
Lift times:
9.00am to 4.30pm

Winter Period:
June to Oct
Lift Passes
Half-day $35
1 Day pass - NZ$45
Season $329
Hire
Board & Boots $40 per day
Board School
Group lessons $15 per hour
Private lessons $45 per hour

Annual Snowfall:
2.6m
Snowmaking:
none

Fly
to Christchurch airport 2 hours away.
Bus
Bus services from Christchurch with changes at Culverden and Waiau, tel 03 388 8987 or (03) 315 6178
Car
From Christchurch, take highway 7 north and highway 70 via Culverden and Waiau to reach My Lyford.

NEW new for 05
120m halfpipe & piste groomer

303

	POOR	FAIR	GOOD	TOP
FREERIDE				
FREESTYLE				
PISTES				

FREERIDE
No trees but good off-piste

FREESTYLE
Bring a shovel

PISTES
go find freshies

6
OUT OF 10

Really fun for a few days especially with new snow

N E W Z E A L A N D

Laying in a south-facing basin, Mt Olympus usually traps more snow than most other club fields. As with those other fields, **Mt Olympus** is by no means a big area, however there are fun times to be had as very little people ride at these areas and fresh tracks are usually plentiful.

FREERIDING. The club fields are a freeriders paradise. There's no grooming but plenty of interesting terrain from wide open faces like **Main Face** to the cool chutes coming down the areas' namesake. The off-piste possibilities are unlimited, but make sure you have a chat with patrol to find out about current avalanche conditions before heading off.

FREESTYLERS. There's no traditional terrain park but the whole area has cool places to build kickers to launch you skyward.

BEGINNERS. There is a short beginner's tow but it is located near the lodge which is accessible by either a more advanced rope tow or by walking! Beginner riders are better off learning to ride at one of the commercial ski areas like **Mt Hutt** or **Porter Heights**.

OFF THE SLOPES
The best way to experience the club fields are to stay the night before riding. That way you can get the latest on the snow conditions and in the morning you just walk out the front door right on to the snow. The **Top Hut** is a very cosy lodge with 10 bunk styled rooms with hot showers! $55 is what it will cost you for accommodation, dinner and breakfast. There's even a qualified chef! There's also the Bottom Hut which costs $25 but you have to supply your own food. The nearest town is **Methven** 58km away, its not exactly lively there, but there are some reasonable places to stay and most importantly a pub.

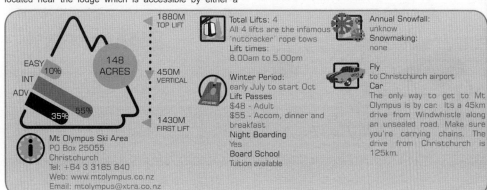

EASY 10%
INT
ADV
35%
55%

148 ACRES

1880M TOP LIFT
450M VERTICAL
1430M FIRST LIFT

Mt Olympus Ski Area
PO Box 25055
Christchurch
Tel: +64 3 3185 840
Web: www.mtolympus.co.nz
Email: mtolympus@xtra.co.nz

Total Lifts: 4
All 4 lifts are the infamous 'nutcracker' rope tows
Lift times:
8.00am to 5.00pm

Winter Period:
early July to start Oct
Lift Passes
$48 - Adult
$55 - Accom, dinner and breakfast
Night Boarding
Yes
Board School
Tuition available

Annual Snowfall:
unknow
Snowmaking:
none

Fly
to Christchurch airport
Car
The only way to get to Mt Olympus is by car. Its a 45km drive from Windwhistle along an unsealed road. Make sure you're carrying chains. The drive from Christchurch is 125km.

POOR FAIR GOOD TOP

FREERIDE
No trees but pure virgin backcountry

FREESTYLE
Huge natural playground

PISTES
none

Fresh lines, no people, awesome terrain

8 OUT OF 10

staging area you get a flight in the heli! There's terrain to suit all abilities and you will get in as much vertical as if you went heli-boarding. Riders do 12-14 runs for a total of 18,000ft of vert. Perhaps the best run of the day is the last run which is a 2km cruise down to the helicopter which flies you back to the lodge and some après drinks.

HELI-BOARDING started at Mt Potts during the winter of 2005. The great advantage of it being a 'new' operation is that the vast majority of terrain (i.e. pretty much all of it!) has never seen a pair of skis or a board!! On our visit there we were doing runs that had never been ridden before... and that's fairly common!

pics - mtpotts backcountry

Since Mt Potts is good enough for the Burton and Salomon Teams, then you know it's definitely good enough for you! Mt Potts is currently the only catboarding operation in New Zealand. They now also offer some great heli-boarding. The worst part about staying there is trying to choose which to do! Mt Potts is located in the **Canterbury** region of the South Island, about 2 hours from Christchurch, an hour from **Methven** and not far from the more famous commercial ski area of **Mt Hutt**. You'll need to be at least an intermediate boarder to enjoy things, and it's a good idea to need to book in advance. Mt Potts receives a hell of a lot of snow... and it helps being the highest 'resort' in the South Island.

Heli and catboarding is all about freeriding and Mt Potts delivers. The Mt Potts guides can get you to pretty much any type of terrain you desire. From wide open bowls to sphincter tight chutes you can find it in Mt Potts lease area. The great thing about heli/catboarding in New Zealand is that the heli, and therefore groups, tend to be small, therefore it's easy for the guides to keep watch over everyone, so if you have an advanced group you can explore the terrain more so than if you were in Canada where they strictly enforce where you can and can't ride (this may also be due to the higher risk of avalanche there).

CATS. They've been cat-boarding at Mt Potts since 1999. To get from the lodge to the cat-boarding

BEGINNERS need to go to Mt Hutt! Heli/catboarding should be done by riders of at least an intermediate level.

OFF THE SLOPES
It's strongly recommended to stay at **Mt Potts Station** (lodge) the night before you fly. That way you can meet the guides and fellow riders and be ready for the day's adventures. Dinner, bed and breakfast and staying in a Shared Room is $89pp and for a Twin Room it's $99pp.

Even though dinner is a set menu the food is really good! You can even see the menu on the Mt Potts website. Breakfast is really good to, with a choice of cereals, fruits, juice and a cooked breakfast.

N E W   Z E A L A N D

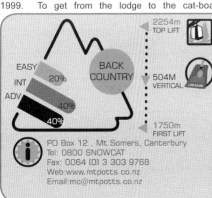

2254m TOP LIFT	Total Lifts: none - only CAT boarding & heli available Mountain Cafes: 1
504M VERTICAL	Winter Period: end July to late Sept CAT Boarding NZ$350 for full days CAT boarding (12-14 runs), includes helicopter return to Mt Potts lodge, transiever and lunch
1750m FIRST LIFT	Heli-Boarding Pure Heli - 5 runs in the Two Thumbs Range, 17,000 vertical feet - $765 Heli Max - 8 runs around Mt Potts, 22,000 vertical feet - $650 Hire Board & Boots $35 / day

EASY
INT 20%
ADV
40%
40%

BACK COUNTRY

PO Box 12 , Mt. Somers, Canterbury
Tel: 0800 SNOWCAT
Fax: 0064 (0) 3 303 9768
Web:www.mtpotts.co.nz
Email:mc@mtpotts.co.nz

Annual Snowfall:
11m
Snowmaking:
none

Fly
includes helicopter pick up from Mt.Potts lodge and heli back to the lodge at the end of the day.

Private flights available from Queenstown or Christchurch, 2 day package $950.Just return flight from Christchurch to Mt.Potts from $198

Car
Drive to Mt.Potts lodge, 1 hour from Methven near Christchurch.

FREERIDE
No trees but some good off-piste

FREESTYLE
A few rock drops

PISTES
A few fast slopes

POOR FAIR GOOD TOP

Good overall resort

7
OUT OF 10

RIDGE RUN

WEDDING KNOB

BOULEVARD

SUN RUN

LUGE

SHIRT FRONT

TOWERS

ESCALATOR

- BEGINNER
- INTERMEDIATE
- ADVANCED
- CAFE
- SKI PATROL
- LIFT
  A - LEARNERS
  B - PLATTER
  C - CHAIR
- SEASON RUNS FROM
  JULY - SEPTEMBER

CAFE

A

B

OHĀU
SNOW FIELDS

pic - Oahu Tourism

The strong-nerved should consider traversing further than Escalator, past the **Rock Bluff** and ride down to the Platter lift. The face above the day lodge, with the **Sun Run trail** on it, offers some steep runs and because it gets sun early in the day, it's often the best place to ride in the morning. On the other face, the **Exhibition** and **Escalator** runs, remain in the shade until late in the day.

FREESTYLERS will have to make do with natural hits, if getting high on a board is you're type of fix, nothing is laid on here.

CARVERS may at first feel left out, however after some close examination, you will soon see that there is enough pisted carving trails to shine on, with runs like the **Shirt Front,** where you can give some style at speed.

Some would say that you haven't truly snowboarded in New Zealand until you have spent a day at **Ohau Ski Area** and a night at the Ohau Lodge. Seemingly in the middle of nowhere, about half way between **Queenstown** and **Christchurch**, most people make the mistake of only visiting Ohau for a day en-route between other resorts.

The views alone here are amazing with **Mount Cook,** NZ's highest mountain, in sight all around the area. This internationally renowned snowboarders resort offers some excellent riding for all levels on amazingly crowd free slopes with a fair share of good powder days. Riders come here because they know that this place cuts it, without any hype of bull shit, just a damn fine mountain that will please hardcore freeriders with a good choice of steeps.

FREERIDERS are most at home here. Apart from the two learner areas at the base and the wide groomed Boulevard Run, the terrain is generally steep. Left of the T-bar, is the steepest part of the area with the **Escalator trail** being the steepest run on the mountain.

BEGINNERS tend to hang out on the **Boulevard** run although it does get a little steep in places (below Top Flat). Boulevard does give less confident riders a good reign of the mountain and a few ski areas have such an easy run from there highest point.

STAYING
The Ohau experience is best enjoyed by staying at the **Ohau Lodge**, situated at the base of the mountain. Food and booze are available in the Lodge on back down in the town of **Twizel**. Wherever you decide to chill out, there's a good choice of cool hangouts with reasonable prices for booze.

NEW ZEALAND

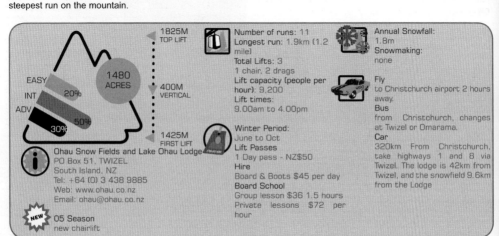

EASY

1480 ACRES

INT 20%

ADV 50%

30%

1825M TOP LIFT

400M VERTICAL

1425M FIRST LIFT

Ohau Snow Fields and Lake Ohau Lodge
PO Box 51, TWIZEL
South Island, NZ
Tel: +64 (0) 3 438 9885
Web: www.ohau.co.nz
Email: ohau@ohau.co.nz

NEW
05 Season
new chairlift

Number of runs: 11
Longest run: 1.9km (1.2 mile)
Total Lifts: 3
1 chair, 2 drags
Lift capacity (people per hour): 9,200
Lift times:
9.00am to 4.00pm

Winter Period:
June to Oct
Lift Passes
1 Day pass - NZ$50
Hire
Board & Boots $45 per day
Board School
Group lesson $36 1.5 hours
Private lessons $72 per hour

Annual Snowfall:
1.8m
Snowmaking:
none

Fly
to Christchurch airport 2 hours away.
Bus
from Christchurch, changes at Twizel or Omarama.
Car
320km From Christchurch, take highways 1 and 8 via Twizel. The lodge is 42km from Twizel, and the snowfield 9.6km from the Lodge

POOR FAIR GOOD TOP

FREERIDE
No trees but some x-treme off-piste
FREESTYLE
No park, but good natural
PISTES
Short but okay pistes

6 OUT OF 10

Good place to ride

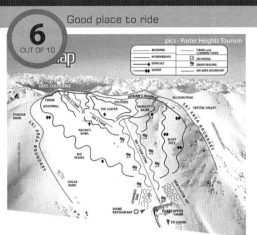

pics - Porter Heights Tourism

BEGINNER	T BARS and LEARNERS TOWS
INTERMEDIATE	SKI PATROL
DIFFICULT	SNOW RACING
EXPERT	SKI AREA BOUNDARY

Porters Heights is situated in the **Craigieburn Range** and is the closest boarding area to **Christchurch**. The whole area is likened to a large terrain park with heaps of runs that can't be beaten on a powder day with cool challenging chutes and hits. Legendary runs like **Big Mama** (one of the largest in the Southern Hemisphere) and **Bluff Face** (NZ's steepest) help to make this an extremely interesting and challenging resort for any snowboarder.

FREERIDERS should go to the top of the No 3 T-bar, because from here the mountain is yours. The view of **Lake Coleridge** and surrounding mountain ranges is spectacular. Don't hang around sightseeing for too long though - the first tracks on Big Mama aren't available all day. It is a reasonably easy traverse (with a little climbing) along a ridge line to the top of Big Mama, but it's not until you're standing at the top of the slope that you realise just how long the run is. It is a huge 620 vertical metres from top to bottom - one of the largest vertical drops in a lift accessed area in NZ. If you're fit enough to enjoy long powder runs, **Big Mama** is heaven. If you prefer chutes, traverse to the left from the top of lift No 3 T-bar to **Aorangi Chutes** and the Leapers, where the terrain is steep and the

chutes are narrow. **Bluff Face** is another cool place to ride reached via a traverse down to McNulty's cat-track and hike up to the summit of Allison Peak. The **Powder Bowl** and **Crystal Valley** runs are both outside the ski boundary. There is a great boarding to be had on both, but the hike can be a mission. For reasons of safety, inform the ski patrol if you intend to go into any of these areas.

FREESTYLERS have a lot here to check out here if man made stuff isn't your bag with heaps of good natural hits dotted around the whole area.

PISTES. Riders will find the runs down either side of the No 1 T-bar have a reasonably consistent gradient and make excellent cruising runs for intermediate boarders

BEGINNERS will find the runs limited to a few short flats at the base area which are serviced by a couple of easy to use lifts.

THE TOWN
The best place to base yourself for local services, is in nearby **Springfield**, where there's some good lodging options, good eating out and great night time happenings shared with friendly locals.

N E W   Z E A L A N D

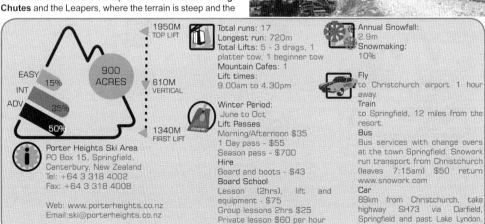

EASY **15%**
INT
ADV **35%**
50%

900 ACRES

1950M TOP LIFT
610M VERTICAL
1340M FIRST LIFT

i Porter Heights Ski Area
PO Box 15, Springfield,
Canterbury, New Zealand
Tel: +64 3 318 4002
Fax: +64 3 318 4008

Web: www.porterheights.co.nz
Email: ski@porterheights.co.nz

Total runs: 17
Longest run: 720m
Total Lifts: 5 - 3 drags, 1 platter tow, 1 beginner tow
Mountain Cafes: 1
Lift times:
9.00am to 4.30pm

Winter Period:
June to Oct
Lift Passes
Morning/Afternoon $35
1 Day pass - $55
Season pass - $700
Hire
Board and boots - $43
Board School
Lesson (2hrs), lift and equipment - $75
Group lessons 2hrs $25
Private lesson $60 per hour

Annual Snowfall:
2.9m
Snowmaking:
10%

Fly
to Christchurch airport 1 hour away.
Train
to Springfield, 12 miles from the resort.
Bus
Bus services with change overs at the town Springfield. Snowork run transport from Christchurch (leaves 7:15am) $50 return www.snowork.com
Car
89km from Christchurch, take highway SH73 via Darfield, Springfield and past Lake Lyndon, take porter heights turn-off

POOR FAIR GOOD TOP

FREERIDE
No trees but some good off-piste

FREESTYLE
Pipe & park

PISTES
Some okay slopes

7 OUT OF 10

Good place to ride!

BASE AREA

The Remarkables lies within sight of the **Cornet Peak** resort. Higher in altitude, the car park is the same level as Cornet's summit, with the result being that the mountain is very craggy and rocky. The Remarkables tends to be a lot quieter than Cornet Peak with fewer skiers. It also gets some incredible powder days and offers terrain to suit every style and grade of rider. The area is some what sheltered but still gives out plenty of sun and loads of natural snow. The **Homeward** runs are the place to shred some deep powder where you can ride some long floating turns with an amazing back drop. The Homewards take you right down to the access road to catch the shuttle bus back to the base building in order to do the whole thing again. The runs here are accessed by three chairlifts. The **Alta** double chair services the best intermediate terrain to suit carvers or freeriders. The **Sugar quad** is the lift to take to get access to some good advance terrain and competent intermediate stuff. However, advanced riders looking to cut it in style and be pushed to the fore should check out the runs found off **Shadow lift.**

FREERIDERS prepared to do some hiking, and after checking the snow conditions with the patrol, can reach some major dogs bollocks terrain with big chutes and scary steeps. Turn left off the Shadow and hike 20 minutes up to the ridge to access the area known as **Elevator** above **Lake Alta**. If you continue up along the ridge then the chutes get narrower and more extreme, so be bloody careful if you don't want this to be your last ever run. Go left off Sugar for the Toilet Bowl a freeriders heaven, which again takes you to the access road and the shuttle bus.

FREESTYLERS will find a new **Xbox Terrain Park** that has tripled the size of the old terrain park, and includes a 150m superpipe. Riders will find plenty of cliffs and rock drops to get air from, especially in areas around Sugar and Alta. There are also plenty of cat-tracks to drop off.

PISTES. Riders will find a number of runs to laying out big super G turns on but in truth this is not a groomed piste lovers home.

BEGINNERS have two superb learner areas with fixed grip tows and an excellent snowboard school that will soon get you sorted out and cutting the mountain up in style.

THE TOWN. Read the **Queenstown** section in the **Coronet peak** review

pic - WSG

EASY
INT 30%
ADV 40%
30%

550 ACRES

1935M TOP LIFT

357M VERTICAL

1603M FIRST LIFT

The Remarkables Ski Area
PO Box 359, Queenstown
New Zealand
Tel: +64 (0) 64-3-4424615
Fax: +64 (0) 64-3-442 4619

Web:www.nzski.com/remarkables
Email:service@theremarkables.co.nz

Longest run: 1.6km (1 mile)
Total Lifts: 5
2 chairs, 3 drags
Lift capacity (people per hour): 3000
Lift times:
9.00am to 4.00pm
Mountain Cafes: 1

Winter Period:
June to Oct
Lift Passes
Half day $49
1 Day pass - $74
5 Day pass - $337
Season pass - $1699
Hire
Board & Boots NZ$51 per day
Board School
Group lessons 1hr50 NZ$47
Freestyle lessons $85 1hr50
from 10:20am

Annual Snowfall:
2.7m
Snowmaking:
10% of slopes

Fly
to Christchurch or Queenstown.
Bus
Bus services from Queenstown to the resort are available on an hourly basis (4 times in morning) $18 return Contact skishuttle@coachline.co.nz or tel +64 3 442 8106
Car
From Christchurch, take highways 1, 8, 8A and 89. Approx 6 hours.

wsg SNOWPARK

Exactly what it says on the tin.

	POOR	FAIR	GOOD	TOP
FREERIDE				
Forget it				
FREESTYLE				
2 pipes and huge park				
PISTES				
Not what its about				

8 OUT OF 10

pics - Snowpark Tourism

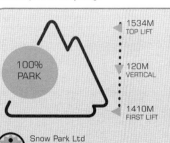

This place is packed with features, and is perfect for the pro as much as the novice taking their first steps into the park. Most of the major features are dug out of the landscape, so they should be open all season.

The Super Pipe is designed to full World Cup spec, and theres another suitable for beginners. Theres a 50x8m 1/4 pipe, this year they're looking at 40+ rails, boxes and hits of varying sizes for all abilities. To ease progression they have 3-4 sizes of each rail, and a similar setup for the boxes. Theres an increase in the number of beginners jumps this year, and its graded to get you ready for some of the monsters such as the 100ft kicker they built for Burton.

Behind the back of the 1/4 pipe theres also a skate park to try out, you can rent the equipment if necessary or for $10 a day just enjoy the skatepark.

Snowpark is New Zealands latest resort, only opening a couple of seasons ago, and is the only one dedicated to freestyling. You'll find it on the **South Island,** about 35km from **Wanaka.** Natural terrain wise this place will not get your pulse racing, but natural is not was this place is. What you get is a resort packed with pipes, rails, hips, boxes the lot; and a team dedicated to making it happen and happen big. There's no equipment hire so make sure you turn up with everything.

N E W   Z E A L A N D

100% PARK

- 1534M TOP LIFT
- 120M VERTICAL
- 1410M FIRST LIFT

Snow Park Ltd
Cardrona Valley, RD1
Wanaka 9192, New Zealand
Phone : +64 3 443 9991
Fax: +64 3 443 9990

Web: www.snowparknz.com
Email: info@snowparknz.com

New for 05 season
new cafe, expanded terrain & new pipe specifically for camps and pro teams.

Total runs: 1
Total Lifts: 1 - 3 drags, 1 platter tow, 1 beginner tow
Mountain Cafes: 1
Lift times: 9.00am to 4.30pm

Winter Period: June to Oct
Lift Passes
1 Day NZ$55, Season $999
Hire
NO rental equipment, some demo equipment available.
Board School
4 day pipe camps on offer throughout the season for $375 (ex. passes)
Night Boarding
Floodlighting covering both pipes and a selection of rails/kickers.
Heliboarding
available in Wanaka and Queenstown. Expect to pay $500-600 for 4-5 drops.

Annual Snowfall: 0.5m
Snowmaking: 100%
Fly to Queenstown (55km) or Wanaka (35km)
Train to Springfield, 12 miles from the resort.
Bus Daily to the Park from Queenstown contact snowbus@paradise.net.nz, or from Wanaka contact 03 443 8422 or email ewa@adventure.net.nz. From Christchurch to Wanaka/Queenstown contact www.atomictravel.co.nz, price $45/50
Car From Lake Wanaka its 35km up the Cardrona Valley. From Queenstown its 1 hr.

FREERIDE
No trees but some good backcountry
FREESTYLE
Natural half-pipes & a park
PISTES
Some good pisted slopes

POOR FAIR GOOD TOP

Good overall resort

7
OUT OF 10

pic - Treble Cone Tourism

Pete's Treat is loaded with rails and boxes and if you're still not satisfied and in need of an adrenaline rush, there are loads of big drops offs and rocks of all sizes dotted all over the mountain.

PISTES. Carvers need not feel left out as Treble Cone has done lots of work developing a series of well groomed runs down the face of the mountain which are ideal for laying down some big wide arcs.

BEGINNERS may note that although Treble Cone is not known as a beginners mountain don't be put off, as there is still enough to try out without killing yourself on the first day. Its skiers who can't handle it here, not fast learning boarders.

Treble Cone is half an hour from the town of **Wanaka** and provides some incredible terrain, on and off piste in a major scenic place. Some would say that Treble Cone gets more than its fair share of dry southern snow as well as the resort boasting a vert un-matched in the rest of the country. With 50% advanced terrain, Treble is known as one of New Zealand's more testing and challenging resorts that competent freeriders and freestylers should love and be able to go home with a few stories to tell after tackling some major steeps, long chutes and deep powder bowls on some gnarly black faces

FREERIDERS will like it here especially when there has been some fresh snow. A particular good area to drop into is **Powder Bowl**. A wide open slope leading into the lower gullies for some big powder turns and super floating glides. For the more adventurous the off-piste in the **Matukituki Basin** is the place to check out.

FREESTYLERS should head to the top and from the summit, drop into the **Saddle Basin** alongside the Saddle double chair, to take advantage of loads of natural hits and halfpipes to gain maximum air time. The **Gun Barrel**, which is also reached from the summit, is another legendary, long natural halfpipe where banked slalom events are regularly held. The terrain park on

THE TOWN Away from the slopes local services are provided down in **Wanaka**, a quiet and relaxed place that provides good places to kip and a few bars popular with snowboarders. For some decent food why not try *Kai Ahaka* for a tasty treat and great coffee. The *Pot Belly Stove* also serves decent local food. Places to check out for a beer are the likes of the *Barrows*, which is the locals haunt, or *Outback bar* which has a pool table and serves booze until late.

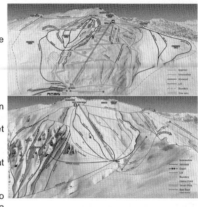

N
E
W

Z
E
A
L
A
N
D

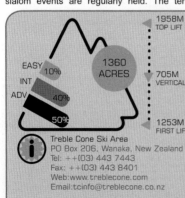

EASY 10%
INT
ADV 40%
50%

1360 ACRES

1958M
TOP LIFT

705M
VERTICAL

1253M
FIRST LIFT

Treble Cone Ski Area
PO Box 206, Wanaka, New Zealand
Tel: ++(03) 443 7443
Fax: ++(03) 443 8401
Web: www.treblecone.com
Email: tcinfo@treblecone.co.nz

05 Season
NEW new chairlift extends the accessible height of the resort and opens up the Saddle basin more. New piste groomer purchased.

Number of runs: 60
Longest run: 4km
Total Lifts: 7
2 chairs, 3 drags, 1 Magic carpet
Lift capacity (people per hour): 6,905
Lift times:
9.00am to 4.00pm

Winter Period:
June to Oct
Lift Passes
1 Day pass - NZ$80
Full Seasons Pass NZ$ 1299
Weekday Seasons NZ$ 950
Hire
Board & Boots NZ$46 per day
Board School
Group NZ$45 ph, private from $75 ph

Annual Snowfall:
2.5m
Snowmaking:
21 Snow Guns

Fly
to Christchurch or Queenstown or direct to Wanaka (NEW direct Air NZ flight)
Bus
from Queenstown to resort available on an hourly basis. Shuttles from Wanaka by Edgewater Adventures and Alpine Coachlines NZ$27 return
Car
From Christchurch, take highways 1, 8, 8A and 89 to Wanaka. The drive time is around 5 hours.
30 minutes drive from Wanaka, 1.5hours from Queenstown via Crown range

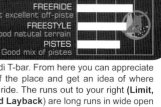

FREERIDE
No trees but excellent off-piste
FREESTYLE
A park & good natutal terrain
PISTES
Good mix of pistes

POOR FAIR GOOD TOP

Simple but good resort

6 OUT OF 10

pic - Turoa Tourism

Turoa is now joined with **Whakapapa** creating, at 2,500 acres, New Zealands largest resort. Turoa is covered with gullies, bowls, walls and wide slopes: the type of terrain only found on a volcano. This can vary incredibly from year to year, depending on the amount of snow cover. Because the area is so large and conditions can vary so much, it is worthwhile spending time in the bars down in **Okakune**, meeting the locals first hand and finding out where the current best spots are. The runs marked on the trail map are really of little more than aesthetics value. There are countless possible routes and like Whakapapa on the other side of the mountain, the fun of riding at Turoa is finding them.

FREERIDERS of an advanced level should get to the top

of the Bacardi T-bar. From here you can appreciate the scope of the place and get an idea of where you'd like to ride. The runs out to your right (**Limit, Solitude and Layback**) are long runs in wide open spaces, where the thrill of riding down an active volcano can be fully realised. The runs way out to your left (Speedtrack, Main Face and Triangle) are a little steeper. There is nowhere on Turoa where the urge to climb Ruapehu's Peak is stronger than when viewing **Mangaheuheu Glacier**, from the Glacier Entrance run. If you want to hike to the top, check with the ski patrol on the best route and do not go without telling them. They'll also appreciate it if you can report to them on your return. It doesn't matter which route you take from the peak back to the ski area, they are 475 of the most unforgettable vertical metres in New Zealand.

FREESTYLERS have a decent park, however on a powder day, which don't occur with great frequency in the North Island, Turoa's walls and gullies beckon you to charge hard. There's nothing like launching off **Clays Leap** or the **Mangawhero Headwall** and landing in the safe hands of powder.

BEGINNERS will find the Alpine Meadows area beside the car park the place to start out on. The cafeteria is right beside it so its never too far to go for a bit of a warm up .

THE TOWN.
There is an abundance of local facilities in **Ohakume**, only 10 miles away. **Accommodation** is provided as cheap B&B's, inexpensive motels and pricey hotels. **Food** and drinking is plentiful, *Clinches Cafe* is the place for breakfast.

N **NEW ZEALAND**

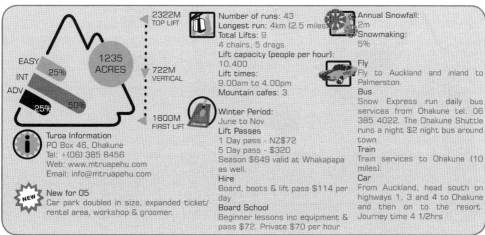

2322M TOP LIFT	Number of runs: 43
	Longest run: 4km (2.5 miles)
	Total Lifts: 9
	4 chairs, 5 drags
	Lift capacity (people per hour):
1235 ACRES	10,400
EASY 25%	**722M** VERTICAL
INT	Lift times:
ADV 25% 50%	9.00am to 4.00pm
	Mountain cafes: 3
	1600M FIRST LIFT
	Winter Period:
	June to Nov
	Lift Passes
Turoa Information	1 Day pass - NZ$72
PO Box 46, Ohakune	5 Day pass - $320
Tel: +(06) 385 8456	Season $649 valid at Whakapapa
Web: www.mtruapehu.com	as well.
Email: info@mtruapehu.com	Hire
	Board, boots & lift pass $114 per day
NEW **New for 05**	Board School
Car park doubled in size, expanded ticket/ rental area, workshop & groomer.	Beginner lessons inc equipment & pass $72. Private $70 per hour

Annual Snowfall: 2m
Snowmaking: 5%

Fly
Fly to Auckland and inland to Palmerston.

Bus
Snow Express run daily bus services from Ohakune tel: 06 385 4022. The Ohakune Shuttle runs a night $2 night bus around town

Train
Train services to Ohakune (10 miles).

Car
From Auckland, head south on highways 1, 3 and 4 to Ohakune and then on to the resort. Journey time 4 1/2hrs

wsg WHAKAPAPA

	POOR	FAIR	GOOD	TOP
FREERIDE No trees but some serious off-piste				
FREESTYLE Terrain park & halfpipe				
PISTES Some well pisted slopes				

6
OUT OF 10

Good freeriding

management have, in the last few years, splashed out thousands of big bucks on a new Pipemaster. Having now learned how to turn it on, the halfpipe can boast perfectly groomed walls with a nice big vert and good transitions allowing for great smooth take offs.

PISTES. Riders can carve away for days on well groomed trails and take a week to do them all a few times over, with a number to test the best of the edge merchants.

THE TOWN
Heaps of good local facilities exist in varying villages all in easy reach of the slopes. Prices vary, but on the whole well affordable and worth the effort of a weeks stay.

pic - WSG

N E W Z E A L A N D

Whakapapa is located near Tuora, on the slopes of Mount Rauapehu. The diversity of the terrain here is caused by the way the underlying volcano has formed over millions of years. As the largest recognised ski resort in the country, Whakapapa has something for everyone, with steeps, cliffs, fast chutes gullies and big natural banks allowing for some big air. The Mt Ruapehu lift pass covers both Whakapapa and Turoa.

FREERIDERS who know what's what, will be aware of the awesome area known as the Pinnacles. Simply put, if you're not a damn good advanced rider, then stay away. The Pinnacles are a series of cliff runs that will wipe the lights out for good if any rider mucks up!

FREESTYLERS will be pleased to learn that

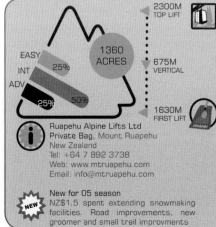

2300M TOP LIFT

EASY | **1360 ACRES**
INT 25%
ADV 25% 50%

675M VERTICAL

1630M FIRST LIFT

(i) Ruapehu Alpine Lifts Ltd
Private Bag, Mount Ruapehu
New Zealand
Tel: +64 7 892 3738
Web: www.mtruapehu.com
Email: info@mtruapehu.com

NEW New for 05 season
NZ$1.5 spent extending snowmaking facilities. Road improvements, new groomer and small trail improvments

Number of runs: 30
Longest run: 2.8km
Total Lifts: 13
7 chairs, 6 drags, 1 learner rope
Lift capacity (people per hour): 23,000
Lift times:
9.00am to 3.30pm
Mountain cafes: 6

Winter Period:
June to Nov
Lift Passes
1 Day pass - NZ$72
5 Day pass - $320
Season $649 valid at Turoa as well.
Hire
Board, boots & lift pass $114 per day
Board School
Beginner lessons inc equipment & pass $72. Private $70 per hour

Annual Snowfall:
2.5m
Snowmaking:
20% of pistes

Fly
Fly to Auckland airport and inland to Taupo airport.
Bus
Sno shuttle run daily from Taupo (7.15am) and Turangi (7.50am) tel: 07 377 0435.
Train
Train services are possible to National Park, which is 12 miles away.
Car
From Auckland, head south on highways 1 to Taupo and then on to Whakapapa (4hrs journey time)

pic: Location Trysil (c) Ute foto /IN

Norway is famous for it's cross country skiing which is reflected in the fact that although there are over 160 resorts dotted around the country, 80% are simply not ridable. The terrain in the suitable areas is best for novices and intermediates, with little long term interest for advanced riders due to the lack of steep terrain.

Travelling around Norway is made easy by the country's excellent road and rail network, connecting well with international airports. The main gateway airport with regular international flights is Oslo, but onward travel usually means an extra 2 to 3 hours of travel.

If you're visiting Norway by car, you can take ferry crossings via ports in the UK, or short crossings from northern ports in Germany and Denmark. Driving in Norway is easy, but snow chains are a must in remote resorts.

The one common factor is Norway is its costs (super expensive in fact). Accommodation is pretty good with the most affordable type being cabins, which cater for groups. Hotels will burn a massive hole in your pocket. Beer prices are so high that evenings in the average bar are out of the question. The best advice is to bring heaps of duty free, or buy your drinks at the off licenses, but note, you have to be 18 to drink beer and 20 to buy or drink spirits.

Overall, Norway is really good but it does have some major drawbacks, like its total lack of music talent, stupidly expensive booze and the world's worst knitwear. On the other hand, the women in this part of the world are to die for.

N O R W A Y

Capital City: Oslo
Population: 4.5 Million
Highest Peak: Galdhopiggen 2472m
Language: Norwegian
Legal Drink Age: 18/20 spirits
Drug Laws: Cannabis is illegal and frowned upon
Age of consent: 16
Electricity: 240 Volts AC 2-pin
International Dialing Code: +47

Norwegian Snowboard Federation
Bentsebrugata 13 B
Oslo, Norway
Tel: +47 22 09 88 40
web: www.nsbf.no

Bus connections
www.fjord1.no - run transfers from Oslo to Geilo, Hemsedal, Stryn
www.nor-way.no - connections to many resorts including Styrn and Tromso
Trains
www.nsb.no - Website for the Norwegian state railway
Airports
www.osl.no - Oslo Airport

Driving Guide
All vehicles drive on the right hand side of the road
Speed limits:
Motorways-80kph (50mph)
Highways-90kph (56mph)
Towns-50kph (31mph)
Emergency
Fire - 110
Police - 112
Ambulance - 113
Tolls
Payable when entering a few cities. Documentation
Driving licence and motor insurance must be carried.
Speeding
On the spot fines are payable if caught speeding.

Time Zone
UTC/GMT +1 hour
Daylight saving time: +1 hour

Currency: Krone
Exchange Rate:
UK£1 = 12.7
US$1 = 7
EURO = 8.4

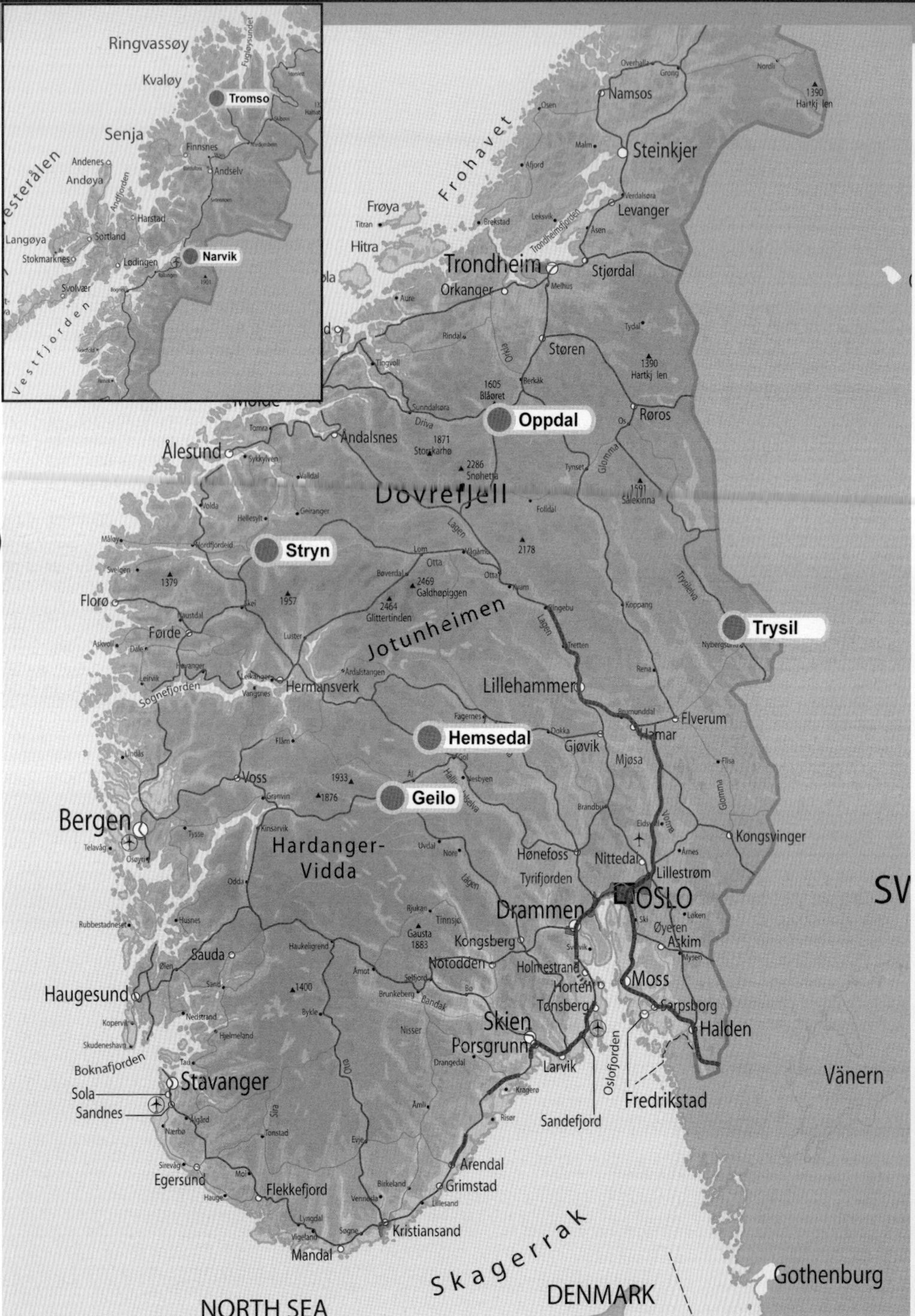

N
N O R W A Y

Inset map

Ringvassøy
Kvaløy
Tromso
Senja
Finnsnes
Andenes
Andøya
Andselv
esterålen
Langøya
Harstad
Sortland
Stokmarknes
Lødingen
Narvik
Svolvær
Vestfjorden

Main map

Grong
Nordli
1590
Hartkj len
Namsos
Chen
Frohavet
Malm
Steinkjer
Fjord
Verdalsøra
Frøya
Titran
Brekstad
Leksvik
Levanger
Asen
Hitra
Trondheimsfjord
Trondheim
Stjørdal
Orkanger
Melhus
Aure
Tydal
Rindal
Støren
Orkla
1390
Hartkj len
1605
Berkåk
Blåøret
Surnadalsøra
Røros
Tromsa
Driva
Oppdal
Os
Andalsnes
1871
Stranggkarhø
Valldal
2286
Snøhetta
Ålesund
Sykkylven
Tynset
1591
Salekinna
Volda
Hellesylt
Geiranger
Dovrefjell
Folldal
Måløy
Nordfjordeid
Lom
Otta
Vågåmo
2178
Stryn
1379
1957
Bøverdal
2469
Galdhøpiggen
Ottra
Vinstra
Kvam
Ringebu
Kvinnarva
Krøppang
Florø
2464
Glittertinden
Jotunheimen
Tretten
Trysil
Førde
Luster
Lagen
Nybergsund
Dale
Levik
Leikanger
Hermansverk
Rena
Askøy
Sogndal
Sognefjorden
Vangsnes
Fagernes
Lillehammer
Elverum
Film
Dokka
Hemsedal
Gjøvik
Hamar
Voss
Nesbyen
Mjøsa
Elisa
Granvin
1933
Al
Gol
Kinsarvik
1876
Geilo
Brandbu
Glomma
Kongsvinger
Bergen
Tysse
Eidsvoll
Arnes
Telavåg
Osøyro
Hardanger-Vidda
Uvdal
Nore
Hønefoss
Nittedal
Oddi
Tyrifjorden
Lillestrøm
Rubbestadneset
Husnes
Rjukan
Tinnsjø
Drammen
OSLO
SV
Sauda
Haukeligrend
Gausta
1883
Kongsberg
Sylling
Ski
Løken
Øyeren
Sand
Åmot
Notodden
Askim
Haugesund
1400
Brunkeberg
Bø
Holmestrand
Myern
Kopervik
Neslandvatn
Randal
Horten
Moss
Skudeneshavn
Hjelmeland
Nisser
Skien
Tønsberg
Sarpsborg
Boknafjorden
Tau
Porsgrunn
Halden
Sola
Stavanger
Sira
Drangedal
Larvik
Oslofjorden
Vänern
Sandnes
Ålgård
Tonstad
Eve
Åmli
Kragerø
Risør
Fredrikstad
Sirevåg
Moi
Sandefjord
Egersund
Flekkefjord
Biskeland
Arendal
Lyngdal
Sogne
Vennesla
Grimstad
Ålgelana
Lillesand
Ågelana
Kristiansand
Mandal
Skagerrak
Gothenburg

NORTH SEA   **DENMARK**

314

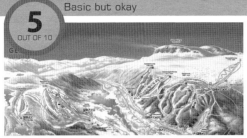

Basic but okay

5 OUT OF 10

	POOR	FAIR	GOOD	TOP
FREERIDE Trees but no real off-piste				
FREESTYLE Terrain park & halfpipe				
PISTES Well groomed short pistes				

Located roughly 4 hours from **Oslo** and situated in the **Hallingdal Valley**, the largest mountain area in Europe, Geilo is the oldest resort in Norway. The well laid out town is easy to get around and lies close to the slopes, making for an easy attack of the runs first thing in the morning. The slopes rise up on two sides of the valley, with terrain that is well maintained, leaving lots of corduroy tracks to mess up in the early hours. Geilo's slopes will suit intermediate and novice riders mostly, with little to set the heart racing for advanced or even competent riders, although there are a few black graded runs. The two separate areas (which aren't connected) rise up to give a maximum lift height of 1173 metres. If you want to ride both places, you'll have to take a snow taxi, which is not included in your lift pass. The Vestila area, which is actually the smaller of the two, has the longer runs, with a mixture of blues, reds and a couple of blacks.

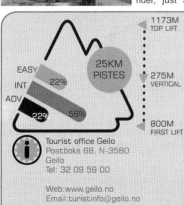

FREERIDERS who pick a resort for powder and fast long adventurous trails, will not be satisfied here. There is no great adrenaline rush if you're a competent rider, just a couple of challenging runs to tackle and only a small amount of good powder terrain to seek out, but there are some trees to shred off the Heissen lift.

FREESTYLERS Theres a huge 150m Super Pipe at **Fugleleiken**; Northern Europe's largest. They spent NK1.2million last season upgrading the park and getting all the toys needed to maintain it, so expect a well cut pipe and plenty of booters.

BEGINNERS are presented with an excellent choice of easy slopes to tackle, starting out at the base area with good flats higher up and easy runs back into the village

THE TOWN

pics: (c) Geilo tourism

Geilo also offers loads of things to do, you can try ice climbing, snow rafting or if you fancy reducing your balls to the size of two peas, you can sign up for a night in a snow hole. Geilo is a sprawling affair with good **accommodation**, but nothing comes cheap. Eating here is simple but even a basic pizza will set you back 70Kr. **Night life** will sting you if you plan to drink heavily or chat up a good looking Norwegian lass. *Hos John's, Laverb* and the *Bardola* are the places to try your luck.

N
NORWAY

1173M TOP LIFT

275M VERTICAL

800M FIRST LIFT

EASY
INT 22%
ADV 22% 56%

25KM PISTES

Tourist office Geilo
Postboks 68, N-3580
Geilo
Tel: 32 09 59 00

Web:www.geilo.no
Email:turistinfo@geilo.no

Number of runs: 39
Longest run: 2.0km
Total Lifts: 19
4 chairs, 14 drags, 5 Children's lifts
Lift capacity (people per hour)
22,000
Lift times:
9:30 – 16:30

Winter Period:
Nov to May
Lift Passes
Afternoon pass - 255
1 Day 295, 2 Days 575
6 Day pass 1225
Hire
Board & boots 310 per day
Board School
Private lesson 390 for 55 mins
Night Boarding
5 evenings a week until 20:00
from 2 January - 11 April.

Annual Snowfall:
1.25m
Snowmaking:
50% of slopes

Bus
Bus transfer from Oslo airport every Friday and Sunday, visit www.fjord1.no
Fly
Oslo airport is 4 hours away.
Train
services are possible direct to Geilo from Oslo and take around 3 1/2 hours. Bergen is 3hrs by train.
Car
Via Oslo , head north on highway 7 via Honefos, Gol and Hol to reach Geilo. The distance is aound 150 miles (240 km) and will take 3 hours .

POOR FAIR GOOD TOP

FREERIDE
Trees & some good backcountry
FREESTYLE
3 Terrain parks & 2 pipes
PISTES
Well pisted easy & short slopes

7
OUT OF 10

Pics - Hemsedal tourism

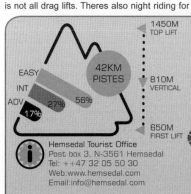

N O R W A Y

Hemsedal has the claim of being the most photographed resort by the snowboarding press, and is no stranger to snowboarding having hosted major events for years. The Artic Challenge was held here in 2001, and recently Mads Jonsson flew in the record books with a 57m jump off a mssive 40m table top built in Hemsedal's backcountry (check the Burton ad - inside cover). Its height, location and use of snow cannons all help to ensure a good snow record and a long season. The slopes lie about 3 kilometres from the main town and are reached by a free shuttle bus. The terrain will appeal to all standards, with 40 kilometres of well prepared piste for freeriders to carve up as well as being ideal for beginners. Freestylers will get to enjoy one of the best parks in Europe, and there's a load of good accessible back country routes. The runs are serviced by a good lift system which, unlike some neighbouring resorts, is not all drag lifts. Theres also night riding for most of the

season during the week until 9pm, useful if you're trying to avoid the expensive bars.

FREERIDERS. Theres a healthy attitude towards going off piste; it's your responsibility plain and simple. So with that in mind, grab a guide or a local and head off to the **Totten** or **Røgjin** Summits. From the back of the Totten Summit, you're treated to some excellent cliffs and powder, which will test even the advanced rider. Make a bee-line for the run known locally as the Annus, a long, steep couloir that should be treated with respect. From the top of Røgjin take the sign for 13 but head for the back of the mountain and follow round, for a run known as the rubber forest. You'll start off in a great powder field, but quickly heading into the trees, and they're thick and deep. These runs should lead you straight to main roads, where those canny Norwegian taxi drivers are ready to take you back to the base. Staying within the boundary line, if you like trees you'll have no complaints here. Theres some concealed tree rails in the woods off run 7.

FREESTYLERS. There's 2 terrain parks and small beginner/kids park. The intermediate park on run 33 consists of series of jumps, and a good variety of rails once you turn the corner. The main park's built well and high with a great selection of jumps, quarter pipes, rails and boxes catering for good intermediates to experts. There's 2 half pipes including a well cut super pipe. Freestylers looking for some natural hits, should take the **Holdeskarheisen** and **Roniheisen** chairs to reach some cool terrain, including a tight gully to pull air in.

PISTES. Any carvers will find the runs known as the **Hemsedalsloypa** and **Kuleloyas** the place to lay out turns. These may not be the longest runs in the world, but they're not for wimps. The **Sahaugloypa** is also a decent run on which to get some speed together. In many of Norway's resorts the runs are usually very short, so it comes as a big relief to find a trail that lasts more than two seconds. The **Turistloypa** is the longest descent and

---

1450M TOP LIFT
810M VERTICAL
650M FIRST LIFT

EASY
INT
ADV 17% 27% 56%
42KM PISTES

Hemsedal Tourist Office
Post box 3, N-3561 Hemsedal
Tel: ++47 32 05 50 30
Web: www.hemsedal.com
Email: info@hemsedal.com

NEW New for 05/06 season
Blue line intermediate park is now twice as wide with more features including a half-pipe.

Number of runs: 34
Longest run: 6.0km
Total Lifts: 17
6 chairs, 11 drags
Lift capacity (people per hour):
22,600
Lift times:
9.30am to 9.30pm
Mountain cafes:
6

Annual Snowfall:
3m
Snowmaking:
15% of slopes

Winter Period:
Nov to May
Lift Passes:
Half-day 285
1 Day pass - 320
2 Day pass - 640
6 Day pass - 1320
Season 4295
Hire
Several companies in town. Hemsedal Sport Skiservice charge 310 per day for board and boots
Board School
90 min lesson 420 (weekend)
5x90mins lesson 595 (week)
Private lesson 430 for 50mins
Night Boarding
Tuesday-friday until 9pm. 5 slopes lit.

although it's easy (even for novices still in nappies), it's worth a blast if only to avoid being on a lift again.

BEGINNERS seem to fare well wherever they go in Norway. Hemsedal is no exception; the only difference is that at least there is something worth progressing onto after mastering the easy flats at the base and those higher up. Instructors tend to avoid the intimidating drags at the bottom, and head up lift F, where theres a nice green all the way back down, it can get a bit busy though. Instructors do speak good english, group and 50 minute private lessons are available. Last season saw the expansion of the beginners/family area. Theres waves, a mini quarter pipe, jumps, rails, self timer slope, and a path in the forest with animals made of wood all serviced by 2 new platter lifts.

THE TOWN

If you plan to put Hemsedal on your calling card, only do so if you have a bank balance akin to that of Richard Branson. Put simply, Hemsedal is very expensive; however it is possible to do it on a budget, just watch the alcohol and taxis and the rest is surprisingly affordable. If you need to check your email then head for the Hemsedal Cafe in town, or the restaurant at the base near the Holvinheisen lift, and its free!

Accommodation can be had near the slopes, either at *Veslestølen* or *Skarsnuten* thats serviced by its own lift. The only trouble being that you're left with an expensive taxi if you want to get to/from the main town as buses to the resort finish early, but you can easily get quality apartment for a week for about £150 based on 8 sharing. Alternativley theres plenty of accomodation in town, or if the budgets really tight then opt for a cabin or the campsite. Hemsedal Cafe does some good food at lunch, enormous portions.

Night life. Things kick off at the outside bar at the base where they'll often have live music from 4pm, then its after ski in the village. A beer will set you back at least UK£5, so hold on to it tightly. The main snowboard hang out for evening madness is the *Hemsedal Cafe*, which is expensive, cool, and full of gorgeous Norwegians. The *skogstad* hotel has a nightclub open late.

CAR
Via Oslo, head north on highway 7 via Honefos and Gol and on to Hemsedal. Oslo to resort is 137 miles (220km).
FLY
to Oslo airport, about 2 1/4 hours away. Direct sunday service from/to hemsedal NOK 375 return contact resort
TRAIN
services are possible to Gol from Oslo and Bergen take around 2 1/4 hours.
BUS
Direct from Oslo & Bergen, www.nor-way.no and www.bergenekspressen.no. Local bus services from Gol

N O R W A Y

POOR FAIR GOOD TOP

FREERIDE
A couple of trees & great off-piste
FREESTYLE
Nothing laid on, but some natural
PISTES
What there is is ok

Ghost town with good terrain if prepared to hike

6 OUT OF 10

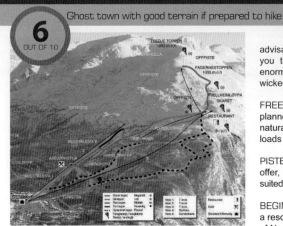

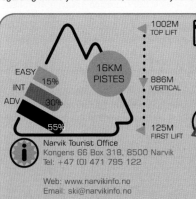

About 1 hour west of the Swedish resort of **Riksgransen** lies Narvik, a hidden treasure in snowboard circles. With only 5 lifts and a summit that only just gets over 1000 metres, Narvik isn't your typical holiday resort: it's a small-town situated at the foot of a superb mountain, with lifts only opening in the afternoons on weekdays and all day on weekends and holidays. The busiest times are in February and Easter, but other than that, lift lines are practically non-existent and being located so far north, tour groups have never heard of this place. This helps to keep the slopes free of sad two plank numpties.

FREERIDERS should get the most out of this area. Much of the riding terrain is above the tree-line, but the lack of tree runs is fully compensated by plenty of natural pipes, bowls, cornices and cliffs to fly off. For fat lazy riders or those who prefer not to exhaust themselves with hiking, you'll be able to have a good blast within the lift covered area. The area known as **Fagernesfjellet** is a paradise for relatively advanced freeriders. The lifts only cover a small percentage of actual terrain available and as heli-boarding is forbidden in Norway, heaven is waiting if you're prepared to hike. There are no rules regarding where you can board, but before you take off, it's

advisable to hook up with one of the locals who will show you the secret spots. In addition to Morkolla, with its enormous amount of snow, Narvik's backcountry offers wicked extreme terrain.

FREESTYLERS don't have a fun park, although one is planned for the future. There is, however, plenty of good natural terrain for getting air and the flat stuff allows for loads of ground spinning.

PISTES. Theres not much in the way of pisted trails on offer, the pistes of Fagernesfjellet are steep, wavy and suited to a bit of carving, but pistes aren't the reason to visit.

BEGINNERS will probably have a better time in **Ankernes**, a resort which is 3 miles away, rather than the main slopes of Narvik.

THE TOWN
Narvik is at the base of the slopes and everything is within walking distance. Expensive is the key word around here, but lodging in a cabin or a room at Breidablikk Inn is one of the easiest on the pocket. As for night life and partying, things happen at the Fossestua which has a pool table and is good for a beer and a late night session.

Narvik Tourism

1002M TOP LIFT

886M VERTICAL

125M FIRST LIFT

EASY
INT **15%**
ADV **30%**
55%

16KM PISTES

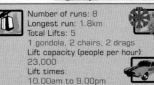

Number of runs: 8
Longest run: 1.8km
Total Lifts: 5
1 gondola, 2 chairs, 2 drags
Lift capacity (people per hour):
23,000
Lift times:
10.00am to 9.00pm

Winter Period:
Nov to May
Lift Passes
1 Day 230, 2 Day 410, 6 Day 890
Hire
Board & boots 210 per day
Board School
Group lessons from 150 for 90mins. Private lesson 235 for 60 mins
Night Boarding
Yes

Annual Snowfall:
Unknown
Snowmaking:
30% of slopes

Bus
Direct buses available from Tromso
Fly
to Oslo airport and then to Evenes which is 50 miles on.
Train
to Narvik from Oslo will take 20 hrs.
Car
Drive via Oslo , head north on E6 all the way up to Narvik, which is at least a 20 hour drive.

Narvik Tourist Office
Kongens 66 Box 318, 8500 Narvik
Tel: +47 (0) 471 795 122

Web: www.narvikinfo.no
Email: ski@narvikinfo.no

	POOR	FAIR	GOOD	TOP
FREERIDE Some trees & decent off-piste				
FREESTYLE Terrain park & halfpipe				
PISTES Lots of easy slopes				

Nothing too pulse racing

5
OUT OF 10

Oppdal is situated 93 miles south of the town of **Trondheim**, where three valleys (originating in different parts of the country) meet. The resort is divided into four main areas, providing something for all riders with some of the best off-piste Norway has to offer. The snowboard scene is expanding in **Oppdal** (as everywhere else in the world) and most weekends the place is 'invaded' by boarders from the city of Trondheim. During the usual winter holiday period, the population doubles, so if you're not particularly fond of lines and crowds, try to stay clear. As one of Norway's biggest areas, Oppdal will appeal (as with much of this country) to easy going, piste loving freeriders. The 80 km of piste are for beginners mainly as there's nothing for advanced riders to get too excited about, and even intermediates will soon tire of the place. At the top of Vangslia there's a black run, but the mountain flattens out at the bottom making it a short and uneventful trail, unless you're a beginner joining at the top of lift A, where it becomes an excellent easy area.

FREERIDERS are kept interested with some particularly good freeride terrain to explore that includes trees, steeps and powder. The stuff found in Stolen Valley is pretty good, but due to avalanche danger, the area is often closed. However, the runs on the Vangslia mountain offer the best time, with some nice terrain features to ride, including steeps.

FREESTYLERS have a pipe (not a hot one, though) and a snowpark. The Adalen area is a natural snowpark which should keep air heads aroused for a day or two. Ground grommets will find the uneven slopes great for flatland tricks.

CARVERS can experience what it's like to fly, by cutting some lines on the Downhill World Cup arena. What's more, Oppdal's longest run reaches a respectable 2.5 miles, offering a long ride.

BEGINNERS are well catered for, with loads of novice trails stretched across the 4 connected areas all accessed with one lift pass. Snowboard instruction is also very good.

pic - Oppdal Tourism

NORWAY

THE TOWN

In the main, local services are varied but expensive. For a convenient place to sleep, stay at the Hellaugstol camp ground, about 100 metres from the slopes, or at Landsbytorget in Stolen where a group can share an apartment. At night, check out 'The Jaeger Pub' or go skating.

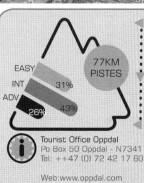

EASY
INT 31%
ADV 26% 43%

77KM PISTES

1350M TOP LIFT
790M VERTICAL
545M FIRST LIFT

Number of runs: 28
Longest run: 4km
Total Lifts: 19
2 chairs, 14 drags
Lift capacity (people per hour):
22,000
Lift times:
9:30 – 16:30

Winter Period:
Nov to May
Lift Passes
1 Day 280, 2 Day 495, 6 Days 1135
Night Boarding
Yes

Annual Snowfall:
Unknown
Snowmaking:
45% of slopes

Bus
services available from Bergen, Oslo, Trondheim, tel: +47 815 44 444
Fly
to Oslo airport, about 4 hours away, nearest airport is at Trondheim
Train
services go direct to Oppdal from Trondheim, Oslo and Bodø. Night trains also available tel: +47 815 00 888
Car
via Oslo, head north on E6 all the way up to Oppdal (420km). 120km from Trondheim

Tourist Office Oppdal
Po Box 50 Oppdal - N7341
Tel: ++47 (0) 72 42 17 60

Web: www.oppdal.com
Email: post@oppdal.com

POOR FAIR GOOD TOP

FREERIDE
Nothing pulse racing
FREESTYLE
Various kickers & rails
PISTES
Short pistes

Good summer riding area

4
OUT OF 10

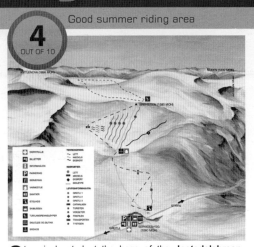

S tryn is located at the base of the **Jostedalsbreen** glacier and is Norway's most famous summer resort (in fact the only one of note). The glacier gets so much snow during the winter (five metres plus), that the lifts are usually totally buried and as they couldn't run them even if they wanted to. Although this is a popular snowboarder's hangout, it should be pointed out that Stryn is also very popular with skiers, resulting in fairly long lift queues. What's more, a number of ski teams spend time on the slopes doing training sessions, swelling the numbers further. Still, leaving the two plankers aside, what you have is a small glacier mountain offering some interesting and steep riding on slopes where snow holds its condition all day. A lot of Norwegians simply come up to strip off and sunbathe (an often enjoyable sight). However, for those wanting to snowboard, the 10 kilometres of terrain are serviced by just two lifts; a double chair and a drag lift. A lot of snowboard camps are held here each year with lots of pros on the teaching staff.

FREERIDERS coming here in search of big powder bowls, dense trees and limitless off piste should forget it, Stryn has none of that. In the main, you are presented with some steep, but featureless terrain.

FREESTYLERS are the ones who are going to benefit from a trip to Stryn the most, apart from the natural hits and the famous road jumps (as seen in many a video), the man made kickers are superb.

BEGINNERS that are easily intimidated may find this place a little daunting as the slopes are steep, but there are some areas to play about on if you really want to ride here.

THE TOWN
Stryn is located along a road that is littered with campsites offering cheap places to sleep. The main hangout is the village of **Hjelle**, 15 minutes from the slopes, where you can rent a shared cabin from 420 Kr. The main **local pub** is where the only action takes place with numerous late night drinking sessions happening place on a daily basis (although it costs).

(c) Stryn tourism

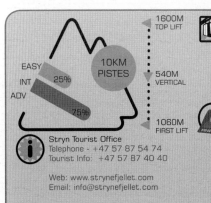

1600M
TOP LIFT

EASY
INT
ADV

10KM
PISTES

25%

75%

540M
VERTICAL

1060M
FIRST LIFT

Stryn Tourist Office
Telephone - +47 57 87 54 74
Tourist Info: +47 57 87 40 40

Web: www.strynefjellet.com
Email: info@strynefjellet.com

Number of runs: 8
Longest run: 2.0km
Total Lifts: 2
1 chair, 1 drag
Lift capacity (people per hour):
1,000
Lift times:
9.00am to 9.30pm

Winter Period:
Feb to March
Summer Period:
April to August
Lift Passes
1 Day 280, 3 of 4 Days 780
6 of 7 Days 1200, Season pass 3000
Hire
Board & boots 270 per day
Night Boarding
Yes till 9:30

Annual Snowfall:
5m
Snowmaking:
none

Fly
to Oslo airport & inland to Trondheim airport.
Train
to Trondheim from Oslo.
Car
via Oslo, head north on route 7 to Gol and then take the 52 to Signol onto the route 1 and route 60 via Olden to Stryn.

FREERIDE
Some trees but limited off-piste
FREESTYLE
Terrain park & 2 halfpipes
PISTES
Great place to learn

POOR FAIR GOOD TOP

Not bad at all for a few days

6
OUT OF 10

pic - Jakob Hertz /IN

Trysil is supposed to be Norway's largest resort and is definitely big by most Norwegian standards, and a very good place to snowboard. Situated just over two hours from **Oslo**, Trysil is a resort that caters well for its visitors, no matter what time of year. Snowboarding is possible here between the months of November and May, on slopes that cover a large percentage of the **Trysilfjellet Mountain**, which is predominately suited to beginners and basic intermediate riders. There are runs for advanced riders which will keep them interested for some time. Strangely the higher you go, the easier things get, notably at the top section of the slopes, where a wide open and somewhat flat snow field opens up above the tree line

FREERIDERS who venture here will find some okay tree riding and a bit of powder, but in the main the terrain is a bit dull and featureless. The runs up from **Hogegga** are the most challenging, with a series of interconnecting black runs that snake through the trees to the base.

FREESTYLERS make up a large number of the riders seen ripping up Trysil. To keep the air heads happy the management have provided them with a well looked after fun park and two halfpipes that are dotted around at various locations.

PISTES Old school carvers note, Trysil allows you ample opportunity to put in some extremely wide turns (especially on the higher sections) but don't come here expecting a mass of long, super fast trails.

BEGINNERS. There are two types of orgasm, one with a good looking Norwegian chick and the other is learning to snowboard at Trysil. The place is learner heaven, with a mass of easy slopes that are well linked and well serviced by the lift system.

THE TOWN
The village of **Trysil** is 2 km from the slopes and offers good local facilities, although what is on offer is stupidly expensive and would make a weeks stay a struggle with funds, and impossible on a low budget.
Accommodation is offered in a huge number of cabins and hotels, (all will burn deep into the pocket). Still, a few beers will help dampen the shock of prices (once pissed, you no longer care what the next things costs).

NORWAY

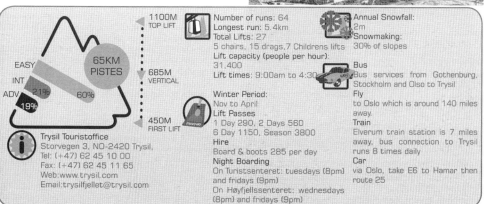

1100M
TOP LIFT

EASY
INT
ADV 21%
19%
60%

65KM
PISTES

685M
VERTICAL

450M
FIRST LIFT

Trysil Touristoffice
Storvegen 3, NO-2420 Trysil,
Tel: (+47) 62 45 10 00
Fax: (+47) 62 45 11 65
Web:www.trysil.com
Email:trysilfjellet@trysil.com

Number of runs: 64
Longest run: 5.4km
Total Lifts: 27
5 chairs, 15 drags, 7 Childrens lifts
Lift capacity (people per hour):
31,400
Lift times: 9:00am to 4:30

Winter Period:
Nov to April
Lift Passes
1 Day 290, 2 Days 560
6 Day 1150, Season 3800
Hire
Board & boots 285 per day
Night Boarding
On Turistsenteret: tuesdays (8pm) and fridays (9pm)
On Høyfjellssenteret: wednesdays (8pm) and fridays (9pm)

Annual Snowfall:
2m
Snowmaking:
30% of slopes

Bus
Bus services from Gothenburg, Stockholm and Olso to Trysil
Fly
to Oslo which is around 140 miles away.
Train
Elverum train station is 7 miles away, bus connection to Trysil runs 8 times daily
Car
via Oslo, take E6 to Hamar then route 25

ROUND-UP

AI
Super boring place, 2 1/2hrs from Oslo

FILEFJELL SKIHEISER
This is one of Norways smallest resorts and also one of the most boring. There is very little on offer, other than a few over rated intermediate and beginner runs. There is a small terrain park with an equally small halfpipe. In its defense its well looked after by local riders. The nearby village offers very basic lodging and other services all of which come at a high price.

Ride area: 8km Top Lift: 1125m
Total Lifts:3
Contact:
Tyin-Filefjell Skisenter
N-2985 Tyinkrysset
Tel +47 (0) 613 675 75
Fax +47 (0) 613 675 76
How to get there: Fly to: Fagerness 2 hours away

GAUSDAL
A bit dull, but okay. 9 lifts, 20 runs

GAUSTABLIKK
A few okay runs, 5 lifts, 8 runs

GOL
Total waste of time, about 20mins from Hemsedal

GRONG
Forget it altogther, 6 lifts, 10 runs.

HOVEN
Okay night riding. 4 lifts & 12 runs

HAFJELL/LILLEHAMMER
This is Norway's famous resort if for know other reason other than it once hosted the winter Olympics. However, just because they flew the '5 rings', doesn't mean that its a good measure of what's on offer. What you get here is a narrow cluster of runs with an okay mixture of all ability terrain that includes a long black run from almost the top to the bottom.

Freestylers have an much improved halfpipe for catching air. Theres a good variety of jumps and rails for all levels. **Beginners** have a few easy to reach novice slopes although crowded

Ride area: 33km Runs: 29
Easy 30% Intermediate 41% Advanced 18% Expert 11%
Longest run: 7km
Top Lift: 1050m Vertical Drop: 830m
Total Lifts:22 - 3 chairs, 18 drags, 1 Magic Carpet
Lifts Open:9.30am to 3.30pm 9.30am to 4.30pm (floodlit slopes)
Contact:
Hafjell Alpinsenter
AS 2636 Øyer Norway
Tel.: +47 61 27 47 00
www.hafjell.no
How to get there: FLY: Fly to: Oslo 2 hours away.
BUS: Free shuttle bus from Lillehammer, and good local bus service www.opplandstrafikk.no
DRIVING: 15km from Lillehammer, follow exit to Hafjell. 200 km (2.55 hrs) from Oslo, follow E6 north.

KVITFELL
2 good halfpipes, 7 lifts 20 runs, 60 minutes from Oslo

RUSTADHØGDA
Small pipe, but nothing else. 3 lifts, 3hrs from Oslo

SJUSJOEN
Only good for no hopers, 1 lifts, 80mins from Oslo

STRANDA
Okay for slow beginners, 5 lifts, 2hrs from Oslo

TROMSO
Famous for holding the finale of the TTR series, the Artic Challenge. Very basic resort, miles from anywhere, but they have the capacity to build a good park & pipe.

www.tromsoalpinsenter.com
www.ttrprosnowboarding.com

pic - Tromso Tourism

VALDRES
Valdres is a small unassuming typical Norwegian resort with a good reputation amongst Norway's snowboard population. The tree lined runs will suit intermediate freeriders and air heads.There is some extreme terrain with trees to check out that should keep the average freerider happy for a day or two.
Grommets will find enough logs to slide down. The fun park and pipe are also good and offer the best chance of pulling some good air.
Carvers looking for lots of wide open flats will be disappointed, as will advanced riders looking for major hits or deep gullies

First timers should have no problem here, the flats at the base area are full-on for collecting the first bruises with ease.
Lodging is the usual Norwegian offerings, with a number of decent chalets or apartments to choose from. **Night wise**, simply crank up the walkman and down your duty free booze.

Ride area: 10km Longest run: 7km
Top Lift: 1050m

ROUND-UP

Total Lifts:4
Contact:
Valdres Tourist Office
P.O.Box 203, N-2901 Fagernes
Tel - (+47) 61 35 94 10
Fax - (+47) 61 35 94 15
www.valdres.com
How to get there: Fly to: Oslo 2 hours away

VASSFJELLET

Vassfjellet is not a tourist resort perched way up high on a mountain and boasting millions of square miles of ridabe piste backed up with a modern base complex decked out with purpose built hotels and other tourist traps. No, this is a locals place and serves the masses from neighbouring towns and the city of Trondheim a few miles away. If you're on a road trip and fancy something different then check this place out, it's pretty cool and very snowboard friendly, with a large number of student riders from Trondheim's University. They are given student concessions on lift passes, so if you're doing the college or Uni number, be sure to carry your student card. The terrain is fairly well matched in terms of level and styles and although the slopes here can be described as dull, most riders will find something to keep them content for an

hour. By most standards this is a very small resort with only around 6 miles of piste (half of which is flood lit for night riding). This place is by no means going to hold the attention of advanced riders for too long, especially if you're looking for big powder bowls and large cliff drops. Still there is a 2 mile run to keep you occupied for a few minutes, (which offers the opportunity to ride at speed and take out a few skiers en route). If you really want to find out where the best ride areas are, contact the guys at the local snowboard club, there are no guides here but they will give you a few pointers.

pic - Vassfjellet Tourism

Freeriders have a few wooded sections to cut through, but they won't take long to ride through.
Freestylers roaming around will find some banked walls to

check out, as well as a well kept pipe and park littered with kickers, rails and a quarter pipe   .
Carvers who can will have the whole area done in five minutes.
Beginners will find this place more than adequate with a good selection of easy runs.

At the end of the day, every one heads off back to Trondheim by a regular bus service. There's a good selection of places to sleep, eat and drink at almost affordable prices.

Night-life is also pretty good but booze will cost you dearly.

Ride area: 10km
Easy 25%
Intermediate 25%
Advanced 30%
Expert 20%
Longest run: 3.5km
Top Lift: 670m
Vertical Drop: 460m
Total Lifts:6
Contact:
Vassfjellet Skiheiser AS
P.b. 6079, 7003 Trondheim
Tel: ++47 (0) 72830200
www.vassfjellet.com
How to get there: Fly to: Oslo 3 hours away

VOSS

Voss is a very popular resort with over 40km of well groomed trails that will please carvers and basic freeriders.
The limited off-piste on offer is not bad and allows the chance to go steep and deep above and below the tree line in a number of spots.

Freestylers should avoid trying to catch air out of the permanent ski jump here, as you're not allowed too. Instead check out the pipe or the numerous natural hits dotted around the whole area

Ride area: 40km
Top Lift: 945m
Total Lifts:10
Contact:
www.voss-fjellheisar.no
++47 (0) 56 51 12 12
How to get there: Fly to: Bergen 2 1/2 hours away

ᴡꜱɢRUSSIA

The West's influence has taken over and Russia is not the place it used to be. Snowboarding, especially freestyle, is becoming increasingly popular. Almost every major region has its own snowboard resort and almost every resort has some sort of snowboard terrain park or at least a half-pipe. Specialized magazines and websites appear almost every month and you see more and more snowboards around every winter.

The main advantages of snowboarding in Russia are the huge amounts of snow, lower prices, and exotic locations. Add to this some great sightseeing to be made along the way and you'll get an unforgettable experience.
The disadvantages are that the resorts are quite small (the largest has only 35 km of runs) and some have long lift queues.

Most of the better resorts in Russia are very suitable for freeriders. The best and perhaps the most known places to snowboard in Russia are Elbrus and Cheget mountain, Kamchatka, and Sheregesh.
The first, Elbrus (southern Russia), is the highest peak in Europe and offers a lot of great off-piste terrain. It is also easily accessible with a plane from Russia or Europe and can be quite cheap.
Kamchatka is the exotic volcano land located close to Alaska (USA), on the east coast of Russia. It will be like a paradise for advanced riders who will love doing heli-boarding and riding the beautiful terrain along the volcanoes. It is quite remote, though, and even though helicopter rent and living costs are not too high, the overall price of the trip can be quite steep.
Sheregesh is a major Siberian resort, which offers lots of super powder snow terrain for freeriders. It can be accessed via Trans-Siberian or with a plane and is quite cheap. A real rough, cold, but enjoyable Siberian experience.

A few resorts at Urals -- Abzakovo, Bannoe and Zavyalikha -- are more suitable for freestylers. The riding area is quite small, there's not too much snow at times, but the natural hits and occasional snowboard parks can occupy you for a couple of days.

If you ever thought about taking a Trans-Siberian railway, then Baikalsk is your chance to "kill two rabbits with one shot". This small, but well maintained resort on the shore of the biggest and deepest lake in the world -
Baikal - is located just a few hundred meters from a Trans-Siberian stop (just after Irkutsk) and can be a refreshing stop after a 4-day train journey.

Krasnaya Polyana is the Russian version of Sierra Nevada: the Black sea is less than an hour drive away. It is also the

R
U
S
S
I
A

324

Capital City: Moscow
Population: 143.8 million
Highest Peak: Gora El'brus 5633 m
Language: Russian
Legal Drink Age: 18
Drug Laws: Cannabis is illegal
Age of consent: 16
Electricity: 220 Volts AC 2-pin, 50hz
International Dialing Code: +7

Currency: Ruble
Exchange Rate: UK£1 = 51 EURO = 35 US$1 = 28

Driving Guide
All vehicles drive on the right hand side of the road
Speed limits:
60km (37mph) towns
90km (55mph) outside towns
Speeding fines payable, "unofficial" payment not uncommon
Emergency
01 - Fire 02 -Police 03 - Ambulance
Info
Very few car hire companys rent cars without a driver for you. Some very dodgy roads, less than half of roads are sealed
Documentation
Home driving licence and a russian translation of it. Passport.

 Trains
Train services around the country are okay and very affordable. The metro trains in Moscow are superb with stations that are a work of art. It is also possible to take trains from the west to the east, but you will need to change trains on route as Russia uses a different rail gauge.

Bus
Buses services in Russia are cheap and on the whole good but they are also notoriously slow and time tables are a myth.

Fly
Gateway international airport is,Moscow (Sheremetevo). The airport is 18 miles out of the city.

Approximate global air travel times to Moscow:
from: London 5$^{1/2}$ hours
Los Angles 17$^{1/2}$ hours, New York 14 hours

Russian snowboard federation
Ananyevskiy pereulok, 5/12, office 161
Moscow 125502
www.snbrd.ru

 Time Zone
UTC/GMT +3 hours
Daylight saving time: +1 hour

most comfortable and the most westernized resort, but the most expensive in Russia.

The capital city Moscow has quite a few snowboard areas in the city and around. The most notable are Volen and Stepanovo, Sorochany, and Ya-Park (features a terrain park and a half-pipe). They are all located very close to each other 1.5 hours drive to the north of Moscow. Kant is only a 30-minute metro ride from the center, but it's too small.

The "northern capital" of Russia, St. Petersburg, also has an area about 1.5 hours to the north of the city, where you can find similar resorts: Snezhny, Zolotaya Dolina, and Krasnoe Ozero. They all have something to offer to snowboarders: terrain parks, half-pipes, big-airs, and cheap self-catering accommodation.

All resorts have a good range of accommodation for any budget and demands (except Moscow, where everything is too expensive), and lots of cafes and restaurants. All the resorts listed here provide snowboards for hire (but some resorts have a poor choice) and the board leashes are never required. Snowboarding is possible from mid-November to late April (till August at Elbrus), but the temperatures can go as low as -25 in mid February. English is spoken by some Russians in Moscow and St. Petersburg, but not much elsewhere, so learning at least the Russian cyrillic alphabet will make things a lot easier.

R
R
U
S
S
I
A

325

	POOR	FAIR	GOOD	TOP
FREERIDE Trees & lots of off-piste				
FREESTYLE Nothing laid on				
PISTES Bumpy				

6 OUT OF 10

Crowded but has a pioneering feel to it

Set amongst the **Caucasus Mountains** near the **Georgian border** is Dombai. It has a unique atmosphere and is often visited by Russian tourists and locals who tend to go up the mountain to eat, view the peaks and drink Vodka as opposed to boarding. The riding is good with plenty to suit all. The lower slopes provide some runs through the trees which are gentle and ideal for beginners. Even though the mountain has three piste bashers, grooming is infrequent and piste markings generally range from poor to non-existent. There are lots of hiking options available although Russians are not big on going off-piste. The chair lifts and cable cars are from the bygone era and nothing is new. You will see some of the most ingenious repair work undertaken. Take for instance the broken perspex windows of the gondola car, they have drilled holes either side of the crack and then sewn it together. The lifts are interesting with a "pay as you ride" system. When lifts are down, some of the piste basher drivers charge each person to ride on a Cat Track tour. Safety is not high on the list of priorities, but it has to be remembered that this is Russia and anything goes.

FREERIDERS will get the most out of this place. Due to the limited number of snowboarders (about 5%) who come here you can be sure when the powder falls it can be ridden for days with no chance of being tracked out.

FREESTYLERS. There's nothing laid on during the winter season. Facilities arise only at the end of March for the Spring Snowboard Camp when dozens of Russian freestylers come here to practice.

BEGINNERS. The runs are not recommended for beginners, you'll find them steep and often icy except for a few lower runs. Besides, there are no markings on the runs and too many people riding in all directions

THE TOWN. Dombai is a relatively small settlement, so in terms of entertainment and apres-ski it's quite a dull place, but the mountains are really beautiful. Most of the people who live at Dombai earn money for the whole year during the winter time renting out their apartments to tourists. The locals are friendly and are very pleased to meet foreigners, especially English speakers, as they like to practice their language skills and love to share their drink with you. Overall the place is very interesting and has a very pioneering feel to it. If you are planning a trip to Russia bring your snowboard with you and have an adventure in the Caucussus.

Accomodation. There are two large hotels - *"Gornie Vershiny"*, tel +7(87864)58236, 58230, 58192 - rooms 800-1000R per night) which is 50-150 m from the lifts, and *"Dombai"* ($30-$100 per night for a double), which is 100-150 m from the lifts. Among smaller and nicer hotels are *"Zolotoy Mustang"* (tel +7(87872) 5-83-33, +7(928) 945-6504 - shared accommodation 500R ($18) per person per night, rooms start at $70 per night) and *"Solnechnaya Dolina"* (tel +7(87864)58269, 58291 - $30 per person per night), 100 m from the lifts. There are also about 15 other small hotels and many private apartments to rent. During the high season and official holidays (29 December - 8 January, 4-8 March) it is hard to find an available room and you have to book two weeks beforehand.

Food. There are many cafes and restaurants. A meal costs $10. The most popular cafe is *"U Zuly"* - you have to book the table a day before. Food is filling, try the Georgian hot cheesebread called 'Khachapuri.

Night time madness is best sampled in the **Hotel Gornye Vershiny.** There are two disco/bars and a few places to eat. The ground floor disco is generally more fun with a mixture of European and old Russian "Pop". Snowboard videos are shown behind the DJ's stand and the place has a distinct 70's feel purely by accident. A swimming pool and a sauna is also available in the hotel but you may need a health card to get in.

EASY
INT 35%
ADV
25% 40%

3012M

1382M VERTICAL

1630M

Tourist Office Dombai
Dombai
Tel: +7 (0) 86522 78168
Accommodation Tel: +7 (0) 865 58 279
Web: www.dombai.ru
Email: mail@dombai.ru

Annual Snowfall:
Unknown
Snowmaking:
none

Number of runs: 10
Longest run: 5km
Total Lifts: 12
1 Gondolas, 5 chairs, 6 drags
Mountain Cafes: 5
Lift times:
9am to 4.30pm

Winter Period:
Nov to May
Lift Passes
1 day pass : 600R
6 day pass: 3200R
10 day pass: 5000R
Hire
Board & boots 300R per day
Board School
300R for 1 hour
Night Boarding
Yes

Bus
from Mineralnie Vody bus station to Teberda (20 km from Dombai). The price is 150 R ($5), takes 7 hours. The timetable is changing frequently and is totally unpredictable.
Fly
Aeroflot Airlines & Siberia Airlines fly to the region. You can fly from Moscow Domodedovo or Moscow Sheremetyevo to Mineralnie Vody. A return costs $200-$350 inc taxes and takes 2.5 hrs.
Train
Train from Moscow to Mineralnie Vody or Cherkessk (takes about 25 hours, costs 1500 R ($59) one way. Then take a bus to Teberda or a taxi to Dombai.
Car
Via Mineral nye, you need to head south for a few kms along the M29, cutting off at Essentuki on to the A157 and the A155 via Teberda and to Dombai. It is not recommended to go by car all the way from Moscow. The road is in a poor condition and the trip can be dangerous in the Caucasus area.

R
R
U
S
S
I
A

	POOR	FAIR	GOOD	TOP
FREERIDE Few trees but huge off-piste				
FREESTYLE Summer park				
PISTES Rutted & rarely bashed				

7
OUT OF 10

Freerider's dream but nightmare lifts queues

Elbrus is the highest ski & snowboard resort in Europe (Val Thorens eat your heart out). It's located in **Kabardino Balkaria** republic in Russia, between the Black and Caspian seas at Elbrusie National Park, close to the **Georgian** border. The centre of it all is the famous mountain Elbrus which with its 5643 m is the highest in Europe. This place is the local freeriders' mecca, offering lots of clear, open powder snow terrain, as well as the opportunity to snowboard until as late into August (on Elbrus). Elbrus actually has two main riding areas: **Elbrus** itself, and the lower **Cheget**, which is about 2 km to the south. **Cheget** is known to be a skier's paradise, and is very underestimated for boarders; the terrain is steeper and more technical than Elbrus's powder trails. Most of area at **Elbrus** is unmarked and people are simply too scared to explore the unmarked trails, and with its better snow record its more of pure Freeriders destination.

The main problem with the resort are the long lift queues (especially on Elbrus - people can spend literally hours queuing) and the bad maintenance of the pisted runs; plenty of ice, stones, bumps etc. So get to the lifts as early as you can and keep clear of the pistes. New lifts at Elbrus are a fairytale, cash flows into the local lefties pockets as long as the old lift is the only way up so they're not exactly interested in changing the status quo; it's a mafia thing no less.

The local people are very friendly and hospitable, but have the southern temperament, so if you are nice to them, they will be nice to you. If you look like an arrogant rich foreigner showing off the latest gear, you'll get it all broken against your head. Officially, the season starts in December and ends in May, but it's recommended to go in February when there's the most snow.

FREERIDING. Elbrus is perfect if you're after some off-piste terrain with clear views and powder snow, but the majority of the terrain is above tree level. As with any place, you need to have a clear idea where you're heading when venturing off piste. A good but tough place to start is **Garabashi** (aka "Bochka" - the highest lift point on Elbrus - 3780 m) from where you can go down towards **Stary Krugozor.** You will also find some very good freeriding at the top of

Cheget (after the last 300-m drag lift, but keep close to the Ai Café). There's also heli-boarding tours available all over the mountain, ask the Terskol travel agency about this. If you are on a tight budget, you can get a near heli-boarding experience by renting a snow cat, which can take you to **Priyut 11** (4800 m). It'll cost $150 for 15 people, so if it's full it'll only cost you $10.

FREESTYLE. The **KingSizePark** at 3750m is easily Europes highest park, but is only built for the summer camps that are run by SPC (see summer boarding section), so in the winter you'll have to seek out your own fun, but theres plenty of air opportunities on both mountains.

BEGINNERS. This is not a beginners' resort, as most piste runs are for intermediates and are not looked too well after. Besides, you're risking spending 4 hours a day in queues.

THE TOWN

The main settlement is **Terskol** which is at the bottom of Elbrus mountain. Azau station is about 4 km which is where the lifts to Elbrus are located. **Cheget** is about 4 km from Terskol. Terskol is a small southern settlement and is very hospitable with a lot of accommodation, cafes, and services. Nightlife it might get a bit rowdy. . If you are worried about terrorism with Chechnya not far away then don't worry about it. There's 500 km and a huge mountain range in between and no problem has ever been reported even during the war.

If you want to stay as close to the **Elbrus** lifts as possible try *Azau hotel* (tel +7 928 2796212) or *Krugozor hotel* (same tel). Both are wooden cottages with all the amenities , and will cost 500R per person. Also try "*Logovo*" at **Azau plain** (tel +7 866 38 7 11 12). Close to the **Cheget** lifts, is *Cheget tourbase* (+7 866 38 71339), from $35 for a room. You can book through www.go-elbrus.com if your Russian isn't too hot. There are a lot of cafes and restaurants in the main village Terskol, as well as Azau and Cheget tourbases. There are also some stands both on Elbrus and Cheget mountains, don't be put off by their run-down looks: the food in most of them is great and cheap.

R

R
U
S
S
I
A

3780M TOP LIFT

EASY

35KM PISTES

INT 25%

ADV

25% 50%

1680M VERTICAL

2100M FIRST LIFT

Number of runs: 21 Longest run: 7km
Total Lifts: 8 - 2 cable-cars, 2 chairs, 4 drags

Winter Period: Dec to May
Summer Period: June to August
Lift Passes 50-70R single, 350R per day
Board School. freeride course $40 per day or $180 6-day course

Bus
All depart from Mineralnye Vody. The journey takes 2-3 hours, costs about 200 R ($7) by bus, about 1000 R ($35) by taxi. Beware of local taxis, as their main entertainment is to bargain, so you'll have to chat for half an hour, before you can drive. Welcome to southern Russia.

Fly
Aeroflot and Sibir Airlines have direct daily flights from Moscow to Mineralnye Vody, which take 2.5 hours and cost about $200 return.

Train
station is Mineralnye Vody. Daily train #34 from Moscow Kazansky station to Vladikavkaz bring you to Mineralnye Vody in about 28 hours. A better train is from Moscow Kursky to Kislovodsk (#27) also takes about 28 hours. The price is about 2200 R ($80) one way in 2nd class.

Car
Long and it poor road quality. However, if you're up for it, you need to go along the federal route from Moscow to Rostov-na-Donu, then drive to Mineralnye Vody and from there it is a 2-3 hour jouney by car to Terskol.

Experience of a lifetime

pic: (c) Kamchatka parks

Kamchatka is a peninsula at the Far East of Russia close to Alaska. Apart from volcanoes and geysers the region is famous for great heliboarding opportunities. Advanced riders from all over the world come to Kamchatka from December to March to experience the untouched snow-fields set in the land of volcanoes. Kamchatka is a top destination for all Russian riders, but you have to know what you're doing and have a guide who can help you find your way back to the helicopter waiting somewhere down the mountain for you.

Most of the boarders prefer to ride at Viluchinskiy (2173 m), Mutnovskiy (2323 m), Avachinskiy (2741 m), Goreliy (1826 m), Opala (2460 m) volcanoes. The average route lengths is 6 km, the average vertical drop is 1500 m. The helicopters are paid on a flight time basis. The price per flight hour is $500 - $1800 depending on type of helicopter. There are several agencies which provide heliboarding tours, but you need to book it at least a month before. Helicopters take off from Elizovo, a village 30 km from the local city Petropavlovsk-Kamchatky. The only local company which hires helicopters is Krechet Ltd, http://krechet.farhost.ru . The helicopters are paid on flight time basis. The price per flight hour is $500 - $1700 depending on the type of helicopter. Maximum capacity (with equipment) is usually 12-20 people, so if you're in a group it can be relatively cheap.

www.kamchatka-parks.com run 8 day heliboarding trips, it costs 575 euros for everything except getting there and the helicopter. You can expect to pay around 1200 euros for the helicopter based on a group of 10 people sharing. www.helipro.ru also offer tours.

Away from heli-boarding there are a couple of tiny resorts dotted around the area, but none of them of any real note. The 3 main resorts are Krasnaya Sopka, Morosnaya and Edelveis. Each resort has nothing more than a couple of drags serving 3 or 4 slopes, the longest of any of the slopes here are just over 1km, and there are certainly no terrain parks.

THE TOWN

There are several hotels in Elizovo, the most popular is "Golubaya Laguna", it has a small aqua park and a natural hot springs (doubles costs $50). In the centre of Petropavlovsk-Kamchatsky, usually occupied by American hunters and Japanese tourists is the Petropavlovsk hotel. Recently renovated, all the staff speak English. There is a bowling alley and a bar in the building. Double- $88 in brekfast. Tel.: +7 4152 5-03-74 or visit www.petropavlovsk-hotel.ru for more details. The Avacha Hotel charges $76 for a nice clean Double. The only casino "Collisem" in the city is in the same building. This hotel located in the middle of the city – not far from ocean, there are daily shops near and many restaurants, market is in front of it. There are TV-sets, fridges and phones in the rooms. They have a travel agency and a DHL courier office. English-speaking staff. Address: Leningradskaya str., 61

There are numerous restaurants and cafes in the city. A meal costs $5-$10 per person. There's virtually nothing going on in the evenings, but if you manage to hang out with local skateboarders and snowboarders (of which there are many), you're guaranteed to have good time Russian style.

pic: Russian Heli Project photo: Maxim Balakhovskiy

Flight is the only option (except occasional ferries) to get to the region. There are no roads to connect peninsula with the mainland of Russia.
Aeroflot Airlines, Siberia (S7), and Transaero Airlines can be used to get in to the region. You should fly to Petropavlovsk-Kamchatsky. A return flight from Moscow costs $500-$700 with taxes and takes about 9 hours. The best offers are usually by Siberia (S7) which offers specials to snowboarders.

POOR FAIR GOOD TOP

FREERIDE
Trees but no real off-piste
FREESTYLE
Nothing except the odd bump
PISTES
Good place to learn

5
OUT OF 10

Earliest powder in Russia but expensive

resort in terms of the run lengths or variety. Its not going to be too challenging for advanced boarders, however there is some good treeriding to be had.

FREESTYLERS are rare guests. Bring a shovel and find somewhere off the main pistes to build something as you won't find anything laid on by the resort

BEGINNERS.

Most of the runs are not too steep and are suitable for those getting their snowboard legs, this is a good place for easy boarding and to work on technique. Unlike most of the Russian resorts the runs are maintained in a good condition.

THE TOWN

Sheregesh is a medium sized miners settlement, so it's not really a great party place, unless you're lucky enough to get together with some locals to experience a few-day long vodka marathon (which is sure to end badly). There's a number of snowboard competitions taking place at the mountain every year, during which there's a good chance to hang out with some snowboarders.

The nearest hotel to the mountain is "*Gubernskaya*" hotel. The rooms cost $100 / night (for a double) over there. The other expensive option is "*Elena*" hotel for the same price. There are many small budget hotels around the mountain, where you can find a room for $50 per night. Rooms are available even during the high season, so is not necessary to book ahead. Most of Russian tourists prefer to rent apartments due to relatively low prices. Prices start at 600 R ($23) per apartment (up to 6 persons). To find a place, go to **Dzerjinskogo ulitsa** (the central street of the Sheregesh settlement) and ask for available rent ("arenda kvartiry"). There are several cafes and restaurants which are located mostly in hotels. More cafes can be found at the bottom of the mountain, where you can have a meal for 200-400 R ($6-$12).

If you are not a Siberian probably the only single reason to go to **Sheregesh** is the local snow. Starting from the beginning of November until the beginning of March there's at least 1 m of high quality snow. The local powder is dry and fast and is considered to be the best snow in Russia. It's only the dedicated that make it to Sheregesh. You'll have to endure an 8-hour trek from Moscow, the famous Siberian frost, and almost as importantly a lack of après ski. Sheregesh is a remote miners settlement in Siberia near **Novokuznetsk** (Kuzbass mines). About twenty years ago the ski resort was built at the nearby **Zelenaya mountain**. With the growing popularity of ski and snowboard in Russia the town itself has been transforming gradually. It is expanding with new cafes and hotels, catering for more and more tourists each year. The resort itself is developing rapidly with new lifts being built every season. Sheregesh is the only place in Russia where one can find a lot of snow as early as November, which is why it attracts many snowboarders from all over the country. The Russian snowboard team trains in this region as well.

FREERIDERS will find conditions more to your liking than the

R

R
U
S
S
I
A

1270M
TOP LIFT

600M
VERTICAL

670M
FIRST LIFT

EASY

INT

ADV

6KM
PISTES

55%

45%

Number of runs: 5
Longest run: 2.5km
Total Lifts: 6
2 chairs, 4 drags
Lift times:
9.30am - 5pm
Mountain Cafes:
1

Winter Period:
Nov to March
Lift Passes
1 ride pass chair: 70R
1 ride pass drag: 30R
1 day pass: 600R
Board School
300 R ($12) for 1 hour
Rental
Board & Boots 500R
(16$) per day

Sheregesh
Web: www.sheregesh.ru
email: admin@sheregesh.ru

Annual Snowfall:
Unknown
Snowmaking:
none

Car
is not recommended all the way from Moscow. The road is about 6000 km with little infrustracture along the way.
Fly
Aeroflot Airlines, Siberia Airlines and Transaero Airlines fly to the region. You can fly from Moscow Domodedovo or Moscow Sheremetyevo to Novokuznetsk (preferably) or Novosibirsk. A return flight costs $250-$400 with taxes and takes about 4hrs.
Train
Direct from Moscow to Novokuznetsk (about 60 hours, costs 1800 R one way). Direct from Moscow to Novosibirsk (48 hours and costs 1200 R one way).
Bus
too far from Moscow to take a bus. From Novokuznetsk 200R one way takes 3hrs from Novosibirsk - 300 R ($11) one way, 6-8hrs journey (depends on the route).
There are more frequent buses to Tashtagol the town just in 17 km from Sheregesh. You can go to Tashtagol first, and then take a local bus form Tashtagol to Sheregesh or take a taxi for 200 R.

wsgVOLEN AND STEPANOVO

POOR FAIR GOOD TOP

FREERIDE
A few trees but no off-piste
FREESTYLE
Occasional park
PISTES
Fine for beginners but too short

Fine for beginners or to escape Moscow

5
OUT OF 10

pic: Volen Tourism

FREESTYLER. The **Flammable Park** is located in Volen, but it's kind of abandoned just a few bumps unless theres an event on. On busy days snowboarders usually gather with shovels and make hits for themselves on one of the slopes. You can also choose the areas between the runs to practice your skills, which is what most snowboarders end up doing there anyway.

BEGINNERS. If you are just starting to snowboard, Volen and Stepanovo might be a good place, as there is a good snowboard school and snowboard equipment hire (quite pricey, though), the instructors hold the Russian Ski & Snowboard Federation certificates and were trained by the French, but probably won't speak English. Most of the slopes are easy and on a weekday they are quite deserted, so you will feel more confident learning.

Volen & Stepanovo are probably the best resorts in **Moscow** region and located about 60 km north from the city. Over the last few years four new ski & snowboard parks have opened in the area; Volen, Stepanovo, Sorochany and Yakhroma. Volen has two main ski areas: the Volen park itself and Stepanovo, which is Volen's small appendix about 5km away. **Volen** has quite short runs (the longest one is 450m) and is full of drag lifts, so the place is good for occasional riding if you are in Moscow, but is quite unexciting if you are after some real snowboarding. **Stepanovo** (which is a 5km or a 10-minute ride by bus from Volen) is worth visiting because, at 1km, it has the longest run of all the slopes around Moscow. Even though it is marked as red, it is pretty easy and is completely empty on weekdays. There's quite a lot of snow during winter in Russia and snowmaking facilities ensure you can ride from December up to the beginning of April.

FREERIDING.Both Volen & Stepanovo are mostly man-made hills, so there's no possibility of long runs or off-piste

THE TOWN

There is one hotel and a few houses for rent. The **accommodation** is good, but expensive ranging from 2000R ($70) to 3400 R ($120) per night. You can usually just except if there's a holiday. **Food.**There is a Swiss, Italian, and Japanese restaurant, but at 650R for a meal it's quite expensive.Weekend brunch is 1400R. Pizzeria Trattoria has lower prices from 300-400R.

The park has quite a lot of facilities including a hotel and is supposed to look like a small Alpine village. There are as many snowboarders as skiers, so it's quite a snowboard-friendly place. The bars are not really worth visiting, however, if you need a break or a beer, there are two of them on top of the hills, and there's a silly disco every night from 10pm.

R
U
S
S
I
A

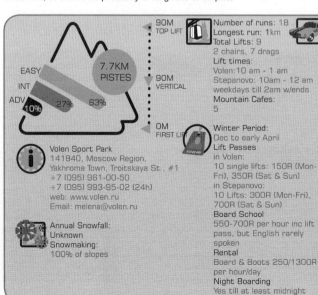

90M
TOP LIFT

90M
VERTICAL

0M
FIRST LIFT

EASY
INT
ADV

**7.7KM
PISTES**

10%   27%   63%

Number of runs: 18
Longest run: 1km
Total Lifts: 9
2 chairs, 7 drags
Lift times:
Volen:10 am - 1 am
Stepanovo: 10am - 12 am
weekdays till 2am w/ends
Mountain Cafes:
5

Winter Period:
Dec to early April
Lift Passes
in Volen:
10 single lifts: 150R (Mon-Fri), 350R (Sat & Sun)
in Stepanovo:
10 Lifts: 300R (Mon-Fri), 700R (Sat & Sun)
Board School
550-700R per hour inc lift pass, but English rarely spoken
Rental
Board & Boots 250/1300R per hour/day
Night Boarding
Yes till at least midnight

i Volen Sport Park
141840, Moscow Region,
Yakhroma Town, Troitskaya St., #1
+7 (095) 961-00-50
+7 (095) 993-95-02 (24h)
web: www.volen.ru
Email: melena@volen.ru

Annual Snowfall:
Unknown
Snowmaking:
100% of slopes

Car
Take Dmitrovskoe Shosse and head north out of Moscow. Drive 46 km, 3 km after Dedenevo village turn left (there will be a sign and a huge billboard). After you cross the river, turn right to Volen through Yakhroma town. If you turn left after the river, you'll get to Stepanovo, but the road is a bit dodgy, so drive carefully.
Takes 1.5-2hrs. Print out this map before driving: http://www.volen.ru/about/way/
Fly
To Moscow (46km away), Riga (Latvia) or Tallin (Estonia), where you can take a train to Moscow for about $50 US one way.
Train
go to Savelovsky station in Moscow (metro Savelovskaya, grey line, center) and take a train to Yakhroma. It takes about 1 hour 15 from where you can take a taxi (about $3) or use a daily mini-shuttle that departs every Tuesday, Wednesday and Thursday at 10.45, 12.05, 15.10, 17.10 and 19.20
Bus
every hour from 8am until 8pm departing from Altufievo metro station (grey line, North-West Moscow), which goes to Dmitrov. You need to get off before Dmitrov in Yakhroma town and take a taxi/shuttle from there. About 2.5 hours total.

ABZAKOVO

Abzakovo is considered to be one of the best developed resorts in Ural mountains, which divide Europe and Asia. Even though the number of slopes is minimal comparing to European resorts and the total riding area is not that large, it might be very suitable for beginners and can be a nice and refreshing stop if you're riding along the Trans-Siberian railway (which passes 400 km away). The nearby Bannoe resort has another 15 km of piste riding area with 2.5 km runs and might be interesting for freestylers, who will find lots of tree-covered terrain there as well as a halfpipe. The local snowboarders (who come from Urals) consider Abzakovo the best mountain in their region, because it provides some freeride and freestyle opportunities, and the prices are relatively low. However, as there's not much snow, you will often see rocks sticking out, so you can freeride, but it will kill your board. Off the slope you will find lots of accommodation, restaurants, and entertainment, suitable for any budget. Because Abzakovo is visited by the Russian president Putin every year, it tends to get a lot of investment, making it stand out among other Russian resorts. However, this does not make it over-expensive, as you can still find accommodation for $10 per night, and a meal won't cost you more than $5.

Freeriders

Freeriders will find some off piste terrain here, but as there's not much snow, the rocks and stones that stick out can be annoying. Many people come back from Abzakovo with scratched boards, so be careful

Freestylers will find some interesting areas in between the runs, but it's not really the place, unless you find some local snowboarders and build a few hits together. Most of the runs are very suitable for **beginners** and as they are not steep, this is a good place for easy boarding and to work on technique. Relatively long runs are usually well-maintained, except if there's too many people in which case it can get a bit hard. Watch out the drag lifts though, as some of them are really steep

Abzakovo base is very close to the mountain and it costs about 300R ($11) per night if you stay in a basic shared room, and 750 R ($25) if you need a better quality private accommodation. There are also some cottages for rent and a hotel all quite close to the mountain. You might get a free room if you just show up, but it's better to contact the resort to book beforehand. There are also some hotels in town and a good choice of more comfortable accommodation in the nearby Bannoe resort, which is 25 km away. There are lots of cafes and restaurants at the bottom of the mountain and in town, where you can have a meal for about $5-$10. There are some clubs and bars, but the nightlife has a peculiar Russian way to it, which means a lot of vodka and funny music.

Ride area: 18km Longest run: 2.8km
Total runs: 13 75% easy, 23% intermediate
Night boading: till 11pm
Contact:
www.abzakovo.ru
Email:info@abzakovo.ru

BANNOE

Bannoe is one of the newest resorts in the Russian Ural mountains, which divide Europe and Asia. Although it is not an especially exciting place to snowboard (the longest runs in the area are 2,5 km and there are only 3-4 runs at every resort), it is considered to be the most modern resort in the region and this year they are planning to open 3 more pistes, 2 of which will be 3km long with 450m drop, bringing the total ride area to 15 km. It has also one of the biggest vertical drops of all resorts at Urals. Even though the riding area is quite small, it will keep you occupied for a day or two, and you can always go to the nearby Abzakovo, which has more runs. However, the tree-lined runs in Bannoe are quite picturesque at times and you might be tempted to stay longer. Also, the resort was built not so long ago you can use its lift system to get to some nice areas, which were not yet turned into piste runs. Be careful though, as there's not much snow, there's lots of rocks and you might kill your board.

Bannoe is located on the shore of Yakty Kul lake in Bashkortostan republic of Russia, 40 km from Magnitogorsk, 25 km from Abzakovo resort. Like nearly all resorts in Urals, Bannoe was originally built by one of the steel producers of the area for its employees, but despite this fact it's not only for skiers: in 2004 they built a 60-meter long halfpipe

331

for snowboarders. Russian snowboarders like the Urals, as it is not too far from the European part of the country and provides a good level of comfort. Bannoe resort claims the first gondola lift in Russia and has ambitious plans to expand. The apres-ski here is determined to compete with the Alpine resorts for the skiers' money, however, as it is just starting you won't find a lot of entertainment here yet. If you get bored, you can always go to the nearby Abzakovo resort which has livelier nightlife. The season normally starts at the end of November and with the help of snow machines continues until the end of April. However, the best riding is between January and March.

Top: 940m Bottom: 490m
Ride area: 7km Longest run: 2.5km
Total runs: 4 50% easy, 50% intermediate
Total Lifts: 2 - 1 gondola and 1 drag
Hire: Board & Boots 1000R per day, 5800 for 7 days
Lift passes:
1 day: 1000R 3 days: 2000R 7 days: 4000R
Night-boarding:
until 11pm
Contact:
Metallurg-Magnitogorsk Ski Center on Bannoe Lake
Russia, Magnitogorsk, 455002, Kirova St., #74
Telephones: +7 (3519) 255-457, 255-601, Bookings: +7 (3519) 24-39-79
Web:ski-bannoe.mgn.ru
Email:bannoe@mgn.ru
Location:
Fly to Magnitogorsk from Moscow in 2hrs (40km from Bannoe) or take a 24hr train for 200R. Local bus from Magnitogorsk towards Ufa (about 100 R ($3) for this 1-hour journey). A taxi from the airport is about 900R ($30).

KRASNAYA POLYANA

Krasnaya Polyana is the most sophisticated ski and snowboard resort in Russia. Sometimes called the "Russian Courchevel", this resort is famous for its well-maintained pistes, quality apres-ski, and overly high prices. The lifts are fast and convenient, the runs are in a very good condition, the local rescue team is considered to be the best in Russia, plus lots of comfortable mini hotels at the village and cozy apres-ski bars. Krasnaya Polyana is located just 45 km from Adler city (a famous summer destination in Russia on the shore of Black Sea) where there is a recently renovated airport and a train station making it the most accessible mountain resort in the European part of Russia. A flight from Moscow takes 2.5 hours, and a transfer to the ski station takes 1.5 hours more. Easy access makes hundreds of Moscow riders spend week-ends at Kransya Polyana during the season (middle of December - begging of March). The locals are very friendly and the resort is completely safe. The only disadvantages of the resort are its small size and mild climate (affected by the nearby sea), which means that there is a risk to find too little snow at the lower runs even in January. Always check the level of snowfall at the resort before going there (their website usually has the up-to-date information). The prices for the lifts are too high and the accommodation is more expensive than at other Russian resorts (although cheaper than in Europe). However, if you want to ride in the Russian mountains and have the western standard of service, that's the best place to go.

Besides, there are plans of massive expansion, so who knows, maybe in a few years this place will be one of the greatest destinations.

Freeriders can explore snow fields along higher runs or ride through the forest along lower runs. Remote snow fileds can be accessed by a helicopter. No snowboard park and no halfpipe. Freestylers usually come in groups of 8-10 and build all the facilities by themselves. Runs are very good for beginners - wide, snowy and not steep. The best resort in Russia if you're just starting.

Krasnaya Polyana is a small village. Dozens of B&B, chalets and several large hotels can be found around there. There is no specific entertainment center in the village, so the riders spend their apres ski in the nearest bars and cafes. "Munhgausen" is the most famous bar located just near the bottom lift. A meal at local cafes and restaurants costs about 150-400 R ($5 - $15). The largest and the most expensive hotel is Radisson SAS Peak hotel where you can always find a room for $200. Medium priced mini-hotels, such as "Tri Vershiny" and "Rodnik" will cost around $30-$50 per night per person including breakfast. For budget travellers renting a room or apartment at a private house is the best option (around $15 per night).

Top: 2228m Bottom: 540m
Ride area: 25km Longest run: 13km
Total runs: 5 55% easy, 40% intermediate , 5% advanced
Total Lifts: 4 chairs
Hire: Board & Boots 500R per day
Lessons: 1000R for 2hrs
Lift passes:
1 day:650R 3 days: 2000R 7 days: 4500R
Contact:
Web:www.kraspol.ru
Email:admin@kraspol.ru
Location:
Fly to Adler from Moscow in 2 1/2hrs (45km from resort) or take a 24-50hr train for 1900R. Regular buses from Adler to resort. Alternatively a taxi ride will cost about $20-$30.

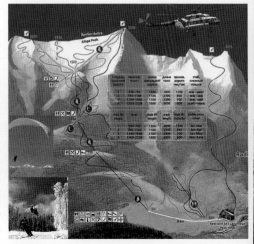

Pic - The back corries in Nevis, page 339. Nevis Tourism

but resorts will try and build a terrain park when there is snow. . But the most notable point about Scotland is the costs: lift tickets are a total rip off and offer very bad value for money. However getting to any of the areas should pose no problems with good air, rail and road links.

You can choose one of the five real snow areas, the many artificial ski slopes dotted around the country, or the new indoor real-snow slope in Glasgow.

Scotland's conditions are extremely variable and snow conditions can be poor, and the wind can blow so hard that it hurts as it hits you at 70 miles an hour. All the resorts are similar: low level hills, with uneven trails that get stupidly crowded. Halfpipes are rare due to the weather conditions,

Season riders will find employment and lodging easily. If you want to teach snowboarding, you can do it legally without an instructor's certificate. However, it may help you get work.

In short, Scotland is a great country for its scenery, natural beauty and history, but due to the weather not a great destination for boarding or skiing.

Capital City: Edinburgh
Population: 5 Million
Highest Peak: Ben Nevis 1347m
Language: English
Legal Drink Age: 18
Drug Laws: Cannabis is illegal and frowned upon
Age of consent: 16
Electricity: 240 Volts AC 3-pin
International Dialing Code: +44

Currency: Pounds Sterling
Exchange Rate:
US$1 = 0.6
EURO = 0.7

Driving Guide
All vehicles drive on the left hand side of the road
Speed limits:
Motorways-70mph (113kph)
Highways-60mph (97kph)
Towns-30mph (51kph)
Emergency
Fire, Police & Ambulance - 999
Tolls
Payable on some bridges
Documentation
A driving licence must be carried as well as insurance.

Time Zone
No UTC/GMT
Daylight saving time: +1 hour

National Associations
Web: www.snowsportscotland.org
www.snowsportgb.com

Visit Scotland
23 Ravelston Terrace
Edinburgh
EH4 3TP
Tel: 0845 22 55 121
www.visitscotland.com

Bus/coach services
www.citylink.co.uk - local buses
www.nationalexpress.co.uk - national

Rail services
www.scotrail.co.uk
www.thetrainline.com
Tel: 08457 48 49 50

Airports
www.glasgowairport.com
www.edinburghairport.com
www.invernessairport.com

POOR FAIR GOOD TOP

FREERIDE
No trees or real off-piste
FREESTYLE
Terrain park on a good day
PISTES
Short & often icy slopes

Okay when theres snow

3 OUT OF 10

CHAIRLIFTS AND TOWS

ZONES
Beginner Zone | Car Park Zone

riddled with moguls.

FREESTYLERS who like to go big off natural hits, forget it. However, when the conditions are good there is a terrain park which has a series of big hits, and some rails.

BEGINNERS, this place is definitely not for you. There are hardly any nursery slopes, and the ones you do find are sandwiched between snow fences and choked up with ski classes. Beginners are far better off going to 'The Lecht', 40 minutes away.

pic - Paul Tomkins/STB

The Cairngorms is a unique place for all sorts of reasons. For some this is a great place to visit to see some of Scotland's wild life, while others venture to these hostile hills to walk along some of the well worn paths. But this is not a proper ski/board destination and doesn't even begin to compare with resorts on main land Europe. The Cairngorms will give locals, those who live close and the casual visitor the chance to have a few hours fun on snow. If you live far away, check on conditions before leaving. This region has a poor annual snow record and suffers from very harsh winters which entail strong winds and ever changing weather patterns. The mountain layout also leaves a lot to be desired, however the introduction the funicular train makes getting around the runs a lot easier but the cost of using the train and the other lifts is horrendous. However, its not all bad news on Cairngorm, and when it has snowed and the sun is out, you can have a great days riding. What's more, local boarders are very friendly and will be happy to show you were the best spots are to ride.

FREERIDERS won't find any trees, bowls or powder and experienced riders used to long testing steeps won't find anything to tackle apart from the West Wall, the only black run. The White Lady run can be good when it's not

THE TOWN

Spey Valley is home to a number of good local villages. For a small village Aviemore has a good choice of restaurants. The *Cairngorm Hotel* is very good, *Harkai's* restaurant does a great hangover breakfast. Nightlife in Aviemore is simple, there are no fancy clubs just a handful of bars, try the Mambo Cafe.

1080M TOP LIFT
530M VERTICAL
550M FIRST LIFT

14KM PISTES

EASY
INT 34%
ADV 4%
62%

Number of runs: 28
Longest run: 2.9km
Total Lifts: 17
1 Funicular Train, 2 chairs, 14 drags
Lift capacity (people per hour): 12,000
Lift times: 8.30am to 4.30pm
Mountain cafes: 3

Winter Period: Jan to April
Lift Passes
Half day £20
1 Day pass £26
5 Days pass £106
Season £350
Hire
1 day £15.50, 5 days £50.50
Board School
Group lessons £35/day (4hrs), half-day £31
Full day including 4hrs tuition, pass & rental £63
Private £135 full day, £75 for half

Annual Snowfall: Unknown
Snowmaking: none

Fly to Glasgow international. Transfer time to resort is 2 1/2 hours. Inverness airport is 30 miles (45 minutes) away
Train services are possible to the centre of Aviemore, 9 miles or 15 mins from the slopes. visit. www.scotrail.co.uk
Bus Bus services from Glasgow airport are available on a daily basis to Aviemore.
Car from Inverness, head south on the A9 and travel to Aviemore. From London, head north via the M1, M6, A74, M8 to Perth and the A9 to Aviemore, 9 hours 535 miles.

Tourist office Aviemore
Grampian Road,
Aviemore. Inverness-shire
Tel: +44 (0) 1479 810 363
Cairngorm info: +44 (0) 1479 861 261

Web: www.cairngormmountain.com

335

GLENCOE

Glencoe is **Scotland's** oldest resort and the best place to ride in the country. Unlike other Scottish resorts, this is not a poor alpine imitation and okay, Glencoe may have very harsh weather patterns, but who cares, they do things the right way here and don't try and make out that they are something that they're not. This may not be a big place, but it is exactly what Scottish snowboarding should be about: simple, friendly and without an attitude. It also has the best natural terrain. In general, the runs will suit all levels, although not testing. Glencoe's remoteness means it is far less crowded than other resorts. People who come here do so because they don't want the bull of the other places.

FREERIDERS will find some okay terrain in the main basin off either the top T-bar or top button lift. Off the top button lift you will find a couple of reds and an interesting black trail that bases out into an easy green run.
FREESTYLERS have a cool natural freestyle area, but the weather prevents the building or lasting of a halfpipe. However, ask the management and they'll happily do what they can to build you a decent series of hits.
BEGINNERS should have no problems learning here as there are some excellent short runs to try out which are easily reached.

Local services can be found in the small village of **Glencoe**, a 6 mile drive away. It offers limited, but good, accommodation with a number of cheap B & B'. Alternatively, the village of **Onich** is 12 miles away and

has a bigger selection of services, including a bunkhouse with a bar. **Fort William** is 30 miles away and has an even bigger offering.

Area size: 500 acres, 20km of pistes
Runs: total 19 - 53% easy, 37% intermediate, 10% advanced
Top: 1058m Bottom: 475m
Total Lifts: 7 - 2 chairs, 4 drags, 1 learner tow
Hire: 1 day £18 5 days £48
Lessons: 2 Hour lesson £15, Private £22/hr
Lift passes:
Half day £15, 1 Day £24, 5 Days £95, Season 225
Contact: Tel: 01855 851226 www.glencoemountain.com
Getting There:
Fly to Glasgow airport 2 hours away. Prestwich & Inverness possible
Train services are possible to Fort William & Bridge of Orchy 30 minutes from Glencoe.
Bus. Citylink run regular coaches from Glasgow to nearby Fort William, White Corries is the access road nearest to the resort. Tel. 08705 50 50 50
Car via Glasgow, head north on the A82, via Dumbarton and Tyndrun to Glencoe. From London, head north via the M1, M6, A74, to Glasgow.

GLENSHEE

With 2000 acres of terrain, **Glenshee** is Scotland's biggest resort. This place was first to use snow cannons, but in truth, they haven't really helped to improve what largely is a disappointment. The runs are spread out over varying slopes and on a good day, you will find some off-piste powder. The majority of runs are short novice trails with only two steep sections.

Freeriders have no trees, but a bit of powder on Glas Maol area. **Freestylers** don't bother. **Carvers**, can crank a it down the **Cairnwell** but not for long. **Beginners** will hate the way the lifts are set out, however, the novice runs will provide some fun.

Local facilities don't exist. Within a large area there are places to stay in and villages to get a meal but nothing near the slopes.
Area size: 2000 acres, 40km of pistes
Runs: total 38 - 60% easy, 34% intermediate, 8% advanced
Top: 1058m Bottom: 650m
Total Lifts: 23 - 2 chairs, 4 drags, 1 learner tow

Hire: 1 day £18 5 days £48
Lessons: 2 Hour lesson £15, Private £22/hr
Lift passes: 1/2 Day £14.50, Day £19.50,5 Day £78
Contact: Tel: 013397 41320 www.ski-glenshee.co.uk
Getting There:
Fly Aberdeen 1 1/2 hours away (69 miles). Edinburgh (84 miles) or Glasgow (101 miles)

ROUND-UP

Train The nearest stations are Aberdeen, Perth, Dundee or Pitlochry.

Bus. Take a bus from Dundee, Aberdeen or Perth to Braemar or Blairgowrie both about 9miles from the resort. Tel: 08705 50 50 50

Car Glenshee is situated on the A93, 9 miles south of Braemar and 25 miles north of Blairgowrie

NEVIS

Nevis Range opened in 1989. The mountain has a modern lift system to rival anything in **the Alps**, but where its no match for Alps, is the weather which is often a mixture of high winds, driving sleet and rain and heavy blizzards. And Nevis gets its fair share of the lot. However, the people who run the place shrug off the problems related to the weather and do their best to look after visitors. Weekends are often very busy, while week days are generally very quite. The resort try and build a terrain park when ever the conditions allow. What they have managed to achieve is a fairly well balanced mixture of short runs that will mainly appeal to beginners, even though most of the novice runs are serviced by drag lifts. Overall the terrain here is pretty unadventurous and an expert rider will tire of this mountain within an hour or two of being here.

FREESTYLERS . Theres usually a park at the summit, depending on conditions there's usually at least some rails, and sometimes a couple of kickers. The gully under the main chairlift provides a small natural halfpipe for a bit of air time.

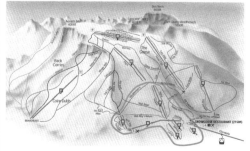

FREERIDERS have a couple of good areas by **Scottish**

standards to ride, namely the back bowl area which has a series of steeps. When its open, the Back Corries present Scotlands trickiest test.

CARVERS will find that the **Snowgoose Gully** is the area to lay some lines on. But overall Nevis is not a cruiser's resort.

BEGINNERS have a number of easy slopes located at the lower areas not far from the top gondola station.

THE TOWN.

The town of **Fort William**, 6 miles away, has a big choice of accommodation and eating spots. There is some accommodation near the slopes but it's limited and isolated. Evenings are not hot but with plenty of pubs to try out, you can have a rowdy time.

Area size: 20km of pistes, 35km of piste runs
Runs: total 35 - 65% easy, 25% intermediate, 10% advanced
Top: 1221m Bottom: 91m
Total Lifts: 12 - 1 Gondola, 3 chairs, 8 drags
Hire: board and boots £17.50,6 days £65
Lessons: 4 Hour group lesson £20, private £22/hr
Lift passes:
1/2 Day Pass £16, Full day £23, 5 days £85, Season £245
Contact: Tel - +44 (0) 1397 705 825 www.nevisrange.co.uk
Getting There: Fly Glasgow 2 hours away.
Train Train services to Fort William, 10 minutes away.
Bus. take a regualr CityLink bus to Fort William
Car From Glasgow, head north on the A82, via Dumbarton and Glencoe, approx 2.5hrs. Nevis Range is 7miles from Fort William

LECHT

The Lecht is by far the smallest resort in Scotland, however, this is also one of the friendliest and quite simply the best beginner's resort. This value for money area, only has a handful of runs that rise up from the car park allowing for good easy access by foot to the well maintained novice runs. This is not a place for those who want long testing steeps, but it is a place with a cool attitude towards snowboarding and a genuine and welcoming feel to it.

FREERIDERS could have the whole place licked in an hour or two.

FREESTYLERS, they always try and build a park and pipe here, with locals from Aberdeen using this as a fun weekend hangout.

CARVERS of beginner to basic intermediate only.

BEGINNERS, this place is perfect for novices, the best in Scotland.

Basic but affordable local facilities can be found in Tomintoul, 15 minutes away.

Area size: 6km of pistes
Runs: total 20 - 70% easy, 25% intermediate, 5% advanced
Top: 777m Bottom: 637m
Total Lifts: 11 - 1 chairs, 9 drags
Hire: 1 day £17
Lessons: 2days hire, pass and group lesson £75
Lift passes:
1/2 Day £15,1 Day pass £20, 5 Days pass £84
Contact: Tel: (01975) 651440 www.lecht.co.uk
Getting There: Fly Aberdeen 2 hours away.
Car On the A939 Cockbridge to Tomintoul Road. West of Aberdeen

S

S
C
O
T
L
A
N
D

337

with little or no snowboard facilities, poor options for places to sleep and limited snowboard hire options.

However, this is generalising because the big areas like Sierra Nevada are an easy match for the rest of Europe, indeed it will put a lot of northern places to shame.

The Spanish tend to be a bit like their Italian cousins, they love to pose and in doing so end up looking stupid in designer ski suits. Snowboarding is, however, fairly well received throughout the country.

S
P
A
I
N

If you thought Spain was only about bull fighting and tacky seaside resorts inhabited by Europe's finest villains, then think again. Spain is also about snowboarding and while it's not as intense as other parts of Europe, it's certainly worth more than a mention as well as a visit.

Spain has some thirty resorts offering every type of terrain possible and to suit all style's of riding and abilities.

Spain hasn't always had the greatest snow record and with many of the resorts not being the most up to date, there's very little artificial snowmaking to help out when the real stuff is lacking. Resort facilities are not the greatest either,

The majority of the resorts are situated in the north of the country and can prove tricky to reach with a hit and miss public transport service. Your best bet is to hire a car at airport and drive, this way you can leave quickly if you dislike a place.

One last point, Spanish snowboarding is not as cheap as you may think. Don't think of it as just a cheap alternative to France or Austria, although Spain is certainly cheaper than Switzerland.

Capital City: Madrid
Population: 40 Million
Highest Peak: Mulhacen 3478m
Language: Spanish
Legal Drink Age: 18
Drug Laws: Cannabis is illegal
Age of consent: 16
Electricity: 240 Volts AC 2-pin
International Dialing Code: +34

Currency: Euro
Exchange Rate:
UK£1 = 1.5
US$1 = 0.8
AU$1 = 0.6
CAN$1 = 0.6

Time Zone
UTC/GMT +1 hours
Daylight saving time: +1 hour

Driving Guide
All vehicles drive on the right hand side of the road
Speed limits:
Motorways   120kph (74mph)
Highways   90kph (56mph)
Towns   50kph (31mph)
Emergency
Fire - 080 Police - 091 Ambulance - 092
Tolls
Payable on a number of main roads
Documentation
Driving licence and motor insurance must be carried.

Spanish Snowboard Association
Web: www.a-e-s.jazztel.es
Email: infoaes@telefonica.net

Rail services
www.renfe.es

Coach services
www.eurolines.es

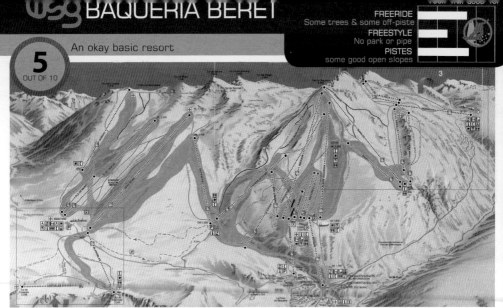

FREERIDE
Some trees & some off-piste
FREESTYLE
No park or pipe
PISTES
some good open slopes

An okay basic resort

5
OUT OF 10

3

S

**S
P
A
I
N**

Baqueria Beret is Spain's biggest and possibly most glamorous resort, but don't let that put you off because when the snow is good (which it usually is) this purpose built haunt is not too bad to ride. Last season (4/5) saw a new chairlift and 4 news pistes open and an increase in snowmaking. The terrain is spread out over four connecting areas, all of which are easy to reach and will largely appeal to intermediate piste loving carvers.

FREERIDERS looking for some cool off-piste to ride will be pleasantly surprised, with some great powder riding to be had well away from the chicken sticks in bad suits. Check out the areas on the Tuc De Dossal that are reached by chair lift, or hit the stuff up at La Bonaiqua. Advanced riders are the ones who will be most disappointed, apart from two black graded runs there's not a great deal of testing stuff.

FREESTYLERS have a rather limited amount of good natural freestyle terrain, but there is the odd good hit to get air from, plus a few drop offs to try out.

PISTES. Carvers take over on the slopes here with terrain that is ideal for hard alpine riding. The resort is mainly suited to intermediates with some nice red runs but not many expert trails. For the less talented edge merchants, there are some easy blue runs.

BEGINNERS will take kindly to this place as this is a good resort to start out on and progress steadily with. Much of the terrain is easily reached by chair lifts and if you don't like Pomas or T-Bars then you'll be happy to know that you can get around the whole area without having to use them.

THE TOWN

Accommodation is close to the slopes, but eating and entertainment is not of a snowboard related nature. Still there is a supermarket for food and loads of Tapas (bar snacks). **Evenings** are OK and drinks are cheap (well compared to say drinks in France) apart from in the clubs where drinks are a flat rate of 10 euros each). Check out *Lobo* first, then *Tiffany's*, where the music is as crap and old as the name, but when you're drunk at four in the morning, who cares?

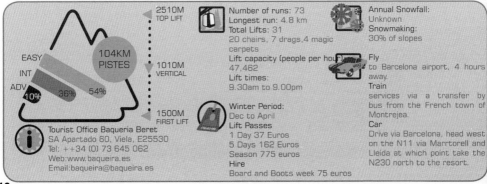

2510M
TOP LIFT

EASY
INT
ADV
10%   36%   54%

104KM
PISTES

1010M
VERTICAL

1500M
FIRST LIFT

Tourist Office Baqueria Beret
SA Apartado 60, Viela, E25530
Tel: ++34 (0) 73 645 062
Web:www.baqueira.es
Email:baqueira@baqueira.es

Number of runs: 73
Longest run: 4.8 km
Total Lifts: 31
20 chairs, 7 drags,4 magic carpets
Lift capacity (people per hour)
47,462
Lift times:
9.30am to 9.00pm

Winter Period:
Dec to April
Lift Passes
1 Day 37 Euros
5 Days 162 Euros
Season 775 euros
Hire
Board and Boots week 75 euros

Annual Snowfall:
Unknown
Snowmaking:
30% of slopes

Fly
to Barcelona airport, 4 hours away.
Train
services via a transfer by bus from the French town of Montrejea.
Car
Drive via Barcelona, head west on the N11 via Marrtorell and Lleida at which point take the N230 north to the resort.

	POOR	FAIR	GOOD	TOP
FREERIDE Trees and some good off-piste				
FREESTYLE park in linked resort				
PISTES Well groomed quiet pistes				

Okay fun resort

5 OUT OF 10

La Molina is located at the end of the Moixero mountain range in the Pyrenees. Its slopes descend from the summit of the Tosa de Alp peak and connect to the neighbouring resort of Masella to form the ALP 2500 area providing access to 111km of pistes. These are both welcome alternatives to big resorts scattered around the northern alps simply because mid-week, lift queues don't exist and the slopes are blissfully crowd free. The people of La Molina make you feel very welcome and coupled with neighbouring Masella, both areas have great terrain to shred, with slopes that are covered by trees up to the midway point and then clear pistes up to the summit. The terrain will capture the imagination of most intermediate riders, no matter what their style is, but advanced riders may feel a little left out.

FREERIDERS in search of extremes that require helmets should forget it, but for the rest, there's ample to search out. Off-piste opportunities present you with loads of trees, with some nice back bowls and good powder stashes on the Marsella.

FREESTYLERS you'll need to get over to Marsella as theres little laid on these days at La Molina. The park on La Pleta has beginner and advanced lines consisting of some kickers and rails.

PISTES. Riders get the chance to polish up their skills on well groomed pistes and because this place isn't busy, you can go completely balls out without the worry of running over small children.

BEGINNERS in La Molina or Marsella will find that the nursery slopes are wide and spacious. Instruction services are excellent, with foreign speaking instructors available (which helps).

THE TOWN

Off the slopes, this is not a resort designed for package groups of clueless skiers without manners. No, **La Molina** is a laid back place with a simple appeal offering affordable accommodation with the chance of staying close to the slopes. Local services are very basic; however, there are enough good facilities to keep you amused with a further selection of amenities down in the village of **Puigcerda**, which is only 10 minutes away. The *El Bodegon* restaurant is the place to check out if you want to try some local dishes while night life in La Molina is what you make of it. There's no great action here but you can have a good rocking time in such places as the *Sommy Bar*.

pic - La Molina Tourism

S

SPAIN

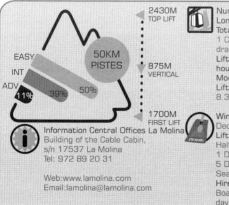

EASY

50KM PISTES

INT

ADV 11% 39% 50%

2430M TOP LIFT

875M VERTICAL

1700M FIRST LIFT La Molina

Information Central Offices
Building of the Cable Cabin,
s/n 17537 La Molina
Tel: 972 89 20 31

Web:www.lamolina.com
Email:lamolina@lamolina.com

Number of runs: 42
Longest run: 4km
Total Lifts: 16
1 Cable-car, 6 chairs, 7 drags, 2 baby lifts
Lift Capacity : (people per hour): 25,000
Mountain Cafes: 6
Lift times:
8.30am to 4.30pm

Winter Period:
Dec to April
Lift Passes
Half day pass 25 euros
1 Day pass 31 euros
5 Days 122.5 euros
Season 460 euros
Hire
Board and Boots 22 euros a day

Annual Snowfall:
Unknown
Snowmaking:
42% of slopes

Fly
Barcelona airport 2 1/2 hrs away
Train
Station at La Molina
Bus
Eurolines run coaches from Barcelona which take 2 1/2hrs. Day trips from Barcelona possible leaving 06:15 returning 20:30 and costs 39.80 inc lift pass. Tel: 902 40 50 40. Local bus runs services run through town, and the train station. 1.9euro single
Car
Drive via Barcelona, head north on the N152 via Granollers, Ripoli and Ribes de Freser.

SIERRA NEVADA

FREERIDE
A couple of trees & some off-piste
FREESTYLE
Park and occasional pipe
PISTES
Lots of easy wide slopes

7
OUT OF 10

Okay terrain for easy going piste lovers

pic - Trey Tomsik/Dutone Snowboards

S
P
A
I
N

It seems amazing, wrong even, that you can quite easily snowboard in the morning in deep powder snow, then pop down to the beach just over an hour away for a huge seafood meal, a swim in the **Mediterranean** sea and a relax on a sun soaked coast, but that's exactly what you can do from here in this most southern resort of **Sierra Nevada,** located a short distance form the town of **Granada**. It's possible from the high point of Veleta to see the **Atlas Mountains** of Morocco across the Mediterranean. Sierra Nevada is an OK place to ride and is particularly well suited to beginners and hard boot carvers, as well as offering some cool off-piste freeriding in powder bowls. The purpose built resort is well located for the slopes. These are first accessed by the main gondola which deposits you in **Borreguilles**, directly onto fantastic beginner's piste. Go up higher and you will be on slopes whose angles are great for free carving - just that perfect angle to really lay 'em out in perfect control. Night-riding is done on the Rio slope, a 2 mile run that provides one of the best lit night trails anywhere. Last season (04/05) saw some major improvements and piste extensions as well as more snowmaking facilties.

FREERIDERS should check out the stuff just below the peak of **Veleta** at 3398m. To do this, traverse to the **Olimpica** and where this crosses the Diagonal, kick hard to your left and travel off piste on an itinerary known as **Tajos de la Virgen**. The view above you is truly stunning, (a bowl edged with dramatic cliffs). The **Dilar chair** takes you towards the Radio Telescope, where after a walk along the ridge you can see below a huge expanse of off-piste which you have just travelled over on the chair. Take any line, the slope is a good safe angle with an easy traverse back to the **Solana** piste and the Dilar chair.

FREESTYLERS have to make do most of the time, with an array of unusual natural hits. They do build a pipe when snow conditions permit it. However, if you ride over to **Tajos de la Virgen** run, you'll find rolling jumps verging into vertical kickers. Kick back again towards the **Cartujo piste** and make use of the piste edge with it's many varied banked sides to gain more air time.

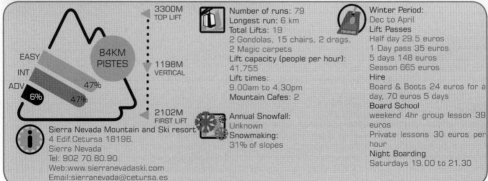

3300M
TOP LIFT

EASY
INT
ADV

84KM PISTES

47%
6%
47%

1198M
VERTICAL

2102M
FIRST LIFT

Sierra Nevada Mountain and Ski resort
4 Edif. Cetursa 18196.
Sierra Nevada
Tel: 902 70.80.90
Web:www.sierranevadaski.com
Email:sierranevada@cetursa.es

Number of runs: 79
Longest run: 6 km
Total Lifts: 19
2 Gondolas, 15 chairs, 2 drags,
2 Magic carpets
Lift capacity (people per hour):
41,755
Lift times:
9.00am to 4.30pm
Mountain Cafes: 2

Annual Snowfall:
Unknown
Snowmaking:
31% of slopes

Winter Period:
Dec to April
Lift Passes
Half day 29.5 euros
1 Day pass 35 euros
5 days 148 euros
Season 665 euros
Hire
Board & Boots 24 euros for a day, 70 euros 5 days
Board School
weekend 4hr group lesson 39 euros
Private lessons 30 euros per hour
Night Boarding
Saturdays 19.00 to 21.30

is located within easy reach of the base lifts and is pretty good, with some accommodation options at affordable prices. For budget riders, there's a hostel offering cheap beds with joint lift pass package rates.

Food. If you don't like Spanish food then don't fret, this place serves up all kinds of affordable grub from Chinese to Mexican. The main thing to watch out for, is that because this is a busy place, restaurants fill up early on in the evening and so a lot of waiting for a table is common place. Still, a meal, at a price, can be had in the likes of the Ruta del Veleta, (very posh and expensive but good). Tito Luigi is good for a cheap meal.

Night Life. If you like hard, fast and drunken action, there is plenty of it here but nothing happens until late. Bars and clubs don't get going until at least midnight, then it rocks and you'll have no trouble staying out late, drinking until you drop at 5 in the morning. The Soho Bar and La Chicle are your main late hangouts, where Senorita's are in plentiful supply all night long.

CARVERS are much in evidence here as the slopes lend themselves really well to edging a board over at speed, especially on the fast black trails. Particular good blacks for this are down from the **Borreguilles.**

BEGINNERS; the Borreguilles area is full on for learning the art of hurtling down a mountain on a board, but not the only place to go. Much of this resort is excellent for novices with good snowboard instruction facilities.

THE TOWN
Off the slopes, Sierra Nevada is a cool place with a lot going on. Getting around the village, which is extremely steep, is pretty tough on foot though (especially once you have had a few beers). There is a bus service that runs until midnight, or alternatively, a chair lift that links the various levels to the centre of the village, for which you will need a valid lift pass to get on. The main set back for this place is the high cost of everything, which may have something to with the fact that the Sierra Nevada attracts a lot of the Spanish elite, and all the baggage that clings on to them. However, what is on offer is of a high standard with locals making you welcome.

Accommodation comes in all manner of styles and prices starting at super expensive. Most of the accommodation

pic -Sierra Nevada Tourism

**S
P
A
I
N**

CAR
Madrid to Sierra Nevada is 270 miles (435km). Drive time is about 6 1/2 hours. From Calais, 1257 miles (2022Km), drive time is around 24 hours.
FLY
Malaga airport is 90mins away. Granada airport is 48km away with connections from Barcelona and Madrid.
TRAIN
Trains to Granada 33km away.
BUS
Bus services from Madrid via a change over at Granada, on a daily basis. Bus services from Granada tel: +34 958 18 54 80

ROUND-UP

ALTO CAMPOO

Very small resort located in the Cantabrian Mountains, in the far north of Spain. The area has a series of short trails mainly of intermediate level with nothing challenging for advanced riders. Overall, this is a simple retreat that will please carvers, bore freestylers but suit novices. **Off the slopes** there is a couple of small hotels and limited basic local services near the base area.

pic. - Alto Campo Tourism

Ride area: 19km
Number runs: 16
Top Lift: 2175m Bottom Lift: 1650m
Total Lifts:13
Contact:
Alto Campoo Tourist Office
Codigo de pais, Spain (34)
Tel: ++34 (0) 942/77 92 23
www.altocampoo.com
How to get there: Fly to: Madrid 3 hours away

ASTUN

Astun is a fairly decent resort which lies in the Astun Valley in the north of Spain. Although a rather featureless resort, Astun nevertheless has some interesting terrain that will keep freeriders of all levels happy for a few days and intermediates content for a week. **Carvers** have a number of long sweeping trails to do their thing on. **Beginners** have a good series of easy slopes. **Local services** at the base area are basic and affordable.

Number runs: 28
Top Lift: 2324m Total Lifts:14
Contact:
Astun Tourist Office
22889 Valle de Astun, Huesca
Tel: ++34 (0) 34974373088
www.astun.com
How to get there: Fly to: Pamplona 1-1/2 hours away

BOI TAULL

A resort in the far north that will bore the tits off you if you know how to ride and spend more than two days here.There is also the odd natural hit for freestylers to gain some air off. There is still a couple of fast blacks for carvers to try out.Not to say this place is no good, its just that its a bit limited unless you're a total beginner. However, there are no convenient local services

Ride area: 1359 acres Number runs: 41
Top Lift: 2750m Bottom Lift: 2020m

Total Lifts:15 - 6 chairs, 9 drags
Contact:
Amigs, 14-16
08021 Barcelona
Tel: 902 40 66 40
www.boitaullresort.e
How to get there: Fly to: Madrid 3 hours away

CERLER

Although not a very big resort, with only 30km of marked piste, Cerler is one of Spain's best natural freeride/ freestyle resorts. it is laid out above the ancient village of Benasque up in the Pinneos Mountains in the north of Spain. On the slopes, **freeriders** will

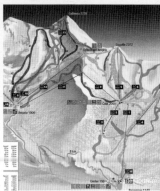

find an abundance of fast trails both on and off the piste with numerous areas where its possible to shred through some tight trees and down some deep powder. Most of the runs are graded red and will appeal to intermediate riders, however advanced riders wanting an easy time with a bit of a challenge, will also like it here especially on the runs that descend from the Cogulla peak. **Freestylers** will find some nice hits. **Beginners** will find this place is perfect.

Good local facilities are provided a short distance from the main base area, with hotels and shops

Number runs: 21
Top Lift: 2364m
Total Lifts:13
Contact:
Cerler Tourist Office
Estacion de Esqui de Cerler
telesilla B-1, 22449 CERLER
Tel: ++34 (0) 974 55 10 12
www.cerler.com
How to get there: Fly to: Barcelona 2 hours away

EL FORMIGAL

Located way up in the north of the country on the French border, El Formigal is a modern purpose built affair. It offers some very good snowboarding on its wide open crowd frees slope that will appeal to piste loving carvers and beginners mostly. Fast riding freeriders and hard core freestylers are not going to be tested too much. There is no pipe or park but there is a lot of good natural freestyle terrain to get air from. Off the slopes you will find a good selection of affordable slopeside services

Number runs:48 - Easy 29% Intermediate 46% Advanced 25%
Top Lift: 2200m Vertical Drop: 377m
Total Lifts:21 - 1 Gondola, 5 chairs, 15 drags
Contact:
Tel - ++34 (0) 974 490 000
www.formigal.com
How to get there: Fly to: Barcelona 3 hours away

S
P
A
I
N

pic - Resort Are (page 349) Mats Olofsson/Are Tourism

Sweden emulates Norway in almost every aspect; cold climate, short winter days and expensive beer. Like Norway, Sweden has a lot of listed resorts - approximately 150. However, 80% cater just for cross country skiing, so most Swedes head down to France and Austria to ride, leaving their own resorts generally crowd free, which helps when you see the size of them.

In general, 99.9% of all resorts are small and at a low level. Terrain will suit mainly intermediate freeriders and freestylers with treeriding and excellent off piste opportunities. Many resorts have built decent terrain parks to try and lure the boarder in. Fast carvers won't be too impressed and advanced boarders may find things a bit limiting, but novices will have a good time on loads of easy slopes.

Getting around the country is easy, although you may have to do some travelling to reach some of the far flung resorts. Air, bus and rail services are damn good, but all are very expensive.
Sweden has the reputation of being very expensive, especially booze. Resort facilities and services are of a high standard. Accommodation is in the form of hotels, little wooden cabins or hostels. A basic Bed and Breakfast home costs from 350kr per night while a bunk in a hostel is around 150kr or a cabin from 170Kr a night.

Over all, Sweden may not be the most adventurous country in which to ride, but it's worth a road trip in June when you can still ride in T-shirts: What's more, Swedes are cool people and the girls are gorgeous and absolutely stunning.

S

S
W
E
D
E
N

Capital City: Stockholm
Population: 8.9 million
Highest Peak: Kebnekaise 2111m
Language: Swedish
Legal Drink Age: 18/20 spirits
Drug Laws: Cannabis is illegal
Age of consent: 16
Electricity: 240 Volts AC 2-pin
International Dialing Code: +46

Time Zone
UTC/GMT +1 hours
Daylight saving time: +1 hour

Driving Guide
All vehicles drive on the right hand side of the road
Speed limits:
Motorways-110kph
Highways-90kph
Towns-50kph
Emergency
Fire/Police/Ambulance - 112
Documentation
Driving licence, insurance certificate and vehicle registration, passport

Currency: Krona
Exchange Rate:
UK£1 = 13.6
EURO - 9
US$1 = 7.5

Swedish Snowboard Association
www.svensksnowboard.net

Sweden Tourist Board
Swedish Travel & Tourism Council
P O Box 3030
Kungsgatan 36
SE-103 61 Stockholm
www.swetourism.se
www.visit-sweden.com

Trains
www.sj.se

Buses
www.ltnbd.se

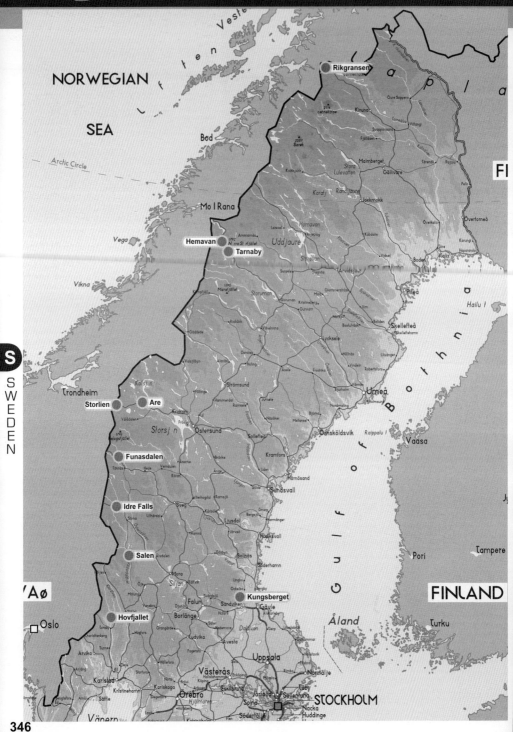

NORWEGIAN

SEA

Arctic Circle

Bod

Vega

Vikna

Mo I Rana

Hemavan
Tarnaby

Trondheim

Storlien   **Are**

Östersund

Funasdalen

Idre Falls

Salen

Oslo

Hovfjallet

Falun

Borlange

Ludvika

Uppsala

Västerås

Örebro

Vänern

Rikgransen

Kiruna

Gällivare

Jokkmokk

Övertorneå

Boden   Kalix

Piteå

Skellefteå

Umeå

Örnsköldsvik

Vaasa

Kramfors

Härnösand

Sundsvall

Ljusdal

Hudiksvall

Bollnäs

Söderhamn

Kungsberget

Gävle

FINLAND

Åland

Turku

Pori

Tampere

STOCKHOLM

Nacka
Huddinge

Södertälje

FI

Gulf of Bothnia

POOR FAIR GOOD TOP

FREERIDE
Trees and some good off-piste

FREESTYLE
Good park & pipe

PISTES
Well groomed slopes

7 OUT OF 10

Very good resort

Mats Olofsson/Åre Tourism

Åre is the biggest and most developed resort in the whole of Scandinavia and unlike many Swedish resorts, this isn't a poxy little hill ! This is a good sized mountain that will give all rider levels a good time. It is situated in the middle of Sweden, near the town of **Östersund**. The runs here cover three main mountains all accessed by one lift pass, although the lifts themselves don't link up. Åre is the largest area with the most challenging terrain while runs on **Duved** and **Bjornange** are a lot shorter and will appeal mostly to novices and intermediates.

FREERIDERS will find a lot of varied terrain, from cornices and wind lips to steeps, as well as some cool tree runs. You can catch a lift on a piste basher or hike up 5mins up to the top of Åre's Areskuten 1400m summit. This allows you to descend some excellent terrain that goes off in different directions but still allows you to get back to the base (study a lift map first).

FREESTYLERS have a great funpark known as The Snowboard Land Park, which is next to the Bräcke lift and comes loaded with a number of big hits to gain maximum air from. There are 2 lines for beginners and experts. The pipe's pretty good and has 3 metre plus walls and is regularly used to host international competitions that attract the worlds top pros.

PISTES. Any carvers who like laying out big arcs will find the well groomed pistes ideal for leaving a signature in the snow. The long red run from the top of the Kabinbanan cable car that eventually takes you home via some wood, is perfect for this.

BEGINNERS should not feel left out here, there are plenty of easy slopes which run from the top lift to the base area. The of runs on the Duvedsomradet area are cool with varying terrain features.

THE TOWN
Off the slopes, what you get here is similar to what you would find in any top resort in the Alps. However, this will hurt the wallet and you shouldn't bother trying to do a week here on a tight budget, you won't last. Still, you won't be disappointed with the level of services and convenience of the accommodation. For **food**, check out *Broken Dreams* for a burger and local grub or *Bykrogens* for a pizza. **Nightlife** is very pricey, but don't hold back, spend and be merry as you can have a great night out here in places like the *Sundial* or *the Diplomats*.

S
S W E D E N

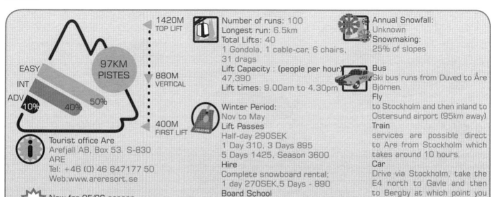

1420M TOP LIFT

880M VERTICAL

400M FIRST LIFT

EASY
INT
ADV
10% 40% 50%

97KM PISTES

Tourist office Are
Arefjall AB, Box 53. S-830 ARE
Tel: +46 (0) 46 647177 50
Web:www.areresort.se

NEW New for 05/06 season
2 new lifts. A 6 person chairlift and a quad

Number of runs: 100
Longest run: 6.5km
Total Lifts: 40
1 Gondola, 1 cable-car, 6 chairs, 31 drags
Lift Capacity : (people per hour) 47,390
Lift times: 9.00am to 4.30pm

Winter Period:
Nov to May
Lift Passes
Half-day 290SEK
1 Day 310, 3 Days 895
5 Days 1425, Season 3600
Hire
Complete snowboard rental;
1 day 270SEK,5 Days - 890
Board School
range of instruction including freestyle, private and off piste.
Night Boarding

Annual Snowfall:
Unknown
Snowmaking:
25% of slopes

Bus
Ski bus runs from Duved to Åre Bjornen.
Fly
to Stockholm and then inland to Ostersund airport (95km away).
Train
services are possible direct to Are from Stockholm which takes around 10 hours.
Car
Drive via Stockholm, take the E4 north to Gavle and then to Bergby at which point you head north west along the E14 via Ostersund to Are. (approx 7hrs).

347

	POOR	FAIR	GOOD	TOP
FREERIDE				
No trees but great off-piste				
FREESTYLE				
No park, but good natural				
PISTES				
Short & sweet				

Midnight freeriding, beat that

8 OUT OF 10

FREERIDERS will find some good off piste with steeps, windlips, and cool hits for getting air born. In addition to the 16 pistes, you'll find another 18 established off-piste runs. There's a huge number of serious routes which usually involve a small hike to start with but are well worth it, try the **Lilla Ölturen** run from the top of the mountain all the way down to **Björnfjell** railway station, or hike to the top of **Norddalsbranten** for some great steep runs. If you sign up for heli-boarding you get the chance to see the best of Lapland's backcountry terrain.

FREESTYLERS are attracted to Riksgränsen in big numbers. The Swedes love their hits and Riksgränsen has an abundance of natural terrain. Get your thinking hat on and search out some of the best freestyle terrain in Scandinavia, or try and claim a backcountry booter left by the pro's.

PISTES. The terrain is not really that good for laying out big turns on, however, via the Ovre lift you do get access to a decent red that joins up to a black.

BEGINNERS do make it up here, but in truth, it's a long way to come just for a couple of small easy flats.

THE TOWN

Riksgränsen Hotel is where it all happens off the slopes. Beds and food are offered at reasonable prices. . Summer up here is for riders in a van, equipped with a tent, loads of duty free booze and a copy of Penthouse. There's no airport in Riksgränsen you should fly to **Kiruna** it's an hour from resort. You can also pig out at *Lappis cafe*. There's no night-life as such here. However, you can have a very good drinking session in the Riksgränsen Hotel which often last all night and après ski can kick off in *Grönans*

**S
W
E
D
E
N**

In the far north of Sweden close to the Norwegian border lies the remote resort of **Riksgränsen**. A place with one of the most unusual seasons in Europe and one that has become a snowboarder's favourite for summer road trips. In late May film crews and an abundance of pros flock here to do some last minute filming. Riksgränsen is located just 300km north of the **Arctic Circle** which would suggest that this is a cold place, but because of its proximity to the Gulf Stream and the Atlantic Ocean, riding in a T-shirt is quite normal in the latter months of the season. Un-like most resorts in Europe, Riksgränsen doesn't open until mid February and stays open until late June, or as long as the snow allows the lifts to be used. You can ride all day in a T-shirt, and strangely enough you can still snowboard right up until midnight when there is still bright natural day light and the lift are sometimes still open. Although no one tends to hang out here for more than a week to ten days, you won't be too disappointed if you're a no-nonsense freerider, or a full on freestyler.

900M TOP LIFT

400M VERTICAL

500M FIRST LIFT

24KM PISTES

EASY
INT
ADV 44%
10%
50%

Riksgransen Tourist Office
S-980 28 Riksgransen
Tel: ++46 (0) 980 400 80

Web:www.riksgransen.nu
Email:info@riksgransen.nu

Number of runs: 16+18 off-piste
Longest run: 1.6 km
Total Lifts: 6
2 chairs, 4 drags
Lift capacity (people per hour): 7,500
Lift times:
9.30am to 11.59pm!

Winter Period:
Feb to late June
Lift Passes
Afternoon 30 euros
1 Day pass - 32.5 euros
5 Day pass - 131 euros
Hire
Board & Boots 35 euros per day, 109 for 5 days.
A Transceiver will cost 55 euros for 5 days
Night Boarding
In perfect daylight until midnight (midsumer)

Annual Snowfall:
5m
Snowmaking:
none

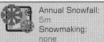

Bus
from Narvik in Norway to Kiruna (www.nordtrafikk.no) or take the number 91 (www.ltnbd.se). Taxis available from Kiruna tel: 0980-12020
Fly
to Stockholm then inland to Kiruna airport about 1hr away.
Train
services direct to Riksgransen which is a 20hr journey from Stockholm visit www.connex. info to book tickets
Car
located close to the Swedish/ Norweigan border east of the Norweigan town of Narvik off the E6 and E10 routes.

BJORKLIDEN

By any stretch of the imagination, Bjorkliden is a small resort with a mixture of basic beginner terrain to simple intermediate carving slopes. Still, overall it?s not a bad resort and offers a lot of interesting opportunities, just not of a very advanced level.

Freeriders who find the marked out runs a bit of a bore could sign up for a heli-board trip and enjoy some cool backcountry riding. **Freestylers** can make do with a decent sized terrain park with a good halfpipe and hits. Nothing local near the slopes but what is available a few miles away is okay but pricey.

BJORNRIKE

Small resort that offers the average rider an afternoons okay carving on a number of trails which include a couple of fast blacks. But in the main, this is a resort to please beginners with a low IQ. Slope side lodging and accommodation and other resort facilities are expensive but okay.

BYDALEN

Overall, this is not a bad place to spend a few days if you are beginner wanting nice and easy runs or a freerider looking for easy to negotiate tree runs. Riders who rate themselves can see if it's justified with a good selection of black runs to try out. **Freestylers** don't have too much to test them, but as with most Swedish resorts, locals build their own hits and session them all day long.

There is also some fast **carving** runs to suit the carvers.

Ride area: 50km
Top Lift: 1010m
Total Lifts:11
Contact:
Tel: +46 (0) 643 32011
How to get there: Fly to: Stockholm 51/4 hours away

FUNASDALEN

Fundasdalen is rated by many as one of Sweden's best resorts, offering a good level of varied terrain and with plenty to keep expert and beginner riders happy for a good few days. Riders who like to go fast can do so here on a series of black runs and a great selection of red intermediate trails.t If back country riding without the hiking is your thing, heli-boarding is available to those with sufficient means. **Freestylers** don't need to go heli-boarding as they are provided with 2 halfpipes and a number of terrain parks that all house some mighty big hits with spines, gaps and quarter pipes. **Beginners** have an equally good number of basic trails. About town theres okay slope side lodging and services

Ride area: 90km
Top Lift: 1200m
Total Lifts:34
Contact:
S-840 95 Fundsdalen
Tel: +46-(0)684-164 10
Fax: +46-(0)684-290 26
www.funasdalsfjall.se
How to get there: Reach Funasdalen via Roros airport in Norway 1 hour away

HEMAVAN

Hemavan is a rather unusual resort that has a reasonable marked out ride area and an even bigger unmarked backcountry terrain accessible by helicopter. For those freeriders who can't fly off to secret powder bowls, there are some nice areas close to the lifts including lots of trees at the lower section of the slopes. This is not a resort noted for its advanced terrain, indeed there is only a couple of advanced graded runs, but for intermediates and first timers, this is a fine place to check out and spend a few days. If you do decide to visit this place then be prepared to put yourself out as there are no local facilities on the slopes and although accommodation and other amenities are not too far away, it's very spread out and will require a car.

Ride area: 30km
Top Lift: 1135m
Total Lifts:7
Contact:
Hemavan-Vaxholm AB
Hemavans Hvgfjdllshotell
Box 162
S- 920 66 Hemavan
Tel: +46 (0)954-301 50
Fax: +46 (0)954-303 08
How to get there: Fly to: Stockholm 12 hours away

HOVFJALLETT

Hovfjallett is basically a waste of time unless you are aged 80, wearing a hearing aid and excel at speeds of one mile an hour. Although the area has a few black runs and half a dozen red trails, all can be licked by an average rider in the time it takes to have a curry induced crap. However, the place is friendly and provides a good halfpipe for air heads.

www.hovfjallet.se

IDRE FJALL

In the top ten ranking of Sweden's resorts Idre Fjall is a place that will suit all levels and rider styles. The area has a combination of easy runs and a number of testing black runs. Nothing here is all that long, indeed the longest trail measures just under 3km, however, with 42 trails this is a place that can take a good few days to explore, especially if you sign up for a heli-board trip. **Freestylers** have a terrain park and a halfpipe which the locals take great pride in and keep in good condition. **Off the slopes** you will find a good choice of slope side lodging and places to eat and drink in.

Idre Fjäll

www.idrefjall.se

KUNGSBERGET

Located 2 1/2hrs South of Stockholm and not far from Sweden's western coast lies the small resort of Kungsberget. With 17 runs, the longest being 1.6km it would bore you stupid after a day or so if it wasn't for the excellent terrain park. Its loaded with some huge tables and kickers, and an array of rails and boxes including a wall ride. Theres night riding every Wednesday till 9pm

Lift Passes:
Half day pass 200SEK
Day pass 240
5 day 860
Season 995
Contact:
www.kungsberget.se
How to get there: Fly to: Stockholm 2 1.2 hours away

Ski Bus leaves from Cityterminalen in Stockholm at 7am weekend and costs SEK 340 including lift pass Tel: +46-290-622 10. Pickups also from Uppsala & Gävle

SALEN

Salen is about as big as they get in Sweden, with 108 pistes serviced by 77 lifts spread out over four areas; they offer every thing you could want both on the slopes and off. Of the four mountain areas Lindvallen and Högfjället are connected by lifts, as are Tandådalen and Hundfjället, so you'll need to take a ski bus to see the whole area.

The terrain is split evenly between all levels and with a host of advanced runs that will have the hardest of riders tested to the limits and needing a week to conquer what is on offer. Freeriders will be pleased to find lots of cool areas to get a fix with deep powder stashes and fast steeps off-piste.
For those wanting to go high off man made hits, then there is a host of terrain parks and halfpipes to satisfy your needs. In Tandådalen theres 2 terrain excellent parks with 2 halfpipes and various spines, kickers, rails and boxes. Theres another park at Lindvallen

Resort services are extreme with literally dozens of hotels, restaurants and night time hangouts much of which is either on the slopes or very close to them.

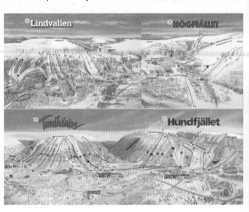

STORLIEN

Storlien is a small affair with nothing great to shout about unless you are a novice or intermediate rider who looks for simple slopes. There is nothing much here to please advanced riders, with only a couple of black runs. Freeriders will find that this place has some nice off-piste areas although very limited. Freestylers have numerous natural hits to get air from and a pipe. Basic lodging is available but none of it is that cheap

www.storlienfjallen.se

PIC - SWITZERLAND TOURISM

The Swiss have gained their riches by shrewdness and getting in on the act early. So it's no wonder their resorts have been welcoming snowboarders for some time and providing them with a huge variety of services. It's never been a big deal for Swiss areas to build halfpipes and fun parks.

What you find in Switzerland is a decent mixture of the old and new. Many resorts are made up of old chalets that look the part, while others are sprawling modern affairs. Verbier is a huge and very impressive place, spoilt only by the fact that it's damn expensive and that it attracts Royalty and idiots on Big Foot skis.

Travelling around the country is made easy with a good road network that links up well with the rest of Europe. To drive on Swiss motorways you need to buy a road tax called the Vignette, which costs around Sfr 30 and can be purchased from Automobile Associations or at border crossings. The tax disc must be shown in the window and fines are payable if you are caught without it.

Flying options are excellent in Switzerland, with most resorts reachable within a 3 hour transfer from the main gateway airports. For such a small country with so many high mountainous areas, it's amazing how good and how many direct train routes there are to resorts. Trains wind their way up to some of the smallest places, travelling up such steep inclines that you're left wondering just how good the brakes are! Few resorts don't have their own train station, or one more than 15 km from away. Bus services are also good, especially from airports, but although they're cheaper than the trains, the buses are slower and less frequent.

Switzerland is not a member of the EU, so all foreign nationals need a passport. However, visas are not required for many nationals, but you must obtain proper permits if you want to work, even as a kitchen porter. You can get cash in hand work with no questions asked, so long as you don't draw attention to yourself.

When it comes to money, Switzerland is costly - budget riders be warned nothing is cheap, and this is not a country where you can scam your way around easily, although thankfully a lot of resorts have bunk houses and youth hostels that help to keep costs down.

S
SWITZERLAND

Capital City: Bern
Population: 7.3 Million
Highest Peak: Mont Rosa 4634m
Language: German/French/Italian
Legal Drink Age: 18
Drug Laws: Cannabis is illegal but laws are slack
Age of consent: 16
Electricity: 240 Volts AC 2-pin
International Dialing Code: +41

Driving Guide
All vehicles drive on the right hand side of the road
Speed limits:
Motorways-120kph (74mph)
Highways-80kph (50mph)
Towns-50kph (31mph)
Emergency
Fire - 118
Police - 117
Ambulance - 117
Tolls
Drivers on motorways must have permit which costs
CHF40 available from most garages. & service stations
Documentation
Driving licence, vehicle registration document and motor
insurance must be carried. Passport will be needed for
photo ID

Currency: Swiss Franc (CHF)
Exchange Rate:
UK£1 = 2.3
EURO = 1.5
US$1 = 1.3

Swiss Snowboard Association
Webereistrasse 47,
Postfach 8134
Adliswil 1
Switzerland
Tel: +41 1 711 82 82
Web: www.swisssnowboard.ch
Email: info@swisssnowboard.ch

Railways
www.sbb.ch
www.zentralbahn.ch
www.tpc.ch (Bus & train)
www.glacierexpress.ch - Glacier Express
www.rhone-express.ch - Rhone Express

Bus Services
www.zvv.ch

Time Zone
UTC/GMT +1 hours
Daylight saving time: +1 hour

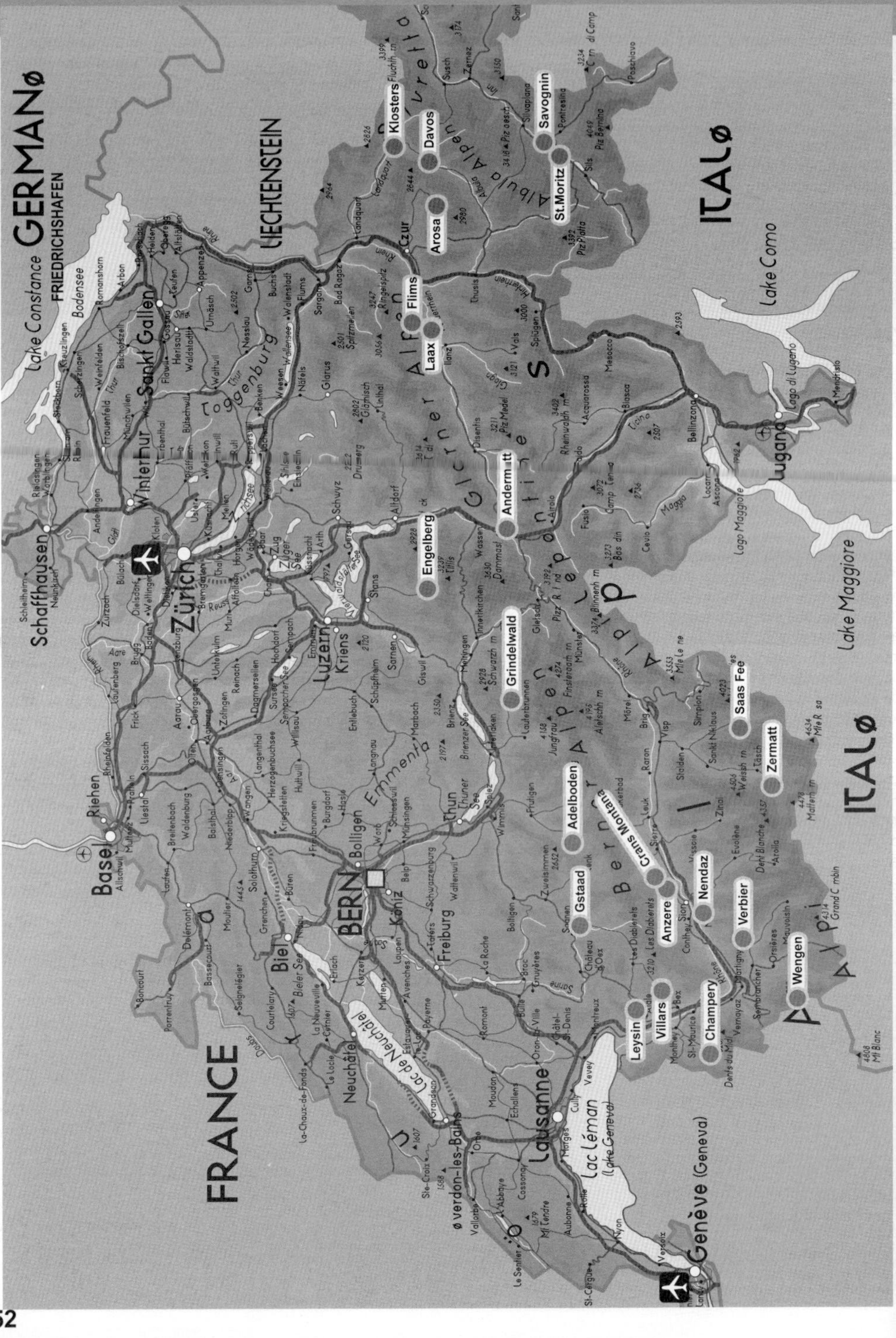

GERMANY

FRIEDRICHSHAFEN

Lake Constance / Bodensee

LIECHENSTEIN

ITALY

Lake Como

Klosters
Davos
Savognin
St.Moritz
Arosa
Chur
Flims
Laax

Sankt Gallen
Schaffhausen
Winterthur
Zürich
Luzern
Krens

Andermatt

Lugano
Lago di Lugano

Engelberg
Grindelwald

Lake Maggiore
Lago Maggiore

Saas Fee
Zermatt

Basel
Riehen
Biel

BERN
Köniz
Freiburg

Adelboden
Gstaad
Anzere
Nendaz
Verbier
Wengen

ITALY

Leysin
Villars
Champery

Neuchâtel
Lac de Neuchâtel

Lausanne
Lac Léman (Lake Geneva)

Genève (Geneva)

FRANCE

S

SWITZERLAND

FREERIDE
Some trees and good off-piste
FREESTYLE
Park & pipe & good natural
PISTES
Nice wide slopes

6
OUT OF 10

Okay but basic resort

pic Adelboden-Lenk - (PHOTOPRESS -Adelboden)

Adelboden, which links with Lenk, is a decent sized picture postcard Swiss resort, located a short distance from the resort of **Gstaad** and close to the glitzy resorts of **Wengen Grindelwald** and **Murren**. However, unlike its neighbours, this is a less popular place making it that bit quieter with crowd free slopes. This is also not a resort favoured by tour operators, although a few do bus in the two plankers to mess things up. What you get to ride here is split into 6 areas all linked by lifts. Collectively, all the areas provide terrain that will keep novices and intermediates happy for a week, while expert riders will have things sorted in a few days after tackling the blacks on the **Geils** area. The mountain has some nice diverse terrain that will bring a smile to most freeriders. It also has some okay backcountry riding offering a few powder stashes and some fun pisted areas.

FREERIDERS will find plenty to keep themselves occupied with here. The Geils area offers some good off-piste riding coupled with a series of black runs that will test the best and draw tears if you fail to respect the terrain.

FREESTYLERS are spoilt for choice here, with the option to ride the Gran Masta Park. The park come equipped with a good selection of gaps and some nice kickers. There's also a cool man made half-pipe and various naturally formed pipes with big walls for getting maximum air. Locals here like to ride the natural hits and have a number of secret spring boards that are tucked away, so hitch up with a local and go big.

PISTES. Boarders who want to stick to the piste will find that Adelboden will suit their needs perfectly, especially competent intermediate boarder who like to give it a turn of speed in the snow on wide open trails.

BEGINNERS have a mountain that caters for them in every aspect, good novice areas with easy access from the village, excellent snowboard tuition at the local snowboard school and runs serviced by easy to use lifts, although many are drag lifts.

THE TOWN. Off the slopes, Adelboden offers plenty of slope side accommodation with various hotels and a number of chalets to choose from, all in a relaxed setting. **Eating** out here is mixed with affordable options coming from traditional swiss style restaurants.
Night life is also okay, but on the whole, not rocking. Check out such bars as the *Alpenrosli* and *Lohner*.

S

S
W
I
T
Z
E
R
L
A
N
D

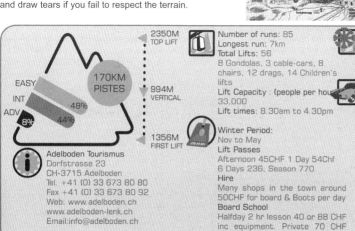

2350M TOP LIFT	**Number of runs:** 85	**Annual Snowfall:** Unknown
	Longest run: 7km	**Snowmaking:** 5% of slopes
	Total Lifts: 56	
170KM PISTES	8 Gondolas, 3 cable-cars, 8 chairs, 12 drags, 14 Children's lifts	**Bus** Taxis: Tel. +41 (0)33 673 28 48 and +41 (0)33 673 15 15
EASY	**Lift Capacity** : (people per hou 33,000	**Fly** to Stockholm and then inland to Ostersund airport (95km away)
INT 48%	**Lift times:** 8.30am to 4.30pm	**Train**
ADV 8% 44%		Train services are possible to Frutigen station (15 minutes).
994M VERTICAL	**Winter Period:** Nov to May	**Car** From Austria/E.Switzerland take the A1 Zurich-Berne, motorway, A6 Berne-Spiez, then take main road for Frutigen-Adelboden
1356M FIRST LIFT	**Lift Passes** Afternoon 45CHF 1 Day 54Chf 6 Days 236, Season 770	
	Hire Many shops in the town around 50CHF for board & Boots per day	
Adelboden Tourismus Dorfstrasse 23 CH-3715 Adelboden Tel. +41 (0) 33 673 80 80 Fax +41 (0) 33 673 80 92 Web: www.adelboden.ch www.adelboden-lenk.ch Email:info@adelboden.ch	**Board School** Halfday 2 hr lesson 40 or 88 CHF inc equipment. Private 70 CHF per hour	

POOR FAIR GOOD TOP

FREERIDE
A few trees & some off-piste
FREESTYLE
Terrain park & halfpipe
PISTES
Good slopes

7 OUT OF 10

Very good resort

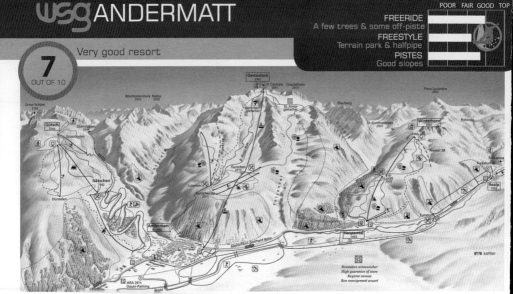

Andermatt is a very small resort, located close to the **St.Gotthard Pass tunnel** with a reputation for excellent powder snow that other resorts can only dream about. This may not be a massive resort, but what it does have is a respectable 1500 metres of vertical with some damn fine steeps, lots of off-piste and crowd-free slopes that are generally also skier free (apart from major holiday times) making **Andermatt** a great place to snowboard There is excellent terrain for advanced riders in soft boots and is noted for its testing runs that also appeal to intermediates who are beginning to sort out their riding. The area is split into four areas with the most testing terrain to be found on the **Gemsstock** slopes, easily reached from Andermatt by a two stage cable ride. From the top, you get to ride down some serious open steep bowls that eventually make their way to the base. However, to guarantee that you do get back to the base, you are well advised to use the services of a local guide.

FREERIDERS have an excellent resort to explore, with great off-piste riding in big powder areas. If your thing is fast steeps and banked walls, Andermatt is a resort that will serve your needs well and will easily keep you interested for a week or so.

FREESTYLERS are provided with a fun park and half-pipe on the Gemsstock area, but they're not particularly hot. However, there is plenty of good natural terrain to get from with big naturally formed banks and some cool drop offs.

PISTES. Riders who like to perform will be pleased to find that there's plenty of fast sections to really crank some big turns on. The **Sonnenpiste** is a decent run to try out before hitting some of the blacks on the **Gemsstock** area.

BEGINNERS usually head for the **Natschen** area, but if you're a slow learner this may not be your resort The slope graduation goes quickly from easy to very hard.

THE TOWN
Good **accommodation** can be found in chalets or in one of the hotels, with access to the slopes very easy by foot. The old village is as Swiss as they come: somewhat boring and somewhat basic. However, it's not as expensive as some other Swiss resorts and as you can ride hard all day, who needs major night-life?
A few beers in a **bar** free of moaning package tour apres numpties should do the trick. Nights can rock and the locals help to make the action take off, but don't expect lots of it.

S
SWITZERLAND

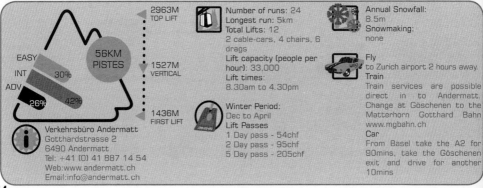

2963M TOP LIFT

1527M VERTICAL

1436M FIRST LIFT

56KM PISTES

EASY
INT 30%
ADV 26% 42%

Number of runs: 24
Longest run: 5km
Total Lifts: 12
2 cable-cars, 4 chairs, 6 drags
Lift capacity (people per hour): 33,000
Lift times:
8.30am to 4.30pm

Winter Period:
Dec to April
Lift Passes
1 Day pass - 54chf
2 Day pass - 95chf
5 Day pass - 205chf

Annual Snowfall:
8.5m
Snowmaking:
none

Fly
to Zurich airport 2 hours away.
Train
Train services are possible direct in to Andermatt. Change at Göschenen to the Matterhorn Gotthard Bahn www.mgbahn.ch
Car
From Basel take the A2 for 90mins, take the Göschenen exit and drive for another 10mins

Verkehrsbüro Andermatt
Gotthardstrasse 2
6490 Andermatt
Tel: +41 (0) 41 887 14 54
Web:www.andermatt.ch
Email:info@andermatt.ch

POOR FAIR GOOD TOP

FREERIDE
Some trees and ok off-piste
FREESTYLE
Boardercross
PISTES
Easy slopes

Good basic resort

6
OUT OF 10

FREESTYLERS can spin off a number of natural hits and there are ample areas for practising your switch stance, especially on the runs frequented by the oldies who are leisurely sliding around on their two wooden planks. There's permanent boardercross on the Pâtres piste.

PISTES. Competent riders will find the black under the Pas-de-**Maimbre** gondola worth a visit. It should be said that this run could be a red, but it's OK and allows for a few quick turns.

BEGINNERS should achieve the most on the well matched and easy slopes which can be tackled by taking the **Pralan-Tsalan** chair lift and then by using the drags (hold on tight, wimps).

Anzere is one of **Switzerland's** custom built resorts that dates back to the sixties. This small resort with a modest 25 miles of piste, sits at an altitude of 1500m. This has helped to ensure a good annual snow record of over 800 centimetres a season on slopes that get a lot of sun. This allows for plenty of tanning as you ride the slopes or sip a beer at a mountain bar. Overall, Anzere is a fun, happy-go-lucky place that will appeal to the laid back snowboarder. A lot of families and older skiers hang out here, but snowboarders can mingle with ease with both and riders are not ignored or snubbed. The 25 miles of runs are simple and all styles will find something to keep them happy, but it appeals mostly to novices and riders just getting things dialled. **Anzere** would be worth a visit for a few days if you're on a road trip, but a two week trip will prove to be a bit of a bore for those riders who rate themselves at an advanced level.

FREERIDERS in soft boots will fair well on the areas found off the **Les Rousses** and **Le Bate** chair lifts. The trees at the lower parts although not extensive, do offer some pine shredding. The Swiss don't particularly like the woods being cut up, so beware, you may encounter a few sharp tongues from the locals.

THE TOWN
Anzere is a well laid out village, with a good choice of accommodation (mostly expensive) but budget snowboarders will find affordable beds in a selection of apartments and chalets. *Village Camp* offers decent priced lodgings while the *Avenir* does the best pizza. For evenings, it's best to check out *La Grange* or the *Rendezvous*.

pic - Anzere Tourism

S

S
W
I
T
Z
E
R
L
A
N
D

2420M TOP LIFT	Number of runs: 24
	Longest run: 4km
	Total Lifts: 11
40KM PISTES	1 Gondolas, 2 chairs, 8 drags
	Lift Capacity : (people per hour):
EASY	9,000
920M VERTICAL	Lift times: 8.30am to 4.30pm
INT 40%	
ADV 10% / 50%	Winter Period:
	Nov to April
	Lift Passes
1500M FIRST LIFT	Half day 31CHF Full Day pass 45
	5 days 188 chf, Season 635
	Board School
	Private lessons 1hr 50CHF, day 260
	Full day group 45CHF, 5 days 165
	Hire
	Board & Boots 38CHF, 6 days 136

Annual Snowfall:
8m
Snowmaking:
5% of slopes

Taxis
+41 27 398 3545 and +41 79 433 4815
Fly
to Geneva airport, 3 hours away. Zurich also close
Train
to Sion station (15min). TGV from paris.
Car
via Geneva, east on the N1 and N9 to Sion and turn left and then drive up the steep road to Anzere.

Office du Tourisme de Anzere
Route du Nord
1972 Anzère
Telephone : +41 27 399 2800
web:www.anzere.ch
email: infos@anzere.ch

	POOR	FAIR	GOOD	TOP
FREERIDE Trees & some good off-piste				
FREESTYLE Terrain park & halfpipe				
PISTES Good for intermediates				

Good freeriding

6
OUT OF 10

S

S W I T Z E R L A N D

A rosa is all Swiss, and a place that fits in perfectly in with how the Swiss marketing chiefs would have you see it. This is one of those cosy Swiss hamlets perched high above the tree drenched valley floor. This is a high altitude resort which sits above 1800 metres and is located in the eastern sector of the country not far from the town of **Chur** and the better known resort of **Davos**. However, unlike Davos, this is not a massive sprawling mountain town, Arosa is a quiet traditional swiss village loaded with all the charm you could hope for, although spoilt slightly by its glitzy stuck up image. Still, the area offers some good snowboarding opportunities and will make a week's trip a good one if you're a novice or intermediate rider. Advanced riders have very little to keep them interested beyond a day or so. The 40 plus miles of open wide trails are serviced by a modern and well appointed lift system that can shift over 22,000 people an hour uphill with just 16 lifts Although Arosa is not on the calling card of every tour operator, the few that do use this place help to cause a few lift lines and the odd bottle neck on certain slopes. The runs are spread out over two areas, that of **Hornli** and **Weisshorn** where the most challenging terrain is located.

FREERIDERS who want to sample some tracks at speed, should check out the black on the **Weisshorn**. If you want to get into some freshies then take the off-piste track to the resort **Lenzerheide** via the Hornli slopes, but do so only with a guide.

FREESTYLERS have a good half-pipe located at **Carmennahue**. This is also the location for the fun park which is equipped with a standard series of hits including one or two nice kickers. However, this is also a place that offers some good natural freestyling, but you have to look for it.

PISTES. Riders who like to slide around on gentle well prepared slopes and without any surprises, will find Arosa ideal for their needs.

BEGINNERS in Arosa could do a lot worse. The slopes here provide novices an easy time and allow for some quick progression.

THE TOWN
Off the slopes you will find a limited selection of facilities, but enough to get by with. **Accommodation** is well stationed for the lifts and comes in the standard grade Swiss hotel format. Warm, cosy, charming and costly. **Eating out** and night time action is not hot at all, but if you're only out for a quiet time away from the crowds, this place will do nicely.

pics ·AROSA Tourism

2653M TOP LIFT

914M VERTICAL

1740M FIRST LIFT

EASY
INT 38%
ADV 6%
56%

64KM PISTES

Arosa Tourist Office. Arosa. Ch-7050
Tel: +41 81 378 70 20
Fax: +41 81 378 70 21
Web: www.arosa.ch
Email: arosa@arosa.ch

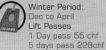

Number of runs: 55
Longest run: 5.5km
Total Lifts: 16
3 cable-cars, 7 chairs, 6 drags
Lift capacity (people per hour): 22,000
Lift times:
8.30am to 4.30pm

Winter Period:
Dec to April
Lift Passes
1 Day pass 55 chf
5 days pass 228chf

Annual Snowfall:
unknown
Snowmaking:
10% of slopes

Fly
to Zurich airport about 3 hours away.
Train
Train services are possible direct into Arosa via Chur.
Car
Drive via Zurich, head south on the N3 to Chur and then take the winding road up to Arosa (30km) , a total distance of around 100 miles (160km).

wsg CRANS MONTANA

POOR FAIR GOOD TOP

FREERIDE
Trees and good off-piste
FREESTYLE
Park & pipe
PISTES
Some good long runs

Offers something for everyone

8
OUT OF 10

PIC -CRANS MONTANA TOURISME

morning runs. Still, for all the area has to offer, advanced riders are not always tested, with the terrain largely covering intermediate or novice levels. The hardest listed run is the black that runs down from the **Toula chair**, which is best tackled in softs as the unevenness in parts is better ridden in something where you can easily absorb the bumps at speed.

FREERIDERS in search of off-piste and fresh powder need to hook up with a guide and set off to areas around the **Plaine Morte Glacier**, where you can make your way to nearby **Anzere**. The route goes through some tunnels, which makes it well worth the effort. The area known as the **Faverges** is cool and for riders with some idea of what they're doing, there are some decent steeps to tackle - but watch out for the thigh burning traverse on the way back. For those who can afford it, you can do some cool heli-boarding on some major terrain.

PIC -CRANS MONTANA TOURISME

One of Switzerland's top snowboard areas is made up of two linking towns, that of **Crans** and **Montana**. Both of which are pretty outstanding and make a totally full-on place with plenty of interest for all. Both areas fuse together to provide over 100 miles (160km) of all-level and all-rider style terrain. Snowboarders have been cutting up these slopes for years, which has lead to a resort with some of the best snowboard instruction and facilities anywhere in Europe. Unfortunately the popularity of this area does mean some stupidly long lift queues with skier cluttered slopes. A lot of tour operators throughout Europe come here with package groups (especially from the UK) and so there's a lot of idiots messing up early

FREESTYLERS are well catered for, with a good pipe on Pas du Loup, which can be reached by the **Montana-Arnouvaz** gondola. The fun park at Aminona is loaded with rails spines and gaps, so new schoolers will love it and for those who want to find out how to ride a pipe correctly or to get big air, there is a number of schools that will help out, all of which offer some of the highest levels of snowboard tuition in Europe (they practically invented snowboard instruction here).

S

SWITZERLAND

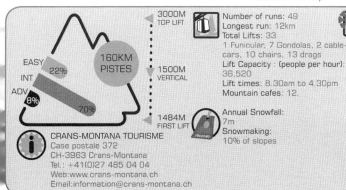

Number of runs: 49
Longest run: 12km
Total Lifts: 33
1 Funicular, 7 Gondolas, 2 cable-cars, 10 chairs, 13 drags
Lift Capacity : (people per hour):
36,520
Lift times: 8.30am to 4.30pm
Mountain cafes: 12.

Annual Snowfall:
7m
Snowmaking:
10% of slopes

3000M
TOP LIFT

1500M
VERTICAL

1484M
FIRST LIFT

EASY
INT
ADV
22%
8%
70%

160KM
PISTES

Winter Period:
Dec to April
Lift Passes
Half-day 47CHF
1 Day 56chf
5 Days 240 chf
Hire
Board & Boots from 28 CHF.
Board School
Lesson, Lift & hire from 40 CHF a day
Night Boarding
3.5 km floodlit every friday 7-10pm, CHF15
Heliboarding
in mont blanc area

CRANS-MONTANA TOURISME
Case postale 372
CH-3963 Crans-Montana
Tel.: +41(0)27 485 04 04
Web:www.crans-montana.ch
Email:information@crans-montana.ch

357

PIC -CRANS MONTANA TOURISME

PISTES. Riders have plenty of long reds to check out. In particular the red run that drops away from the **Plaine Morte** down to the village of **Les Barzettes**, is perfect to lay out some big lines and with a length of 7.5 miles, you have plenty of time to get it right.

BEGINNERS are treated to a variety of no nonsense blues which may require some navigation to avoid drag lifts. That said, this is a good novices resort, apart from the sometimes busy slopes. What really stands out is the superb level of snowboard tuition available, with a 3 hour group lesson costing from 40 Cfr.

THE TOWN
As well as supposedly having the largest linked resort in Switzerland, Crans-Montana also said to have the largest number of hotels and accommodation options of any mountain resort in the country. However, you could actually be forgiven for not classing this place as resort at all, but rather a large bustling town which in effect is what it is. The whole area is serviced by a regular bus service which is the best way to get around if you don't have a car (taxi prices are criminal). There are loads of sporting outlets, dozens of shops, (check out *The Avalanche* ++41 (0) 402 2424 for snowboard hire) a cinema and if you are feeling really lucky, a casino.

ACCOMMODATION. The 40,000 plus tourist beds are spread throughout a large area with the option to stay in either Crans or Montana Lodging options are fairly extensive with a good choice of slope side hotels or a large selection of self catering apartment blocks for groups, but on the whole nothing comes cheap wherever you stay.

FOOD. Around town you are spoilt for choice when it comes to restaurants with a selection of over 80 eateries no one need starve here. This place is blessed with simply loads of places to get a meal and even though this is an expensive resort, there are affordable joints such *San Nick's*, which offers some good pub grub or *Mamamias* for a slice of pizza or a bowl of pasta at just about affordable prices. If you wish to splash out, try *Le Sporting's*

NIGHT LIFE is pretty damn good here and well in tune with snowboard lifestyle, although it is carried out along side some very sad Swiss style après ski nonsense (simply to please holiday crowds who don't know how to have a good time). Cool hangouts to have a beer in include The *Amadeus Bar* and *Constellation*, both with a party mood and loud music. The *Memphis Bar* is a good bar.

SUMMARY
A big snowboarders resort offering something for everyone. Great carving and excellent freeriding areas. Lots of local services but a very busy place.
On the slopes: Excellent
Off the slopes: Very good
Money wise: Overall, a very expensive resort but well worth the money.

S

S W I T Z E R L A N D

CAR: A9 to Sierre then 15 km to resort
FLY: 2.5 hours from Geneva, Zurich 4hrs. Sion nearest airport, 40 mins away.
TRAIN: To Sierre then Funicular 12 mins or 30min drive
BUS: Buses between Sierre-Montana-Crans via Chermignon or Mollens

POOR FAIR GOOD TOP

FREERIDE
Trees and excellent off-piste
FREESTYLE
Park & 2 halfpipes
PISTES
Good variety of runs

10
OUT OF 10

Great pistes & excellent freeriding, but pricey

pic ·San Tang

Davos is not just a major snowboard resort, it's also a massive town that offers just about all you need to have a cool time. This very happening place offers the lot; tons of deep powder, loads of trees, big natural hits, half-pipes and fun parks. All this on 200 miles (320km) of fantastic snowboard terrain, on slopes that hold the snow well. The **O'Neil SB Jam** is held here every turn of the year, and attracts many a top name to ride the excellent pipe at the bottom of town at Bolgen.

Davos sprawls along the bottom the Davos valley with the 5 mountain areas either side. The main Davos Dorf/Platz area services the **Parsenn** and **Jakobshorn** mountains. Nearby **Klosters** is next to the Madrisa and **Parsenn** mountains. The other 2 mountains **Pischa** and **Rinerhorn** will involve a 20 minute bus or a train to get to. Davos itself, has a bit of an attitude when it comes to money, but it's a working town of 13,000 and so far less snobby than other similar places. It plays host the World Economic Conference at the end of January when all the World

leaders and billionaires gather to schmooze and pretend they care in front of the cameras; a security nightmare and a week to avoid. Klosters is much prettier and compact, but does stink of money and poodles.

Davos provides a great location to explore. The main park is located on the Jakobshorn mountain, but it also has a few great backcountry routes. The other side of town provides access to Parsenn, which is by far the biggest mountain and you can board all the way into Klosters.

FREERIDERS will wet themselves when they see the off-piste opportunities, which are mega and best checked out with the services of a guide. The run down to **Teufi** from **Jakobshorn** is pretty cool, but you will have to bus back to Davos. From the top station (which is well above the tree lines), advanced or intermediate freeriders will find a number of testing blacks which mellow out into reds as they lead straight back down to the **Ischalp** mid-section. From here you could carry on down through the trees to the base or if you want an easy final descent, there's an easy blue that snakes it's way home, ideal for novice freeriders.

FREESTYLERS have long been provided with a good pipe and park area, however, they weren't always well maintained, apart from at competition times. Now that has changed and the earth shaped pipe at the foot of the **Jakobshorn** is pretty faultless and shaped twice a week. The main park, the **Sunrise park** is located off the **Jatz Junior lift** and has 2 kickers, a quarter pipe, rollers and various rails. There's also a 110m superpipe up there. Away from the parks you'll find an abundance of good natural freestyle terrain.

PISTES. Theres plenty of slopes to keep everyone happy, but the piste map is pretty dreadful. The leg burning 6 mile red run into the village of **Serneus** is full-on and you should be carving big style at the end of this one.

BEGINNERS wanting to get to grips with things should go see the guys at the '*Top Secret snowboard school*', the instructors really know how to turn you from a side standing fool into a powder hound. At the top station of

S

S W I T Z E R L A N D

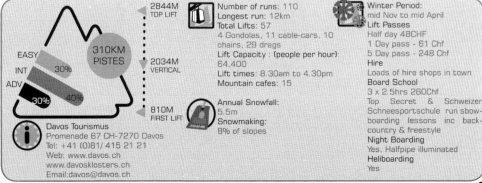

2844M TOP LIFT	Number of runs: 110	Winter Period: mid Nov to mid April
	Longest run: 12km	Lift Passes
	Total Lifts: 57	Half day 48CHF
EASY	4 Gondolas, 11 cable-cars, 10 chairs, 29 drags	1 Day pass - 61 Chf
310KM PISTES	2034M VERTICAL	Lift Capacity : (people per hour): 64,400	5 Day pass - 248 Chf
INT 30%	Lift times: 8.30am to 4.30pm	Hire Loads of hire shops in town
ADV	Mountain cafes: 15	Board School 3 x 2.5hrs 260Chf
30% 40%	810M FIRST LIFT	Annual Snowfall: 5.5m	Top Secret & Schweizer Schneesportschule run sbow-boarding lessons inc back-country & freestyle
	Snowmaking: 8% of slopes	Night Boarding Yes, Halfpipe illuminated
Davos Tourismus Promenade 67 CH-7270 Davos Tel: +41 (0)81/ 415 21 21 Web: www.davos.ch www.davosklosters.ch Email:davos@davos.ch		Heliboarding Yes

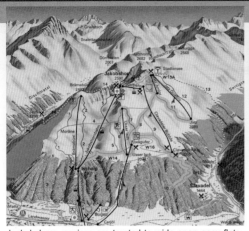

Jackobshorn, novices are treated to wide open easy flats which are serviced by drag lifts or a short cable car ride. Alternatively, there are plenty of very easy runs lower down on the **Parsenn** slopes.

THE TOWN
If you're the sort of individual that wants to be housed, fed and watered in a charming sweet little village with cow bells hanging from rickety old sheds, don't bother with this place. Despite its some- what glitzy image, off the slopes, Davos doesn't muck around, lacks style, doesn't come cheap nor is this a visually pleasing joint. What you have here is a massive drab mountain town offering a huge choice of everything. Although this is a super expensive place that attracts international conferences and all that goes with them, you still get a large slice of snowboard lifestyle. Local facilities include sports centres, lots of shops, and even a Casino

Accommodation in Davos is second to none, for a 3*

you'll be looking at a minimum of 80CHF a night. On top of there being loads of expensive hotels, Davos also has an affordable snowboarders hostel come hotel called the The *Bolgenschanze*, www.bolgenschanze.ch. It offers a number of ride and stay packages at reasonable prices, a weekend package inc 2 nights, food, lift pass will cost 270CHF. (tel: +41 (0)81 413 71 01) . The town also boast a host of bed and breakfast joints.

Food. Two words that don't go together in Davos, cheap and eating out, but if you have the cash then the options for dining high on the hog are excellent. There is a good choice of restaurants offering every type of cuisine, ranging from local dishes to Chinese. You will also find a few fast food joints serving cardboard burgers and horrid euro style fries (chips should be fat and greasy UK style). Theres a good 24hr café on the promenade in Davos Platz.

Night life in Davos rocks despite being so damn expensive, but you'll have to ask around to find the best bars. There is a good choice of bars and late night clubs, with live bands and artists playing seven nights a week. Most places pump out modern music but a few play sickening euro pop to please the après skiing nerds. The Bolgenschanze Hotel is one of the best hangouts, providing the full snowboard lifestyle package and gets packed out with loads of chicks.

CAR
From Zurich take motorway A3/A13 towards Chur, take the Landquart exit and continue to Davos. 145km total
FLY
Fly to Zurich international 155km away, transfer time to resort is 2 1/2 hours. Friedrichshafen airport 145km away
TRAIN
to Davos centre. Train from Zurich via Landquart takes 2 1/2hrs. Train from Geneva will take 5hr20
BUS
Kessler Carreisen AG run transfer from Zurich airport 4 times every saturday, 70 single, 120 return
tel: +41 (0)81 417 07 07. Local bus service timetables on www.vbd.ch

POOR FAIR GOOD TOP

FREERIDE
Some trees and good off-piste
FREESTYLE
All year round park
PISTES
Uncrowded slopes

6
OUT OF 10

No hype and good for a week

are common here. Some of the best off-piste terrain can be found having taken the **Jochstock** drag lift to reach the slopes on the **Alpstublii**, where you will find some amazing runs. Another easy to reach gem is the **Laub area**, which bases out conveniently to allow you to do it again. But this pleaser should not be tried out unless you know the score and can handle fast steeps, because this one will wipe your lights out for good if you balls up. Guide services are available here so use them, and stay alive.

FREESTYLERS who like it done for them will find the park on the **Jochpass area** (www.terrainpark.ch) the place to head for. Theres a some big kickers and a rail line that they usually keep nicely in shape. Dotted around the area are plenty of good natural hits to check out.

Engelberg is a cool resort located slap bang in the middle of the country, not far from the town of **Lucerne** or the resort of **Andermatt**. By any standards, Engelberg has a very impressive rideable vertical drop which is said to be the longest in Switzerland. The beauty of this place is that it's left alone by mass ski crowds so the place has a cool laid back feel about it, without the hype. The ride area is a bit unusual and spread out from the village area. This is a resort noted for its avalanches so lots of attention is called for before trying out any of the slopes. The main happenings are offered on the Titlis area noted for its intermediate terrain but somewhat lacking for those who like to shine. The **Gerschnialp** area is for those sucking on a dummy (beginners). Theres is some summer boarding and a terrain on the **Titlis glacier**.

FREERIDERS have a very good mountain here with some great off-piste to check out, but be warned, avalanches

PISTES. Riders have a fair selection of well looked after pisted runs or some fine unpisted slopes. Check out the Jachpass trails for a burner.

BEGINNERS, 30% of the slopes are said to be easy terrain, but in truth if you're a fast learner, then you soon get to ride a further 60% of slopes which are rated intermediate.

THE TOWN
Local services at the base area are of a high standard located in a traditional Swiss setting. The village offers some affordable **accommodation** but don't expect cheap digs near the slopes. There is a number of restaurants here which are all similar in style and price, but as for **night life**, it's a bit dull.

S

EASY
INT   30%
ADV
10%
60%

82KM PISTES

3020M TOP LIFT

1970M VERTICAL

1050M FIRST LIFT

Engelberg-Titlis Tourismus AG
Tourist Center, Klosterstrasse 3
6390 Engelberg
Tel: +41 (0)41 639 77 77

Web: www.engelberg.ch
www.titlis.ch
Email: welcome@engelberg.ch

Number of runs: 44
Longest run: 4km
Total Lifts: 27
1 Funicular train, 7 Gondolas, 7 chairs, 12 drags
Lift Capacity : (people per hour) 23,000
Lift times: 8.30am to 4.30pm

Winter Period:
Nov to April
Summer Period:
June to August
Lift Passes
Half day 49CHF, 1 Day 58 Chf
5 Days 219 Season 1100
Board School
Swiss Snowboard School (www.skischule-engelberg.ch)& boardlocal (lucerne@boardlocal.ch) run lessons
Hire
board and boots from 45 Chf/day

Annual Snowfall:
3m
Snowmaking:
5% of slopes

Taxis
+41 (0)78 666 57 57 or 41 (0)41 637 33 88
Fly
to Zurich airport, about 2 hours train away.
Train
from Lucerne there is a direct hourly service to Engelberg operated by the LSE. Direct trains available from Zurich to Lucerne.
Car
Via Zurich, head south on the routes A123/N4a/N14/N2 to Stans and turn off at signs for Engelberg.

POOR FAIR GOOD TOP

FREERIDE
Trees & some good off-piste
FREESTYLE
2 terrain parks & 2 halfpipes
PISTES
Great condition & variety

Excellent riding area

9
OUT OF 10

shoots down from the Cassons and arrives to connect up with the **Grauberg trail**. The Cassons area is a specific freeride area, that rarely opens but when it does you need to make a bee-line for it. The cable-car only holds 20 people so you'll find yourself almost alone at the top. Below that the area from Naraus to Foppa is great after a good dump for beginner and intermediate freeriders.

FREESTYLERS wanting a fix from a well shaped half-pipe wall, will need to make their way up to the Crap Sogn area above Laax. Here you find an extremely well maintained pipe and park shaped by a pipe dragon.

PISTES. Riders sticking to the pistes will not have themselves overtaxed, but there is a nice series of good red runs below Narus that will make for a few good lines at a controlled speed. The **Heini** is a long red that starts out as a black down from the Cassons and will sort out the boys from the men (or birds from the skirt).

BEGINNERS have a well set out series of novice trails from the base area of **Flims Dorf.** The easy blues start out from the Narus and allow first timers a good choice of easy to negotiate descents back down to the base area.

THE TOWN
Flims runs along the road in and out of town and offers a good choice of slope side **accommodation** and places to eat. Riders on a budget, book in at *Gliders* which is a cool backpackers place where a bed will cost around 45 CHF a night with breakfast available for an extra fee. Food wise La Dolcha Vita serves good pizzas for 18CHF

Night life in Flims is not too hot, but what's on offer is okay but doesn't start to get going until after 9. *The Iglu* at Flims Dort is open till 1am, as is the *Stenna bar* oppositite. Theres a nightclub open till 6am in Flims Waldhaus towards Laax.

Flims is often over shadowed by its bigger brother, **Laax**. However, this gem of a place deserves to be given a platform of its own and although Laax is far bigger with more rideable terrain, **Flims** can hold its own. What's more, being the junior partner, Flims tends to be a little less crowded even though the two resorts link up on the slopes by lifts and share a joint lift pass. Flims sits at a slightly higher altitude than Laax but on the whole, the slopes are the same in both areas. Indeed on the mountain you would be forgiven for thinking that this was two resorts although in many ways it's not. Both places share a lift pass and the series of pisted runs connect well with each other. The trails above Flims are well prepared and offer a mixture ranging from gentle blues, to a fast black trail running down the **Cassons slopes** which falls away sharply.

FREERIDERS, have for a number of years been aware of what is on offer here, whether up on Flims or over on the Laax slopes. For a nice long freeride trail that's not over testing, try out the **Segnes trail** which is a red run that

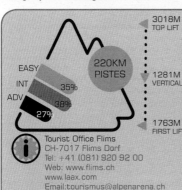

3018M
TOP LIFT

1281M
VERTICAL

1763M
FIRST LIFT

EASY
220KM
PISTES
INT   35%
ADV   38%
27%

Tourist Office Flims
CH-7017 Flims Dorf
Tel: +41 (081) 920 92 00
Web: www.flims.ch
www.laax.com
Email:tourismus@alpenarena.ch

Number of runs: 58
Longest run: 14km
Total Lifts: 29 - 7
Gondolas, 4 cable-cars, 7 chairs,8 drags, 3 kids lifts
Lift capacity (people per hour): 42,000
Lift times:
8.30am to 4.30pm

Winter Period:
Nov to April
Lift Passes
Half day 50CHF
1 Day pass 62Chf
5 Days 273
Lessons
Various group & private lessons as well as special-ised freestyle and freeride courses

Annual Snowfall:
7.2m
Snowmaking:
20% of slopes

Bus
Bus services from Zurich take around 2 1/2 hours direct to Laax via Chur. Buses from Chur run 8 times a day from 06:49 until 22:15 visit www.zvv.ch/ postauto for timetables
Fly
to Zurich about 3 hours away Milan 3 1/2hr away
Train
to Chur, 40 mins away.
Car
Zurich via Chur to Laax is 90 miles (145 km). Drive time is about 2 1/2 hours.

wsg GRINDELWALD

Good carvers resort

6 OUT OF 10

	POOR	FAIR	GOOD	TOP
FREERIDE Some trees and limited off-piste				
FREESTYLE Terrain park & halfpipe				
PISTES Crowded slopes but long				

Grindelwald Tourism

Grindelwald is one of the resorts that helps form the area more commonly known as the **Jungfrau Region**. The other resorts that make up this sector are Wengen (very posh and super up its arse attitude), and **Murren** the most laid back and snowboard friendly of the three. **Grindelwald** sits up at an altitude of some 1034 metres and scenically, is an impressive place. However, the same can't be said of the rideable terrain that is immediately on offer from the base village, for this is not an adventurous mountain resort and freeriders will soon get bored of the place, although it is a very good carvers resort. The 200 plus kilometres of marked piste stretch out across two large wide open plateaus that stretch up from both sides of the village, with the slopes on the **Mannlichen** and **Kl.Scheidegg** side linking up with the runs that descend back down into Wengen. You can also reach Murren via the slopes but in truth, it can be a bit of a pain the arse. Grindelwald is a large sprawling resort that attracts a lot of visitors, there is no such thing as a good time to visit to avoid crowds, the place is always packed. The main access lifts are not only slow but the queues for them can be hellish and can often mean a 50 minute wait in line. Still, once you do get up on the slopes and the conditions prove to be favourable, provided you do not want to be tested, you will be able to have a good time.

FREERIDERS who stick to Grindelwald are not going to find a great deal to keep them entertained, not because it's crap, there's just not that much to appeal. The best freeriding terrain is in Murren

FREESTYLERS. Theres a terrain park at Bärgelegg featuring a number of kickers and various kinked, straight and rainbow rails and boxes as well as a wallride. There's a superpipe located on Schreckfeld and a boardercross at Oberjoch. Visit www.stoneland.ch for details.

PISTES. The slopes may be busy, but there is still plenty of piste to lay out lots of wide linked turns on if thats your thing.

BEGINNERS have a host of nice gentle open slopes to learn on, the only draw back being that the access to them is not convenient.

THE TOWN
The village at the base of the slopes has a number of hotels and chalets to choose from, but nothing comes cheap as this place is stupidly expensive. Not all the **accommodation** is close to the slopes so expect to do some hiking to and from the base lifts. The resort has a host of sporting attractions, a lot of hotel restaurants but little or no cheap fast food, the night-life also sucks.

S

S W I T Z E R L A N D

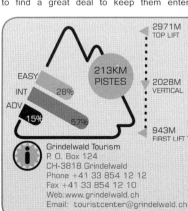

2971M TOP LIFT

2028M VERTICAL

943M FIRST LIFT

213KM PISTES

EASY

INT 28%

ADV

15% 57%

Grindelwald Tourism
P. O. Box 124
CH-3818 Grindelwald
Phone +41 33 854 12 12
Fax +41 33 854 12 10
Web:www.grindelwald.ch
Email: touristcenter@grindelwald.ch

Number of runs: 35
Longest run: 15km
Total Lifts: 45
10 Gondolas, 6 cable-cars, 16 chairs,13 drags
Lift Capacity : (people per hour) 42,000
Lift times: 8.30am to 4.30pm

Winter Period:
Dec to April
Lift Passes
Half day 42 CHF Full day 56 CHF
5 day 233 CHF. 2 day for entire Jungfrau region 120, 6 days 288
Board School
Private lesson CHF 320 for full day
Group 3 day 185 CHF, 1 week 255
Hire
6 days Snowboard & boots 219

Annual Snowfall:
5.3m
Snowmaking:
10% of slopes

Fly
Zurich Kloten and Geneva Cointrin have rail services to Interlaken. Bern Belp have airport taxis available to take you to the train station.
Train
to Interlaken Ostthere, then train to Grindelwald (approx 35min)
Car
Motorway to Bâle, Geneva or Zurich to Spiez, then to Grindelwald via interlaken

363

POOR FAIR GOOD TOP

FREERIDE
Some trees & good off-piste
FREESTYLE
Terrain park & good natural
PISTES
Well groomed slopes

6
OUT OF 10

pic - Gstaad Tourism

S W I T Z E R L A N D

G staad is part of a massive slope linked area void of the mass holiday groups. What you get here is crowd free snowboarding with miles of backcountry adventures and over 150 well prepared pistes covered by a single lift pass. Welcome to Gstaad, a place where snowboarding comes as second nature and a place that despite its appeal for attracting far too many poncy image junkies with designer eye-wear, is a place that has a good snowboard feel to it and one where you can ride hard. Despite the sad gits that flock here, the area has long allowed snowboarders freedom to roam its slopes, which are split between a number of areas with Gstaad sitting mid-way between them. The areas most favoured by snowboarders are **Saanenmoser** and **Schonried** which can be reached without any hassle from Gstaad. Further a field is **Les Diablerets** which is a glacier that's open in the summer months.

FREERIDERS are somewhat spoilt for choice here with some notable freeriding terrain over on the Saanen area where with aid of a guide, you can ride out some great powder fields. Alternatively, for something a little more testing you should head up to the **Les Diablerets** glacier.

FREESTYLERS have a number of terrain parks to choose from, with the best offering on the **Sanserloch** area (www.vanillaz.com), where you'll find some big jumps, gaps and rails. A bit of a trek away is a park on the Glacier 3000 with various kicker and rail lines, and a halfpipe. However, constructed half-pipes are not always necessary here as there is a lot of diverse natural terrain with some notable cliffs and big wind lips. Check out the cliffs up at **Huhnerspiel**.

BEGINNERS have the biggest percentage of easy slopes around here much of which is not linked and spread out between the areas with some of the best runs on the **Saanenmoser** slopes.

THE TOWN
Gstaad is not for those with a weak stomach as on the snobbish, fur clad scale, this joint rates high and therefore is very expensive. Good affordable **lodging** can be had in places like the *Snoeb Hotel*, a specialist riders hangout. **Night life** here can also be good with an okay selection of bars that allow for some hard core drinking sessions.

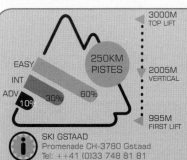

250KM PISTES

EASY
INT
ADV

10% 30% 60%

3000M
TOP LIFT

2005M
VERTICAL

995M
FIRST LIFT

SKI GSTAAD
Promenade CH-3780 Gstaad
Tel: ++41 (0)33 748 81 81
www.glacier3000.ch
Web:www.gstaad.ch
Email:gst@gstaad.ch

Number of runs: 60
Longest run: 15km
Total Lifts: 69 - 14
Gondolas, 3 cable-cars, 38 chairs,14 drags
Lift capacity (people per hour): 42,000
Lift times:
8.30am to 4.30pm

Winter Period:
Nov to April
Lift Passes
Half day 47
1 Day pass - 55Chf
5 Days pass - 232Chf

Annual Snowfall:
Unknown
Snowmaking:
5% of slopes

Fly
to Geneva airport 2 1/2 hours away. Berne-Belp Airport 91 km away.
Train
Train services are possible to Gstaad/Vevey station.
Car
From Geneva, take the N1/N9 via Lusanne to Aigle at which point turn of on to the A11 to Gstaad just after the village of Saanen.

	POOR	FAIR	GOOD	TOP
FREERIDE Trees & some good off-piste				
FREESTYLE 2 terrain parks & 2 halfpipes				
PISTES Great condition & variety				

9 OUT OF 10

Excellent resort

pic - Laax Tourism

S

SWITZERLAND

aax and its smaller brother **Flims** are Swiss national treasures and pure snowboard heaven. This place is highly regarded by those snowboarders who know about it and what you have here is a full on snowboarder's resort that links up with the more sedate Flims. Together they form an area regarded as one of the most snowboard friendly places in Switzerland. The resort bosses go out of their way to help snowboarders and it's no wonder that when there's a boarder event, the world pro's all seem to make it here. The **Burton European Open** moved here from Livigno last season, and plays host again this season in mid January. The **Orange AIM** series finals are also now hosted here in mid March. When events are held here, it's not just the top riders that come to perform, some big name pop stars and DJ's also put in an appearance.

The **Vorab Glacier** opens in October with a decent terrain park and a halfpipe, however it can take up to an hour to get up from the base. When the season opens fully in December the park relocates to its main place under the **Crap Sogn Gion**, and the Vorab area becomes a great

freeriding area.

It is notable that not many tour operators plague these slopes; if ever there was a mountain meant for snowboarders free of two plankers, this is it. Laax also has one of the best lift systems in Europe with lots of fast Gondolas whisking you up to the peaks, and you are seldom queuing for long. Beginners will also enjoy the fact that although there are some drag lifts, they can be easily avoided without restricting yourself too much.

FREERIDERS are tempted by some amazing off-piste opportunities with some cool tree riding and full-on powder. The ride down from **La Siala summit** is a real pleasure and can be tackled by most intermediates. Alternatively, for some easy to reach, classic off-piste riding, check out the **Cassons area** when its open, which is on the slopes above Flims and forms the top area, but it's not for the faint-hearted. Theres some good tree riding accessed from the **Nagens Gondola** by picking up the black 18 run. Its quite a narrow path as it snakes around the mountain,

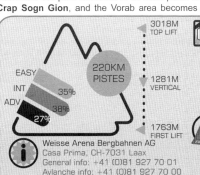

3018M TOP LIFT	
EASY	**220KM PISTES**
INT 35%	**1281M** VERTICAL
ADV 38%	
27%	
	1763M FIRST LIFT

Number of runs: 58
Longest run: 14km
Total Lifts: 29 - 7
Gondolas, 4 cable-cars, 8 chairs, 7 drags, 3 kids lifts
Lift capacity (people per hour): 42,000
Lift times:
8.30am to 4.30pm

Annual Snowfall:
7.2m
Snowmaking:
20% of slopes

Autumn Period (Vorab Glacier):
end Oct to mid Dec
Winter Period:
mid Dec to end April
Lift Passes
Autum day pass 50CHF
Winter: Half day 50CHF
1 Day pass 62Chf
5 Days 273
Lessons
Various group & private lessons as well as specialised freestyle and freeride courses contact: fahrschule@laax.com
Hire
Plenty of hire shops, some allowing a try before you buy.

Weisse Arena Bergbahnen AG
Casa Prima, CH-7031 Laax
General info: +41 (0)81 927 70 01
Avlanche info: +41 (0)81 927 70 00
Web: www.laax.com
Email: bergbahnen@laax.com

allowing you to hop off the side and (hopefully) pick the path up again after some tree shredding.

FREESTYLERS are coaxed here with an excellent park and pipe situated on the **Crap Sogn Gion**. The 140m earth shaped monsterpipe is impeccable and is usually joined by a 80m version. The terrain park has separate kicker and rail lines, but again they are well shaped and when the parks in full flow you'll find at least 6 kickers and up to 20 rails of various shapes and sizes. Early season you'll need to head onto the **Vorab Glacier** where they build a park during the Autumn months

PISTES. There's a good variety of pistes from open slopes at the top to the ones lower down that cut through the trees. They are all very open and wide, but there's nothing too testing but those with balls should try out the long black race run, Crap Sogn, back down to the base station of Murschetg.

BEGINNERS have a great mountain where learning the basics is a joy on simple, hassle free slopes, which are easy to reach from all parts of the resort.

THE TOWN
Both the villages of Laax and Flims (which are 10 minutes apart by road) sit at different levels and offer a host of good local facilities that will make a two weeks stay well worth the effort. Mind you, neither come cheaply and two weeks will burn a big hole in your wallet. Laax has a host of attractions from squash courts to an outdoor ice rink.

Accomodation. Some 6000 visitors are offered somewhere to sleep here, and although the choice of lodging and the prices are good, most places are a little spread out and for most, may entail a walk to the slopes. The trendy and well located *Riders Palace*, www.riderspalace.ch has 5 bunk dorms at 70CHF per night (based on a week, peak season) or you can pay triple that for a room with a plasma TV and a playstation. They often do special packages including lift passes.

Food is much the same as in any other high mountain retreat, that is lots of hotel restaurants all serving up generally bland, traditional Swiss meals at very high prices. Still, there are a number of notable places to get a good meal including the odd pizza, try the Pomodoro in Flims. If you fancy a fish meal then look no further than Crap Ner restaurant in Laax, which is noted for its food (and its prices).

Night-life in either Laax or Flims is pretty good and fairly well suited to snowboard lifestyle (apart form the cost of a beer – approx 7CHF). Nothing here is of mega status but the bars on offer are good for getting messy in while listening to some good tunes. The *Crap bar* in Murschetg at the bottom of the slopes is easily the pick of the bunch for some après or late on. It's a cool place that plays some good tunes, and luckily you'll find most of the skiers Oompah'ing up in the Umbrella bar opposite. The *Riders palace* has a bar that's open till 4am and they always have some boarding films showing on the big screen. There's a huge club underneath that's lively when the big stars are out. Around the Murschetg area is also the *Casa Veglia* nightclub that's open till the early hours.

CAR
Zurich via Chur to Laax is 90 miles (145 km). Drive time is about 2 1/2 hours.
FLY
to Zurich about 3 hours away, Milan 3 1/2hr away
TRAIN
to Chur, 40 mins away.
BUS
Bus services from Zurich take around 2 1/2 hours direct to Laax via Chur.
Buses from Chur run 8 times a day from 06:49 until 22:15 visit www.zvv.ch/postauto for timetables
Ski buses run between Flims & Laax and run every 20mins until 6pm, takes about 15mins.

	POOR	FAIR	GOOD	TOP
FREERIDE Trees & great off-piste				
FREESTYLE Parks & halfpipe				
PISTES Very quiet slopes				

10 OUT OF 10

First class ultra friendly snowboard resort

pics - Leysin Tourism

Leysin is located in the French speaking part of Switzerland and has become one of the best and most happening snowboard haunts in the country. Unlike many more popular ski resorts, this place isn't really known for its skiing which has allowed it to be adopted by snowboarders. This has helped to ensure that the place has a low key friendly appeal about it with- out any bull or hype. Leysin connects with the two alpine villages of Villars and Les Diablerets to create a very acceptable 60 km of piste.

This resort has gone out of its way to be snowboard friendly for years , back in 92 it played host an ISF tour event, and these days the TTR Nescafe Camps Open is held here (Beginning Feb 06 - www.nescafechamps.ch) where the world's top riding fight it out in the pipe & park.

Leysin is in fact an old and rather large sprawling mountain town and not a modern purpose built resort like some found nearby. What you get here is a high up mountain that in a good winter, offers everything to keep adventure seeking advanced riders happy, while also appealing to first timers who don't want to use a drag lift straight away. A notable point about Leysin is that it's not a popular resort with holiday companies, which is a good thing as the slopes don't get clogged up although weekends can still be a bit busy with locals and punters from Geneva. However, once you do get up on the slopes, you can roam freely over acres of great terrain without seeing another soul for hours

FREERIDERS have plenty of great terrain to explore, with tree runs down to the village, or extreme terrain with bowls and cliffs which you can reach by dropping in to your right on the Berneuse. You should also check out the official off-piste runs that give you the feeling of backcountry riding, for example try the route behind Tour D' Ai, starting at the top of Chaux de Mont.

FREESTYLERS will be able to spin huge airs in the huge pipe, which is normally maintained, but don't be shy to ask for a shovel at the nearby lift hut. As well as the pipe, the fun park (located between Berneuse and Mayen) has quarter pipes

S

SWITZERLAND

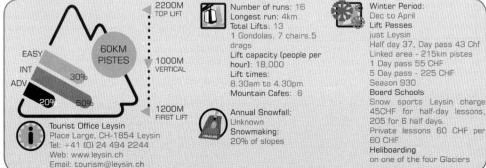

2200M TOP LIFT

1000M VERTICAL

1200M FIRST LIFT

EASY
INT
ADV

60KM PISTES

30%
20%
50%

Tourist Office Leysin
Place Large, CH-1854 Leysin
Tel: +41 (0) 24 494 2244
Web: www.leysin.ch
Email: tourism@leysin.ch

Number of runs: 16
Longest run: 4km
Total Lifts: 13
1 Gondolas, 7 chairs,5 drags
Lift capacity (people per hour): 18,000
Lift times:
8.30am to 4.30pm
Mountain Cafes: 6

Annual Snowfall:
Unknown
Snowmaking:
20% of slopes

Winter Period:
Dec to April
Lift Passes
just Leysin
Half day 37, Day pass 43 Chf
Linked area - 215km pistes
1 Day pass 55 CHF
5 Day pass - 225 CHF
Season 930
Board Schools
Snow sports Leysin charge 45CHF for half-day lessons, 205 for 6 half days.
Private lessons 60 CHF per 60 CHF
Heliboarding
on one of the four Glaciers

LEYSIN

and gaps to ride. Mind you, it's not usually built until the end of February.

PISTES. Carvers will enjoy The Berneuse which is a good place to lay out some big turns.

BEGINNERS can get going at the nursery slopes which have easy to use rope tows, before venturing up to slopes on the Berneuse. The drag lift at the Chaux de Mont will

pic - © Nescafé CHAMPS OPEN Leysin- Jeff Webb

be difficult for first timer and beginners should not use this lift, even for the lower section, as the exit point is on a very steep piece of terrain. The local ski schools handle all the snowboard tuition here.

THE TOWN
Being such a spread out place means that depending on where you're booked into, you could end up doing a lot of hard walking, unless you have a car. Around the town, life is very easy going with a lot of Americans hanging around due to the American colleges based here. Local services

are basic but acceptable, offering a well located sports centre equipped with a swimming pool and indoor tennis and squash courts. If you happen to speak the language (French and German) you could even while away your evening at the cinema. Anyone who fancies a skate can check out the ramps down in Aigle, about 40 minutes away, however there's plenty of street in Leysin which the locals will happily share with you.

Accomodation. The options for a bed range from a classy hotel to the normal array of pensions along the main high street. One of the best options is the really cool bunk house called The Vagabond, which offers cheap nightly rates and has a cool bar. Alternatively, Chalet Ermina is a really good bed and breakfast place and great value.

Food. Plenty of restaurants to choose from, but a few of them are tucked away so you will need to study your tourist guide to search them all out. Generally, prices are in the middle to high bracket but affordable food is available, especially if you check out the offerings at the cool bunk house called Club Vagabound which is located away up on the back road. The town also has a couple of cheap pizza restaurants.

Night-life in Leysin is just as it should be nothing major but plenty going down with a lively crowd that's always ready to party. The partying is aided by a lot of young American students (none of whom can drink anything like the amounts the Europeans sup). The main spots are Club Vagabound, although on Saturday nights it gets way too busy, and Top Pub which is much quieter.

SUMMARY
First class ultra friendly snowboard resort with terrain to suit all levels and styles. Great freestyle terrain and ok for novices. Great local services.
On the slopes: Fantastic - Great
Off the slopes: Very good

CAR
Take the A9 from Geneva, take the Aigle exit to Leysin. 100km. Drive time is about 2 hours.
FLY
to Geneva international. Transfer time to resort is 2 3/4 hours, 100km away. Nearest airport is Sion, 50km away.
TRAIN
Take a train to Aigle then change for Leysin. Takes 35mins and departs every hour. TGV from Paris takes 4:25hs
BUS
services from Geneva take around 2 hours direct to Leysin via Aigle. Taxis 024 493 22 93 or 024 494 25 55

S
W
I
T
Z
E
R
L
A
N
D

Great ride area

7 OUT OF 10

pic - © francois panchard

top, this place is one of only a few locations in Europe to offer Heli-boarding with passenger collection and mountain guides. You can fly to the heart of the **Rosablanche glacier** to ride major backcountry powder spots.

FREERIDERS will be pleasantly surprised when they arrive and see what this area has to offer both on and off-piste. Both advanced and timed riders will find a weeks stay a pleasure while thrill seekers can test themselves to the limits.

FREESTYLERS are provided with loads of possibilities for gaining air (and not just in a helicopter).There are loads of banks, gullies and cool areas with logs to grind. Park wise you'll have to head over to **Thyon**. The **Jean Pierre** parks for beginners and the **Tracouet** is the expert park, they're located either side of the Theytaz drag. There are various kickers and rails, and they burried a car there last season.

Being in the shadow of a big brother can often have its draw-backs, and the little guy may get left out and dismissed as not worth the effort. Not in this case. Nendaz is the lesser known relation of **Verbier** and along with a number of other resorts, forms the collective 425km 'Les 4 Vallees', located 2 1/2 hours east of Geneva just up from the town of Sion. Although linked by lift with Verbier, Nendaz offers an entirely different experience and is a lot less formal and populated. What you have here is a resort with a selection of runs starting right from it's base. It then connects up with the neighbouring hamlets and slopes of **Veysonnaz, Thyon and Siviez**. What's more, with the **Mont Fort** area offering some great summer snowboarding, this place becomes a bit of an all year round treasure. Apart from Nendaz's unique piste markings and the fact that they have installed snowmaking facilities all the way to the

PISTES. Carvers have as much here as any other style of rider, particularly on the series of red trails above **Siviez** and on **Veysonnaz** slopes where you can shine on your edges at speed.

BEGINNERS should leave after a week's visit at a new level. The gentle slopes directly above Nendaz will suit you're every need.

THE TOWN
Off the slopes, Nendaz offers a quality selection of places to sleep, eat and drink in at prices to suit everyone, not just the elite, as is often the case in many resorts. Furthermore, basic local services are well appointed and you can sleep close to the slopes. Locals make you very welcome which helps to give this place a good snowboard vibe and these are some good night posts to check out.

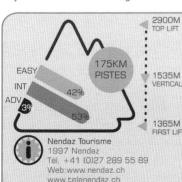

EASY
INT
ADV 3%
42%
53%

175KM PISTES

2900M TOP LIFT

1535M VERTICAL

1365M FIRST LIFT

Nendaz Tourisme
1997 Nendaz
Tél. +41 (0)27 289 55 89
Web:www.nendaz.ch
www.telenendaz.ch
Email:info@nendaz.ch

New for 05/06 season
new 1522m 4 seater chairlift from Siviez to Combatzeline.

Number of runs: 45
Longest run: 15km
Total Lifts:22 - 3 Gondolas, 1 cable cars, 5 chairs,13 drags, 3 Magic Carpets
Lift Capacity : (people per hour) 22,190
Lift times: 8.30am to 4.30pm

Winter Period:
Nov to April
Lift Passes
4 Valleys area: Half day 52CHF
1 Day 62, 5 Days 274, Season 820
Local area: Half day 40CHF
Day pass 48, 5 Days 211
Board School
3 schools offering the usual group & private lessons.
Ski Nendez offers half day lessons (3hrs) for 39 CHF, 5 full days 340 CHF. 90min privcate lesson 85 CHF.
Freeride & Freestyle lessons available
Heliboarding
Available through Ski Nendez

Annual Snowfall:
5.3m
Snowmaking:
15% of slopes

Fly
to Geneva airport, about 1 1/2 hours away 165km. Zürich, 2 1/2 hrs, Bâle 2 1/2 hrs. Nearest airport is Sion, 15km from resort
Train
services possible to Sion (15 minutes). Direct services available from Geneva & Zurich.
Car
Motorway A9 to Sion, exit Sion-Ouest in the direction of Nendaz. Then 15 minutes drive (15km) up to the center of the resort.
*Drive time from Calais is 9 1/2 hours. 544 miles
Bus
from Sion Airport to Nendaz. Taxis , Taxi Praz tel: +41 (0)79 409 32 15

POOR FAIR GOOD TOP

FREERIDE
Some trees but little good off-piste
FREESTYLE
All year terrain park
PISTES
Some flats but ok slopes

7
OUT OF 10

pic – Saas-Fee Tourism

SWITZERLAND

Saas-Fee has been a resort well known to snowboarders for many years. They have been building half-pipes, parks and other obstacles since way back and before many others areas had even heard of snowboarding. With its high altitude glacier, Saas-Fee also provides a mountain where you can ride fast and hard in the summer months, indeed for some, this is the only time worth visiting. Winter or summer, this is still a cool place that stages numerous competitions in both seasons and snowboard manufactures do a lot of product testing. Saas Fee is a resort with two faces. In summer the small glacier area has a snowboard park which boasts two half pipes, a boardercross course, and various hits. However, in winter the snowboard park relocates and the resort focuses itself more on family skiers. Most of the mountain is geared to skiers and possibly hard-booters. There's a

variety of red and black runs, as well as nursery slopes and top to bottom blue runs, but nothing to really test you (although the runs off the Hinterallalin - when open - are supposed to be more challenging). Pisting is somewhat haphazard away from the main stations at the mid point and top glacier, so expect moguls on red and black runs

FREERIDERS will be disappointed to find that the off-piste is limited by crevasse danger around the glacier - but there are some nice tree runs off **Platjen**. Alternatively, the runs off the **Hinterallalin** drag lift will sort out the wimps, with some cool freeriding to be had and some fast steep sections to try out.

FREESTYLERS. There's a park on **Morenia** which has a pro and normal kicker line and a few rails. The halfpipe's located up there as well. Away from the park you may find some hits off the **Mittaghorn** and **Langfluh** lifts, but they are far between. You will find a few drop offs near the **Langfluh** and **Platjen** areas.

PISTES. There's a host of pisted runs on which to lay out some wide tracks. No matter what your level, you'll soon be weaving in and out of the two plankers in style on graded runs from steep blacks to tame blues. The runs under the **Mittelallalin** restaurant are a great area for carvers.

BEGINNERS are not left out, Saas Fee has plenty of novice runs, but some of the blue pistes have long flat sections to catch you out, resulting in a fair bit of skating along. You'll also get really used to T-bars by the time you leave this place. The lower runs have a reputation for rocks and worn patches, so take care when you first head out. However, the best way to find out what's what, is to call in on the boys at the Paradise Snowboard School, they'll show you how to get around any obstructions

THE TOWN
Saas Fee is a car-free place where you get around by either electric vehicles or on foot. However, everything is located close to each other and the slopes. The town is a cool place, with options to sleep close to the slopes in hotels or chalets. Money wise, Saas-Fee can be very expensive if

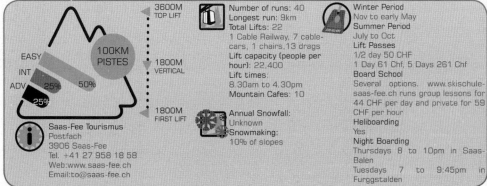

EASY
INT
ADV 25% 50%
25%

100KM
PISTES

3600M
TOP LIFT

1800M
VERTICAL

1800M
FIRST LIFT

Saas-Fee Tourismus
Postfach
3906 Saas-Fee
Tel. +41 27 958 18 58
Web:www.saas-fee.ch
Email:to@saas-fee.ch

Number of runs: 40
Longest run: 9km
Total Lifts: 22
1 Cable Railway, 7 cable-cars, 1 chairs,13 drags
Lift capacity (people per hour): 22,400
Lift times:
8.30am to 4.30pm
Mountain Cafes: 10

Annual Snowfall:
Unknown
Snowmaking:
10% of slopes

Winter Period
Nov to early May
Summer Period
July to Oct
Lift Passes
1/2 day 50 CHF
1 Day 61 Chf, 5 Days 261 Chf
Board School
Several options. www.skischule-saas-fee.ch runs group lessons for 44 CHF per day and private for 59 CHF per hour
Heliboarding
Yes
Night Boarding
Thursdays 8 to 10pm in Saas-Balen
Tuesdays 7 to 9:45pm in Furggstalden

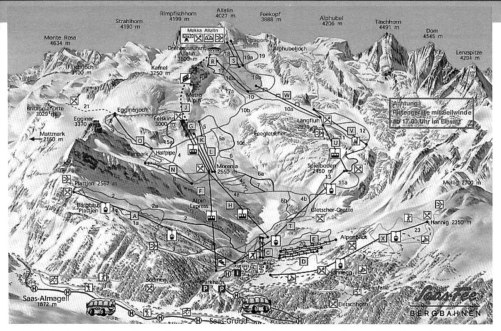

you're staying in a hotel and eating out in restaurants, but on the other hand, you can do things cheaply by staying in an apartment and feasting on supermarket produce. The resort crams in loads of amenities, from swimming pools, a cinema, a museum, an ice rink to heaps of shops, including a couple of cool snowboard shops centrally located; Popcorn +41 (0) 958 19 14 and Powder Tools +41 (0) 89 220 7792.

Accommodation: 7500 visitors can be housed here. Hotels come as one would expect, standard Swiss and expensive. However, with this place comes a good number of affordable bed and breakfast places apartment and chalets for those wanting to go self catering. Whereever you stay, nothing is too far from the slopes.

Food. Being a modern and popular resort, Saas Fee is well equipped to feed all its visitors no matter what their chosen diet is. There are well over 50 restaurants here many based in hotels but also a good number of independent ones. Notable places to pig out in are the Boccalino for pizza or the Lavern for traditional Swiss food. Hotel Allalin is a good restaurant with affordable meals set in a rustic style.

Night life is very good here despite there being a few places offering the ski après crap. Snowboard life-style centres around the Popcorn bar and snowboard shop, but the Happy bar is cheaper (especially at happy hour 7:30 - 8:30 daily). There are a few other bars worth checking out. If you decide to stay in and party, watch out for the 'hush police' - too much noise after 10pm and you'll get fined around 120 Sfr.

CAR
Geneva via Aigle, Saas Fee is 145 miles (235 km, drive time is about 3 hours. Travelling from the east you'll need to take the Furka pass or jump on a car-train.
Resort is car free so you'll park up (CHF 8 per day) and get an electric shuttle to your hotel.
FLY
Fly to Geneva international, Transfer time to resort 2 hours.
TRAIN
to Brigg or Visp (20 minutes) then take the post bus.
BUS
services from Geneva take 3hrs direct to Saas-Fee via Brigg. Buses from Brigg and Visp run hourly until 8pm

ᴡꜱɢ SAVOGNIN

	POOR	FAIR	GOOD	TOP
FREERIDE Some trees & a bit of off-piste				
FREESTYLE Terrain park & halfpipe				
PISTES Very well groomed slopes				

Okay for a few days

6
OUT OF 10

pic - Savognin Tourism

pipe or in the fun park which is tooled up with fun boxes, gaps, spines, rails and a quarter pipe. For some natural hits there are a few cliff drops and some air to be had on the area called Tiem.

PISTES. Riders have some particularly well groomed runs A good piste to suit all levels whether you're in soft or hard boots, is the **Cresta Ota**, which runs down from the **Piz Cartas** summit and makes for a good time.

BEGINNERS are looked after with a number of easy blues and the option of being able to slide back to base at the end of the day on easy to handle runs. However, uplift is mainly via drag lifts.

Two hours south of **Zurich** lies the relatively unknown resort of **Savognin** that is fast becoming a magnet for snowboarders out for a good time and for riders who want to steer clear of the big resorts because they don't want to get caught up in the hustle and bustle of large ski crowds. Fortunately the ski press don't mention Savognin, which helps to keep this gem a small secret for snowboarders to do as they please with. The natives are super friendly and happy to have snowboarders on their slopes. The local snowboard scene is cool with its own riders club where you can find out all there is to know about this place, such as the best hits or runs and where to get messy in the evenings when the lifts are closed. The 50 miles of piste will make a weeks stay well worth it, appealing to novice carvers

FREERIDERS of an advanced level are going to be disappointed if its testing stuff you crave for, there is none really. You can have a bit of excitement on the black run known as the **Pro Spinatsch**, running down from the **Tiggignas** chair lift, it is also the location of Savognin's fun park. It doesn't take too long to conquer if you know what you're doing on your edges.

FREESTYLERS will find the best air to be had is either off the nicely shaped walls in the 90m half-

THE TOWN
Savognin is a small village with nothing major going on, although it's affordable and doesn't come infested with apres ski crowds. **Accommodation** is a mixture of Swiss pensions and hotels, all of which are well located for the slopes. There are one or two good evening haunts, with the best place to get a **beer** being the *Zerbratent Paulin*.

S

S W I T Z E R L A N D

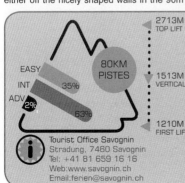

2713M TOP LIFT		
1513M VERTICAL		
1210M FIRST LIFT		

EASY
INT 35%
ADV 2%
63%

80KM PISTES

Number of runs: 27
Longest run: 7km
Total Lifts: 10
3 chairs, 7 drags, 3 magic carpets, 1 cat
Lift capacity (people per hour): 16,000
Lift times:
8.30am to 4.30pm

Winter Period:
Dec to April
Lift Passes
Half Day 41CHF
1 Day pass - 50Chf
5 Day pass - 216Chf
Season 705

Annual Snowfall:
4m
Snowmaking:
10% of slopes

Fly
to Zurich airport, 2 hours away.
Train
to Chur then take the local bus to Savognin
Car
Via Zurich, head south on the N3 to Chur and take the A3 via Tiefencastelt to Savognin.

Tourist Office Savognin
Stradung, 7460 Savognin
Tel: +41 81 659 16 16
Web:www.savognin.ch
Email:ferien@savognin.ch

372

	POOR	FAIR	GOOD	TOP
FREERIDE Trees & great off-piste				
FREESTYLE Parks & halfpipe				
PISTES Very quiet slopes				

Way too poncy but great riding

8
OUT OF 10

pics - St Moritz Tourism

St Moritz has two classic distinctions, on the one hand this has to be one of the finest natural backcountry freeride places to ride in **Switzerland**, but on the other hand, St Moritz happens to be top of the league when it comes to snobbery. With out doubt this is one of the most expensive resorts on the planet, and not with-standing the outrageous costs here, the place attracts so many stuck-up rich idiots, that you can smell the fur clad sods a mile away. St Moritz is a high altitude resort that along with the areas of

Pontresina and **Diavolezza**, form the Upper Engadine region. Diavolezza is another glacier on the shrink that used to host summer snowboarding, but now offers only hiking. St Moritz, which gives access to the slopes on the **Corviglia** and **Marguns**, is an area that is largely made up of intermediate pisted runs which get stupidly busy on most days and unfortunately there are not too many expert pisted trails to escape the hordes of learning skiers. However, there is heaps of adventurous off piste terrain to check out, but only do so with the advice and services of a local guide

FREERIDERS have a huge amount of great backcountry terrain will blow you're mind beyond, with lots of steeps, gullies, cliffs and virgin powder to seek out. Some of the best freeriding can be found up on the **Diavolezza glacier**, which is for serious riders only. St Moritz's number steep is the slope that drops down from the **Piz Nair summit** of the top cable car.

FREESTYLERS The Mellowpark is located below Corviglia. There's usually a table-top, some kickers, a spine and a

Piste map of Corvatsch/Furtschellas

S

SWITZERLAND

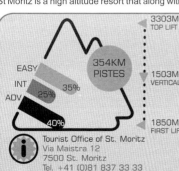

3303M TOP LIFT		
354KM PISTES		
EASY		
INT 35%		1503M VERTICAL
ADV 25%		
40%		1850M FIRST LIFT

i Tourist Office of St. Moritz
Via Maistra 12
7500 St. Moritz
Tel. +41 (0)81 837 33 33
Web:www.stmoritz.ch
www.bergbahnenengadin.ch
Email:information@stmoritz.ch

Number of runs: 88
Longest run: 8km
Total Lifts: 56
3 Funiculars, 1 cable railway, 6 Gondolas, 7 cable-cars, 18 chairs,27 drags
Lift capacity (people per hour): 65,000
Lift times:
8.30am to 4.30pm
Mountain Cafes: 37

Annual Snowfall:
3.5m
Snowmaking:
15% of slopes

Winter Period:
Nov to April
Lift Passes
Half-day 48/54CHF normal/ high season
1 Day Pass - 59/66Chf
5 Day Pass - 265/291Chf
Board School
group 1/2 day lesson from 45CHF
6 half-day lessons from 230CHF
Private lesson half-day 180CHF
Heliboarding
No
Night Boarding
Every friday 19pm till 2am!

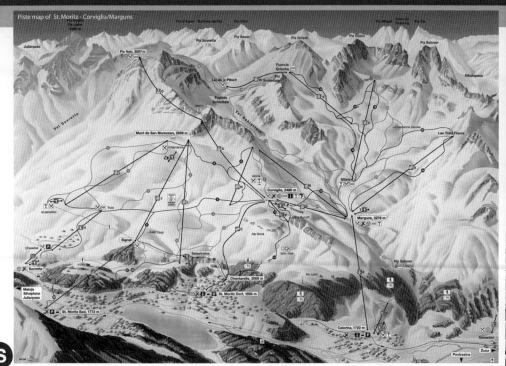

Piste map of St. Moritz - Corviglia/Marguns

number of rails and boxes. For the junior grommets there's some easy jumps and rollers.

CARVERS will find lots of fairly easy and ordinary well pisted runs to cruise down. But really you should freeride only at this place.

BEGINNERS may not have the best selection of novice trails to start out with, but what is on offer is superb if only too busy.

THE TOWN
Off the slopes St Moritz can easily be summed up as an over priced, over hyped ugly sham that rips you off big style for everything and attracts some very sad gits in designer wear and fur hats.

Accommodation, which is provided by an array of hotels and chalets, is available in a spread out area.

Food. There are plenty of places to get a meal, but you have to look hard to find an inexpensive burger bar.

Night-life.As for having a good night out and a few beers, unless you're a brain dead mutant who owns a platinum credit card, forget it, it's sucks big style.

CAR
From Zurich, head south on the N3. Turn off at Landquart on to the route 28 to Zernez and then take the R-28 down to St mortiz (200km)
From Calais the journey is 9 1/2 hours. 516 miles (830 km)
FLY
Fly to Zurich/Milan airport, 3 hours drive away. Munic h/Basel, 4 hrs away. Local airport is Samedan - St. Moritz, most airports offer connecting flights
TRAIN
Take a train to Chur, then take Rhätische Bahn direct to resort. www.rhb.ch for more info

wsg VERBIER

Some of the best extreme terrain in Switzerland

	POOR	FAIR	GOOD	TOP
FREERIDE				
Some trees & major off-piste				
FREESTYLE				
Terrain park & good natural				
PISTES				
Some good long runs				

10 OUT OF 10

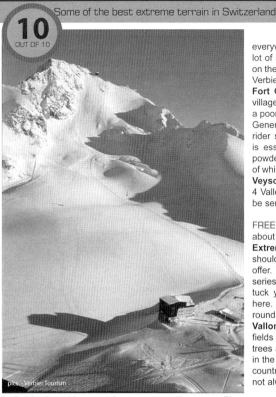

pics - Verbier Tourism

Verbier is a big resort in more ways than one: Big slope area, big mountain and big on extreme terrain. However, Verbier is also big on the stuck and poncy scale being a resort that goes out of its way to attract the rich, the stuck up elite, disposed European royals and their side kicks. Despite its great terrain and summer snowboarding opportunities, this is also a resort where snowboarding is still fairly small (less than 5% of slope users) but don't fret, the attitude is pretty cool and snowboarders are welcome everywhere, although you have to share the slopes with a lot of scum bags in fur hats poncing around the mountain on their stupid Big Foot skis. Still, on the plus side of things Verbier offers all year round snowboarding up on the **Mont Fort Glacier,** although you won't be riding down to the village in June. The snow record here is good and even in a poor season it's still possible to ride to the resort in April. Generally, the terrain gives over to all levels, offering every rider something to get their teeth into. However, Verbier is essentially a freerider's resort, with easily accessible powder, trees, hard-pack, cliffs, hits and extremes, some of which necessitate a hike first. Verbier joins with **Nendas, Veysonnaz, La Tzoumaz** and **Val de Bagnas** to crate the 4 Vallees with 94 lifts and over 400km of piste, which can be serviced by one lift pass.

FREERIDERS who know just what snowboarding is all about will be very impressed with Verbier. The **Verbier Extreme** competition is now regularly held here which should give you an idea of what awesome terrain is on offer. The **Mont Gele** cable car serves no piste, just a series of off-piste runs and couloirs of varying extremity; tuck your balls (or equivalent) away before you get up here. The less squeamish should check out the areas round the back of **Lac des Vaux!** The **Col des Mines,** and **Vallon d' Arbi** routes steer you towards wide open powder fields with the words 'session me' written all over them. If trees are your thing, Verbier has loads of them, especially in the **Bruson** area, but remember, Switzerland is the one country that protects its forests, so shredding the spruce is not always appreciated.

FREESTYLERS have the decent 1936 Neipark to play in, located up at La Chaux. Theres 3 kicker lines depending on your ability and an additional rail line. Visit www.mysnowpark.ch for more info. The natural stuff around **La Chaux** and **Lac des Vaux** lifts, are the other places to get air.

PISTES. Carvers and those after some speed will fine the best is undoubtedly the long, wide red piste that goes from the top of Attelas all the way back to the **Medran** lifts.

S W I T Z E R L A N D

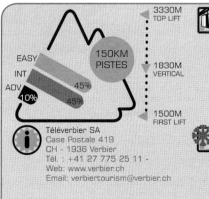

3330M TOP LIFT	
EASY	150KM PISTES
INT	
ADV 45%	
10% 45%	1830M VERTICAL
	1500M FIRST LIFT

Téléverbier SA
Case Postale 419
CH - 1936 Verbier
Tél. : +41 27 775 25 11 -
Web: www.verbier.ch
Email: verbiertourism@verbier.ch

Number of runs: 56
Longest run: 15km
Total Lifts: 38
8 Gondolas, 2 cable-cars, 18 chairs,10 drags
Lift capacity (people per hour): 26,000
Lift times:
8.30am to 4.30pm
Mountain Cafes: 10

Annual Snowfall:
3.5m
Snowmaking:
5% of slopes

Winter Period:
Nov to April
Lift Passes
Verbier only
Half day 45CHF, Day pass - 54Chf
5 Day pass - 237Chf, Season 1107
4 Valleys (400km)
Day 67, 5 days 274
Board School
La Fantastique have Mountain Guides available 440 CHF per day, Full day private lesson 370 CHF per day
Hire
Board & Boots froom 43CHF per day (verbier.com)
Heliboarding
www.lafantastique.com offer heliboarding from 360 CHF each based on 4 people
Night Boarding
Yes

There's also some cool stuff at **Savoleyres and Ruinettes**.

BEGINNERS will find that the main areas are actually closed to snowboarders, which means that first timers are faced with steeper slopes. The best option is the runs at **Savoleyres**, where you are certain to be end up doing a few 180 butt spins. Some lifts can be tricky, so keep to the slower chair lifts. Lift pass checking is slack, so think on, but don't get caught as they jail you here.

THE TOWN

S

**S
W
I
T
Z
E
R
L
A
N
D**

Off the slopes, Verbier is a Royals, city slickers & lottery winner's only place, with prices that exclude everyone else. There's no such thing as a cool scene unless you can pay for it. The place is over populated with farts and their spoilt off spring (rich kids with attitude but no brains). Bedding down is costly and if you get caught scamming on someone's floor, you could face a 200 Swiss Franc fine. However, the resort is well set out and can sleep over 15,000 rich skiers. Overall, Verbier simply is not a place to visit on a tight budget, unless you have a degree in scamming. To get the information on Verbier, check with the guys at 'No Bounds' or 'Extreme' snowboard shops.

Accomodation. There are 15,000 beds on offer in Verbier but as

**VERBIER &
ELSEWHERE**

For the most suitable
accomodation and
no-hassle holidays call
Mountain Beds for
expert advice

Mountain BEDS
Ski Resorts

**Tel: 07000 780 333
Fax: 07000 780 334
www.mountainbeds.com**

with everything else its at a high price, but thats not io say you won't be able to get a bed somewhere. The best two options open to you are **1)** take a package tour, or **2)** hook up with a local bird, no matter

how ugly, and promise her the earth in order to get in her bed.

Food. Bring stacks of tins of baked beans with you and a cooker, as unless your name is Princess Lucky, you simply won't be able to afford any of the restaurants or even the supermarkets. Food in a town that attracts the super rich, is not easy to come by cheaply, although there are loads of restaurants to choose from with a cross the board range of menus from Chinese to bland Swiss fondues.

Night life, take a fork lift truck and ram in through the doors of the main bank, then take you're spoils to any one of the bars and if your lucky, you may just have enough francs to get a fruit juice. Night-time costs the earth here unless you can scam your way into a club pretending that you're Sara Ferguson's lap dog. The clubs are not only costly but play crap music to please the lame heads who don't know any better.

CAR
Geneva via Martigny to Verbier = 104 miles (167 km) Drive time is about 2 hours.
FLY
Fly to Geneva international, 3hr transfer to resort . Local airport is Sion
TRAIN
Trains to Le Chable (10 minutes). More info www.rail.ch
BUS
Bus services from Geneva take around 3 hours direct to Verbier via Martigny. and cost 55CHF, its 95CHF and 4 1/2 hours from Zurich. Taxis +41 (0)27/776.16.33

POOR FAIR GOOD TOP

FREERIDE
Some trees & a little off-piste
FREESTYLE
Small terrain park
PISTES
Good variety

6 OUT OF 10
Basic but okay

Villars - Gryon - Les Diablerets

Villars, in the French speaking part of Switzerland, is a simple place that sits in view of the high peaks of the **Les Diablerets Glacier**, where you can snowboard winter and summer. Villars is a popular place that gets its fair share of visitors throughout the season. The slopes are well spread out covering the **Les Chaux** and **Bretaye** areas and linked after some careful navigation, with the base area at Les Diablerets. Overall the place is not noted for being a hardcore destination; in fact, it's true to say that this is a resort that favours piste loving hard boot carvers and family ski groups. However, the resort has a good attitude towards snowboarding and regularly allows its slopes to be used for various competitions. If you get a bit tired of it here and fancy something a more challenging, you can easily head up to Les Diablerets and ride harder and faster.

FREERIDERS are not known for flocking to this place because although there is some okay freeriding terrain, it's not that extensive in terms of steep blacks on or off-piste. That said, the black trail running down from **Les Chaux** is a real pleaser which if you stick to the left, can also be tackled by intermediates as it mellows out the further it spreads across the slope. The place for some great freeriding is up on the Les Diablerets slopes.

FREESTYLERS can either decide to ride the park areas that are split between the Bretaye slopes and Les Chaux slopes. However, this is not one of those resorts where one can get too excited about the man made frills, and coupled with the fact that this place is not as snow sure as the slopes up on Les Diablerets, sculptured hits are not always guaranteed.

PISTES. Carvers have the best of the slopes here from the long gentle blues and a couple of steep blacks on the Les Chaux area, to the excellent pisted reds on the Bretaye area.

BEGINNER'S slopes are out numbered by intermediate ones, but don't be put off, this is a good first time resort although the place has a lot of drag lifts.

THE TOWN
Local services and **accommodation** options are comfortably provided in the setting of a traditional Swiss village located close to the slopes. The amenities on offer are some what basic but perfectly adequate for a weeks family fun holiday; In general an affordable week can be had. **Night-life** is on the dull side with only a few okay bars and the odd disco.

pic : Villars Tourism

S

S
W
I
T
Z
E
R
L
A
N
D

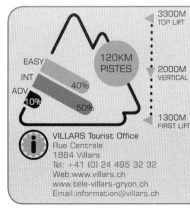

EASY	120KM PISTES	
INT		40%
ADV	10%	
	50%	

3300M TOP LIFT

2000M VERTICAL

1300M FIRST LIFT

Number of runs: 52
Longest run: 5km
Total Lifts:45
1 Funicular train, 3 Gondolas, 3 cable-cars, 11 chairs,27 drags
Lift Capacity : (people per hour) 36,000
Lift times: 9.00am to 4.30pm

Winter Period:
Dec to April
Lift Passes
local area: Day 47, half-day 36
whole area:
1 Day pass - 55 Chf
5 Day pass - 225 Chf
Season pass - 930Chf
Night Boarding
No

Annual Snowfall:
Unknown
Snowmaking:
8% of slopes

Fly
to Geneva airport, 2 hours away 110km, Zurich 210km.
Train
Major train services are possible to Aigle or Bex, then take bus/mountain train respectivley. Villars station tel: +41(0)24/495.21.15
Car
From Geneva, head along the N1 and N9 and turn off at Aigle on route A9 towards Monthey turning left for Villars and drive for another 30mins

VILLARS Tourist Office
Rue Centrale
1884 Villars
Tel: +41 (0) 24 495 32 32
Web:www.villars.ch
www.tele-villars-gryon.ch
Email:information@villars.ch

wsg WENGEN

	POOR	FAIR	GOOD	TOP
FREERIDE Trees & some good off-piste				
FREESTYLE Terrain park				
PISTES Plenty of slopes				

6 OUT OF 10

Spoilt by the stuck-up attitude

pic - Wengen Tourism

Wengen, which is part of the **Jungfrau Region**, is one of Switzerlands more famous resorts, but why it should be is a mystery really, it can't just be for the terrain on offer, which although not bad, is not major, nor can it be for the welcome you get here. No Wengen has simply become well known because the idle rich deposed European royals and a certain class of scum bag skiers from Britain who frequent this resort en-mass. The place reeks of snobbery, which is a bit of a shame because this is not a crap resort, far from it, with the slopes on offer here and at **Grindelwald** and at neighbouring Murren, a rider can have a good weeks riding on terrain that have something for all, although not a great deal for expert riders. Wengen, which shares direct slope access with Grindewald, lies at an altitude of 1274 metres and is reached via the village of **Lauterbrunnen**, which is also the main access point for **Murren**. Wengen and Grindewald are much the same, with Wengen having a few more interesting spots to try out. You can also decent from a height of 2971 metres, which is higher than Grindewald, but in truth there is not much

to separate the two places. However, Murren, the least crowded of the three resorts, offers the most challenging terrain and out of the three areas, it is also the most snowboard friendly. Wengen hasn't got a clue what its policy is towards snowboarding. A couple of seasons ago, the management set up a really good terrain park with loads of features, then the following year they decided not to build a thing for freestylers preferring to make a euro carvers (David Seaman look-alikes in hard boots and head bands) area.

FREERIDERS are best off on the runs at Murren, off the **Schilthon**. Great powder stashes are can be found in a number of spots.

FREESTYLERS have pipe and park up on the **Oberjoch area** via Grindewald. Wengen also has some natural hits.

PISTES. Any carvers will blend in well here as there's a lot of Euro's with head bands and one piece suits posing on Wengen's slopes.

BEGINNERS will only be put off by the crowds of skiers falling around on the gentle slopes. Wengen has the best novice terrain, while Murren has the worst.

THE TOWN
Wengen offers a lot of local facilities with lodging close to the slopes. However, if you decide to stay here, it's going to cost you dearly with night-life totally geared around après-ski rich gits.

S W I T Z E R L A N D

2971M TOP LIFT

2028M VERTICAL

943M FIRST LIFT

EASY

INT 28%

ADV 15% 57%

213KM PISTES

Tourist Information Wengen
CH-3823 Wengen
Tel +41 (0)33 855 14 14
Fax +41 (0)33 855 30 60
Web:www.wengen-muerren.ch
Email:info@wengen.ch

Number of runs: 35
Longest run: 15km
Total Lifts: 45
10 Gondolas, 6 cable-cars,
16 chairs,13 drags
Lift Capacity : (people per hour): 42.000
Lift times: 8.30am to 4.30pm

Winter Period:
Dec to April
Lift Passes
Half day 42 CHF Full day
56 CHF
5 day 233 CHF. 2 day for
entire Jungfrau region 120,
6 days 288
Board School
private lesson 65 CHF per
hour

Annual Snowfall:
5.3m
Snowmaking:
10% of slopes

Fly
to Zurich airport, about 2 hours
away. Nearest airport is Berne
which run a shuttle bus to the
train station
Train
services are possible to Interlaken
then take the Bernese-Oberland-
Railway to Lauterbrunnen
Car
From Zurich, head south on the
E41, N4a/N14 via Hergiswil and
then the N8 to Interlaken. From
here follow the Lauterbrunnen and
then signs for Wengen.

POOR FAIR GOOD TOP

FREERIDE
Some trees & good off-piste
FREESTYLE
2 Terrain parks
PISTES
Good variety of runs

8
OUT OF 10

Extremely good resort with terrain for all

pics - Zermatt Tourism

Zermatt is one of the highest resorts in Europe. It has great snow conditions throughout the winter and, thanks to the **Theodul Glacier** (Klein Matterhorn), the summer months too. The main access is via mountain railway from Brigg or Tasch; the most practical way being via the excellent Swiss railway service from **Geneva** or **Zurich** airports. Zermatt is expensive, but its picture-postcard looks with its breathtaking views of the Matterhorn and its vast boarding area makes it worth spending a little more.

Zermatt, and its neighbour, the Italian resort of **Cervinia**, has an impressive 250 kilometres of marked piste and countless acres of backcountry terrain covering 3 main areas. Heli-boarding trips are available up to the

Monte Rosa at 4250 metres, the **Alphubeljoch** at 3782 metres and up to the **Plateau Rosa** at 3479 metres, but they are not cheap with trips costing over 450 Chf. Riding off the glacier will of course need a guide. However, a helicopter is not necessary to explore Zermatt's fantastic terrain, because once you have made the hike to the first lifts from the main town, or in some cases taken the bus, and hit the slopes the array of lifts will whisk you up the mountain to numerous start points. The mountain layout is Swiss efficiency at its best with lifts connecting effortlessly across the mountains, pistes groomed immaculately and even tri-lingual announcements in the major lifts informing its passengers of how to avoid congested areas. Your lift pass will take you to **Schwarzsee**, up the glacier at 3899 metres, which can be extremely cold in the winter months, over to Cervina in Italy and across the other side of the valley to **Rothorn**. Soon these 2 valleys will be connected via lifts, rather than via the village as is current in 2005.

FREERIDERS on the lookout for open powder bowls and couloirs to ride will be kept busy in a number of areas. Zermatt offers a lot of advanced off-piste riding, with some excellent runs on the **Stockhorn** or over at the **Schwarzsee** areas. If riding trees is your thing, note that Zermatt totally restricts riding through the forest areas. If you have the money, you can also take a day's heli-boarding. Air Zermatt, but it is very expensive: two flights over the **Monte Rosa** will cost you around 440 Chf.

FREESTYLERS are provided with 2 ever improving half-pipes, but as there is so much good natural terrain, it's not that important. Two fun parks have been built in recent years.

PISTES. Carvers are still in evidence here, preferring to cut up the number of good and long testing runs that descend en-route to the village via some extremely crowded lower novice trails.

BEGINNERS may find Zermatt a bit tricky but not a big problem, just a bit tainted with too many first timers on skis

EASY		**3820M** TOP LIFT
INT 23%	**245KM PISTES**	
ADV 44%		**2200M** VERTICAL
33%		**1620M** FIRST LIFT

i Tourist Office of Zermatt
3920 Zermatt
Switzerland
Tel +41 27 966 81 00
Fax +41 27 966 81 01
Web:www.zermatt.ch
Email:zermatt@wallis.ch

Number of runs: 73
Longest run: 13km
Total Lifts: 57
1 Funicular trains, 7
Gondolas,12 cable-cars, 20 chairs, 17
drags
Lift capacity (people
per hour): 64,500
Lift times:
8.30am to 4.30pm
Mountain Cafes: 38

Annual Snowfall:
3m
Snowmaking:
25% of slopes

Winter Period:
Nov to April
Summer Period:
May to Sept
Lift Passes
Zermatt only:
Half day 52, Day pass 67Chf
5 Days pass 286Chf
Zermatt/Cervinia
Half-day 58, Day pass 75, 5 days
322CHF, season 151.
Summer day pass 62CHF
Board School
Group lessons from - 40CHF
Hire
Board & Boots daily rates from - 28CHF
(Kids from 22CHF)
Heliboarding
www.air-zermatt.ch
Night Boarding
No

cheap eateries and for many a diet of crisps, biscuits, mars bar and cheap beer is enough. There is a McDonalds for a cheap Mac attack

Night life varies from the après ski of the rich – there are some exclusive and expensive bars, to more casual bars and cafes. There is a cool snowboarder's bar located on the bridge en-route to the Matterhorn lift in the Swartzee area. Around town there is a large selection of bars offering different themes and some being quite lively. There are also a number of late night discos such as the *Pink Elephant*, *Grampis* or *Le Broken*

clogging up the easy trails, particularly on the long blue run into Cervinia. However, you can ride easily higher up the mountain, certainly on the glacier, making for some long, easy runs to progress on.

THE TOWN

Off the slopes, Zermatt is a large, car free town that can be pricey which may call for some major scamming to get by. A useful tip when travelling here from abroad is, if you fly in to Geneva and plan to take the train down to Zermatt, buy your train ticket at a Swiss Tourist office in your home country before you enter Switzerland, as it can be cheaper. Around the town you are presented with loads of shops, various sporting centres and other visitor attractions. Getting around the main part of town is easy, but in parts you will find that a lot of walking is required. Cars are banned to protect Zermatt's environment and microclimate, so there are free electric buses and more costly taxis (tuk tuks) to shuttle you around. Do be aware that the buses are silent so take a good look left before you cross any roads.

Accommodation can be expensive. However, there is a youth hostel located about 400 metres from the main lifts in the centre of town, which is cheap and offers half board accommodation.

Food. The supermarket located near the train station offers

SUMMARY

Zermatt is an extremely good resort with terrain for all styles and levels. It is more expensive than the average resort, but the slopes, lifts and town are all more remarkable than the average resort.

CAR
From Geneva, take the N1/N9 via Sion to Sierre. Then take the E62 to Visp at which point turn right and travel via Stalden to Zermatt. Resort is car free, so you'll need to park in Täsch, 5km away.
FLY
Fly to Geneva airport 3 hours away, Zurich 3 1/2hrs. Sion nearest airport, 2hrs away.
TRAIN
Take a train to Brig or Visp and then transfer onto the Matterhorn Gotthard railway for the 90min train to Zermatt. You can take the GlacierExpress train from Davos/St. Moritz straight to Zermatt www.glacierexpress.ch
BUS
services from Geneva take around 4 1/2 to 5 hours direct to Zermatt. Electro carts provide a bus service around Zermatt, Taxis: 0848 11 12 12

BEATENBERG

Beatenberg is a blip of a place not far from Interlarken and above Lake Thun. The 10 miles of beginner friendly, intermediate dull and advanced crap terrain is spread out over a slope area unspoilt by mass crowds. In truth this is not a snowboarders destination unless you're recovering from piles and need somewhere out of the way to convalesce in peace.

Local services are very basic but at the same time offer more than what is on the slopes.

Ride area: 16km
Top Lift: 1905m
Total Lifts:5
Contact:
www.beatenberg.ch
+41 (0) 33 841 1818
How to get there: Fly to: Zurich 2 hours away.

BETTMERALP

pic - Bettmeralp Tourism

On its own, Bettmeralp offers a mere 20 miles of basic carving terrain, but by linking with the Aletsch area, you suddenly have a more respectable 60 plus miles of okay freeride terrain in an area that also has a number half-pipes and a couple of fun parks for big air possibilities. Generally, the slopes here will suit beginners and mid way merchants as well as giving advanced riders something to look forward too. Okay local services but costly

Ride area: 32km
Top Lift: 2710m
Total Lifts:12
Contact:
Tel: +41 (0)27 928 60 60
Fax: +41 (0)27 928 60 61
How to get there: Fly to: Zurich 2 1/2 hours away

BRAUNWALD

Braunwald is located two hours from Zurich. This small place has gained a reputation as a friendly freestyle outpost where locals and those in the know spend the weekend getting air.t The terrain itself is nothing to shout about but is still cool and rarely attracts more than a 5 minute lift queue. They regularly build decent half-pipes and parks here for which they stage various events in. **Off the slopes** things are laid back, good but basic.

Ride area: 24km
Top Lift: 1900m
Total Lifts:8
Contact:
Tel: +41 (0)55 643 30 30
Fax: +41 (0)55 643 10 00
How to get there: Fly to: Zurich 1 hour away

CHAMPERY

Champrey is a resort that forms part of the massive Portes du Soleil area, which boast a lift linked area of over 400 miles. Champery itself has 62 miles of terrain, with something for all but nothing that outstanding. An intermediate freerider will like this place although the slopes do get busy. They have a good sized park and half-pipe here. (www.superpark.ch) . Local services are very good in a village full of character.

Ride area: 99km
Top Lift: 2277m
Total Lifts:35
Contact:
www.champery.ch
Tel: +41 (0) 24 479 20 20
Fax: +41 (0) 24 479 20 21

381

How to get there: Fly to: Geneva 1 1/2 hours away

CHAMPOUSSIN

Champoussin is yet another resort that helps to make up the Portes du Soleil area. This is a major plus because you would by no means want to get stuck with what's on offer here. A rider who knows what?s will have this place done and dusted in an hour, even a quick learning novice could lick the place in a day or two. This a resort that old timers wanting to find their youth will like, but any- one else will find it dull. Local services near the slopes

Ride area: 24km
Top Lift: 2150m
Total Lifts:8
Contact:
Tel - +41 24 477 20 77
Fax - +41 24 477 37 73
How to get there: Fly to: Geneva 1 1/2 hours away

CHATEAU D'OEX

Chateau d'Oex is a place that is relatively unknown by the masses. When you see what's on offer its soon clear to see why. Famed more for balloon races, the slopes here are very ordinary and won't take a good rider that long to conquer. However with a further 150 miles of terrain in the area to check out, a week's visit here will be worth the effort. Freestylers get to ride a pipe and beginners have some good slopes. Good slope side services

Ride area: 48km
Top Lift: 1800m
Total Lifts:10
Contact:
Chateau-d'Oex Tourist Office
Tel: +41 (0) 26 924 25 25
Fax: +41 (0) 26 924 25 26
How to get there: Fly to: Geneva 2 hours away

KLOSTERS

pic - Klosters/ Swiss Tourism

Forget the reason for Klosters fame, this resort offers any rider a challenging time with good off-piste that will please freeriders. Carvers have some excellent runs to try out and freestylers have a fun park (not hot mind, better to use the one at nearby Davos). Great also for beginners. The biggest let down here is the brown nosed ski snobs from the UK, hoping to be seen with a royal. Okay local services but pricey

Ride area: 160km
Top Lift: 2844m
Total Lifts:12
Contact:
Tourist Office Klosters
Alte Bahnhofstrasse 6
CH-7250 Klosters
Tel: +41 (0) 81 410 20 20
Fax: +41 (0) 81 410 20 10
How to get there: Fly to: Zurich 2 hours away

LENZERHEIDE

pic - Lenzerheide Tourism

Lenzerheide is a big place that covers two mountain slopes, offering some really nice open riding with tree line trails to the base area. Intermediate freeriders and carvers are in for a treat here, with the biggest cluster of runs to be found on the Statzerhorn slopes.**Freestylers** have an okay half-pipe and park on the Rothorn slopes. **Beginners** should love this place with easy trails all over the place high and low. Good laid back local services slope side.

Ride area: 152km
Easy 46%
Intermediate 41%
Advanced 13%
Top Lift: 2865m
Total Lifts:35
Contact:
www.lenzerheide.ch
Lenzerheid Tourist Office
CH-7078 Lenzerheide
Tel: +41 (0)81 385 11 20
Fax: +41 (0)81 385 11 21
How to get there: Fly to: Zurich 2 hours away

LES DIABLERETS

Les Diablerets is a cool snowboarders hangout that offers summer riding on the glacier. This is not a place for piste

S
SWITZERLAND

loving carvers, no, this is a freeriders retreat offering some great backcountry riding in deep powder, but not for the fainthearted, some of this stuff will take you out quick style if you balls up. Although not a big place, this is a good unspoilt haunt that caters well for freestylers and novices. Good slope side services.

Ride area: 125km
Runs: 77
Easy 50%
Intermediate 42%
Advanced 8%
Top Lift: 3000m
Bottom Lift: 1200m
Vertical: 1800m
Total Lifts: 46 - 3 Cable Cars, 3 Gondolas, 11 Chair Lifts & 28 Drags
Lift Pass: 1 day 39 euros for Isenau 1 day 46 euros Diablerets 1 day 54 euros Glacier 920 euros season
Board School: 1 morning (adult) 35 CHF 4 mornings 120 CHF private lesson 60/250 per hour/day
Contact:
Les Diablerets Tourist Office
1865 Les Diablerets
Tel: +41(0)24-492.33.58
Fax: +41(0)24-492.23.48

How to get there: FLY: Geneva : 120 km Zürich : 250 km Bâle : 200 km
BUS: Shuttle bus runs everyday during winter when Glacier 3000 is open. The stops are situated at the hotel Le Chamois, at the train station, at the bottom of the Meilleret area, at the Sport Center, at the bottom of Isenau, at the hotel Les Diablotins, at the Belvédère and at the Col du Pillon.
TRAIN: direct trains to Aigle and then a mountain train to Les Diablerets. Lausanne - Aigle : 30 min Aigle – Les Diablerets : 50 min
DRIVING: Motorway A9, direction Grand St Bernard, exit Aigle. Then, road Aigle - Les Diablerets (20 km).

MEIRINGEN-HASLIBERG

Meiringen-Hasliberg has a history related to Sherlock Holmes, but today what you have is great snowboarders out back close to the Jungfrau Region. There?s no hype here, no mass holiday crowds, just a cool mountain with something for everyone. There are wide powder fields, gullies and big cliffs on a mountain that is majorly snowboard friendly providing a very decent park and good beginner areas. Visit freestyle-park.ch for info on the terrain park. Good lodging and local services close by.

Ride area: 64km
Top Lift: 3000m

Total Lifts: 28
Contact:
www.meiringen-hasliberg.ch
Meiringen Haslital Tourism
CH-3860
Meiringen
Tel: +41 (0)33 972 50 50
Fax: +41 (0)33 972 50 55
How to get there: Fly to: Zurich 1 1/2 hours away

MORGINS

Morgins, on the Swiss side, is yet another resort that forms part of the massive Portes du Soleil area which crosses into France. On the Swiss side, Morgins is the highest resort and not a modern imitation of some of its cousins. What this place has to offer is easy access to over 40 miles of direct terrain and a further 360 miles of linked terrain. Collectively, there is something for everyone. Good slope side local services

Ride area: 67km
Top Lift: 2000m
Total Lifts: 16
Contact:
www.morgins.ch
Morgins Tourist Office
Tel - +41 24 477 23 61
Fax - +41 24 477 37 08
How to get there: Fly to: Geneva 11/2 hours away

ROUGEMONT

Rougemont is a tiny place that links indirectly with its bigger and more famous cousin Gstaad. This helps boost the 12 miles of terrain on offer here to a respectable 150 miles plus. Rougemont on its own is not a place that you would book a week's holiday at, indeed only a rider so stoned that an inch seems like a mile will enjoy this place. However, there is a small half-pipe and an 80 year old beginner will fair well. There are slope side facilities, but over all, this place is very dull.

Ride area: 19km
Top Lift: 2156m
Total Lifts: 3
Contact:
Website: www.rougemont.ch
Email:info@rougemont.ch
Rougemont Tourist Office
Batiment Communal
CH - 1838 Rougemont
Tel: +41 (0)26 925-83-33
Fax: +41 (0)26 925-89-67
How to get there: Fly to: Geneva 21/2 hours away

There are hundreds of resorts in the US spread out over the northern eastern states, the central Rockie states and the north western states, however, many are no more than a backyard affair operated by a dollar-hungry hillbilly.

The usual season lasts from November until mid-April, with a few northern areas staying open until mid-May. US resorts are generally much smaller than ones in Europe. However, the Rockies do have peaks that rise up to 3,000 metres.

Flights to US cities are frequent, with many having transfer flights to resorts. From various airports you can reach the resorts by bus (sometimes a free shuttle service), or by hire car. If you're touring around the US, you can fly very cheaply using an Air Pass costing from $375.

Travel to a resort by **train** is limited in terms of direct routes. In most cases you will need to take a train to the nearest city and then transfer by bus. East coast resorts are the easiest to reach by train from international airports. A 30 day rail pass for unlimited travel costs from $400.

Greyhound **Buses** operate the largest cross-country network of routes, with dozens of options. Like trains, it may be necessary to take a Greyhound bus to a city and then transfer by a local bus. A 30-day adult Ameripass costs from $450.

Visa requirements vary, but generally, Europeans can enter without a visa and stay for 90 days. All foreigners need a valid passport. If you want to work in the US, you will need to obtain a work visa, which is difficult. If you are caught working without a visa, you will be deported.

Accommodation comes in the form of hotels, motels, guest houses and condominiums (apartments), which are reasonably priced and usually of a very high standards. A low cost option would be to stay in a youth hostel or a ski dorm.

Restaurants vary considerably in price from cheap to ridiculous, and remember that you are expected to tip in restaurants.

Proof of age is constantly required when buying alcohol, so keep some form of ID on you wherever you go. Baby-faced snowboarders forget it.

Capital City: Washington D.C.
Population: 293 million
Highest Peak: Mt. Mckinley 6194m
Language: English
Legal Drink Age: 21 (most states)
Drug Laws: Cannabis is illegal and frowned upon
Age of consent: 16
Electricity: 110 Volts AC 2-pin
International Dialing Code: +1

USA Snowboard Association
PO Box 3927
Truckee, CA 96160
Tel: (800)404-9213
email: karen@usasa.org
web: www.usasa.org

Trains
www.amtrak.com
Tel: 1-800-872-7245
Bus/Coach
www.greyhound.com
Tel: 1-800-231-2222

Currency: US Dollar (US$)
Exchange Rate:
UK£1 = 1.8
EURO = 1.2
AU$1 = 0.76
CD$ = 0.8
NZ$ = 0.7

Time Zone
5 time zones (see states)
UTC/GMT -5 to -10 hours

Driving Guide
All vehicles drive on the right hand side of the road
Speed limits:
Varies per state
Emergency
Police/Fire/Ambulance - 911
General police enquiries 625-5011
Tolls
Called Turnpikes and payable on many highways
Documentation
Driving licence and motor insurance must be carried.

U
S
A

If you mention the name Alaska to most people, they will shiver with the thought of huge icebergs, wild snow cape mountain ranges and ridiculously cold temperatures.

In terms of terrain for snowboarding, most believe that the only people who can snowboard in **Alaska** are expert riders who know how to ride high altitude, steep, extreme back- country areas. While much of this is true with some 90% of the ridable terrain only accessible via a helicopter or by long hikes form barren and remote out-posts, Alaska is infact not just for a select few of big headed sponsored riders doing a video shoot, its a place that welcomes all

riders no matter what you're ability, and although this is a very cold state with recorded low temperatures of -70°C, don't be put of. Alaska has all the modern resort facilities found in any other US snowboard/ski resort. The only difference is that what Alaska offering are a lot more limited with infact only one major developed resort, **Alyeska** which is a fully developed resort with some 62 runs and many purpose built facilities at the base of the slopes (see next page). As well as Alyeska, there are a number of smaller ridable areas, but the remainder are very basic and are not resorts as we know them. They are more or less for locals and run by clubs and private companies. One thing to put

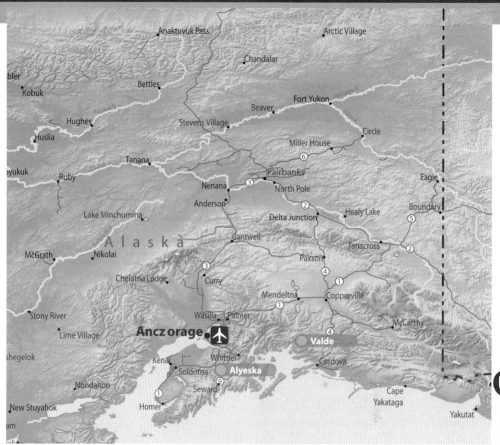

a big smile on your face is the 20 metres of snow most of the resorts get on average.

Where you won't get any of the standard resort set up style of services is in **Valdez**, which lies some 300 miles east of **Anchorage**. Valdez, which is actually a busy oil port, is the snowboarders heaven and for the place for purist only. This is where backcountry, means 'Backcountry'. There are no lifts with lines of skiers in sad clothing and headbands moaning about snowboarders, no groups of ski classes getting in the way all over the place, no ski patrols, no marked runs, no pisted runs. Nothing other than pure virgin terrain that should only be ridden if one, you can ride, and two, you only ride in a group and with a local guide and are properly equipped with backcountry clothing and safety equipment.

A number of established and professional companies are based here and operate proper backcountry tours with local guides who know the mountains and are fully trained in mountain safety and rescue. Organised trips in areas such as the **Chugach Mountains** and the **Thompson Pass** can be arranged with travel options that range from

flying in by helicopter, snow-plane, snow-cat or on foot by hiking. Its even said that if you can show that you are the first to ride a particular slope, you get the honour of naming the slope or face, after your self or what ever name you choose.

Fully inclusive trips that include travel, accommodation, food and guiding are available all year round and although a weeks all in tour will cost you dearly, it will be a trip of a life time. Valdez Heli-Camps, www.valdezhelicamps.com offer numerous heli and snowcat packages.

As for local amenities, accommodation and restaurants, Valdez is a hard town that is home to oil workers who can drink stupid amounts of alcohol and who don't give a shit what snowboard you ride. The town has a number of lodges and bed and breakfast homes with affordable rates. The *Totem Inn* is one of the main places to hang out in the evenings, where you can get a decent meal, shoot some pool or drink yourself stupid well into the night trying to keep up with the locals.

387

POOR FAIR GOOD TOP

FREERIDE
Trees & excellent off-piste

FREESTYLE
Terrain park & good natural

PISTES
for the more advanced riders

8
OUT OF 10

Excellent resort with great freeriding

pic - Alyeska Resort

U

U S A

A L A S K A

T ravel 40 miles south west of **Anchorage** and you will eventually arrive at the somewhat unusual, but interesting resort of **Alyeska**. It happens to be **Alaska's** only traditional purpose-built resort which, now celebrating its 40th year and has a lot going for it. Forget the impression of severe weather conditions and ice slabs that one normally associates with Alaska. What you find here is a great mountain, with excellent terrain serviced by a

modern lift system and is spread out over a series of slopes that begin at almost sea-level. Over the years, places like Alyeska have been largely left alone by the mass holiday crowds. Hardly any ski guides or magazines feature this resort, which is a shame because despite its location in the far northern reaches of the US and Canada, Alyeska has as much to offer, if not more, than many Rocky Mountain-based resorts. A huge plus for this resort is not only its excellent snow record, with average yearly dumps of 20m, but also the fact that you can ride deep powder in early and late spring. The 1000 acres are excellent and offer something for every style and ability, especially advanced riders. The double black diamond runs on the **North Face** are a match for anything found anywhere else in the US. There's plenty of diverse terrain with a number of damn good bowls and gullies. Across the lower slopes are glades, while higher up you will find nice open slopes and well groomed trails.

FREERIDERS who know the score, have a damn fine mountain to check out with some very challenging terrain on offer. The double blacks on **North Face** will give you the chance to go wild at speed, as will the double black listed as **Max's**. There is also plenty of intermediate freeride terrain with lots of okay red and blue trails both on and off-piste. If you hike to the summit, you can gain access to the **Glacier Bowl** which has a superb descent down a wide, open expanse of deep snow. For those not content with the easy access slopes there is heli-boarding and snowcats tours in the **Chugach** mountain range, where you will get to see Alaska as it should be, wild, un-tamed, spectacular, orgasmic.

FREESTYLERS are well catered for here with an abundance of natural hits to get air, such as the nice banks on the **Mambo**. The resort also has a good terrain park located on the Prince Run which is furnished with a a few kickers and an arrary of rails and boxes. The park is floodlit.

BEGINNERS don't have a vast area of novice slopes but what is on offer is not bad especially on the lower areas off Lift 3. Avoid this area at the end of the day as it becomes the busy homebound route for everyone coming down off

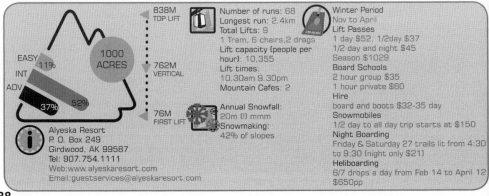

838M
TOP LIFT

762M
VERTICAL

76M
FIRST LIFT

EASY
11%

INT

ADV

37% 52%

1000 ACRES

Alyeska Resort
P. O. Box 249
Girdwood, AK 99587
Tel: 907.754.1111
Web:www.alyeskaresort.com
Email:guestservices@alyeskaresort.com

Number of runs: 68
Longest run: 2.4km
Total Lifts: 9
1 Tram, 6 chairs,2 drags
Lift capacity (people per hour): 10,355
Lift times:
10.30am 9.30pm
Mountain Cafes: 2

Annual Snowfall:
20m (0 mmm
Snowmaking:
42% of slopes

Winter Period
Nov to April
Lift Passes
1 day $52, 1/2day $37
1/2 day and night $45
Season $1029
Board Schools
2 hour group $35
1 hour private $60
Hire
board and boots $32-35 day
Snowmobiles
1/2 day to all day trip starts at $150
Night Boarding
Friday & Saturday 27 trails lit from 4:30 to 9:30 (night only $21)
Heliboarding
6/7 drops a day from Feb 14 to April 12
$650pp

the mountain.

THE TOWN

Off the slopes you will find all the creature comforts required to make your stay a pleasant one and although not extensive, local services are very good. There is a good choice of lodging and eating joints conveniently located either at the base of the slopes or in the small town of **Gridwood**, a few minutes away by shuttle bus. The area also boasts an array of local activities ranging from river rafting, to para -gliding on skis or a board. You can even do a cruise around some of the glaciers or try your hand at salmon fishing.

Accomodation. You can lodge at the base of the slopes, most notably in the *Westin Alyeska Prince* Hotel which is located just yards from the cable car's base station. Around **Gridwood** there's a good selection of condos and B&B's, but it's not the cheapest place to stay. The cheaper option is to lodge in **Anchorage**, which has a far bigger selection.

Food. Alaska my not be world renowned for its culinary

skills, however, the choice and quality of restaurants along with fast-food outlets is particularly good in and around the resort. You can pig out on fine Cajun food at *Double Dusky's* Inn, or sample some well-prepared sea food at *Simon's Saloon*. The *Bake Shop* is a local's favourite for quick snacks, whilst the *Teppanyaki Katsura* offers traditional Japanese nosh, but at a price.

Night-life around Gridwood is somewhat tame, but nevertheless not bad. There is a decent selection of laid back hangouts. The *Sitzmark* and *Aurora* bars are well visited and lively spots. But if you want some real late night action, check out what's going down 40 miles away in **Anchorage**, where you are able to party hard.

U

**S
A**

**A
L
A
S
K
A**

CAR
from Anchorage take New Seward Highway , take left to Alyeska Highway at mile 90 (after approx 40miles) and continue for another 3 miles until you see the sign. Total distance 45 miles (72km), drive time is about 50 minutes.
FLY
to Anchorage International (64km), transfer time to resort is 50 mins.
TRAIN
Train Direct to Girdwood (Alyeska)
BUS
There is a daily bus service between Alyeska and Anchorage run by Gray Line Buses. A return ticket cost from $12 or $8 single.

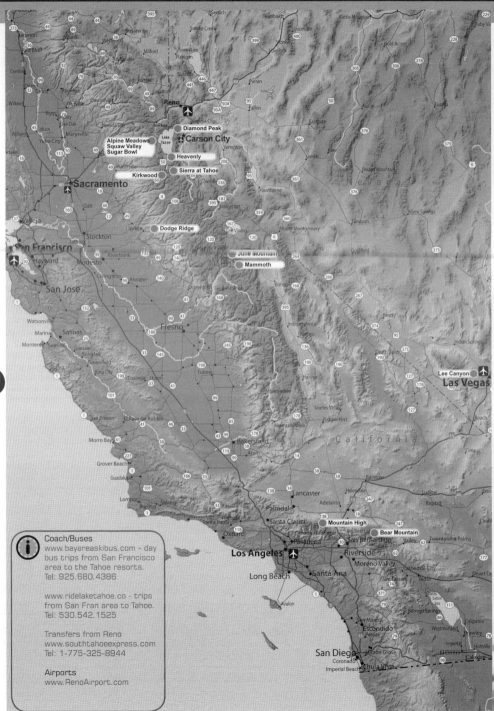

Coach/Buses
www.bayareaskibus.com - day bus trips from San Francisco area to the Tahoe resorts.
Tel: 925.680.4386

www.ridelaketahoe.co - trips from San Fran area to Tahoe.
Tel: 530.542.1525

Transfers from Reno
www.southtahoeexpress.com
Tel: 1-775-325-8944

Airports
www.RenoAirport.com

U
S
A

C
A
L
I
F
O
R
N
I
A

POOR FAIR GOOD TOP

FREERIDE
Trees & good off-piste
FREESTYLE
2 parks & halfpipe
PISTES
Pistes suitable for all

Great freeriding and natural freestyle resort

8
OUT OF 10

pic - Martin Robinson

chair takes you to over 70% of the mountains terrain in just six minutes and also access to the back bowl which offers some nice hiking to some black diamond chutes. Alpine Meadows is also home of some of the best open tree runs in the area with some nice cliff drops if it takes your fancy. On powder days check out some awesome off-piste available from **Scott chair** and **Lake View**. Unlike other nearby resorts, Alpine has an 'open boundary' policy, meaning that providing the area boundary is marked 'OPEN', you can ride wherever you desire. However, you must observe all 'CLOSED' signs, or risk riding in dangerous areas and losing both your lift pass and your life. If you are prepared to explore at Alpine you will find some excellent powder, long after a storm - it's worth hiring a guide for the day. Intermediates can enjoy long cruises from the Roundhouse detachable quad, and also over the back of Alpine on **Sherwood**, where the best early sun can be found.

Alpine Meadows has some of **North Tahoe**'s best terrain and should be an essential stop when ever you visit Tahoe. This is a no frills resort with only a car park, a restaurant and lots of high speed lifts, but what more do you need. Terrain is a big thing here and they have it big time, and what's even better, is they run an open boundary policy which is hard to find in North America.

Alpine Meadows has all sorts of natural terrain that lends itself to the specific needs of snowboarders. There is a wide variety of trails from beginner to expert, lots of tree runs, great off-piste with amazing views of **Lake Tahoe**, if you care to stand and stare. On a week-day, you will hardly ever stand in line for the lifts, giving maximum riding time and ample reason to rest and chill at one of the mountain restaurants. Combine all this with a very snowboard-friendly and generally mellow attitude, and you've got simply a magic place for all snowboarders.

FREERIDERS look no further this resort has everything to keep you smiling for many days. The **summit six**

FREESTYLE Alpine has two terrain parks which are well maintained by the mountain and the local boys who are super friendly. The super pipe is also well looked after with a daily cut. The rails are all standard orientated with a long C rail for the big boys. For those who like their hits spread naturally across the mountain, you may need to ask a local where the best ones are located as they are not always obvious but are in abundance. Be sure to use a spotter for reasons of safety.

THE PISTES are just great with super smooth corduroy slopes all over the mountain. The best advanced and intermediate stuff is off the **Summit chair** lift, where you will find some nice blacks that mellow out into blue trails for some real fast descents.

U
S
A

C
A
L
I
F
O
R
N
I
A

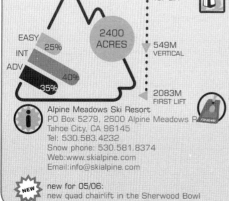

2632M
TOP LIFT

2400 ACRES

549M
VERTICAL

2083M
FIRST LIFT

EASY
INT
ADV
25%
40%
35%

Alpine Meadows Ski Resort
PO Box 5279, 2600 Alpine Meadows R
Tahoe City, CA 96145
Tel: 530.583.4232
Snow phone: 530.581.8374
Web:www.skialpine.com
Email:info@skialpine.com

NEW
new for 05/06:
new quad chairlift in the Sherwood Bowl

Number of runs: 100
Longest run: 4km
Total Lifts: 14
11 chairs,2 drags, 1 magic carpet
Lift capacity (people per hour): 15,000
Lift times:
9.00am to 4.00pm
Mountain Cafes: 3

Annual Snowfall:
11.6m
Snowmaking:
80% of slopes

Winter Period:
mid Nov to early May
Lift Passes
1 Day pass $39
1 Day High season $59
Season $1240
Board Schools
Group inc hire day@$79
Private 1hr $85
2/4 people 3hrs@$135
Hire
Standard package 1day $35
additional day $30. Premium $50 addit day @$45
Snowmobiles
Yes
Night Boarding
Friday & Saturday 27 trails lit from 4:30 to 9:30 (night only $21)

391

There are loads of shops, including loads of souvenir outlets so beloved by tourists and skiers. With the Tahoe area being so popular, it is quite possible that you could be hanging out, on or off the slopes, with some of the biggest names in snowboarding as a number of pros live in the area.

Accommodation can be found in **Truckee** and **Tahoe City,** 6 miles away. It's a bit of a trek but you can often get great deals in **Reno** also known as the "mini Vegas". *Cal-Nev resort* at $79 per person is quite expensive, but this place has history and used to be owned by old blue eyes himself. You also get great views over lake Tahoe www.calnevaresort.com . In Reno, the *Circus Hotel* (www.circusreno.com) and *Harrah's* (www.harrahs. com) are good. Many hotels offer excellent room & lift pass deals, especially mid-week.

Food. If you can't find anywhere in this area to suit your taste buds, then you have a serious medical problem. There are loads of eating outlets in every price range - the choice and range are excellent. For a decent breakfast before hitting the slopes, check out *The Alpine Riverside* Cafe. For good food at reasonable prices, check out *Bridgetender* or the *Mandrian Villa* in Tahoe City. *Jasons Saloon* also serves up some decent nosh.

Night-life here is pretty cool with lots of night spots in the area. Partying options are great, with excessive drinking and chatting up of local birds made easy. Some of the best talent can be found in places such as Naughty Dog, Pierce St Annex, or Humpty's. The River Ranch, which is en-route to Alpine, is also noted for being a lively place.

BEGINNERS once you've managed to link your turns you have a good area to take things that little bit further. The hot wheels chair takes you to some easy going terrain. The beginner's slopes are found at the base station which is handy to grab a quick a beer on the massive balcony if you need a break. The local ski-school offers a high level of tuition, with a full day's package costing from $56. Novice's can even have freestyle lessons

THE TOWN
Alpine Meadows, doesn't have any real slope side services. However, just about anything you need can be found in nearby Tahoe City. **Tahoe City** has a surplus of accommodation, eating out and sporting facilities.

CAR
From Reno take Interstate 80-West to Truckee (45 miles) then State Route 89-South exit (10miles), then right onto Alpine Meadows Road (3 miles). Drive time is about 1 1/2 hours.
FLY
Fly to Reno International, transfer time to resort 1 1/2 hours. 4 hrs from San Francisco
TRAIN
Trains: to Truckee, 6 miles away
BUS
A bus from Reno takes around 1 hour. A Grey Hound bus from San Francisco takes 5 hours via Tahoe City, 6 miles away. Free Ski shuttle buses run from most Tahoe towns (tel 530.581.8341.)

BEAR MOUNTAIN

Okay slopes, great park but dull off

7 OUT OF 10

POOR FAIR GOOD TOP

FREERIDE
Some trees but little off-piste
FREESTYLE
4 Terrain parks & 2 halfpipes
PISTES
Short and sweet

pic - Bear Mtn Resort

station. The **Outlaw Snowboard Park** features enormous table tops, and the famous Serpentine. There's 117 jumps, 57 jibs and 2 pipes set in 195 acres.

PISTES. Lovers of the groomed slopes have a number of good trails to cruise, although in fairness the resorts not the best for super fast cranking it over trails. For a quick burst plus a show-off, check out Grizzly, a short but steep trail.

BEGINNERS, Bear is an excellent place to learn. The local snowboard school offers an introduction to Snowboarding scheme, and a Vertical Improvement Program for riders who want to enhance their carving and jumping skills. Kids under 9 can also sign up for the **magic Minors** Snowboard Camp.

THE TOWN. There is a huge range of accommodation available at Big Bear Lake with apartments to rent at the base of the slopes. Local services are varied, with hundreds of places to eat and drink. The Grizzly Manor Cafe is the place for breakfast or lunch, whilst Village Pizza is the place for a take-away. As for night-life, with a choice of over 50 bars, no-one should miss out.

Bear Mountain Valley is home to two mountain resorts, **Big Bear** and **Snow Summit.** Both play host to numerous top snowboarding events including the Annual Board Aid Festival at Snow Summit. As a rule, resorts' marketing slogans are trite and meaningless, but Bear Mountain's billing as a 'Good Time' place is quite accurate. Anyone who has ridden the parks or pipes, and afterwards sat in the sun on the outdoor deck for lunch, would be hard-pressed to dispute this claim. Part of the deck's inherent allure is the fact that riders need a place to kick back after spending time on Bear's slopes, where vertical is the name of the game. The high speed quad, Big Bear Express, reaches the top of **Goldmine Mountain** in about seven minutes, where you can ride the Claim Jumper trail to notch up over 500 vertical metres. Bear Mountain offers riding for all abilities, from carving to freestyle and all species in-between. Big Bear is a black diamond bliss but also okay for intermediates.

FREERIDERS have a good choice of areas to ride. The double black diamond **Geronimo run** is a real tester, however **Gambler**, a nugget most riders never find off the top of **Showdown Mountain**, is also super cool.

FREESTYLERS now have four big terrain parks and halfpipes. **The Zone** is located immediately above the deck. There is a snack shack at the top of the pipes called **The Yurt** with a judging stand and a DJ

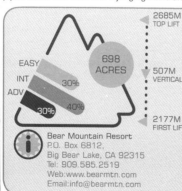

2685M
TOP LIFT

698 ACRES

EASY
INT   30%
ADV
    30%   40%

507M
VERTICAL

2177M
FIRST LIFT

Number of runs: 32
Longest run: 3m
Total Lifts: 12
9 chairs, 3 drags
Lift times: 8.30am to 4.00pm

Winter Period:
Dec to April
Lift Passes
1/2 Day Pass $39/49
full day $49/59
Board School
2 hours $30 group
1 hour private $85
Rental
board and boots $30/day
Night Boarding
Yes

Annual Snowfall:
2.54m
Snowmaking:
100% of slopes

Fly
Fly to Los Angeles, with a transfer time of around 2 hours.
Bus
Bus services from Los Angeles can be taken to the resort.
Car
From Los Angeles, use Interstate 10 east to Redlands. Then Hwy 15 north to San Bernardino and west on route 18. Los Angles to resort, 99 miles, 2 hrs drive.

Bear Mountain Resort
P.O. Box 6812,
Big Bear Lake, CA 92315
Tel: 909.585.2519
Web: www.bearmtn.com
Email: info@bearmtn.com

POOR FAIR GOOD TOP

FREERIDE
Trees & small amount of off-piste

FREESTYLE
Small terrain park & halfpipe

PISTES
Wide but short slopes

Great views of the lake but a day's enough

5
OUT OF 10

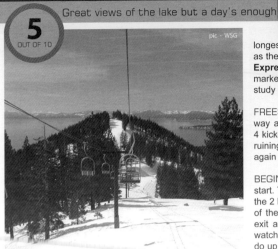

pic - WSG

longest and most challenging terrain up in the area known as the **Solitude Canyon**, which is reached off the **Crystal Express** chair. But note you are not allowed to go past the marked boundary and if you do you will be prosecuted, so study your lift map.

FREESTYLERS head for the new terrain park located half way along **Spillway**. It has a badly maintained pipe and 4 kickers. Its not fenced off so you get a lot of idiot skiers ruining your approach. Up at **Lakeview** theres a rail park, again nothing too taxing.

BEGINNERS, the **school yard** run the obvious place to start. There is a special lift pass available that only covers the 2 beginner lifts and will save you a lot of money. Some of the other lifts have such as **Ridge** have a nice steep exit as you leave the lift, so its worth spending a while watching the beginners clatter into each other while you do up your bindings.

Of all the resorts in **Tahoe**, Diamond Peak doesn't quite mix it with the likes of Squaw and Heavenly but that's not necessarily a bad thing; as the weekends swell the other resorts, Diamond Peak promise amazing views, no crowds and good value. Built after Squaw hosted the Winter Olympics in 1960, and extended to its current size in the 80's. Diamond Peak is a resort that places a strong emphasis on fun, families and snow, and they succeed in many ways as this is a cool hang-out that attracts all ages with the slopes getting a good annual snow covering. The slopes are set out in a simple manner with a good mixture of runs spread out over the whole mountain. Being a quiet resort, the trails don't get busy and there aren't long lift lines. The 2003/4 season saw the replacement of its longest chair with a high speed quad, and boy did it need it. The rest of the lifts are still painfully slow, but does give you plenty of opportunity to sample the amazing views of Tahoe. If you're up there on a Sunday and missed your regular church service then they hold a special service up and Snowflake lodge.

FREERIDERS who can cut the mustard, will find the

THE TOWN. There's no accommodation at the resort but **incline village** has the closest hotels. There's plenty of accommodation to choose from around Tahoe though, plenty of parking and there is a free shuttle bus available.

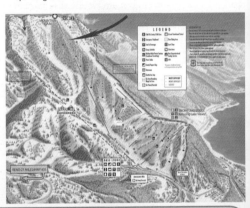

U
S
A
C
A
L
I
F
O
R
N
I
A

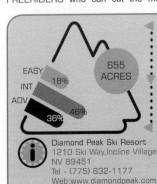

2603M
TOP LIFT

655 ACRES

560M
VERTICAL

2042M
FIRST LIFT

EASY
INT
ADV
18%
46%
36%

Number of runs: 30
Longest run: 4km
Total Lifts: 6 - all chairs
Lift times:
9.00am to 4.00pm
Mountain cafes: 2

Winter Period:
Dec to April
Lift Passes
Half day $35
$46 adult day,
$535 adult season,
$58 family day ticket
Board School
Private lessons from $75ph
groups $55 - $72 for 1.45hrs.
Hire
All boards have Rossignol step-in bindings. 34$ per day for full kit

Annual Snowfall:
7.5m
Snowmaking:
75% of slopes

Bus
Ski buses pick up from many locations around Tahoe
Fly
35 miles from Reno/Tahoe Airport
Car
From San Francisco or Sacramento - Take I-80 East to Truckee. Take HWY 267 exit to North Shore Lake Tahoe. At HWY 28 junction, turn east to Incline Village. Turn left on Country Club Drive. Take Ski Way to the top.

Diamond Peak Ski Resort
1210 Ski Way, Incline Village
NV 89451
Tel - (775) 832-1177
Web: www.diamondpeak.com
Email: info@diamondpeak.com

wsg DODGE RIDGE

	POOR	FAIR	GOOD	TOP
FREERIDE Some trees but little off-piste				
FREESTYLE 4 Terrain parks & halfpipe				
PISTES Some good steep slopes				

Small and pefectly formed

6 OUT OF 10

Dodge Ridge is not one of those resorts that springs to mind when one is thinking about where to go for a few days riding. Come to think about it, Dodge Ridge is almost unknown outside of those who live in the area or by a few hardcore riders who travel around in a van searching out the small haunts. Anyway, why would this relatively new resort be of much interest? After all, it's only been going for 15 years. Well Dodge Ridge has some 60 trails with 12 lifts which take you over a mountain that has a lot to offer, especially advanced riders, with a good series of double black diamond runs such as the trails that can be found going off of lift 3. The slopes are well maintained and well set out offering something for all levels with a good mixture of trails.

FREERIDERS who like to experience rough, hard core and fast terrain will like what they find here. There is a good selection of expert runs to take on with the most interesting being the **Six Shooter** and the **Sonora Glades**, which is a tricky steep section with heaps of trees. Little more sedate trails to try out are the **Sunrise** or the **Exhibition** while the **Gentle Ben** is even easier.

FREESTYLERS have had a halfpipe and terrain park here for years. The **Discovery way park** is set up for beginners located just off chair 6 while half pipe at **Center Bowl** off of Chair 5 is 300 foot long. For jibbing head to Rockys road top of chair 7 and if board cross is your thing then **Ry's Run** under chair 3 will tickle your fancy. All the hardend freestyles hang out at the **Sunrise park** off chair 8 where there's some mean arse hits.

PISTES. Fast riders have a couple of cracking trails to let loose on, namely the **Sunrise** if you have the balls or the **Quicksilver** which is a nice long blue trail off lift 8. **Fools Gold** is another cool fast trail.

BEGINNERS will find the best areas to take on are located at the lower sections of lifts 2 and 1. Please note that these are novice areas and although tame, should not be at speed.

pic - Dodge Ridge Resort

THE TOWN

Off the slopes things suddenly change and become a little different as well as very basic indeed. Local services, provided in nearby town of **Pinecrest** are very good with good rates for accommodation and other services. There are a number of good eating joints but don't expect a lot of night life. There is none of note really, which is not to say that you can't have a good time out.

USA CALIFORNIA

EASY
INT 20%
ADV
40%
40%

815 ACRES

2500M TOP LIFT

487M VERTICAL

2011M FIRST LIFT

Number of runs: 50
Longest run: 3.2m
Total Lifts: 11
9 chairs, 2 drags
Lift capacity (people per hour):
15,700
Lift times: 9.00am to 4.00pm

Winter Period:
Dec to April
Lift Passes
Day Pass $46
1/2 day $38
Hire
board and boots from $35/day
helmet $10/day

Annual Snowfall:
7.5m-12m
Snowmaking:
unknown

Fly
to San Francisco, transfer is 2 1/2 hrs
Bus
services from San Francisco available.
Car
30 minutes from Sonora; 90 minutes from the Central Valley; 3 hours from the Bay Area. Directions: 580 East to the 205 East past I-5 and 99. At Manteca take 120 East toward Sonora. Stay on the 120/108 through Escalon to Oakdale. At Oakdale turn left on 108 East to Sonora. Stay on 108 East through Sonora to Pinecrest (30 miles). Turn right on Dodge Ridge Road.

Dodge Ridge
P.O. Box 1188
#1 Dodge Ridge Road
Pinecrest, CA. 95364
Tel: 209.965.3474
Fax: 209.965.4437
Web: www.dodgeridge.com
Email: info@dodgeridge.com

POOR FAIR GOOD TOP

FREERIDE
Trees & good off-piste

FREESTYLE
4 Terrain parks & halfpipe

PISTES
Huge number of excellent slopes

Great all-round resort with some excellent steeps

8
OUT OF 10

pic - Steve Barker

Snowboard Federation has held world cup events that have attracted riders from around the world, who came for the challenge of a big mountain with hardcore terrain. However, Heavenly is not just for the pro's - there is something here for everyone - but the slopes do favour riders of intermediate and advanced levels, with steeps and big air possibilities on double black diamond runs, like those of Mott & Killebrew Canyons and the Gunbarrel.

FREERIDERS will find the most challenging terrain is located on the **Nevada** side of the resort in the **Milky Way bowl**. However, it does become tracked out very quickly and would be best left until just after a fresh dump. Still, the Milky Way Bowl is major and offers some great powder. Advanced riders who like their slopes steep and covered with trees should check out the **North Bowl**. But for those who really want to fill their pants should make for the white-knuckle rides on the **Mott & Killebrew Canyon** area. Here you will find a series of expert double black diamond runs through a series of chutes. For something a little less intimidating try the blues off **Tamarack** and **Sky chairs**.

FREESTYLERS. Well kick my free style arse into space , freestylers are not only provided for but are welcomed with a big hug. Four claimed to be new but really just improved parks where opened last year. Spreading out across both sides of the mountain the parks can offer all level of riders a place to hang out and progress slowly. The **Groove Terrain Park** is the perfect stomping grounds to learn the basics. **Cascade Terrain Park** is the intermediate park the stepping stone between the **Groove park** and the high flying hits of the **High Roller** Terrain Park. Jibbers have there own hang out in the **Rail Yard Terrain Park** which evolves as the season progress's

PISTES. Riders of the piste are not to be outdone, since Heavenly is a highly rated as a groomed resort. There are plenty of well prepared pistes for laying out big tracks on, such as Liz's and Big Dipper

BEGINNERS may at first feel a little left out with the lack of green runs. However, there are plenty of excellent blue trails to check out. Be aware that in various areas there are a number of blacks that turn off and drop away from

U
S
A

C
A
L
I
F
O
R
N
I
A

This is an over hyped resort, but its the only one where you jump on a Gondola straight from town without need for any transport. The gondola that runs from downtown **South Lake Tahoe** makes access to the mountain so much easier, but you still can't board back down . **Heavenly** is a large resort that stretches across the two states of **California** and **Nevada**. Heavenly has over 40 years of operation under its belt, as well as some of the largest snowboard/ski acreage in the US, and by far the biggest vertical out of the **Lake Tahoe** resorts. Snowboarders are drawn from afar, especially at weekends and during holidays. In the past, the International

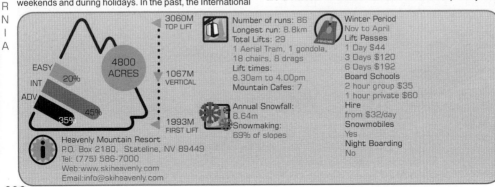

EASY
INT 20%
ADV
35% 45%

4800 ACRES

3060M TOP LIFT

1067M VERTICAL

1993M FIRST LIFT

Number of runs: 86
Longest run: 8.8km
Total Lifts: 29
1 Aerial Tram, 1 gondola,
18 chairs, 8 drags
Lift times:
8.30am to 4.00pm
Mountain Cafes: 7

Annual Snowfall:
8.64m
Snowmaking:
69% of slopes

Winter Period
Nov to April
Lift Passes
1 Day $44
3 Days $120
6 Days $192
Board Schools
2 hour group $35
1 hour private $60
Hire
from $32/day
Snowmobiles
Yes
Night Boarding
No

Heavenly Mountain Resort
P.O. Box 2180, Stateline, NV 89449
Tel: (775) 586-7000
Web:www.skiheavenly.com
Email:info@skiheavenly.com

pic s - Heavenly Resort

some of the easier trails, so check your piste map. The cluster of greens off the **Waterfall lift**, on runs like **Mombo Meadows**, are good for whetting the appetite before trying the blues off **Ridge** and **Canyon lifts.**

THE TOWN
Off the mountain, local action is lively and plentiful. The choice of accommodation, eating and booze joints is massive and many within easy reach of the slopes. However, local services are a bit spread out and having a car here is a must. Locals make you feel at home and services are of a very high standard. However, the popularity of the area does mean that the place can be excessively busy, especially at weekends. South Lake Tahoe has heaps of shops and loads of sporting facilities

Accommodation: Although there is lodging within walking distance of the slopes, it is very expensive. South Lake Tahoe is heaving with hotels and motels from very cheap to very expensive. If you are on a budget try 'Doug's Mellow Mountain Retreat' (916) 544 8065 at $13-$15 per night for a small dormitory. The Blu Zu Hostel 4140 Pine Park (916) 541 9502 $15 per night for a bed in the dormitory.

Restaurants are plentiful and at prices to please everyone,

there are also various fast-food joints. Every type of food is available here from Chinese, Italian, Mexican to standard American fair. It's all on offer. The list of good eating places is too long to mention in this short journal, but loacls will point you in the right direction if you ask for some recommendations. In the meantime Red Hutt or Chris's are both good.

Nightlife in Heavenly is dull. However in South Lake Tahoe there is plenty of gambling if that is your thing and many of the casinos have nightclubs. Some of the better ones are Club Z and Nero's. Hoss Hogs host some great band nights and Mulligans Irish bar is always a favourite for late night drinking.

CAR
From Reno take highway 395 to Carson City, then highway 50 & folllow the signs (58 miles)
From San Francisco take highway 80 through Sacramento, then highway 50 to tahoe
FLY
Reno via Carson City, Heavenly = 58 miles (93). Drive time is about 1 hour.
TRAIN
Nearest station at Reno
BUS
A bus from Reno takes 1 1/2 hours. A Grey Hound bus from San Francisco takes 6 hours via South Lake Tahoe, 6 miles away. Ski buses do a morning pick-up from many towns & hotels around Tahoe area.

U
S A C A L I F O R N I A

	POOR	FAIR	GOOD	TOP
FREERIDE Trees & some off-piste				
FREESTYLE 3 terrain park & halfpipe				
PISTES quiet slopes				

Small but perfectly formed

9 OUT OF 10

pic - June Mountain Resort

June Mountain is located in the **Eastern High Sierra**, 17 miles north of its sister resort **Mammoth**. For an area of such modest size, June offers a richness of riding terrain that is often not found in even in many larger resorts. It's as though some of the best mountain features have been selectively picked and welded together to form a neat package that is user-friendly to a multitude of disciplines. This place has something to offer carvers, freestylers or freeriders of any level. There is a welcome blend of energy-sapping steeps and mellower stuff perfect for cruising. Because of the small size of June it doesn't have package tour status and it has a minimal number of ski schools, making the place a bit of a secret for those in the know and leaving you without lift queues even in peak periods. This all makes the place sound a bit like something resembling heaven, and in many respects it is, especially if there's been a dump and if the park and pipe have been recently re-shaped. Having said that, June can't offer the variety of the decent larger resorts. Nevertheless, if you don't mind riding the odd run more than once and having to take one foot out along some of the flat green runs, you will get a lot out of the relaxed attitude here, away from the big resort experience.

FREERIDERS can feel free to use any of the perfectly good pistes if they wish, but when there's trees-a-plenty to circumnavigate like there is here, you'd be mad to limit yourself. At June **Mountain Summit** are some steep natural chutes and bowls. From the June Meadows Chalet those who can should be sure to drop off blind in to **Gull Ridge** for a tasty black run or two back down to June Lake.

FREESTYLERS fortunate enough to find themselves at June have at their disposal a world class half pipe in front of June Meadows Chalet and the **Boarder Town Snowboard Park** located on Gunsmoke off of lift J4. This fantastic board park is out of bounds to bi-plankers, a testament to June's snowboard policy, and consists of about 20 hits, tabletops and banks of all sizes plus another half pipe upon which those skills can be honed. **Mambo park** is good for the beginner while **Sunrise park** is a mile and a quarter of mid sized hits and rails. In total we're talking 40 acres of dedicated freestyle terrain.

PISTES. The resort has a lot of well-groomed slopes to take advantage of, suiting an array of styles. The selection of black rated slopes from June Mountain Summit are great for the speed freaks to let loose, while the green and blue runs down from Rainbow Summit offer something far less daunting. Beware of some very flat green sections around the middle elevations.

BEGINNER freeriders can take their time on a few gentle, un-crowded slopes. This can be attempted alone or under the laid back tuition of the instructors available. For those novice freestylers who wish to learn the art of the pipe there are also instructors around to teach you what you need to know. In fact, not just the novices need benefit from their guidance as upper level tuition is offered too.

THE TOWN. June Lake is the residential area of the June Mountain resort; the population is a mere 600. It's a very relaxed community and there are a number of cabins and motels at which to stay, as well as plenty of fine eateries.

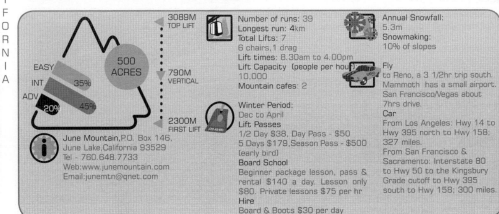

3089M TOP LIFT

790M VERTICAL

2300M FIRST LIFT

500 ACRES

EASY
INT 35%
ADV 20% 45%

June Mountain, P.O. Box 146, June Lake, California 93529
Tel - 760.648.7733
Web: www.junemountain.com
Email: junemtn@qnet.com

Number of runs: 39
Longest run: 4km
Total Lifts: 7
6 chairs, 1 drag
Lift times: 8.30am to 4.00pm
Lift Capacity (people per hour) 10,000
Mountain cafes: 2

Winter Period:
Dec to April
Lift Passes
1/2 Day $38, Day Pass - $50
5 Days $179, Season Pass - $500 (early bird)
Board School
Beginner package lesson, pass & rental $140 a day. Lesson only $80. Private lessons $75 per hr
Hire
Board & Boots $30 per day

Annual Snowfall:
5.3m
Snowmaking:
10% of slopes

Fly
to Reno, a 3 1/2hr trip south. Mammoth has a small airport. San Francisco/Vegas about 7hrs drive.
Car
From Los Angeles: Hwy 14 to Hwy 395 north to Hwy 158; 327 miles.
From San Francisco & Sacramento: Interstate 80 to Hwy 50 to the Kingsbury Grade cutoff to Hwy 395 south to Hwy 158; 300 miles.

U S A   C A L I F O R N I A

	POOR	FAIR	GOOD	TOP
FREERIDE Some trees & good off-piste				
FREESTYLE Terrain park & halfpipe				
PISTES Some good quiet steep slopes				

A real advanced riders heaven

7 OUT OF 10

Kirkwood has the reputation of being an advanced rider's mountain, as proved by their hosting of the North American Freeride Championship. In 2005 Kirkwood (and most of Tahoe's resorts) boasted having "The biggest snow base in the WORLD"!; a truly epic season with over 20m of snowfall. With an array of double-black diamond trails, good back country access gates, and the highest base elevation in the area, this resort is a 'powder hounds' dream. Although Kirkwood has some rather long, slow chair lifts, it is far less crowded than any other resort in Tahoe, leaving fresh lines to be had all day long. In addition to its amazing 'fill-ya-pants' freeriding, Kirkwood has excellent pistes and some full-on freestyle terrain. It is located a little south of Lake Tahoe, along Highways 88 and 89, and is about a half-hour drive from the resort of Heavenly.

FREERIDERS in particular will get stoked with the natural terrain Kirkwood has to offer. Areas like **The Wall** and **The Sisters** reachable from Chair 10, accessing some very serious drops and chutes, in addition to an abundance of other black and double black diamond runs, will make those hardcore freeriders feel like a kid in a candy store. If it's big open bowls you enjoy the most, head out towards **The Wave** and **Larry's Lip** accessible from Chair 4. And if that's not enough to get your whistle wet Kirkwood now offer back country Powder Cat Riding tours at very reasonable prices. Do be careful not to venture into these areas if you're not up to the mark as they are strictly for experienced riders only.

FREESTYLERS will be more than happy with Kirkwood's **Stomping Grounds terrain park**. Accessible from Chairs 5 and 6, here you will find a range of advanced features with different jump and jib lines continuing on to the **Sierra Mist Super Pipe**. There is also a good beginner's terrain park found off of Chair 7, called the **Terrain Garden**. Those freestylers that like to explore will discover plenty of natural hits and drops all over the place.

PISTE riders are presented with some first class carving terrain that is a match for anywhere else in the Tahoe region. If you like long, steep groomers, runs like **Zachary** and **Olympic** from Chair 6 will keep the heart pumping. For something a little less daunting check out some of the blue runs off of Chair 2.

BEGINNERS need to get their act together fast if they want to appreciate Kirkwood's offerings to the full. Although Kirkwood only has a small percentage of easy trails, there are some good 'learn-to-turn' areas to be found over on Chair 9, like Graduation which has its own easy-to-use lift. If you're feeling up for a bit more of a challenge head up Chair 7 for some easy blue runs. When you make it back down to the Timber Creek Lodge have a killer hot-dog at the cafe whilst enjoying the view.

THE TOWN
There isn't much in the Kirkwood Mountain Village itself, apart from a few quiet bars, small eateries and some rather expensive accommodation. Your best bet is to stay in **South Lake Tahoe** town, where you can find something to suit all holiday budgets, and rent a car to drive the short distance to Kirkwood, but don't get caught out in a snow storm as the road can close very quickly. They do also operate a daily $5 bus service with pickup points around Tahoe.

pic - Kirkwood Resort

U S A   C A L I F O R N I A

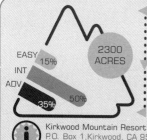

2987M TOP LIFT

EASY 15%
INT
ADV 35%
50%

2300 ACRES

609M VERTICAL

2377M FIRST LIFT

Kirkwood Mountain Resort
P.O. Box 1, Kirkwood, CA 95646
Tel: (209)258-6000

Web: www.skikirkwood.com
Email: info@kirkwood.com

Number of runs: 65
Longest run: 4m
Total Lifts: 12
10 chairs, 2 drags
Lift capacity: 17,905
Lift times: 9-3.30pm

Winter Period:
Dec to April
Lift Passes
1/2 Day $24, 1 Day
$47, Season $900
Board School
Beginners day package
(pass, lesson, hire) $80.
2hr group $40. Private
$90 per hour. Pipe &
park lesson $25
Hire
board & boots $41 day

Annual Snowfall: 12m
Snowmaking: 10%

Bus
Day trips from San Fran possible,
shuttle buses run from Tahoe $5
Fly
to Reno, 70 miles from the resort
Bus
Bus journeys from Reno, take 90 mins
Car
From Reno take the US route 395
south and then state route 88 west
to Kirkwood. Reno to resort is 70 miles.
From S.Tahoe, take US50 (Lake Tahoe
Blvd.) West. Turn left onto US50W/Hwy
89S(Emerald Bay Rd) approx 5miles
to Meyers. Continue Hwy 89South for
11miles then onto Hwy 88 West for
14miles then, turn Left onto Kirkwood
Meadows Drive.

Come on, you're in Vegas man

POOR FAIR GOOD TOP

FREERIDE
Trees but no decent off-piste

FREESTYLE
Basic Ttrrain park & halfpipe

PISTES
short & rutted slopes

EASIER   MORE   MOST

Not many people will know this or indeed will believe it, but yes it's true, it's a fact, it exists: a snow-capped mountain to ski and ride on just outside the world's gambling heaven **Las Vegas**. Lee Canyon is a tiny resort only 45 miles from the Las Vegas Strip. To give some perspective, its total 40 acres are about half the area of Mammoths terrain parks. It is weird to drive up from the heat of the desert to arrive in just 20 minutes at altitude with snowdrifts all around. The mountains get regular snow throughout the winter with an average of 3m a year, The resort can also cover 60% of the slopes with artificial snow should the real stuff be lacking. Set at 8500ft in the **Spring Mountains** to the north west of Las Vegas, what you actually get is a slope area offering a respectable 1000ft of vertical drop. There are three slow chairlifts, one on the nursery slopes accessing a total of 10 trails, one of them dotted with ramps and kickers (plus a sign that says "No aerial flips allowed" (most people seemed to ignore it!). All standards from beginner to snowgod would find something here to keep them amused for a while - if only an afternoon or two. What's more, this place never gets too crowded. The car park often seems full yet the slopes never seem to number more than 50 people at a time. At the slopes you can get full snowboard hire but like most hire kit the quality varies - getting there early gets you better equipment. There is also a shop, bar and cafe for your standard burger hit.

FREERIDERS should find the 4 black runs, which are not groomed and are basically mogul fields, a cool place to ride offering a fun challenge. Two of the blacks descend through some trees which only adds to the fun. There are a few bits where you can get off piste but the powder soon gets shredded out so don't expect any hardcore backcountry terrain.

FREESTYLERS are best looking out for natural hits as the man made offerings are a bit lame. The snowboard park, which is designed as a long trail, has a pretty mundane halfpipe but money has been spent to improve things.

PISTES. Riders who stick to the piste will find that this is not a place for them due to the lack of well maintained trails. The terrain is often too bumpy to hold a good edge and the runs are short.

BEGINNERS only have a few rather dull areas to slide around on. A new 150' Magic Carpet will help increase uphill capacity and make learning easier.

THE TOWN. To find out what's going on off the slopes, get your self a guide book on **Las Vegas** as there is no way that we can even begin to tell you all that is on offer in this massive gambling city.

pic - Vegas Resort

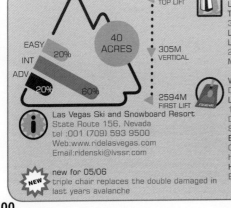

40 ACRES

EASY   20%
INT
ADV
20%   60%

2899M TOP LIFT
305M VERTICAL
2594M FIRST LIFT

Las Vegas Ski and Snowboard Resort
State Route 156, Nevada
tel :001 (709) 593 9500
Web:www.ridelasvegas.com
Email:ridenski@lvssr.com

NEW new for 05/06
triple chair replaces the double damaged in last years avalanche

Number of runs: 10
Longest run: 914m
Total Lifts: 4
3 chairs,1 drag
Lift times: 9am - 4pm
Lift Capacity (people per hour)
2,500
Mountain cafes: 1

Winter Period:
Dec to April
Lift Passes
1/2 day $28
Day pass $38
Season $319-499
Board Schools
Group lessons $25 for 1 1/2 hours. Private lessons $70 ph
Hire
Boards & Boots $25 per day

Annual Snowfall:
3m
Snowmaking:
60% of slopes

Bus
from Las Vegas take around 1 hour.
Fly
to Reno or Las Vegas International
Drive
Route 95 out of Las Vegas towards Reno. After 30 miles turn left onto Route 156, then15 miles or so to Lee Canyon.

wsg MAMMOTH MOUNTAIN

	POOR	FAIR	GOOD	TOP
FREERIDE Trees & good off-piste				
FREESTYLE 3 parks & 3 halfpipe				
PISTES Imaculate & varied runs				

Award winning parks & great freeriding

10 OUT OF 10

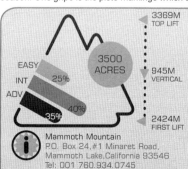

pic - WSG

California has given us Hollywood, Daffy Duck and thankfully, **Mammoth Mountain**. Located in the **Eastern Sierra** region, Mammoth has welcomed snowboarders onto its slopes for many years, and with a good snow record (a record 15.4m in 2004/5 season), riding is often possible into June. The past few years have seen huge investment by Intrawest (owners of Whistler & Squaw), much of this evident in the huge terrain parks and fast lift system, but also the construction of the new village resort that opened last season. The new village sits on the edge of town with a Gondola taking you to **Canyon Lodge**, this season should see a trail back to the village completed. Mammoth's slopes can often get busy at weekends when the place fills up with California's city dwellers. Don't let that put you off though as by normal American standards, Mammoth is a pretty big place. In fact, it's one of the biggest resorts in America, with over 150 trails set out on a long-since dead volcano; no matter what your style or ability, there's plenty to do. Mammoth's terrain parks have achieved legendary status, for the third year running picking up **Transworlds best pipe award**, and runner up to Whistler for best terrain park. Its not just for the pro's either, there's parks and pipes designed for every ability. Overall Mammoth is a great resort for boarders, there's good variety in terrain from trees to open bowls, an efficient lift system; the last drag lift was removed last season. One gripe is the piste markings which are a bit of a nightmare as they seem to just disappear.

FREERIDERS have a great mountain to ride with trees, big bowls and loads of natural hits to catch air, especially in areas such as **Huevos Grande** and **Hangman's Hollow**. Experienced riders normally head up to the ridge reached by **Gondola 2** Here there is a host of chutes that lead into a wide bowl, perfect for freeriders to show what they're made of. The **Cornice** run is the one to go for - it's awesome and will give you a major buzz. If you really have the balls, check out **Wipe Out**, a double black run off Chair 23. If you emulate the name of this run, not only will it make your eyes water, but everyone on the chair lift above will be able to watch and laugh as you wipe out in style (give them two fingers and then get on your way).

FREESTYLERS have a resort that is well in tune with their needs, whether you're after natural hits or purpose built jumps. A good spot to check out is the area known as **Lower Dry Creek** which is a natural halfpipe. Alternatively, the **Dragon's Back** gives the advanced freestyler plenty of air time. Theres 3 terrain parks suitable for all levels. The family park near **Canyon Lodge** has a beginner's half-pipe (10ft walls) and a few boxes, but the real fun starts on the unbound parks. The unbound team keep the parks & pipes maintained perfectly all season. Depending on the snow conditions there's a huge number and variety of rails and the awesome 16'x36' wall ride. **Unbound south** is a great long park full of intermediate to advanced jumps, rails and boxes with lifts to take you straight back up. The **main unbound** park is across by the main lodge with great views of the park as you ascend on the lifts crossing it. Here you'll find the super pipe with its 15ft walls and next to it the massive super duper pipe. They try and open the pipes as soon as the resort opens, and when things start getting slushy in April, they build a spring pipe in the saddle bowl off the face lift express. You'll also find some huge table tops, and jumps up to 80 foot in length. To the side of the main unbound is a good run through the trees full of

U
S
A

C
A
L
I
F
O
R
N
I
A

3369M TOP LIFT	Number of runs: 150
	Longest run: 4.8km
	Total Lifts: 27
3500 ACRES	3 gondolas, 24 chairs
	Lift capacity (people per hour): 50,000
945M VERTICAL	Lift times: 8.30am to 4.00pm
	Mountain Cafes: 9

EASY

INT 25%

ADV

40%

35%

2424M FIRST LIFT

Annual Snowfall: 11m
Snowmaking: 33% of slopes

Winter Period:
Nov to June
Lift Passes
Half day $50
1 Day $63, 4 Days - $206
Season Pass - $1300
Board Schools
Group lessons $60 for 3hrs
Private lesson $75 per hour, half-day $225, $450 per day
Hire
Board & boots $30 per day, $25 half-day
Snowmobiles
Yes
Night Boarding
No

Mammoth Mountain
P.O. Box 24, #1 Minaret Road,
Mammoth Lake, California 93546
Tel: 001 760.934.0745
Web: www.mammothmountain.com
Email: info@mammoth-mtn.com

NEW new for 05/06:
Main Lodge gets a refit, 2 new shuttle buses, new snowcat

easy jumps on the right and tables to the left. Jump straight back on the lift and you can easily get up and down in 10 minutes. For complete beginners check out the area under

pic - WSG

the lift between the **sesame street** runs. There are some bumps to get some credit card air on, and some boxes. If you're still not happy then **June Mountain** is only a 30 drive away.

PISTES. The runs are super-well pisted and make for good terrain, both for those wanting to go at speed or for the more sedate carver. Check out the trail known as the **Saddle Bowl,** where you will find a nice, tame, long blue run.

BEGINNERS, if you can't learn or improve at Mammoth, then you're into the wrong sport. The area is perfect for novices, with plenty of green and easy progression blue runs at the lower sections and excellent snowboard tuition available. **Sesame Street** run off chair 11 near the main lodge is perfect for beginners, theres no pistes joining it so you won't get flustered by other riders, and under the chairlift are a series of bumps and boxes to try if you're not

bruised enough already. Special beginner packages including lesson, lift and gear start from $87 and are well worth the money and the local snowboard school has a good reputation.

THE TOWN
At the base area you will find some accommodation and basic facilities. However, the best value is to stay down in the town of **Mammoth Lakes** which is 4 miles from the mountain. Mammoth Lakes has a huge selection of good local services and although the area is not noted for being affordable, riders on a budget will still be able to swing it with a number of cheap supermarkets and low priced dorms to lodge at. For all your snowboard needs, Mammoth has a number of snowboard shops, such as *Stormriders* tel (760) 934 2471 and *Mountain Riders,* tel (760) 934 0679.

Accommodation. There's plenty of accommodation to be found in the town of Mammoth Lakes which is about 4 miles from the main lodge, but note on the whole most are very expensive. You will find condo-overload plus a few B&B joints and a hostel. The *Ullr Lodge* on Minaret Rd is a

pic - main unbound park - (c) Mammoth Resort

pic - WSG

reasonable priced hostel with beds from $20 a night. The new village on the edge of town has various apartments available and means you can practically ski-in/out every day, but at a cost. The *Mammoth Mountain Inn* is situated near the main lodge and offers some good room and lift deals, but the development work going on nearer town however leaves it feeling increasingly isolated. The rooms have been refurbished and a free night bus now runs into town, so it's not a bad choice if you want to be one of the first on the slopes.

Food. You can get almost any type of food here, ranging from expensive to mega bucks. There are a number of cheaper food-stops such as Berger's, where you can dine

on chicken or burgers. The Breakfast Club is the place for early starters, while *Roberto's* serves hot Mexican nosh. If pizzas are your thing, then try a slice at *Nik-N-Willie's* which is noted for its food. *Grumpy's* is noted for chicken served up in a sporting setting. *Hennessey's* in the new village is ok, but if you fancy something that's not in breadcrumbs then take a look along the old Mammoth road, the *Alpenrose* comes highly recommended. For a great coffee and to check your email go to *Looney Beans*, 3280 Main Street.

Night-life hits off in **Mammoth Lakes** and while not fantastic; it is still pretty good with bars playing up-to-date sounds. Amongst the more popular hangouts are

pic - WSG

Whiskey Creek and the *Stonehouse Brewery*. *Grumpy's* is a cool place that serves booze and burgers, set to a back drop of TV screens showing the latest slope action. In the new village *Dublins* does the beer/TV thing well, and has a nightclub called *Fever* next door, but pick of the bunch is *Lakanuki's*. The *Innsbruck* near the main lodge is good for a beer after a long day.

U
S
A

C
A
L
I
F
O
R
N
I
A

CAR
From LA follow US 395 north to Hwy. 203 (at Mammoth Lakes Junction) - 307 miles.
Reno - US 395 south, to Hwy. 203 - 168 miles.
San Francisco Area - Interstate 80 or Interstate 50 to US 395 south, to Hwy. 203 - 320 miles.
FLY
Fly to Reno International, transfer time to resort is 4 hours, Local airport is Mammoth Lakes, 20 miles away. There are plans to upgrade airport to handle larger planes.
BUS
A bus from Reno takes 3 1/2 hours. CREST bus service from Reno/Tahoe 3 days a week, call (800) 922-1930 for info.

FREERIDE
Trees & small amount off-piste

FREESTYLE
2 Terrain parks & halfpipe

PISTES
Well laid out trails

POOR FAIR GOOD TOP

A small fun resort offering something for all

7
OUT OF 10

pic · Mountain High Resort

U
S
A

C
A
L
I
F
O
R
N
I
A

Have you heard about the resort that although located in the southern reaches of **California** and only ninety minutes from **Los Angeles**, boasts at having five terrain parks, two half pipes, forty-seven named trails, twelve lifts and night riding seven days a week over seventeen flood lit slopes? No? Well let me introduce to you **Mountain High**, a no nonsense resort with riding over two mountain areas with a summit of over 2499 metres. By no means is this a big resort, indeed Mountain High is relatively small when compared to the likes of its more northern neighbour **Mammoth Mountain**. However, unlike Mammoth Mountain this place is far less over-hyped, far less crowded and a lot more affordable. There may only be just over 200 acres of ridable terrain, but as the saying goes, 'size doesn't always matter, it's what you do with the size that counts.

And to be fair, Mountain High does very nicely with what it has with tow mountain areas covered in tight trees and offering a good selection of well laid out trails. The **East Resort** mountain has the highest summit elevation of 2499 metres but the smallest selection of trails, while the **West Resort** has the largest selection of trails. Both mountain areas have terrain parks and halfpipes however, the two areas are not connected by mountain lifts and you can't ride between the two, instead you will need to take the resort shuttle bus to reach either. They have been doing things here on the mountains since 1937 so in that time the management have learnt a thing or two. Along with standard tickets they operate lift ticket schemes such as the Flexi ticket system where you buy a pass for a certain number of hours or the Point system which is a system

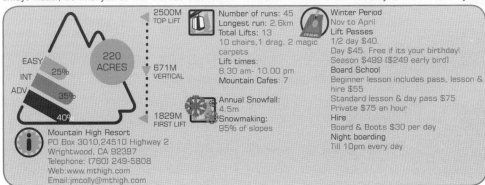

2500M TOP LIFT

EASY
INT
ADV

220 ACRES

25%
35%
40%

671M VERTICAL

1829M FIRST LIFT

Number of runs: 45
Longest run: 2.6km
Total Lifts: 13
10 chairs, 1 drag, 2 magic carpets
Lift times:
8.30 am- 10.00 pm
Mountain Cafes: 7

Annual Snowfall:
4.5m
Snowmaking:
95% of slopes

Winter Period
Nov to April
Lift Passes
1/2 day $40.
Day $45. Free if its your birthday!
Season $499 ($249 early bird)
Board School
Beginner lesson includes pass, lesson & hire $55
Standard lesson & day pass $75
Private $75 an hour
Hire
Board & Boots $30 per day
Night boarding
Till 10pm every day

Mountain High Resort
PO Box 3010,24510 Highway 2
Wrightwood, CA 92397
Telephone: (760) 249-5808
Web:www.mthigh.com
Email:jmcolly@mthigh.com

East Resort
El 8,200'

West Resort
El 8,000'

East Base

West Base

U
S
A

C
A
L
I
F
O
R
N
I
A

FREESTYLERS are extremely well looked after here with choice of five terrain parks and two halfpipes as well as loads of natural hits from which to get air from. The terrain parks, which are sponsored by Vans are spread across both mountains and known as the **Faultline**. Two of the parks are for beginners while both half pipes have their own drags lifts.

PISTES. Riders will find that the **East Resort** offers some of the best cruising with a good selection of runs from the top.

where you buy points that let you ride whenever you want throughout the season. You can even transfer the points to a friend.

FREERIDERS will no doubt find the slopes on the East Resort to there liking, especially the **Olympic Bowl** which is a double black diamond stretch. On the West Resort there are a number of nice trails to check out with lots of trees and some fine steeps. The runs off the **Inferno Ridge** are particularly good as is the **Vertigo**. For those who like to take it easy then the Upper and Lower **Chisolm trails** are first class trails.

BEGINNERS should like Mountain High with a nice selection of gentle slopes laid out at the base areas with the best runs on the **West Mountain** off the **Coyote** and **Roadrunner** lifts.

THE TOWN
Off the slopes things are somewhat different and not what you would totally expect. The resort itself, doesn't own or provide any slope linking accommodation or provide a multi complex resort with all the normal holiday attractions. Around the base areas are a few sport shops and snowboard hire outlets and cafeterias, but that's about it. However, Mountain High is located next to the town of Wrightwood which provides a host of local facilities from lodges to bed and breakfast joints. Los Angeles is only 90 minutes away so you could even base yourself there or at any one of the many towns en route. Where you eat depends basically on where you decided to stay. Most lodges and hotels in the area have restaurants or are close to one. There are also loads of fast food joints to seek out all the way back to Los Angeles.
Nightlife and other evening entertainments vary from place to place, but basically things in Wrightwood are laid back and not very exciting while Los Angeles rocks big style and offers millions of things to do.

pic - Mountain High Resort

CAR
From LA, take Interstate 10, Freeway 60 or 210 freeway south. Exit Highway 138 West, take left onto Highway 2, resort 3 miles past Wrightwood. Approx 90mins total
FLY
to Ontario airport with a transfer time to the resort of 45 minutes, also 90mins from LA
BUS
from Ontario airport takes around 45 mins to Mountain High. Buses from Los Angeles take around 90 hours and from Orange County the time is 75 minutes.

POOR FAIR GOOD TOP

FREERIDE
Trees & some off-piste
FREESTYLE
4 terrain parks & halfpipe
PISTES
lots of bumpy gladed runs

Okay freestylers place

6
OUT OF 10

pic - Sierra at Tahoe Reesort

PISTES. Riders who look only for perfectly flat, bump less slopes may not be too impressed. This is not a resort that can lay claim to having lots of great piste on which to lay some fast turns. In general the terrain is a little unforgiving. However, there is some quite good riding to be had on the **West Bowl** Slopes where carvers can show off in style and at speed.

BEGINNERS will find plenty of easy slopes, with the chance of riding from the summit down the green **Sugar 'n' Spice** trail. Other cool novice trails are off **Rock Garden** and **Nob Hill** lifts. **Broadway**, located at the base area, is good for the total beginner and it even has its own beginner chair so you won't have to suffer the embarrassment of continually falling off a drag lift.

Sierra-at-Tahoe is located south-west of **Lake Tahoe** and is one of the lesser known or visited resorts in the Lake Tahoe Region. This means that the 2,000 acres of freeriding and freestyle terrain is left relatively crowd-free. 46 trails cut through thick trees that spread out over three areas, offering excellent snowboarding for all abilities, but mainly favouring intermediates. Advanced riders are provided with some very challenging riding on a number of good black trails, especially those found under the **Grand View Express**.

FREERIDERS who get their fix by shredding trees will love this resort. Sierra is covered with tight trees that will rip you apart if you drop down the wrong line. However, much of the area is rated as intermediate standard.

FREESTYLERS will find this mountain a bit of a gem but instead of having one mail park, theres lots of smaller parks dotted over the mountain depending on the conditions. The main park is on **Broadway**, but don't forget Upper Main, The Alley and Bashful, and theres a beginners park on Smokey. Hey and don't forget **Pipeline** which is a long, well looked after superpipe. For those who like their hits to come naturally, you will find plenty of banks and big walls to ride, especially where snow banks up alongside the trees.

THE TOWN. There is some basic slopeside accommodation, but for the best local happenings and night-life, head back down to the **South Lake Tahoe** area, only 12 miles away. Get the free shuttle bus if you don't have car. Around town you will find every thing you could possibly want to make your stay a worth while one.

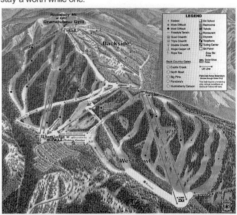

U
S
A

C
A
L
I
F
O
R
N
I
A

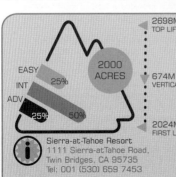

2698M
TOP LIFT

674M
VERTICAL

2024M
FIRST LIFT

EASY
25%
INT
25% 50%
ADV

2000
ACRES

Sierra-at-Tahoe Resort
1111 Sierra-atTahoe Road,
Twin Bridges, CA 95735
Tel: 001 (530) 659 7453

Web:www. sierratahoe.com
Email:sierra@boothcreek.com

Number of runs: 46
Longest run: 4km
Total Lifts:
9 Chairs, 1 magic carpet
Lift times: 8.30am to 4.00pm
Lift Capacity (people per hour)
14,920
Mountain cafes: 2

Winter Period:
Nov to April
Lift Passes
Half day $49, 1 Day pass - $59
3 Days $117, Season pass - $689
(unlimited Northstar & Sierra)
Board Schools
Burton LTR centre - $74 for 2hr
lesson package or $40 for just the
2hr lesson.
private $90/285 hour/day
Hire
board and boots $34 per day

Annual Snowfall:
12.2m
Snowmaking:
20% of slopes

Bus
from Reno to South Lake
Tahoe.
Fly
to Reno, with a transfer time
of around 2hrs. San Francisco
airport approx 3 1/2hrs away.
Drive
From Reno, take I-395 south
through Carson City to US
Highway 50 west over Echo
Summit and turn left onto
Sierra-at-Tahoe Road. 1 3/4hrs,
78miles

	POOR	FAIR	GOOD	TOP
FREERIDE Trees & some extreme off-piste				
FREESTYLE 2 parks & halfpipe				
PISTES good go anywhere runs				

9 OUT OF 10

pics - Squaw Resort

Squaw Valley is full-on and has been snowboard-friendly for many years. Squaw is a total snowboarder's resort in every sense and is one of the best known in the **Tahoe** area. With its European-alpine feel, and its history in hosting the 1960 Winter Olympics, Squaw is well used to looking after its visitors, with a substantial mountain on which to do so. 4000 acres of open bowl riding, 6 peaks, 30 lifts, a total capacity of 49,500 people per hour, 3 fun-parks and a halfpipe, combined with an average of 450 inches of snow a year (with massive amounts of snowmaking too), makes Squaw a great riders' hangout. Countless snowboard action videos feature the slopes of Squaw and it's easy to see why. Located a stone's throw from its neighbour **Alpine Meadows**, Squaw has heaps of

terrain for all styles of rider to conquer - steeps, trees, long chutes, as well as easy flats for novices. Like many of the resorts in the Tahoe region, Squaw serves the weekend city dweller. Don't despair though as the slopes can still be fairly quiet during the week-days leaving plenty of powder and open runs to shred.

FREESTYLERS have been able to ride Squaw's excellent halfpipes and parks for a good number of years. The **Central Park** fun-park features many obstacles to catch air and is one the best kept terrain parks in the US. The halfpipe is shaped with a Pipe Dragon and has perfectly cut walls that most resorts only dream about. You can also ride the park and pipe at night until 9 pm. Squaw also has a fast Boarder Cross circuit. **Belmont Park** is the place for novice freestylers while the Ford Freestyle Superpipe & Terrain Park has hits and a 550foot pipe!

FREERIDERS wanting an adrenalin rush will be able to get it in an area known as the **KT22**. This particular area is rated double expert, and it's for no mean reason. Lose it up here and its all over - your own dear mother wouldn't even recognise your body, so be warned. Powder-seekers will find some nice offerings around **Headwall**, or over at **Granite Chief** which is a black graded area (not for wimps) with well spread out trees.

piste-PISTES. loving freeriders, will not want to leave the amazingly well groomed slopes at Squaw. The runs off Squaw and Siberia Express are superb for laying big edged turns and can be tackled by all levels. Gold Coast is a long trail that will leave you breathless if do it in one.

BEGINNERS have a great resort to start mastering the art of staying upright. Much of the novice terrain is to be found at the base area, while the bulk of easy trails are located further up the slopes and reached off Super Gondola or the cable car. Once up, the smattering of greens and blues are serviced by a number of chair lifts, so you can avoid the T-bars during the early stages of snowboarding.

U S A   C A L I F O R N I A

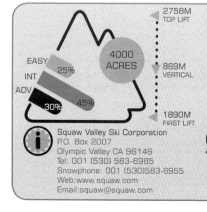

EASY
INT
ADV
25%
30%
45%

4000 ACRES

2758M TOP LIFT
869M VERTICAL
1890M FIRST LIFT

Squaw Valley Ski Corporation
P.O. Box 2007
Olympic Valley CA 96146
Tel: 001 (530) 583-6985
Snowphone: 001 (530)583-6955
Web:www.squaw.com
Email:squaw@squaw.com

Number of runs: 100
Longest run: 4.8km
Total Lifts: 33
2 Gondolas, 1 cable-car, 35 chairs, 4 drags, 1 Magic carpet
Lift capacity (people per hour): 49,500
Lift times: 8.30am to 9.00pm
Mountain Cafes: 3

Annual Snowfall: 11m
Snowmaking: 50% of slopes

Winter Period:
Nov to May
Lift Passes
1 Day pass - $62
1/2 day $45
Night pass - $20,
2 Days $108, 5 Days $256
Season pass - $1,495
with 1 day and afternoon pass you get free night boarding
Board Schools
group $43/2hr
private $90/hr
Hire
board & boots $37/day, 5 days/$148
Night Boarding
4pm-9pm, costs $20. Pipe & lit

THE TOWN

Away from the slopes, Squaw has gained a reputation of being both expensive and a bit snobbish, and in both cases, it's true. But don't be put off as the place has a good buzz about it, and the locals are really friendly. Lodging, feeding, partying and all other local services are convenient for the slopes. The village packs in a raft of activities with ice skating, climbing walls and a games hall. Getting around is easy, although having a car would allow you to travel around at your own leisure.

Food. Like any dollar-hungry mountain resort, expect to notch up some mileage on the credit card. Even a burger can set you back a small fortune. But as there are so many eating options, even the tightest of tight riders will be able to grab some affordable scram.

Night-life is aimed at the rich, so if you find that Squaw's local offerings are not your style, then try out the far more extensive facilities on offer in nearby **Truckee** or **Tahoe City** where you'll find the best night spots and local talent. You can either drive down, or catch a bus or taxi. Check out *Red Dog* or *Naughty bar*.

Accommodation is offered with a number of places close to the slopes. But it will cost you. Condo's are plentiful and well equipped, but not all affordable. For a cheap and comfortable place to stay, check out the *Youth Hostel* - it has bunks at happy prices but bring your own sleeping bag. Check Squaws web site for the latest deals.

CAR
42 miles from Reno, NV, 96 miles from Sacramento, and 196 miles from San Francisco via Interstate 80. Resort is 8 miles from Truckee and 6 miles from Tahoe City and the North Shore of Lake Tahoe, on Hwy 89
FLY
to Reno International (42miles), transfer time to resort is 1 hour
TRAIN
Amtrak to Truckee, 6 miles away
BUS
from Reno takes around 1 hour. A Grey Hound bus from San Francisco takes 5 hours via Tahoe City, 6 miles away. Local service runs between Truckee/Tahoe to Squaw. Call (530) 550-1212

wsg SUGAR BOWL

	POOR	FAIR	GOOD	TOP
FREERIDE Trees & some good off-piste				
FREESTYLE 3 Terrain parks & halfpipe				
PISTES Some okay slopes				

Mickey Mouse it isn't

6 OUT OF 10

Sugar Bowl has numerous points that it likes to draw to people's attention, such as the fact that it is one of the oldest resorts in **California** and was fathered by no less than **Walt Disney** 60 years ago. However, don't be alarmed; Donald Duck and Mickey Mouse are nowhere to be seen, although many of the skiers here are a right bunch of Dumbos. Sugar Bowl is a nice little gem of a place that should keep you amused for a few days, but it should be pointed out that this place can become a little crowded over holiday periods etc. The terrain is evenly split over three main areas that are connected, **Lincoln, Mt Judah**, and **Mt Disney**. Lincoln and Mt Disney offer some of the most testing runs with a cool selection of black trails and a couple of double black diamonds. Mt Judah has the most sedate terrain and best for beginners and intermediates. The resort offers base facilities where you can get snowboard hire.

FREERIDERS will be pleased with Sugar's nice offering of trees, back bowls and morning powder trails. The black runs on **Mt Disney** will sort out the wimps from the men, with some very challenging trails especially the area off the **Silver Belt** chair lift where you will find a steep cliff section.

FREESTYLERS are more than welcome here and have full access to all three areas. From the top of the Mt.Judah lift you can access the Coldstream Terrain Park then the huge Golden Gate park. They are littered with tables, quarters, kickers and numerous rails and boxes for the jibbers. The Nob Hill Park is great for beginners and has a few rollers and boxes. The x-games/FIS standard superpipe's located at the bottom the Lincoln express, and is usually in fine condition.

PISTES. Most of the runs are fairly short and can be a little uneven, but that said Sugar Bowl is still okay with a few good cruising trails.

BEGINNERS will find that the best laid out easy terrain is available on **Mt Judah**, which has a particularly good easy section for novices to shine on. The section of the **Christmas tree** chair is also noted for being a good easy area.

THE TOWN
Off the slopes there is some very limited accommodation in the base lodge, which houses a hotel and can be reached via the gondola. However, the best option and biggest choice of local services can be found in the nearby town of **Truckee** which is only 10 miles away.

U S A C A L I F O R N I A

EASY 17% INT ADV 43% 40%	**2083 ACRES**	

2555M TOP LIFT

457M VERTICAL

2083M FIRST LIFT

Number of runs: 80
Longest run: 3 miles
Total Lifts: 13
1 gondola, 10 chairs, 2 drags
Lift times: 9am - 4pm

Winter Period:
Nov to April
Lift Passes
1/2 Day Pass - $35
Day Pass - $50
Season Pass - $900
Board Schools
private $90/hr
Hire
Boards & Boots from $39/day

Annual Snowfall:
12.7m
Snowmaking:
13% of slopes

Bus
from Reno to the resort. Bus pickups from San Fran area $99 inc lift pass visit www.bayareaskibus.com
Shuttles from Truckee to resort run every hour
Fly
to Reno, transfer time is 40 minutes.
Drive
From San Francisco - Take Bay Bridge to Interstate 80, head east toward Sacramento/Reno, exit at the Norden/Soda Springs off ramp. Turn right on Highway 40 eastbound, continue 3 miles

Sugar Bowl
629 Sugar Bowl Road
Norden, CA 95724
Phone: (530) 426-9000
Web:www.skisugarbowl.com
Email:info@sugarbowl.com

NEW New for 05/06 season
Christmas Tree Lift being replaced with a new highspeed quad chair. Mt. Judah Day Lodge being extended

ROUND-UP

BOREAL

Small resort, but has 5 terrain parks and a halfpipe. One of the parks is floodlit and open till 9pm every night

Ride area: 380 acres Number runs: 41

30% easy, 55% intermediate, 15% advanced

Total Lifts:9 chairs, 1 magic carpet

Lift pass:1/2 Day, $22 Day $36

Contact:

Tel: (530) 426-3666

www.borealski.com

How to get there: Truckee 8 miles, San Francisco 175 miles Reno 45 miles. On the I-80 take the Boreal / Castle Peak exit

HOMEWOOD

Number runs: 56

15% easy, 50% intermediate, 35% advanced

Total Lifts:8

Lift pass:1/2 Day, $32 Day $42

Contact:

www.skihomewood.com

Email:smile@skihomewood.com

How to get there: Nearest airport is the South Lake Tahoe airport that services Tahoe Air. The Reno Tahoe International airport has just a 1hr drive time

MT.ROSE

The nearest resort to the lively gambling den that is Reno. The ski-bus from Reno will have you on the slopes within an hour. There's been a lot of money put into this resort of late and there's now 2 good size terrain parks and 60 runs. They get around 10m of snow in a season, and theres a whole line of double D shoots to drop into.

Number runs: 60

20% easy, 30% intermediate, 50   % advanced

Top Lift: 2956m Bottom Lift: 2408m Vert: 549m

Total Lifts:7 - 6 chairs, 1 drag

Lift pass:1/2 Day, $42 Day $62

Contact: Mt. Rose - Ski Tahoe

22222 Mt. Rose Hwy

Reno, Nevada 89511

Tel: (775) 849-0704

How to get there: Fly to Reno, 25mins away by car, Located on Mt. Rose Hwy SR431 22 miles from Reno.

NORTH STAR

Northstar (piste map above)   opened its slopes to snowboarders in 1997 and its quickly become one of the most boarder friendly resorts. The terrain is awesome the amount of rails on offer is beyond. The vibe is so mellow it has been remarked as a little Whistler village. The resort is found on the north side of the lake and a few minutes from the old cowboy trading post Truckee. The resort is under going a big development project which will be complete very soon. Check out "Totally Board snowboard shop" for some bargains, you'll find the shop in truckee. Northstar is a resort not to be missed.

Freerider it's going to take you some time to cover all the 70 recognised routes. All the trails are cut through the trees so tree runs are a must. Don't expect any cliff drops or wide open bowls to bang in some big powder turns. The whole area is well covered with obstacles to please all standards.

Freestyle Northstar has a team of park staff who keep the 6 terrain parks in good order. The parks cater for everyone what ever the standard. So if you are planning to expand your book of trips into the rail chapter then head to Northstar, I lost count the amount of rails on offer. If you are into pipe riding the northstar has a well maintained 400 ft super pipe.

Beginners Northstar has an excellent starters pack with everything included in the price. The area also has some gentle terrain if you are starting out or shaking off the cob webs. If you ability is intermediate or advanced why not hook up to a free 75 min lesson which are held in the afternoon

Accommodation   with   the   new   development accommodation can be found, dead centre of the lifts or a few minutes away in Truckee

Ride area: 2420 acres Number runs: 70

25% easy, 50% intermediate, 25% advanced

Top Lift: 2624m Bottom Lift: 1929m Vert: 695m

Total Lifts:17 - 10 chairs, 6 drags, 1 tubing lift

Lift pass:1/2 Day, $47 Day $61

Contact: Northstar-at-Tahoe

P.O. Box 129, Truckee CA, 96160

Tel: 1-800-GO-NORTH

www.skinorthstar.com

How to get there: Fly to Reno, 45mins away

U
S
A

C
A
L
I
F
O
R
N
I
A

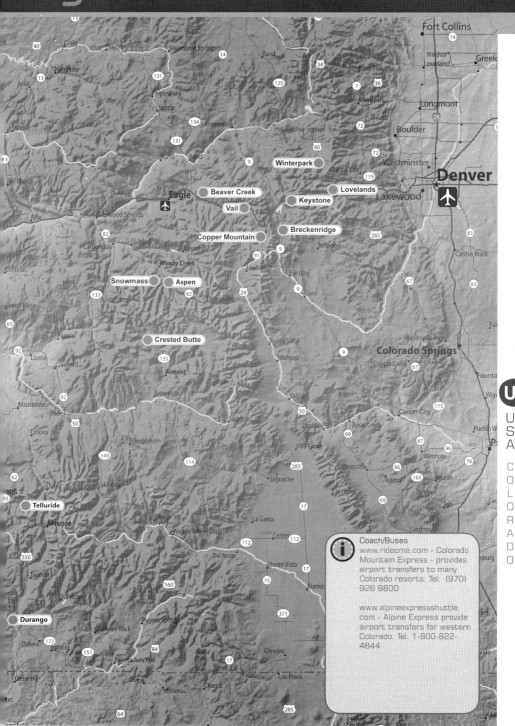

Coach/Buses
www.ridecme.com - Colorado Mountain Express - provides airport transfers to many Colorado resorts. Tel: (970) 926 9800

www.alpineexpresssshuttle.com - Alpine Express provide airport transfers for western Colorado. Tel: 1-800-822-4844

U
USA COLORADO

BEAVER CREEK

FREERIDE
Trees & good off-piste
FREESTYLE
4 Terrain parks & 2 halfpipes
PISTES
Imaculate gladed slopes

8 OUT OF 10

Good riders resort but not cheap

plc - Jack ... k Resort

Beaver Creek, a short distance from its more famous cousin **Vail**, has a classy and expensive reputation - an ex-US President even has a house here. But don't let that put you off as this is a resort that has come of age with a really healthy attitude towards snowboarding, as seen by the provision of so many snowboard services. Even some of the local riders give up their time to form what they call the

USA COLORADO

Snowboard Courtesy Patrol, which is a group of snowboarders that patrol the area's slopes to offer assistance and keep everyone in check. **Beaver Creek** is a relatively new resort, but unlike some old timers, it has managed to get things right. The well set out lift system is located on four areas, with runs that favour intermediate riders for the most part. The trails, which are cut through thick wooded areas, are shaped in a way that allows you to get around with ease, making riding here an ideal experience

FREERIDERS are presented with a series of slopes, covered in trees from top to bottom. If you like to ride hard and fast, then the double black diamonds on **Grouse Mountain** off the Grouse chair will satisfy you. Here you can drop down a line of four steep trails, where the longest, **Royal Elk,** sweeps in an arc through trees, whilst **Osprey** is the shorter of the four. Alternatively, the **Half Hitch** and single black trails found off the **Centennial** chair are less daunting, but just as much fun. If you prefer tree runs, make sure to check out the areas in the **Bachelor Gulch** & **Arrowhead Villages**. Enjoy established runs such as **Coyote Glade** and **Renegade**, or carve your own runs through the powder-filled trees in both Villages. To ride the best spots, hook up with a local snowboard guide.

FREESTYLERS will find plenty of big natural hits to float air. If you're a park rider, then head for any of the three parks Beaver Creek has to offer depending on your ability. For the 03/04 season, Beaver Creek introduced a new park system with it's "**Park-ology.**" The new system features three parks, beginning with **Park 101** for those new to the park that features rollers, dots and other terrain features that will allow lower level riders of all ages to learn. For intermediate park riders, **Zoom Room** features small rollers, tables and rails, and moves to progressively larger features and rails throughout. The most advanced park, **Moonshine,** is designed to be user friendly for intermediate to expert riders looking to improve their skills on a wide variety of features, including tables, hips, spines,

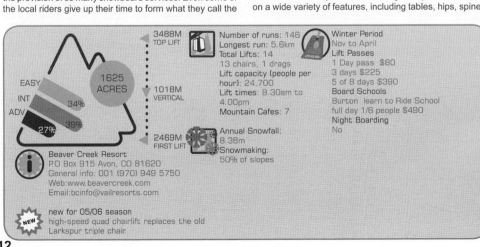

3488M TOP LIFT
1018M VERTICAL
2469M FIRST LIFT

1625 ACRES

EASY
INT 34%
ADV 39%
27%

Number of runs: 146
Longest run: 5.6km
Total Lifts: 14
13 chairs, 1 drags
Lift capacity (people per hour): 24,700
Lift times: 8.30am to 4.00pm
Mountain Cafes: 7

Annual Snowfall: 8.38m
Snowmaking: 50% of slopes

Winter Period
Nov to April
Lift Passes
1 Day pass $80
3 days $225
5 of 8 days $390
Board Schools
Burton learn to Ride School full day 1/6 people $490
Night Boarding
No

Beaver Creek Resort
PO Box 915 Avon, CO 81620
General info: 001 (970) 949 5750
Web:www.beavercreek.com
Email:bcinfo@vailresorts.com

NEW new for 05/06 season
high-speed quad chairlift replaces the old Larkspur triple chair

412

pic - Jack Affleck/Beaver Creek Resort

Snowboard Shop at 001 (970) 845- 8969

Accomodation. There are no real cheap options for lodging in Beaver - in short, prices start at silly and go up to downright criminal. There are plenty of beds with many close to the slopes, but for budget riders, you are better looking for somewhere to kip in the small, nearby hamlet of Avon.

Food. If your sole reason for visiting Beaver is the food, you will find a variety of mostly costly, but good restaurants to choose from. Vegetarians, vegans, or monster meat lovers will find their every desire well catered for from one end of the village to the other. The Coyote Cafe, which is near the lift ticket office, is noted for good food at okay prices. Other good eateries to try, are The Saddleridge, the Mirabelle or On The Fly for great sandwiches.

Night-life: put simply, is dull and basically non-existent. The bars cater in the main for rich ski-types in expensive cowboy boots, who prefer to sit around log fires talking bull. However, the Coyote Cafe is good and worth a visit for a few beers. The best thing to do is head for **Vail** - but remember to have plenty of dollars on you.

rails, logslides and half-pipe.

PISTE riders are well catered for here with many good trails. Edge-to-edge stylers are attracted by the extremely well groomed trails that descend from all areas of the resort, which twist and wind their way through the tree-lined trails. The **Centennial trail** is an extremely popular run that starts off at the top of the Centennial lift. Starting as a black run and descending into a more sedate blue down to the base area, it can be done in a short space of time if you can hang on at the start.

BEGINNERS will find the best easy trails are to be found at the top of the **Cinch Express** Lift. To get down from the beginner area, take the Cinch green run back to the village. A nice touch at Beaver Creek is the kid's fun-park, **Chaos Canyon** Adventure Zone, which has a series of small hits. Riders who have never been on a snowboard will learn quickly if they visit the local snowboard school, which has a high reputation. Burton runs a learn to ride Method Center here.

THE TOWN

Beaver Creek is a major in terms of dullness. However, the village is a laid back place and locals are very friendly. Beaver is a much quieter hangout than nearby Vail, which may be why the place attracts nice family groups that walk around holding hands and smiling as they go. The resort offers all the normal **Colorado** tourist attractions from hot air baloon rides to sleigh rides and an attraction called the Adventure Ridge. You can hire full snowboard equipment at Beaver or in Vail with prices much the same wherever you go, from around $35 a day. Check out the Otherside

U

S
A

C
O
L
O
R
A
D
O

pic - Jack Affleck/Beaver Creek Resort

CAR
Denver via Interstate 70. Beaver Creek = 120 miles. Drive time is about 2 1/4 hours. Exit Avon
FLY
Fly to Denver International. Transfer time to resort is 2 1/4 hours. Local airport is Eagle County, 10 miles away.
BUS
There are daily bus services from both Denver and Vail/Eagle County airports direct to Beaver Creek. visit www.airlinkshuttle.com for transport from Eagle county or tel: (800)-554-VAIL. Taxis (970) 476-8294

POOR FAIR GOOD TOP

FREERIDE
Trees & excellent off-piste
FREESTYLE
4 Terrain parks & 3 halfpipes
PISTES
Some great challenging slopes

Despite the price, a great resort

8
OUT OF 10

– Jack Affleck/Breckenridge Resort

snowboard. At the top of Chair 6, you'll find loads of good hits and drop offs, while lower down there are some wicked tree runs. You'll find good powder here, even after everywhere else has been tracked out. The **Imperial Bowl** on Peak 8 has over 1,000 metres of vert to tackle, and new for this season is a chair that'll take you to the top.

FREESTYLERS should have no reason to complain as apart from having some fantastic natural freestyle terrain, there are also four terrain parks and four pipes of competition standard. The latest addition to Breckenridge is what they call a 'Super Pipe Dragon', the only one in the US which can cut perfectly smooth deep walls. The **Lechman** trail is known for being one of the best natural freestyle runs on the mountain, with loads of hits formed from big wind-lips running down the sides of certain sections. Head for Peak 9 and you'll find the **Gold King** fun-park which is pretty awesome and well-maintained: there are some big, big jumps to go for and thankfully it's groomed at least twice a week, although it does gets icy. There is also a halfpipe, located just above the park, which is shaped with the Pipe Dragon every Thursday and is therefore closed on that day. However, when it's re-opened on Friday mornings, it's perfect - but get up early because everyone wants to get there first. Peak 8 is home to another park and pipe on the **Fairway** area.

PISTES. Riders have a mountain here that will allow for some very fast and challenging riding on well groomed alpine trails. Speed-freaks should try out the **Centennial trail,** which is a long flat and perfect for cranking out some big turns. Intermediates will find the runs off Peak 10 the place to be, in particular the **Crystal.**

BEGINNERS have plenty of easy runs, many of which can be found on Peaks 8 and 9. The fact that novice trails like **Silverthorne** are wide enough for all newcomers helps to make this a great beginners' resort, especially around the **Quicksilver** lift.

THE TOWN
As with many of Colorado's resorts, **Breckenridge** can be

Breckenridge is a true snowboard classic, and has been for many years, having played a leading role in the development of snowboarding in the US. The resort is constantly improving by adding new features to the mountain and around town. Located off Interstate 70, to the west of **Denver** and part of the **Ten Mile Range**, Breckenridge is a big and impressive area with terrain that spreads over four excellent snowboarding peaks, all offering something different for everyone. Some say that the 'new school' style of snowboarding started here, but whether you're from the new or the old, you should have no problems cutting big turns on the mainly wide, open flats

FREERIDERS with their powder-searching heads on will not have to hunt for long when they see what's available in the Back Bowls off **Peak 8** and off **Peak 9**'s North Face. Here you'll find plenty of terrain for riders who know how to

U
S
A

C
O
L
O
R
A
D
O

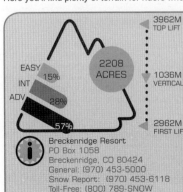

EASY 15%
INT
ADV 28%
57%

2208 ACRES

3962M
TOP LIFT

1036M
VERTICAL

2962M
FIRST LIFT

Number of runs: 146
Longest run: 5.6km
Total Lifts: 27
15 chairs, 5 drags, 7 Magic carpet
Lift capacity (people per hour): 36,680
Lift times: 8.30am to 4.00pm
Mountain Cafes: 9

Annual Snowfall: 7.5m
Snowmaking: 25% of slopes

i Breckenridge Resort
PO Box 1058
Breckenridge, CO 80424
General: (970) 453-5000
Snow Report: (970) 453-6118
Toll-Free: (800) 789-SNOW
Web:www.breckenridge.com
Email:breckguest@vailresorts.com

Winter Period
End Nov to end April
Lift Passes
1 Day $45-75 (low to high season)
3 Day pass - $135-225
5 of 8 days $225-375
Board Schools
3 days of lessons from $165 with beginers lift pass for $11/day
park and pipe lasson $60/75
Night Boarding
No

new for 05/06 season
new quad chairlift to the top of Peak 8. At 3913m it claims to be the highest lift in N.America. The Imperial Express provides access to 400 acres of terrain that you used to had to hike 45mins to get to.

uncomfortably expensive. However, for riders on a tight budget, providing you shop around for accommodation and other local services, you will be able to stay here. The town is spread out, and has a rustic wild west feel about it. You can spend until you drop here with a staggering 225 plus shops, including a number of good outlets for snowboard hire with the option to rent demo boards and step-in set. Other attractions include a new 5 million dollar ice ring and a cool area for skateboarders to do their thing.

Accommodation options are vast with some 23,000 visitor beds up for grabs. Those on a tight budget will manage to find a cheap B&B, while those wanting some luxury will be able to chill out in a lodge or classy hotel. Breckenridge Mountain Lodge is an okay and affordable place. The Great Divide Lodge is an expensive alternative.

Food, Around town you will find a massive selection of good restaurants and fast food joints ranging from cheap to steep with over 100 places to choose from. Breakfast is dished up in numerous places. The *Prospect* does a nice sunny side up as does the *Mountain Lodge Cafe* . Veggies should head to *Noodle & Bean* for the very same, while meat lovers may want to try a grill at '*Breckenridge Cattle Co*' which is also noted for its fish food.

Night-life is pretty good and rocks until late. There's plenty of beer, dancing and fine local talent to check out, including four main nightclubs and some 80 ood bars. Head to the *Underworld Club*, or *Jake T Pounders* which is young, trendy, fun and one of the main hangouts that has darts, football and pool tables. *Eric's* is another cool hangout.

SUMMARY
Despite being an expensive location, this is a super good resort with great snowboard terrain, and excellent local services.

pic - Jack Affleck/Brekenridge Resort

U S A   C O L O R A D O

CAR
Denver via Interstate 70 & Hwy 9. Breckenridge is 81 miles. Drive time is about 1 1/2 hours.
FLY
Fly to Denver International, Transfer time to resort is 1 1/2 hours. Local airport is Eagle Airport (Vail). 63 Miles away.
BUS
Colorado Mountain Express run bus services from both Denver and Vail/Eagle County airports direct to Breckenridge. Taxis - (970) 468-2266

415

POOR FAIR GOOD TOP

FREERIDE
Trees & great off-piste
FREESTYLE
3 Terrain parks & halfpipe
PISTES
Groomed to perfection

One of Colorado's best resorts

9
OUT OF 10

pics - Copper Mtn Resort

U
S
A

C
O
L
O
R
A
D
O

Most of the main chairs take around ten minutes to reach their drop off points, although it seems double that time when you're dangling hundreds of feet in the air, with wind driving snow up your nose and down your neck. Still, the lifts are modern and connect well with the runs. Once you get to the top of each run, you will not regret the chair ride as you are presented with a mountain that is lovingly pisted, and well marked out and will make for a great time.

FREERIDERS, welcome to sex on snow! Copper has it all for you. Powder, deep bowls and trees all on offer from expert double blacks to tame piste trails. Take the Flyer chair to reach the Flyer area where you will find a series of blue runs that cut through trees. Alternatively ride the **Sierra lift** to get a powder fix. More advanced riders should take **Lift E** to take on a cluster of short blacks. These are perfect for freeriders, especially the **Union Bowl**. If you keep right off the E-lift, you hit some decent trees. Intermediate freeriders will find plenty to interest them on the run known as **Andy's Encore,** reached off the B-1 chair.

FREESTYLERS have a great mountain to explore with great natural terrain and numerous parks that always make it onto the top ten lists of best parks in N.America. The main park **Catalyst** is located on the Loverly trail and features 3 separate ability lines. The beginner line has a series of rollers and simple rails, for the expert line we're talking huge tabletops, spines and a quarterpipe. At the bottom of the park is the competition 130m superpipe. Junior grommets have their own park and they've added a special floodlit jib park near the base. Natural terrain seekers should find **Union** and **Spaulding Bowls** the areas to check out for wind-lips, rock jumps and hits galore. Copper has a programme called the Team. If you volunteer to help look after the park and pipe, you will get a free season pass. tel 001 970 968 2318 for details.

Copper Mountain is considered by many to be one of the best mountains in the USA and since being bought by Intrawest Resorts, the whole place has seen heavy investment to greatly improve a place that was good before. Copper's crowd free slopes with long trails and few traverses appeal to tree-riding fans, and those looking for something interesting to tackle. Powder is in abundance here with four big bowls holding massive amounts of it.

PISTE riders will find that this is definitely a place for them, with plenty of advanced and intermediate wide open trails to choose from. Trails are groomed to perfection and runs

3767M
TOP LIFT

2433
ACRES

EASY
INT   21%
ADV   25%
          54%

793M
VERTICAL

2926M
FIRST LIFT

Number of runs: 125
Longest run: 5km
Total Lifts: 21
15 chairs, 9 drags
Lift capacity (people per hour): 30,600
Lift times: 8.30am to 3:30pm
Mountain Cafes: 2

Annual Snowfall:
7.1m
Snowmaking:
15% of slopes

Copper Mountain Resort
PO Box 3001 (USPS)
209 Ten Mile Circle (FedEx, UPS)
Copper Mountain, CO 80443
Tel: 866-841-2481
Web:www.ride-copper.com

Winter Period
Nov to April
Lift Passes
1 Day pass - $49-69 (early to regular season)
Half-day $44-$50
5 Day pass - $225
Season pass - $1000
Board Schools
Various beginner, progression, park & freeride lesson packages available
Hire
Board & Boots package $37/day
Heliboarding
Yes
Night Boarding
Friday & Saturdays open till 9pm, the jib park is floodlit

like **Bittersweet** are a speed demons dream

BEGINNERS who come here won't be disappointed. Copper has more than sufficient areas for learning the basics and progressing onwards. There are plenty of easy green trails. The tree-lined runs of the American Flyer Quad are a real joy. The flats of K and L lifts are also perfect for first timers.

THE TOWN
Copper Mountain is very much a snowboard-friendly place and the locals will make your stay a good one. However, **Copper** has the usual pitfalls of many Colorado resorts -

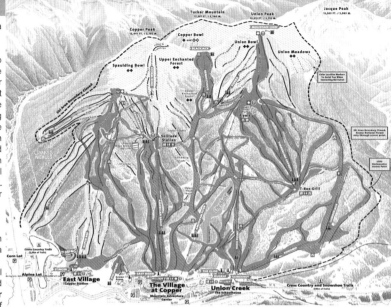

it can be painfully expensive. But if you're a good scammer, you can stay here on a low budget if you put yourself about and get to know the locals. The resort facilities are very good and un-like many resorts, Copper isn't overloaded with dozens of soppy tourist shops, but rather a need to have selection. There is also a sports centre a swimming pool and gym.

Accommodation in Copper offers slopeside beds, but prices range enormously from $20 up to $800 a night. Staying in nearby Dillon or Frisco would be a good alternative if you're on a tight budget , both have a good selection of cheaper accommodation. For all your lodging needs, contact Copper Mountain Lodging Services.

Food. The menus on offer here are perfect for the holiday crowds, but nothing comes cheap - a burger and a coke at Copper Commons is about $6. Still, Farley's does do an affordable steak, while O'Shea's serves up killer breakfasts at very reasonable prices. Pesce

Fresco's is another noted eatery with a big menu to choose from. However, for a burger and other light snacks, check out the B-Lift Pub, a favourite with locals and visitors alike.

Night-life around Copper is somewhat tame. The main hang outs being B-Lift Pub, O'Shea's and Farleys. However, the better option for a night out drinking or pulling a local bit of skirt, is in nearby Breckenridge or Vail. The choice of bars is much better, but unless you're 21+, and have ID to prove it, you're going to be seriously bored.

U
S
A

C
O
L
O
R
A
D
O

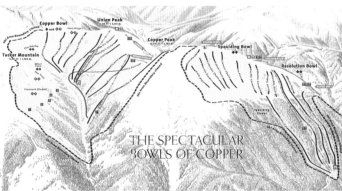

THE SPECTACULAR BOWLS OF COPPER

CAR
Denver via Interstate 70, Copper Mountain is 78 miles, drive time is about 1 1/2 hours.
FLY
Fly to Denver International Transfer time to resort 1 1/2 hours. Local airport is Eagle County, 20 miles away.
BUS
Colorado Mountain Express run transfers from Denver airport to resort every 90 minutes. Price is $108 return and takes 2 hours. Call 970-241-1822 for details

CRESTED BUTTE

FREERIDE
Trees & good off-piste
FREESTYLE
Terrain park
PISTES
Not always groomed

The dog's balls for backcountry riding

8
OUT OF 10

All Pics - Joseph Rehana

Butte's extreme terrain, you are strongly advised to get a copy of the **Extreme Limits Guide**, which is a separate lift and trail guide, pinpointing how and where to ride. Ignore its advice, and you may not live to regret it. However, don't simply read the guide and head off, you **MUST also seek the services of a local snowboard or ski guide** as well.

FREESTYLERS will find that a two week stay would still not be enough time to check out all the natural options for going airborn. Check out Crested Butte's gnarly fun-park, which has rails, logs, table-tops, quarter-pipes and is also skier-free. To get to the park, take the Silver Queen or Keystone lift.

Crested Butte is one of Colorado's ex-mining haunts and well worth a visit. It has gained a good reputation as a snowboard-friendly resort, but is best known for is its extreme and hard core terrain. Indeed, you could call this place the extreme frorider's heaven in the USA, as it has successfully staged several US Extreme Snowboarding Championships. The resort was bought in 2004 by the Muellers who also own **Okemo Mountain Resort** in Vermont. They are planning some huge investments in the resort, with the long term aim to expand terrain to nearby **Snodgrass Mountain**. Crested Butte easily offers some of the most challenging snowboarding in America. What you get is a serious mountain for serious riders, and not your typical dollar-hungry **Colorado** destination. If you like your mountain high with steeps, couloirs, trees, major off-piste in big bowls, then Crested Butte is for you. With 88 runs, spread over 1000 acres, no-one needs to feel left out, on crowd-free slopes, with a good average snow record.

FREERIDERS are in command here, with much of the terrain best suited to riders who know how to handle a board and prefer off-piste. Extreme Limits is a gnarly, un-pisted heaven for extreme lovers wanting big hits and steeps. Check out **Headwall** and **North Face** for some serious double black diamond trails, offering cliffs, couloirs and trees. In order to stay safe and appreciate Crested

PISTES. Riders who choose a resort because of its motorway-wide, perfectly groomed slopes without a bump in sight, may feel a bit left out, but not too disappointed. You can still carve hard on a number of selected trails. For a fast trail, give **Ruby** a try, or check out the flats on the **Paradise Bowl.**

BEGINNERS cutting their first runs would do best to ride on the lower slopes near the village, before trying out **Poverty** or **Mineral Point** off the Keystone lift. There are

U
S
A

C
O
L
O
R
A
D
O

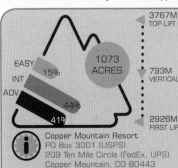

3767M TOP LIFT	Number of runs: 88
	Longest run: 4.2km
	Total Lifts: 15
	10 chairs, 3 drags, 2 Magic carpets
EASY 15%	Lift capacity (people per hour): 19,160
1073 ACRES	Lift times: 9:00 a.m. – 4:00 p.m
INT	Mountain Cafes: 5
ADV 44%	793M VERTICAL
41%	
	2926M FIRST LIFT

Winter Period
Mid Nov to end April
Lift Passes
Half-day $52
1 day $69
5 of 7 days $315
Season $739-1109
Board Schools
Private lesson $225for 2hrs. Varrious 2hr group workshops around $80 for beginners to advanced.
Beginners day package inc lift pass & 5hr lesson $115
Hire
Board & boots $23.40 per day. Top demo kit available for $32.40 per day

Annual Snowfall:
6.1m
Snowmaking:
30% of slopes

Copper Mountain Resort
PO Box 3001 (USPS)
209 Ten Mile Circle (FedEx, UPS)
Copper Mountain, CO 80443
Tel: 866-841-2481
Web:www.ride-copper.com

NEW new for 05/06 season
Carrying on from last season, this season sees a new quad chair replaces the t-bar. New base village and groomers, and various improvements to the resort in general.

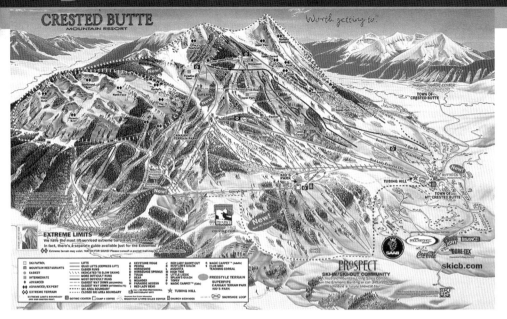

CRESTED BUTTE MOUNTAIN RESORT

Worth getting to.

EXTREME LIMITS
We have the most lift-serviced extreme terrain on the continent. In fact, there's a separate guide available just for the Extreme!

skicb.com

PROSPECT
SKI-IN/SKI-OUT COMMUNITY

a number of green runs to tackle before trying some of the easy connecting blues. The runs off **Gold Link** lift are pretty cool and worth a go. A beginners learn to snowboard programme with lift, lessons and hire, costs from around $80.

THE TOWN
Visitors coming here expecting to find the all too often horrible Colorado-style, glitzy ski-tourist trap, will be pleased to note that **Crested Butte** is none of that. This is a friendly and welcoming place with services located at the base area or in the old town, a short bus journey away. Wherever you stay, there is plenty to keep you entertained at prices that don't always hurt. Local facilities include basic sporting outlets, a swimming pool, a gym, and an ice rink. There is also a cinema with the latest movies on show. But note, this is not a place loaded with attractions, but more of a place where you can sit back and relax without being over pampered. Colorado Boarders Shop is the place for hire and snowboard sales.

Accommodation is available at the slopes or in the old town, and together they can sleep 5,000 visitors in a choice of condos, hotels and B&B's. Prices vary, with rates as low as $25 a night in a B&B, or as high as $300 in a fancy hotel. The nearer you stay to the slopes, the more costly things are, making the old town the cheapest option.
Food. Fatties on a mission to eat fast, hard and cheaply, welcome - you have arrived in heaven. This place is littered with eateries in every price range. For a hearty breakfast,

there are a number of good places to visit such as *Forest Queen*, The *Woodstone Grill* or the *Timberline Cafe*, all three open early. Later on in the day, check out *Idle Spur* where they serve damn fine steaks cooked exactly to the way you like it.

Night-life comes with a cowboy theme without the flashiness or bright lights. You can drink in a relaxed atmosphere at a number of joints that go on until the early hours. *Talk of the Town* has a punkish reputation and worth a visit. The *Idle Spur* is another cool hang which offers a good selection of beers and often has live music.

U S A
C O L O R A D O

CAR
From Denver take Highway 285 south to Poncha Springs ,Highway 50 west to Gunnison , then Highway 135 north into Crested Butte, total 233 miles, drive time is about 6 1/2 hours.
FLY
Fly to Denver International, transfer time to resort is 6 1/2 hours. Local airport = Gunnison, 30 miles south.
BUS
Alpine Express run bus services from both Denver and Gunnison airports direct to Crested Butte.

POOR FAIR GOOD TOP

FREERIDE
Trees & some off-piste
FREESTYLE
2 terrain parks & halfpipe
PISTES
some good trails

Good resort for all

7
OUT OF 10

Durango Mountain Resort was formerly known has **Purgatory** and changed its name when it was taken over in 2000.
Its a fantastic place and one that doesn't come with all the razzamatazz and ponciness that many of **Colorado's** other resorts have. What's more, this place is not an over priced hunt designed for Dot.Com millionaires, this is a place where riders who like to ride hard and then relax with ease, can do so at resort that is friendly and extremely well set out. This can be said for both on and off the mountain and down town in Durango, which is 25 miles away. Although Durango is under new management, there has been a ski centre here for the past 36 years, and the future looks good for this place with a number of major developments taking place up on the slopes and down in the base village of Purgatory. On the slopes you have a surprisingly well laid out selection of runs that provide something for everyone with a good choice of advanced and excellent intermediate slopes.

FREERIDERS have a wonderful mountain to play on. A weeks visit won't be wasted here with a good selection of runs to choose from with some very fast descents through trees and some fine powder stashes to seek out. The runs located under and around the **Grizzly chair** lift are cool and will offer the advanced rider a good time. The **Bull Run** is especially good but be warned, the lower section is not for the faint hearted. For some less daunting descents try the runs off the **Hermosa** Quad. Snowcat boarding is a good option to find some great untracked lines.

FREESTYLERS have plenty to do here with a choice of terrain parks and halfpipes. **Paradise Terrain Park** has a 450ft half-pipe, hits, rails & drops. **Pitchfork Terrain Park** features hips, rails, table tops, gaps, big air hit.

THE PISTES here are ok and you have a series of cool cruising trails but in truth this place is more of a freerider's resort. Still, runs like the **Path of Peace** is a good intermediate cruising trail.

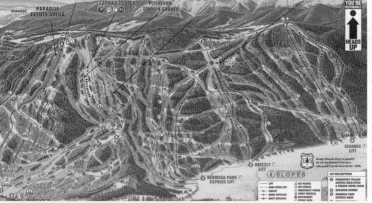

BEGINNERS can almost ride from the top to the bottom on a nice cluster of easy green trails reached off the Hermosda lift.

THE TOWN
If you wish to lodge close to the slopes, then theres 3,120 beds near the resort , but a cheaper bet is to head 25 miles over to **Durango**. Theres 7,000 beds there, as well as okay restaurants and bars.

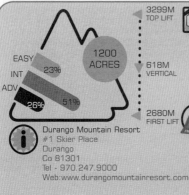

3299M
TOP LIFT

618M
VERTICAL

2680M
FIRST LIFT

EASY
INT 23%
ADV
26% 51%

1200
ACRES

Durango Mountain Resort
#1 Skier Place
Durango
Co 81301
Tel - 970.247.9000
Web:www.durangomountainresort.com

Number of runs: 86
Longest run: 3.2km
Total Lifts: 11
9 Chairs, 2 drags
Lift times: 8.30am to 4.00pm
Lift Capacity (people per hour): 15,600
Mountain cafes: 3

Winter Period:
Nov to April
Lift Passes
Day $55/59, 4 Days $200/216
Board Schools
Group $40 2.5 hours
Private lessons $140 for 2hrs, $300 all day.
Snowmobiles
$50 1 hour, $170 4 hours
Hire
board & boots $28/32 a day

Annual Snowfall:
6.6m
Snowmaking:
20% of slopes

Bus
from Denver but not direct.
Fly
American Airlines offers daily nonstop jet service from Dallas to Durango which means a one-stop connection from most anywhere in the country. Additionally, connecting flights into Durango are offered from Denver on United Express, from Phoenix on America West Express, and from Albuquerque on Rio Grande
Drive
30min drive from downtown Durango. Albuquerque is a 3 1/2 hour drive to the south, Denver is 6hrs northeast, and even Phoenix is an easy day's drive.

U
S
A
C
O
L
O
R
A
D
O

wsg KEYSTONE

Making a move on the rest of the Colorado resorts

POOR FAIR GOOD TOP

FREERIDE
Some trees & good backcountry
FREESTYLE
2 Terrain parks & halfpipe
PISTES
Well maintained slopes

7 OUT OF 10

pic - Tim Axe/Keystone Resort

Keystone has been a ski resort since 1970, but it was only in 1997 that the management finally allowed snowboarders to use their mountain. Since then Keystone seems to have embraced snowboarding whole-heartedly, with the recently revived terrain park (named **Area-51** after its 51 different features) proving their commitment to the sport. Keystone is owned by **Vail Resorts**, who also own Vail, Beaver Creek, Breckenridge and Heavenly - all these resorts offer a multi-area pass allowing additional access to the smaller resort of Arapahoe Basin. Having the only gondola access (2 of them actually) in Summit County, in addition to offering the county's only night-boarding area (15 lit trails including the park and pipe) Keystone has started to attract boarders from all around.

FREERIDERS can roam freely over Keystone's three connected mountains: **Keystone Mountain, North Peak** and **The Outback.** Keystone is the front mountain and is laden with jib runs like **Mozart** and **Spring Dipper.** It's a good idea to have someone to spot your blind landings off the big rollers as it can get real busy. **North Peak** (the second mountain) offers some good steeps and open tree runs. However The Outback is the place to go with newly available Cat Riding Tours providing unique, guided services in the new expansion of **Erickson Bowl** and **Bergman Bowl.** Along with a shuttle service in the Outback Bowls and a bit of dry pow pow it makes Keystone a freeriders playground.

FREESTYLERS will not be disappointed with the perfectly crafted park known as **A51**, with a 400-foot Super Pipe and as many different rail features as the mind can imagine. Located in the **Packsaddle Bowl,** Keystone have just added a quarter of a million dollars of improvements tripling the parks size. Sitting on a perfect aspect allowing just the right amount of sun to both walls, the pipe is excellent, with walls reaching 5m in high season. They have a new snow-bowl feature (super fun to play in), wall ride and some really aggressive advanced rails including a 50 foot flat bar and a gigantic rainbow that they light on fire at night. There is now also a great beginner/intermediate freestyle area known as the **Incubator Terrain Park** on **Freda's Way** loaded with heaps of intro features, an intermediate fun box line and intermediate rail line.

PISTES lovers will be delighted to know that Keystone grooms some of their runs twice a day, leaving lots of terrain to lay out big turns. Check out runs like **Wild Irishman** and **Frenchmans** if you want to crank out some turns.

BEGINNERS are well catered for with two good ski schools and some reasonable learning areas and good long green runs like **Schoolmarm.** However you may find that there are a few too many flats.

THE TOWN
Keystone has recently completed a multi-million dollar redevelopment plan so theres a lot of expensive condos and a handfull of hotels. Eating and drinking options are plentiful, although night time action can be a bit lame to say the least. Head to the local towns of **Silverthorne** and **Frisco** for some cheap backpacker options. If you're after some good pub grub head to the *Great Northern Tavern* for a good steak and a handcrafted microbrew. *Piasano's* does great Italian and *Summit Seafood* for 'guess what'. Nothing really on the fast food end until you get closer to the town of **Dillon.** Party people will have a good variety of choice including some local haunts like *Dos Locos, The Goat, Great Northern Tavern* and nightclub *Greenlight.*

3782M TOP LIFT

2722 ACRES

EASY 12%
INT
ADV 29%
55%

953M VERTICAL

2829M FIRST LIFT

Keystone Resort
PO Box 38
Keystone, CO 80435
Tel: 001-970-496-2316

Web:www.keystoneresort.com
Email:keystoneinfo@vailresorts.com

Number of runs: 116
Longest run: 5km
Total Lifts:20
2 Gondolas, 12 Chairs, 2 drags
4 magic carpet
Lift capacity: 35,175
Lift times: 8.30am to 8.00pm

Winter Period:
mid Nov to end April
Lift Passes
1 Day $75, 2 of 3 Days $150
5 of 7 days $375
Board Schools
Burton LTR 2hr group lesson
$70+$11 for lift pass. Terrain park lessons $70 2hrs
Private 2hrs $205, full day $430
Hire
board and boots $28 per day
Night Boarding
Until 8.00pm 15 trails, half pipe & park lit

Annual Snowfall:
5.84m
Snowmaking:
35% of slopes

Bus
Colorado Mountain Express run transfers from Denver airport and take 1 1/4 hours
Fly
Fly to Denver Int which with a 1,3/4 hours transfer time. Vail/Eagle airport is 65 miles away
Drive
From Denver, head west on I-70 via the Eisenhower tunnel to Dillon. Exit at the junction 205 to Hwy 6 onto Keystone, a further 6 miles.

U
USA COLORADO

POOR FAIR GOOD TOP

FREERIDE
Trees & some off-piste
FREESTYLE
Terrain park
PISTES
Well laid out

6 OUT OF 10

Good compact resort

Lovelands is a resort that has a reputation for good snow, a long season, and a claim to have the world's highest quad chair lift which lets you off at an elevation of 3871 metres. Located close to **Denver**, is definitely a place that is worth a visit and a great one for day trippers, especially for the city slickers from Denver. Despite being close to Denver, however, overcrowding is not a problem and both the lift lines and pistes are often deserted. The resort has recently been investing a lot of dollars in expanding the terrain with the addition of another 400 acres of extreme slopes at the area known as **the Ridge**. A lot of money has also been spent on upgrading the snowmaking facilities to help boost the snow cover. Loveland is not the biggest hill in **Colorado**, but what you get is more than adequate and there are certainly smaller places than this one. What you have is a ridable area that stretches up from two points, Loveland Valley and Loveland Basin that are linked by chairlift and road. Loveland Valley is the smaller of the two areas with a cluster of runs that rise up through some thick wooded glade's that eventually thin out the further up you go. **Loveland Basin**, who's slopes stretched out around a high bowl above the entrance to the **Eisenhower Tunnel**, is the main area to ride with a good choice of runs from basic intermediate trails to some hardcore extreme runs with a few double black diamond extreme slopes.

FREERIDERS should grab the number 2 lift and head up to the Ptarmigan area where you will find lots of cool freeriding terrain. However, some of the best freeride terrain can be found off lift 8 in the **Zip Basin**. Here you will find some nice backcountry type terrain with a few gullies and bowls.

FREESTYLERS have an okay terrain park with a series of kickers and numerous rails, but in truth some of the natural features are better for air.

PISTES. The resort has a number of well maintained trails that are nicely laid out. Some of the best carving trails are off the number 6 lift.

BEGINNERS can take a lesson here to help then tackle what is largely not a beginner's resort. That's not to say novices should stay away, it's just that the resort is more of an intermediate level.

THE TOWN
While there area boasts a few shops and places to eat, this is not a resort as such. One okay option would be to stay down in Denver where you can't fail to find good local facilities.

pics - Lovelands Resort

U
S
A

C
O
L
O
R
A
D
O

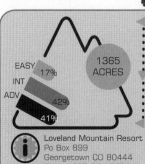

EASY 17%
INT
ADV 42%
41%

1365 ACRES

Loveland Mountain Resort
Po Box 899
Georgetown CO 80444
Phone: 303-571-5580
Web:www.skiloveland.com
Email:loveland@skiloveland.com

3965M
TOP LIFT

734M
VERTICAL

3230M
FIRST LIFT

Number of runs: 70
Longest run: 3.2km
Total Lifts: 11
9 Chairs, 2 drags
Lift times: 9am - 4pm
Lift Capacity (people per hour):
15,600

Winter Period:
Nov to April
Lift Passes
Day $55. Late season day $39
Board Schools
Group lessons $40 for 2 1/2 hrs,
packages available that include
hire & lift pass from $63. Private
lessons from $70 per hour
Hire
Board & Boots $28 per day

Annual Snowfall:
10m
Snowmaking:
12% of slopes

Bus
from Denver available by
arrangement.
Fly
to Denver, transfer time 1 hour.
Drive
From Denver, head west on I-70 via
Idaho Springs and turning left onto
the route 6 past Georgetown, to
reach Loveland. The distance from
Denver is 56 miles.

POOR FAIR GOOD TOP

FREERIDE
Trees & some good off-piste
FREESTYLE
3 Terrain parks & 2 halfpipes
PISTES
Well maintained slopes

6 OUT OF 10

Okay, but expensive

pic - Aspen/Snowmasse Resort

and **Cirque** for some double black steeps and powder bowls. The run known as **Baby Ruth** is also where advanced riders will get a real buzz. Snowmass offers plenty of backcountry riding with organised tours: Aspen Powder Tours runs trips for riders wanting the ultimate thrill, from around $230 a day.

FREESTYLERS have two halfpipes and a three terrain park, as well as a mountain riddled with natural hits. The main pipe is some 500ft long, with big walls and perfect transitions for getting massive amounts of air. The pipe was originally designed by pro Jimi Scott, and is easily reached off the Funnel lift. There is also a very good fun-park reached off the **Coney Glade** chair lift.

PISTES. There's a good selection of wide, open motorway flats for putting in some big carves, with an array of all-level, well groomed trails set out across the area. Big Burn reached off Lift Number 4 is a good intermediate trail.

Snowmass is the biggest of the resorts that make up the Aspen area, and the second largest resort in **Colorado**. With its four separate peaks, Snowmass is an impressive resort with a lot going for it and warmly welcomes snowboarders. This has not always been the case within the Aspen group, where snobbish areas such as **Aspen Mountain**, still ban snowboarders. However, the 1,246 metres of vertical available here, means you don't have to go anywhere else. Snowmass is mainly an advanced/intermediate rider's retreat, with a good choice of double black diamond runs and trails through trees, steeps and awesome powder making this a place where everyone can get a fix.

FREERIDERS will go crazy here. Snowmass is a real pleasure and offers fantastic riding. Those wanting to cut some serious terrain should check out **Hanging Valley**

BEGINNERS cutting their first snow should start at the base area from the Fanny Hill chair lift, before trying out the steeper stuff on the Big Burn. The local ski-school has a 3 day beginner's programme that guarantees you will learn to ride: if you don't, you get an extra day's tuition free.

THE TOWN
The base village has dozens of lodging options, with beds within easy reach of the bottom runs. Evenings are not up to much, but there is a lot more going on in nearby Aspen. For a drink, check out the *Copper Street Pier*, or *Eric's* for a game of pool. Be aware that **Aspen** is super $$$ dollar-hungry.

U
USA COLORADO

EASY **7%**
INT
ADV **38%** **55%**

3100 ACRES

3813M TOP LIFT

1343M VERTICAL

2473M FIRST LIFT

Aspen Skiing Company
Post Office Box 1248, Aspen, CO 81612
Tel - 800-308-6935
Web:www.aspensnowmass.com

new for 05/06
New intermediate level terrain park on Velvet Falls. The existing Fanny Hill chairlift will be replaced with a six-passenger lift - the Village Express. new Sky Cab gondola to connect Snowmass Mall with base village

Number of runs: 84
Longest run: 8.2km
Total Lifts:21
17 Chairs, 2 drags,2 magic carpets
Lift capacity (people/hr): 27,978
Lift times: 8.30am to 4.00pm

Winter Period:
Nov to April
Lift Passes
1 day pass $72
6 day pass $432
Season $1,879
Board Schools
Full day private $479
Full Day Group $109
Hire
Number of hire shops on mountain

Annual Snowfall:
7.62m
Snowmaking:
5% of slopes

Bus
Bus journeys from Denver, take around 2 1/4 hours. Buses run between aspen and snowmass until 2am
Fly
to Denver, with a 3 1/2 hour transfer, local airport is Aspen, 3miles
Train
Nearest station is Glenwood Springs about (64 km) from Aspen. www.amtrak.com
Drive
Snowmass Village is located 5 miles off Colorado 82 via Brush Creek Road. Aspen is located 5 miles past Brush Creek road via Colorado 82

usg STEAMBOAT

Excellent treeriding, but stuck up off the slopes

	POOR	FAIR	GOOD	TOP
FREERIDE Trees & some good off-piste				
FREESTYLE 3 Terrain parks & 2 halfpipes				
PISTES Lots of good gladed ,long runs				

8
OUT OF 10

PIC- Steamboat /Larry Pierce

S teamboat is a curious place in more ways than one. What you get is an old mining town with a seemingly laid back approach coupled with a mountain that offers some great riding with over 2939 acres of terrain that is spread out over four tree-lined mountain peaks. Unfortunately, many will find Steamboat is certainly not the best place to spend a weeks vacation. Although this is not a bad place to visit in terms of the riding opportunities and the good annual snow record, its tacky dollar hungry, fur-clad ski-cowboy image will make most normal snowboarders want to throw up.

However, Steamboat has a growing snowboard population and has made a real effort to drag itself into the 21st century (although having live bands playing on the lower slopes on a Friday afternoon is hardly ground breaking stuff). Still, the resort has several things in its favour. The resort offers some fantastic tree-riding, there's ample deep powder and some great carving slopes. There is also a couple of double black diamond trails offering extreme slopes for advanced riders to tackle along with some over-rated blacks for intermediate riders to try out. What is most notable here, are the trees and the options for backcountry snowboarding, which can be explored by taking a snowcat trip organised locally.

FREERIDERS can have a good time at Steamboat. If you're up to the grade, try riding the steeps on the Meadows of Storm Peak, where **Christmas Tree Bowl** and the neighbouring chutes will give you a good challenge. Alternatively, try cutting some deep powder tracks in areas like **Toutes**.

FREESTYLERS can catch some decent natural air or sample the man-made hits in the **Maverick terrain park** on **Big Meadow**. The Maverick park claims to have the biggest park in North America 650 foot long ending in a 50foot 1/4pipe. There's also a great park, called the **Sobe Park**, with a 200foot pipe and numerous rails and kickers. **The Beehive**, is a small fun-park with a series of mini-hits for kids only, located on the Spike trail reachable off the South Peak lift.

THE PISTES here are very good with good long descents on which to perfect their technique. Steamboat is also noted for its Olympic race runs, which can be used by snowboarders. Further more, this is also a place where speed skiers, and indeed extreme down hill mountain bikers, often come to practice their thing. Which means the mountain certainly has a number of very gnarly slopes where you can cut it at great speed, but don't go racing down fast runs in an out of control or dangerous manner, because not only will someone get seriously hurt, but the ski patrol will take a very dim view of your actions and throw you off the mountain.

U
S
A

C
O
L
O
R
A
D
O

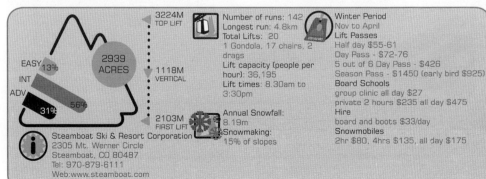

EASY 13%
INT
ADV
56%
31%

2939 ACRES

3224M TOP LIFT

1118M VERTICAL

2103M FIRST LIFT

Steamboat Ski & Resort Corporation
2305 Mt. Werner Circle
Steamboat, CO 80487
Tel: 970-879-6111
Web:www.steamboat.com
Email:info@steamboat.com

Number of runs: 142
Longest run: 4.8km
Total Lifts: 20
1 Gondola, 17 chairs, 2 drags
Lift capacity (people per hour): 36,195
Lift times: 8.30am to 3:30pm

Annual Snowfall:
8.19m
Snowmaking:
15% of slopes

Winter Period
Nov to April
Lift Passes
Half day $55-61
Day Pass - $72-76
5 out of 6 Day Pass - $426
Season Pass - $1450 (early bird $925)
Board Schools
group clinic all day $27
private 2 hours $235 all day $475
Hire
board and boots $33/day
Snowmobiles
2hr $80, 4hrs $135, all day $175

ʊsɠ STEAMBOAT

BEGINNERS and total novices will feel most left out here, for apart from some green runs snaking in and out of the higher grade trails, the easy stuff at the base area is often very tiresome. Steamboat has an excellent ski and snowboard school.

THE TOWN

Steamboat is a welcoming town even if it has a poncy feel about it. The town is loaded with all manner of attractions and is well equipped for making your stay a good one. You can choose to stay on or close to the slopes and the main resort facilities are well located to each other and for the slopes. However, being a dollar-hungry place, those of you on a tight budget may not be able to survive beyond a couple of days here. The cost of most things is unjustifiably high. Which is a shame (perhaps its a deliberate resort policy so they can attract dot.com millionaire's and keep low-lifes away). Around town you will find a host of things to do, from a climbing gym to an indoor ice rink. The town also has a number of shops, with most now catering for snowboarders, some even offer good deals on board sales.

Accomodation. Steamboat has a very good selection of

accommodation with loads of lodges, chalets and condo's to choose from.

Food. Steamboat has a good selection of restaurants from fancy dining out joints to a number of fast food places, whether you have a steak or a burger, one thing is for sure, you can guarantee it will be top notch (mind you so will the price). You can eat out in style on the mountain at places like the *Bear River Bar & Grill* or the *Rendezvous Saddle* cafeteria.

Night-life in this over hyped town leaves a lot to be desired and can be best described as crap and aimed at middle-aged skiers with sad dress sense. They have way too much après-ski nonsense here. However, the *Cellar bar* has a good deal going. For $12 you get to drink as much as you can for two hours.

SUMMARY

On the mountain this a great place to ride with some excellent treeriding to try out and some cool carving runs. But off the slopes the place is way too stuck up

U

USA

COLORADO

CAR
From Denver, head west on I-70 via the Eisenhower tunnel, leave the Silverthrone exit. Then head north along Hwy 9 and Hwy 40. Denver to resort is 167 miles.
FLY
Fly to Denver, with a 4 hour transfer. Yampa Valley airport is 22miles from the resort, theres 5 flights daily from Denver & Houston
BUS
Buses from Denver take around 3 hours 20 mins from Yampa.

425

usg TELLURIDE

	POOR	FAIR	GOOD	TOP
FREERIDE Trees & some good off-piste				
FREESTYLE Terrain park & halfpipe				
PISTES many short trails				

8 OUT OF 10

Great no nonsense freeriders resort

bruised if you bail, or make you feel like a god if you complete them in style. These are serious double black diamond trails and not for wimps.

FREESTYLERS who are happy to roam around riding off natural hits are in for a pleasant surprise. The mountain has a number of natural pipes and banks. The **West Drain** slope offers some cool riding due in part to it being a natural half pipe. The **Air Garden Terrain Park** covers 10 acres and features a number of boxes, rails, kickers, table tops and a halfpipe designed for a variety of abilities. You'll find it on **Lower See Forever** area.

Telluride sticks two fingers up to convention when it comes to the norm in **Colorado**! Why? Well it's simple, no tackiness, no bull, no hype, no snotty nose yuppies; none of it, what you have here is easily summed up as 'superb'. Telluride, which is said to have been robbed over a hundred years ago by Butch Cassady, is full on, but unlike other resorts in Colorado, this Wild West town won't rob you blind. Telluride, which is an old mining town, is set in the **San Juan Mountains** and is a skiers and snowboarders' heaven that offers every style and ability of rider something to saviour, especially beginners as this place has to be one of the best novices resort in the whole state. Now in it's forth year and $14mill later the **Prospect Bowl** area is great, accessed by three high speed quad lifts which lead you to varied runs and the **Ute Park**; It's really opened up this hill.

FREERIDERS who like fast hard steeps will love it here as Telluride offers some fantastic riding. The **Kant-Mak-M**, the **Spiral** and the **Plunge** runs are a series of really challenging steeps that will either leave you seriously

designed for a variety of abilities. You'll find it on **Lower See Forever** area.

PISTES, This resort lends itself perfectly well to cruising at speed, although it should be said that many of the trails are a bit short. Note also that some runs are only pisted on oneside, which means one side being smooth and the other bumpy

BEGINNERS are probably the one group who will feel most pleased here and most at ease because Telluride not only has a good percentage of easy trails, they are also well set out and very easy to negotiate.

OFF THE SLOPES things are just as good as on them. There are two options to choose from for lodging and local facilities in either **Telluride's** main town or up in the **Mountain Village.** Which every you choose you wont be disappointed as both offer good accommodation, great places to dine and a number of cool bars.

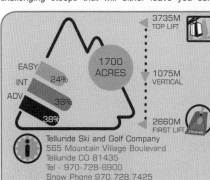

3735M TOP LIFT

1075M VERTICAL

2660M FIRST LIFT

EASY
INT 24%
ADV 38%
38%

1700 ACRES

Number of runs: 84
Longest run: 7.36km
Total Lifts: 16
2 Gondolas, 11 Chairs, 2 drags,1 Magic Carpet
Lift times: 9am - 4pm
Lift Capacity (people per hour): 21,186

Winter Period:
Nov to April
Lift Passes
Day Pass - $74
6 days $414
Season Pass - $1375
Board Schools
Beginners and various clinics available 800-801-4832
Hire
Board & Boots $33 per day

Annual Snowfall: 7.9m
Snowmaking: 15% of slopes

Fly
Montrose Airport is 65 miles away flights from Chicago, Dallas, Houston & Newark. Telluride Airport is 6 miles away & connecting flights from Denver and Phoenix
Drive
From Denver by way of Grand Junction - Take Interstate 70 West to Grand Junction, go South on Route 50 to Montrose. Continue South on Route 550 to Ridgway then turn right onto Route 62. Follow this to Route 145 and turn left. Follow the signs into Telluride. Travel time - 7 hours

Telluride Ski and Golf Company
565 Mountain Village Boulevard
Telluride CO 81435
Tel - 970-728-6900
Snow Phone 970.728.7425
Web:www.telski.com
Email: info@tellurideskiresort.com

U
S
A

C
O
L
O
R
A
D
O

	POOR	FAIR	GOOD	TOP
FREERIDE Trees & some good off-piste				
FREESTYLE 3 parks & halfpipe				
PISTES confusing layout but immaculate				

10 OUT OF 10

PIC- Jack Affleck / Vail Resorts

Vail has the reputation of being one of America's most prestigious (ie snobbish) ski resorts, and in some respects it's true. The town of Vail, a bizarre imitation of a 'typical' Swiss alpine village, is centred around the base of the resort and is hellishly expensive. However, there are loads of good reasons to visit Vail, which include the large amount of terrain on offer (over 4,000 acres) and Vail's extremely healthy and positive attitude towards snowboarding. The terrain park has 3 halfpipes and 12 runs, and is also open to skiers although thankfully, it's frequented almost exclusively by snowboarders. One major point regarding Vail is that it is a very popular resort resulting in some long lift queues throughout the season. But in terms of climate and cost, a good time to visit is late season when the snow is soft and the price of lift tickets drop dramatically.

FREESTYLERS are extremely well catered for on Vail's slopes. Vail also provides a major half pipe and terrain park known as the **Golden Peak**. Both park and pipe are groomed to perfection. The pipe has huge walls offering great transitions while the park is loaded with not only a major series of gaps, spines etc, but also a chill out area that has video screens, pumping music and drink vending services.

PISTES. Vail has some excellent blue trails and some challenging fast blacks. Many of the runs start out as one grade and then suddenly become another, so study a lift map in order to negotiate the best spots with ease. The **Avanti lift** gives access to some really good fast trails. The **Mountain Top lift** also allows you to ride in style on a number of extremely good trails.

FREERIDERS will find this place heaven. Vail's Back Bowls will stoke you beyond belief when you see what is on offer. In order to find out where the best places are, you should pick up a copy of the free pocket-sized snowboard mountain map which will point you in the direction of the best boarding trails and hits. The most popular backcountry includes **Ptarmigan Ridge**, a 25ft cornice jump and **Kengis Khan**, another cornice not suitable for sufferers of vertigo. The cliffs under Chair 4 are easier to access, as long as you don't mind your slams being applauded by everyone on the lift. The tree run **Cheeta Gully** is marked as one of the special snowboard trails and will test the most proficient rider.

BEGINNERS have a mountain with so many easy trails and excellent progression possibilities, that if you fail here, you must be a complete loser. The areas of **Golden Peak** are perfect for learning the basics, although it can become a little clustered around midday, especially at weekends and holidays. Vail's snowboard school is excellent and has a number of instruction programmes.

U S A   C O L O R A D O

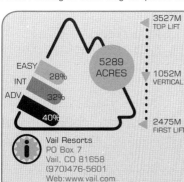

3527M TOP LIFT

5289 ACRES

EASY 28%
INT
ADV 32%
40%

1052M VERTICAL

2475M FIRST LIFT

Vail Resorts
PO Box 7
Vail, CO 81658
(970)476-5601
Web:www.vail.com
Email:vailinfo@vailresorts.com

Number of runs: 193
Longest run: 5.4km
Total Lifts: 34
1 Gondola, 23 chairs, 10 drags
Lift capacity (people per hour): 53,281
Lift times: 8.30am to 4.00pm
Mountain Cafes: 20

Annual Snowfall: 8.5m
Snowmaking: 5% of slopes

Winter Period:
mid Nov to end April
Lift Passes
Day pass $80
3 of 5 days $237
5 of 8 days $395
Better deals if you book in advance via their website
Board Schools
one day group $90/100
Full day inc pass & rental $190-202
1 Hour Private Lesson - $110
3 hours park lesson $80
Hire
board and boots $27/day
Snowmobiles
1 hour from $62
Night Boarding
Yes

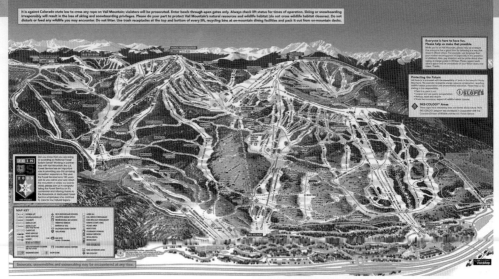

It is against Colorado state law to cross any rope on Vail Mountain; violators will be prosecuted. Enter bowls through open gates only. Always check lift status for times of operation. Skiing or snowboarding irresponsibly will result in the loss of skiing and snowboarding privileges. Please do your part to protect Vail Mountain's natural resources and wildlife habitat (do not cross wildlife habitat closures). Do not disturb or feed any wildlife you may encounter. Do not litter. Use trash receptacles at the top and bottom of every lift, recycling bins at on-mountain dining facilities and pack it out from on-mountain decks.

THE TOWN

If you reckon that **Vail** is just about the slopes, think again as there are heaps of things going on with an amazing amount of great local services. The area is huge, so use of the free shuttle bus may be necessary depending on where you base yourself. Recently, merchants & restaurant owners have taken a much-needed approach to offering lower priced options for visitors, including apres, dinner & drink specials. Do your homework before making a choice and you will save much more $$ than you thought. Locals know exactly what to do to make your stay a good one. They offer a high level of service whether you're buying a burger or checking in to a hotel.

Accommodation consists of a selection of some 30,000 visitor beds and providing you don't mind not being slopeside, you will find affordable lodging. Many opt to stay out in one of the nearby villages with cheaper housing and on average, only a 20 minute 'commute' to the slope. Check Vails web site for a full listing of accommodation.

Food. Eating in the resort or around the main area may destroy your bank balance or father's credit card if you don't choose carefully. Some prices are silly, but there are plenty of semi-affordable, fast-food joints to check out. To tickle your taste buds, why not check out *Pazzo's*, which serves a good helping of cheap pasta or where you can have a 'do it yourself pizza'. The *Red Lion* also features good, cheap burgers, sandwiches & fries in one of the most convenient, frequently visited village locations (On Bridge Street,

in the heart of all the action).

Night-life, as you'd hope, is extremely good. The offerings are excellent, with good bars and okay places to boogie well into the early hours. Contrary to popular belief, you CAN find cheap drink specials in the heart of the village. Two frequented stops this season included *Fubar* and *8150*, which both featured a $10(US $) all-you-can-drink special on Sunday & Monday nights (we hope to see the return of this unbelievable deal in the 04/05 season). You can also checkout the many après specials, which include $3 beers and discounted appetizers.

PIC- Jack Affleck / Vail Resorts

CAR
Denver via Interstate 70, take Main Vail Exit (176), 97 miles (156km). Drive time is about 1 3/4 hours.
FLY
Fly to Denver International (110 miles), transfer time to resort is 2 hours. Local airport is Eagle County, 30 miles away, 13 airports offer connection
BUS
There are daily bus services from both Denver and Vail/Eagle County airports direct to Vail.

POOR FAIR GOOD TOP

FREERIDE
Trees & some good off-piste
FREESTYLE
3 Terrain parks & a halfpipe
PISTES
Very tame slopes

Slopes ideal for pensioners, luckily saved by the parks

6 OUT OF 10

pic - Winterpark Resort

W inter Park - a mere 67 miles from **Denver,** nestling at the base of Berthoud Pass at an altitude of 2,743 feet, is said to be the fifth largest resort in the USA, with over 2886 acres of terrain. The old saying that 'size always matters' doesn't ring true at winter, since although this place is vast, it is not as great as the hype dictates. However, Colorado is famous for its powder snow and in fairness; Winter Park snags more than its fair share, with an average annual snowfall of 350 inches and plenty of blue sky days. The high tree line of Winter Park means that even when there is low cloud, visibility is still good. Winter Park is actually two mountains, **Winter Park** and **Mary Jane.** Winter Park has trails for all standards of rider and is well groomed. What makes this place somewhat dull is that it is really tame, with hardly any fast, challenging terrain. The best runs (if such exist) are on the Mary Jane slopes and are mostly black trails. There have been some big improvements in the terrain parks last season.

FREERIDERS will find plenty of okay tree runs around both mountains with near perfect spaced trees. However, don't expect to ride all the ferns at any great speed. There is some good riding to be had in **Parsenn Bowl** on June Mountain, and on the runs of the **Challenger**.

FREESTYLERS are presented with three fun-parks. The **Rail yard** is the big one designed for the advnaced rider. Conditions depending it has 25 rails, 16 jumps and a super-pipe organised into various lines. The **Jack Kendrick park** is set-up for more intermediate riders it has a number of rails and kickers and a less intemidating halfpipe.

Kendrick is designed for the Freerider looking to hone their skills before going to Rail Yard. Apparently Kendrick's jumps have more flow than the Mississippi River. The **Discovery Park** is the place to learn how to navigate rollers, catch air, and slide on foreign surfaces! This beginner terrain park is designed to be a great place to learn skills for the first time.

PISTES. Riders looking for wide pistes where they can pose doing big arcs, will find Winter Park right up their street. Much of what you find on Winter Park mountain will suit piste lovers.

BEGINNERS also fair well here. The easy trails, and indeed some of those classed as intermediate, can be ridden within a few days if you put your mind to it.

THE TOWN
Winter Park's lodging is 6 miles down the valley, where you can find a good selection of places to stay at affordable prices. The evenings are not too hectic, but you can party. Check out *Lord Gore Arms* which shows videos every night with DJ's and bands, or The Pub for Sunday night disco mayhem.

U

U S A

C O L O R A D O

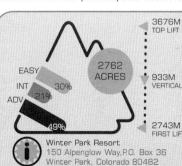

EASY

2762 ACRES

INT 30%

ADV 21%

49%

3676M
TOP LIFT

933M
VERTICAL

2743M
FIRST LIFT

Number of runs: 134
Longest run: 8.2km
Total Lifts:21
18 chairs, 2 Magic Carpets, 1 Rope tow
Lift capacity (people/hr):
35,030
Lift times: 8.30am to 4.00pm

Winter Period:
Nov to April
Lift Passes
Half-day $48-50
1 Day pass - $64-69
Board Schools
Beginners package lift, hire & 2 1/2hr lesson $89/99 per day.
Various group lessons 2 1/2hrs $49/59 Hire
Beginners Board & Boots $28/32
Demo Board & Boots $40/44

Annual Snowfall:
9.1m
Snowmaking:
20% of slopes

Bus
Bus journeys from Denver take 1 hour
Fly
to Denver Int, transfer 1 1/2 hours
Drive
From Denver, head west on I-70 via the Eisenhower tunnel to exit 232 on Hwy 40 direction Granby.. 67 miles. 1 1/2 hours drive time.
Train
Amtrak's California Zephyr goes to Winter Park daily from Chicago & LA. Ski train weekends from Denver

Winter Park Resort
150 Alpenglow Way,P.O. Box 36
Winter Park, Colorado 80482
tel: (970) 726-5514
Web:www.skiwinterpark.com
Email: wpinfo@skiwinterpark.com

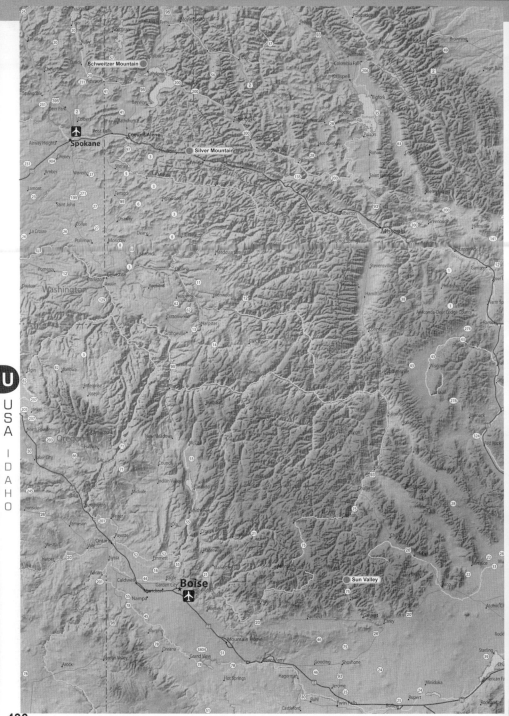

wsg SCHWEITZER MTN

Really cool resort

POOR FAIR GOOD TOP

FREERIDE
Trees & some good off-piste
FREESTYLE
2 Terrain parks
PISTES
Lots of well groomed quiet slopes

7
OUT OF 10

chutes on the west side of the front half of the mountain, to an amazingly long (and tiring) blue run that starts from one of several high speed, no-queue lifts about 100 feet from the day-lodge. The ridge that links the runs together along the top of the mountain also provides a breathtaking view of Lake Pend O'Reille.

FREESTYLERS have a magical mountain do to their tricks on. A favourite with local students, this overlooked mountain has not 1 but 2 terrain parks. There's the Freestyle Garden that is perfect for novices with assorted rails and jumps. If you want something more substantial check out the **Stomping Grounds Park** which features a rail garden, booters and competitions that are held throughout the winter.

Lying about an hour's drive north of **Couer D'Alene**, Idaho, (and about an hour and a half south of the **Canadian border**) is the town of Sandpoint. Sandpoint is in the lucky position of having one of the coolest snowboarding spots in the North-western United States. A mere 10 minutes drive up a beautiful wooded ascent takes you to the Schweitzer basin. Probably unheard of by anyone that hasn't spent time in the area. On top of the amazingly laid back atmosphere of the Northwest in general, Schweitzer enjoys a very low "I snowboard so I'm great" bullshit factor, a problem that needs addressing both in the UK and central states like Utah and Colorado. The resort has a good lift system with reasonably priced lift tickets at $35 a day for the whole mountain - this may also include some excellent night riding on one of the many well lit runs. If you haggle, you might get some bargains for multi-day tickets, or if you are with a group.

FREERIDERS are assured plenty of powder days and an enormously varied selection of terrain from the super steep

PISTES. There's plenty of groomed stuff on offer and speed perverts can make good on runs such as **Cathedral** and **Zip**

BEGINNERS have no need to worry here as all the novice runs are well away from the main runs so helping to prevent mass collisions, and serviced by a separate chair lift

THE TOWN
All your local needs are mainly provided down in Sandpoint 2 miles away. There is some accommodation available at the base area close to the slopes such as *The Green Gables Lodge* or in one of the condos. Far cheaper lodging can be found in **Sandpoint** where you will find a basic but okay selection of shops, restaurants and bars. For a burger try the *Powder House* and for a beer give *Roxy's* a try

U
S
A

I
D
A
H
O

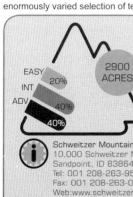

1951M
TOP LIFT

732M
VERTICAL

1217M
FIRST LIFT

EASY
INT 20%
ADV 40%
40%

2900 ACRES

Number of runs: 64
Longest run: 4.3km
Total Lifts: 10
6 chairs, 3 drags, 1 Rope tow
Rope tow
Lift capacity (people/hr):
8,092
Lift times: 9.00am to 4.00pm

Winter Period:
Nov to April
Lift Passes
1 Day pass - $44/49, Night pass - $12
Season pass - $709 (early bird discounts available)
Board Schools
One day with pass and board/boots $59
Three days with pass & board/boots $99
Hire
Board & Boots $30/40 day, Helmets $7
Night Boarding
Friday/Sat 3pm till 8pm 19 Dec-13Mar
CAT/Snowmobiles
www.selkirkpowderco.com run cat and
snowmobile tours tel: 208.263.6959

Annual Snowfall:
7.6m
Snowmaking:
10% of slopes

Bus
from Spokane to resort
takes 90 mins
Fly
to Spokane Int, 86 miles
south west is served by
most carriers. Sandpoint
airports handles the
seriously minted
Drive
From Spokane, take I-90
east and then Hwy 95
north via the town of
Sandpoint. Schweitzer is
another 2 miles on.
Train
Sandpoint is nearest
station. Amtrak has trains
from Chicago & Seattle, 2
miles from resort

Schweitzer Mountain Resort
10,000 Schweitzer Mountain Road
Sandpoint, ID 83864
Tel: 001 208-263-9555
Fax: 001 208-263-0775
Web:www.schweitzer.com
Email:ski@schweitzer.com

NEW new for 05/06 season
new surface lift from Siberia to the ridge
which will expose 400acres of new terrain
and 5 new pistes.

431

	POOR	FAIR	GOOD	TOP
FREERIDE Trees & a little off-piste				
FREESTYLE Terrain park & halfpipe				
PISTES They have a grooming guarantee				

5 OUT OF 10

pic -Silver Mountain Resort

on a board. However, to be fair to the resort management, they are dealing with the problem by getting rid of a lot of the cat tracks. Overall, the mountain offers a fair selection of long steeps with generally great snow and weather conditions. The seven lifts are quick and easy to negotiate and mercifully lift lines are tiny. Slope facilities are a bit suspect, the day lodge is far less impressive than that at Schweitzer, and the food is both mediocre and extortionate. But a major plus is the very low lift prices, with a day pass from only $24 bucks during the week.)

FREERIDERS will find that the backcountry stuff is thin on the ground - unlike tree stumps, grit, and large rocks, which seem to litter a good deal of the area outside the fences. However, some very nice, but challenging, freeriding can be had on areas like the **Rendezvous** or down the **Warner Peak**.

FREESTYLERS note that this is not a place loaded with natural freestyle terrain. However, to counter this there is a good terrain park and halfpipe called the **Trench** which is built and shaped to conform with competition standards located up on Noah's.

PISTES. You can lick it down the slopes here with some degree of style. There are a number of long cruising trails that are groomed to perfection. The **Tamarack** is a fantastic two and a half mile long trail to try out.

BEGINNERS have a mountain that is well suited to their needs, with a host of novice trails offering easy sedate descents.

THE TOWN
You can lodge close to the slopes, but in general the main thing to do is base yourself down **Kellogg**, which is 2 minutes away. The town offers a good choice of local facilities with very reasonable prices for lodging and general living. The *Silver Ridge Mountain Lodge* offers some good packages.

A smaller resort than **Schweitzer**, and much closer to civilisation, is **Kellogg, Idaho**. A small mining town in north central Idaho, about 40 minutes from Couer **D'Alene**, Kellogg has the honour of running the longest gondola ride in the world, which culminates at the day lodge of Silver Mountain. Essentially composed of two resorts, the new Silver Mountain lift system and the incorporated **Jackass Ski Bowl** provide a superb set of runs, although the intermediate rider is better catered for than freestylers or super euro-carvers. In fact, the only real downside to this hidden gem of a mountain is the fact that it is infested with cat tracks linking one run to the next. Easy on skis, a real drag

U S A

I D A H O

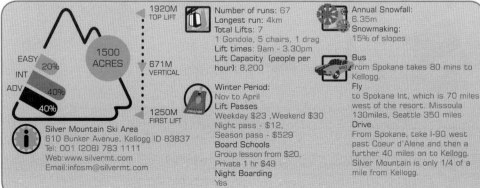

1920M TOP LIFT

671M VERTICAL

1250M FIRST LIFT

1500 ACRES

EASY 20%
INT
ADV 40%
40%

Number of runs: 67
Longest run: 4km
Total Lifts: 7
1 Gondola, 5 chairs, 1 drag
Lift times: 9am - 3.30pm
Lift Capacity (people per hour): 8,200

Winter Period:
Nov to April
Lift Passes
Weekday $23 ,Weekend $30
Night pass - $12,
Season pass - $529
Board Schools
Group lesson from $20,
Private 1 hr $49
Night Boarding
Yes

Annual Snowfall:
6.35m
Snowmaking:
15% of slopes

Bus
from Spokane takes 80 mins to Kellogg.
Fly
to Spokane Int, which is 70 miles west of the resort. Missoula 130miles, Seattle 350 miles
Drive
From Spokane, take I-90 west past Coeur d'Alene and then a further 40 miles on to Kellogg. Silver Mountain is only 1/4 of a mile from Kellogg.

i Silver Mountain Ski Area
610 Bunker Avenue, Kellogg ID 83837
Tel: 001 (208) 783 1111
Web:www.silvermt.com
Email:infosm@silvermt.com

	POOR	FAIR	GOOD	TOP
FREERIDE Trees & some some off-piste				
FREESTYLE Terrain park & halfpipe				
PISTES Excellent groomed quiet slopes				

A resort that will suit all riders

8 OUT OF 10

pic · Sun Valley Resort

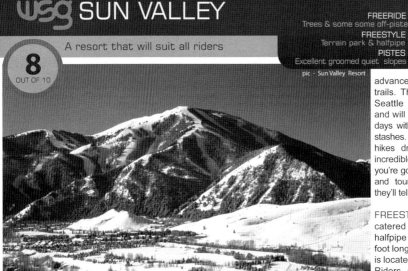

Sun Valley dates back decades and comes with a fair share of its own history. Said to be the USA's oldest ski resorts, Sun Valley has managed stay up with the times and today is a resort that is a match for any other destination in the country. Located in the southern part of Idaho and east of the capital **Bosie**, what you have here is a resort for every one from advanced air heads to total first timers, although it's fair to say that the beginner terrain is a bit limited. On and off the slopes the whole area has a rather strange feel to it with a mixture of the Old Wild West and a hint of Europe thrown in. Its set to a back drop of a large rideable area which covers over 2000 acres and split over two main areas known as **Dollar/Elkhorn** and **Bald Mountain**. Dollar/Elkhorn area the smaller and best for beginners while Bald Mountain is the place to head for to ride some advanced steeps. Whichever area you try out, you will be met with excellent slope facilities which incorporates a high tech automated snowmaking system that covers over 78% of the slopes.

FREERIDERS who know what life is about and can handle a board at speed will be able to prove it on the slopes up on Bald Mountain which has a good selection of advanced and intermediate trails. The bowls below the Seattle Ridge are superb and will keep you amused for days with some nice powder stashes. There's some great hikes dropping in to some incredible backcountry, but you're gonna have to kidnap and tourture a local before they'll tell you.

FREESTYLERS are well catered for here with a halfpipe that measures 350 foot long by 80 foot wide and is located on the Dollar area. Riders can also purchase a budget priced lift ticket that covers Dollar and the pipe area. Around the whole area freestylers will find loads of awesome natural hits to get air off.

PISTES, Nutters who consider themselves to be of the advanced grade, should look no further than the slopes off Bald Mountain where you'll find a first class selection of long, well pitched cruising runs

BEGINNERS should be aware of the difference between the main areas. If you are a total first timer to snowboarding then stay away from Bald Mountain and check out the offerings on Dollar. The local ski school offers clinics from $45 a session for all grades.

THE TOWN
Off the slopes, **Sun Valley** is a resort that is fully geared up to handle visitors needs. There is a good selection of slope-side accommodation and excellent resort services with some nice restaurants and good bars, but note this is not a cheap resort. The town of **Ketchum** is only a mile away, but is the cheaper option. Bars of note are the *Roosevelt Tavern* and *Whiskey Jacques*

USA IDAHO

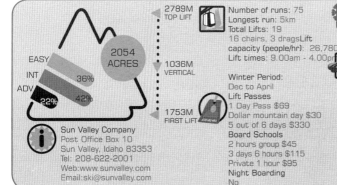

2789M TOP LIFT

EASY

2054 ACRES

INT 36%

ADV 22% 42%

1036M VERTICAL

1753M FIRST LIFT

Sun Valley Company
Post Office Box 10
Sun Valley, Idaho 83353
Tel: 208-622-2001
Web:www.sunvalley.com
Email:ski@sunvalley.com

Number of runs: 75
Longest run: 5km
Total Lifts: 19
16 chairs, 3 dragsLift capacity (people/hr): 26,780
Lift times: 9.00am - 4.00pm

Winter Period:
Dec to April
Lift Passes
1 Day Pass $69
Dollar mountain day $30
5 out of 6 days $330
Board Schools
2 hours group $45
3 days 6 hours $115
Private 1 hour $95
Night Boarding
No

Annual Snowfall:
6m
Snowmaking:
78% of slopes

Bus
Shuttle bus from Boise, Twin Falls, Pocatello and Idaho falls
Fly
into Sun Valley/Friedman Memorial Airport in Hailey, connections from Salt Lake City,Boise & Utah
Drive
From Boise, head south on I-84 and then via hwy 20 at Mountain Home to hwy 75 heading north following signs for Ketchum and then onto Sun Valley.

433

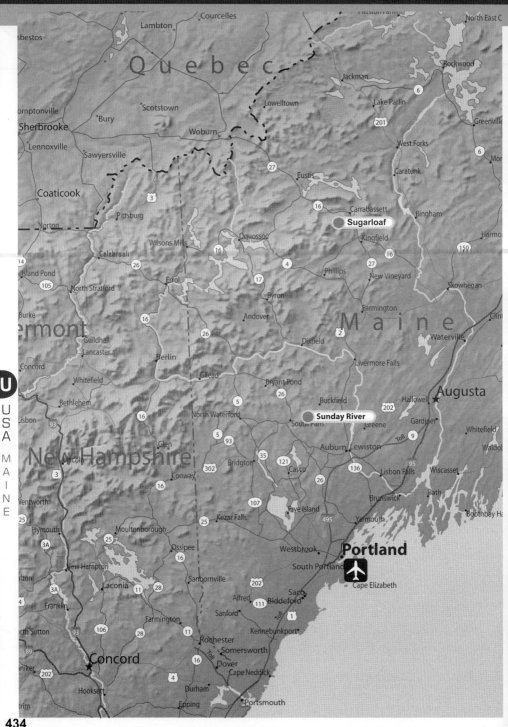

wsg SUGAR LOAF

FREERIDE
Trees & some good off-piste
FREESTYLE
3 Terrain parks & halfpipe
PISTES
Some good longish runs

Some good challenging terrain

7
OUT OF 10

FREERIDERS are going to feel very much at home here, with a good choice of descents that include acres of **summit bowl** riding and over 500 acres of treeriding terrain. Some of the most challenging terrain to check out can be found off the **Spillway chair** lift, while for a less stressing descent, the **Gauge** is okay.

FREESTYLERS can be seen kicking off natural hits all over this mountain as the place lends itself very nicely to natural freestyling. If you can't find a decent hit to please your desires, than Sugarloaf/USA has 3 terrain parks and large halfpipe with huge walls and nice transitions. The main n park, **Pipeline** comes loaded with hits galore with rails, spines and big gaps. Beginners can get their first air in the **Quarantine Zone**, before progressing to the **Stomping Grounds** on the double diamon Chaser run.

By east coast standards, Sugarloaf/USA is a big resort and a highly rated one that is well worth taking the time to visit. Located around two and a half hours drive time from **Portland**, this is a relatively easy place to get to and one could quite easily spend a week riding here on a mountain that has the only treeless summit with lift access in the east. Another notable point is that unlike many other east coast resorts, Sugarloaf/USA manages a longer season than many other east coast destinations as the resort is able to keep hold of its snow very well. What's more, they back up their real snow with snowmaking facilities that cover almost 94% of the mountain. In truth this is a mountain that will mainly appeal to freeriders and carvers. The 131 well groomed and well set out runs offer some very challenging runs with the option to ride down some extreme steeps and fast double diamond black trails.

PISTES. Riders of all levels will find an abundance of runs to choose from which are laid out all over the mountain starting out at the summit and allowing for long cruising runs all the way back home

BEGINNERS are presented with numerous trails that are mainly laid out across the lower section of the mountain and although the resort has a lot of good novice areas, the main section is often clogged up with skiers and others using the routes as access to the base, and base lifts.

THE TOWN
Local facilities are well placed for the slopes with lots of condo's available for letting at reasonable rates. Around the resort you will find a good selection of restaurants and a number of nightspots.

U
S
A

M
A
I
N
E

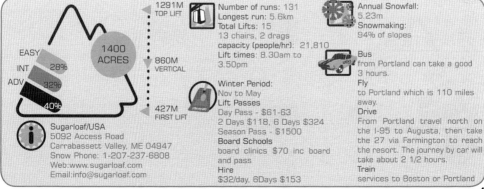

EASY		1400 ACRES	1291M TOP LIFT
INT	28%		860M VERTICAL
ADV	32%		
	40%		427M FIRST LIFT

Sugarloaf/USA
5092 Access Road
Carrabassett Valley, ME 04947
Snow Phone: 1-207-237-6808
Web:www.sugarloaf.com
Email:info@sugarloaf.com

Number of runs: 131
Longest run: 5.6km
Total Lifts: 15
13 chairs, 2 drags
capacity (people/hr): 21,810
Lift times: 8.30am to 3.50pm

Winter Period:
Nov to May
Lift Passes
Day Pass - $61-63
2 Days $118, 6 Days $324
Season Pass - $1500
Board Schools
board clinics $70 inc board and pass
Hire
$32/day, 6Days $153

Annual Snowfall:
5.23m
Snowmaking:
94% of slopes

Bus
from Portland can take a good 3 hours.
Fly
to Portland which is 110 miles away.
Drive
From Portland travel north on the I-95 to Augusta, then take the 27 via Farmington to reach the resort. The journey by car will take about 2 1/2 hours.
Train
services to Boston or Portland

POOR FAIR GOOD TOP

FREERIDE
Trees & small off-piste

FREESTYLE
4 Terrain parks & 2 halfpipes

PISTES
Lots of little runs

Some good treeriding and terrain parks

7 OUT OF 10

pic - John Quigley

U S A

M A I N E

from **Portland** and other nearby towns, to its simple but extremely well laid out slopes that cover eight linked mountains with three resort base areas. Once you arrive, it's not long before you appreciate just why this place is a popular destination with many of Maine's snowboarders and skiers alike as this is an excellent east coast resort which is thick with trees from the top to bottom on all the mountains. All the runs are hacked out from the dense pine to form a cluster of trails suitable for all styles and level of rider, in particular freeriders who know how to go for it. The eight mountain peaks are all open to snowboarders, with over 120 well looked after runs that get a good annual covering of real snow and are backed up by major snowmaking facilities that covers nearly all of the trails. The one off putting point is the crowds, particularly at weekends when the whole mountain can become a bit busy.

FREERIDERS will find that a week's stay here will not be wasted provided you get out and explore all eight mountains. Each one offers something a little different to the last, although in the main they don't vary too much. Still, the resort management have planned the runs and offer different slope pitches and terrain features that will catch you out if you are not concentrating on what you are doing. For those riders who can handle fast steeps, the double blacks on **Oz Peak** and **Jordan Bowl** (especially the double black **Caramba**) are the places to head for. However, beware of **Kansas**, a long, flat muscle-pumping traverse used to get you back to the main area, the trick here is to keep you speed up. Some good tree-riding can be found on the **Baker Mountain**.

Sunday River, which happens to be one of the major resorts in the American Skiing Co's portfolio, has rapidly grown from a local snowboarder's haunt to a fairly happening place in a very short space of time. Located a stone's throw away from the state border with **New Hampshire**, Sunday River attracts a lot of city dwellers

FREESTYLERS will find lots of natural hits to catch air, and plenty of places for jibbing off logs and other obstacles. However, for those who like things laid on, Sunday offers a lot more than many other resorts by providing four terrain parks loaded with all sorts of hits, a boardercross circuit and two halfpipes.

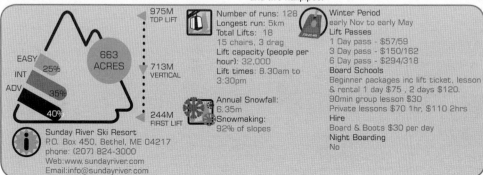

975M TOP LIFT

663 ACRES

EASY
INT 25%
ADV 35%
40%

713M VERTICAL

244M FIRST LIFT

Number of runs: 128
Longest run: 5km
Total Lifts: 18
15 chairs, 3 drag
Lift capacity (people per hour): 32,000
Lift times: 8.30am to 3:30pm

Annual Snowfall: 6.35m
Snowmaking: 92% of slopes

Winter Period
early Nov to early May
Lift Passes
1 Day pass - $57/59
3 Day pass - $150/162
6 Day pass - $294/318
Board Schools
Beginner packages inc lift ticket, lesson & rental 1 day $75 , 2 days $120.
90min group lesson $30
Private lessons $70 1hr, $110 2hrs
Hire
Board & Boots $30 per day
Night Boarding
No

Sunday River Ski Resort
P.O. Box 450, Bethel, ME 04217
phone: (207) 824-3000
Web: www.sundayriver.com
Email: info@sundayriver.com

PISTES, People who like speed and steeps mixed in together can crank some fast turns on the **White Heat** trails, which is one of the steepest runs on the east coast. The trails on the **North Peak** are ideal for intermediate riders who like to take it easy.

BEGINNERS here have a resort that is superb for learning at with a large choice of easy runs to try out. The local ski-school offers a great teaching programme called the 'Perfect Turn Snowboard 'Clinic', where they guarantee to teach you to ride in a day, with a maximum of six people in a class.

THE TOWN
Off the slopes, local services are initially provided in the base areas where you will find a good selection of slope side lodging with condo's being the main choice. However, you may find it better to take the four mile drive back down to **Bethel** which plays host to all your needs. This is an easy-going and laid back kind of place that offers far more options for lodging, eating out or going for a beer. Bethel also offers cheaper facilities because as with most resorts, if you stay on or near the slopes, prices go up, and this place is no exception.

Good **accommodation** exists at the base of Sunday's slopes with a big choice of condo's. For riders on a budget then The *Snow Cap Lodge* Dorm is a good place to stay. On the other hand, if you have the cash then the *Jordan Grand Hotel*, which is on the slopes, is the place. Here they have all the facilities of a hotel which include a swimming and health club, bar lounge and dining room.

Food. Sunday River hasn't always had a good reputation for it's eating out. But things are changing with a good selection of restaurants on the slopes, or close by. In many of the lodges or hotel-condo's one is able to fine something that will please. You can get a decent steak in places like the *Hill Trading restaurant*, or a good Italian meal at *Rosett's*.

Nightlife is probably Sunday River's main let down. This is basically a place for lame heads into apres and all the horrible stuff that comes with it. There are a number of okay bars such as *Bumps*, the *Foggy Goggle* or *Suds Pub* and the *Sunday River Brewery*, but they all seem to think that sad music and silly games are cool.

SUMMARY
This is a place that offers some great all round freeriding to suit all levels. There is some excellent treeriding to be had and good beginner areas.

pic - Sunday River Resort

U

U
S
A

M
A
I
N
E

CAR
From Portland, head north on I-95 to exit 63 and then take Hwy 26 to Bethel which is 6 miles from Sunday. Follow Route 2 East for 2.6 miles then left onto Sunday River Road. Total 65miles, 1 1/2hrs
FLY
Fly to Portland Int, with a transfer time of 1 3/4 hours. Boston 172 miles, 3hrs away.
BUS
Bus services from Portland can take 1 3/4 hours.
TRAIN
to Portland

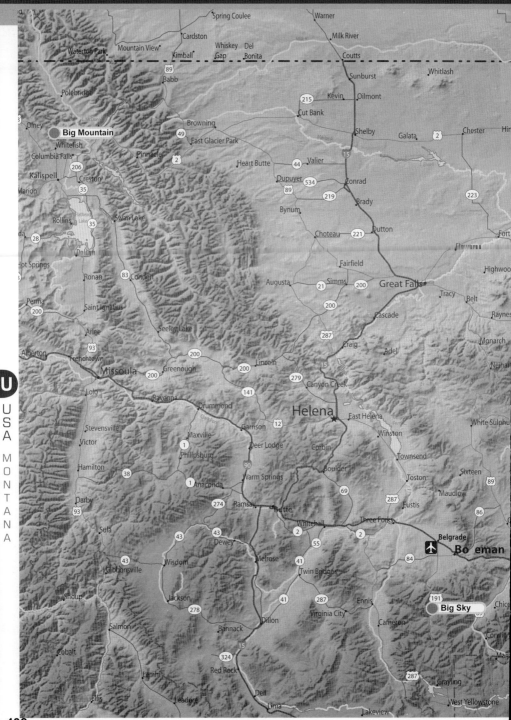

U

USA

MONTANA

POOR FAIR GOOD TOP

FREERIDE
Trees & some good off-piste
FREESTYLE
Terrain park
PISTES
Courduroy 'tastic

8
OUT OF 10

pic - Big Mountain Resort

haunts visited by fur clad skiers out to pose as is so often the case in many of Colorado's resorts. No, this is a purist's resort, a place where you come to ride and take it easy without gimmicks.

Big Mountain, which is closely linked to the nearby town of Whitefish, attracts visitors from places such as Seattle and up in neighbouring **Canada**. However, it doesn't attract too many of them so it never becomes overpopulated here. Some riders combine a trip to Big Mountain with a trip to Fernie, Canada which is only 2 hours away. Excellent transport links exist making this an easy place to get to either by plane or by train. Amtrax runs a daily service to **Whitefish**, called the *Empire Builder Passenger service* to and from major cities like **Seattle** and even **Chicago**. Overall this is a place that keeps things simple and affordable, both on the mountain and around town. The slopes operate a good lift system and provide heaps of annual snow. They don't bother with snowmaking here as they simply don't need it. The real stuff covers a mountain that offers a mixture of wide open bowls, wooded glades and great cruising runs.

FREERIDERS are in for a major treat at this place with a fantastic offering of deep powder, big bowls, lots of trees and great natural terrain features. Recently the resort has installed a new T-bar which has not only opened up more terrain but also provided better access to some existing runs. Basically, the mountain splits into three marked out areas. There's the Main Mountain, which has the most trails and something for every level, the North Side, which has a splattering of tree line black and blue runs and the **Hellroaring Basin**, which is an area mainly suited to advanced freeriders with riding on black and double black trails.

FREESTYLERS can have lots of fun here and any rider that doesn't appreciate this mountain should give up boarding and become a girl guide. This place is ideal for freestylers. Apart from lots of natural features, there is a massive terrain park off the **Silvertip chair** complete with table tops, berms, gap jumps etc.

THE PISTES are long and wide corduroy trails, that can be

Question, Big Mountain, have you heard of it? Answer no? Well other than those in the area and those from surrounding states, not many people have, and those in the know who have discovered this gem, may want to keep this place a secret. But it could be said that to not tell others about this rider's heaven could be criminal. Located in the far north of **Montana**, Big Mountain has attracted a lot of attention recently and is steadily growing in popularity due to it not only having great riding available, but also because of the resort's super laid back attitude and no nonsense approach. This place isn't one of those horrible glitzy

U
S
A

M
O
N
T
A
N
A

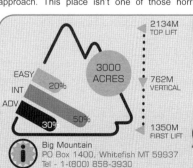

2134M TOP LIFT	
3000 ACRES	762M VERTICAL
EASY	
INT 20%	
ADV	
50%	1350M FIRST LIFT
30%	

Big Mountain
PO Box 1400, Whitefish MT 59937
Tel - 1-(800) 858-3930
Web: www.bigmtn.com
Email: bigmtn@bigmtn.com

Number of runs: 91
Longest run: 5.3km
Total Lifts: 11
9 chairs, 2 dragsLift capacity (people per hour): 13,800
Lift times:
9.00am to 9.00pm
Mountain Cafes: 10

Annual Snowfall:
7.62m
Snowmaking:
5% of slopes

Winter Period:
Nov to April
Lift Passes
1/2 Day Pass - $41
Day Pass - $49
Season Pass - $690
Board Schools
Full day group $50 Half Day $35
Full Day Private $310 Half Day $160
Hire
Board and boots $20/30, Helmet $5
Snowmobiles
1/2 day $130, Full day $230
Night Boarding
4pm to 9pm Fri and Sat. Pass $14

found all over the mountain. It's ideal for riders who want to turn into white van man, or just fancy some easy cruising. Beginners have a great mountain with lots of easy trails especially at the lower sections. There's a number of the blues are suitable for quick learners and novices to ride from the top of the mountain all the way to bottom.

THE TOWN

Big Mountain offers a good choice of local services with a wide range of options for lodging, eating and having a good night out. The facilities at the base of the slopes are very good and will provide you with most of your basic needs with condo's that have restaurants and bars. Around the base village you will also find a few shops, but in truth the biggest choice of shops and all other local services can be found back down in the sprawling and old fashioned town of **Whitefish**. Here you will find a place where locals treat you with respect.

Accommodation is provided at the slopes or in Whitefish. If you stay near the slopes you will be able to find a condo or a bed in one of the lodges at reasonable prices however if you base yourself down in **Whitefish**, you will be able to get better deals. There is a hostel called the *Non Hostile Hostel* that offers cheap bunks 001 (406) 862 7383.

Food. Big Mountain and Whitefish provide good and simple choices for going out and filling your stomach at a price to please everyone. You can pig out at The *Stube &*

Chuckwagon Grill which serves excellent food all day long. *The Moguls Bar and Grill* is an ideal place to get breakfast before hitting the slopes and is located near the base of **Swift Creek chair lift**. In **Whitefish** the *Buffalo Cafe* is a good place to eat.

Nightlife here is very laid back, but that's not to say that you can't have a stomping time. Highly rated by the visiting ski groups is the *Stube & Chuckwagon Grill* which goes in for too much après ski stuff, is still a cool bar. The *Great Northern* in Whitefish is not a bad joint which has a good selection of beers.

pics - Big Mountain Resort

CAR
In the US, take Interstate 90 until you're eight miles west of Missoula. Take US Highway 93 north 110 miles to Kalispell. From US-93 toward Whitefish, turn RIGHT (North) onto Baker Ave. City Hall will be on your right. Head (North) over the Viaduct, go straight onto Wisconsin Ave through the lights. 3 miles ahead, turn RIGHT (North) onto Big Mountain Rd. 8 miles up the road you'll find Big Mountain Village.
FLY
Glacier Park International Airport (FCA) has non-stop flights from Salt Lake (Delta), Minneapolis (Northwest), Spokane and Seattle (Horizon) arriving daily.
BUS
services from Calgary, but not direct. Local bus services are available from Glacier and nearby towns of Browning and Whitefish.
TRAIN
take Amtrak from Seattle, Portland and points east, including Minneapolis and Chicago. Multi-night package deals, including lodgings and ski tickets, are available by calling (800) 858-3930. Shuttle services ferry skiers from the Whitefish station to Big Mountain.

FREERIDE
Trees & some good backcountry
FREESTYLE
2 Terrain parks & halfpipe
PISTES
Lots of wide & easy slopes

POOR FAIR GOOD TOP

Good freeriding area

6
OUT OF 10

pic - Big Sky Resort

Big Sky is a typical corporate style resort which only goes back to around 1973, when the place was first built aided by millions of corporate dollars. Located just south of **Bozeman** in the **northern Rockies**, Big Sky is an impressive place, where you can do some serious riding on crowd-free slopes that rise above the tree lines. The rideable area is reached by Big Sky's tram and is spread over **Andesite Mountain** and **Lone Mountain**, which rise up to 3,400 meters. This has led to the claim that Big Sky has the largest vertical in the US. The two mountains, with a total of 100 trails, are connected by just seventeen lifts, consisting of some very fast chair lifts that can move 20,000

people uphill per hour. For the new 05/06 season, your lift pass is now accepted in nearby **Moonlight Basin.**

FREERIDERS will find this is a great place to get a fix. A good trail is the **Big Horn** which begins as an unchallenging trail that passes through woods, before dropping sharply into a bowl with banks and some good hits. Some of the most challenging terrain can be found if you first take the **Lone Peak** chair, and then hike up to reach the ridge off the south-facing summit. For those who know what they're doing, you get the option to go for it down loads of chutes.

FREESTYLERS looking for some natural hits, would do well to check out the gully formed down the side of **Lower Morning Star,** which is pretty cool. And if this is not enough, then Big Sky has a wheel-carved halfpipe and a good series of hits in the two terrain parks, **Swiftcurrent** and **Ambush Park**, which will both keep grommets happy for days on end

PISTE. Riders of the piste should get a good buzz out of these slopes, with plenty of wide open groomed trails that allow for some serious cranking it over turns. Check out the stuff off the **Ram Charger quad**, where you can descend at speed. Intermediates will dig the wide terrain on **Elk Park Ridge**, where you can crank some wide turns and take some easily stoppable spills

BEGINNERS will find plenty of easy terrain to practice their first moves, with the best novice stuff on the south side of **Andesite**, off **Southern Comfort chair** lift. The local ski-school handles all levels of tuition with full beginner programmes.

THE TOWN
Big Sky is not a place for the budget conscious. The modern town is a friendly place which looks after its visitors well and offers all the things you would expect of a tourist trap. Lodging is a mixture of condos and hotels along with a number of expensive restaurants and a few okay bars.

U
S
A

M
O
N
T
A
N
A

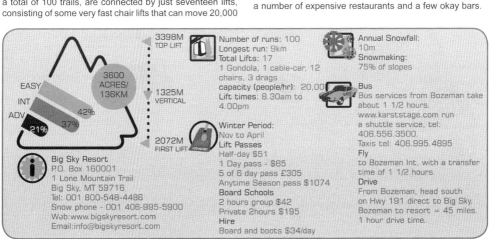

3398M
TOP LIFT

1325M
VERTICAL

2072M
FIRST LIFT

EASY
INT
ADV
21%
37%
42%

3600
ACRES/
136KM

Number of runs: 100
Longest run: 9km
Total Lifts: 17
1 Gondola, 1 cable-car, 12 chairs, 3 drags
capacity (people/hr): 20,000
Lift times: 8.30am to 4.00pm

Winter Period:
Nov to April
Lift Passes
Half-day $51
1 Day pass - $65
5 of 6 day pass £305
Anytime Season pass $1074
Board Schools
2 hours group $42
Private 2hours $195
Hire
Board and boots $34/day

Annual Snowfall:
10m
Snowmaking:
75% of slopes

Bus
Bus services from Bozeman take about 1 1/2 hours.
www.karststage.com run a shuttle service, tel:
406.556.3500.
Taxis tel: 406.995.4895
Fly
to Bozeman Int, with a transfer time of 1 1/2 hours.
Drive
From Bozeman, head south on Hwy 191 direct to Big Sky. Bozeman to resort = 45 miles. 1 hour drive time.

Big Sky Resort
P.O. Box 160001
1 Lone Mountain Trail
Big Sky, MT 59716
Tel: 001 800-548-4486
Snow phone - 001 406-995-5900
Web:www.bigskyresort.com
Email:info@bigskyresort.com

FREERIDE
Trees & some good off-piste
FREESTYLE
small Terrain park
PISTES
Groomed but some flats

Great funky laidback freeriders resort

7
OUT OF 10

feature is the area known as "The Ridge". This is the area at the very top of the resort which is composed of the steepest runs on the mountain and where everyone heads to on powder days. To get there it's a 400ft vertical hike up from the top of the highest lift. The hike is worth it as the area has many steep chutes and the best snow conditions at Bridger. You must carry an avalanche beacon, shovel and probe to access this area.

FREESTYLERS. Bridger Bowl is definitely a freeriders resort as it does not have a terrain park of any description. Having said that though, they are planning to build a small one this season. It'll be located between Bridger and Deer Park lifts above Doot Hill, but even so go freeride!

When people think about snowboarding in Montana they usually picture Big Sky or Big Mountain, but there is another resort that also starts with a "B" and is just as good; Bridger Bowl. Located near the funky college town of **Bozeman**, Bridger Bowl is an undiscovered gem. This small-medium sized resort can be a powder-hounds dream....during the 03/04 winter season Bridger got puked on, receiving over 100 inches in 3 days...that's about 2.5 metres in 3 days! Have you heard the expression "bring your snorkel"? Well, people were actually using them when they were riding the snow was that deep. If you would like a day off the board drive the 90 miles down to the famous **Yellowstone National Park** to checkout Old Faithful Geiser and the buffalo!

FREERIDERS The resort can basically be divided into two bowls, one on the **North side** and the other on the **South side**. Most of the resort has wide open terrain with some areas of wicked gladed runs. The lower half of the resort is fairly mellow, however Bridger's redeeming

PISTES. Riders will enjoy Bridger's beautifully groomed runs, however these are usually of low angles so hardcore carvers may become bored.

BEGINNERS will love Bridger's terrain. The lower runs are a novice's paradise...nothing too scary. As you progress you can move further and further up the mountain as your ability improves.

THE TOWN
All the action after hours takes place in the nearby town of **Bozeman**. It may not be a bustling metropolis, but it is a fun town to spend a few days in. This is mostly likely to do with the large amount of college students who attend Montana State University and who frequent the many bars and cool micro-breweries.There's something to suit all budgets, from backpackers to those with money to spare. **Food** - Find out which bars are having a 'chicken wing' special!

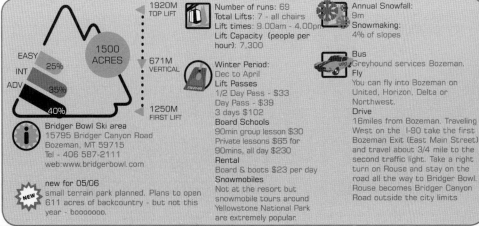

1920M TOP LIFT

671M VERTICAL

1250M FIRST LIFT

EASY 25%
INT
ADV 35%
40%

1500 ACRES

Number of runs: 69
Total Lifts: 7 - all chairs
Lift times: 9.00am - 4.00pm
Lift Capacity (people per hour): 7,300

Winter Period:
Dec to April
Lift Passes
1/2 Day Pass - $33
Day Pass - $39
3 days $102
Board Schools
90min group lesson $30
Private lessons $65 for 90mins, all day $230
Rental
Board & boots $23 per day
Snowmobiles
Not at the resort but snowmobile tours around Yellowstone National Park are extremely popular.

Annual Snowfall:
9m
Snowmaking:
4% of slopes

Bus
Greyhound services Bozeman.
Fly
You can fly into Bozeman on United, Horizon, Delta or Northwest.
Drive
16miles from Bozeman. Traveling West on the I-90 take the first Bozeman Exit (East Main Street) and travel about 3/4 mile to the second traffic light. Take a right turn on Rouse and stay on the road all the way to Bridger Bowl. Rouse becomes Bridger Canyon Road outside the city limits

Bridger Bowl Ski area
15795 Bridger Canyon Road
Bozeman, MT 59715
Tel - 406 587-2111
web:www.bridgerbowl.com

new for 05/06
small terrain park planned. Plans to open 611 acres of backcountry - but not this year - boooooooo.

USA MONTANA

wsg BRETTON WOODS

Simple and unadventurous, good for beginners

POOR FAIR GOOD TOP

FREERIDE
Trees but little off-piste

FREESTYLE
small park & halfpipe

PISTES
Groomed but some flats

4
OUT OF 10

Mountain which is a nice area for advanced riders who like to shred tight trees. All the trails and lifts connect up well and getting around the three slope faces can be done with ease. But that said, riders who prefer steep trails that last more than a few turns, may find that anything more than a couple of days on these slopes may become a bit tedious. On the other hand, a 10 year old kid taking their first snowboard trip with their parents will enjoy a weeks stay.

FREERIDERS do have a mountain that allows for easy going riding which also means taking in some treeriding. But this place is by no means a good freerider's resort, there's nothing that adventurous to take on and the few advanced runs that there are, don't take long to conquer. More terrain was opened last season in Rosebrook Canyon providing some steep gladed runs.

FREESTYLERS are presented a mountain that is basically dull when it comes to finding good natural hits. They do exist but not many. However, there is a 500ft halfpipe to check out.

PISTES. Boarders who like to take it easy will enjoy Brettons Woods. In the main, this is a good simple cruising resort, with a number of decent trails especially those on Mt Rosebrook

THE TOWN. Local attractions and services are provided at the base of the slopes. What you are offered is of a very high standard, the only problem being that the place is very boring and not much fun.

Bretton Woods lies 165 miles north of **Boston** and 100 miles north of **Manchester** and claims to be the largest resort in **New Hampshire**. However, claiming to be the biggest at something is not always an indicator of how good you are. What you have here is a respectable mountain that by east coast standards is fairly decent. Some 93 runs are hacked out of dense trees that cover the whole mountain from the summit to base. The slopes, which are in view of **Mt Washington**, are currently spread out over two peaks, **Mt Rosebrook** and **West Mountain** with the trails all working their way back down into one main base area. Soon to open will be another ridable area, that of **Mt Stickney.** What Bretton seems to be about to the casual observer, is a place that likes to keep things simple and one that attracts a lot of family ski groups. Constantly expanding, this is a resort that is best suited to beginners and intermediate carvers although freeriders who like easy slopes with trees will also fair well here. In recent years major expansion plans have lead to the area almost doubling in size with the opening of the West

U S A N E W H A M P S H I R E

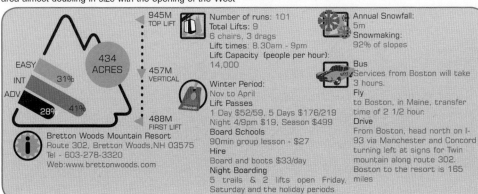

945M TOP LIFT

457M VERTICAL

488M FIRST LIFT

434 ACRES

EASY
INT 31%
ADV
28% 41%

Number of runs: 101
Total Lifts: 9
6 chairs, 3 drags
Lift times: 8.30am - 9pm
Lift Capacity (people per hour):
14,000

Winter Period:
Nov to April
Lift Passes
1 Day $52/59, 5 Days $176/219
Night 4/9pm $19, Season $499
Board Schools
90min group lesson - $27
Hire
Board and boots $33/day
Night Boarding
5 trails & 2 lifts open Friday,
Saturday and the holiday periods

Annual Snowfall:
5m
Snowmaking:
92% of slopes

Bus
Services from Boston will take
3 hours.
Fly
to Boston, in Maine, transfer
time of 2 1/2 hour.
Drive
From Boston, head north on I-93 via Manchester and Concord turning left at signs for Twin mountain along route 302. Boston to the resort is 165 miles

Bretton Woods Mountain Resort
Route 302, Bretton Woods,NH 03575
Tel - 603-278-3320
Web:www.brettonwoods.com

wsg LOON MOUNTAIN

FREERIDE
Trees but very little off-piste

FREESTYLE
Terrain park & halfpipe

PISTES
Well groomed easy slopes

Pretty dull but a good park

6
OUT OF 10

New Hampshire breeds a lot of resorts, most of which are frankly crap. However, Loon Mountain is one of the state's better offerings with a good friendly snowboard attitude. Located in **White Mountain National Forest**, Loon is the highest mountain in New Hampshire and a very popular resort that attracts a lot of punters. The resort has been going through a multi-million dollar expansion programme and has recently expanded the ride area with new lifts and services. The 275 acres of terrain is nearly all covered by snow cannons, so when the real stuff is lacking, they can still ensure good coverage. Despite Loon's small size and the odd lift line, it's a good place to ride, with a mixture of varied terrain to appeal to most recreational boarders of intermediate standard

FREERIDERS have a tree-covered mountain that allows for some good riding experiences. The **Kissin' Cousin** is a popular warm-up area, before trying out the likes of **Speakeasy**, reached by the **Kancamagus** chair. The **East Basin** is also a popular freeride area, where you'll find some decent wind-lips to track up.

FREESTYLERS have a full-on fun-park called **Skid Road**, which

snowboarders travel a long way to ride. Located on **Lower Flying Fox** and approximately 1,500m long, the park has plenty of very big hits including a 100 metre halfpipe, and was voted 16th best park in the US. Not bad for an east coast resort

PISTES. Riders of the piste will soon realise that Loon is the mountain for them. It offers great pistes for you to carve out some big turns on long, well prepared trails. Some of the best runs are the **Flume** and the Upper and Lower **Walking Boss**, an area that offers some well maintained pistes on either blue or black trails. There is also plenty for novice and intermediate riders

BEGINNERS will find plenty here. The best and easiest stuff is found on the **West Basin**, while the mid-section of the **Seven Brothers** chair offers something a little more testing. Loon Ski School offers a very good learning snowboard clinic

THE TOWN. Local services are plentiful in either **Loon**, **Lincoln** or **down** in the famous hippy hangout of **Woodstock**. All three towns are friendly and look after their visitors well. **Food** around the area caters well for all tastes and pockets. The *Old Mill* is good for seafood, while *Elvios* is the pizza place, and The *Woodstock Inn* is good for bar food. There are also a few good late-night hangouts in either Loon, Lincoln or Woodstock.

pics - Loon Mountain Resort

U

USA

NEW HAMPSHIRE

930M TOP LIFT	Number of runs: 45
	Longest run: 4km
EASY	Total Lifts: 10
275 ACRES	1 Gondola, 6 chairs, 2 drags, 1 magic carpet
INT 20%	capacity (people/hr): 11,865
640M VERTICAL	Lift times: 8.30am to 4.00pm
ADV 16%	Winter Period:
04%	Oct to May
289M FIRST LIFT	Lift Passes
	1 Day pass $52/59
	5 Days $212/259

Annual Snowfall: 3m
Snowmaking: 96% of slopes

Bus
Bus services from Boston can take 21/4 hours to Loon.
Fly
to Boston, with a transfer time of 2 1/4 hours.
Drive
From Boston, head north on I-93 to exit 32 at Lincoln. Then go east along R-122 to Loon Mountain. Boston to resort is 132 miles. 2 hours drive time.

Board Schools
Half day Group $35/39
Full Day Group $74/79
Hire
Board and boots $38/day, 5 days $180

i Loon Mountain Resort
RR1, Box 41, Kancamagus Hwy
Lincoln, NH 03251
Tel: 603-745-8111
Fax: 603-745-8214
Web:www.loonmtn.com
Email:info@loonmtn.com

POOR FAIR GOOD TOP

FREERIDE
Trees but little off-piste
FREESTYLE
3 terrain parks & halfpipe
PISTES
busy but smple slopes

Not hot, but not bad

6 OUT OF 10

Pics -(c) Waterville Valley Resort

FREESTYLERS and trick merchants have three fun-parks and a massive halfpipe to play in. The parks (shamefully open to skiers), are spread out around the slopes and offer something for all levels. The **Exhibition Terrain Park** (located near the base) is a pro-level park and features quarter-pipes, rail slides, table-tops and gaps and the superpipe. The **Boneyard** (located on Periphery) is a step down for more intermediate riders. The **little Slammer** is for junior grommets, and has some 8-10ft jumps of various guises and a few wide rails.

PISTES. People who can handle a board on its side have just one steep double black to go for - **True Grit**. Alternatively, the cluster of blues that descend from the summit make for nice easy riding on pleasant and well groomed trails

BEGINNERS only have a couple of dull green trails at the base, with a number of over-rated blues higher up that can be tackled quite easily by those with a few days under their belt.

THE TOWN. Local facilities, a few minutes from the slopes, are without frills. **Accommodation** covers condos, hotels and an array of B&B's. Prices are affordable and a number of weekly packages are available at reduced rates. **Dining out** offers no great surprises, with a simple choice of restaurants providing local dishes, fast-food and deli stuff. For some decent food check out *Chile Peppers* or *Alpine Pizza*. **Night action** is dull, but the *Zoo Station* and *Legends 1291* are okay for a beer.

Waterville is an easy-going, laid back place that is part of a programme called the Peaks of Excitement, a group of resorts working together. This means that your lift pass can be used at over 20 other places, giving a combined area of around 2,000 acres. The resort is only two hours from **Boston** and can be easily reached by bus or car. The slopes are a two minute drive from the village and serviced by a regular shuttle bus to the lifts. Waterville really tries hard to please snowboarders, with four fun-parks. However, the resort is a busy place at weekends, and being quite small, it can feel a bit cluttered at times. Advanced riders don't have a host of challenging trails, in the main this is an intermediate's and fast learning novice's resort.

FREERIDERS may not have the biggest or most happening playground at **Waterville**, but you still have areas to cut, with plenty of trees to shred like **Lower Bobby's**

U S A

N E W

H A M P S H I R E

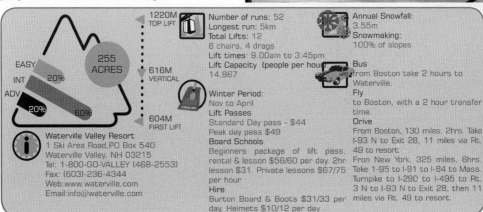

Number of runs: 52
Longest run: 5km
Total Lifts: 12
8 chairs, 4 drags
Lift times: 9.00am to 3:45pm
Lift Capacity (people per hour)
14,867

1220M
TOP LIFT

616M
VERTICAL

604M
FIRST LIFT

EASY
INT 20%
ADV
20%   60%

255 ACRES

Winter Period:
Nov to April
Lift Passes
Standard Day pass - $44
Peak day pass $49
Board Schools
Beginners package of lift pass, rental & lesson $56/60 per day. 2hr lesson $31. Private lessons $67/75 per hour
Hire
Burton Board & Boots $31/33 per day. Helmets $10/12 per day

Annual Snowfall:
3.55m
Snowmaking:
100% of slopes

Bus
From Boston take 2 hours to Waterville.
Fly
to Boston, with a 2 hour transfer time.
Drive
From Boston, 130 miles, 2hrs. Take I-93 N to Exit 28, 11 miles via Rt. 49 to resort.
Fron New York, 325 miles, 6hrs. Take 1-95 to I-91 to I-84 to Mass. Turnpike to I-290 to I-495 to Rt. 3 N to I-93 N to Exit 28, then 11 miles via Rt. 49 to resort.

Waterville Valley Resort
1 Ski Area Road, PO Box 540
Waterville Valley, NH 03215
Tel: 1-800-GO-VALLEY (468-2553)
Fax: (603)-236-4344
Web:www. waterville.com
Email:info@waterville.com

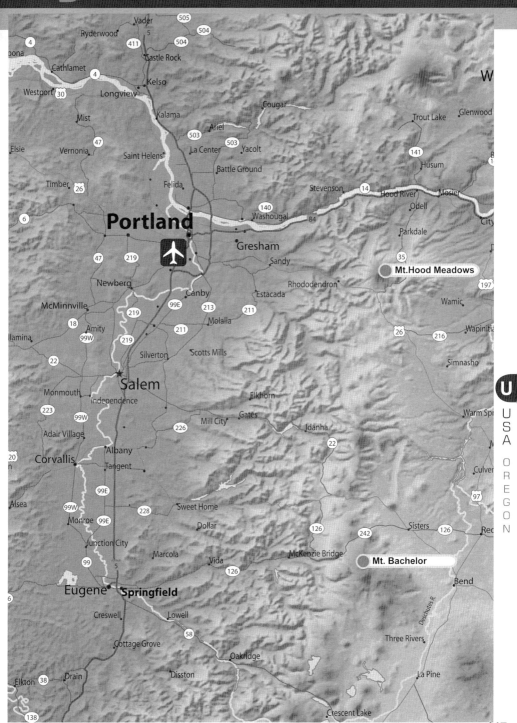

usg MT BACHELOR

Full-on freeriders resort; top open tree-lined riding

10
OUT OF 10

	POOR	FAIR	GOOD	TOP
FREERIDE Trees & good off-piste				
FREESTYLE 3 Terrain parks & a halfpipe				
PISTES Lots of well pisted long trails				

feet) and the infamous **Jamo Jump**, where you can fling yourself silly. Also accessible from the summit chair is Mt Bachelor's Backside, where you are sure to find fresh snow and solitude. You can use the new 2 mile long **Northwest Express** chair to access a vast amount of steep bowls and perfect tree runs. There are minimal man-made runs here, and the ones that are cut are narrow and winding.

FREESTYLERS-the **Outback** has many BMX and skate park-like runs that are easy to find by following the tracks. On crowded days, head over to **Rainbow chair**, which unfortunately is as slow as shit, but there are many natural quarter-pipes and rollers untouched by the weekend crowd. If you're man enough, ask some local jackass about the Compression jump, which on good days allows you to travel an unlimited distance before shooting up the side of the Cindercone. If natural terrain is not for you, Mt Bachelor maintains Mt Bachelor maintains four terrain parks, and a Superpipe which has been reshaped for a 2006 Olympic Qualifier.

PISTES. Riders who don't like bumps on the piste will find that Bachelor has them in mind and has grooms its trails to perfection. The runs off Skyliner and Pine Marten chairs are great intermediate and novice trails, but if you have the bottle then head to the summit and ride the unpisted open steeps of the Cirque - but don't bail!

BEGINNERS-this is a mountain that you'll appreciate, with its selection of good, easy green runs that can be ridden from the mid-section of the **Pine Marten** chair. The runs descend in a manner that allow you to steer onto a more

Pic -Peter Butsch/Mt Bachelor

Mt Bachelor is located in the **Cascade Mountains** of **Central Oregon**, 20 miles from the booming resort town of **Bend**. The snow-capped, dormant volcano is unique in that it is conical-shaped with seven high-speed quads, offering 360 access to the whole area. Chutes and gullies created long ago by lava flows, gives the terrain a shape and contour found in few other places. Combine 370 inches of annual snowfall, howling winds that create fairy-tale wind-lips, and you're left with acres of terrain that rival the best of any man-made park. Weekly storms rock the mountains, forcing you to frequently use force to steer through the dense weather systems. But even before the clouds clear and the sky is blue again, Mt Bachelor is damn fun!

FREERIDERS-if the summit is open, be sure to make the 10 minute hike to the top of the **Cirque Bowl**. You will find here an extra large cornice (that grows to 45

U S A

O R E G O N

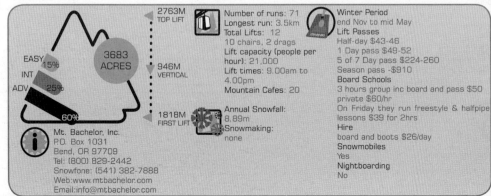

2763M TOP LIFT

EASY 15%
INT
ADV 25%
60%

3683 ACRES

946M VERTICAL

1818M FIRST LIFT

Mt. Bachelor, Inc.
P.O. Box 1031
Bend, OR 97709
Tel: (800) 829-2442
Snowfone: (541) 382-7888
Web:www.mtbachelor.com
Email:info@mtbachelor.com

Number of runs: 71
Longest run: 3.5km
Total Lifts: 12
10 chairs, 2 drags
Lift capacity (people per hour): 21,000
Lift times: 9.00am to 4.00pm
Mountain Cafes: 20

Annual Snowfall:
8.89m
Snowmaking:
none

Winter Period
end Nov to mid May
Lift Passes
Half-day $43-46
1 Day pass $49-52
5 of 7 Day pass $224-260
Season pass -$910
Board Schools
3 hours group inc board and pass $50
private $60/hr
On Friday they run freestyle & halfpipe lessons $39 for 2hrs
Hire
board and boots $26/day
Snowmobiles
Yes
Nightboarding
No

448

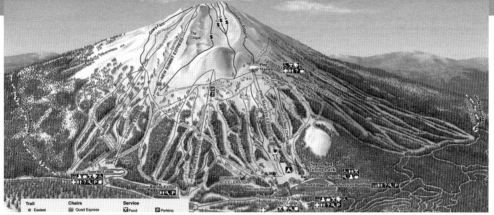

interesting and challenging blue as you gain confidence. The local snowboard school is really good, and the staff know how to turn you into a fast freeriding god within a day or two. A day's all-in programme will set you back just $40, and for those who want to make it big, sign up for one of High Cascade's winter camps.

THE TOWN

Mt Bachelor doesn't offer any substantial slopeside facilities. However, excellent laid back local services with a warm welcome are available 20 miles away in **Bend** or **Sunriver**. A free, daily and regular shuttle bus service runs to and from the slopes. Hitching to the mountain is also a good bet and cars do stop to pick you up. Bend and the surrounding area has everything you need for your stay, shops, banks, postal services and a huge array of in and out-door sporting attractions. Good snowboard hire services are at Bachelor Ski & Sport and Side Effects Snowboard Shop.

Accomodation.

The area can accommodate over 7,500 visitors, but nothing directly on the slopes. The nearest lodging is only a few miles from the slopes at the Inn of The *Seventh Mountain*, but the best choice of condos, B&B's and lodges can be found in the town of Bend, 20 miles away from Bachelor.

Food. There are no big surprises when it comes to restaurants. What you are offered is a good, but somewhat basic selection of eatries where you can wine and dine down in Bend, or have a snack attack up on Bachelor. The *Taco Stand* is the place to fill yourself with a burrito bomber: this beauty will clog up any 15 gallon pressure-locked toilet. *Stuft Pizza* is the place for pasta dishes. On the Mountain locals call *Scapolo's* in the Pine Marten Lodge from the chairlift and have pizza waiting when they arrive.

Night-life at Bachelor is not exactly the most happening. However, things liven up in **Bend** where there are enough joints to drink and dance in until you drop. Try *Evil Sister Saloon* if you're inclined to the 'alternative' end of the spectrum. *Legends* is also a cool hangout with large screens and a decent beer.

CAR
Portland via Madras & Bend. Mt Bachelor is 203 miles. Drive time is about 3 1/2 hours.
FLY
Fly to Portland International, transfer time to resort is 3 1/2 hours. Local airport is Redmond, 15 miles from Bend
BUS
There are daily bus services from both Portland airport and Redmond domestic airport. 4 shuttles a morning leave from the Park-N-Ride in Bend (7am, 8:15,9:30,11:15) to the mountain $5 single
TRAIN
to Chemult 60 miles away

U
S
A

O
R
E
G
O
N

POOR FAIR GOOD TOP

FREERIDE
A few tree runs & good off-piste
FREESTYLE
Terrain parks & a halfpipe
PISTES
good mix, but short advanced runs

Full-on fplace for great open terrain freeriding

10 OUT OF 10

There are three main resorts on Mt Hood, a dormant (not extinct!) volcano: **Mt Hood Meadows**, **Ski Bowl** and **Timberline**. Although small, Meadows is the most popular and has a huge range of interesting riding crammed into its space and, joy of joys, virtually no traversing anywhere. It maybe tempting fate, but it is hard to get lost on Hood. You can spend a whole day taking different lines, but know that you are not too far from where you started. This is a very mixed ability mountain, with some nice basic novice terrain to pockets of testing trails for the more advanced rider, but in truth this not the most testing place, Steep descents will only be found in very short doses, like on **Waterfall** or around the back of **Nightmare Knoll** (a 40+ft cliff). The locals have their own names for most of the stuff they ride and are more than happy to show you their favourite little stash(!). The lifties are cool too, and a large proportion ride. If you can't afford the daily rates, the mountain is open for night-riding until March, although not extensively; take advantage of the special offers at Safeway's Supermarkets ($8.50 for Sunday 4pm-10pm) and you can't complain. Meadows is a popular destination for **summer riding**, with *Tim Windell's High Cascade* and *Mt Hood Snowboard Camp,* but you have to be enrolled on a camp to use their facilities.

FREERIDERS-this mountain is very much for you: the terrain, which may not offer a super amount of challenging stuff or be the most extensive in the world, is still perfect wherever you go. The **Super Bowl** is a black graded area, with a series of descents on open terrain. The notable thing about the Super Bowl, is that it's not serviced by a lift line; instead you get up on a snowcat for around $10 a go

FREESTYLERS-there are natural hits everywhere and also a good fun-park off the **Hood River chair**. However, the fact that skiers are allowed in the park with so much good natural terrain on offer, make it hardly worth using. You can have a great time riding the hits around **Chunky Swirl** and the **Texas run**. If you're a pipe hound, then you'll usually find it well maintained but often very busy with local air heads.

U
S
A

O
R
E
G
O
N

pics - Mt.Hood Meadows Resort

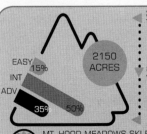

2225M TOP LIFT

2150 ACRES

EASY 15%
INT
ADV

35% 50%

846M VERTICAL

1379M FIRST LIFT

(i) MT. HOOD MEADOWS SKI RESORT
P.O. Box 470
Mt. Hood, OR 97041-0470
Tel: 503.337.2222
Fax:503.337.2217
Web:www.skihood.com
Email:info@skihood.com

Number of runs: 87
Longest run: 5km
Total Lifts: 10
10 chairs
Lift capacity
(people per hour):
16,145
Lift times: 8.00am
to 10.00pm
Mountain Cafes: 2

Annual Snowfall:
9.15m
Snowmaking:
none

Winter Period
mid Nov to June
Winter Period
July to August
Lift Passes
1 Day pass $48-52
Half-day $41-45, Night only $22
4 of 6 Days $160, Season pass $999
Board Schools
Group lessons $35 for 90mins
Beginner package $99 for 3 days lift, lesson & hire. Private lessons $65 hour
Hire
Board & boots $28 per day, demo kit $40
Night Boarding
240 acres including park & pipe. Wednesday, Thurs & Sun nights till 9:00 PM. Fri & Sat nights until 10:00 PM.
Snow CAT
Super Bowl Snow Cat provides 1,700ft vertical dropping into Heather Canyon. Head to top of Cascade Express $10 a trip.

the MOUNTAIN

Top Cascade Express	7,300 ft.
Bottom Hood River Express	4,523 ft.
Vertical Rise	2,777 ft.
Elevation at Base Lodge	5,366 ft.
Snowcat Skiing Additional	1,700 vertical ft.
Top of Snowcat Skiing	9,000 ft.

TERRAIN

15% Beginner	50% Intermediate
20% Advanced	15% Expert
Skiable Acres	2,150
Acres of Night Skiing	240
Longest Run	3 Miles
Annual Snowfall	430"

TRAIL MAP LEGEND

- ●—— EASIER
- ■—— MORE DIFFICULT
- ◆—— MOST DIFFICULT
- ◆◆—— EXPERT
- ◆◆ FREESTYLE TERRAIN
- 🍴 DINING
- 🚡 HIGH SPEED QUADS
- 🚠 SNOWCAT SKIING
- ✚ FIRST AID STATION

opposite **Ski Bowl** which is only a few miles away. Alternatively you could base yourself in the town of **Hood River**, 36 miles away, which has loads of facilities.

Accommodation is provided in various locations, with the more expensive near the slopes at Mt Hood. Mt Hood Hamlet B&B has rates from $95 tel (800) 407 0570. While down on **Hood River** you can get a bed at *Prather's Motel* for around $40 a night. The *Bingen School Hostel* has nightly rates from $15 and is a good budget hangout.

Food. If you're the sort of person that wants to dine out night after night eating fine haute cuisine dressed in a tuxedo, then firstly see a shrink, and secondly visit another resort. This place is for those who like their food served man style, big portions no frills and cheap. Wherever you stay, there are plenty of budget food-stops. *Huckleberry's* does a damn fine breakfast and is open 24 hours. While down in Hood River, *Big City Chicks* is good.

Night Life. Hood may seem to be quiet and tame from the outside, but in fact things can get very lively and in a snowboard way, kick off nightly with a lot of hardcore boozing, especially in the no frills Government Camp or in Mt Hood at the likes of the *Alpenstube*. The biggest selection of night action takes place in **Hood River**.

PISTES. The runs from Cascade are the best in terms of wide, open riding trails, with a couple of decent blue trails down to choose from. There isn't an abundance of steeps for long fast descents, but what is there is excellent

BEGINNERS are treated to a good number of trails that are easy to reach and easy to negotiate. **Mt Hood Express** gives access to some interesting green runs and some tame blues. The local snowboard school has a host of teaching programmes for all levels, including a Mountain Master Programme

THE TOWN
If you're the sort of person that doesn't want the normal, tacky, overpriced tourist facilities found in many resorts, then this place will please you. What you have is a laid back and very basic place where the locals are cool. *Timberline Lodge* (the location for the film 'The Shining') has recently had an overhaul and is the only real slopeside accommodation which is open all year, but prices can be a bit steep. A good option would be to stay down in **Government Camp**

CAR
From Portland take Hwy 26 east to Government Camp; then north on Hwy 35 - 10 miles to Meadows. 75 miles total, drive time is about 1 1/2 hours.
FLY
Fly to Portland International. Transfer time to resort is 1 1/2 hours. Vancouver 74 miles
BUS
There are daily bus services from Portland airport as well as good car hire services.
Weekend day trip specials from Portland, return $20 leaves 6:40am returns 4:00pm tel: 503. BUS. LIFT /287.5438/
TRAIN to Portland 69 miles on

U

U S A   O R E G O N

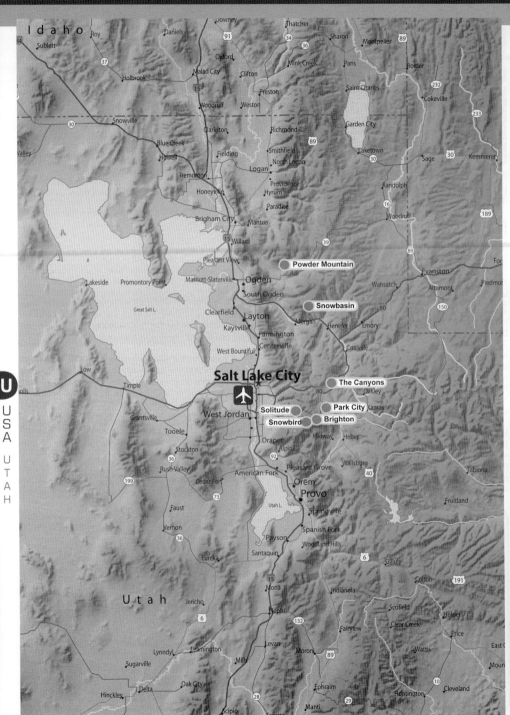

wsg BRIGHTON

Over-rated, some good freeriding if prepared to hike

OUT OF 10

FREERIDE
Trees & some cool backcountry
FREESTYLE
Terrain park & halfpipe
PISTES
many slopes lack pitch

POOR FAIR GOOD TOP

Peak from the **Snake Creek Express** leads to some super tree runs in Snake Bowl. **Hidden Country** backcountry also has a limitless possibility of tree runs and powder shoots after a good storm, but it tends to get tracked out pretty fast.

FREESTYLERS will be disappointed with the pipe but the park is very well maintained. It has a bunch of decent table tops and spine jumps and is not usually crowded during the week.

Brighton is generally talked of as the snowboarding capital of **Utah**, but that is over-rated. **Brighton** is located at the top of **Big Cottonwood Canyon** and most of the mountain is lacking in vertical and challenging terrain. The pipe sucks and the regulars here are not a friendly crowd. There are some really good riders but they don't appreciate visitors crowding the snowboard parks and they will always be the first to let you know it. However, Brighton has been welcoming pleasure seekers to its slopes since 1936 and is fully open to snowboarders. Brighton is also close to the snowboard friendly resort of Solitude.

FREERIDERS will want to head straight for the **Millicent** lift. The **Wolverine Cirque backcountry** is out of this world. This area may require a hike out, but it is well worth the effort. Scree-Slope rocks too. It accesses a sweet cliff/shoot area, which goes all the way over to **Camera Land** and **Mary Chutes** backcountry. An easy hike to the top

THE PISTES of Brighton don't have a lot to offer. There are only a few fast groomers off of Millicent and Evergreen. The rest of the mountain just does not maintain enough vertical

BEGINNERS would really enjoy learning on this mountain. A large portion of the terrain is not too steep or technical. The **Explorer lift** is a great place to start and there are numerous runs off of the **Majestic lift** that beginners would be comfortable with. **Sunshine** off the Snake Creek Express is a long run, but mellow.

THE TOWN
Off the slopes things are remarkably different to on the slopes because in truth there is nothing here other than a couple of basic lodges and a few bed and breakfasts haunts. You should stay in a neighbouring resort or down in **Salt Lake City**.

U
S
A

U
T
A
H

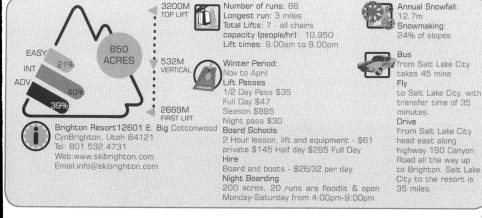

453

FREERIDE
Trees & good off-piste
FREESTYLE
2 terrain parks & a halfpipe
PISTES
Lots of decent slopes

Good freeriders resort

7
OUT OF 10

Pic - Eric Schramm/Park City

FREERIDERS will be wetting themselves once they see what awaits them on these slopes, which stretch out over a number of peaks. If you like backcountry riding then check out **McConkey's bowl** where there are some great double diamond runs that weave through the trees. If riding deep powder in bowls is your thing then this place has some fantastic bowls that involve some hiking and then dropping in, notably the trails on **Jupiter**. Here you will find some black diamond rated trails that can be ridden down to a chair lift, but be warned, this area is for experts.

FREESTYLERS who want to catch big air off natural hits are going to love this place. The mountain is littered with hits galore whether it be up in the bowls or down on the lower pisted areas. The resort also builds numerous terrain parks with man-made hits of every shape. Jonesys Park is great for beginners, while the biggest **Pick n'shovel park is great** for the intermediate. **Kings Crown Super Park** is for the mad and Pros only, and if that's not enough, to cap it all there the serious **Eagle Superpipe** located at the top of the Payday trail. The pipe and the Payday park are flood lit for night riding and are open daily from 9 till 19.30.

PISTE huggers are also in for a good time here. There is a fine choice of good cruising trails such as the runs off the **King Con chair** lift.

BEGINNERS who have never ridden will soon be able to get to grips with things here, as this is a very good first timers resort.

THE TOWN.
Around town there are lots of things to do as well has offering fantastic nightlife. No other resort in Utah packs in as many facilities as this one. There is every imaginable type of accommodation available although not many are aimed at budget riders. However, a good cheap option is the *Park City Youth Hostel* (www.parkcity.com tel 435 655 7255). Don't listen to the stories about the Mormon **drinking** laws, they do exist but they just make things more amusing. Ask a local bartender what the score is on this.

U
S
A

U
T
A
H

Park City, which played host to the 2002 Olympic Winter Games, is by far the most famous resort in Utah and also one of the most expensive. However, don't let the fact that this is a costly place with a bit of an attitude put you off. In terms of what there is to ride and the way the place is laid out, **Park City** is cool. With some 100 named trails and over 3300 acres of linked terrain, no-one is going to feel left out here. For the 2002 Olympic Winter Games, Park City was home to skiing's giant slalom and as well as the snowboard races and when you see this place, it's easy to see why. This is a place that knows how to put on a show, (even if the snow can often be a bit dodgy).

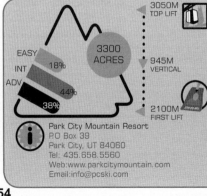

EASY
INT 18%
ADV 44%
38%

3300 ACRES

3050M
TOP LIFT

945M
VERTICAL

2100M
FIRST LIFT

Park City Mountain Resort
P.O. Box 39
Park City, UT 84060
Tel: 435.658.5560
Web:www.parkcitymountain.com
Email:info@pcski.com

Number of runs: 100
Longest run: 5.6km
Total Lifts: 14 - all chairs
Lift times: 9.00am to 9.00pm
Lift Capacity (people per hour):
27,200
Mountain Cafes: 5

Winter Period:
Nov to April
Lift Passes
Day Pass - $61
Season - $1050
Board Schools
Group 3 hours from $70
Hire
Board & Boots $31 per day
Snowmobiles:90 mins $50
Night Boarding:Yes

Annual Snowfall:
8.89m
Snowmaking:
47% of slopes

Fly
to Salt Lake City, 45 mins transfer
Drive
from Salt Lake airpoty head East on Interstate 80 for 4.4miles, then onto I-15 South for 2.5 miles, continue I-80 Eastbound for 21 miles. Take Kimball Junction/Park City exit # 145. Take UT-224 for 6 miles, turn right onto Empire Avenue to resort

wsg POWDER MOUNTAIN

FREERIDE
Trees & HUGE backcountry

FREESTYLE
2 Terrain parks & halfpipe

PISTES
some groomed slopes

Great freeriders resort with some cool cat boarding

7
OUT OF 10

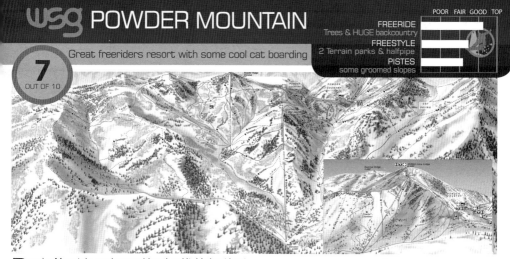

Powder Mountain can be considered as Utah's best kept secret. It is just outside of the small mountain town of **Eden**, north of **Salt Lake City**, and does not attract the crowds like many of the larger resorts near Salt Lake City and Park City. The resort has a decent 2800 acres of lift served terrain, however the real joy of the resort is to make use of the shuttle, snow CAT and the guided tours to give you another 2800 acres of pristine backcountry.

FREERIDERS will be stoked to find that Powder Mountain is one giant playground. Most of the terrain is a variety of tree shots, rock drops, and open powder fields. There are great lines off either side of **Straight Shot** and from the top of **Cobabe Canyon**. . Riders will also fall in love with the backcountry area known as **Powder Country** which is well known throughout the region. These impressive steeps are easily accessible from the **Sundown lift** and drop to the highway where a shuttle service runs for another ride up. Powder has super **cat skiing** from the top of **Lightning Ridge**. There's 700 acres of powder. A 30min hike to James Peak gives access to a number of chutes and bowls. it costs $7 for a trip up. Group tours are available at $80/125 half/full day to these areas. Tel: 801-745-3772

FREESTYLERS If you search a little, you can find plenty of natural hits to play on. The **boulder field** on lower Straight Shot and the trees off of East 40 have some nice kickers. There's the **Sundown Park** off the Confidence lift which is lit at night, and has a half decent pipe (usually open by mid-January). There should be a good selection of features in the new **Hidden Lake terrain park**

BEGINNERS should all learn to ride at this resort with ease. **Sunrise, Sundown**, or **Hidden Lake** lift would be good places to start while the **Picnic** and **Mushroom** runs are nice mellow runs to follow up on.

THE TOWN
Resort lodge restaurants are the only places to eat nearby and the only accommodation at the mountain is the *Columbine Inn,* where rooms and condos are available. The best bet for inexpensive food and accommodations is 19 miles away in the city of **Ogden**. Here you will find a large selection of everything, birds, booze and music, to mention but a few.

U
S
A

U
T
A
H

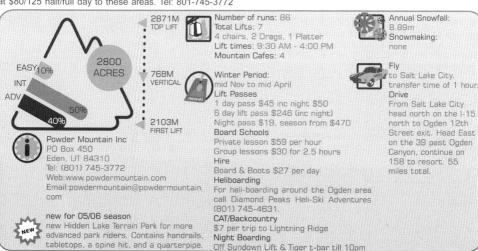

EASY 10%
INT
ADV
50%
40%

2800 ACRES

2871M
TOP LIFT

768M
VERTICAL

2103M
FIRST LIFT

Powder Mountain Inc
PO Box 450
Eden, UT 84310
Tel: (801) 745-3772
Web: www.powdermountain.com
Email: powdermountain@powdermountain.com

new for 05/06 season
new Hidden Lake Terrain Park for more advanced park riders. Contains handrails, tabletops, a spine hit, and a quarterpipe.

Number of runs: 86
Total Lifts: 7
4 chairs, 2 Drags, 1 Platter
Lift times: 9:30 AM - 4:00 PM
Mountain Cafes: 4

Winter Period:
mid Nov to mid April
Lift Passes
1 day pass $45 inc night $50
6 day lift pass $246 (inc night)
Night pass $19. season from $470
Board Schools
Private lesson $59 per hour
Group lessons $30 for 2.5 hours
Hire
Board & Boots $27 per day
Heliboarding
For heli-boarding around the Ogden area call Diamond Peaks Heli-Ski Adventures (801) 745-4631.
CAT/Backcountry
$7 per trip to Lightning Ridge
Night Boarding
Off Sundown Lift & Tiger t-bar till 10pm

Annual Snowfall:
8.89m
Snowmaking:
none

Fly
to Salt Lake City,
transfer time of 1 hour.
Drive
From Salt Lake City
head north on the I-15
north to Ogden 12th
Street exit. Head East
on the 39 past Ogden
Canyon, continue on
158 to resort. 55
miles total.

POOR FAIR GOOD TOP

FREERIDE
A few trees & some off-piste

FREESTYLE
2 terrain parks & a halfpipe

PISTES
Some decent length trails

5 OUT OF 10

Decent terrain, but too commercial

bottom of the **Grizzly downhill** slope

PISTES. Theres some nice steep options like the men's and women's downhill courses when races are not going on. Most of the mountain is intermediate groomers with some nice long trails.

BEGINNERS have a good resort for learning the basics at and although there are not loads of green easy trails, what is on offer is okay, especially the beginner terrain off of **Becker Chair.**

Snowbasin is located north of the city of **Ogden**. Unfortunately, they hold so many races here that the **John Paul Express**, which takes you to the men and women's downhill courses and which accesses a large kick ass part of the mountain, is usually closed of for competitions. Still, there are a lot of other runs to check out with a good supply of black ones at the upper area and a number of intermediate trails leading from the top to the bottom, taking in a few trees en-route. The whole mountain is open to boarders, but only if you have a safety strap on your board. If you arrive without one, you won't be allowed up.

FREERIDERS will like this mountain more than anyone else. In general the mountain is not extensive and a week's stay would be overdoing it. However, there is a good selection of black marked slopes to keep most riders interested for a day or two. The **Strawberry Express** is good for access to backcountry gates.

FREESTYLERS will find 2 terrain parks, one at the base and another on Porky Face. The **Krazy Kat park** at the base has some boxes, a couple of rails and a table top, while the **Apex Park** at the top of Porcupine lift has some bigger jumps and a 1/4 pipe. There's a superpipe at the

THE TOWN

Forget about any slope side facilities, however, **Ogden** has everything you could possibly want. The *Alaskan Inn* 001 (801)-621-8600 is pricey and the rooms fill up fast, but it is fun and is right in *Ogden Canyon*, closer to the resorts.

Pic - John Paul Area at Snowbasin resort

U
S
A

U
T
A
H

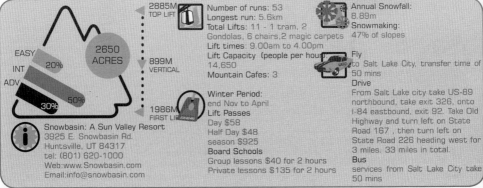

2885M TOP LIFT

899M VERTICAL

1986M FIRST LIFT

2650 ACRES

EASY
INT 20%
ADV 50%
30%

Number of runs: 53
Longest run: 5.6km
Total Lifts: 11 - 1 tram, 2 Gondolas, 6 chairs, 2 magic carpets
Lift times: 9.00am to 4.00pm
Lift Capacity (people per hour) 14,650
Mountain Cafes: 3

Annual Snowfall: 8.89m
Snowmaking: 47% of slopes

Fly
to Salt Lake City, transfer time of 50 mins

Drive
From Salt Lake city take US-89 northbound, take exit 326, onto I-84 eastbound, exit 92. Take Old Highway and turn left on State Road 167 , then turn left on State Road 226 heading west for 3 miles. 33 miles in total.

Bus
services from Salt Lake City take 50 mins

Winter Period:
end Nov to April
Lift Passes
Day $58
Half Day $48
season $925
Board Schools
Group lessons $40 for 2 hours
Private lessons $135 for 2 hours

Snowbasin: A Sun Valley Resort
3925 E. Snowbasin Rd.
Huntsville, UT 84317
tel: (801) 620-1000
Web:www.Snowbasin.com
Email:info@snowbasin.com

Epic mountain for good riders

	POOR	FAIR	GOOD	TOP
FREERIDE Some trees & excellent off-piste				
FREESTYLE 2 Terrain parks & halfpipe				
PISTES get freeriding				

8 OUT OF 10

pic - Credit: Richard Cheski/Snowbird

day there after a good storm and never get bored. On the other hand, once you take the tram to the top of Hidden Mountain, you can't really go wrong no matter what face you drop in off. There are plenty of cool runs like **Silver Fox**, **Great Scott**, and **Upper Cirque**, and **Gad Valley**. It is also not a bad idea to save some quality time for **Thunder Bowl**, accessible by the Gad 2 lift.

FREESTYLERS have a new superpipe located on the **Big Emma** run in Gad Valley which was dug out in the summer of 05. Besides that, you will have to use some creativity to find hits outside of the two parks.   The Beginner Terrain Park is next to the Super Pipe and can be accessed from the Mid-Gad, Gadzoom and Wilbere chairlifts. The Expert Terrain Park is accessed by the **Baby Thunder lift** and has a sires of rails and hits.

Snowbird is unquestionably the choice mountain for intermediate and expert snowboarders. It has the most vertical terrain of any **Utah** resort and a pretty decent halfpipe. Skiers tend to out-number riders on this mountain, but the attitude is not competitive. Over the years, this is a resort that has become well known for its steep terrain and fantastic powder, trees, bowls and gullies along with some okay novice terrain. In all honesty, this place is for riders who can ride, because nearly half of the mountain is rated as advanced. If you like going balls out down serious steeps then Snowbird is your heaven, but be warned, if you fail to respect any of the slopes, you may go home in a body bag.

FREERIDERS should take the **Mineral Basin** lift off the backside of **Hidden Peak** which accesses some of the most epic snow and terrain imaginable. It is easy to spend

BEGINNERS will quickly find that Snowbird is really an intermediate to expert mountain and might get bored on the limited availability of easy runs. However, the easy area known as the Baby Thunder, is good.

THE TOWN
Local services are sparse to say the least. There are a couple of lodges close to the base lifts along with a few restaurants and a couple of bars. But don't expect much, or anything cheap.

U
U
S
A
U
T
A
H

EASY 27%
INT
ADV 38%
35%
2500 ACRES

3352M TOP LIFT
880M VERTICAL
2365M FIRST LIFT

Number of runs: 85
Longest run: 2.5miles
Total Lifts: 12
1 tram, 10 chairs, 2 drags
Lift capacity (people/hour): 16,800
Lift times: 9am to 4:30 pm

Winter Period:
mid Nov to mid April
Lift Passes
Lift pass $58, 5 day pass $225
Board Schools
Half-day improvers workshops $56.
Beginners package inc lift, lesson, hire $99 for 1 day, $149 3 days. Private 3hr $275. Secret spots day for advanced freeriders $90 per day
Hire
Board & Boots $31 a day, $45 demo kit
Heliboarding
7 runs/day $525/770
Night Boarding
Chickadee lift open until 8.30 p.m for night boarding on wednesdays and fridays

Annual Snowfall:
12.7m
Snowmaking:
1% of slopes

Fly
to Salt Lake City,
transfer time 45 mins
Drive
From Salt Lake City head east along I-80 and I-215 south and leave at exit 6 following the route for little Cottonwood Canyon. Salt Lake City to the resort 25 miles.
Bus
Bus services from Salt Lake City takes 45 mins. Contact 1.800.232.9542 to book 40min shuttle to resort from airport.

Snowbird Ski and Summer Resort
P.O. Box 929000
Snowbird, UT 84092-9000
Tel: 1-801-742-2222
Web:www.snowbird.com
Email:info@snowbird.com

	POOR	FAIR	GOOD	TOP
FREERIDE Trees & some good backcountry				
FREESTYLE A small terrain park				
PISTES Some decent length trails				

Super terrain but limited air possibilities

7 OUT OF 10

pic - Solitude Resort

FREESTYLE. Expert Freestylers will probably hate it here as the **Terrain Park** is dedicated solely to beginners. However, everyone was a beginner at some stage and those learning will enjoy the 2 table tops, one fun box and the set of rollers on offer.

THE PISTES accessed by the **Eagle Express** are where there are plenty of fast cruiser runs like the **Challenger**, **Gary's Glade** and **Inspiration**. Riders will also be happy with a handful of smooth runs off of the Summit chair such as **Dynamite** and **Liberty**. The Apex chair will get you to a few short groomers as well.

Solitude is a nice change of pace because Solitude is a nice change of pace because it does not seem to attract hoards of people like the other Salt Lake resorts, plus the mountain kicks ass! There is also a great variety of terrain and a way of spreading out the crowds so that the lines in any one area do not get too long. The attitude is low key and the regulars are super friendly.

FREERIDERS will have no problem having the time of their lives at this resort. The **summit lift** is sure access to some of the sweetest powder country in Utah. **Honeycomb Canyon** is long and extreme and offers freeriding at its best. The **Evergreen area** is a must and the **Headwall Forest** rarely gets tracked out. The best freeriding on this mountain is the Solitude backcountry area, only accessible by hiking. These impressive steeps and powder fields drop down onto **Brighton Ski Resort**, but by staying far left, you will find trails that wrap back around to Solitude.

BEGINNERS will find that this mountain is a great place to first try snowboarding at. There is a good area for learning right off of the **Moonbeam II chair**, where you will find plenty of good easy runs to keep you happy for a while. **North Star** and **South Star,** off the Sunrise lift, are also great beginner runs. First timers can also warm up on **Easy Street** off the Link chair.

THE TOWN. You can stay close to the slopes in one of the lodges or condo units offering a choice rooms at generally high rates. *The Powderhorn* is Solitude's newest place for lodging offering visitors somewhere to stay that is both good and convenient, but it's not cheap. Eating out options are basic, however, the Creekside makes fantastic pizza's. Nightlife's pretty quiet. Riders looking for a bit of a party are best off heading into **Salt Lake City.** You can chose to stay up at the resort, however, if you are on a budget your best bet would be to stay in a cheap hotel near the mouth of the Big Cottonwood Canyon.

U S A

U T A H

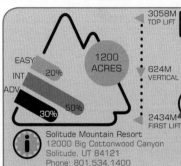

EASY
INT 20%
ADV
30% 50%

1200 ACRES

3058M TOP LIFT

624M VERTICAL

2434M FIRST LIFT

Number of runs: 64
Longest run: 5.6km
Total Lifts: 8 - all chairs
Lift times: 9.00am to 4.00pm
Lift Capacity (people per hour): 12,550
Mountain Cafes: 3

Winter Period: Nov to April
Lift Passes
Morning pass $44, Afternoon $42
Day pass $50, 2 days $96
Board Schools
Beginners package $85 for day hire, lift pass & 2hr lesson
Hire
Board & Boots $20/30 half/day

Annual Snowfall: 12.5m
Snowmaking: 30% of slopes

Fly
to Salt Lake City, transfer time of 50 mins
Drive
From Salt Lake City head east along I-80 and south on I-215 and exit at junction 6 to Wasatch. You'll find the resort 14 miles up Big Cottonwood Canyon
Bus
services from Salt Lake City take 50 mins

i Solitude Mountain Resort
12000 Big Cottonwood Canyon
Solitude, UT 84121
Phone: 801.534.1400
Web:www.skisolitude.com
Email:info@skisolitude.com

NEW new for 05/06 season
Moonbeam Chairlift replaces the current lift and will be positioned higher than is current. New day lodge position next to the Moonbeam Center

great boarders resort, not for absolute beginners

8
OUT OF 10

	POOR	FAIR	GOOD	TOP
FREERIDE Trees & good off-piste				
FREESTYLE Parks but great natural				
PISTES Huge number of gladed slopes				

The Canyons is **Utah's** newest resort and one of the largest with over 3625 acres of fantastic terrain to check out that makes this part of the **Rockies** a pure dream. Newest Canyons may be, but in fact this place has been around for quite some time but under another name, that of **Park West**. However, that's neither here nor there, what this place is about is the future. This massive mountain, which is covered in trees from top to bottom, is constantly expanding by opening new areas all the time and upgrading base facilities year on year off. Indeed Canyons has big ambitions and plans to one day be the biggest resort in the US. And when you see what they have achieved so far, perhaps it could happen. But for now this is a mountain that has everything to turn the aspiring freestyle junkie into a pro air head, or a freeride grommet into a mountain guru. You have deep gullies, massive powder bowls and natural hits galore wherever you go.

FREERIDERS have landed in paradise when they get here. You simply won't believe not only the amount of terrain, but also the diversity of it all. The **Tombstone Express** will take you to some super terrain, but make sure you study your lift map, it would be easy to head off down a steep trail above your ability. However, one of the best areas to visit is the **South Side Chutes** off the Condor chair lift, where you will find a series of steep chutes.

FREESTYLERS who have been wondering which place to check out in Utah, should look no further than this resort. The Canyons is a mega freestylers hangout having loads of natural halfpipes with excellent banked walls. And as if having perfectly formed natural pipes wasn't enough, the resort also has a first class superpipe. For rails and hits take the Sun Peak Express chair to the **Snow Peak area** where you'll find the extensive **Sobe terrain park**.

PISTES. Riders of any level will find that this is a fine resort to practice cranking out some turns at speed. There are loads of carefully prepared pistes that will keep you happy for days on end.

BEGINNERS must study a lift map or seek advice from a local in order to get to the best of the easy terrain, which in truth, is rather limited. However, if you're a quick learner then it's fine.

THE TOWN. The Canyons has some base area accommodation and other local services. However, the best option in terms of choice and prices is either down in **Park City** or back along in **Salt Lake City**.

U

U S A

U T A H

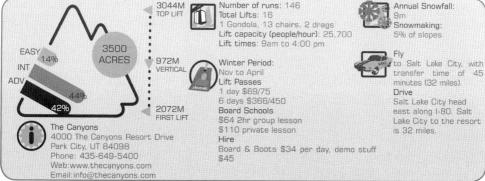

EASY 14%
INT
ADV
44%
42%

3500 ACRES

3044M TOP LIFT

972M VERTICAL

2072M FIRST LIFT

Number of runs: 146
Total Lifts: 16
1 Gondola, 13 chairs, 2 drags
Lift capacity (people/hour): 25,700
Lift times: 9am to 4:00 pm

Winter Period:
Nov to April
Lift Passes
1 day $69/75
6 days $366/450
Board Schools
$64 2hr group lesson
$110 private lesson
Hire
Board & Boots $34 per day, demo stuff
$45

Annual Snowfall:
9m
Snowmaking:
5% of slopes

Fly
to Salt Lake City, with transfer time of 45 minutes (32 miles).
Drive
Salt Lake City head east along I-80. Salt Lake City to the resort is 32 miles.

The Canyons
4000 The Canyons Resort Drive
Park City, UT 84098
Phone: 435-649-5400
Web:www.thecanyons.com
Email:info@thecanyons.com

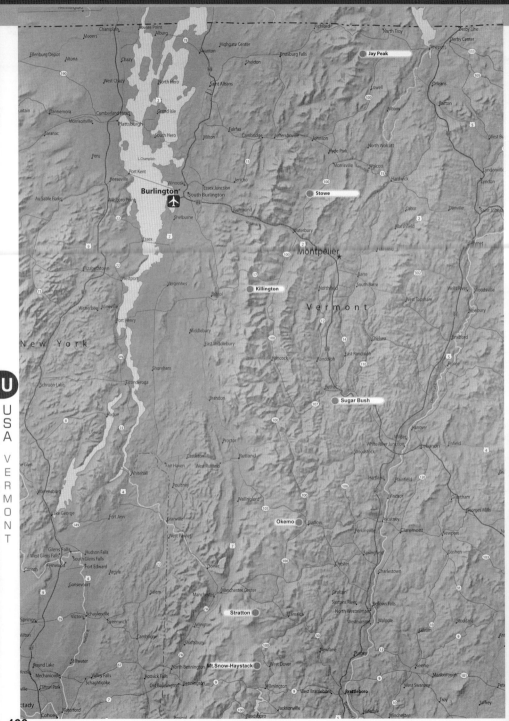

Okay East coast freeriding

	POOR	FAIR	GOOD	TOP
FREERIDE A few trees & some off-piste				
FREESTYLE 4 Parks but great natural				
PISTES Some good slopes				

5 OUT OF 10

Pic - Henry Georgi/Jay Peak

year. It is also notable that although it may not be a very big place, the amount of good hardcore and tree riding stands out's. Much of the mountain is fully open to snowboarders and is rated for advanced and intermediate riders, novice terrain is very limited. The resort has a modern lift system which includes a 60 person tramway and a series of chair lifts and T-bars. The location of Jay Peak may be the chief reason for this place for not becoming overcrowded while lift lines are either nonexistent or very small, except over holiday periods and weekends.

FREERIDERS will find that the offerings on Jay Peak are pretty good and will allow advanced and intermediate riders the chance to ride hard and fast with some excellent powder spots, some very fast chutes and lots of tight trees. Note, the resort has a strict policy when it comes to riding in the woods. Basically you must take responsibility for your own actions if you ride out of bounds, you must be a competent rider and you must not go alone. Areas such as **Buckaroo**, the **Everglade** or the **Beaver Ponds Glades** are pure nectar and will excite all riders.

FREESTYLERS have 4 terrain parks and a boardercross trail. But with so much natural freestyle terrain on offer, the man made hits are almost not needed but great to learn on. The **Canyonland** is home to an amazing natural halfpipe that should keep you amused for hours.

PISTES. Boarders who dig the piste have a nice number of cruising trails set out everywhere

J ay Peak, located in the far northern part of **Vermont** and close to the **Canadian border,** is not a bad place and one that attracts a fair few riders from within the state and across the border in Canada. Indeed the resort is actually owned by a Canadian resort company and you can even use Canadian dollars to pay for your lift ticket. For an east coast resort, Jay has a fairly good annual snow record, and although the amount of snow that falls here is no match for the resorts in the Rocky Mountains, is still good for the east and you can usually be guaranteed some fine powder each

BEGINNERS are the one group who may find this place not for them. There are novice areas but they are very limited.

THE TOWN
Jay Peak is a small town and has a limited amount of accommodation on offer. However, prices are not too bad and around town you will be able to go out and get a good meal with a reasonable choice of restaurants. Night life, however, is tame.

U
U S A   V E R M O N T

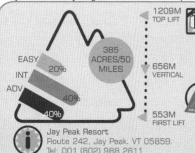

1209M TOP LIFT	
656M VERTICAL	
553M FIRST LIFT	

EASY
INT 20%
ADV 40%
40%

385 ACRES/50 MILES

Number of runs: 76
Longest run: 3miles
Total Lifts: 8
1 Gondola, 5 chairs, 1 drags, 1 magic carpet
Lift capacity (people/hour): 12,175
Lift times: 8.30am to 4.00pm

Winter Period:
Nov to April
Lift Passes
Half day $42, Full Day $58
5 Days $215
Board Schools
Group lesson morning $28, full day $48
Private lesson 1hr for $50, full day $230
Beginner package - pass, rental & lesson $49 for full day
Hire
Board & Boots Day/5 days $58/$215

Annual Snowfall:
9m
Snowmaking:
85% of slopes

Fly
to Monteal in Canada,
transfer time of 1 1/2 hours.
Drive
From Montreal head south on I-10, 35 & 91 & Hwy 100 via Newport. Montreal to the resort = 70 miles. Boston is 3 1/2 hours New York City is 6 1/2 hours.
Bus
services from Montreal takes 1 1/2 hours.
Train
AMTRAK Vermonter to St. Albans, 45 minutes away.

Jay Peak Resort
Route 242, Jay Peak. VT 05859.
Tel: 001 (802) 988 2611
Web:www.jaypeakresort.com
Email:info@jaypeakresort.com

Good boarder's resort with ample, diverse terrain

8
OUT OF 10

U

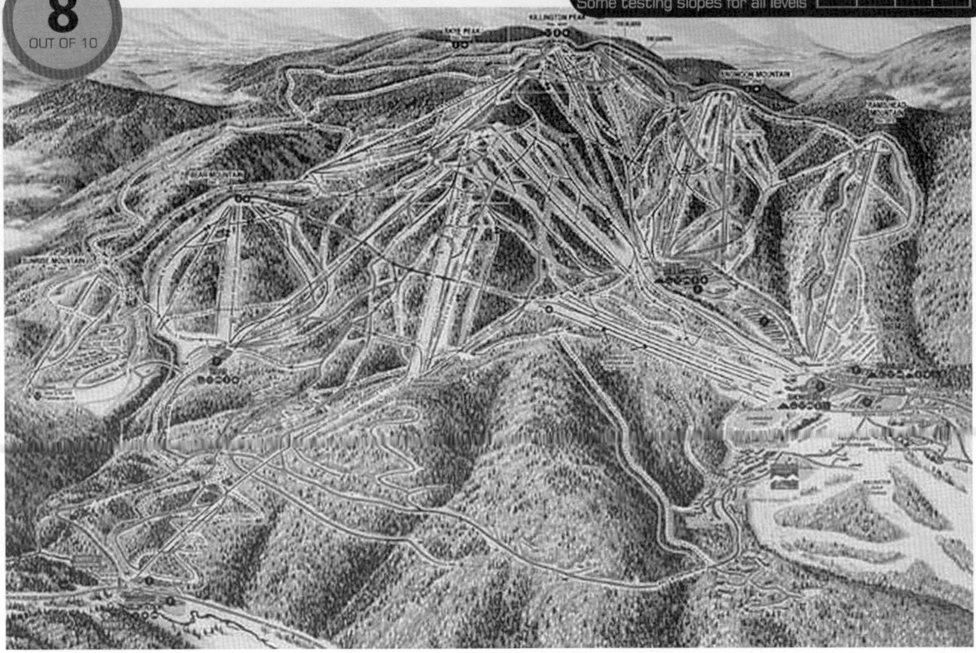

U S A

V E R M O N T

Killington is a big resort - the Beast of the East as the locals like to call it. If you thought the east coast of America was lame and no match for the central or western resorts then think again. Killington has seven mountains of steeps, bumps, mega carving terrain, loads of fun-parks and halfpipes, all serviced by a modern and well equipped lift system that includes an artistically painted and heated gondola. Visitors arriving here thinking that they will have the place licked in a day or two will be surely tested. You will need at least a couple weeks to ride all the runs and then a further month just to get to know what you have just been down. Killington reportedly has the largest snow-making facilities in the east, and like a number of other US resorts, it's a particularly snowboard-friendly place having hosted many snowboard events. The United States Amateur Snowboard Association once chose Killington as

its training ground, and it's easy to see why: the terrain is perfect for all levels and all styles. One thing that boarders should be aware of is traversing, as it's very easy to end up spending a lot of time travelling across the mountain, trying to get around. An excellent tool here is the **free Ride Guide** which tells you everything worth knowing, from a snowboarder's perspective, about the mountain and surrounding town - you can pick up a copy at the ticket office.

FREERIDERS have a mountain that often seems to vary at every turn: you get to ride lots of bumps - Superstar on **Skye Peak** and **Outer Limits** on **Bear Mountain** for instance; plus there are lots of trees to ride in, with numerous 'secret' trails to search out. If you're after a heart tester, check out the steeps at **Killington Peak** off

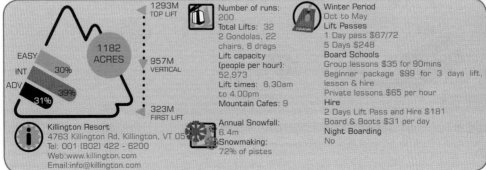

EASY
INT   30%
ADV   39%
31%

1182 ACRES

1293M TOP LIFT

957M VERTICAL

323M FIRST LIFT

Killington Resort
4763 Killington Rd, Killington, VT 05
Tel: 001 (802) 422 - 6200
Web:www.killington.com
Email:info@killington.com

Number of runs: 200
Total Lifts: 32
2 Gondolas, 22 chairs, 8 drags
Lift capacity (people per hour): 52,973
Lift times: 8.30am to 4.00pm
Mountain Cafes: 9

Annual Snowfall: 6.4m
Snowmaking: 72% of pistes

Winter Period
Oct to May
Lift Passes
1 Day pass $67/72
5 Days $248
Board Schools
Group lessons $35 for 90mins
Beginner package $99 for 3 days lift, lesson & hire
Private lessons $65 per hour
Hire
2 Days Lift Pass and Hire $181
Board & Boots $31 per day
Night Boarding
No

Pic -Killgton Resort

the Cascade chair, where you have a choice of tree-lined steep blacks.

FREESTYLERS have four terrain parks and two halfpipes. The main pipe in the **wild fire park** has 18foot walls and is 425 foot long. And as well as the pipe having great transitions and sounds blasting out, you can also get a burrito pipe side. As well as featuring four terrain parks, one of which is now on the Timberline, there is now a boardercross course on the **Dream Maker** area. Killington offers a pipe-only pass for $20

PISTES. Riders who want it steep will love Killington's terrain, which ranges from ultra-wide, straight down trails like **Double Dipper,** to narrower, more traditional runs such as East Fall or Royal Flush. Other notable spots are on Ram's Head, Snowdon or Skye Peak.

BEGINNER'S areas are excellent. However, like a lot of New England resorts, they can get busy at weekends. Stick to mid-week if possible as there are no crowds and empty runs. The *Killington Snowboard School* is excellent and offers every level of tuition, at prices worth paying. A day's ride package costs $65.

THE TOWN
Local facilities are extensive and varied, with a purpose-built village at the base of the slopes. However, by far the bulk of local hospitality is stretched along the access road. If you're prepared to pay for the convenience, then try to stay at the base; the cheaper thing to do is move away from **Killington** and hang out in one of the smaller hamlets. This way you get a better feel of the place and the locals are easier to get to know. Wherever you stay, it's always good to have a car, although there are shuttle bus services. For snowboard services check the *Ride On*

slopeside condos, but they don't come cheap. A full range of lodging options can be found stretched along the five mile access road, and offers dozens of cheap B&B joints to motels.

Food is standard grade, east coast, with big portions, lots of variety with over 60 restaurants throughout the area and in every price bracket. *Churchills* is noted for its steaks but isn't cheap and may entail a drive to get to it along route 4. Also highly rated is *Hemingways*, a super dollar hungry restaurant. For a decent and filling breakfast, why not check out the *Kodiak Cafe*. Or for a reasonably priced burger visit *Peppers bar.*

Night-life in and around Killington is noted for being well suited to snowboarders. There is a host of evening spots where beer and local birds are available to all ,and which can be very lively most evenings while rocking 'til late. The *Pickle Barrel* is known for having a good vibe as is the *Wobbly Barn* with live bands and rowdy crowds.

SUMMARY
Very good snowboarder's resort with ample, diverse terrain to suit all styles and levels. Lots of good local services but not a convenient layout.
Money wise: In the main very pricey but with options for budget riders to make it.

Killgton Resort

CAR
2 3/4 hours from Boston I93 to south of Concord,NH. I89 north to us 4 Rutland, Exit 1 in Vermont. Follow US4 west to Resort
FLY
to Boston, but theres no direct transfers.

wsg MT SNOW-HAYSTACK

FREERIDE
Trees but little off-piste
FREESTYLE
4 terrain parks & a halfpipe
PISTES
scttatered but okay trails

Basic but good riding

6
OUT OF 10

Pic MtSnow Resort

FREERIDERS coming here for the first time will find that the slopes on Mount Snow will offer challenging and difficult terrain. Advanced freeriders should head up to North Face with its series of blacks and double blacks which will test you with a mixture of bumps and groomed terrain. On Haystack, The **Witches** double blacks offer some interesting riding, but they're quite short.

FREESTYLERS are best checking out the slopes on Mount Snow, where you'll find a good series of well constructed man-made hits in the shape of four parks, at Carinthia you have **Inferno** for the air heads, and **El Diablo** for the intermediate, Un Blanco Gulch off Canyon trail is for the beginner while Grommet located on **Beaver Hill** is for the first timer in a park. Also at the base of Carinthia, The Gut Pipe is consistently rated as one of the top 10 pipes in the country, it's 460-feet long with 18-foot walls. All parks are designed by Ken Gaitor once of Brighton Utah. Also of Interest is the Beartrap area which blast music all day.

PISTES. Boarders wanting to lay down some turns at speed can do so with ease on Snowdance, one of the blues from the Summit Cafe. The North Face area on Mount Snow is good for fast full on steep descents

Mount Snow and Haystack are located in the **Green Mountain National Forest**, and like many of the east coast resorts within easy reach of major towns and cities, the area sees plenty of weekend ski-dwellers. Mount Snow and Haystack are, in fact, two separate resorts that are not, unfortunately, linked by lifts or snow trails. However, they are only a few minutes apart via the regular shuttle bus operating between the two areas. Collectively, the two areas have some 145 trails that are sold as one when you buy a lift pass. In the main, the whole place forms a cruisy mountain, best suited to intermediates and novices, with some decent-sized runs and interesting terrain features with hits, rollers, flats and trees. Be warned that at weekends and holiday periods, long lift queues do appear.

BEGINNERS tend to stay on Mount Snow, where there is a good layout of easy trails. Haystack has a complete beginner-only area. Ride On Snowboard School offers a Guaranteed Learn to Ride session, at $50 all-in.

THE TOWN
There is accommodation at the base of the slopes. *Mount Snow Condominiums* offer very good facilities which include a pool, but it's not a cheap option. A far greater selection of services can be found at West Dover or Wilmington, both inside a 10 mile radius. The lifestyle here is nothing amazing: a few bars and a number of places to eat give a laid back feel to the place, without any ego.

U S A
V E R M O N T

1097M TOP LIFT

518M VERTICAL

579M FIRST LIFT

EASY
INT
ADV

771 ACRES
37 MILES
PISTES

16%
22%
62%

Mt Snow
105 Mountain Road
VT 05356
Tel: 001 (802) 464 3333

Web:www.mountsnow.com
Email:info@mountsnow.com

Number of runs: 104
Longest run: 4km
Total Lifts: 19
15 chairs, 1 drag, 3 magic carpet
Lift times: 8.30am to 4.00pm
Lift Capacity (people per hour): 30,370

Winter Period:
Nov to April
Lift Passes
Day pass $57/68 (hi/low season)
6 Day $240-336
Board Schools
private $87/hr 6 hours $360
3 day learner package $175 includes rental, lift pass & 8hrs tuition
Hire
Board and Boots $36/day
5 Days $121

Annual Snowfall:
4.21m
Snowmaking:
76% of slopes

Fly
to Boston Int, or Bradley Int, both with a transfer time of around 2 3/4 hours .
Drive
From Boston, head west along Hwy 2, then north on I-91,west along Rte 9 and then finally north on Rts 100 to Mt Snow. Boston to resort is 134 miles, 2 3/4 hours.
Bus
Greyhound and Vermont Transit, tel: 802-254-6066 run services to Brattleboro. www.adventurenortheast. com run buses from New York City, tel: 718-601-4707
Train
The Amtrak Vermonter to Brattleboro or the Ethan Allen Express to Rensselaer/Albany

big mountain riding for a small mountain

	POOR	FAIR	GOOD	TOP
FREERIDE — lots o tree runs but little off-piste				
FREESTYLE — 3 Parks and 2 halfpipes				
PISTES — Lots of quiet slopes				

6 OUT OF 10

Pic -Okemo Resort

Diamond and Outrage. Both are long, steep and covered by snowmaking machines, which means that they open early and stay open late into the season. Okemo has expanded and now has new glades in the South Face area known as **Forest Bump** offering even more tree riding! Once you're clear of the trees and bumps, you won't believe the huge, ultra-long, rolling trails that are Okemo's trademark. Sapphire, World Cup, Coleman Brook, and Tomahawk are just a few trails that are perfect for going fast and boosting huge airs. For safety's sake, always use a spotter.

FREESTYLERS won't want to miss okemo's snowboard parks, or the massive super pipe, which measures over 500 feet and is served by the Pull surface lift. There's also the **Hot Dog Hill**'s mini pipe ideal beginners. **Nor'Easter Super Park** located on the Nor'Easter trail is by far the resorts biggest park. The **Dew Zone** is next to the superpipe while the **Blind Faith Terrain Park** has some big table tops. Located at Jackson Gore is the **Snowskate Park** with some rails and kickers. The Hot Dog Hill Mini Park is for beginners.

PISTES. Riders have 117 trails to choose from, so every standard of boarder should find something to please them, with the best terrain for fast turns being located on the upper sections.

BEGINNERS are extremely well catered for at Okemo and for those who need to brush up or learn something new,there is an award-winning snowboard school catering for all levels and style of rider, with the beginner terrain being easy to handle. A First Tracks programme costs from $45 a day.

THE TOWN
Off the slopes there are plenty of places to stay, with the usual array of hotels, motels and even a youth hostel. Prices will suit every budget, whether it be a slopeside condo or a giant B&B. To dine in style, *Nikki's* or *DJ's* is the place, whilst *Savannah's* is the joint for burgers. If you want a good drink with your food, then head for the *Black River Brew Pub*.

After spending a couple of days on Okemo, you will notice the incredible core of talented riders who call Okemo home. There is tons of diverse terrain to ride, with over 100 trails, so you can find plenty of room, no matter what type of rider you happen to be. The lift system at Okemo is rarely busy, but if you don't have a leash you won't be welcome, so come equipped

FREERIDERS who like bumps must check out **Ledges, Chief** and **The Plunge**. Recommended gladed runs are Double

U S A V E R M O N T

Number of runs: 117
Longest run: 7.2km
Total Lifts: 18
12 chairs, 5 drags, 1 magic carpet
Lift capacity (people/hour): 32,050
Lift times: 8.00am to 4.00pm

Winter Period:
early Nov to late April
Lift Passes
1 days $61/67
5 Days $245/285
Hire
Group $33hr, Private $80/hr
Board School
Board and Boots $33/day, 5 Days $135

Annual Snowfall: 5.08m
Snowmaking: 95% of slopes

Fly
to Boston, with a transfer time 3 hours. Albany 2Hrs
Drive
From Boston, head north on I-93 to Hwy 89, turning off at junction 9 for route 103 via Ascutney and Ludlow. Boston to resort is 150 miles. 3 hours drive time.
Bus
services from Boston can take 3 hours.

1019M TOP LIFT
655M VERTICAL
364M FIRST LIFT

610 ACRES

EASY
INT 33%
ADV
25% 42%

Okemo Mountain Resort
77 Okemo Ridge Rd, Ludlow VT 05149
Tel - (802) 228-4041
Snow Phone - (802) 228-5222
Web:www.okemo.com
Email:info@okemo.com

POOR FAIR GOOD TOP

FREERIDE
Tree runs but little off-piste
FREESTYLE
4 Terrain parks & a halfpipe
PISTES
Well pisted but can get busy

Where Jake Burton first started selling his boards

8
OUT OF 10

Pics Stratton Resort

U
S
A

V
E
R
M
O
N
T

in a flash, but at the weekend, lift queues appear as everybody from **New York** and **Boston** arrive en-mass. However, with 40 years history as a ski resort, the management know how to keep things moving along to everyone's satisfaction. Riding here will suite everyone although riders who look for extreme or big cliff jumps may be a little disappointed. Still this is a resort that has a good annual snow record and one which offers snowmaking facilities covering over 82% of the terrain on offer.

FREERIDERS who like their terrain carved out of tight trees, won't be disappointed as all the trails are hacked out of thick wood from top to bottom. For a good ride fix, the rollers and banks on the intermediate/novice terrain of **Black Bear** and the **Meadows** should do the trick. Riders with some know-how should check out the **Upper Tamarack** and if you are looking for some open trees, Freefall is the place.

FREESTYLERS hanging around the lower mountain can use the high-speed, six-person chair to access one of four fun-parks and the super pipe. All the parks have a series of table-tops, gaps and ramps, and to keep you interested they regularly build new hits. The superpipe in the **Power Park** also has a loud sound-system, and floodlights for hitting the walls at night. The four parks are set up for Beginner to Expert, so when you enter a specific park you know what you're letting yourself in for. The **East Byrneside park** has a boardcross along side it's jibs.

PISTES. The runs are well pisted and wide enough to allow you to put in some fast, continuous runs, without too much fear of a collision. Pistes of note are North American, Upper Standard and Lifeline. They look after the pistes here but get up early and get them while there still corduroy as there are often ice patches come the afternoon.

Stratton is generally recognised as the home of snowboarding, well at least on the east coast. A decent-sized resort, **Stratton** was one of the first areas in the US to give snowboarders access to its mountain. It is also noted for not only being the original home and test area for **Jake Burton** and his Burton Snowboards, but also as the place where America's first pro-snowboard school was set up and the home to the world's longest running snowboard competition, The US Open, which uses what is reputed to be the best halfpipe on the planet. The Green Mountain Race Series also comes to Stratton for a couple of events. Midweek you are up and down the mountain

BEGINNERS and novice riders will have the whole of the lower mountain to explore, plus easy routes from the summit. The runs are particularly well suited for first timers, but at weekends the flat pitches become crowded, so expect a few collisions. Snowboard tuition is first class at Stratton with loads of lesson programmes.

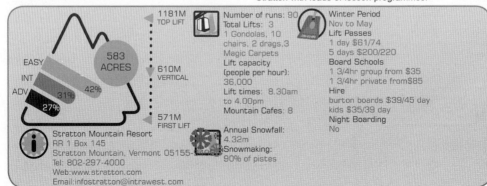

1181M
TOP LIFT

583 ACRES

EASY
INT
ADV   31%   42%
      27%

610M
VERTICAL

571M
FIRST LIFT

Number of runs: 90
Total Lifts: 3
1 Gondolas, 10 chairs, 2 drags,3 Magic Carpets
Lift capacity (people per hour): 36,000
Lift times: 8.30am to 4.00pm
Mountain Cafes: 8

Annual Snowfall: 4.32m
Snowmaking: 90% of pistes

Winter Period
Nov to May
Lift Passes
1 day $61/74
5 days $200/220
Board Schools
1 3/4hr group from $35
1 3/4hr private from$85
Hire
burton boards $39/45 day
kids $35/39 day
Night Boarding
No

Stratton Mountain Resort
RR 1 Box 145
Stratton Mountain, Vermont 05155-
Tel: 802-297-4000
Web:www.stratton.com
Email:infostratton@intrawest.com

Lodge is the first port of call in the early evening hours, where you can play pool, pinball and a juke box pumping out up-to-date sounds. Later on, check out the *Green Door Pub* for a few lively beers, or *North Grill* to sample some blues in a laid back atmosphere.

SUMMARY
Good snowboarder's resort with ample, diverse terrain to suit all styles and levels. Lots of good local services, but a bit hit and miss!

THE TOWN
Whether you're planning a week's trip or a two week stay, you won't be disappointed with what you find both on the slopes and off them. At the base of the mountain is a compact alpine style village with more or less everything you need. The scene can't be described as wild and in your face, but it is out there and with plenty going on. The place has a warm and welcoming atmosphere, and although you pay for it, services are very good. Shopaholics will love it here as there are dozens of stores and malls to help while away your time. There's also a very good sports centre in Stratton, where you can tone up, have a massage, or simply perve at the women doing their exercises.

Accomodation. With nigh on 20,000 visitor beds around the area, lodging options are really good, with the usual offerings of condos, lodges, fancy, over-priced hotels or basic B&B haunts. The Lift Line Lodge has rates from $70, while the Stratton Mountain Inn has rates from $90 and offers good services in the centre of the village.

Food. Eating out options are a little disappointing, with the choice of expensive, bland food in a pompous restaurant, or cheap, bland nosh at a fast-food outlet. However, if you search around, you will find something to please your pallet. The *Sirloin Saloon* fries up some damn fine steaks and the Base Lodge Cafeteria dishes up a decent breakfast. Pizza lovers should check out the offerings from *La Pizzeria* while *Red Fox* is the Italian place.

Night-life in Stratton is okay but not spectacular. The *Base*

U
S
A

V
E
R
M
O
N
T

 CAR
Take Route 2 west to I-91. Go north to exit 2 and follow signs to Route 30 north, then drive 38 miles north to Bondville, VT. Total distance 146 miles, drive time is about 3 1/4 hours.
FLY
Fly to Boston International. Transfer time to resort is 3 1/4 hours. Local airport is Albany 90 miles.
TRAIN
to Brattleboro, 40 miles away
BUS
There are daily bus services from Boston airport and from Albany airport.

Okay fun resort

5
OUT OF 10

FREERIDE
Tree runs but little off-piste
FREESTYLE
3 terrain parks & a halfpipe
PISTES
Busy but good intermediate runs

POOR FAIR GOOD TOP

Pic -SMR/ Landwehrle studio

If you're after some serious east coast riding, then the popular resort of **Stowe** is your place. It's a proper mountain spread over three distinct areas, each one lending itself to a different level of ability: **Spruce Peaks** is the beginner/intermediate area (a little isolated from the main ride area); **Mt Mansfield** is accessed by the fastest 8-person gondola in the world, and is an intermediate's paradise with great cruising terrain, perfect for those who like to carve. The final area is the largest, and a perfect mix for each style in the advanced stages. Because Stowe is a popular hangout with city slickers and weekend tourists, the lifts can get clogged on weekend mornings, but don't be put off - a short wait will be awarded with a good long run.

FREERIDERS may find the area under the gondola fun with heaps of tracks through trees, and plenty of places within the main area to disappear into. Liftline and National are rather tame trails having been widened over the years, and

cool if you are into bumps. **Nosedive** is good for freeride and carving, with the rest of the **Mansfield** area consisting of intermediate terrain, including a few good natural hits and jumps on the trail's edge.

FREESTYLERS are going to kick arse on any mountain after a session in one of three fun-parks at Stowe. The top choice park is the specially designed **Jungle**, located on the **Lower Lord area** which is easily reached from Lift 4. Stowe also has a pipe, and the resort even provides a park for beginners and novices, alongside 20 minute lessons called Quick Trick at £15.

PISTES. There's plenty of piste riders in evidence at Stowe, with the runs on **Mt Mansfield** having some nice, tame trails suitable for picking up speed & cranking over some turns

BEGINNERS will surprise themselves when they see how quickly they can progress on the abundance of easy slopes, especially if they are aided by the teaching staff at the local snowboard school who have more teaching programmes available than you could poke a stick at, ranging from novice to freestyle camps.

THE TOWN
The village is about six miles from the main slopes and is reached by a free shuttle bus. There are plenty of places to lay your head along the road to the lifts, with the usual choice of condos and B&B's. Stowe doesn't have the most radical **night-life**, although you can eat and drink well in a number of restaurants and bars, with the cool, friendly locals. The *Rusty Nail* is a hot spot for beer and music.

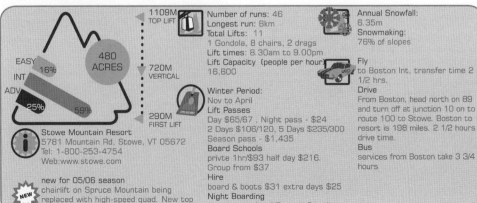

1109M
TOP LIFT

480
ACRES

720M
VERTICAL

290M
FIRST LIFT

EASY 16%
INT
ADV 25% 59%

Number of runs: 46
Longest run: 8km
Total Lifts: 11
1 Gondola, 8 chairs, 2 drags
Lift times: 8.30am to 9.00pm
Lift Capacity (people per hour)
16,600

Winter Period:
Nov to April
Lift Passes
Day $65/67 , Night pass - $24
2 Days $106/120, 5 Days $235/300
Season pass - $1,435
Board Schools
privte 1hr/$93 half day $216.
Group from $37
Hire
board & boots $31 extra days $25
Night Boarding
thurs-saturday 4/9pm on 2 trails

Annual Snowfall:
6.35m
Snowmaking:
76% of slopes

Fly
to Boston Int, transfer time 2 1/2 hrs.
Drive
From Boston, head north on 89 and turn off at junction 10 on to route 100 to Stowe. Boston to resort is 198 miles. 2 1/2 hours drive time.
Bus
services from Boston take 3 3/4 hours

Stowe Mountain Resort
5781 Mountain Rd, Stowe, VT 05672
Tel: 1-800-253-4754
Web:www.stowe.com

new for 05/06 season
chairlift on Spruce Mountain being replaced with high-speed quad. New top to bottom snowmaking installed

	POOR	FAIR	GOOD	TOP
FREERIDE Tree runs but limited off-piste				
FREESTYLE 2 Parks and a halfpipe				
PISTES Some good slopes				

Not a bad series of mountains

6 OUT OF 10

Pic :Sugarbush Resort

some trees, **Mount Ellen**, which is the highest in the resort, **North Lynx Peak** home to a lot of novice terrain and finally **Slide Brook Basin**. You can ride all the areas on one lift pass and all are connected by the array of chair and drag lifts.

FREERIDERS should first make for the **Lincoln Peak** where you will be able to sample some major runs via the Castlerock chair. This area is mainly for riders who know the score, if you are easily frightened, forget it. However, if you are up to it then you won't be disappointed. You can now buy a **Mt. Ellen**-only season's pass for 2004/2005. The pass is designed for people who want access to big-mountain skiing and riding at a cheaper price and will give holders access to over 2,600 vertical feet of terrain, 42 trails, 6 lifts, and new gladed trails

FREESTYLERS have a new Progression Park on **Mount Ellen** for beginners. The pro park has moved to the **Sunny D area** and has it's own lift and a reasonable pipe. Around the resort there is also an abundance of natural hits for catching air off.

THE PISTE riders can pick and choose really what they want. The area has a cool choice of groomers. Some of the runs on Lincoln are ideal for speed.

THE TOWN
Off the slopes Sugarbush offers a large number of accommodation options, from quality hotels to basic bed and breakfast homes. Dining out is also rather good around here, however, the same can't be said for the nightlife, it's very lame indeed.

Located along the **Mad River Valley** is the very snowboard friendly resort of Sugarbush, a mountain resort that is not bad and well worth a visit if you are in the area. Sugarbush is split over six connected mountain areas, all of which offer different features for different abilities. A short distance from Sugarbush is a resort called **Mad River Glen**, however, don't bother with this arse of a place because seven years ago they banned snowboarders due to a dispute with the management. Still, today there's no such problem here at Sugarbush, which has been operating as a resort since 1958. Today Sugarbush is a modern and well equipped resort with state of the art snowmaking facilities that reach almost 70% of the slopes. Mind you the resort has a respectable real annual snow fall of some 716 cm per season, making artificial snow not always so important. The six rideable areas are split up as, **Castlerock Peak,** which is home to some major expert terrain, **Cadd Peak**, which is the location for the Mountain Range Snow Park and good intermediate runs, **Lincoln Peak**, which has a splattering of good carving trails and

U
S
A
V
E
R
M
O
N
T

1260M TOP LIFT	Number of runs: 115 Total Lifts: 17 - 14 chairs, 3 drags Lift capacity (people/hour): 25,463 Lift times: 8.30am to 4.00pm
508 ACRES/ 54 MILES	
EASY 18% INT ADV 39% 43%	807M VERTICAL
	452M FIRST LIFT

Winter Period:
Nov to April
Lift Passes
1 day $62/65
6 days $270/330
season $1319
Board Schools
group 2 hours $37
private 1 hour $82 all day $297
Hire
board and boots $30/day

Annual Snowfall:
6.6m
Snowmaking:
68% of slopes

Fly
to Burlington Airport which is a 45min taxi away from resort. Boston airport approximately 3 hours drive/bus away.
Drive
Southbound: take I-89 south to Exit 10 Waterbury,Route 2 south to Route 100, through Waitsfield then right onto Sugarbush Access Road. Northbound: take I-89 Exit 9 on to Route 100b onto to 100 through Waitsfield, then right onto Sugarbush Access Road.
Bus
services available from Boston
Train
Waterbury and Rutland nearest stations, Amtrak runs trains from Washington DC,Baltimore,Philadelphia and New York

Sugarbush Resort
1840 Sugarbush Access Rd.
Warren, VT 05674
Phone: (802) 583-6300
Web:www.sugarbush.com

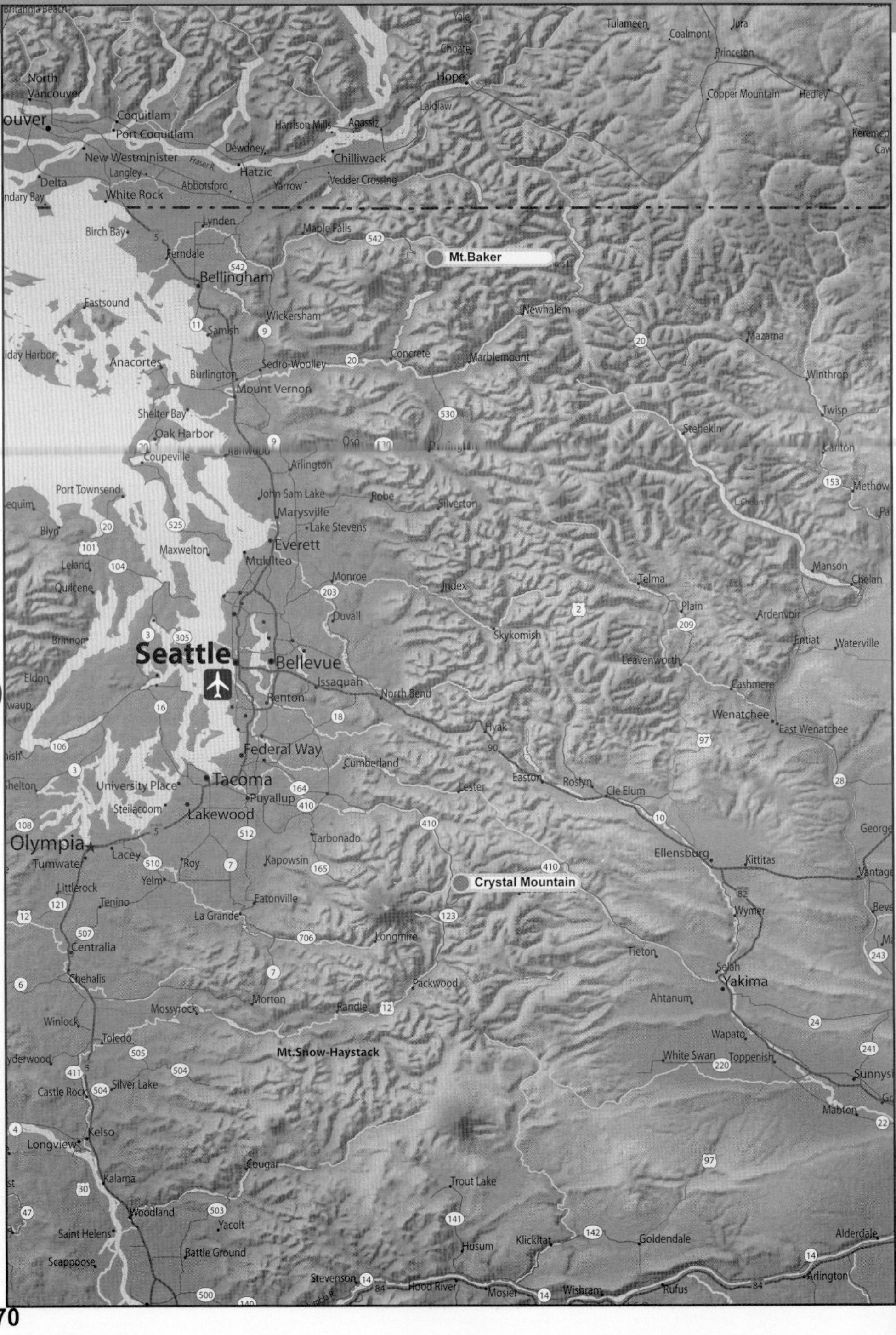

North Vancouver
Brit annia Beach
Yale
Tulameen
Coalmont
Jura
Princeton
Choate
Hope
Copper Mountain
Hedley
Laidlaw
Keremeo
Cav
Coquitlam
Port Coquitlam
Harrison Mills
Agassiz
Dewdney
Chilliwack
New Westminister
Langley
Abbotsford
Hatzic
Yarrow
Vedder Crossing
Delta
ouver
White Rock
ndary Bay
Birch Bay
Lynden
Maple Falls
542
Mt.Baker
542
Newhalem
Ferndale
Bellingham
Fastsound
Wickersham
Mazama
Samish
11
9
Anacortes
Sedro-Woolley
Concrete
Marblemount
20
Winthrop
iday Harbor
Burlington
20
Mount Vernon
Twisp
Shelter Bay
530
Stehekin
Carlton
Oak Harbor
9
Oso
I 10
153
Methow
Coupeville
Arlington
Pa
equim
Port Townsend
John Sam Lake
Robe
Silverton
Manson
Blyn
525
Marysville
Lake Stevens
Chelan
Leland
101
104
Maxwelton
Everett
Mukilteo
Telma
Manson
Emtiat
Waterville
Quilcene
Monroe
Index
Plain
Ardenvoir
Brinnon
203
Duvall
209
Skykomish
Leavenworth
Eldon
305
Seattle
Bellevue
Issaquah
Cashmere
waup
16
Renton
North Bend
Wenatchee
106
Federal Way
18
Hyak
97
East Wenatchee
nish
3
University Place
Cumberland
90
28
Shelton
Tacoma
164
Lester
Easton
Roslyn
Cle Elum
10
Puyallup
410
Lakewood
512
Carbonado
410
Ellensburg
Kittitas
Vantage
Olympia
Roy
7
Kapowsin
165
82
Bev
Lacey
510
Crystal Mountain
410
Wymer
Tumwater
Littlerock
Yelm
Eatonville
123
Tieton
243
Tenino
La Grande
706
Longmire
Selah
Yakima
12
121
507
Centralia
Packwood
Ahtanum
24
Chehalis
7
Morton
Randle
12
Wapato
108
6
Winlock
Mossyrock
White Swan
220
Toppenish
Sunnys
Toledo
Mt.Snow-Haystack
411
505
504
Silver Lake
504
Mabton
22
Castle Rock
4
Kelso
Longview
30
Cougar
97
Kalama
Trout Lake
George
47
Woodland
503
Yacolt
141
Husum
Klickitat
142
Goldendale
Alderdale
Saint Helens
Battle Ground
14
Scappoose
500
Stevenson
84
Hood River
Mosier
14
Wishram
Rufus
84
Arlington
14

	POOR	FAIR	GOOD	TOP
FREERIDE Tree runs & good off-piste				
FREESTYLE Park and a halfpipe				
PISTES Quiet but short slopes				

Good freeriding for this up & coming resort

6
OUT OF 10

Pic -Cyrtal Mountain Resort

Located mid-way into **Washington State**, an hour and twenty minutes from **Seattle**, Crystal is yet another yankee freeride classic, unspoilt by skiers, for riders in the know. The terrain is spread out over four peaks, with an awesome amount of backcountry riding. The resort was taken over in 97 and since then they've added 3 new lifts and other modifications. They've recently had their master plan approved so over the next 8 years there's going to be a huge investment in lifts, trails and base services. Crystal's already rising profile is bound to increase which may have the adverse effect of bringing in more skiers

- presently there is a balanced mix, leaving the slopes crowd-free and lift queues short.

FREERIDERS, miss this place and you're missing out on life; the terrain is pure freeriding and South Back is the place to check out if you're willing to do some hiking. From the summit of **Throne**, you get to ride what can best be described as heaven - unfortunately it is not for wimps being a steep with a double black diamond rating. Less daunting but still a big buzz are the runs off **Summit House**, while the trails in the North Back area on the likes of **Paradise Bowl** are total joy.

FREESTYLERS won't need man-made facilities at Crystal Mountain, as there is plenty of natural freeride terrain to catch big air. However, there is a pipe off the **Rendezvous chair**, but it's not up to much. The Boarder Zone fun-park, located off the **Quicksilver** chair, has a number of hits, but like the halfpipe, it doesn't live up to what nature can offer.

PISTES. Boarders who stick to the piste can have as good a time as those looking for the untamed, with a choice of excellent slopes that will please advanced and intermediate riders, even if some of the trails are not too long.

BEGINNERS can't do much worse than at Crystal. Only 13 of its trails are fine for novices, but what is on offer is excellent and easily reached from the base. And like many US resorts, a number of the higher rated runs are not that tricky, so many of the red trails can be licked by a competent, fast-learning novice.

THE TOWN
No big surprise here, the village at the base of the slopes is simple, basic, but good enough, with affordable places to sleep and eat in to suit all tastes and pockets. For a **bed** check out The *Alpine Inn*, which is close to the slopes and good value. For a feed try the *Cascade Grill* which serves a good breakfast. The main hangout for booze is the *Snorting Elk Cellar,* but unfortunately it's not a place for babes.

U
U S A   W A S H I N G T O N

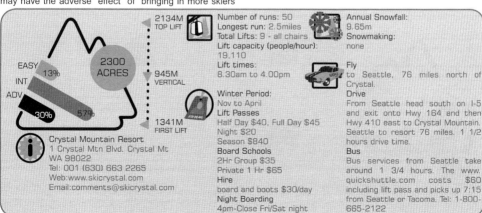

	2134M TOP LIFT	
EASY **13%**	**2300 ACRES**	945M VERTICAL
INT ADV **30%** **57%**		1341M FIRST LIFT

i Crystal Mountain Resort
1 Crystal Mtn Blvd. Crystal Mt
WA 98022
Tel: 001 (630) 663 2265
Web:www.skicrystal.com
Email:comments@skicrystal.com

Number of runs: 50
Longest run: 2.5miles
Total Lifts: 9 - all chairs
Lift capacity (people/hour):
19,110
Lift times:
8.30am to 4.00pm

Winter Period:
Nov to April
Lift Passes
Half Day $40, Full Day $45
Night $20
Season $840
Board Schools
2Hr Group $35
Private 1 Hr $65
Hire
board and boots $30/day
Night Boarding
4pm-Close Fri/Sat night

Annual Snowfall:
9.65m
Snowmaking:
none

Fly
to Seattle, 76 miles north of Crystal.
Drive
From Seattle head south on I-5 and exit onto Hwy 164 and then Hwy 410 east to Crystal Mountain. Seattle to resort 76 miles. 1 1/2 hours drive time.
Bus
Bus services from Seattle take around 1 3/4 hours. The www. quickshuttle.com costs $60 including lift pass and picks up 7:15 from Seattle or Tacoma. Tel: 1-800-665-2122

FREERIDE
Tree runs & epic off-piste

FREESTYLE
2 small parks but top natural

PISTES
Not really what its about

POOR FAIR GOOD TOP

Fantastic snowboarder's resort

10
OUT OF 10

If sex was a mountain, Mt Baker would be the orgasm, because this treasure is pure snowboarding heaven, with a snowboard history that is written in big letters. In the early days when other ski resorts had their heads up their arses and were banning snowboarders, this amazing place took a far different view. That foresight has crowned Baker as one of the best unspoilt snowboard resorts in the world, with a snow record to be envious of. It also holds the world record for most snowfall for a resort in a season, set back in 98/99 with a staggering 29m. On average they get 16m which explains why theres never been any plans, nor will

there be of adding snowmaking to their facilities. Mt Baker is also the home to the legendary Banked Slalom race, which is held every year. Located in the far north of Washington state, Mt Baker was home to the late legend Craig Kelly, who liked riding Baker's terrain so much, he moved there. Due to Baker's isolation it has the added advantage that it doesn't attract hoards of day-tripping skiers, leaving the slopes bare and the lift queues at a big fat 'zero'. The slopes span two mountains - **Mount Shuskan** rising to 2,963m (9,720ft), and **Panorama Dome** with its more modest summit of 1,524m (5,000ft). Both mountains offer the opportunity to ride steeps and deep powder, with the majority of advanced piste set out on the Panorama side. Runs like the **Chute** are set to test anyone, but be warned, parts of it are really steep and carry avalanche warnings. Overall, Baker is a mountain where you need be fully aware of your surroundings and not take any chances. One wrong turn could easily see you returning home to mum in a black body bag!.

FREERIDERS wanting to explore the amazing off-piste should seek the advice of a local rider; it's the only way to locate the best stuff, of which there are heaps. The amazing amount of unrestricted freeriding terrain is truly awesome and will keep you riding happily forever and a day. For the less adventurous, the blue off Number 8 chair in the **Shuskan** area is well worth a ride, offering piste-loving freeriders the opportunity to shine at speed.

FREESTYLERS will love the whole area, particularly the natural halfpipe that runs from the top of the two **Shuskan** chair lifts. This is where the Banked Slalom is held and, apart from beginners, is a must for all freestylers and freeriders. The run drops down a long winding gully and is totally magic. There are 2 small terrain parks off chair 8 and 3 that feature a few kickers and rails.

PISTES. Riders who only want to pose whilst laying fast tracks on perfectly prepared piste should stay away. Mt Baker is not a motherly resort it's a wild freeride place, although there are some runs to blast down. It's best to buckle in with soft boots and go freeriding which this

U
S
A
W
A
S
H
I
N
G
T
O
N

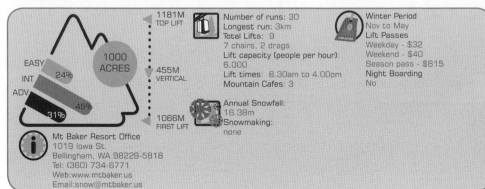

1181M
TOP LIFT

455M
VERTICAL

1066M
FIRST LIFT

1000 ACRES

EASY
INT 24%
ADV
45%
31%

Number of runs: 30
Longest run: 3km
Total Lifts: 9
7 chairs, 2 drags
Lift capacity (people per hour): 6,000
Lift times: 8.30am to 4.00pm
Mountain Cafes: 3

Annual Snowfall: 16.38m
Snowmaking: none

Winter Period
Nov to May
Lift Passes
Weekday - $32
Weekend - $40
Season pass - $615
Night Boarding
No

Mt Baker Resort Office
1019 Iowa St.
Bellingham, WA 98229-5818
Tel: (360) 734-6771
Web:www.mtbaker.us
Email:snow@mtbaker.us

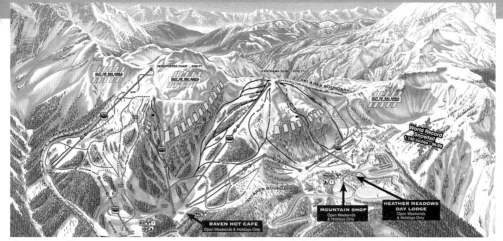

place is meant for,

BEGINNERS won't be disappointed with Mt Baker, with the option of learning on plenty of easy runs that are spread out around the area, the best being located on Shuskan. The local snowboard school is well established and offers a number of teaching programmes for all levels, with an emphasis on general freeriding.

THE TOWN

Riders who like everything on their doorstep will not be happy as the only facility at the base is a car park. Baker is not a gimmick, so you do have to put yourself out which is another reason why it's so good. The slopes of Mt Baker are located 17 miles from the main local services which can be found in the low-key town of **Glacier**, a simple and unspoilt place. Local services may be a bit thin on the ground, but don't let that put you off. What is offered is cheap and damn good value, making a week or even two, well worth the trip up. The town of Bellingham, just over an hour away has an even greater selection of lodgings, sporting facilities and other visitor attractions.

Accommodation is only possible down in **Glacier** which has a number of options at very reasonable prices. Cool places to contact for a bed, are *Glacier Creek Lodge, Mt Baker B&B, Diamond Ridge B&B* or a condo at the Mt Baker Chalets & Condos.

Food. The options for getting a meal on the slopes or down in Glacier may be a bit limited in

terms of choices of restaurants, but what is available will do nicely. During the day you can pig out on the slopes at the White Salmon Day Lodge which has very reasonable rates. The new Raven Hot cafe has fast become a major day time hangout whilst also serving up some wicked food. Down in Glacier, Milano's Cafe is the place to check out, where they do great pasta dishes.

Night-life. One of the beauty's of this place is it's laid back atmosphere, which applies equally to the night life in Glacier, the perfect snowboard scene-laid back and cool. There is no hype, no après-ski crap and no gits in silly hats playing party games. What you get is basic, offering a good laugh and messy late night drinking sessions, resulting in some killer hangovers.

Pics -Mt Baker Resort

CAR
From Seattle take the I-5 South, take exit 255 at Bellingham and continue on the State Hwy 542 for approximately 56 miles. Drive time is about 2 1/2 hours.
FLY
Fly to Seattle International. Transfer time to resort is 2 hours. Local airport is Bellingham 56 miles away.
TRAIN
to Bellingham (56 miles)
BUS
Buses from Seattle take 3 hours and 1 1/4 hours from Bellingham airport.

RESORT ROUND-UP

BLUEWOOD

Ride area: 430acres Number runs: 24

27% easy, 43% intermediate, 30% advanced
Top Lift: 1728m Bottom Lift: 1385m Vert: 343m
Total Lifts:3 - 2 chairs, 1 drag
Lift pass:1/2 Day, $27 Day $34
Contact: P.O. Box 88
Dayton, WA 99328
Phone: 509/382-4725
www.bluewood.com
How to get there: located in the Umatilla National Forest, 21 miles from Dayton

49 DEGREES NORTH

Ride area: 2325 acres Number runs: 42

30% easy, 40% intermediate, 30% advanced
Top Lift: 1759m Bottom Lift: 1195m Vert: 564m

Total Lifts:5 - 4 chairs, 1 drag
Lift pass:1/2 Day, $27 Day $29-35
Rental:Board & Boots $28 per day
Lessons:Private lessons $45 per hour, then £20 ph
Beginner package $39 for 90min lesson, lift pass & rental
Contact: PO Box 166
Chewelah, WA 99109
Tel: 866-376-4949
www.ski49n.com
How to get there: From Spokane take HWY 395 north to Chewelah (42 miles). Turn east (right at stoplight)on to Main Street to Flowery Trail Road.

SUMMIT AT SNOQUALMIE

Ride area: approx 300 acres + 500 backcountry
Number runs: 76
Top Lift: 1597m Bottom Lift: 795m Vert: 695m
Total Lifts:28 - 19 chairs, 6 drags, 3 magic carpets
Freestyle facilities: 4 terrain parks & halfpipe
Annual snowfall: 11.27m
Lift pass:Full 9am - 10pm day pass $45
Half day $36, Night pass 4pm-10pm $28
Night Boarding:Till 10pm
Rental:Board & Boots $32 per day, $26 night
Lessons:Beginner 2hr lesson $37, package including pass & equipment $62
Private lessons $58/$99 for 1/2 hours
Contact: 1001 State Route 906
Snoqualmie Pass
WA 98068
Tel: (425) 434-7669
www.summit-at-snoqualmie.com
How to get there: 52 miles East of Seattle, Washington, via Interstate 90. Take Exit 52 for Summit West and Alpental Exit 53 for Summit Central, Tubing Hill and the Demo Center

Pic Ride Snowboards

FREERIDE
Tree runs & CAT off-piste
FREESTYLE
2 small parks but good natural
PISTES
Not well groomed

POOR FAIR GOOD TOP

A resort for powder hounds

8
OUT OF 10

FREERIDERS will soon work out that this is a resort for them. The terrain on both mountains lends itself perfectly for both piste and backcountry riding. You'll find a number of steep black trails on **Fred's Mountain**, but most of them are quite short.

FREESTYLERS have a naturally formed halfpipe that provides air heads with some interesting walls to ride up. There is also a killer boardercross circuit that needs to be treated with full respect. However, man-made obstacles aren't really necessary in Targhee; the place is riddled with natural hits, many of which are known only to the locals. However, the riders here are cool and will happily take you to the best launch pads and show you how much diverse, natural freestyle terrain there actually is. For those who want it man made there are two small parks, one for total beginners

Freeriders in search of powder and lots of it, will find that Grand Targhee is the perfect place to find it. This fantastic resort is a US powder heaven, with an average snowfall of over 1,280cm a year making riding powder a buy word here, even the piste map shows the powder terrain levels so novices can even try out powder stashes. What you have here in this low key resort are two mountains - **Fred's Mountain** which can be reached via three chair lifts and a drag lift, and **Peaked Mountain** accessible only by snowcats. Both mountains offer the chance to do some full-on freeriding on crowd free slopes that will suit advanced and intermediate riders in the main. The trails on Fred's Mountain are a collection of short blacks that snake through a smattering of trees with a couple of nice, wide open blue runs. If you're the adventurous sort, then Peaked Mountain should be the place to get your fix. This is where you get to ride perfect freeride territory with the help of snowcats - a local company offers snowcat tours for around $299 a day. Tours are accompanied by guides and limited to 10 people per cat; prices include a lunch. Peaked Mountain is not exclusively for advanced riders; in fact most of what is on offer is graded green and blue, with a couple of black descents that take in some thick trees.

PISTES. There's not too much smooth grooming here, the generally uneven slopes will take you out if you edge over without good speed control. This is another US resort that isn't about the piste, so if it's flat and smooth piste you want, you best look elsewhere.

BEGINNERS are the one group who may feel left out here. Although there is some novice areas around the base, there's not much of it. Still, if you're a fast learner then don't be put off.

THE TOWN
Off the slopes what you get is both basic and very limited. There is only a handful of buildings at the base area offering a number of high quality lodges, hotels and a few local shops all close to the slopes. The village has a very relaxed and laid back appeal to it, but if you're the sort that wants a resort loaded with the usual tourist gizmo's, forget it.

U
S
A

W
Y
O
M
I
N
G

EASY 10%
INT
ADV 35%
55%

2500 ACRES

3110M
TOP LIFT

729M
VERTICAL

2438M
FIRST LIFT

Grand Targhee Ski & Summer Resort
Box Ski, Wyoming 83422
Tel: 001 (307)-353-2300
Web:www.grandtarghee.com
Email:info@grandtarghee.com

Number of runs: 62
Longest run: 4km
Total Lifts: 5
4 chairs, 1 Magic Carpet
Lift times: 9.30am to 4.00pm

Winter Period:
Nov to April
Lift Passes
1 Day $55, 3 Days - $159
5 Day pass - $260
Board Schools
2hr group $45, 1 hr private $70
Mountain guide 3 hrs $175
Hire
Board & Boots $29 per day pro kit $40
Snowmobiles
Targhee Snowmobile Tours offer day trips through Yellowstone National Park, www.tetonvalleyadventures.com
Cat Boarding
Full day: $299,Half Day: $225
Reservations and deposit are required, call ext. 1355

Annual Snowfall:
12.8m
Snowmaking:
5% of slopes

Fly
to Salt Lake City International. Transfer time to resort = 5 3/4 hours. Local airport = Teton Peaks 13 miles away.
Drive
Idaho Falls via Driggs.Grand Targhee is 87 miles. Drive time is about 1 3/4 hours. *Salt Lake City is 289 miles, which will take about 5 3/4 hours.
Bus
from Idaho Falls take 1 1/2 hours and 5 3/4 hours from Salt Lake City airport (289 miles). Buses from Jackson or Teton contact www.jacksonholealltrans.com tel: (307) 734-9754. Price $69 including lift pass

	POOR	FAIR	GOOD	TOP
FREERIDE Tree runs & epic off-piste				
FREESTYLE Parks & halfpipe, good natural				
PISTES some good long trails				

8 OUT OF 10

pics - Jackson Hole Resort

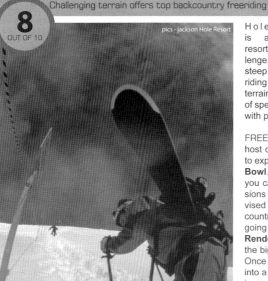

Hole is a resort that will appeal to snowboarders that like a challenge. Much of the terrain is rated black, offering some steep sections with trees and long chutes. Back country riding is also a major option as there are vast amounts of terrain to check out. To get the best of it, there are a number of specialist backcountry tour operators, offering daily tours with prices starting at around $300.

FREERIDERS should love it on Jackson's slopes, with a host of marked out trails and acres of backcountry terrain to explore in areas such as the **Green River Bowl** or **Cody Bowl**. Backcountry guides are on hand to help you, and you can sign up for half day, full, or two day guiding sessions for around $325. But note that you are strongly advised to always check with the areas **Bridger-Teton** Backcountry avalanche hazard and weather forecast before going anywhere. Some of the best riding can be found on **Rendezvous mountain** which was once noted for having the biggest vertical descent in the US, some 1261 metres. Once you get off Rendezvous' old tram, you drop down into a cool playground, offering a great selection of chutes, jumps and big drop-ins, Jackson also features **Corbett's Couloir**, a famous vertical drop into a marked run that will leave you breathless.

FREESTYLERS will certainly appreciate Jackson. From the **Thunder Chair** you will be able to reach a natural pipe. The **Paintbrush** and **Toilet Bowl** also offer loads of hits, where you can ride for hours off and over loads of good natural stuff. If this isn't enough, then check out the man-made park at the bottom of the of **Apres Vous** chair. There's also a beginners area the **Eagle's Rest** mini terrain park along with a 450 foot pipe with a rope tow and sound system

Jackson Hole is a truly all American resort and comes with cowboys, saloon bars and high peaks. Not the typical tree-lined rolling mountains found in a lot of US resorts, Jackson is a high peaked mountain resort that is located in a large valley some 10-40 miles wide and 50 miles long. At the base of the slopes is a small village called **Teton**, 10miles away from the main town of Jackson Hole, which has the much smaller resort of **Snow King** rising out of it. Jackson

PISTES. People who want to push it should check out **Gros Venture** as this is the place for experienced speed merchants. The run is over 3 km long and drops away, forming an excellent testing trail Intermediates (and those not so sure of themselves) should try out **Casper Bowl** or **Moran Face** on Apres Vous Mountain.

U S A W Y O M I N G

EASY 10%

INT

DV 40%

50%

2500 ACRES

3185M TOP LIFT

1216M VERTICAL

1924M FIRST LIFT

Hole Mountain Resort
Box 290, 3395 West Village Drive
Teton Village, WY 83025
Tel: 1-307-733-2292
Web:www.jacksonhole.com
Email:info@jacksonhole.com

Number of runs: 111
Longest run: 7.2km
Total Lifts: 12
1 Aerial tram, 1 Gondola,
9 chairs, 1 Magic Carpet
Lift capacity (people per hour): 12,096
Lift times:
8.30am to 4.00pm
Mountain Cafes: 3

Annual Snowfall:
11.6m
Snowmaking:
10% of slopes

Winter Period:
early Dec to early April
Lift Passes
1 Day pass$70
6 Day pass $390
Season $1595
Board Schools
Private lessons half/all day
$265/$445
3 Day beginner package lesson,
lift pass, hire $210
Group lessons 3hr $80
Hire
Burton Board & Boots $26.5
per day

NEW new for 05/06 season
new triple chair, Sweetwater, to link beginner terrain to mid-mountain. new cafe at base of Bridger Gondola

BEGINNERS will find Jackson's mostly steep and testing terrain a bit daunting, but don't fret; most novices should manage to get around after a few days, although they should probably avoid the **Rendezvous** area. First timers have the chance to progress quickly, especially on the runs found at the bottom of Apres Vous mountain, reached off the Teewinot chair. A high level of instruction is available including halfpipe training run camps for women.

THE TOWN

Immediately at the base area of the slopes lies the resort of **Teton Village** which is more or less your typical horrid ski resort all in set up. That's not to say it's not welcoming, it is, and locals will make your stay a good one. However, the town of **Jackson** which is a 20 minute bus ride away operating on an all-day basis, offers a more sedate time with a heavy dose of pure outback Americana. Around town there is a lot of activities and not all costing the earth, which makes the place cool and worth it. There is a number of good snowboard shops to check out: such as the *Hole in the Wall*, or the *Bomb Shelter*.

Accomodation. The area has a vast array of lodging. There is plenty near the slopes in **Teton Village** where you can kip close to the slopes at the Hostel for around $5 a night. For a bigger selection and cheaper prices check out the offerings in Jackson, 10 miles from the slopes.

Food. If you don't leave here over weight, then see a shrink. The place has dozens of places to get food from, whether it is a supermarket, fast food joint or an up-market restaurant frequented by fur clad clueless city slickers. Prices to suite all are possible but on the whole, dining out is not a cheap experience here. However, *Bubba's* is comes highly recommended and serves some great chicken dishes. The *Snake River* and *Otto Brothers* brew pub are also noted for their good food.

Night life here is just how it should be, with something for all with a snowboard flavour. Options for some night action exist in either **Teton Village** or **Jackson** itself. Tretton is a lot quieter than Jackson, with *Mangy Moose, the Stagecoach* or the *Rancher* all being popular hangouts. As for local talent, the place seems a bit of a guy place but there is some skirt to be had.

pics - Jackson Hole Resort

CAR
Idaho Falls via Victor. Jackson Hole is 111 miles. Drive time is about 1 3/4 hours. *Salt Lake City is 299 miles, which will take about 5 3/4 hours.
FLY
Fly to Salt Lake City International. Transfer time to resort is 5 3/4 hours. Local airport is Jackson, 10 miles away.
BUS
Buses from Idaho Falls take 1 1/2 hours and 5 3/4 hours from Salt Lake City airport (299 miles).
www.jacksonholealltrans.com run shuttles from Salt Lake tel: 800-652-9510

Measurements & Conversions

TEMPERATURES	
°C - Celsius	°F - Fahrenheit
-15	5
-10	14
-5	23
0	32
5	41
10	50
15	59
20	68
25	77
30	86
35	95
40	104
45	113

SPEED	
MPH	KmPH
10	16
20	32
30	48
40	64
50	80
60	96
70	112
80	128
90	145
100	161

SMALL MEASUREMENTS	
CM	INCH
1	0.4
5	2
10	4
15	6
25	10
50	20
75	29
100	39

DISTANCES	
KM	Mile
1	0.6
5	3.1
10	6.2
20	12.4
50	31
75	46.6
100	62
200	124

AREAS	
ACRES	HECTARES
100	40
250	101
500	202
1000	405
1500	607
2000	809
3000	1214
4000	1618

SHOE SIZE (MEN)		
UK	US	EUROPE
6	6 1/2	38 1/2
7	7 1/2	40
8	8 1/2	42
9	9 1/2	43 1/2
10	10 1/2	44 1/2
11	11 1/2	45 1/2

SHOE SIZE (WOMEN)		
UK	US	EUROPE
3	5 1/2	35 1/2
4	6 1/2	37
5	7 1/2	38
6	8 1/2	39
7	9 1/2	41
8	10 1/2	43

200 190 180 170 160 150 140 130 120 110 100 90 80 70 60 50 40 30 20 10

NOTES

To some it's a one week holiday, to others it's a life. Many people spend years and all their cash chasing the winter around the world. To lots it's a living. Some lucky people actually make a living riding fantastic terrain, others make their dollar by helping beginners link a few turns.

Whatever snowboarding is to you and however much you've put into it, be it time, money or blood there's one thing that's true to all of us who snowboard: there's always another mountain to ride. The Alps and Rockies are great but what about putting a few virgin lines down in India and finishing the day with a Vindaloo, or maybe carving it up in Cyprus before heading to the beach? Wherever there's a mountain with snow, you can board.

We at WSG want you to broaden your horizons. Bosnia? Lebanon?? Algeria??? Yes, you can board in all of these places. Some may not be snow sure, and yes, some may have a lift system that looks like it was made during the industrial revolution, but snowboarding and travelling to a far flung place with food and a culture you've never experienced. It's an adventure.

Before you head off the beaten track have a look at **www.`co.gov.uk** for the latest travel advice as some countries can turn from playground to war zone in the time it took you to fly there.

Photo: Frederik & Mads by Jedd Curtes © Burton

FAR - FLUNG

ALGERIA

There's one resort here called Chsea, and it's best to take you own equipment. The capital is Algiers and it's a 3 hour flight from the UK. Travel to the south of Algeria is not recommended due to suspected terrorist groups. Chsea, 70 km from Algiers, has been out of bounds of late so check Foreign Office advice, keep your head down and don't flash your cash. Their season is December to March.

CHSEA
1860 to 2508m
Runs: 4km pistes
50% beginners
50% Intermediate
Lifts: 2

ARMENIA

Reportedly has 2 resorts. Its Capital is Yerevan and the currency is Dram.

TSAKHKADZOR
is situated in the Kotayk region, 50km north of Yerevan, was once a soviet Olympic training ground. Lately a lot of investment has been pumped into the resort and there has been talk of Russian gangster money along with Austrian cash buying new lifts and snow cats. Construction of a new hotel is well under way. Tsakhadzor translates to Valley of Flowers, so why not take your Mum ?

AFGHANISTAN

An English newspaper, The Independent, has reported that an ex-warlord wishes to build a 600 bed resort on the former front line battle field with Russia. After the Russians left they then fought off the Taliban. Let's hope he gets his plans off the ground and, if he does, I wouldn't be the first to explore the back country, as the area has its fair share of mines and the remnants of US cluster bombs. www.independent.co.uk

BOLIVIA
CHACALTAYA
is the highest resort in the World at 5420 metres, with the fastest and hardest drag lift. It's 30km from La Praz. The one run has a vertical drop of 200 metres and is serviced by 1 rope tow. The season is from November until March.

BOSNIA HERZEGOVINA

This country has 16 small resorts. Its Capital is Sarajevo.

BJELASNICA
the main resort, is a 20 minutes drive from Sarajevo. This is where the men's downhill, slalom and giant slalom were held in the 1984 Winter Olympics. The resort has loads of trees up to 1500 metres with the resort summit just over 2000 metres. Things are pretty basic here, as Sarajevo was under siege in the 1990's, and foreign investment is slow to stretch to the winter resorts.

INGMAN
is low in altitude at 1500 metres but can still boast the lowest ever temperature in the region of -43. Thanks to this, Ingman still gets an average snowfall which is enough for them to host the strange Olympic sport of wearing lycra and shooting at little round targets. Ingman is located south west of the Capital and is worth a visit if you're in the area.

TREBEVIC
is known more for fighting over the last decade than boarding. It is higher than it's neighbour Ingman, and offers some fun at 1630 metres. Trebevic hosted the Olympic bob sled in 1984 but due to its vantage point over the surrounding area, in the 1990s it instead hosted a lot of fighting. Although most of the land mines have thankfully been cleared, the infrastructure is still a long way off western European resorts. However, like Ingman, if you're in the area check it out.

CHINA

With the fastest growing economy in the world and a population of 1.28 Billion people, China is starting out on its snowboard development. With high mountains and many new developing resorts, China is high on the list of many adventurous Snowboarders. What a buzz for those used to boarding in Europe: strange food, mad dialects, intriguing history, resort names like "Jade Dragon" and best of all, its very cheap. There are no £10 bowls of spaghetti here. One thing to think about, however, is if you have big feet bring your own kit, as you'll never find large boots for rent. Burton have seen the opportunity of this ever growing market place and set up a LTR school in Nanshan close to Beijing.

ALSHAN ALPINE SKI RESORT
is a small forested resort near the region of Inner Mongolia in China's far north.

BEIJING NANSHAN
is the closest resort to the capital with public transport covering the 50 miles in a little over an hour. Nanshan has 10 pistes and the Country's first Half Pipe. There is 1 chair and 9 drag lifts.

BEIJING SHINGLONG
opened in 2000, has 3 pistes; the longest being 1km and is also about 50 miles from the capital.

BEIJING HUAIBEI
is an hour and a half from Beijing. It has a piste of over 300 metres and is situated alongside the Great Wall.
Another resort close to Beijing is Jindinghu.

CHENGDU XILING MOUNTAIN SKIING RESORT
is situated in central Sichuan Province and is the biggest resort in China. It is a two hour drive from the city of Chengdu, which has a population of almost 10 million. The Xiling resort had a summit of 2400 metres but has a limited snow fall, which can lead to rough conditions after the weekend crowds have visited. When it does snow there are some great tree runs and the longest run of over 2 km can be taken at speed. There even have a gondola to keep you warm on the way back up.

JADE DRAGON MOUNTAIN RESORT
is close to Tibet and has an altitude of 3500 metre which is accessed by a cable car. There are no set out runs and there are plenty of trees to dodge and often loads of snow.

JILIN CHANGBAISHAN SKI RESORT
in the Jilin Province about 400km north of the North Korean border, has 4 runs which wind their way through the dense forest. The cable car is old and the temperatures can be bitter, but pop in if you are passing.

YABULI INTERNATIONAL ALPINE SKI RESORT
is the oldest resort in China, it opened in 1980. The resort is in the far north east of China near the Russian border in the Heilongjiang province. It's not particularly high, at under 1500metres, but can boast Central Asia's longest run at 5km and has an average snow fall. There are 12 runs and 8 lifts but with temperatures as low as -40 you better take a good coat, especially if you want to take advantage of the night boarding. Nearby there is the smaller resort of Erlongshan

CROATIA

SLJEME MOUNTAIN

Resort Sljeme Mountain Medvednica (1035 metres) has 6 runs, 4.5km of slopes, snow making and night boarding. A 1 day pass costs 70,00kn (about £7). It's close to the capital Zagreb and is linked by a good road. Currency: Kuna 10 / £1

CZECH REPUBLIC

Has 22 mostly small resorts. Capital: Prague, Currency: Koruna.
Highest point: Snezka at 1602 metres

HARRACHOV

Harrachov in the far east of the republic centres on the Certova Mountain which has snow making facilities. The resort is limited to low pitch rolling slopes. Its main boast is the array of ski jumps and cross county trails so its best suited to our two plank brothers.

Lifts: 3 chairs 1 drag. **Pistes:** 5 runs. **Total:** 6.3 km. **Longest** 2.2km.

HERLIKOVICE AND BUBAKOV

are resorts with linked runs and lift passes and are close to the major resort of Spindleruv Mlyn. There is a 1.5km cable car and 8 drag lifts. The longest run is 3km, there is good snow making facilities and the chance to board a 2.5km night run. Most impressively there's a terrain park but don't expect too much.

JANSKE LAZNE

is a spa town and has had some recent investment which includes snow making. If you get bored of the small slope area there is always the 3.5km sledging piste.

Lifts: Cable Car: 1. Chair: 1. Drags lifts: 12. **Runs:** 14 **Longest:** 3.5km. **Total** 13km

SPICAK

In the far west of the country near the German boarder in amongst the Bohemian Forest is the resort of Spicak. Its a small resort with only 5.5km of pistes and two snow cats but its a good beginners resort and an intermediate could have fun here for a day or two. It offers night boarding and has snow making facilities and when there's been a dump there are plenty of trees to shred. Open from 8.30 till 16.00 and 18.30 to 21.00. 560czk for a day+night, 200czk for night boarding only.

SPINDLERUV MLYN

Spindleruv Mlyn is one of the best known resorts in the area and its easy to get to as there are plenty of public buses from Prague which take 3 hours. Its located just south of the Polish boarder, and consists of a strip of soviet style concrete hotels set near woods at 780metres. Medvedin to the north west is the highest peak at 1235m while Plan to the south at 1196m sometimes has the better snow as it doesn't get so much sun.

Lifts: Chairs: 4 Drags: 10. **Runs:** 20. **Total km piste:** 25. **Longest Run:** 2.7km.

Night Boarding: 1 run of 1.1km. **Open** 6pm to 9pm and supported by snow making. Lifts: 2 www.skiarealspindl.cz

Photo: Czech Republic

Cyprus Ski Federation
Diagorou & Panteli Katelari 21
Office 101 Libra House
P.O.Box 22185
1518 Nicosia, CYPRUS
Phone: +357 (22) 675340
Web: www.skicyprus.com
Email:info@CyprusDestinations.com

Number of runs: 16 Longest run:900m
Total Lifts: 4 t-bars Mountain Cafes:1

Winter Period: Jan to March
Lift Passes
1 day 9.5 CYP, week 33 CYP
Hire: Board & Boots 7.5CYP per day at the
resort. Mavros Sports & ThreeSixty in Nicosia and
Force 8 Sports in Limassol also hire gear.

Car: From Limassol or Nicosia follow signs for
Troodos, through Moniatis village to Troodos
Square, then follow signs to Mount Olympus. After
1.3km take the steep left for the Sun Valley area
(1km) or continue for 1km to reach the North Face area
Fly: Fly to Larnaca airport

CYPRUS

Right slap in the middle of the Mediterranean island of Cyprus towers Mount Olympus. At just under 2000m it's able to collect enough snowfall from late December to March to have its own resort. Originally built and operated by the British army after the Second World War, the 1960's saw the Cyprus Ski Club take over the resort and since then they installed more lifts and expanded the terrain. It's about an hour to drive from Nicosia and Limassol or a short drive from Troodos village.

Not surprisingly the season is very hit and miss; as the snow doesn't tend to last too long once on the ground, with rocks showing through after about 4 days without snow. However when the snow is good then there are a few trees to board through. The 4 drag lifts are old but keep going all season without a hitch. Unfortunately they seem to have lost the keys to the piste basher as it is seldom used.

The slopes can be busy at the weekends and holidays, but it's normally extremely quiet during the week, with just a few people on the slopes. Locals are only just beginning to recognise snowboarding and at the moment only skis are available to rent from the store situated next to the café which is adjacent to the 'Sun Valley' run. Boards can be purchased from Force Eight Sports in Limassol.

During heavy snowfall, the local police will stop vehicles from reaching the slopes unless you're in a 4x4 or using snow chains. You can have some fun for a few days, find your board legs for the season, get some weird looks from the local (pink all-in-one wearing) skiers, and in the afternoon you can go and sit on the beach.

FREERIDERS. When there is snow the double black diamond (pah) slopes of the Jubilee and Racing runs are as steep as it gets here. There are plenty of trees to shred through.

FREESTYLERS. Not much fun for the freestylers with no park and very few natural hits.

PISTES. You will find the slopes narrow (20/25 m) and badly maintained.

BEGINNERS. Good for beginners to learn the basics.

Photo: SkiCyprus
Photographer: Bernard Musyck

GEORGIA

Home to the fantastic Caucasian Mountains which stretch over the border into Russia. They are better known for climbing and hiking so there are few winter resorts here. All of them are basic and could do with a lot of investment. Georgia had a peaceful revolution in 2003 with the ex-Communist leader running back to his mates in Russia. Foreign investments isn't forthcoming, but with all that dodgy money floating around in Russia, you just don't know what will happen here over the next few years. If you use public transport keep an eye on your bags, as people here are skint and petty crime is a particular problem in the capital Tbilisi.

BAKURIANI

is located in the Minor Caucasian Mountains, about 90 minutes from Tbilisi in the south east of Georgia. It has 2 lifts and a few runs which wind their way through the trees. The highest point is 1800m and the season starts in November, which is early compared to Western Europe. Accommodation is available in local guest houses or a run down 3 star hotel.

GUDAURI RESORT

is at 2000m with 2 chairs taking you up over a thousand metres to 3010m. From the top you have the option of 16km of pistes or a hike to some back country terrain. The resort is good for beginners and intermediates but advanced riders will get bored quickly. The lowest chair starts behind the Sport Hotel allowing you to Board to the door. Gudauri is 120km north of Tbilisi which is 1 ½ hours drive. Heliboarding is also available.

GREECE

Greece, the hot spot where bodies bare all on countless sun drenched beaches, scattered around numerous islands, also has a winter sports industry! Its not well known, and come to think of it not even thought of by most. Nevertheless, you can snowboard at one of fifteen recognised ski resorts, though some are very dubious. There are a number of mountain ranges where enough snow falls on an annual basis for shredding. Athens may be the historic home of the Olympics but just 2 1/2 hours away is the resort of Parassos, where you can ride some 20 runs. Although the Greeks allow snowboarders on to the slopes they're not totally sure about the whole scene yet, and sometimes seem a bit stand-offish but they're cool enough. Greece is definitely not a freestyler's playground; forget about half-pipes or fun-parks. Some areas may have stupidly short runs and be only equipped with an antique single lift system located alongside the resort's only building, and often the terrain is not that great. It's generally flat, not well groomed and not very adventurous, but what the heck, you're riding in Greece!

If you fancy giving Greece a try, remember to contact the resort prior to leaving, to check if the place is actually open and the latest snow forecasts. The resorts are unbelievably basic, many without any facilities. You won't find many places to eat, sleep or drink in, and as for hard-core partying: forget it - this is walkman and duty free territory! You would be well advised to take your own snowboard because hiring options are zero. Getting to the resort is best done by driving yourself as public transport is also poor.

AGIO PNEVMA
Top: 1720m
Runs: 3
Lifts: 2
Contact: 051 835952
Agio Pnevma is located 43km from Drama

KAIMAKTSALAN,
2050m -2480m
Runs: 13,
Lifts: 6
Contact: 0381 82169, 22073
Kaimaktsalan has the highest lifts in Greece and is located 45km outside Edessa. It has a small terrain park.
www.edessacity.gr/VORAS/

ORPHEA VALLEY,
Top:1750m
Runs: 1
Lifts: 1
Contact: 051 835952
Orphea Valley is located 44km from Kavala

SELI,
Top:1500m
Runs: 8
Lifts: 4
1 chair, 3 t-bars
Contact: 0332 71234
Mountain Vermio, Maccedonia

TRIA-PENTE PIGADIA
1402m to 2005m
Runs: 4, Longest 2km
Lifts: 4
1 chair, 3 t-bars
Contact: 0332 44446
Mountain Vermio, Maccedonia

VASILITSA
Top:1750m
Runs: 3,
Lifts: 2 drags
Contact: 0462 26100

VIGLA
Top:1650m
Runs: 3
Lifts: 2
Contact: 0385 22354
Vigla is located 18km from Florina

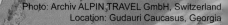
Photo: Archiv ALPIN TRAVEL GmbH, Switzerland
Location: Gudauri Caucasus, Georgia

HOLLAND

Reputedly has 51 dry slopes and a number of indoor real snow slopes, including Europe's longest.

SNOWPLANET

is about 45 mins outside Amsterdam, and features a 230m and a 100m real snow slope.
SnowPlanet Spaarnwoude
Heuvelweg 6-8,
1981 LV Velsen-Zuid,
phone: +31 (0)255-545848,
fax: +31 (0)255-545840,
www.snowplanet.nl

SNOWWORLD

is part owned by the Austrian resort, Sölden, and is in 2 different locations. SnowWorld Landgraaf hosts the World's largest indoor slopes at 500m and 520m. It is located in the Strijthagen Nature Park.
SnowWorld Zoetermeer has 3 slopes and 8 lifts, and is in the Buytenpark Nature Park. For more info see www.snowworld.nl. Prices are around 15 euros an hour.

ICELAND

This Country has 12 resorts which allow snowboarding both in the winter and summer months. None of the resorts are big or offer extensive mountain services, instead there are basic low level mountains with poor road access to them. On the slopes, runs tend to be short and not that well kept. However, Iceland is a very snowboard friendly country and resorts are more than happy to provide hits for freestylers to get air off. Visitors to Iceland will notice that apart from the short day light hours, it is a very expensive country. Visa requirements for entry in to the Country are very liberal but you do need to have return flight tickets on arrival.

KERLINGARFJOLL

is no longer in operation and has been dismantled, but boarders are still welcome whenever there is snow

HLIDARFJALL
Top:1000m
Terrain park and pipe.
Runs:14
Lifts: 4 - 1 chair, 3 drags (2930 ph)
Lift pass: Day 1000/1400 ISK weekday/weekend
Season pass 14,000 ISK
Hire: Board & Boots 2,500 ISK per day from resort
Board School: Lesson, lift & rental 3000 ISK per day
Private lesson 5000 ISK for 3hrs
Contact: www.hlidarfjall.is tel: 462-2280
Location: 10 minute drive from the town of Akureyri
Skálafell
Terrain park and pipe.
Lifts: 5 - 1 chair, 4 drags
Night Boarding: Yes
Contact: www.skidasvaedi.is tel: 354 566 7095

BLAFJOLL
Runs:20
Lifts: 11 - 2 chair, 9 drags
Lift times: Monday - Friday from 14:00-21:00. Weekends and public holidays from 10:00-18:00
Night Boarding: Yes
Contact: www.skidasvaedi.is tel: +354 561 8400
Location: 20 minutes from Reykjavik. Buses run from most towns to resort

Photo: Iceland

INDIA

One of the best areas to ride is the resort known as Auli, near Joshimath in the Garhwal Himalayas, where snowboarding expeditions have taken place. Manali is a place that offers some serious heli-boarding while the areas known as Narkanda and Kufri are only suitable for total beginners and as such they have very little in terms of facilities and are not really recommended. The Indian season is best from mid-December to the end of March. All the areas offer a variety of terrain with a lot of freeriding and backcountry hikes, although you should only go backcountry riding in India with a knowledgeable mountain guide and the full kit.

AULI

is located in the Garhwal Himalayas and lies at an altitude of 2,500-3,048m in the province of Uttaranchal close to both the Chinese and Nepalese borders. It is within sight of Nanda Devi which, at 7816 metres, is one of the world's highest mountains. Boasting 12 miles of wooded piste and an average snow fall of 3 metres, the Winter Games Federation of India holds many events here, and they even have two German built piste bashers. There are some budget huts which are government run near Auli, and a few options for food. At all resorts in India it's important to take your own equipment. The best way to get here is by private car or to take a train from Delhi to Haridwar. From here many buses go to Josimath then you'll have to take a taxi.

GULMARG

is in the disputed region of Kashmir. A ceasefire has tentatively been in place since 2004 but the odd bomb still goes off. Although tourists haven't been targeted recently, in the past Kashmiri separatists have kidnapped and executed a few westerners. There is a new $8million Gondola which will take you to 4150 metres. From there you can take one of the drag lifts or descend the vertical drop of 1400metres. This winter resort was first developed in the late 1940's, and you don't have to look too hard to find traces of the Raj. The golf course is one! The closest airport is Srinagar 60 km from resort.

Other snowboard areas are.
KUFRI
is in the Himachal region 9 miles from Shimla and is a flat place which suites beginners.
NARKANDA
is in the Himachal region, 40 miles from Shimla with, the top lift at 3143m.
MANAII
is also in the Himachal region just 35 miles from Kullu.
MUNDALI AND MUNSIYARI
are in the Uttaranchal region.
ROHTANG
is in the Himachal region just 30 miles from Manali.

All the Indian resorts provide very basic local facilities but are very cheap indeed, and we all love curry, don't we?

ISRAEL

Israel has one major resort Mt. Hermon, located in the Golan Heights near the border between Israel and Syria. The resorts had US$1million recently spent on updating the lifts and other facilities. There are 4 funiculars and 5 chairs covering 45km of pistes, but no sign of any terrain parks

Photo: Kashmir, India

IRAN

Check official travel advice for current conditions before heading there, but Iran is cheap, the food is excellent, you can drink the tap water, and most importantly there are some excellent snowboard resorts.

The Germans, who were building much of Iran's railroads in the early 1930's introduced Iranians to skiing, and the building on the resorts begun. In 1947 the Iranian Ski Federation was formed, and in 1951 the first chair lift was built.

It may be surprising to hear that 30% of all people on Iranian slopes are snowboarders. The ski lifts are well maintained and there have been no accidents in the past twenty years.

Iran has two big ski resorts; Shemshak and Dizin. Both resorts are within 2 hours drive from the capital, Tehran. There are a total of 20 resorts in the Country, although most of them will have little more than a couple of tows.

How to get to these resorts
You will have no problems arriving at Tehran airport with your own snowboard equipment, but make sure it is in a snowboard bag. It is best to get a taxi from the airport into Tehran - it will cost $6 maximum and will take half an hour. You cannot rent cars here so it is best to organise a bus tour from Tehran to the ski resort. This only costs $6-$7. You can either go up for the day or you can leave the tour and stay in the resort for the week then catch a tour bus back down. Go to one of the many sports/ski shops in Tehran to organise a tour.

General information about all resorts
Their season is from the beginning of December to the end of March. You can easily go off piste, and there are vast fields of powder. However, there are no ski patrols recording the avalanche risks nor triggering off avalanches where needed to reduce the risk. It is possible to hire a guide to go off piste for $5-6 per day. The guides are experienced and are usually trained in Austria or Switzerland.

There are also capable mountain rescue teams. There are no heliboarding facilities. Most of the time the weather is reliable so you are sure to get a good weeks riding whenever you go. There are a variety of lifts in these resorts ranging from gondolas and chairlifts to button lifts. Also, it is wise to take your own food to the resorts. Look out for a town called Fasham on the Way to Shemshak – you can buy all your basics there.

Accommodation
The concept of bed and breakfast accommodation is non-existent in Iran. However, because accommodation is cheap why not stay in a 4 star hotel for $50 per night for a double room. Head to the north of the Tehran; this is the safest and has upmarket hotels like the Hilton and Sheraton. You can contact the Iranian tourist board and ask them to organise accommodation for you in Iran.

What to wear
On the slopes it is fine to wear your normal snowboard gear. However, if you are a girl make sure you are wearing a hat. If it is sunny and you are boiling it is not advisable to strip off to your t-shirt on the slopes if you are male or female. At all other times women have to cover their hair and body but you do not need to wear a black cloak or chador. Instead it is fine to wear a colourful thin silk scarf tied under your neck and wear loose trousers, shirts with long sleeves, and a loose thin jacket that reaches down to your knees. It is fine to smoke anywhere except while walking along the street. Guys should nor wear shorts and it is best to wear long sleeved shirts.

The food
The food is unbelievably tasty – with fresh kebabs, amazing rice based dishes, fresh cheese, a lot of vegetarian dishes, amazing sweets, and an array of fruits to choose from. The thing you do have to be careful about are eating salads and herbs that haven't been washed properly. However keep in mind it is absolutely safe to drink the tap water. Also check out Arak – Iranian vodka made with raisins and dried apples containing 35-45% alcohol. It is illegal for Muslims to drink Arak, but not for Armenian Christians to drink it. Therefore as tourists, you can buy Arak from the Armenians for approximately $3 for 2 litres.

More Info
The tourist board can organise accommodation for you, work out an itinerary, give advice on prices and give telephone numbers for places, and its ok, they speak English. Contact Iran Tourism and Touring Organisation by email at info@itto.org

Iran Ski Federation,
Shahid Shirodi Sports Complex,
Varzandeh St., Shahid Mofatteh Ave.,
Tehran, I.R. Iran.
Web: www.skifed.ir

Email: office@skifed.ir
tel: +9821 8825161-2

SHEMSHAK

Shemshak is only a 45-minute drive from **Tehran** and the most popular resort. The route is stunning, with interesting towns to stop at on the way, and if you are hungry try out the amazing kebabs. Shemshak is well known as a resort for advanced skiers and snowboarders. The slopes are steep and funnily enough, have names such as The Wall. There are approximately eight extremely long runs with access to off piste slopes. Iranian slopes are generally long, wide, interconnect and have no trees. This resort is undulating so it is hard to see all the different slopes. There are cafes on the slopes and hotels and chalets at the bottom of the slope. It is extremely easy to find accommodation as a lot of people only come here for the day or they stay at their own chalets. A one day ski-pass costs a measly $12 for an adult. It is also very easy to hire snowboard equipment. A whole setup for a day will cost $15, and don't worry its not second hand Russian stuff, a lot of it is brand new.

2550m to 3050m
Runs: 16
Lifts: 7 - 2 chairs, 5 drags
Location: 57 kilometres north-east of Tehran

If you want to have good après-snowboard sessions this is the place to be. A lot of the Persians who come here are young, rich students studying in America or Europe and are probably on holiday seeing their parents. Practically all of them speak English, they are very western in their outlook and they are up for a damn good party. Shemshak is known as the party resort. It's best to check out a group of snowboarders that look friendly and go up and chat, mention that you have heard that this is the party resort and they are sure to tell you what's going on.

DIZIN

If you continue along the road for another 30mins after **Shemshak** you will reach Dizin. At an altitude of 12,900 feet this is the highest snow resort in Iran and attracts the most amount of snow. Iran gets powder snow by the bucket load - it is common for 50cm to land overnight during a dump in Shemshak, and even more in Dizin. However, because of the huge amount of snow there are a lot of avalanches, and the Iranians just let them happen naturally. There is no dynamite bombing, therefore there is a risk that the road to Dizin might be blocked with snow. However, in the past three years the road has been open most of the time. To be on the safe side check at

Shamshak before driving.
2650m to 3600m
Runs: 16
25% Easy
44% Intermediate
31% Advanced
Lifts: 13 - 3 Gondolas, 2 chairs, 8 drags
Location: Tehran 123km away and Shemshak is 71km

Dizin is a completely different resort to Shemshak. The views are amazing, as you can see unending mountain ranges and there is a clear view of the highest mountain in Iran, the semi-active volcano, **Mount Damavand**. Also, it is possible in this larger resort to see all nine runs. Like Shemshak, the runs are wide, long and interconnecting but there are no trees. However, the slopes are not as steep and thus attract beginners through to advanced riders. The prices for ski pass and hired equipment is the same as in Shemshak. It is also easy to find accommodation here.

KAZAKHSTAN

Kazkhstan is a former part of the Soviet Union that's known for its vast flat steeps and home of the soviet space program. In its far south-east corner lies part of the Tien Shan mountain range known as the celestial mountains, an absolute gem of a place. Its best known peak is Khan Tengri (7010 metres) which is supposedly the World's most beautiful mountain and a Mecca to many a climber. The place has still got all the hang ups of the old Soviet Union with a big police presence, road blocks to look for capitalist spies from the west and a need to carry your passport everywhere you go. If you travel independently you will get hauled off the bus at every check point, by police with bigger hats than a New Orleans pimp. For the best boarding you will need a helicopter (see our heliboarding section).

ALMA-ATA

pronounced Almarty is the Capital. Its a mix of Russian and Kazakh people which has been described as a huge knocking shop no ones heard of. Its a great place to drink vodka and check out the locals, and also a good base for the only real resort Chimbulak, which is home to the soviet ski team and the highest and largest ice rink in the world.

CHIMBULAK

An hour's drive from Alma-Ata at 2200 metres is the village of Chimbulak which has hotels, board hire, bowling and vodka fuelled Russians. It's a good little resort to get your legs ready for that helicopter you're going to get. Other than a few rope drags there are 3 chairs that can handle up to 900 people/hr, taking you from 2200 m to 3160 m. The resort is sheltered by imposing peaks on it's flanks, which helps with the temperature. There are also some trees to head for if the visibility is bad. The fun park has some hits and a few slides and is open from 10 till 5. You can sort out transport to the resort with one of the many agents in Alma-Ata. To save cash take a Lada taxi but make sure you've sorted out the return price before you leave town or once you're up there it'll cost the price of a new Lada to get back.

KYRGSZSTAN

Kyrgyzstan is a place for boarders who like a hike or have loads of cash for a helicopter. The neighbour of Kazakhstan, Kyrgyzstan is a lot more laid back and cheaper. You won't get stopped by the police but you might get taxed by a local if you walk through one of the parks alone at night. Mind you, it kicked off big time in the summer of 2005. Bishkek, the Capital, saw riots with government buildings stormed and shops looted. It eventually calmed down when the President did a runner and a new parliament was formed. Elections are planned for Nov 05 so it might happen again then.

Bishkek has wide tree lined streets which are surrounded by huge snow covered peaks. 80% of this country is mountainous and most of the other 20% is lakes. During Soviet rule most of Kyrgyzstan was out of bounds to foreigners due to missile testing in Lake Issyk Kul and near its border with China. Home to felt hats, goat head polo and wrestling on horse back while covered in goose fat, the Kyrgyz are a hospitable lot. The main drink in the countryside is fermented mare's milk, which tastes like sour yogurt and turns the local men into giggling kids. The food is mostly meat based with horse a favourite. In the countryside you see herds of horses waiting for the pot. Since the break up of the Soviet Union, the Kyrgz have embraced independence, setting up their own currency and welcoming investment from the west. Unfortunately lorry loads of plastic junk and rip off clothes from China have also arrived.

Heliboarding here is basically the same as in Kazakhstan but a little cheaper. You may even find that you'll stay in Karkara camp and use the same helicopter as you would if you booked it in Kazakhstan. The main advantage along with cost is if you start your trip in Kyrgyzstan you will only need a Kyrgyz visa. (See heliboarding section).

ALA-ARCHA

A 30 km Lada drive from Bishkek leads to the Ala-Archa National Park, which is a steep sided treed valley with a small resort at its top. The accommodation is a modern A frame hotel located a few km after the park gate. Last spring the road in was taken out by a huge land slide but they've been working really hard to rebuild it and a temporary route has been set up. The valley is lined with 5000 metre plus peaks and cascading glaciers. There are 4 lifts drag lifts starting at 3400 metres going up to 4000 metres and 4 runs, but basically you can go anywhere you want. The whole resort is on the Ala-Archinsky glacier so watch out for crevasses. The best thing to do is leave the lifts alone and get your board on your back to get some really fresh lines. There are loads of slopes to choose from with hat fulls of snow but there is no reliable mountain rescue so you're on your own.

491

LATVIA

The former Soviet state, Latvia gained independence in 1991 and in April 2004 became full members of the EU along with Greece and Poland.

There are around 30 resorts in Latvia, all within 100 miles of the capital Riga. However only 6 of those have more than 1 lift and the longest run in any resort is a paltry 350m. Valmiera is the biggest and best resort in the country.

Snowboarding in Latvia has taken off and most of the resorts have a terrain park, and there are many national snowboard events held annually. The Latvian Snowboard Association was started back in 1996 and now has over 120 members.

Expect snow quality to be poor, however most resorts posess some snowmaking equipment.

VALMIERA
Valmiera is the main snowboarder's hangout in Latvia, and is located 80 miles (130km) north of the Latvian capital Riga. There are two slopes, the longest measuring a mere 170 metres, serviced by two basic lifts and a snow-cannon. You couldn't split this place into styles or levels. Suffice to say that novices alone will have half an hour's fun. The winter allows for some limited riding on real snow while the summer sees an influx of boarders to ride the only sliding carpet, (better known as a 'Dry Slope'), in the Baltics. During the summer a lot of BMX riders also turn up to ride the BMX dirt track, while others simply come to chill out and take the occasional boat trip on the river Gauja.

Theres a terrain park thats floodlit, which provides a decent number of kickers and rails, although theres no half-pipe. You can hire snowboards and boots at the base and snowboard instruction is also available on request.

Lodging and other local services at the slopes are not for wimps or for those looking for all the creature comforts of an Alpine resort. You can choose to stay in one of the small camping style houses located behind the slopes, which use old wood stoves for heating. Alternatively in the town of Valmiera you will find hotels and other basic cheap lodgings.

Night-life is a Do-It-Yourself job with a Walkman, or check out Multi Klubs, Tirgus iela 5, ph 42 32114 for a party.

Fly to Riga International airport 80 miles away. Bus: A transfer takes 2 /2 hours. Trains: via Riga take 2 /2 hours.
Driving: via Riga, head north on the A2 for 50 miles travelling via Sigulda and turning north via Cesis to reach Valmiera.

Other Latvian resorts of note

RAMKALNI
A tiny hill with a ride area of 400m and only 2 runs. The longest is 200m, and there are 2 drags.

REINA TRASE
is another dinky place with 10 or so very short runs. However, there is a terrain park with a fair number of hits and some rails. It is serviced by 4 drag lifts and a rope tow.

MILZKALNS
60km east from the capital Riga, lies the resort of Milzkalns. There nothing to get exited about here. It's just a small hill with a few pomos and runs that never exceed 300 metres. There are only 5 drag lifts and 8 runs.

ZAGARKALNS
is yet another small hill.

Photo: Zagarkalns resort

LEBANON

Lebanon, bordering Syria and Israel, is not the first place that springs to mind when thinking about a snowboard trip. But think again, Lebanon in the winter gets great snow, its highest point is over 3000meters and it's the first mountain range that all that moisture from the Mediterranean hits. There are six resorts of varying standard, The Cedars is the highest while Faraya has the best infrastructure. Faqra and Zaarour are both private resorts although visits can be arranged outside of peak season holidays. www.skileb.com are experts in skiing in the Lebanon and have a good website and can organise board holidays in all six resorts.

THE CEDARS

The oldest and Highest resort in Lebanon which was founded by the French military in 1935. There's a lot of money going into the Cedars with new chair lifts and even talk of a new Gondola and 400 bed refuge. 122km from Beirut, about a 2 hour dive, The Cedars is open daily from 8.30 till 4, with a maximum height of 2800meters, and a longest run of 1110meters. There's a ski school but no board lessons of any value, 12 hotels and over 300 chalets and lots of bars and night clubs. So with a small slope area and all those beds try not to go on the weekend.

FAQRA CLUB

Opened in 1974 with the help of the Swiss and built on Mount Sannine, the Faqra Club has always had an exclusive reputation, one it still has today. From the slopes you can see the bay of Beirut as it's only 45km from the city, about an hours drive. The resorts has 4 lifts from 1735 to 1980 metrers and visits from non members can be arranged by calling (00 961) 01/257220

FARAYA MZAAR

By far the biggest resort in Lebanon, Faraya Mzaar has 16 lifts, 12 of which are chairlifts; it's built on 3 mountains with a base station on each. 1850 to 2465 meteres above sea level and with a longest run of 1652 meters and around 80 kilometres pistes, Faraya is a great resort for a few days or a good day out from Beirut which is only 46km away. Open daily from 8 till 4 Faraya has the most varied terrain in Lebanon.

KANAT BAKICHE

Is a small family owned resort which is 50km from Beirut near the village of Baskinta. It has a small slope area but things are being developed and the resort is slowly growing. The resort boasts a good snow record and is open daily from 8.30 till 4

LAQLOUQ VILLAGE

With 6 surface lifts and 3 chairs lifts Laqlouq is a good intermediate resort and it's only 62km from Beirut and is reputedly the most beautiful resort in Lebanon. The base at 1650 and resort max is 1950.

ZAAROUR

Zaarour is only 40km from Beirut and has a maximum altitude of 2000meters. It has two new 3 people chair lifts but has a limited slope area so is only really good for a day trip or complete beginners. The slopes are north facing so hold there snow well and are open 8.30 till 4 daily.

Photo: © SKILEB.com
Location: Faraya resort

LIECHTENSTEIN

This tiny country is situated between the borders of Switzerland and Austria. The main resort is Malbun which is just over 2 hours from Zurich airport. The resort is not particularly big, with 20km of pistes and 6 lifts

MALBUN

This is pretty small but does have a terrain park with a few rails & kickers

Lifts: 6 - 2 chair, 4 drags (6800 ph)
Lift pass: Day pass 37 CHF
6 Days 155 CHF, Season 380 CHF
Board School: Ski school Malbun offer 3 day beginners course 120 CHF (2hrs lesson per day), 5 day 170 CHF. Private lessons CHF 60 per hour
Contact:
Mountain Railways, P.O. Box 1063
9497 Triesenberg Malbun
Tel: + 423,265 40 00
Web: www.bergbahnen.li

Location: From Zurich (110 km) head to Valduz via Coffin, approx 1 1/2 hours. Munich, 250km, Innsbruck 170KM. nearest airport is Zurich Kloten, 1 1/2 hr transfer

POLAND

These people have had some shit, the Second World War started there and ended with 20 years of Communist Russian rule. When you arrive in Warsaw or Krakow it's grey. Even when the sun shines, it's grey. Beware of the taxi drivers who will try to rip you off by about 1000%. Look a little deeper past the unsmiling faces and the bastard taxi drivers and you'll find a really wild spot. Renaissance buildings, cheap beer, beautiful people and enough vodka and gherkins to see out any post nuclear war fall out. In the High Tatras the bushes are full of wolves and bears; in the city there full of suit wearing vodka heads who just cant make it home. There are many resorts in Poland but most are tiny, with only one or two lifts. The best is Zakopane, directly south of Krakow, on the Slovakian boarder.

ZAKOPANE

Founded in the seventeenth century, Zakopane is now a collection of wooden chalets, Soviet flats and Western branded shops. It's really a town which services a collection of small resorts. Kasprow Wierch is 3 km away and has the best runs. It has a cable car built in the 1930's that's in two stages which takes you up to 1985 metres and offers some long runs down. There are also two great treeless bowls to play in. Gubalowka which is reached by tram has some shorter runs good for beginners, except it has mostly t bar lifts. Sometimes when they can be arsed, there's also a pipe here. Nosa has night boarding and artificial snow production, a few chairlifts but mainly t-bars.

If you're in Poland over the winter or are on a road trip in eastern Europe then visit Zakopan; but if you're sitting at home planning your one week this season away don't bother; unless you love vodka and gherkins

MEXICO

There are plans to create a resort on a huge volcano in the Iztaccíhuatl-Popocatépetl National Park. The 5000m high volcano, if developed, would become one of the highest resorts in the world - not far behind Chacaltaya Bolivia. If all goes well there will be an $11million investment from businesses in Japan. Let's hope it gets off the ground then we can have Tequila on the slopes, as long as the volcano doesn't erupt.

MOROCCO

Not known as a snowboarding destination, Morocco could surprise some. It is home to the Atlas Ranges and the tallest mountain in North Africa, Jebel Toubkal, at 4167 metres.

From the sun drenched streets of Marrakech you can have a breakfast of croissant and mint tea while your ears ring with the call to prayer, the buzz of street sellers and horse drawn carts. Through the morning haze of 2 stroke oil you can see the snow capped peaks of the central High Atlas.

OUKAIMEDEN

A 76km drive from the city is the resort of Oukaimeden. It claims a 663m vertical drop from 3258metres. There is 1 chair lift, 7 drags and 20km of piste. If you find any of this working or open then you're in luck. Most of the time it's a donkey ride or walk up. From the top there are great views of the Marrakech plain and with good snow, it's a fun ride down. There are some posh hotels and also a few bunk houses. If you don't want to hire a board that's the shape of a bullet bring your own.

JEBEL TOUBKAL

A two hour drive from Marrakech is the small Berber village of Imlil, the last port of call before heading up Jebel Toubkal. It's a good idea to spend the night here to organise a guide, if you haven't done so in Marrakech. It's best to crash in a local's house and bung them some money in the morning. From Imlil you can hike up to the bloody cold Toubkal Refuge. To make it easy hire a porter or a mule. From here it's possible to hike the surrounding slopes and board back to the refuge. There's a good bowl directly behind the refuge. You will need a guide as well as all your own equipment and food, including a very good sleeping bag, ice axe and crampons. Remember to hike slowly and drink plenty of water to stave off altitude sickness. The best snow is normally late Jan early Feb.

MICHLIFEN

In the Middle Atlas, 81km south of Fez, is Michlifen. It's got 1 chair and 1 drag, 4 pistes, a top elevation of 2000m and a drop of 200m. With its low altitude and a strong African sun it's best to get up early before the snow becomes slush. The town of Ifrane is where all the accommodation is and if you hadn't just driven though pine trees with monkeys in and all the men weren't in dresses you wouldn't think you were in Morocco. The King has a mansion here and there are even posh hotels with bell boys. It's a weird hybrid of France and Africa and it isn't cheap.

Morocco doesn't offer great boarding and if you're not prepared to hike it's awful. But it's a cool destination if you want to spice up a visit to Fez and Marrakech. Boarding in Morocco is about the whole experience - meeting the locals, eating the food, and seeing some great mountains. After all whom do you know who's boarded in Africa?

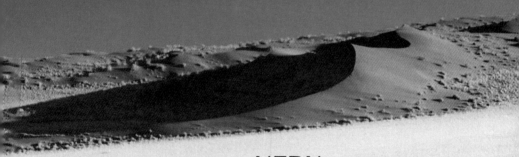

The High Atlas run from the Atlantic east towards the Sahara, and are home to the Berber Tribe, a rock hard group of once nomadic herdsmen. Now semi nomadic they still have thicker skin on their hands than you have on your feet. When the Arabs from the east invaded they couldn't control them and instead persuaded them to take on the Spanish. They made it all the way over the Pyrenees before getting a slap in Martel. When the French were here they thankfully never got control of these beautiful mountains and their inhabitants are still on the wild side but really hospitable as most true mountain people are.

NEPAL

In 2003 permission was granted to the Himalayan Heli Ski Guides (HHMG) to become the first company to operate Heli Skiing in Nepal. It's now possible to board in the Annapurna region and there are plans to open up the Everest area to trips. More info can be found on www.heliskinepal.com

PAKISTAN

MALAM JABBA

is the only real resort in Pakistan. It's 314km from Islamabad with the closest airport being Saidu Sharif 51km away. The resort is in the Swat Valley, at a height of 2896m. It's not the biggest resort in the world, with 2 chairs and a 200m vertical, but it does get a respectable 5m of snow a season, and has fantastic views of the mighty Hindu Kush, the Karakuram and Black Mountains ranges. The resort was built with the assistance of Austrian government and holds events for local ski clubs including the army. The place went up for sale in 2002 but has not yet been sold. The government hopes the resort will help the surrounding Swat Valley known as "The Cradle of Buddhism" to develop and generate some foreign cash, as long as the cease fire with India holds.

PERU

Pasto-Ruri/Huascaran the second highest resort in the World at 4800 metres. The Cordillera Blanca area is the only area where it is possible to board. From the nearby town of Huaraz there are several places where you can hire gear, and some organised trips are possible, or you can grab a local guide. Pastoruri Glacier is the most recognised area

ROMANIA

POIANA BRASOV

was Founded in 1895, is part of the Carpathian range which spreads all over Eastern Europe. It first served as a tourist district for Brasov and the first construction there was in 1904, then in 1909 it hosted its first Romanian ski contest.

It is a small resort with just 9 miles of marked out terrain offering some limited advanced carving on the Valea Lupului trail to basic freeriding through trees up on the Postavarul area. Although the slopes are not noted for having long lift queues, some of the runs can be very busy, especially the beginner areas. Freestylers will have to make do with getting air by building hits and then hiking them as there is no halfpipe here or any good natural kickers.

Runs: 10 (12km of pistes)
Longest 2.3km
34% EASY
34% INTERMEDIATE
33% ADVANCED
Lifts: 11
3 cable-cars, 8 drags
Board School: yes, 120 instructors. English spoken
Contact: www.poiana-brasov.com
Location: 13km from town of Brasov. Fly to Bucharest, 168km or 3 hours by car from resort.
Currency Leu

Off the slopes the purpose built resort is suitable for a few days of hanging out with a few cheap hotels and lots of cheap night-life. There are a some night clubs here and lots of...erm..."Gentleman's Bars", if you know what I mean!

SZCZAWNIK

is the other most recognised resort, but at 520m it's little more than a hill.

Photo: Bran (Dracula's) Castle, Romania

PORTUGAL

Portugal, believe it or not, has a mountain winter sports resort where you can snowboard, complete with uphill lift services. Although **Sierra de Estrela** is no match for the main European Alps, it's still has real snow and is cheap to visit. It's worth noting that the summit is over 2000m, which is higher than anything in Scotland and many Scandinavian resorts. Portugal has a good snowboard following that stems from its influences and links with the big surf scene here. The riding styles favour mostly freeride and freestyle with only a few Alpine/Carvers around. The people are really friendly and if you do decide to do a road trip for a two day visit in winter, remember that even if the snow is miserable, at least the people are not. They are warm and friendly and will show you a cool time, partying and chasing gorgeous women, while waiting for the white stuff to fall. Getting around in winter is best done with your own vehicle as local transport is not so hot.

SIERRA DE ESTRELA

Sierra de Estrela, located in the mid-northern region of the Country. Despite the area's altitude, conditions are not always that favourable. The warm winds that blow in from the Atlantic coast also make it impossible to have snowmaking facilities. Most riders only check the place out at weekends and if the locals want to ride any longer they tend to visit Sierra Nevada in Spain and Val D'isere or Isola 2000 in France. At present it only gives 10 hectares of lift serviced terrain, though there is more to explore if you're willing to do some hiking.

Freeriders will find some amazing off-piste that will appeal as much to intermediate riders as it will to advanced. If you take the lengthy hike over to the area called Covado de Boi at the opposite side of the main area, you'll gain access to a good share of couloirs and some big hits to fly off. The only real draw back is that once at the bottom, if you don't have someone waiting with a car to take you back to the main area, you'll have to hike back. Still work hard, play hard! Another good place to check out is Lagoa Escura; a big slope where the best powder is, in a totally crowd free area that bases out at an amazing lake.

Freestylers should also check out the Covado de Boi area, where there's a 300 metre natural half pipe which, on occasions, has 3 metre walls banked up.

Carvers who like to ride only long wide runs, forget it. This place is not for you. That said, there are some open areas that allow for a few signatures in the snow with your edges.

Beginners this place is absolutely perfect for you, although hopelessly limited.

Accomodation

Because Sierra de Estrela is an ecological natural park, there are a lot of development restrictions on and around the mountain. Although some accommodation is available close by, the best option is in Covilha, 12 miles away where you'll find hotels, restaurants, shops to hire snowboards, bars, discos and places to simply hang out, all at affordable prices.

SLOVAKIA

Slovakians drink more beer per capita than any other country in the World and at 50p a pint who can blame them? It's home to the **High Tatras** mountains (see Poland) part of the Carpathian range. Its best resort is Jasna in the Low Tatras. Slovakia, the eastern half of the former Czechoslovakia, is a beautiful place and is well cheap. The towns are made up of Renaissance architecture and grey Commie high-rise tower blocks. **Bratislava**, the Capital, has an International airport, and makes a great place to start you trip. It's a 3 hour train ride to the hills through some breathtaking scenery. You can also fly to Kosice, or the closest place to Jasna, Tatry-Poprad.

As well as great beer and beautiful women, it has some good riding. If you're an experienced rider and like a road trip then it's a cool place to tour and it's also a good place to learn. The instruction is ok and board hire is available and Burton even have a hire shop in Jasna. If you're a complete beginner then why spend loads of money on a lift pass for a huge area when you're going to spend days on the same slope? A week's pass here is around £50. Most resorts have a lot of drag lifts but you've got to learn to conquer them. There's nothing worse than seeing your mates heading off to that hidden spot while you are on your belly being dragged up the hill holding on for dear life.

Most resorts have really old ski lifts and there are always a few closed when you get up the hill. They look like they've not worked in years, but they are all boarder friendly and most have loads of rail slides and a few wonky hits.

JASNA

Up a dead end road you find Slovakia's best resort of Jasna which is sometimes referred to as **Chopok** (the name of the mountain). A tree laden resort, although a little tight for a full speed tree run, it makes for picture postcard scenery. It can get over loaded at weekends and school holidays with snow ploughing Ukrainians, but has a good choice of terrain for beginners and intermediates. The top is susceptible to high winds and is often closed, and don't believe the map that makes out the resorts of Jasna and Trangoska are linked because it's a good hours walk after the top lift to get up and over. There are plenty of cheap eateries on the hill as long as you like goulash, fried cheese or corn on the cob. Beer is available and drunk everywhere. The fun park, which you can walk to, has loads of rail slides but not much else. Two of the nursery slopes are open at night and frequented by one piece suits bent double, with arses pointed to the heavens and eyes fixed on the tips of their skis. Accommodation is available in hotels and for £18 a night you can get half board in a small room. If you want to live it up there's the newly built **hotel Grand** where the Burton hire and board schools are. The resort is really just a collection of hotels so the only option for a beer is a hotel bar. However, on a Friday night they put up a marquee near the Grand and fill it with Cheeky Girl look-alikes and thump out house music.

VELKA RACA

Is a small resort with 16km of marked down hill piste. There are 3 chair lifts including a new 6 person lift which links with an 8 seater cabin to take you to the resort's highest point 1050metres. You can get to 1236 metres but it's a walk. There is night boarding on one of the longer runs and a few bars and hotels at the resort. Height 630metres.
www.velkaraca.sk

SERBIA

KOPAONIK
1770M TO 2017M
Located on Mt Kopaonik, which is the biggest mountain of the central Serbia is the resort of the same name, which is the largest in the area. The most recent claim to fame is that NATO fired cruise missiles at transmitters on Mt Kopaonik in March 1999.

Runs: 23. 20% beginners,70% intermediate,10% advanced
Total runs 44km. Longest run: 3.5 km
Lifts: 22 lifts - 8 chairs, 14 drag
Getting there: 275 km from Belgrade 3hrs flight from London

SOUTH AFRICA
Capital: Pretoria - Cape Town
Time Zone: GMT + 2 hours
Top peak: MtAuxSources 4165m
Mostly people visit South Africa for safaris but there is a mountain with snow making facilities. Be careful here as crime is rampant, but on the whole you'll find a warm welcome. In Gauteng there's an artificial indoor slope.

TIFFINDELL
Top: 3001M
This is the only place in South Africa with snow making facilities, but its enough to give it a full 100 day season from May to September. They've built a small terrain park this year with a couple of kickers and a rail. In addition to the 450m beginners slope and the 600m intermediate one, theres also access to a chute and about 1.5km of off-piste runs. Located on Southern Drakensberg Mountains on Mt Ben Mc Dhui

SOUTH KOREA
Capital Seoul, Currency Won

17 resorts, best known Seoul Ski Resort with 3 lifts and 4 runs. Seongwoo, Phoenix Park, Daemyeong Vivaldi and Yongpyeong are the largest resorts.

THE ALPS RESORT
The Alps resort is up near the DMZ (De Militarized Zone) about 5 hours drive North East of Seoul; so close you can almost see North Korea from the summit. The surrounding army bases and numerous military checkpoints give the area a frontier feel. In this remote location not far from Seorak San (South Korea's version of the Matterhorn), and only 20 minutes from the East Sea (Sea of Japan), Alps Resort claims to receive the largest natural snowfall in South Korea, a whopping yearly average of 200cm.

It's a small resort even by Korean standards. Seven or Eight pistes cut through trees accessed by 5 of the world's slowest lifts. Four of which don't open any new terrain that can't be reached by taking the Champion chair to the summit.

Don't come here for the freeriding. With more snow than anywhere else in Korea there is the potential for some fun runs down the gullies at Alps but the trees are not well spaced. These runs are usually fenced off and guarded by the resorts army of ski patrollers who seem to make it their mission to eliminate fun. That said, the ski patrol is inexperienced when it comes to trees and powder so if you do take off into these thickly forested gullies they are unlikely to pursue you. Should you be apprehended, speaking quickly in English is usually enough to deter any further reprimand.

Natural hits are fairly limited across the resort but the Champion B run to the skiers right at the summit has some fun little hips before it leads down into the board park. This is known as the "Board Play Zone" and is also serviced by the Alps chair. It contains a variety of small boxes and rails and two poorly maintained table tops. Helmets must be worn.

All of Korea's resorts are immaculately groomed. At Alps speed freaks can cut some nice turns down the steep Paradise and Champion A runs. Even though this resort is extremely small, on weekdays you'll be one of only 5 or 10 people on the mountain and should be able to carve the corduroy for most of the day.

If rookies avoid the Paradise and Champion lifts there isn't much on this mountain that can't be mastered in a day. There is a snowboard school but don't expect to find an English speaking instructor.

The resort hotel is a rip off. Many rooms don't have a bed so you must sleep in the Korean style - wrapped in a blanket on the floor. A much better option if you have a car or don't mind bussing it to the slopes each day is to stay at the Hwangtae village ten minutes down the road. These rooms cost only 40 000 won per night and you can cram as many people in as you like. They're in a really cool setting and there is some OK hiking from your door.

Food wise, don't buy a hamburger anywhere in Korea. But try one of the numerous Dak Galbi restaurants near the resort. It's a delicious chicken stew sort of thing that you eat from the BBQ as it's being cooked in front of you.

TURKEY

Many people only think of Turkey as a place to lye on a beach get a tan, and maybe get harassed by under sexed men with dodge moustaches. Well if you head to some of the tourist beach resorts, that's what you'll get. Cool if you want the chance to buy some cheap fake sun glass's, but if you're looking for some great snowboarding in pine forests then leave the beach behind and head for the hills. With great food, hospitable mountain folk, and some good snow Turkey could just be the place for you.

What you will experience in Turkey is a mixture of good freeriding on mountain slopes that will offer all level of rider something to take on. Advanced riders will need to find out from locals where the best off piste is and it's advisable to hire the services of a local mountain guide. Like all mountains, Turkeys peaks can be very dangerous so extreme caution should be taken. Ski or snowboard patrols are not common and especially not in remote areas where there more or less non existent. For those who can afford it, there are options to go heli-boarding with a guide. Turkey's resorts, which although great value for money are very primitive and not extensive in area with only a few marked out trails and poor mountain facilities. Off the slopes resorts services are very basic, but where there are slope services, they are surprisingly very good with hotels, restaurants, and bars on the slopes allowing for plenty of doorstep snowboarding. The one big feature about Turkey and what it has to offer is the cost of things, 'Cheap', making Turkey an attractive option to other parts of Europe. Travel to Turkey should pose no real problems. It would be a good idea to check with your local travel centre to see which companies offer winter package deals, or just get yourself a flight and use public transport. Onward travel from airports and train stations, for inexperienced travellers, may prove to be the trickiest of all your tasks but ask the locals for advice and you'll get by. Give it a go, as Turkey, despite its sometimes ageing infrastructure, is well worth a visit for a snowboard holiday.

ULUDAG

Located south east of the Istanbul, is the biggest resort in Turkey boasting high altitude riding, heli-boarding and a good lift system. This small resort is also the playground for Turkey's rich. The 16 miles of pistes are well located to the resort with a number of hotels on the slopes, allowing for convenient doorstep riding on a daily basis. In general this is a resort that offers mainly intermediate easy going freeriders a simple time. Although there are a number of black steeps up on the Zivre Peak area, Uludag will not hold the attention of adrenaline seekers for too long.

Freeriders are presented with a mountain that offers the chance of riding some okay off piste in the Kusaklikaya area, reached off the Kusaklikaya chair lift. There is also the chance to shred through trees and ride some decent red runs at speed, especially on the trail that descends from the Zirve summit. Here the run starts out as a fast open black before dropping into a red and tame blue to the base, but be prepared for a 400 metre hike.

Freestylers will have to make do with getting air from the natural hits, as no permanent pipe exists. However, there are some really good gullies to ride up. Log freaks will also find some wood to grind.
Piste lovers will be able to stretch themselves on wide open runs which offer a mixture of fast reds on Kusaklikaya and blues on the Beluv area.

Beginners are best staying on the Beluv area, which has some good novice runs reached by chair or drag lift. Note the easy slopes can get busy at weekends but, like the rest of the mountain, are crowd free on weekdays.

Uludag is a match for many foreign resorts, boasting good slope side hotels and a number of average places to eat and drink. Although this is a place that caters for Turkey's high earners, it's still very affordable, has a lively night life and is well worth a visit.

Photo: Blue Mosque, Istabul

TAIWAN

The Taiwanese invented grass skiing so lets leave them to it. They also produce Hi-Tec boarding wear, goggles etc.

UKRAINE

Capital Kiev, Currency Hryvnia.

This is another ex-Soviet state to have a revolution in 2005, albeit a peaceful one. The streets of Kiev were full of protestors for weeks until a second election was held and the crowd got the result it wanted. So, if people needed to protest for a new government and industrial investment, you can imagine what the mountain resorts are like. Most were built in the 70's and need investment as does the hire kit, so bring you own.

BUKOVEL

has seen some investment of late and has plans for more. It also claims to be the Country's up and coming resort. Theres 10 pistes served by 5 lifts, including one black run www.bukovel.com

DRAGOBRAT

near the Romanian boarder has 2 longer lifts and a few short ones and claims the highest slopes in the country at 1400 metres.

SLAVSKO

in the Carpathian Mountains to the west of the county near Poland, is a popular resort with the locals. Varied terrain on Mt Trostyan is between 900-1250metres.

TYSOVETS

near the resort of Slavsko, is a smaller resort that is ok for beginners. Other resorts to note are Yaremcha and Slavske.

Photo: Stefan Tordenmalm
Landscape, The castle Swallow's Nest near Yalta, Ukraine

VENEZUELA

Capital Caracas, Currency Bolivar
MERIDA
at 1600-4765 metres is truly a high altitude resort with 4 lifts. Well in fact the lifts are one long line of 4 cable cars which take over an hour to reach only 2 runs at 1km each, so it won't keep you busy for long. That's the theory anyway, the reality is that they rarely open, and even rarer theres any snow to board on. Merida is 680 km southwest of Caracas and a good one to tell your mates you've visited, but not one to head to for an action packed season.

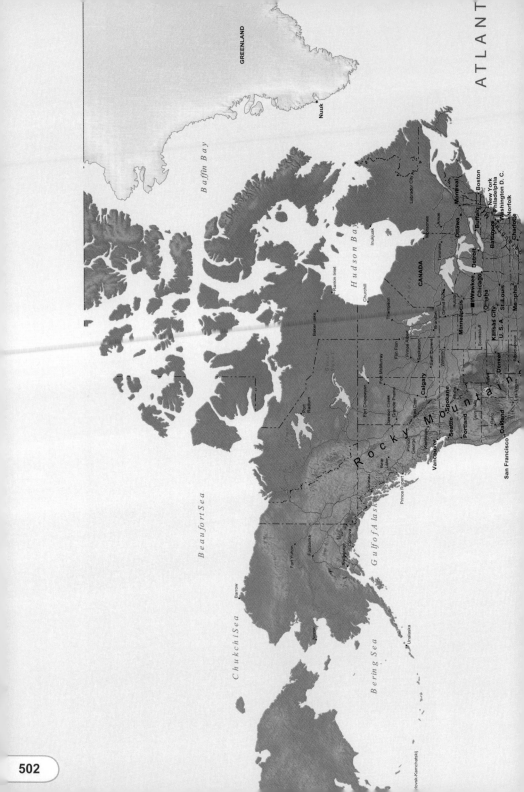

GREENLAND

Nuuk

ATLANT

Baffin Bay

Hudson Bay

CANADA

Rankin Inlet

Churchill

Inukjuak

Labrador City

Moosonee

Amos

Ottawa

Buffalo

Boston

New York

Montreal

Detroit

Battleford

Philadelphia

Washington D. C.

Norfolk

Charlotte

Timmins

Milwaukee

Chicago

St.Louis

Memphis

Grand Forks

Omaha

Minneapolis

Kansas City

U. S. A.

Thompson

Baker Lake

Flin Flon

The Pas

Prince Albert

Saskatoon

Brandon

Winnipeg

Fort McMurray

Grande Prairie

Swift Current

Regina

Fort Chipewyan

Dawson Creek

Red Deer

Calgary

Scottsbluff

Denver

Albuquerque

Port Radium

Prince George

Kamloops

Spokane

Seattle

Portland

Bear Lake

Vancouver

Prince Rupert

San Francisco

Oakland

R o c k y   M o u n t a i n

Beaufort Sea

Gulf of Alaska

Fort Yukon

Fairbanks

Barrow

Chukchi Sea

Nome

Bering Sea

Unalaska

Novosk-Kamchatski

502

ARCTIC OCEAN

Greenland Sea

Norwegian Sea

Leptev Sea

Kara Sea

Barents Sea

North Sea

Baltic Sea

Black Sea

Caspian Sea

Aral Sea

Sea of Okhotsk

Sea of Japan

Yellow Sea

ICELAND

IRELAND
Dublin
Cork

U.K.
London
Sunderland

NORWAY
Oslo

SWEDEN
Stockholm

FINLAND
Helsinki

DENMARK
Copenhagen

NETH.
BELGIUM
LUX.

FRANCE
Paris
Nantes
Toulouse
Bayonne

SPAIN
Madrid
Barcelona
Valladolid
Sevilla

PORTUGAL
Porto
Lisbon

GERMANY
Berlin

POLAND
Warsaw
Gdansk
Krakow

CZECH
SLOVAKIA
AUSTRIA
HUNGARY
SLOVENIA
CROATIA
BOSNIA
SERBIA
MONTENEGRO
MACEDONIA
ALBANIA

ITALY
Rome
Naples

GREECE
Athens

ROMANIA
Bucharest
Constanta

MOLDOVA

BULGARIA

BELARUS
Minsk

LITHUANIA
LATVIA
ESTONIA
Tallinn
Riga

UKRAINE
Kiev
Lviv

St. Petersburg

RUSSIA
Moscow
Rostov
Gorkiy
Yaroslavl
Kazan
Ufa
Saratov
Volgograd
Krasnodar
Perm
Izhevsk
Sverdlovsk
Chelyabinsk
Kuybyshev
Tol'Yatti

Murmansk
Archangelsk
Vologda

Ural Mts

Siberia

Krasnojarsk
Irkutsk
Nov sibirsk
Omsk

TURKEY
Ankara
Izmir
Istanbul
Adana

GEORGIA
ARMENIA
AZERBAIJAN

SYRIA
IRAQ
Tehran

KAZAKHSTAN
Qaraghandy
Almaty
Alma Ata

UZBEKISTAN
TURKMENISTAN
KYRGYZSTAN
TAJIKISTAN

MONGOLIA
Ulaanbaatar

Gobi Desert

CHINA
Beijing
Lanzhou
Xining
Xining
Baotou
Taiyuan
Yinchuan
Urumqi
Hotan

NORTH KOREA
Pyongyang

SOUTH KOREA
Seoul

Harbin
Changchun
Jilin
Qiqihar
Shenyang
Dalian
Fuxin
Qingdao
Jinan

Sapporo
Sendai

Torshavn

504

	October	November	December	January
1				
2				
3			Nokia Air & Style, Munich (Germany)	
4				
5				
6				
7				
8				
9				
10			Nissan X-Trail Jam, Tokyo (Japan)	
11				
12				Honda Session, Vail (USA)
13				
14				
15				
16				Burton European, Laax (Switzerland)
17			Malmi & Oksanen Inv, Finland	
18				
19				
20				
21				
22				
23				O'Neill Pro Freestyle, Avoriaz (France)
24				
25				Snow-board League, Livigno (Italy)
26				
27				
28			O'Neill SB-Jam, Davos (Switzerland)	
29				
30				
31				

2005/2006 TTR Events Calender

	February	March	April	May
1				
2	Nescafé Champs Open, Leysin (Switzerland)			
3		The Artic Challenge, Tromso (Norway)		
4				
5				
6		Billabong Junior Pro, Les Deux Alpes (France)		
7				
8				
9		Ästhetiker Shred Down, Westendorf (Austria)		
10				
11				
12		The Battle, Sweden		
13				
14		Burton US Open, Stratton (USA)		
15				
16				
17		Austrian Masters, Nordpark (Austria)		
18				
19				
20	X-BOX Big Day Out, Val D'isere (France)			
21				
22				
23		Ästhetiker Wangl Tangl, Mayerhofen (Austria)		
24	Nippon Open, ALTS Bandia (Japan)			
25				
26				
27				
28				
29				
30				
31				

* Tour event times correct at going to press, but check **www.ttrworldtour.com** for updates

NOTES

Resort index